DATE DUE

Okanagan Reg Lib due Nov 2 06		

Brodart Co.   Cat. # 55 137 001   Printed in USA

D0769087

The Planting of New Virginia

Creating the North American
Landscape

Gregory Conniff
Edward K. Muller
David Schuyler
Consulting Editors

GEORGE F. THOMPSON
Series Founder and Director

Published in cooperation with
the Center for American Places,
Santa Fe, New Mexico, and
Staunton, Virginia

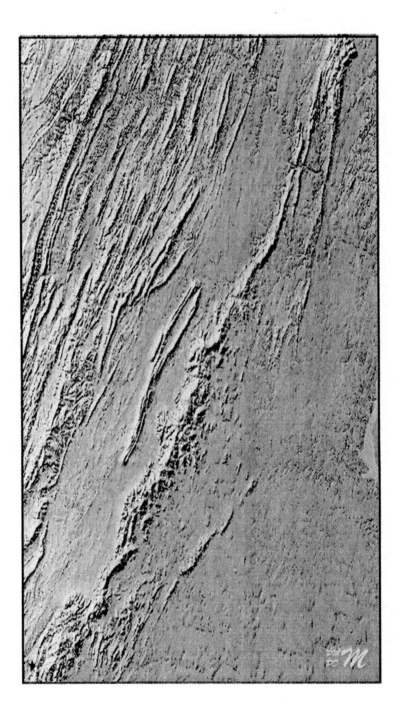

The PLANTING *of* NEW VIRGINIA

Settlement and Landscape in the Shenandoah Valley

WARREN R. HOFSTRA

. ⚗ .

The Johns Hopkins University Press

Baltimore and London

This book was brought to publication
with the generous assistance of
Nancy Chappelear Baird,
Betty Jean Fawcett,
and Robert Woltz.

The Johns Hopkins University Press
2715 North Charles Street
Baltimore, Maryland 21218-4363
www.press.jhu.edu

Library of Congress Cataloging-in-Publication Data
Hofstra, Warren R., 1947–
   The planting of New Virginia : settlement and landscape in the Shenan-
doah Valley / Warren R. Hofstra.
      p. cm.— (Creating the North American landscape)
Includes bibliographical references and index.
   ISBN 0-8018-7418-1 (alk. paper)
      1. Shenandoah River Valley (Va. and W. Va.)—Historical geography.
2. Landscape—Social aspects—Shenandoah River Valley (Va. and W. Va.)—
History—18th century. 3. Frontier and pioneer life – Shenandoah River Val-
ley (Va. and W. Va.). 4. Land settlement—Shenandoah River Valley (Va. and
W. Va.)—History—18th century. 5. Shenandoah River Valley (Va. and W.
Va.) –History—18th century. 6. Frontier and pioneer life– United States.
7. United States—Territorial expansion. I. Title. II. Series.
F232.S5H64 2004
911'.7559 – dc21   2003007658

A catalog record for this book is available from the British Library.

Frontispiece: The Shenandoah Valley. This terrain map was produced using
digital elevation model data supplied by the United States Geological Survey
to generate contour symbolization for portions of six 1:250,000 quadrangles.
This, and all illustrations bearing the PDM and PMM logo, were prepared by
Paul D. McDermott and Phil M. Mobley.

For Mary, Kate, and Andrew

Contents

Illustrations

Acknowledgments

THE COMPLETION of this book is due to support and assistance from many individuals and institutions. To each of them I owe a great debt of gratitude. The National Geographic Society, the Virginia Department of Historic Resources, and the Savannah River Archaeological Research Program funded portions of the research for this project. The summer stipend and research fellowship programs of the National Endowment for the Humanities afforded me extended periods of time, including a year's sabbatical, for research and writing. A fellowship for a semester at the Virginia Center for the Humanities of the Virginia Foundation for the Humanities and Public Policy permitted me to lay the groundwork for this study many years ago. Numerous visits to the Virginia Historical Society, where much of my research was conducted, were made possible through the society's Mellon Fellowship program. A Mednick Fellowship from the Virginia Foundation for Independent Colleges allowed me to spend a week working in the collections of the Historical Society of Pennsylvania. And from time to time the Fund for Excellence of Shenandoah University provided critical support for various aspects of my work.

In many cases the conclusions of the study were the result of collaborative work and joint publications with other scholars. To Leila Boyer, Ed Connor, Galtjo Geertsema, Clarence Geier, Kevin Hardwick, Ken Koons, Deborah Lee, Bob Mitchell, and Joe Whitehorne I am indebted for the pleasures and satisfactions of working together, sometimes under most pressing circumstances. Scholars and friends read the manuscript for me or contributed ideas and perspectives that significantly influenced my thinking. These include Ellen Eslinger, Van Beck Hall, Ed Matthews, Ted Muller, and Mike McConnell. To them I am deeply indebted for wise counsel and help in setting many matters straight. Responsibility for errors is mine alone. Anonymous reviewers of the manuscript will, I hope, see how their suggestions also improved it.

George Thompson, president of the Center for American Places, provided encouragement for this project from its inception, stuck with it as acquisitions editor through many protracted evolutions, and in his own work contributed many invaluable perspectives on studying the North American landscape. Also at the center, Randall Jones supplied both technical and moral support as well as the kind of friendship and collegiality that makes scholarly work a pleasure. To the varied members of the Shenandoah Valley Regional Studies Seminar, whose Friday afternoon discussions once a month got me going on a number of ideas and stratagems, I owe a good round of drinks at a postseminar debriefing. Other friends and colleagues pitched in with advice, assistance, and encouragement. Thus, the breadth of my gratitude includes Paul Davis, Allan Eney, Paddy Fitzgerald, Ann Grogg, Bob Grogg, John Hemphill, Audrey Horning, Maral Kalbian, Brian Lambkin, Evgenia Leonovitch, Turk McCleskey, Melissa McLoud, Phil Mowat, Greg Nobles, Ed Redmond, Gary Stanton, and Brent Tarter.

Behind the conclusions of this volume lie hours of research at libraries and repositories sometimes far from home. At the Virginia Historical Society, Frances Pollard and Janet Schwarz gave freely of their expertise in one of the preeminent manuscript collections for Virginia history. The daunting resources of the Library of Virginia were made accessible to me through the thoughtfulness and skill of staff members such as Conley Edwards, Minor Weisiger, and Marianne McKee. With unparalleled knowledge and skill, Rebecca Ebert revealed to me the unimaginable treasures in the Archives Room of the Handley Regional Library in Winchester, Virginia. Others at the Alderman Library of the University of Virginia, the Swem Library at the College of William and Mary, the Library of Congress, the Maryland State Archives, the John D. Rockefeller Jr. Library at Colonial Williamsburg, the Public Record Offices in London and Belfast, and the British Library have speeded and eased my work immeasurably.

Friends and colleagues at Shenandoah University, where I teach, are responsible for creating a collegial environment in which scholarship is nurtured and appreciated. It has been a pleasure to work over the years with Brandon Beck, James Davis, Tracy Fitzsimmons, Jane Pittman, Catherine Tisinger, Bruce Souders, Joel Stegall, John Warren, and Dutch Van Voorhis. The costs of composing and illustrating a lengthy text have been considerable. My deepest appreciation goes to Nancy Chappelear Baird for meeting subvention expenses of this volume. Betty Jean Fawcett and Robert Woltz also provided vital assistance with various expenditures entailed in manuscript preparation. A constant inspiration to my endeavors has been the dean of Winchester historians, Stewart Bell Jr. His passing in late 2001 left a void in the community but also many legacies, including the title of my position at Shenandoah University.

The original maps in this volume are the product of the hard work and genius of Dan McDermott and Phil Mobley. Without their cartographic talents many of the important geographical relations so vital to my thesis and argument would have been left unillustrated. A logo composed of their initials identifies their maps. To Barbara Lamb, editor on this project, I am deeply indebted for her grace and style in weeding out infelicities and inconsistencies in my manuscript. Perhaps my greatest intellectual obligation is to historical geographer Robert D. Mitchell. As a senior scholar with many path-breaking studies of the Shenandoah Valley behind him, Bob took an interest in my work at its earliest stages. It was Bob who raised the compelling question of why the Shenandoah Valley was town rich in 1800, when the remainder of Virginia was impoverished of urban settlement forms. It was with Bob that this investigation into that and related questions began and it is to him that the satisfaction of many of its attainments belong. When Bob retired from both the University of Maryland and academic life a number of years ago, I undertook solely the realization of many of the inquiries we had begun together. His imprint on this volume, however, is profound.

For the emotional sustenance necessary to undertake a project as substantial as this book, I am wholly indebted to my family. Kate and Andrew have grown up through their teen years with this study and their father's inability to separate his intellectual from his domestic life. They may, however, never know how much I owe to their wit, good sense, and abhorrence of bad ideas. Throughout it all, the love, kindness, and conscience of my wife, Mary, has made light the burden of hard work. To her belongs my ineffable gratitude.

The Planting of New Virginia

The Evolution of New Virginia

A T T H E D A W N I N G of the eighteenth century the Shenandoah Valley of Virginia was an open land—unfamiliar territory to the Europeans who were just beginning to encounter and explore it. According to Franz Louis Michel, a young Swiss merchant on a scouting trip for a colony of his countrymen, a "considerable tract of wild and uncultivated deserts" lay along the lower stretches of the Shenandoah River (fig. I.1). "There is good land," he observed, "where are great forest trees of oak, and where much game abounds. All this country is uninhabited except by some Indians." To Native Americans the Valley was an old land. Although few Indians had dwelt there since the mid-seventeenth century, the area would remain critical to the way native nations reckoned and contended for territory. This fact would escape Europeans of the first immigrant wave and later cause much bloodshed and suffering. Moreover, the changes Native Americans had worked on the land during occupations across twelve previous millennia were discernable to Europeans as only a few clearings, or "Indian old fields." Within seventy years, however, these newcomers would transform the land and rewrite the landscape with a new cultural text.[1]

By 1800 the entire valley had become what Native Americans never envisioned, or perhaps feared the most: private property—divided and subdivided by metes and bounds surveys, endorsed by colonial and state governments in patents and grants, and secured by deeds in local courthouses. On these properties, farmers produced enormous quantities of wheat and livestock. Roads traversed the landscape connecting farms to local mills as well as to markets in Alexandria, Baltimore, and Philadelphia and in such distant destinations as the West Indies and southern Europe. Local market towns like Winchester, the seat of Frederick County in the northern or lower Valley, stood at the center of local road systems. Town merchants retailed goods imported from throughout the world. Winchester, moreover, predominated over a hierarchy of towns, which included lesser villages and smaller settlements consisting often of no more than a shop and a mill or a few houses. Goods and money flowed throughout the region as farmers marketed flour, beef, or wool and purchased fabrics, ceramics, furniture, tools, and whatever else made their lives possible, profitable, and pleasant.[2]

This transformation from a frontier to a settled world was repeated time and again across America west of the Appalachian Mountains. The Bluegrass region of central Kentucky would see these changes completed within the last two decades of the eighteenth century alone. What took place over seventy years in the Shenandoah Valley was replicated in a much shorter time on new frontiers. The Shenandoah Valley backcountry thus became forecountry. What was replicated was a landscape of town and country. This was a world of dispersed, enclosed farms and farm families producing for national and international markets, while towns and townspeople organized the exchange of goods and services. In the nineteenth century, this arrangement would become synonymous with the much-fabled "Main Street" small towns so indelibly associated with the American midlands. Its origins and evolution in the Shenandoah Valley of Virginia—the earliest settled region in the southern backcountry and by 1800 the most developed—are the subject of this book.

· ☙ ·

Because early American history is so often conceived in dichotomous terms—the towns of New England and the rural world of the plantation South—the concept of town and country when applied to the interior backcountry suggests that discrete, if not disjointed, landscape elements defined the region. On the contrary, the people of town and country depended closely upon one another for their survival. Their lives and livelihoods cannot be understood as separate. Town life beat to the rhythms of the agricultural year, and townspeople not only depended directly upon country produce for their sustenance but also cultivated gardens, kept a cow or two, and sometimes operated a nearby farm themselves. Merchants timed their buying trips to coastal port cities so that imported goods arrived at their stores in spring and fall, when seasonal changes dictated new demands for farm families. These families, furthermore, situated their dwellings and farm buildings directly on the roads leading to town in patterns revealing a need to be connected to the markets upon which their livelihoods depended. Stores, streets, roads, and farmsteads created a single pattern of public space that overspread the land, binding together the activities of country and city dwellers. Town and country represented the poles of a settlement continuum, not alternative ways of life.[3]

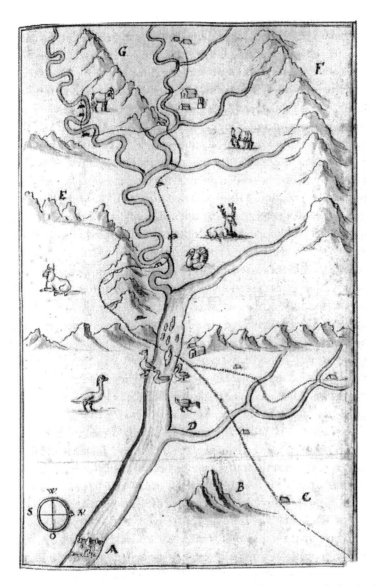

FIG. I.I. Franz Louis Michel's Map of the Shenandoah Valley, 1707. Michel and others filed this map of the Shenandoah Valley with a petition to the English crown to establish a colony of Swiss settlers along the Potomac River in a mountainous region previously uninhabited by Europeans. According to Michel's key, the letters on the map refer to (A) "Rocks in the River called Potomack, as far as one can ascend in barques and beyond in small boats," (B) "A spring which flows 60 miles from Annapolis," (C) "First hut which was made to sleep in on the trail on their route," (D) "A river called Quattaro," (E) "Mountains of Virginia," (F) "Region of the Mesesipi," and (G) "Mountains of Cenuntua" (see Intro., n. 1). CO 5/1316, f. 79, Colonial Office Papers, Public Record Office, London.

The landscape expression of this continuum held a meaning deeper than any particular vista viewed in fixed time and space. Behind and sustaining the arrays of fences and fields, roads and paths, houses and barns, mills and manufactories, villages and towns lay complex regional patterns of social relations and economic activities. The natural environment of uplands and lowlands, woodlands and scrublands, meadows and marshes, grasslands and savannas also underlay the town and country landscape. This foundation was shaped in part by the long span of geological, climatological, and biological change and in part by the briefer impact of previous human occupations. The landscape was, moreover, never the sole creation of the men and women who claimed to possess it at any one time. The distant decisions of those with power to shape the lives of peoples taking up new lands also influenced the emerging landscape. Colonial and imperial officials often set the timing and established the character of the land's taking. They frequently controlled who procured the land and what ethnic or national traditions were brought to it. Sometimes they fixed specific settlement locations and dictated their forms. Just as often the contours of local landscapes reflected patterns of international trade and the demands that distant commerce placed on both producers and consumers.[4]

The emergence of a town and country landscape in the Shenandoah Valley during the last two-thirds of the eighteenth century was, therefore, not simply the consequence of the immediate steps taken by men and women who occupied the region. That landscape also expressed the policies that brought about the occupation, determining how, when, and by whom the Shenandoah Valley would be planted. The term *plantation* customarily applies to the designs that English policy-makers in early-seventeenth-century London developed to impart both impetus and form to the movement of Scottish, English, and some German and French Protestants into the north of Ireland in an effort to wrest the region from the native Irish and reduce the threat of Catholic power to the security of England.[5] The term was never employed so explicitly to describe efforts to occupy the margins of the English colonial world of the eighteenth century with white, Protestant, yeoman farm families amidst a war with French and Spanish colonists, Native Americans, and enslaved Africans. But English officials in colonial capitals and in imperial London did make deliberate decisions to plant communities of these families in broad, arching backcountry buffer zones so as to secure English frontiers not only from the external threats of foreign peoples outside the Crown's control and but also from the internal threats of alien peoples over whom control was all too complete. The movement of people into the eighteenth-century backcountry is most often viewed from the perspective of those who wanted land for the security of their families and offspring.[6] Rarely is it surveyed from the vantage point of those with the power to exchange that form of security for the internal and external security of nation states in global struggle.

· ✞ ·

The term *New Virginia* was used by the end of the eighteenth century to distinguish the region west of the Blue Ridge from *Old Virginia*, to the east. It consciously set off the world of the farmer from the world of the planter, a region rich in towns from one poor in towns, grain and livestock production from tobacco culture, and a free labor society from a slave labor society (fig. 1.2). The distinction cannot be too rigidly drawn because grains were produced throughout Virginia by 1800, and some Shenandoah Valley counties had significant slave populations. But it was strong enough to force a recognition that town and country west of the Blue Ridge was not only different from the rural world of dispersed plantations but also new, that is, more attached to the future and dynamic developments taking place west of the Appalachians and less reflective of the past and of a tobacco economy increasingly mired in economic depression.[7]

· ✞ ·

Three evolutionary phases marked the development of a town and country landscape west of the Blue Ridge. The first, covered in chapters two to four of this volume, concerned the planting time beginning in the 1730s, when Europeans first moved onto the land. Their movements were not solely the consequence of demographic and economic pressures pushing them out from the settled regions of mid-Atlantic North America. Certainly, these pressures were at work, and the men and women who moved to the Shenandoah Valley were seeking new lands and new opportunities, but their search would have ended far short of this isolated region had it not been for the land policies of Virginia's colonial government under its governor William Gooch.[8]

Gooch faced a variety of problems in the late 1720s, problems that white, Protestant, yeoman farm settlement in the Shenandoah Valley could address. He was well aware of the delicate balance that held the English colonial world in peril between the Catholic empires of Spain to the south and France to the west. Moreover, the northern portion of the Valley lay under the contrary claims of both the neighboring colony of Maryland and of Thomas, sixth lord Fairfax's Northern Neck Proprietary. A culture of persistent warfare that pitted northern and southern Indian nations against one another regularly brought Native American war parties through the Shenandoah Valley and dis-

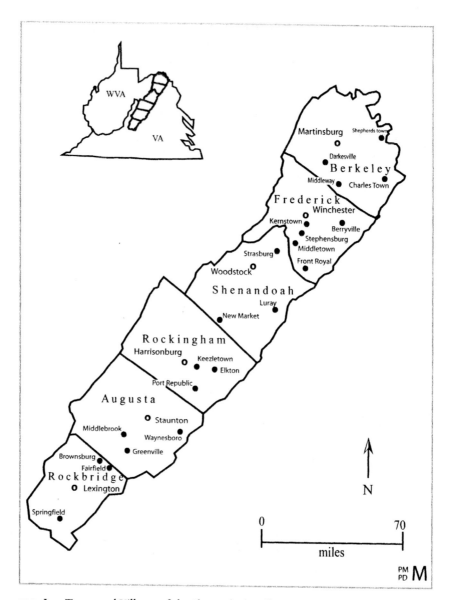

FIG. I.2. Towns and Villages of the Shenandoah Valley, 1800. By 1800 the Shenandoah Valley was rich in market towns and smaller villages. Tidewater Virginia, by comparison, was poor in these settlement forms. Based on Robert D. Mitchell, *Commercialism and Frontier: Perspectives on the Early Shenandoah Valley* (Charlottesville: UP of Virginia, 1977), 192, fig. 25.

rupted Virginia's relations with Indians long settled within the colony. Finally, Gooch readily compared the haven Virginia's mountains offered to bands of escaped slaves with the mountain fastnesses so conducive to slave uprisings in England's Caribbean colonies. The land policy the governor and his advisory Council subsequently devised was designed to buffer the Virginia colony from the external threats of French encroachments, Indian incursions, and conflicting land claims as well as the internal threat of slave uprisings.

Virginia was not alone in initiating backcountry settlement for these reasons. The efforts of the Virginia government were one element of a loosely coordinated series of measures taken across the settlement frontiers of eighteenth-century North America designed to move white Protestants into sensitive and contested regions for the security of established settlements and the advancement of English colonial interests. The origins of these measures can be traced to the early eighteenth century and the inception of imperial conflicts involving Indian and European nations over the interior of North America. By the 1730s new frontiers extended from South Carolina, where the royal governor organized the backcountry into townships, across the mountains of Virginia and Pennsylvania to New York, where fortifications were constructed along the lakes bordering New France, and finally to New England, where planned settlements of German and Scots-Irish immigrants were established in the northern reaches of English claims so as to secure land against the movements of French colonists.

These developments bore profound consequences for the Shenandoah Valley and what came to be called the Opequon settlement, which emerged there during the 1730s (fig. I.3). According to Virginia land policy, frontier buffers allowed for the initial dispersal of farm families occupying land holdings averaging three to four hundred acres. The actual pattern of dispersal was closely adjusted to both environmental conditions and family aspirations for capturing the mix of environments essential for economic competency. In addition to land and natural resources, a competency consisted of those assets in labor, skills, tools, and capital necessary to live independently, that is, free from the will of others. A mentality of competency therefore permeated the settlement landscape.[9]

Dispersal, moreover, generated rural communities, or open-country neighborhoods, critical as the first stage in the narrative of evolving centrality in backcountry areas. To these areas Virginia land policy brought a mix of ethnic and national groups in which the English and Anglo-Americans significantly constituted only a minority among predominantly Scots-Irish and German populations. That Scots-Irish and German peoples responded to Virginia initiatives was not entirely an accident, because these were peoples who had occupied the contested ground of European imperial and religious conflicts for nearly two centuries and were enured to seeking opportunity amid the devastation of warfare and the expropriation of native inhabitants. In Europe, however, they would remain dependent peoples. In the Virginia backcountry, as elsewhere on English settlement frontiers, they sought competency and independence.

That the governor and his Council conceived buffer settlements in the form of loosely occupied agricultural landscapes also meant that these settlements needed to be organized within the institutional framework of the county. The settlement frontiers of Virginia had conventionally been marked by the founding of new counties as the means for converting wilderness or waste land into private property. The political, legal, and military institutions of the county served to protect individual landholdings. Developments leading toward the creation of a town and country landscape were thus set in motion with the establishment of Frederick and Augusta Counties in 1738 and the laying out of county towns in 1744 and 1745, within months of the outbreak of hostilities between England and France in the War of the Austrian Succession. With the establishment of counties and the commissioning of their courts, the first phase of landscape evolution in the Shenandoah Valley drew to a close, and the founding of county towns initiated the second phase, which is treated in chapters five and six in this volume.

Winchester, as the new town in Frederick County came to be called, maintained many of the aspects of a garrison town throughout the 1750s and the Seven Years' War. It benefitted from the economic stimulus of military demand but remained poorly integrated into the economies of surrounding open-country neighborhoods. These still functioned within the decentralized world of household production and local exchange facilitated by a system of keeping accounts through the double or single entry and periodic balancing of debits and credits. Bookkeeping, not money, provided the medium of exchange in what can be called an exchange economy. The flow of goods and services through the reckoning of debits and credits over time allowed men and women to disperse across the landscape, maintain extensive trade among scattered households, and, through numerous and constant exchanges, achieve the competency that no single family could attain alone. The alternative political cultures that flourished in the independence of the resulting open-country neighborhoods also help explain clashes between local militiamen and colonial leaders in the imperial conflicts of the 1740s and 1750s.[10]

The closing years of the Seven Years' War, however, unleashed a flurry of new economic activity in backcountry areas as merchants in coastal ports

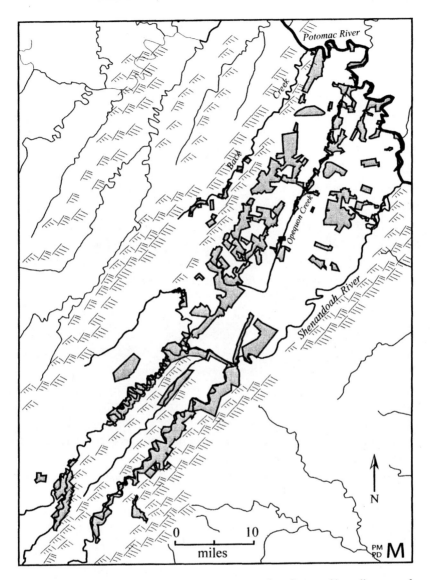

FIG. I.3. The Opequon Settlement, 1735. European settlers dispersed broadly across the Shenandoah Valley in establishing the Opequon settlement, depicted here by the extent of land patented by 1735. In search of natural resources, they created a landscape reflecting the values and mentality of economic competence. Based on maps by Galtjo Geertsema, in Cecil O'Dell, *Pioneers of Old Frederick County, Virginia* (Marceline, Mo.: Walsworth, 1995).

sought to capitalize on opportunities opened up by expanded sources of credit, new supplies of money, more concentrated settlements, and transportation improvements brought about by war and military demands. Winchester soon found itself within the market orbit of Philadelphia merchants, so the town began to assume economic functions more central and integral to surrounding neighborhoods.[11]

The landscape elements of open-country neighborhoods and a county town took root, therefore, as a consequence of political events that permeated the entire Atlantic world. After 1760, however, Atlantic-wide economic developments would produce a closer integration of town and country in the backcountry. These developments and their outcome in a coherent town and country landscape define the third phase of landscape evolution, traced to 1800 in the seventh chapter of this volume. During this period the European economy was transformed by dramatic increases in population, the beginning stages of the Industrial Revolution, the declining capacity of European agriculture to supply the needs of a growing, dependent population, and the consequent worldwide rise in the price of food, especially grains. By the late 1760s flour prices in Atlantic ports were sufficient for the first time to offset transportation costs from inland areas and allow backcountry farmers a profit from the flour they had long produced for home use and local exchange.[12]

The commercialization of the countryside, when combined with the so-called consumer revolution sweeping the Atlantic world, dramatically increased the interdependency of town and country in the Shenandoah Valley and expanded the economic functions of Winchester as a market town. Landscape change came to be driven by people wanting a better life. Flour exports, most destined for Alexandria, continued to leave this inland region from farms and mills in decentralized patterns long established in household economies. Profits, however, increased consumer demand in the countryside and directed the attention of farm families to market towns. There, merchants drawing upon commercial links dating to the Seven Years' War organized the import trade in consumer goods flowing through coastal ports, primarily Philadelphia. Because the long-distance trade depended increasingly on cash in the balance of payments, a commercial economy slowly began to replace the exchange economy, and towns developed as commercial centers. Thus town and country became linked in an integrated regional economy in which the export trade in provisions and the import trade in consumer goods remained spatially distinct but economically interdependent.[13]

The development of commercial agriculture and the establishment of market-town functions not only created what can be called a settlement system out of disparate rural communities and a county town, but these trends also had a profound impact on the visible landscape. Roads, which previously extended an irregular web across rural space, increasingly took on a new pattern linking rural communities to market towns as spokes of a wheel to the hub. Industrial enterprises, especially flour mills and iron furnaces, grew in number and significance. The local system of communications and trade became better linked to external markets and Atlantic ports. As goods and commodities began to move more rapidly through the system, so did people seeking backcountry lands farther and farther south, into the Carolinas and Georgia. More migrants meant more trade.

Transportation improvements and the greater profitability of Shenandoah Valley agriculture after the American Revolution also help explain the appearance of a new element in the settlement system—people whose primary cultural experience and social connections were with the plantation world of Tidewater Virginia. Onto lands claimed under the auspices of the Northern Neck Proprietary came tenants, overseers, and slaves, followed eventually by prominent and well-connected planter families. Although most of these men and women remained within the plantation orb of eastern Virginia, they introduced into the small-farm world of the Shenandoah Valley a social experience distinctive in its emphasis on deference and dependence, power and wealth, and international high culture. I have examined this encounter between Old and New Virginia within the Shenandoah Valley elsewhere, and because plantation economies suppressed town development, it will not play a prominent role in the analysis of town and country landscapes that follows.[14]

The decade of the 1780s brought peace in the struggle for political independence with Great Britain and if not immediate prosperity, at least an expansion of commercial agriculture that laid the foundation for sustained economic growth in the 1790s. Winchester had been incorporated in 1779 as the largest Virginia town west of the Blue Ridge, and the Kentucky Land Act of that year marked the passing of the Shenandoah Valley from backcountry to forecountry.[15] The retail sale of consumer goods increasingly locked town and country together as the export trade in agricultural commodities stimulated consumer demand in the countryside and inland merchants perfected methods of investment, credit, and cash accumulation to increase the flow of imports from coastal cities to towns like Winchester and, through them, to new western settlements. The landscape consequences were profound. Winchester remained the primary market town in the region, but more and more smaller-order places emerged, including crossroads hamlets with a store, mill, or shop and a few houses. Somewhat larger villages contained a multiple of functions and structures to house them but no regular market. These were not detached settlements. Instead, they were arrayed in a continuum extending from dispersed farms on one end to the market town of Winchester on the other. Rural producers and a hierarchy of central places were linked by an elaborating trade network in which Winchester merchants both organized the import retail trade in consumer goods and wholesaled these goods to merchants in smaller communities. As the backcountry now overspread the trans-Appalachian interior, Winchester merchants also retailed goods to rapidly growing numbers of migrants and managed a wholesale trade with merchants as far west as Kentucky and Tennessee.

Commodity production, the consumer revolution, and the retail and wholesale trades yielded a substantial increase in wealth, the pursuit of which in turn produced an increasing articulation of social classes, including an expanding slave population. By the end of the eighteenth century, 24 percent of the men and women of Frederick County were slaves.[16] Rising wealth also helped precipitate a comprehensive rebuilding of the landscape during the last decades of the century. Older dwellings in both town and country, often constructed in various folk vernaculars, gave way to new structures that reflected the international design tendencies of the Georgian and neoclassical periods. Field and road patterns were rationalized to make farm operations more efficient and transportation more effective. Winchester took on the characteristics of a "civic community." Not only were dwellings and shops rebuilt to express commercial respectability, but new institutions, such as a borough corporation, churches, schools, and newspapers, began to characterize a distinctive town life. Town life in the eighteenth century, however, was never alienated from its country context as the modern antithesis of urban and rural ways of life might suggest. Rebuilding was a process that drew town and country together as streets merged directly into roads, and dwellings throughout the countryside bore the same immediate relation to roads as town houses did to streets. Town and country remained a continuum.

· ☙ ·

As portrayed in this volume, the scope of the evolutionary process yielding a town and country landscape concerns all of the Shenandoah Valley. In the largest sense, political and economic developments encompassing the entire Atlantic world of the eighteenth century came to bear on this process. Yet as the analysis proceeds, its focus narrows from the whole Valley to the lower Valley settlement system, which, by 1800, had emerged around the primary town of Winchester and a functional continuum of surrounding villages, hamlets, and open-country neighborhoods. What happened here can serve as a model for comparable developments in town and country landscapes throughout the Shenandoah Valley and the broad swath of the North American interior for which the Valley served as forecountry well into the nineteenth century.

· ℔ ·

Historians and geographers have long been fascinated by the rural quality of early American life and challenged to explain the development of towns and town life within various rural contexts. The eighteenth-century backcountry and the recent attention focused upon it provide a new occasion for the study of how dispersed settlement populations evolved into complex settlement systems integrating the functions of self-sufficiency, commodity production, and rural consumption with the development of urban markets and market places. The principal theoretical question here concerns the work of centralizing forces in decentralized settlement economies and the emerging landscape of town and country.

The classic formula explaining centrality and urban functions is central-place theory. As worked out by Walter Christaller in the 1930s and modified later by August Lösch and others, central-place theory explains the concentration of economic activities in settlement clusters as a function of the retail trade in consumer goods. Centrality increases with the "surplus importance of a place, or the ability of a place to provide goods and services in excess of the needs of its own residents." The marketing of goods and services produces certain spatial regularities in ordering central places across a landscape. Furthermore, the different market ranges of goods and services in a sequence from nonspecialized to specialized explains the generation and function of an urban hierarchy. Shops specializing in imported goods and artisans producing high-style furniture or metal wares concentrate in larger places commanding larger market areas; blacksmiths and stores marketing country produce, in lower-order places.[17]

Certainly a central-place system had come to "nest" in the town and country landscape of Frederick County, Virginia, by the last two decades of the eighteenth century. Deprived of a handling trade in agricultural commodities, Winchester merchants organized the retail import trade, and market town became marketplace to a large region. In lower-order places, shopkeepers depended on these merchants for a stock in trade and on a smaller market area for customers. Central-place theory, however, fails to describe the emergence of this landscape. It does not account for how Winchester rose to the top of the urban hierarchy, nor does it explain the timing of the town's growth.

The town-rich landscape of the late-eighteenth-century Shenandoah Valley was also a material expression of the region's grain economy. The town-

poor landscape east of the Blue Ridge stood in stark contrast. Grain economies quite clearly generated a greater demand for auxiliary goods and services than did tobacco economies. Tobacco processing and packaging were
conducted independently by each producer. Grain farmers, however, brought
their wheat or rye to mills for grinding and barreling. Millers often arranged
for further transportation to market or sometimes took ownership of all or a
portion of the product and assumed additional costs of transportation, storage, and merchant commissions otherwise borne by the farmer. In either case,
grains called forth the services of numerous auxiliary specialists, including
millwrights, teamsters or carters, wagon makers, harness makers, wheelwrights, coopers, and numerous other tradesmen associated with the processing, storage, and transportation of flour. In theory, at least, these artisans clustered in backcountry towns, where merchants also collected shipments of flour
for consignment to coastal ports. Towns thus grew apace with the expansion
of the grain trade.[18]

In the Shenandoah Valley, however, the export of flour remained rooted in
the decentralized household economies established during the first phase of
settlement. Flour departed the region from mills dispersed by necessity across
the local system of rivers and creeks. Possessing only a weak and unreliable
water source, Winchester was separated from the nearest mill by more than a
mile. Many farmers, moreover, mixed a trade with crop and livestock production. The intensive service economies generated by staple agriculture neither
produced nor depended upon towns.

The problem here is not simply one of describing how urban functions
were performed in dispersed rural contexts; urban form cannot be divorced
from urban function, just as the town cannot be subsumed by the countryside.
Not only did the town-rich environment of the Shenandoah Valley and its
westward replications yield a hierarchy of central places, but towns themselves assumed a characteristic morphology of streets, grids, marketplaces,
civic spaces, and public buildings. Moreover, the thesis of this study maintains
that the systematic quality of interactions between farm families in rural communities and the purveyors of goods and services in towns gave form to a
town and country landscape. Form and function united in the creation of this
landscape.[19]

The missing link necessary to describe the mechanism supporting the town
and country landscape and explain its evolution can be found by enlarging the
scale of central-place analysis beyond the immediate terrain of the retail trade
to encompass the worldwide, long-distance wholesale trade. From this perspective, settlement formation in inland North America began not within the backcountry, as central-place theory would suggest, but outside it, as European co-

lonial trades established points of attachment along the Atlantic coast. Port merchants then redistributed goods to inland locations, or "unraveling points," as economic geographer James Vance called them. The distribution of wholesale imported goods was the first economic activity conducted in newly settled areas, according to Vance. The business of itinerant traders and peddlers was gradually taken over by merchants who imported and distributed manufactured goods. Eventually, a central-place system emerged from the settlement and transportation structure established initially by long-distance trade.[20]

The long-distance trade as a link between an integrated system of town-country exchanges and the larger framework of import and export functions successfully shifts the focus of attention from local relations to regional, colonial, imperial, and Atlantic-wide commercial connections. It also provides a mechanism for relating the timing of town formation in inland areas to the initiation of long-distance trade relations. Unfortunately, in the Shenandoah Valley, as throughout the southern backcountry, dispersed open-country neighborhoods preceded the establishment of towns, and the mechanisms of the exchange economy allowed for goods and services to flow readily throughout these neighborhoods with only tenuous connection to the Atlantic economy. Town formation had as much to do with the achievement of certain thresholds in rural productivity as it did with the wholesale trade.

· ☫ ·

Ultimately, an interpretation of the evolution and function of a town and country settlement landscape can best be told as a narrative that takes into account the various economic models provided by central-place, staple, functionalist, and long-distance trade theories and also looks at the more conventional historical fare—land policy, imperial relations, local and colonial government, war, capitalism, and consumerism. A narrative braiding contingent events into a complex story of landscape change possesses greater power to explain the progressive integration of town and country than do any of these theories. It begins with settlement dispersal, traces the growing influence of centrality through the various phases of settlement system integration, and concludes by linking town and country in a highly effective mechanism of Anglo-American expansionism and a powerful symbol of cultural imperialism.

Although this narrative unfolds according to schematic tensions between dispersal and centrality, it was driven at each point by human agency. What made the global strategies of territorial expansion work for imperial and colonial officials were the aspirations for independence pursued by Protestant families and the mentality of competency they infused into a new landscape. Behind the development of an Atlantic grain economy and an international consumer revolution lay the desires of people to translate agricultural profits into a fuller material life. Prosperity initially represented the fulfillment of collective aspirations in a republican society, and for many European travelers in the late eighteenth century, the Shenandoah Valley came to represent the moral independence and good life freehold-farm families could achieve when liberated from the oppressive hand of aristocracy. Only later, in the liberal economic state of the nineteenth century, did the pursuit of wealth betray a growing conviction that aggregated self-interest defined the public good.

This narrative of process and agency adds significant new elements to our understanding of the motive forces and meaning of landscape evolution during the eighteenth century. First, it enlarges the settlement story from a quest for land into an account of the regional consequences of struggles among European empires and American Indian nations for dominance and domain in the North American interior. Second, it looks at the ways various European ethnic and national groups organized a landscape of discrete open-country neighborhoods as a material outcome of a drive to achieve economic competency within the limits and opportunities of an exchange economy. Third, it attributes the evolution of more complex landscapes and the formation of towns to political processes in which the traditional institutions of county government reoriented dispersed communities first in relation to colonial garrisons and second to market towns. Fourth, it accounts for the elaboration and integration of town and country settlement forms in terms of worldwide movements in expanding grain markets, which penetrated deep into the production and consumption activities of men and women throughout the American backcountry. And finally, this narrative attributes the formation of integrated town and country landscapes to a growing American sophistication in the differential marketing of export commodities and import goods within the large trading regions that structured the geography of nineteenth-century American life. The world of town and country that would come to characterize, and in many ways epitomize, middle America had its inception not only in the motives of those who laid out and built its various landscape elements but also in the economic, social, and political forces pervading the entire Atlantic world in the final century of European expansion and conflict in North America.

Chapter 1

Empire and Encounter

A PROLOGUE

URING THE LATE FALL of 1742 a party of thirty Indians, mostly
Oneidas and Onondagas from the Six Nations Iroquois, departed
their homelands in New York and turned south along the Susquehanna River. They were headed for the Carolinas to raid long-standing enemies, the Catawbas. By October 10 they had reached some shallows along the
Susquehanna River where John Harris operated a ferry. There their leader, a
warrior named Jonnhaty, received a pass for safe travel through Pennsylvania
from Lancaster County magistrate John Hoge. Hoge shared some advice with
them: "The back Inhabitants of Virginia might perhaps Use them ill if they
travelled that Way, as there was no good Understanding between them." Hoge
would know; his father was a prominent landholder in what people in Pennsylvania and Virginia knew as the "opickin Settlement." Native Americans
called the region Jonontore. Encounters between Indians and settlers there
late that fall reveal many of the themes of this book.[1]

From Harris's ferry the Indian party headed south and west along the Great
Valley of the Appalachians (fig. 1.1). Beginning in the uplands of New England, this valley extended along the eastern fringe of Iroquoia and would
eventually lead the Indians to the Carolinas. West of the Susquehanna, however, they encountered few European settlers. Moravian missionaries traveling this same route one year later reported that they "found only two houses
within twenty miles" after passing through an uninhabited stretch of twenty-
five miles. Even the Moravians could get "nothing to eat, because the people
themselves had no bread." Living off the land, the Indians probably fared
better. If they followed the Conococheague Creek, they could have stopped at
the settlement of Charles Friend. Friend was well known to Native Americans, partly through his brother, Israel, who had once been designated by the

governor of Maryland as an emissary to them. Several years earlier Charles had preserved the life of a lone Delaware survivor of a Catawba attack. As the legend was carried down for a century in the area, a "most bloody battle was fought at the mouth of Conococheague, on Friend's land, in which but one Delaware escaped death, and he ran in to Friend's house, when the family shut the door, and kept the Catawbas out."[2]

When the Indians crossed the Potomac River is not known, but they probably entered Opequon sometime in late October or early November. They were moving slowly, covering in two months the same ground they would later recross in about three weeks under the press of a gathering crisis. For now, however, they paused to hunt, fish, and spend time in the settlements. In 1742 there were somewhat fewer than five thousand people living in Jonontore, an area the English also called the Shenandoah Valley. Twenty or so miles at its widest and seventy-five miles long, it was framed by the Blue Ridge on the east and the Allegheny Front on the west. Through this valley flowed the Shenandoah River and the Opequon Creek. Native Americans had occupied this gently rolling land for more than a hundred centuries before the arrival of Europeans. Indigenous societies had seen a long, slow evolution from the nomadic, big-game hunters of the Paleo-Indian Period, which lasted until about 8000 B.C., through the development of more settled societies, as the climate warmed and the environment diversified across the next six millennia of the Archaic Period, and finally to the emergence of agricultural villages during the Woodland Period. Conflicts over trade and territory between the Iroquois and their counterparts living throughout the upper Ohio–upper Potomac region, however, had led to the abandonment of the Shenandoah Valley in the seventeenth century and to its appearance as vacant land to European settlers.[3]

Most settlements in the northern, or lower Shenandoah Valley, were clustered along the Opequon. Farther south settlers had taken up the bottomlands along the Shenandoah's forks. Dispersal was Opequon's salient feature. There were no forts (or stations, as they were later called in Kentucky) and no large areas of contiguous settlement. Settlers often tucked four, five, or six holdings together, with as many as thirty to forty along the creek's fanlike drainages. Families nonetheless decided to build their dwellings and farmsteads according to which bottomland terrace provided the best access to water and also the greatest protection from floods. Three-hundred- to four-hundred-acre tracts of land thus allowed for a quarter to a half mile between dwellings. Separating these open-country neighborhoods of adjoining tracts were large areas of unoccupied land.[4]

From the point of view of Indian travelers, this selfsame dispersal linked Opequon to the world they knew. In the seventeenth century Indian towns

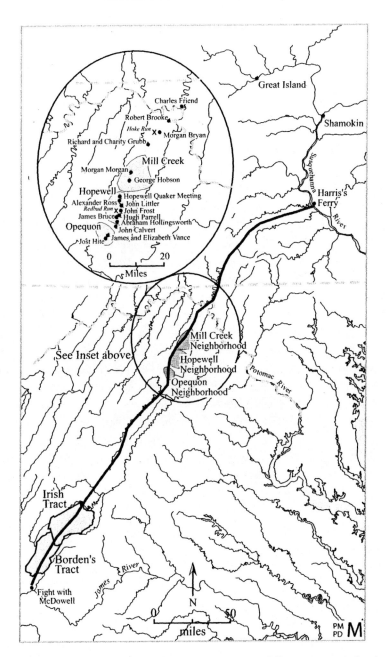

FIG. 1.1. Jonnhaty's Journey through Jonontore. During fall 1742 Iroquois headman Jonnhaty led a party of thirty Oneidas and Onondagas through central Pennsylvania to the Shenandoah Valley of Virginia, a region the Indians called Jonontore. After a skirmish with armed settlers along the James River, the Indians beat a hasty retreat to Great Island and along the West Branch of the Susquehanna River.

were tightly clustered settlements often surrounded by palisades and called castles by the English. Neutrality in the Anglo-French imperial wars of the eighteenth century, however, had allowed Indians to spread out. Onondaga, at the very heart of Iroquoia, was, according to Philadelphia botanist John Bartram, a town "about 2 or 3 miles long, yet the scattered cabins on both sides the water, are not above 40 in number, many of them hold 2 families, but all stand single, and rarely above 4 or 5 near one another." Moravians visiting Onondaga in 1750, eight years after Bartram, described it as "very much scattered, . . . 5 small towns beside the single scattered huts." And Bartram said that Shamokin, through which the Indians had passed on their trek down the Susquehanna, was nothing more than "eight cabbins near the river's bank."[5]

Dispersal of the Indian villages had, in fact, alarmed the English. Only a few months prior to the departure of the Oneidas and Onondagas, the lieutenant governor of New York, George Clarke, had castigated their leaders, declaring: "It is with much concern I hear that most of the six Nations have of late years lived dispersed forgetting their Ancient Custom of dwelling together in Castles. I cannot let slip this opportunity of exhorting you to return to your Primitive way of liveing together as your Ancestors did . . . whereas a scattered people will soon become contemptible in the eyes of the world and the common interest and safety of the Community will give place to private Views." The Indians were evidently intent upon pursuing private views, and conditions in new Delaware and Shawnee settlements farther west along the Allegheny and Ohio Rivers were much the same. Kittanning, for instance, consisted of seven clusters of dwellings, which housed related lineages and stretched a quarter mile along terraces overlooking the Allegheny River. Fields were scattered on bottomlands below. Essential to the community, but not central in the town, was a longhouse, for "frolicks and War Dances." Because westward migration occurred in fragments made up of families or single men, not whole villages, western towns tended to be multiethnic combinations of diverse tribal groupings.[6]

Dispersal throughout the Indian towns and the Opequon settlement does not mean that the landscapes created by Indians and Europeans looked the same but only that Native American travelers may have found more that was familiar at Opequon than was strange or alien. Native Americans knew what the landscape changes attending European settlement meant for their way of life. Reckoning the extent and quality of land for its capacity to sustain life for bands and tribes, Indians feared the signs of land surveys, which signified the private property of individuals or families claiming exclusive access to nature's resources. Indians called a surveyor's compass the "land stealer." Lacking domesticated animals of their own, Native Americans saw fences not only as an impediment to their travel but also as a symbol of the fragmentation of land that otherwise meant wholeness and identity to them. Roads granting public access across private property seemed incongruous to people who moved freely across terrain, frequently navigating by natural landmarks alone. But roads more often than not traversed property holdings instead of running along their boundaries. Because surveyors marked only property corners, which could be some distance from roads, and because settlers fenced small fields around their dwellings to keep cattle out instead of fencing their property lines to keep cattle in, few signs were visible from the road to distinguish one holding from the next.[7]

Even the log houses many settlers had erected might not have impressed the Indian visitors as an exclusive mark of Europeanness. By 1740 many Iroquois lived in cabins, with only a central, open hearth and smoke hole to distinguish them from the dwellings of Europeans. Like Indian towns, the open-country neighborhoods consisted of kin groups living close together. Nevertheless, these neighborhoods were ethnically varied. Settlers with English ancestry were in a minority everywhere west of the Blue Ridge. Far more numerous were Germans and Scots-Irish immigrants who had passed through Philadelphia, often stopping in Pennsylvania for several years before heading to the Virginia backcountry.

· ✛ ·

If the Indians followed the path—or road, as it was designated for Iroquois travel a few years later—they would have moved south and west, crossing the land of Robert Brooke at Falling Water. Brooke had been designated surveyor of the "Lands on Sherrando River" some ten years earlier. In 1716, however, he had joined one of the first exploring parties of Europeans in the Shenandoah Valley. Alexander Spotswood, governor of Virginia from 1710 to 1722, had just been apprised of newly found passes over the Blue Ridge. Wanting to see these discoveries and fearful that they might speed hostile French or Indian warriors across one of Virginia's natural defenses, Spotswood assembled a troop of sixty-three horsemen, including Brooke, and left Williamsburg in August. The party crossed the Blue Ridge and arrived on the banks of the Shenandoah River in early September. Although Spotswood and his men tarried in the Valley only long enough to claim the land for King George I and raise a few toasts with volleys of gunfire, what Brooke saw must have whetted his appetite for frontier land. Brooke later served as deputy clerk for Essex County and surveyor for Essex and Caroline Counties in the East, but by 1732 he was back in the Shenandoah Valley. During the next two years he surveyed eighty-two tracts for land-hungry settlers. He probably did not live on the Falling Water tract but held it in hope of selling it in the future.[8]

While in the vicinity of the Potomac River the Indians were not far from the scene of yet earlier explorations by Europeans. In 1707 Franz Louis Michel had spent sufficient time here to map most of the lower Shenandoah Valley. Michel also left the earliest account of the environment that Jonnhaty and his party encountered. In addition to oak forests abounding with game, Michel described "land that is dry and barren and where it is difficult to pass through the wild brush-wood." In choosing oaks for about two-thirds of their witness trees at property corners, later surveyors such as Brooke confirmed Michel's observation that oak trees dominated the forest cover. The Iroquois would also have passed under a canopy of numerous hickories in a woodland ensemble that included walnuts, poplars, maples, sycamores, linden, and box elder. Michel's "dry and barren" land probably lay in the center of the Shenandoah Valley, where a band of thin, infertile soil supported a poorer forest of chestnut oak and various pines, including Virginia, pitch, and short leaf. Michel, however, might also have been referring to the natural openings that characterized much of the land between the Blue Ridge and the Allegheny Front. Seventeenth-century explorers traveling along the east slopes of the Blue Ridge called them "savanae." A later traveler crossing the Great Valley of the Appalachians in Pennsylvania passed through "large Plains, or as the Inhabitants call them, Glades, quite bare of Timber, & covered with Shrubs, Ground-Oak, Hazles, &c."[9]

What caused these openings in the forests is not clear. Indians throughout eastern North America burned the land less to level forests than to hold back the understory and facilitate both travel and hunting. They did clear land around villages for farming and left what settlers often called Indian "old fields." The Pennsylvania traveler observed that the "large open Plains" he found were "cleared either by the Indians, or by accidental Fire." But many years earlier, when asked by John Smith of Jamestown what was "beyond the mountaines," an Indian interpreter had responded "the Sunne: but of any thing els he knew nothing; because the woods were not burnt," and thus Indians had not traveled there. Many meadows, however, flanked streams and were maintained by periodic flooding. Traveling along the Opequon Creek our Pennsylvanian found "large & rich Meadows—Many have good Grass on the Uplands." Whatever the natural or cultural mechanisms maintaining meadows and glades, the environment Jonnhaty and his party encountered would have been varied—a mosaic of forest and open land. Edge habitat thus characterized much of the Shenandoah Valley. Many native animals favored this forest-grassland boundary, which in turn attracted early hunters, both Indian and white.[10]

To European settlers streamside meadows meant good land they did not have to clear. Here access to water combined quite conveniently with the vistas required for defense and the grasslands needed for livestock. As the Iroquois proceeded south, keeping the Opequon Creek on their left, they would cross every few miles stream after stream flowing eastward to mingle waters with the Opequon. Complex geologic forces at work for hundreds of millions of years on the earth's crust had left exposed bands of limestone with a central ribbon of shale all aligned with the strike of the Valley. The Opequon itself flowed northward along the line where shale and limestone formations met. Conforming to structural weaknesses in the shale bedrock, the creek's tributaries extended westward in the geometry of a gardener's trellis. So the journey of Jonnhaty and his party was one of ups and downs—long traverses over wooded, seemingly unoccupied uplands and brief descents to a string of cabins lining a stream and its bordering meadows.[11]

· ⚜ ·

Following the road for another three miles the Indians would eventually have dropped down along Hoke Run, which emptied into the Opequon near the Potomac River. Here they would have encountered Morgan Bryan and his family. Bryan operated a mill along the stream and lived nearby. Of Irish descent but born in Denmark, the septuagenarian Bryan had previously lived along Brandywine Creek in Chester County, Pennsylvania. There he had been a member of the New Garden meeting of the Society of Friends and husband to Dutch-born Martha Strode. But Bryan possessed a restless streak. In 1724 he moved west to Pequea Creek, in territory later to become Lancaster County. Then he heard of even greater opportunities in Virginia. Having "set forth that they & divers other Families of the sd Province [of Pennsylvania] amounting to one hundred are desirous to remove from thence & Settle them Selves in the Government [of Virginia]," Bryan, with fellow New Garden Quaker Alexander Ross, received orders from the governor and Council on October 28, 1730, for "100[,]000 Acres of land lying on the west & North Side of the River Opeckan." Two years after Jonnhaty's passage, Bryan would relocate more than a hundred miles south in the Shenandoah Valley. Ever on the move, however, he ended his days as the patriarch of the Bryan settlement along the Yadkin River in North Carolina. Bryan's roving interests in acquiring land and founding new settlements placed him among those quintessentially rootless frontiersmen so common in the later history of the United States.[12]

Bryan's Quaker identity also imposed upon him the status of outsider in the Anglo-American culture of the colonies to which he was migrating. So too did the hunting culture, which pervaded the Opequon settlement. John Bartram commented, while traveling through Opequon in 1738 on a botanizing venture to Virginia, that the "mountains is very thinly inhabited with [people] that is lately settled there & lives A lazy life & subsists by hunting." Bryan was, in fact, connected closely with the family of America's most famous frontier hunter, Daniel Boone. Bryan's son William married Boone's sister, and Boone's own wife was Bryan's granddaughter. The Boones lived a few miles down the Yadkin from the Bryans in North Carolina and hunted there, as well as later in Kentucky. Hunters set their sights on a variety of game, including bear, raccoon, and opossum, all of which were abundant on the Virginia and Carolina frontiers. But white-tailed deer constituted the principal quarry. So predacious were hunters in their quest for deer and their valuable skins that in the same year Bartram passed through Opequon, the Virginia Assembly took steps to protect the colony's deer population. The "Act, for better preservation of the breed of Deer, and preventing unlawful Hunting" was, as Governor William Gooch put it, designed to check the "unaccountable Practices of many idle vagrant Fellows, near the Frontiers." Their "sucy pernicious Doings" such as "watching . . . [deer] in their retreats in the Rivers, and killing them there," letting hounds "go at large," "Fire Hunting which is setting the woods on Fire in large Circles inclosing a number of Deer therein, and then Shooting them when forced together by the Violence of the Flames," and "Hunt[ing] on his Neighbour's Land without Licenes" were destroying the planters' game.[13]

These practices were precisely those that frontier hunters had borrowed from Native Americans; indeed, the hunting culture of the frontier was a fusion of European and Indian practices. Few immigrants to the English colonies in the eighteenth century would have possessed much familiarity with hunting. For most Europeans, to hunt was to poach, because what few game animals remained in western Europe were the personal property of the upper classes and considered the object of sport, not survival or profit. To the culture of hunting in America, Europeans brought metallurgy and firearms. Muskets, shotguns, and steel knives were essential, but most valued of all was the long rifle. Accurate at distances up to five times greater than the range of the musket, the long rifle was the innovation of Pennsylvania gunsmiths and the preeminent weapon of the frontier deer slayer.

The techniques of the hunt, however, were borrowed from the Indians. First and foremost the Indians studied their prey—learning their habits, searching out their haunts, appeasing their spirits. For the Indians, to hunt was to enter the world of animals, to watch them "in their retreats," and to antic-ipate their fears. Driving game with fire was not simply a crude means to the slaughter but a communion of the hunter and the hunted in the presence of nature's most awesome force. Some Europeans came to understand this world. As Joseph Doddridge put it in his "Notes . . . on the manners of the first settlers" of western Virginia and Pennsylvania, "the whole business of the hunter consists of a succession of intrigues. From morning 'till night he was on the alert to *gain the* wind of his game, and approach them without be-ing discovered. . . . It should seem that after hunting awhile on the same ground, the hunters became acquainted with nearly all the gangs of deer within their range, so as to know each flock of them when they saw them."[14]

Frontier hunters dressed like their Indian counterparts. They wore mocca-sins, hunting shirts, breechclouts, leggings, and fur caps. They hung their belts with powder horns, bullet pouches, knives, and tomahawks. "Our young men became more enamoured of the indian dress throughout," observed Dodd-ridge, "The drawers were laid aside and the leggins made longer, so as to reach the upper part of the thigh. The indian breech clout was adopted. . . . The young warrior instead of being abashed by this nudity was proud of his indian like dress." Thus the people who offended Bartram when he passed through Opequon possessed habits and manners familiar to those of Jonnhaty and his men. No doubt their farmsteads were littered with the signs of out-door life—skins tacked to walls or stretched on frames to dry, rough tables or boards set out for slaughtering, animal bones strewn across yards, and open-air fires for cooking, rendering, or boiling. Bartram saw Opequon in October. Men would have been resting for the hunt—many would be in the woods from late fall to early spring. By mid-fall much of the work of harvesting winter grains was finished and next year's crop was already in the ground. Women performed the daily tasks of dairying, milling, and preparing food. Thus, what seemed a "lazy life" to Bartram may have been nothing more than a res-pite before the hard work of the hunt to come. Europeans often made the same observation about Indian men, who, when not hunting, fighting, or politick-ing, seemed to lie around with little to do while abandoning to women what in European culture were the manly duties of farming.[15]

· ⚶ ·

Jonnhaty's visit with Bryan is, of course, only hypothetical. But whether the two hunted together, conversed over a fire, or shared a meal, their possible en-counter need not be thought of as one between people strange to each other's ways. Misunderstanding and hostility always lurked in the background, as events would soon prove, but as the Oneidas and Onondagas proceeded south, there was as much familiar in what they experienced as foreign or threatening. They next encountered European settlements along Tuscarora Creek, where the road forked. If the Indians took the west branch of the road they would have traveled through the lands of the Beeson family. Richard and his wife, Charity Grubb, were Quakers who had removed from the New Garden Meeting to Virginia in 1736 and the next year purchased 1,650 acres along the Tuscarora. In the year and a half following Jonnhaty's journey, this couple divided their lands among their sons Richard, Edward, Benjamin, John, and William, and their son-in-law Mordecai Mendenhall. Each family possessed a roughly rectangular tract that spanned the creek. The proximity of kin in dwellings strung along a creek would have struck the Oneidas and Onondagas as a community similar to their own.[16]

Several miles farther down the road the Indians would have passed through the much larger open-country community that had developed along the banks of Middle and Mill Creeks. Here they may have been looking for George Hobson or Morgan Morgan. Both were justices of the peace, and the Indians needed their services. The pass acquired from John Hoge in Pennsylvania no longer served to authenticate their presence. In their own words, "they wanted to go to some Justice to have their Pass renewed." Hobson and Morgan were important men at Opequon; they sat on the court of Orange County, which convened monthly across the Blue Ridge in a small courthouse near Raccoon Ford on the Rapidan River. There the justices heard civil and criminal cases, registered deeds and wills, probated estates, and performed administrative functions such as establishing roads, designating mill seats, or setting rates charged at taverns and ferries. The appointment of Hobson and Morgan had come in 1734 from the governor and Council in answer to a petition from the people of Opequon "praying that some persons may be appointed as Magistrates to determine Differences and punish Offenders in regard the Petitioners live far remote from any of the established Counties within the Colony." Having a great distance to travel to court, Hobson and Morgan were not "oblidged to give their Attendance as Justices" at court sessions.[17]

Justices such as Hobson and Morgan did much of their work not from the magistrates bench but in their own homes. Here they settled suits for small debts—the most numerous kind in an economy that worked on credit. A creditor, fearing the imminent departure of a debtor, could appear before a justice of the peace for a writ instructing the sheriff to attach sufficient goods of the debtor to secure the debt. Justices also worked to keep the peace. They could protect those threatened with assault by binding the accused with surety for good behavior. When someone broke the law, justices could bond the offender to keep the peace or face the court's indictment. Those who resisted could be jailed. According to the laws of Virginia, justices could exercise these powers "if a Man do affront any Court of Justice" or against "Night-Walkers . . . who are suspected to steal any Thing in the Night," against "such who frequent Gaming Houses . . . and have no Estates to support themselves," against "those who contrive, procure, or publish, scandalous Letters, or Libels, whether true or false," against "a Woman that is a common Scold," against "those who lie in Wait, or attempt to rob another," and so on. Even those suspected of "mis-behaviour of any Kind whatsoever" could come under the powers of the justice of the peace.[18]

Native Americans distinguished their own leaders by a variety of nonhereditary titles or simply by recognition on merit. Headmen gained influence by the number and kin of their followers or by their sway over domestic concerns, warfare, and diplomacy. The kind of power that men such as Hobson and Morgan exerted over people at Opequon was vastly different from the power held by Iroquois headmen. Like justices throughout Virginia, they held their powers by appointment from the governor, who, as the designate of the king, represented the royal prerogative in the colony. By virtue of their position in a political hierarchy, justices exercised power through the law and through the will of the state to use force in upholding that law. Thus, if an accused person broke the peace or failed to appear in court, the sheriff could throw him or her in jail. The office of magistrate existed above and beyond the particular qualities or character of the officeholder.

To Iroquois headmen, however, power existed only in the ability to influence the thoughts or actions of others; power resided more in the person than in the office. Men achieved power not by appointment but through their ability to persuade, to gather a following, to act on kinship responsibilities, and to bestow gifts or privileges. Headmen often led, collectively and individually, by building a consensus among themselves and their followers. What they lacked was the ability to coerce. No leader could impose his will on the people by force. Personal disputes, even crimes against persons, were reconciled by retribution or compensation under pain of retribution. Women held real power in Iroquois society. As matriarchs in a matrilineal and matrilocal world, in which identity and place followed female associations, women held property in food, houses, and fields, they dominated the affairs of villages, and they not only selected male leaders but also influenced them through women's councils. The men who followed Jonnhaty through Jonontore would, therefore, have sought out Opequon's headmen with expectations about power and leadership very different from the nature of the power Hobson and Morgan wielded.

Nonetheless, Jonnhaty and other headmen among the Iroquois warriors would have regarded Hobson, Morgan, and their fellow justices as equals from whom could be expected the civilities due a visitor, such as food, shelter, or a pass of safe conduct. In some respects the position of Hobson and Morgan in their community may not have differed too radically from that of their Iroquois counterparts. For headmen in both cultures power was negotiated. Their wealth certainly distinguished Hobson and Morgan from their neighbors and identified them as likely justices in 1734. Hobson controlled 5,098 acres and Morgan 1,000, when the average landholding at Opequon stood at approximately 330 acres. But affluence in Anglo-American society was based as much on a man's ability to draw upon the obligations of neighbors as on money or possessions. In fact, the European fixation on the conspicuous display of tangible wealth had much to do with the inconspicuous nature of these obligations. A merchant could live well not on income as money but on the credit earned by distributing goods on account. A large landowner could literally transform land into labor. The capacity to build and furnish a large or fine house, for example, did not depend solely on the capital a wealthy person controlled but upon the goods and artisanal services the affluent could call in to balance long-standing accounts. The mason paid for dry goods by laying stone, the carpenter retired his debt on a small holding by setting window frames or raising a roof, the blacksmith fashioned hinges and latches, and so on, until the house was built and furnished. Few erected fine houses on the frontier in the 1740s, but the role of debits, credits, and keeping accounts would have been doubly important in the cash-poor economy there. So wealth was always relative to what others could pay or, more importantly, do. It had to be constantly negotiated in a network of obligations. To be wealthy meant to have considerably more than an average share of credit to draw upon. Insofar as wealth meant status and status could be converted to power in the office of the magistrate, the power of men such as Hobson and Morgan at Opequon rested upon the influence they could exert among neighbors and the mutual influences that bound neighbors into a community. Jonnhaty and his followers could readily understand this kind of power.

What Hobson and Morgan could do that Jonnhaty could not was to exercise the coercive power of the state to enforce written laws and abstract justice. There were no sheriffs, constables, or jails in Iroquois society; no writs, summonses, sentences, or executions. Armed force could be exerted at any place and any time for any purpose by any warriors with the will to fight, the ability to gather a following, and the political skills to justify violence. Jonnhaty had no doubt raised his war party through just this kind of personal influence. In Virginia, armed force to be lawful had to be contained within the county militias or, in times of emergency, within duly constituted regiments of a colonial army. No one was free to use personal violence in seeking to right wrongs, either against individuals or society. But there were no sheriffs, constables, or jails in the Shenandoah Valley in the fall of 1742. The court met sixty-five miles away. Morgan had been appointed captain in the Orange Militia on February 17, 1735, but no militia units in the Shenandoah Valley were mustering regularly. For Hobson and Morgan, the coercive power of the state bordered on an abstraction. They could not rely upon it to reinforce their positions as justices. Individuals could be bound to answer indictments at court, but justices possessed no investigative powers. They could act only if conflicts or crimes were brought to their attention or if "any Person, who, in his Presence, or Hearing, shall mis-behave himself in some outrageous Manner of Force, or Fraud." Many offenses were resolved by the parties themselves or through mediation within families or religious congregations. Here too the powers of the magistrates were not pervasive but were constantly negotiated in the give and take of daily affairs within their communities. Just as Jonnhaty and his warriors understood the kind of power Hobson and Morgan possessed, so the cultural experience of the Indians would have led them to comprehend the limitations of power on the Anglo-American frontier.[19]

· ☙ ·

The Indians may never have located Hobson, Morgan, or "some Justice" for the sake of a pass. At least they admitted they "could find none." But they probably encountered an alternative source of authority in the Opequon community when, continuing southwest on any of several paths, they would soon have passed by or near the Hopewell Meeting House of the Society of Friends on the lands of Alexander Ross. Ross had used his land orders from the colonial government to acquire 2,373 acres for himself, and he built his home not far from a gently flowing stream that emptied into the Opequon Creek. Sometime before the spring of 1734 he proposed "on behalf of ffriends att Opeckon that a Meeting for worship may be Settled among'st them." The Quakers who gathered at Hopewell composed an open-country community dispersed along streams and roads throughout a surrounding sixteen-square-mile area. Ross was in his early fifties when he established the meeting. He had been born in Ireland, and when or how he became a Quaker is not known. He was still a boy when he migrated to Pennsylvania, where he was apprenticed to a last maker. By his early twenties he was working as a joiner and married to Katherine Chambers. The young family moved west, first to Radnor, then to a five-hundred-acre farm on the Conowingo Creek near the Susquehanna River, and finally to Opequon in the early 1730s. Ross and his partner, Morgan Bryan, had promised the Virginia government one hundred settlers for the Shenandoah Valley frontier; by 1734 they had brought in seventy.[20]

Quakers lived largely according to their own, self-constituted authority. Steadfastly refusing to swear oaths in recognition of the state's or any power over their lives but God's, they had gained the right through Pennsylvania and parliamentary legislation simply to affirm their loyalty to the crown as a prerequisite to holding office, serving on a jury, or testifying in court. In practice Quakers avoided the judicial institutions of local government whenever possible. Most Quakers chose instead to reconcile their differences before peers in their own meeting. At Hopewell in 1748, for example, Evan Thomas and William Jolliffe admitted to "having transgressed the rules of our Discipline . . . through carelessness & unwatchfulness have–suffered ourselves to be so far overcome with passion & anger which tended to fighting & quarreling with each other." The two men condemned their actions and promised in the presence of fellow Quakers "to be more careful & circumspect in our lives and—Conversations for the time to come." Thomas and Jolliffe thereby assumed joint responsibility for their behavior, and eschewing blame, they bound themselves in the witness of equals to keep the peace in the future. A resolution of their conflict through the English common law of magistrates such as Hobson and Morgan would have required one to be plaintiff or accuser, the other, defendant or the accused. An end to their strife would have come only with the triumph of one over the other in exoneration or in guilt and punishment.[21]

Quaker attitudes toward self and community had real consequences for the landscape. Quakers denied the world by living plainly but embraced worldly success as a sign of right living, hard work, and God's blessing. Strong advocates of private property, they viewed personal wealth as a trust for the welfare of the community. Wherever possible they supported, sustained, and worked with or for one another. Mutual assistance had helped place Quakers among the wealthiest people in Pennsylvania. Likewise, these traits would allow them to do very well in Virginia. Quakers also possessed a profound respect for the original inhabitants of the land. Quaker elders had admonished the Hopewell settlers that they must "be very careful (being far and back inhabitants) to keep a friendly correspondence with the native Indians, giving them no occasion for offense; they being a cruel and merciless enemy, where they think they are wronged or defrauded of their rights."[22]

Ross and the Hopewell Quakers may or may not have discussed matters of right—especially rights to land—with Jonnhaty, but if the Iroquois continued along the road toward the Carolinas, they would soon have encountered another Quaker who had already demonstrated his impartiality, if not openness, in dealings with the Indians. About three miles from Hopewell Meeting House and on a tributary of Opequon Creek named Redbud Run lived Hugh Parrell. At about the same time that the Hopewell Quakers had been cautioned about honesty in Indian affairs, a group of Delawares called at Parrell's house. They were returning home from raiding among the Catawbas and "exulted much at their success." What happened next passed into the folklore of the Shenandoah Valley as collected and recorded in the early nineteenth century by writer and historian Samuel Kercheval. "The next day a party of ten Catawbas called at Mr. Perrill's in pursuit. They inquired when their enemy had passed. Being informed, they pushed off at a brisk step, overtook the thirty Delawares at the Cohongoruton (Potomac), killed every man, recovered their prisoner, called at Mr. Perrill's on their return, and told what they had done."[23]

· ☙ ·

Parrell's troubled encounter with the Delawares and Catawbas revealed an intriguing feature of the landscape. Parrell lived along a path that, according to a survey by Robert Brooke in late October 1734, led "from John Littlers to Abraham Hollensworths." During the year before Jonnhaty's party traveled this route, the Orange County Court had made it into a public road. Littler, Hollingsworth, and Parrell all belonged to the Hopewell Meeting. So did John Frost, James Bruce, and John Calvert, who lived along the six miles between Littler and Hollingsworth. These men and their families were bound by kinship as well as religious ties. Littler was Alexander Ross's son-in-law and Parrell, Bruce, and Calvert were all related to one another by marriage. That these men settled adjacent tracts of land is no surprise. Their line of tracts, however, conformed to two features of the landscape, one natural and the other cultural.[24]

Each of the tracts along the path from Littler's to Hollingsworth's straddled the contact between the shale and limestone beds that stretched the length of the Shenandoah Valley (fig. 1.2). In other words, these properties contained some limestone land and some shale land. Shale and limestone created not only distinct topographies but different soils as well. Limestone weathered into rounded uplands and low ridges aligned with the Valley. These landforms enclosed broad and sinuous streams flanked by numerous terraces and benches. Since much of the land drained through underground solution channels, springs were common. Deep and fertile limestone soils made for the "good land" Michel described and supported the "great forest trees" he found on it. Shale, on the other hand, drained water across its surface and yielded a deeply dissected landscape of steep, V-shaped valleys with narrow bottomlands exhibiting few features conducive to agricultural settlement. Soils on the uplands were thin and infertile. These were Michel's "dry and barren" lands, where pines predominated.[25]

Did Littler, Frost, Parrell, Bruce, Calvert, and Hollingsworth cast their land claims so as to capture a diversity of landscapes, soils, and resources characteristic of shale and limestone lands? Aside from the varying topographies of shale and limestone, could these men tell much about the different soil qualities? Most likely they could. Europeans commonly read the merits of soils and their potential for agriculture from the trees. According to John Bartram, "ye woods Consisting at first of Oaks Hicories Poplars Walnuts & c. . . . mark . . . much better land than what bears pines." That better soils supported a mixed oak-hickory forest and poor soils, pine, was also suggested by

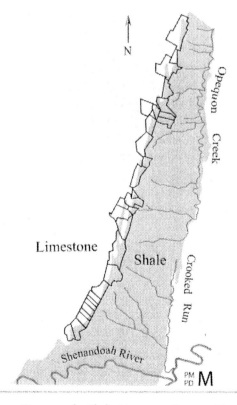

FIG. 1.2. Settlement Tracts on the Shale-Limestone Contact. Many of the earliest settlers in the Shenandoah Valley devised tracts that engrossed both productive limestone and less-fertile shale land. Based on maps by Geertsema, in O'Dell, *Pioneers of Old Frederick County*.

other visitors to the southern backcountry late in the eighteenth century. John F. D. Smyth observed that "by the different species and growth . . . the quality and excellence of the soil is easily discovered; for those grounds which bear the oak, the poplar, the walnut, the sassafras and the hickory, are extremely, fertile; . . . The pine barren is the worst of all." Nicholas Cresswell, a contemporary of Smyth who once contemplated establishing a farm not far from Hopewell Meeting, also made the link between forest cover and soil fertility. "Limestone in general," he said "abounds with Shumack, Walnut, and Locust trees which are certain indications that the Lands are rich." If shale soils were demonstrably poorer, why would early settlers, who had their pick of new lands, select any on shale? They may have eyed the comparatively level uplands as ideal pasturage. Or as one Opequon settler asserted, shale was regarded as superior for the cultivation of flax.[26]

The other feature of the land that might have influenced where Littler, Frost, and the others placed their settlements was the path itself. Most likely the route from Littler's to Hollingsworth's was only one segment of the much longer Indian path that led from Pennsylvania to the Carolinas. During 1744 treaty negotiations at Lancaster, Pennsylvania, representatives of the Six Nations pointed out that they "had not been long in the Use of this new Road, before your People came like Flocks of Birds, and sat down on both Sides of it." If a preexisting Indian road or path determined where at least some Europeans settled, then why the Indian route followed the contact between shale and limestone formations requires explanation. East of the contact the land grew more and more deeply cleaved by steep-sided stream valleys. This was land for even the foot traveler to avoid. Limestone lands to the west of the contact, however, offered many convenient routes. But forest openings, edge habitats, environmental variation, and species diversity predominated where one type of forest on shale land gave way to another on limestone. What was evidently good hunting for Indian travelers might therefore also have meant cleared land prized by Europeans for settlements. Whether cultural factors such as road placement or the ecologies of shale and limestone land influenced the settlement choices of Europeans may never be determined, but European actions on the land leave little doubt that there was a system to their settlement that was closely attuned to a combination of cultural and natural features.[27]

· ⚘ ·

From Hugh Parrell's the road continued southwest, leading Jonnhaty and his party of Indian warriors across a level upland between the drainages of Redbud Run and Abrams Creek. After three miles they would have reached Abraham Hollingsworth's mill, and proceeding another five miles, the home of Jost

Hite (fig. 1.3). Hite, like Hobson and Morgan, was a justice of the peace. If Jonnhaty was still seeking a pass, he probably would have made a point of calling at Hite's. Hite was a hard man to miss on any account. A native of Bonfeld in the Kraichgau region of south-central Germany, Hite had been in the English colonies for more than three decades. Under the auspices of Queen Anne he had joined thirteen thousand Palatinates seeking refuge in England in 1709 from devastations worked along the Rhine by poverty, crop failures, and the War of the Spanish Succession. Twenty-five hundred of these people, including Hite, left London the next year for New York under an agreement to produce naval stores, such as tar and pitch, until the costs of their support and transportation had been paid. Colonial officials also sent along instructions to the governor of New York, Robert Hunter, to locate the Germans on the fringes of English and Dutch settlement, where these foreign immigrants could provide a buffer against the French. Supplies furnished the settlement included six hundred guns. The naval stores project never paid off, and locating lands for the Germans troubled the New York government for years. The experience, however, provided valuable lessons for Hite about settling the English frontier and the imperial purposes of extending it toward French settlements and Indian lands. Hite, in fact, belonged to a cohort of German immigrants, including Conrad Weiser, Jacob Stover, and other men, who would play a critical role in defining and expanding that frontier in the years to come.[28]

Hite soon married and moved to a "very valuable piece of Land" on Perkiomen Creek in Pennsylvania. About 1730, however, he heard reports "that the Government of Virginia proposed to give Encouragement for the Settlement of the Frontiers of that Colony which were much exposed to the Incursions of the Indians and other enemies." Taking the cue from previous experiences, Hite, with partner Robert McKay, petitioned the Virginia government "that they & divers others Families to the number of one hundred are desirous to remove from thence & seat themselves on the back of the great Mountains." Hite was soon in possession of land orders for 140,000 acres in the Shenandoah Valley and an obligation to recruit and settle 140 families for the Virginia frontier. By the end of 1735 he had secured close to one hundred.[29]

Under these orders Hite acquired 5,018 acres of limestone land that engrossed the entire headwaters of the Opequon Creek. Where the Indian path crossed the Opequon, he built a dwelling that came to be called Hite's Fort, although no evidence exists to suggest that it was ever fortified or used for the defense of the community that sprang up around it. By 1738 Hite was operating an ordinary or tavern, probably in his house, and he had constructed a mill several hundred yards upstream. That year he and forty-five of his neighbors

FIG. 1.3. Jost Hite's House. Jost Hite constructed this *Flürkuchenhaus,* or *Ernhaus,* shortly after helping to found the Opequon settlement. Its remains, depicted in a nineteenth-century photograph, lie along the trace of the Philadelphia Wagon Road where it crosses the Opequon Creek. From Thomas K. Cartmell, *Shenandoah Valley Pioneers and Their Descendants: A History of Frederick County, Virginia* (Winchester, Va.: Eddy Press, 1909), 7.

petitioned the court of Orange County to designate a public road eastward from this mill to a ford in the Shenandoah River below a gap in the Blue Ridge.[30]

Thus, by the time the thirty Iroquois warriors crossed the Opequon a small compound of structures had developed at Hite's settlement. Even though Hite sold land west of the Blue Ridge for the English government and administered justice under the English common law in his own home, his dwelling was distinctively Germanic. Called a *Flürkuchenhaus,* or *Ernhaus,* today, the structure stood long side to the road and was entered by a door directly into the *Küche,* or kitchen (fig. 1.4). A large cooking hearth stood on the left separating the *Küche* from the *Stube,* a room that Germans sometimes furnished with a table and benches for dining but generally used for formal occasions. Hite's tavern guests would have been entertained in this room. If Hite kept to German traditions, then his *Stube* would have been heated by an iron-plate stove stoked through an opening into the kitchen hearth. A *Kammer,* or unheated sleeping chamber, may have been partitioned from the *Stube* by a vertical plank wall. The first floor stood upon a cellar, which probably accommodated a spring. Under the rafters above were additional chambers. Replaced by a larger merchant mill in the 1780s, Hite's original mill structure might have supported nothing more complex than a horizontal, fanlike tub wheel driven directly by the force of water falling only a few feet. Surrounding the house and mill with its race and headwater dam would have been a complex of farm buildings, including barns, granaries, stables, dairies, and other outbuildings. If the Opequon settlement had produced a central place by 1742, it would have been at Hite's, for it was there that the Pennsylvania road crossed the creek and intersected the only established route east across the Blue Ridge.[31]

Hite maintained an open and inviting manner suiting such a place. One German family from Pennsylvania seeking Shenandoah Valley land in 1737 encountered him "sitting at his door." These visitors stayed several hours talking about his lands—which could be had, and where they lay. Five years later, Moravian missionaries reported that they "came to a German innkeeper, Jost Hayd, a rich man, well known in this region." "He was very courteous," one said, "when he heard that I was a minister." Hite also extended hospitality to sojourning Indians. His grandson told the story that "numerous parties of Indians, in passing and repassing, frequently called at his grandfather's house, on Opequon, and that but one instance of theft was ever committed. On that occasion a pretty considerable party had called, and on their leaving the house some article of inconsiderable value was missing. A messenger was sent after them, and information of the theft given to the chiefs. Search was immediately made, the article found in the possession of one of them and restored to its owner."[32]

Despite Hite's hospitality, his house, the mill, and the tavern never became anything more than a simple country crossroad during his lifetime or at anytime since. Between March 1736 and the time of Jonnhaty's visit, Hite sold twelve tracts of land ranging from one hundred to slightly more than one thousand acres to twelve families from his five thousand surrounding acres.

Facing page

FIG. 1.4. Andrew Keyser House. This house on the Shenandoah River in present-day Rockingham County is typical of central-chimney, three- or four-room houses constructed by first-generation Germanic peoples throughout the Opequon settlement. Photo: Library of Virginia. Plan: Based on Edward A. Chappell, "Acculturation in the Shenandoah Valley: Rhenish Houses of the Massanutten Settlement," *Proceedings of the American Philosophical Society* 124 (1980): 74.

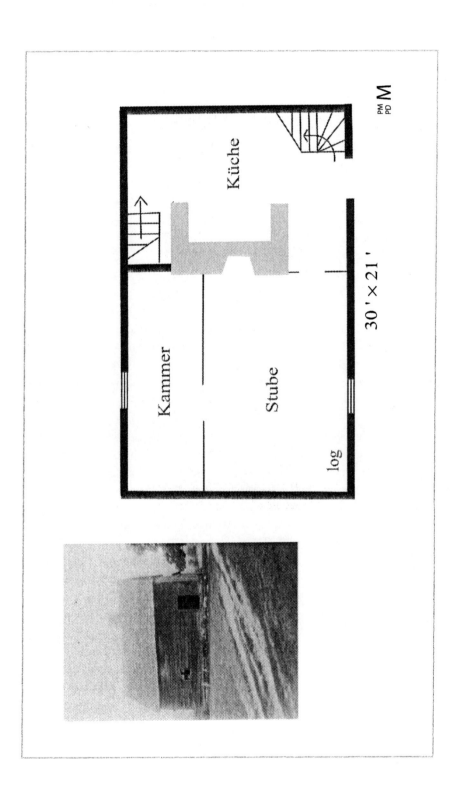

Kammer

Stube

Küche

log

30' × 21'

With an additional tract sold one year later and another in 1750, these proper-ties grew into an open-country neighborhood covering about thirty-five square miles and containing more than thirty homesteads.[33]

Hunting, visiting, or curiosity could have led Jonnhaty and his companions through portions of this community on the upper Opequon. Unlike the Hope-well settlers between Littler's and Hollingsworth's, those who took up Hite's land oriented their farmsteads to the creek, not a road. Each of the settlement parcels either bordered or straddled the Opequon or its tributaries. Linking roads extended trellislike from the old Indian path, soon to be a wagon road. Along the creek were marshes, whose constant damp and periodic floods kept bottomlands in grass. Surveyors often recorded that they ran their lines from the creek "thence out in the woods" suggesting that the "big timbers" on the uplands reached only to the flood plain.[34]

Dwellings along the Opequon stood about every one-quarter to one-half mile apart on tracts that were all roughly rectangular. Archaeological remains of foundation stones or earthen mounds indicate that these structures were small, approximately square, and between sixteen to twenty feet on a side. They were by all accounts single-room cabins. Where they survived, they were often incorporated into later structures. When Samuel Kercheval lived in the area at the turn of the next century, a sufficient number remained standing for him to note that "the first houses erected by the primitive settlers were log cabins, with covers of split clapboards, and weight poles to keep them in place. They were frequently seen with earthen floors; or if wood floors were used, they were made of split puncheons, a little smoothed with the broad-axe." De-spite the log cabin myth of the early frontier, many of the earliest structures were built of stone. In December 1744, two years after Jonnhaty and his party had passed through the Shenandoah Valley, Duncan O'Gullion, for instance, agreed to build a house for a hatter, William Dobbins, with "stone walls & wrought with lime . . . Twenty four foot square from out to out Ten foot high in the walls." Many of these structures would also have been roofed with thatch.[35]

Surrounding each dwelling would have been a patchwork of small fields. Some contained gardens, and others, crops. Opequon settlers raised practi-cally every grain in the repertoire of European agriculture. James Vance, for instance, grew wheat, rye, barley, oats, and corn. He also had fields of flax and hemp for cloth or cordage. Buckwheat and spelt, a variety of wheat popular among Germans, might also have been seen in the fields of other farmers. Fences protected crops from free-roving livestock. Bottomlands, already clear of forests, became meadows. Vance kept cattle, horses, sheep, and swine on his land, but these animals probably roamed the fairly large, effectively open range that existed across properties. Vance was typical; surviving probate inventories show that even during the earliest frontier period, most families at Opequon kept horses, cattle, sheep, and pigs.[36]

One of the most striking characteristics of the open-country neighborhood that grew up along the banks of the Opequon's headwaters was its mixture of ethnic groups. Of Hite's settlers whose ethnicity can be determined, five were German and seven were Scots-Irish. Each settler, moreover, had at least one neighbor with a different cultural background. Nonetheless, ethnicity and family were powerful forces in these peoples' lives. All of twenty-two Scots-Irish settlers from eleven nuclear families that acquired land in and around Hite's holdings were related. In nearly four out of every five marriages, children of these pioneer families found mates among these or other Scots-Irish families living nearby. Thus the kin group grew but stayed Scots-Irish. Land, too, bound the members of this community. Nineteen individuals among the first two generations acquired twenty-five tracts totaling 8,193 acres. Ninety-five percent of this land passed from fathers to sons or sons-in-law, from brother to brother, or friend to friend.[37]

Take, as an example of the importance of family, ethnicity, and land at Opequon, the case of Elizabeth Vance, the wife of James Vance. She became a widow early in the 1750s, when her husband died after "having one of my Members to be Cut off in a short time," as he said in his will. Pregnant at the time, she was also left with the care of four children aged eight to seventeen. Of undoubted assistance and comfort to her, however, were both her parents, four brothers, a sister, and six brothers-in-law. All lived nearby. As executors of James's will, her brother Robert and brother-in-law William were to insure that the children provide for her as they came of age. Each child, moreover, married and remained within the community. Elizabeth Vance kept control of the family's land. She acquired an additional 338 acres of her own, and on her death in the early 1780s she left property to each of her children.[38]

Kinship patterns among eleven German families along the Opequon were not as discernable as those of the Scots-Irish, but Germans acted in a variety of ways to bind families together and to the land. Several, including the Snapps, Mauks, Hotsinpillers, and Nisewangers, traveled to America on the same ship and married into the same families. Intermarriage between Germans and the Scots-Irish was very rare, and the only known instance among early settlers ended in separation. Germans, however, took numerous actions in support of one another. Itinerant Lutheran minister John Casper Stoever Jr. made eleven visits to Opequon between 1734 and 1741, noting the baptisms he performed. Members of the Hite, Wiseman, Snapp, and Poker families often stood forth to sponsor one another's children. Germans also wrote wills that reinforced the ties of family and land. They divided their land among sons and provided for widows through a life interest in the home place and the care required from children.[39]

The stories of these German families, of Elizabeth Vance, and of her numerous Scots-Irish relatives jump far ahead of whatever encounter these men and women may have had with Jonnhaty and his men, but they demonstrate that the world through which the Indians passed was no helter-skelter congeries of frontier misfits spoiling for a fight. Deep ties to kin, land, and ethnic group gave structure and meaning to life for Opequon families that Native American travelers would have understood from their own experience, in which kinship determined living patterns and shaped social obligations. Tribal identities, moreover, formed a rough counterpart to what distinguished Germans from the Scots-Irish.

· ⚲ ·

However long the Oneidas and Onondagas spent along the Opequon, they eventually moved on as days grew shorter and colder during the fall of 1742. Heading southwest from Hite's house their path led through a string of settlements carved out of several of Hite's other large tracts. Here lived more Germans, with names such as *Nisewanger, Writtenhouse, Stephens,* and *Chrissman.* After crossing Cedar Creek, a tributary of the North Fork of the Shenandoah, the path struck slightly westward and away from the river's numerous bottomland bends, where other Europeans were taking up lands. For the first time since crossing the Potomac River, the Indians would have been away from the settlements. The land was poorer here. Moravians traveling this route some ten years later commented that they found it "pretty barren, overgrown with pine trees." At the time of the American Revolution travelers still remarked that the "Valley here is narrow; the Soil sandy; The Timber mostly Pine." The Indians would have encountered few Europeans for more than a hundred miles until early December, when they reached the "Irish tract."[40]

Jost Hite, himself, used the term *Irish tract* when giving directions to visiting Moravians headed for North Carolina in 1743. Also called Beverley Manor, the tract belonged to prominent Essex County planter William Beverley by virtue of a grant of 118,491 acres in September 1736. A year earlier Benjamin Borden, a New Jersey native who had been living in the Shenandoah Valley for some time, had acquired 100,000 acres from the Virginia government immediately to the south of Beverley Manor. European settlement on these lands proceeded slowly. Borden promised to find one hundred settlers in two years as a condition of the grant, but in 1737 he was forced to beg the indulgence of the Virginia Council for more time to fill his quota. By 1738 Beverley had made only two grants, both to an Ulster sea captain, James Patton. Patton subsequently transported many families from the north of Ireland to Beverley's tract, giving it the name by which it was known to Hite. About three hundred and twenty-five families held land there by 1750. When Jonn-haty's party arrived, there were probably several score families living on dispersed holdings much as at Opequon.[41]

Among the first places Jonnhaty stopped after arriving in Borden's Tract on December 14 was the home of John McDowell. McDowell, a militia captain and justice of the peace, treated his visitors well, plying them with food and drink for the better part of a day. Afterward the Indians retired to the James River, where they camped for several more days. Where the trouble started is not clear. While on the James, the Indians killed at least one hog and shot several horses. Although ranging freely over a largely unfenced landscape, these were animals the settlers considered private property. December, moreover, was the time they slaughtered hogs to put up for winter provisions. The loss represented not only theft in the settlers' minds but a major threat to survival.[42]

Living off the land had been a problem for the Indians since their arrival in Virginia. They later stated that when they "got over Potomack River no body would give them a mouthful of Vicutals. . . . There was no more Deer to be killed, and they had been Starved to Death if they not killed a Hog now and then." These actions, however, did not always lead to conflict. "Tradition informs us, and the oral statements of several aged individuals of respectable character confirm the fact," Samuel Kercheval wrote, "that the Indians and white people resided in the same neighborhood for several years after the first settlement commenced, and that the Indians were entirely peaceable and friendly." The ideal of Anglo-Indian accommodation survived even though "their traveling parties would, if they needed provisions and could not otherwise procure them, kill fat hogs or fat cattle in the woods in order to supply themselves with food. This they did not consider stealing. Every animal running at large they considered lawful game."[43]

· ☙ ·

But Shenandoah Valley settlers were up in arms in the fall of 1742 and wary of traveling Indians. Earlier in the year they had received a warning from William Gooch, the governor of Virginia, "to be on their Guard, to Seize and examine all Indians they shall find Stragling or in Parties." Frontier militia companies had been ordered to "keep Constant Patroles in large Bodys to prevent Surprise." The governor had backed his warning with supplies of "Powder and Ball."[44]

Why Gooch raised the alarm and what happened as a result need some explanation. To Europeans the Indians from the north were visitors, often unwanted. Native Americans, however, saw the settlers as trespassers. Europeans never understood the origin of claims laid by the Six Nations to the Shenandoah Valley, but Iroquois assertions probably rested on victories over the Susquehannocks in the 1670s. At least the Six Nations insisted that the Shenandoah was theirs by "right of Conquest." Representatives had pressed this point before the Pennsylvania Council in October 1736, asserting that "all the Lands on Sasquehannah & at Chanandowa were theirs, & they must be satisfied for them." The Pennsylvania Council puzzled over the Indians' request to "write to the Governors of Maryland & Virginia, to make them Satisfaction for the Lands." Council members admitted that they did "not clearly understand this Matter" or "know not how this [claim] is supported." James Logan, president of the Council, apparently did write to the governor of Maryland, but he never received an answer. Although put off for the time being, the Indians never forgot their claims, and William Gooch remained ignorant of them.[45]

Then, in May 1742, a party of twenty or so Shawnees appeared in Dorset County on Maryland's eastern shore. After a brief visit they departed in company with several local Nanticokes. Soon, as one militia colonel reported to Samuel Ogle, governor of Maryland, there was "not One Indian of Either Sex or Size in Dorchester County." All the towns had been abandoned, and suspiciously the "Indians are drawn together at Pocomoke Swamp at a Place called Winnasoccum." The governor and Council immediately suspected that the Indians had "entered into a Conspiracy to do Mischief" and ordered the militia officers to interrogate the Indians camping in the swamp. By July 10, Maryland officials revealed what to their minds was a conspiracy of "several Nations of Our own Indians to rise and cut off the English, . . . assisted with 500 of the Shawan & Northern Indians [Iroquois], and about the same time the French with the Assistance of other Indians were to attack the back Inhabitants of Maryland and Pensilvania." This fear governed subsequent events. Of immediate concern was additional evidence that the northern Indians were soon going to Pennsylvania to dispose of part of their lands for arms and ammunition.[46]

Unaware of events in Maryland, the lieutenant governor of Pennsylvania, George Thomas, and the Pennsylvania Council had opened negotiations with headmen of the Six Nations joined by the Delawares and Shawnees on July 2 in Philadelphia. The purpose of the meeting was to confirm the previous release of Indian lands to the west of the Susquehanna River. After receiving a wide range of goods, which included match coats, blankets, kettles, shirts, hats, looking glasses, and most significantly, five hundred pounds of powder and six hundred of lead, and forty-five guns, the "Solemn Cry by way of Approbation was repeated by the Indians as many times as there were Nations present." The Onondaga headman Canasetego then promised to respond the next day to Thomas's further requests that the alliance with the Six Nations known as the Covenant Chain be renewed and that "utmost care therefore ought mutually to be taken by Us on both sides, that the Road between Us be kept perfectly clear and open." On the afternoon of July 7, Canasetego reported that after deliberating on the matter, the Indian nations were committed to "brightening of the Chain of friendship," but complained that the goods exchanged for land were sufficient only for the two hundred or so Indians present. "If you consider what Numbers are left behind, equally intitled with us to a Share, there will be extremely little," he added, with a request that "if you have the Keys of the Proprietor's Chest, you will open it and take out a little more for us." Included in the Indians' wants were additional guns.[47]

More ominous, however, was the implied threat that followed. Canasetego pointed out that south of Pennsylvania were the lands occupied by Europeans "from whom we have never received any Consideration." Canasetego reminded Thomas of the request six years earlier for assistance in receiving satisfaction from Maryland and Virginia. To discourage further delays the Indian spokesman added that, short of compensation, "we are able to do ourselves Justice." Thomas understood what was at stake and warned his visitors "to be careful not to Exercise any Acts of Violence towards his [the Maryland governor's] people, as they likewise are our Brethren, and Subjects of the same great King, and therefore Violence towards them must be productive of very evil Consequences." The next day the Council ordered Thomas to write Ogle of these matters without delay. The letter went out by special messenger on July 10, the same day Maryland officials concluded the investigation into their Indian conspiracy.[48]

News of negotiations with Pennsylvania authorities and threats of violence against Maryland settlers must have confirmed Ogle's fears of a coordinated Indian attack on the eastern and western frontiers of the middle-Atlantic colonies. By July 13 he had responded to Thomas, describing the Indian conspiracy with the French "to Cut off and Destroy all the English Inhabitants of Maryland & Pennsylvania." To substantiate his suspicions, he enclosed all the depositions taken from the Indians. Explicating the strategy of trading land for weapons in Philadelphia, these documents were in the hands of Thomas and the Pennsylvania Council by July 19, six days after the Indians had departed with additional presents, exceeding the initial supply of ammunition and including twenty-four more guns. Even more significant for subsequent events in Virginia, Ogle wrote William Gooch about the matter, passing on additional copies of the depositions. With this evidence in hand Gooch, too, became convinced that a continental war was imminent. He quickly convened the Virginia Council, which on July 26 ordered that the powder and ball be sent to the frontier and that militia forces there keep close watch on suspicious parties of Indians.[49]

· ✿ ·

It was into this net of suspicion and fear, then, that Jonnhaty and his men walked. This was the "no good Understanding" about which Justice Hoge had warned them. More than customary disagreements or misunderstandings over free-ranging livestock and private property would upset the delicate balance of Indian-white relations on the Virginia frontier that fall. Precisely where tensions surfaced is not clear, but at one point on the Indians' journey south three of them left the others to search out the road. They soon encountered an equal number of white men, whose attempt to seize their guns was foiled only when one of the Indians brandished a large knife. The white men, however, raised the alarm, and the Indians quickly found themselves accompanied by a harrying force of about ten settlers outfitted with hay forks. Violence almost erupted at one plantation, probably McDowell's, where the Indians were invited unarmed into the "big House." Some of the older men entered, but those outside, "suspecting the Designs of the white People," soon "called to their ffriends to come away." Detaining the Indians in the house, the whites, one of them flourishing a sword, attempted to dissuade those outside from continuing their journey. "Commanded by their Captain to be quiet til they were hurt," the Indians managed to slip away without a fight.[50]

It was probably to buy some time for "consulting what to do" that the Indians retreated to the camp on the nearby James River. There they "hunted for Deer," as they said, but whites reported the losses of roaming hogs and horses. Visits to settlers' houses, moreover, "scared the women and Children." Growing more and more alarmed, the whites complained to county lieutenant James Patton. Observing that the "law of nature and Nations obliged us to repel an Enemy force by force," Patton ordered John McDowell to muster his militia unit and escort the Indians through the settlements. Sensing trouble, the Indians abruptly broke camp and headed south. But McDowell and his men came up to the Indians on the evening of December 17 and bivouacked about a quarter mile away. The next morning the Indians got a jump on McDowell, but they were soon overtaken. What happened next was the subject of considerable dispute. Not surprisingly, two versions of events have survived, one from the white point of view, the other from the Indian. Receiving the white version first, Virginia's governor William Gooch acted consistently with fears of a continental struggle with the Indians and the French. Circumstances and the arguments of those wiser in Indian affairs than he was proved him wrong. Either way, however, subsequent events would have a profound impact on the planting of New Virginia.[51]

Late in the day on December 18, James Patton penned a letter to William Gooch reporting that when McDowell approached Jonnhaty's party, he first dispatched a messenger with a "Signal of Peace." Without warning the Indians killed the man "on the Spot" and opened fire on the militia. After a brisk exchange lasting about forty-five minutes, the Indians fled, leaving McDowell and ten militiamen dead along with eleven of their own. Patton himself came up with additional forces, but not until two or three hours after the battle was over. In a postscript Patton added that "there are some white men (whom we believe to be French) among the Indians." A few days later Patton wrote again, observing that it had been two of McDowell's men who carried a white flag to the Indians. Before firing, the intruders had proclaimed "O Friends are you there, have we found you?" In this version, Patton did not arrive with reinforcements until the next day, but he quickly ordered out patrols "on all our Frontiers well equipp'd." Moreover, he "drafted out certain number of young men out of each Company" as a rapid-response force "to be in readiness to reinforce any party or place that first needs help." Because "we have certain news of one Hundred and fifty Indians seen seventy Miles above me, and about the same number lately crost Patowmack on their way up here," Patton established strongholds "where each neighbourhood may draw to an occasion, and . . . call'd in the stragling Families that lived at a Distance."[52]

Forewarned, frontier men and women were up in arms and prepared to meet what was rapidly appearing to be an all-out attack by the northern Indians. In Williamsburg, Gooch responded in kind. Within days of receiving Patton's first communication, he convened the Council. After a briefing that emphasized French involvement in the fight, the Council promptly ordered that an "immediate Supply of Arms & Ammunition be sent to Colo Patton . . . in Case the Indians should be so hardy as to make another Attempt upon them." The Council took two additional steps, commanding the militia forces of Orange and Fairfax Counties "to hold themselves in Readiness" and directing Gooch write New York governor George Clarke to determine what claims the Indians had on Virginia land. In this letter Gooch described the "murder" of McDowell and complained of "how barbarously our Inhabitants in a Settlement beyond the Mountains have been insulted and attackt by a Party of the Northern Indians." The governor did not "expect any other satisfaction from Savages bred up to delight in nothing so much as shedding of blood, than the giving of them speedy Information of our Resentment." But he did ask the "favour of your Interposition" to inquire what Indian nation "dared to treat His Majesties subjects in so insolent and outragious a manner" and "what part of this Government it is they dispute." Virginia would be willing "upon reasonable terms to purchase our safety and free ourselves for the future from the desperate attempts of men void of humanity."[53]

Gooch portrayed events in a similar manner to the Board of Trade—the London government's advisory body on colonial affairs. Writing in February 1743, he protested against the Indians' "cruel outrage," which forced "our People, in their own Defence, to take up arms and repel them." By this time, however, another version of events had surfaced. Immediately after the fight the Indians had retreated a short distance, built a fire, and treated their wounded. Realizing the seriousness of the affair, Jonnhaty divided his party and dispatched ten warriors directly to Onondaga to give "account of the Usage they had met with." Jonnhaty, with the remainder, would usher the wounded along a safer route home through the westward mountains. Although harassed by Virginians, the lead party arrived at Great Island, a Shawnee Indian town on the west branch of the Susquehanna River, on January 12 or 13. Alerting the Shawnees of their presence and woeful tidings with the "Dead Hallow" cry, the party of ten then gave an account of the unfortunate events in Virginia. Among the listeners was Pennsylvania trader Thomas McKee. It was McKee's deposition that Lieutenant Governor George Thomas presented before the Pennsylvania Council on January 24.[54]

Thomas and the Council recognized that McKee's was the "Indian side of the Story" and that the Indians "have no doubt been Artful enough to make their own Cause as good as they could." The Council also had before them an account of "some White People lately come down from Lancaster, & who say they had it from some that live near the Place where the Action happen'd." Not surprisingly, this version recounted Patton's report. The Indians, by contrast, emphasized their attempts to avoid confrontations in Virginia and depicted themselves as victims in the encounter with McDowell. Recognizing that the peace of Pennsylvania and perhaps the lives of backcountry inhabitants depended upon getting to the bottom of the story, the governor and Council dispatched Conrad Weiser to Shamokin. As Pennsylvania's interpreter and chief ambassador to the Six Nations, he was to consult with Iroquois spokesman Shikellamy and reassure the Indians of Pennsylvania's peaceful intentions. The Indian view of events in Virginia can be pieced together from McKee's deposition and the report Weiser subsequently submitted to Thomas and the Pennsylvania Council on April 5, 1743.[55]

After having traveled seven or eight miles from their camp on the morning of December 18, the Indians were overtaken by McDowell and his militiamen, half of whom were on horseback with flying colors that included a white flag. While the footmen stayed in the rear, McDowell rode to the front of the Indian column and joined Jonnhaty, whom he, of course, knew. The two leaders fell into conversation. Meanwhile, one of the Indian boys, who was either lame or in need of relieving himself, drifted behind and into the woods. Perhaps fearing some intrigue or diversion, a militiaman fired on the boy. At this point accounts differed as to whether the Indians returned fire immediately or waited until additional shots killed two of their number "upon the Spott." In either case the Indians then threw down their bundles and fired at the white militiamen, killing McDowell in the first volley. Resorting to hatchets and hand-to-hand combat, the Indians soon routed the whites. In all, ten white men and four Indians lost their lives. After removing their own dead and treating the wounded, the Indians stripped the whites, divided their forces, and departed for home, hoping to make the best of a bad affair.[56]

· ⚘ ·

That Samuel McDowell, in relating the story of his father's death, blamed white militiamen for opening fire lends credence to the Indian version of events. Regardless, the Indians' journey through Virginia, which had lasted the better part of two months, was over—ending in what both sides recognized as a tragedy. Indian and white leaders realized as well that this tragedy could escalate into full-blown warfare across the frontier. "It will be a very nice affair should the Indians attempt to pass through any of the inhabited parts of this Province to make War upon our fellow Subjects in Virginia," observed the governor of Pennsylvania. "They will expect provisions, &t., as usual from the Inhabitants, and if they are denied them, which it will be the Duty of every Man in that Case to do, it is not improbable but they may resent it in their usual Barbarous manner, and force Us into the War too." Pennsylvanians might not be blameless if war broke out. Recognizing that "our back Inhabitants are very much alarmed at the late unhappy Skirimish in Virginia," Thomas also feared "their falling upon some of the Indians as they did once before." On the advice of his legislature Thomas then wrote Gooch with an "Account of the manner in which the Indians represent this Action, to Point out . . . the necessity of an Enquire therein, that Justice may be done, and the ill Consequences which otherwise might happen to the back parts of most of the British Colonies in America be prevented."[57]

The colonial government of New York and the Iroquois councils at Onondaga were also drawn into the unfolding crisis. The letter Gooch had written to George Clarke in early January 1743, shortly after receiving word of hostil-

ities on the frontier, did not arrive until April 5. New York's Commissioners of
Indian Affairs, however, had already received word about events in Virginia,
probably from the *Pennsylvania Gazette,* which printed both versions in late
January. In March the commissioners sent their own representative to Onondaga and learned "that as the Indians tell the story of the Fight to the Southward, the English fired first upon them & that four Indians were killed, & that
the other twenty six are all returned home." Clarke, however, initially accepted Gooch's account of the hostilities, describing them as an "act of the
highest treachery & breach of faith." He asked the commissioners to send an
interpreter to the Six Nations "that I may know more fully the Indians
pretences." The report he received, however, disabused him about Indian
"pretence." It asserted that even James Patton "knows what they [the Indians]
say to be truth, and that he could not deny it in their presence." Clarke then
wrote to Gooch in mid-June 1743 urging reason and caution in a way that
helps explain why Jonnhaty's journey and its outcomes are so important for
understanding Virginia's frontier and the emerging settlements at Opequon:

> I am persuaded you will not be hasty to take any steps that may lead to widen a
> breach that may involve all the Colonies in a warr, which in its consequences may
> plunge them into inextricable miseries, and procure to our natural enemy the French,
> what they are incessantly labouring to accomplish.
>
> The Sachims you see (and I am well assured of it) endeavour all they can to re-
> strain their youth from these Excursions, but it is next to impossible, the Nations are
> resolved on their part to preserve the union I made and will be sorry to see it violated
> by a sharp resentment of the injuries committed by a few of their licentious youth
> (and they forced to it by hunger) over whom by the nature of their government they
> have no coercive power: reason and persuasion being their only authority. Your
> people and they differ widely in an essential point. vizt Who fired first, be that as it
> will, I hope some amicable end will be made of the business, & next to your treating
> with them in person, I realy think your sending some prudent person with one or
> two of each Indian nation depending on Virginia, Carolina & Georgia to Albany
> there to treat with the Six Nations, will have a very happy effect not only in healing
> this breach, but for preventing the like for the future. We are not I presume to insist
> on punctilio's with such people we are to consider them as they are or may be usefull
> or prejudicial to us, and if you look upon them in that light, they will appear to be the
> best barrier, against Canada, to all the Provinces, Wherefore I think we ought to pre-
> serve their friendship by all the means we can, If we lose them and the French gain
> them what will become of all the Provinces is but too obvious to every one.[58]

The reconciliation of the two versions of what happened on the Virginia
frontier is central to the story of life and landscape at Opequon. That reconciliation, however, would take some time. What is significant for the narrative at this point is that participants and everyone who received news of the

fight in Virginia understood that the consequences might mean war between the Six Nations and Virginia–and few doubted that such a conflict would soon engulf all the surrounding English colonies and bring the French into the fray as well. This was a war that no one, neither American nor Indian, wanted. For the Six Nations a war of retribution carried on by young warriors without the sanction of headmen would mean sacrificing a policy of neutrality in the colonial wars of England and France that had brought peace and power for nearly half a century. English colonists were in an even more precarious situation because England was at war with France in spring 1743 while maintaining the fiction of Covenant Chain diplomacy and a presumed English-Iroquois alliance. To sacrifice this coalition and thrust the Iroquois into the hands of the French would drive the English colonies to the brink of disaster.

How the affair in Virginia was resolved demonstrates the role of imperial politics and Indian diplomacy in shaping settlement and material conditions on the Virginia frontier. These factors would impose new political forms upon the people and their landscape. The establishment of the first local government would lead to the creation of the first town. Imperial policy and Indian diplomacy thus produced the first centralizing tendencies in the otherwise dispersed settlement that Jonnhaty and his party encountered. Conflict among European and Indian nations would ultimately stimulate trade in both town and country, linking town to country and merging a rapidly developing town-country settlement system on the frontier with the eighteenth century's Atlantic economy.

But the story of the journey of thirty Iroquois warriors across the interior of Virginia in 1742 raises other questions of equal importance for explaining the planting of a settlement in so isolated a region of the colony. Even though it is doubtful that Jonnhaty's party was in Virginia to attack settlers over Iroquois land claims and was more likely on its way to assault other Indians much farther south, its presence immediately provoked fears about these claims and what the Six Nations might do to assert them. Suspicions of an Indian conspiracy with the French to destroy frontier settlements in fact led to hostilities as a form of self-fulfillment. The incident in Jonontore therefore calls for an inquiry into why *Europeans* settled in the region west of Virginia's Blue Ridge in the first place. Why, in other words, had the Opequon settlement been established? Why was it so dispersed at the time of Jonnhaty's arrival? Was that why the Virginia government was so jumpy in its defense? Why had authorities in Maryland, Pennsylvania, Virginia, and New York leapt to the conclusion that a general war with Native Americans was imminent? The answers to these questions begin to unfold in events that took place almost half a century earlier and in England's growing consciousness of its imperial frontiers and issues of their defense and security.

Chapter 2

Peopling an Empire

THE ENCOUNTERS among Jonnhaty, his twenty-nine Oneida and Onondaga companions, and people such as Charles Friend, Morgan Bryan, Richard and Charity Beeson, Morgan Morgan, George Hobson, Alexander Ross, Hugh Parrell, and Jost Hite are, of course, only hypothetical—a vehicle for introducing and discussing important themes that shaped the first and all subsequent phases of landscape evolution and cultural history in the early Shenandoah Valley. But encounters such as these must have occurred during the Indians' rather leisurely journey through the Opequon settlement, with about six weeks to spare in time not required for traveling. Jonnhaty's journey has been so cast as to reveal what was similar and what was different in the cultures of Native and immigrant Americans recently arrived on the periphery of European colonization. Where these two cultures intersected, they borrowed from each other. Certainly, the "lazy life" led by Opequon hunters owed much to Indian life ways. Indian and European cultures were similar in other ways, too, as both adapted to conditions of the forested interior of North America. Anglo-American political forms, such as the system of county courts and magistrates, were clearly cultural imports. But that justices, despite their offices and ascribed powers, had to negotiate much of their authority over those for whom they bore legal responsibility suggests that dispersal and cultural pluralism on the frontier positioned the European world much closer to the Indian than might be expected.[1]

It is important to identify what was borrowed and what was shared in the experiences of Indians and Europeans because of the long tradition of regarding the frontier from the Anglo-American perspective. In this view, the frontier was a wilderness of "free," or available, land, which Europeans claimed. They built new communities, new societies, new economies, new towns, and ultimately a new politics and a new nation. Jonnhaty's journey, by contrast, reminds us that the landscape of Opequon and many places like it on the eighteenth-century frontier were not simply new. The glades that settlers preferred for their homesteads were often Indian "old fields," that is, the sites of previous dwellings or patches of cleared and cultivated ground. Similarly, the grasslands Europeans valued for pasture frequently resulted from Indian burnings intended to improve a landscape for hunting. In another sense, of course, landscapes are never new, because they always have a history. What people do to change the land and the natural or cultural environments it supports is inevitably based on experience—experience often drawn from the work of generations. The landscapes of Opequon and places like it were, then, the product of complex historical forces born and disseminated in innumerable actions taken on both sides of the Atlantic.[2]

To any visitor or resident a landscape is certainly the composite of woodlands, meadows, fields, waterways, mills, dwellings, barns, fences, roads, streets, courthouses, shops, stores, and so forth. Long practice in living on the land teaches any careful observer that these and many other elements come together in distinct patterns at specific times and places. But any landscape—in this case the landscape of New Virginia—is much more than the sum of its parts. Encoded in the landscape is the story of its origins. American landscapes differ from European in what appears as a specific moment of origin— the first episode of European settlement. Breaking the landscape code, however, reveals that the aggregate patterns of fields and houses, streets and buildings, roads and mills are intricately connected not only to Native American precedents but also to elaborate European landscape lineages. The social mechanisms of community formation, the developing economies of farming, trade, and manufacture, the technological changes underpinning economic activity, the evolving structures of society, the alterations in the politics of human relations from the local to the national, and the changing roles of religion and ideas in all aspects of life—all are engraved on the land.

· ⌘ ·

Reading the land or landscape at any time and place in the past is therefore a way of writing history. Even an area as small as the Opequon settlement reveals the action of large-scale social, economic, political, or intellectual forces on the land. What, then, does Jonnhaty's journey tell us about cultural manifestations on the land of Opequon?

Jonnhaty and his party traveled through scattered settlements arrayed along the road the Indians had themselves established or along the drainages of the Opequon Creek. The pattern of settlement dispersal the Indians encountered was the result of choices each settler or family had made about where best to fix a dwelling, a farmstead, or a property line to utilize fully the natural resources necessary for the way they lived off the land. As one Virginia governor put it, they "scattered for the Benefit of the best Lands." The influence of Alexander Ross, Jost Hite, Lord Fairfax, or other men with responsibility for organizing settlements also affected these choices. So did colonial laws. Collectively, nonetheless, settlement decisions gave rise to communities, or open-country neighborhoods, as they have been called. They were open because they were dispersed but also because, encoded in the pattern of dispersal, were settler aspirations to be free from the land and social systems of Europe and America that enforced dependence—to be rid of tenancy, peonage, and servitude. A landholding secured as private property and developed through family labor meant self-sovereignty and competence in the affairs of life.[3]

Europeans brought with them to backcountry communities the diverse agricultural regimes of farm life in Europe. They grew a wide variety of crops but devoted the bulk of their labor to small grains, like wheat and rye, and to livestock, among which cattle, horses, and pigs were the most important. As a group, backcountry settlers were not opposed or indifferent to slavery, and many acquired slaves, but small-farm agriculture produced neither plantation economies nor black majorities. On the other hand, predominantly white backcountry communities were ethnically pluralistic. West of the Blue Ridge, people with English or Anglo-American ancestry were everywhere a minority in a society composed of immigrants from the north of Ireland or the Palatinate region of central Germany. There were also small numbers of Swiss, Welsh, Dutch, and French Huguenot settlers. Westerners were overwhelmingly Protestant and identified mainly with dissenting or sectarian traditions. Presbyterian, Reformed, Quaker, Mennonite, and Dunker meetinghouses were the religious landmarks of western Virginia.[4]

Insofar as economic, ethnic, and religious diversity prevailed in the freehold-farm, open-country communities of the Opequon settlement, the Virginia frontier came to typify the emerging backcountry, which, during the second and third quarters of the eighteenth century, extended from Pennsylvania to the Georgia highlands. What was striking about Opequon, however, was its distinctiveness in the larger social context of Virginia. East of the Blue Ridge, a great majority of white people traced their ancestry to England. They worshiped in the Anglican Church and lived under the authority of the deferential social practices of both the established church and the colonial government. Most made their living in one way or another through the cultivation, processing, or marketing of tobacco. Tobacco combined with African American slavery had created a plantation culture in which whites on plantations increasingly found themselves outnumbered by the blacks they held in bondage. Many of these black men and women had been born in Africa and preserved African life ways within slave communities.

The distinctiveness of the backcountry would have profound consequences for the future development of Virginia. By effectively extending political order and county government to its backcountry frontiers—partly as an outcome of Jonnhaty's troubled journey, as later chapters make clear—Virginia successfully avoided the sectional strife and hostilities that so violently divided North and South Carolina during the Regulator controversies of the 1760s and 1770s or that wrenched western Pennsylvania apart during the Whiskey Rebellion of the 1790s. But the ethnic, religious, and economic differences that divided Virginia along the Blue Ridge would, in the nineteenth century, break out in political controversies destroying the Old Dominion during the Civil War and leading to the creation of West Virginia. Although in the 1730s no one, from Governor William Gooch to Alexander Ross and Jost Hite or the hundreds of settlers they brought to Opequon, could foresee these outcomes, the original distinctiveness of the backcountry and its consequences raises an important question: Why did a society develop on the Virginia frontier whose social and economic construction profoundly altered the identity, landscape, and future of the colony?

Traditional answers to this question have relied on the perspectives of those who took up new land in the backcountry and those who profited by selling it. Arriving from what were often impoverished circumstances and dependent conditions in Europe, new immigrants went wherever land was available, the explanation goes. Frustrated by high land prices in Pennsylvania and discouraged by disputes among colonists, Indians, and the Pennsylvania proprietors that limited the available land, these men and women turned south along the Great Valley of the Appalachians to Virginia, where speculators among the gentry were eager to sell land to them. Viewing frontier settlement through the eyes or aspirations of pioneers became the perspective of the great frontier historian Frederick Jackson Turner. "The most significant thing about the American frontier," Turner stated in 1893, "is, that it lies at the hither edge of free land." There, at first the "wilderness masters the colonists," but "little by little he transforms the wilderness." Uniquely American character traits and democratic political institutions were the result of the transformation, but Turner also taught that the frontier was the self-creation of those who settled it. It was an American story. The idea that the ambitions of settlers drove frontier expansion dominated later studies of the Shenandoah Valley, especially those of Turner's student Freeman H. Hart in the 1940s and historical geographer Robert D. Mitchell in the 1970s.[5]

The concept that land-hungry immigrants were welcomed in Virginia by land speculators among the gentry has had a long historiography and a profound influence. Writing in the 1940s—ironically, to discredit Turner—Thomas Perkins Abernethy argued that "it was easier for Virginians to secure titles in the Valley than it was for Pennsylvanians, and it is not likely that many of the latter would have established themselves there had not the speculators paved the way for them. . . . How different would have been the settlement of our early West had it been carried forward by bands of free spirits setting out upon their own initiative, equipped only with the rifle and the axe, to take possession of unoccupied lands, with no thought of speculators or surveyors!" Twenty years later, the dean of Virginia history, Richard Lee Morton, reinforced the idea that the Virginia backcountry developed as land speculators met the demands of settlers. "Western lands," he wrote, "were now opened up to settlement by the planters of eastern Virginia who had the enterprise, the venturesome spirit, and the money to explore and survey large tracts in the wilderness and to plant them with settlers. These gentlemen of eighteenth-century Virginia, like those of the seventeenth century, did not wait for obscure backwoods hunters, fur traders, cattlemen, and small farmers to blaze the trails to the West and subdue the forests for them; they were themselves pioneers in those ventures."[6]

Although Turner, his followers, and Virginia historians such as Abernethy and Morton may have differed over who came first, settlers or speculators, and who ultimately shaped society on the frontier, both schools argued that land desired either for farms or for profits drove frontier settlement and that the material interests of colonists shaped American society. Certainly, a coincidence of interests existed between settlers and speculators, but from these perspectives alone the movement of peoples into the Shenandoah Valley in the 1730s and the evolution of a distinctive society is difficult to explain. Virginia had never had a frontier of free land; land had never been available simply for the taking. Virginia history had been the story of the engrossment of land in larger and larger quantities by a coterie of powerful men becoming more and more closely allied through intermarriage, inheritance, and political dominance in Williamsburg. They had always controlled land in their own interests and had spent much of the 1720s amassing huge tracts in Virginia's Piedmont to the east of the Blue Ridge. William Gooch had defended the practice, writing the Board of Trade that "where the greatest Tracts have been granted & possessed" by "men of substance," the "meaner sort of People [have been encouraged] to seat themselves as it were under the Shade & Protection of the Greater." He could have added: to the enrichment of the greater. These were men who, in one instance in May 1741, denied a petition for three thousand acres because the "Petitioner is not known to any of the Board [Council] and therefore [this quantity is] thought too much for so obscure a Person."[7]

If settler ambitions alone could not have driven settlement beyond the Blue Ridge, neither could speculation. In the early 1730s the region lay outside the bounds of any Virginia county—beyond the pale of colonial government. No deeds to land there could be recorded with a county court. Land could not be conveyed with certainty of title or seized for debt. No sheriff's writ ran there, nor did a justice preside over property disputes. No sane land speculator would have invested in the Shenandoah Valley. Virginia authorities may have provoked a migration to the marshlands of the colony but not in the interests of its gentleman speculators and only by coincidence in the interests of settlers.[8]

· ⚐ ·

Explaining the peopling of the Virginia backcountry and the origins of its landscapes in the distinctive social, economic, and political cultures of its people therefore requires a new and much larger perspective. What happened on the Virginia frontier in the fall of 1742 and its aftermath points the way. A scuffle—even one in which fifteen to twenty Indians and whites lost their lives—could have passed relatively unnoticed in the councils of colonial affairs. Nonetheless, colonial leaders understood immediately that a continental war between Indians and whites, and possibly involving the French, was at stake. It took the combined efforts of the governors of Pennsylvania and New York to calm William Gooch and head off precipitous and possibly tragic actions. In April 1743 George Thomas tried to assuage the Virginia governor's fears that the Indians had "design'd Hostilities." If so, he said, "it is not probable they would have trusted themselves in any of the white Inhabitant's Houses." The following month George Clarke pleaded with Gooch to "listen to overtures of Reconciliation than to the sanguine impulses of revenge." As Clarke explained, "it may be very fatal if an open rupture [with the Iroquois] should ensue, and they be thereby driven to the necessity of throwing themselves into the arms and power of our natural Enemy the French, who only want the advantage of such an event to open an uninterrupted way to annoy all the Colonies and render the Settlements therein very precarious." The following year the Board of Trade admonished Gooch to settle the affair with the Indians on "so good a foundation as to leave no room for future Quarrels."[9]

The reaction to the violence in the Virginia backcountry throughout colonial capitals and in the chambers of colonial administration at Whitehall in London suggests that what settlers were doing on the frontier had as much to do with imperial affairs as with their own interests or the profits of land speculators. Clearly, British authorities had invested backcountry settlements with

a strategic importance far beyond the activities of either settlers or speculators. Accounts of frontier settlement by peoples strange to the cultural norms
of Virginia must subsume their concerns and the interests of speculators
under the geopolitical forces that defined strategic frontiers in colonial North
America and made their settlement expedient. Williamsburg and London
ought to supply the best viewpoint, then, for explaining the initial settlement
of that frontier and its cultural distinctiveness. This is an imperial story.

From this perspective, the fight on the Virginia frontier in December 1742
provoked widespread fear of a continental war because frontier settlements
were conceived in the early 1730s as part of an imperial effort to keep the
French from surrounding Britain's North American colonies, to extend the
reach of British power across the Appalachian Divide, and to secure a frontier
destabilized by conflicts with Indians. In the minds of British and colonial officials, frontier settlements in a mountainous region, which otherwise could
provide a haven for runaway slaves, also helped check the internal threat of
slave rebellion and flight, which was growing more and more menacing during the first quarter of the eighteenth century. The moment in 1716 when the
Virginia governor learned that passes had been found over the Blue Ridge
mountains provides a good starting point in the story of Shenandoah Valley
settlement because it was also its turning point.

· ♏ ·

On June 12, 1716, Alexander Spotswood appeared before his Council and announced that "some discoverys have lately been made by the Rangers of a
Passage over the great mountains to the westward." Rangers were small units
of scouts employed by the Williamsburg government to rove Virginia's frontiers and warn militia forces about signs of Indian attack. Sometime in late
April or early May 1716, a party of rangers had apparently happened on one of
the water gaps across the Blue Ridge. Not only had the ridge "always been
look'd upon as unpassable" by the Council, but the Virginia authorities had a
special reason to worry about the colony's security that spring. The previous
year Yamasee Indians, outraged by white attempts to enslave them and take
their lands, had attacked settlements in South Carolina and nearly destroyed
England's southernmost province. Although Virginia sent troops to its belea-
guered neighbor, it was Cherokee support that eventually saved the colony.
Throughout the conflict Spotswood and the Council had fretted that Virginia
was "in danger of being also invaded."[10]

Spotswood and the Council had an additional reason to take a special interest in the newfound passes: The Virginia government was seeking to expand

the reach of the colony's Indian traders. "Their great Aim has been to endeav'r at a Trade with the Nations on ye other side of the Mountains," Spotswood observed, crediting the rangers' discovery partly to the "encouragement" of the traders. Thus Spotswood promised the Council to dispatch a "greater Body of the Rangers upon further discoverys which he Judges may be of great advantage to this Country." Spotswood, as we shall see, soon kept his promise, leading the rangers himself on a new western expedition, but that he saw both threat and opportunity in gaining access across the Blue Ridge requires further explanation.[11]

The links between imperial strategy, colonial defense, the Indian trade, and ultimately, settlement, had a significant history in Virginia. It extends back to the turn of the eighteenth century, when France established its first Louisiana colonies, Native Americans resumed disruptive wars stretching across the North American interior, and African slavery became the basis of the southern colonial labor system. More specifically, this story can be traced to three developments of the European peace of 1697–1702. This brief interlude between the War of the League of Augsburg and the War of the Spanish Succession saw the significant expansion of Virginia settlement along the Chesapeake Bay, the growth of French power along the Mississippi and Ohio River Valleys, and the intensification of Indian movement through the mountainous interior separating the English and the French.

Virginia enjoyed considerable prosperity during the five years of peace. A boom in the tobacco economy encouraged Virginians to take up more than a million acres of land and bring three thousand African slaves to the colony. During the next two decades the plantation economy created by tobacco would come to depend increasingly on the bound labor of blacks, increasing the slave population of the colony by more than 60 percent. Territorial expansion, however, forced the colony to adopt a number of defensive measures by 1702, including the establishment and arming of a settlement of French Huguenots at Manakin Town, improvements in militia organization, and a new land act that encouraged companies of armed men to take up land on the frontier.[12]

What happened in Virginia was only part of a broader pattern of European commercial and settlement expansion during the years of peace. Alarmed by reports that English traders were forging ties with Indian tribes west of the Appalachian Mountains and that English colonies were planned at the mouth of the Mississippi River, Louis XIV established the first French settlements of the Louisiana colony at Mobile Bay, followed closely by new posts along the Mississippi River, in the Illinois Country, and on the Great Lakes at Detroit.

Worrying the English in return were French proposals for a "communication" between Canada and Louisiana that would encircle the seaboard colonies and possibly drive the English from North America.[13]

Thus, what the Five Nations of the Iroquois accomplished at that time had ominous consequences for the English colonies. During much of the last half of the seventeenth century the Five Nations had pursued a series of conflicts designed to establish Iroquois hegemony in both trade and politics throughout much of the St. Lawrence and Ohio River Valleys. Mixed success at great cost forced the Five Nations to embark on a new policy of neutrality in the imperial struggles of France and England with the so-called Grand Agreement of 1701. Established with separate treaties in Montreal and Albany, neutrality allowed the Iroquois to resume mourning wars with southern Indians—Cherokees, Creeks, Catawbas, and Yamasees. Conducted by small raiding parties traversing the North American interior, these struggles provided new opportunities to revitalize tribal leadership in the exploits of young warriors and to rebuild kinship networks with the addition of southern captives. Captives replaced fallen warriors in grieving families, hence the name *mourning wars*. At the same time, the movement of northern Indians and southern counterparts across the Virginia frontier created all too many opportunities for conflict with the native tribes of the colony and with whites, who were pushing the plantation economy westward. What frightened English authorities most was a combination of Iroquois and French power that the colonies could not resist. In playing their neutral card carefully, the Iroquois became the key to Virginia's security.[14]

The significance of Iroquois power was at no time more plain to the Virginia government than in 1711, when the Tuscarora Indians attacked English colonists in neighboring North Carolina. Outraged by encroachments on their land and enslavement of their people, the Tuscaroras lashed out against settlements in the Albemarle Sound area, killing 120 colonists in initial attacks. Internal political disputes prevented Virginia from providing more than nominal assistance, but the involvement of Virginia Indians in the conflict and the Tuscaroras's ties to the Five Nations inflamed fears that Virginia would be caught in a pan-Indian war engulfing the entire English colonial world. As Spotswood pointed out, the Iroquois had made the Tuscaroras "large offers of Assistance to revenge themselves on the English." Meanwhile, Virginia's own defenses proved inadequate. Raising an effective military force proved too costly for either the resolve or the pocketbook of the Burgesses, and ranger units were powerless before a cunning, mobile enemy.[15]

In crafting a defense policy for Virginia, Governor Alexander Spotswood sought the root of the problems with the Indians. In November 1714 he informed the Burgesses that he had "discovered enough to convince me that the Mischiefs We have of late years Suffered from the Indians are chiefly owing to the Clandestine Trade carryed on by some ill men." The Assembly complied with an "Act for the better Regulation of the Indian Trade," confining commerce with the natives to Fort Christanna and granting a monopoly to the Virginia Indian Company. The company, however, was never successful, and opposition to its privileges led to the law's disallowance in 1717. Although Virginians conducted a significant private trade with southern Indians, a virtual trade war with South Carolina, in which Native Americans successfully played off competing parties, meant that Virginia was unable to exploit Indian dependence on English goods as a diplomatic tool for forging alliances, buying peace, and stabilizing the frontier. Trade gave Virginia no diplomatic leverage with the Five Nations either, and the southern trade declined precipitously in the 1720s.[16]

From the story of Spotswood's Indian trade policy, however, arose a more enduring lesson for the settlement of the Virginia backcountry. In addition to regulating the Indian trade, Fort Christanna was supposed to facilitate the formation of Indian settlement buffers against just the kind of incursions by the Tuscaroras that had proved so costly to settlers on the southern frontier. "I have begun to try what may be done for their Safety by way of treaty," Spotswood announced to the Assembly shortly after the conclusion of the Tuscarora War, "and I am perswaded that the Setling [Virginia Indians] Along our Frontiers without all our Inhabitants . . . would be a better and cheaper Safe guard to the Country than the old Method of Rangers." Nottoways and Meherrins would be situated between the Roanoke and James Rivers, the Saponies would settle on the Roanoke, and the defeated Tuscaroras would find a new home between the James and Rappahannock. With each group, twelve to fifteen armed Englishmen would settle to "observe all their motions & . . . go out constantly with their hunting Parties."[17]

In his opening address to the Burgesses in fall 1714 Spotswood described a very important addendum to his program for frontier security: "I have began a Settlement of Protestant Strangers, Several Miles without our Inhabitants." The governor had fixed a community of German miners at Germanna, near the forks of the Rappahannock River, to produce bar iron and fortify a northern counterpart to Christanna. Although these immigrants were "of the Same Nation with our present Sovereign" (George I of Hanover in Germany), they, like the Indians, were marginal peoples, to be shuffled about the frontiers of the colony as human buffers for the protection of English-occupied areas. Having discovered that "our People are not disposed for Warlike undertakings," Spotswood now concluded that the "Security, I have provided for the

Country to be of Such a nature, that if half the pains be used to improve it, which I have taken to Settle it, the Strength of your Barrier may with time be encreasing and the Expence Decreasing."[18]

The Indians, however, refused to cooperate. By early 1715 Nottoways and Meherrins were already resisting forced relocation, and the Council had to command that if they did not move soon, women and children would be seized and brought to Christanna until the men complied. Three months later the Council openly suspected the Nottoways of "evil intentions towards his Majesties Subjects, by their continual disobedience" and ordered them disarmed. By 1718 the Indian buffer policy was in shambles. In May, Spotswood complained to the Assembly: "If these Tributarys had all of them Complyed with their Engagements I cannot but think your frontiers might have been constantly provided with a Standing Guard at a very moderate Expence." What endured, however, was the Germanna idea of settlement by foreign peoples for the defense of Virginia.[19]

Thus, in August 1716, when Spotswood was preparing for the expedition to the passes over the Blue Ridge, much would have been on his mind about their strategic significance to Virginia. Since the Virginia Indian Company was still a going concern, ready access across the mountains would be to the "advantage" of its efforts to extend the Indian trade westward. Considering the French "communication" and fears of French encirclement, however, the passes represented a threat to Virginia's security. Rangers certainly could not stem the French tide if an attack came, and Virginia had no permanent military force. Nor was it likely the Assembly would fund one or erect forts at the passes. Establishing good relations with western Indians through honest trading could supply some allies against the French and perhaps a timely warning of an attack, but the passes nonetheless rendered Virginia vulnerable, and both northern and southern Indians were moving across western territory for warfare, not for trade. Experience with existing settlement treaties was proving that Virginia Indians could not be relied upon as a first line of defense. Spotswood's expedition departed for the mountains from the Germanna settlement. Surely the governor might be considering ways of extending European settlement toward the passes as Virginia's surest protection against the incursions of the French.

Spotswood's party came to be called the Knights of the Golden Horseshoe, after the memento the governor gave to each gentleman who accompanied him. But "party" the journey has often been dubbed by historians. When the fourteen rangers, four Indians, and dozen gentlemen with their servants, numbering sixty-three in all, reached the peak of the Blue Ridge on September 6,

1716, they drank "King George's health here and all the Royal Family." Although some of the men wanted to return, Spotswood continued on, descending the ridge and the next day crossing a river he named the *Euphrates*. That evening, on the banks of what was later called the Shenandoah, the governor "got the men all together and loaded all their arms and we drunk the King's health in Champagne, and fired a volley; the Prince's health in Burgundy, and fired a volley; and all the rest of the Royal Family in Claret, and a volley. We drunk the Governor's health and fired another volley. We had several sorts of liquors, namely Virginia Red Wine and White Wine, Irish Usquebaugh, Brandy, Shrub, two sorts of Rum, Champagne, Canary, Cherry punch, Cider, water &c." Celebrate Spotswood and his company did, but their carryings on had a deeper meaning. Toasting the royal family's health on a distant river was a way of proclaiming the power, scope, and magnitude of the British empire as well as invoking its longevity. Naming that river *Euphrates* cast that empire as an agent of civilization in what the English called the wilderness.[20]

Various motives have been assigned to Spotswood's journey. It was a prospecting expedition in search of silver mines or a desperate attempt by the governor to rehabilitate his political reputation, which had been badly damaged in struggles with the Assembly. South Carolinians, still in the grips of war with the Yamasees, complained that Spotswood was taking advantage of their dire straits to extend Virginia's Indian trade into Cherokee territory previously dominated by their traders. Modern historians have claimed that Spotswood's purpose was to "stage a public-relations event to dramatize for Virginians the opening of the West" and to stimulate investment or speculation in western lands. Two years after the expedition Spotswood himself asserted that the "Chief Aim of my Expedition over the great Montains in 1716, was to satisfye my Self whether it was practicable to come at the Lakes."[21]

In Spotswood's mind the Great Lakes represented the centers of French power in Canada. Like many of his fellow Virginians, the governor believed that across the Blue Ridge all the rivers flowed westward to the Mississippi. He "regretted that after so many Years as these Countrys have been Seated, no Attempts have been made to discover the Sources of Our Rivers." So seriously did he misunderstand trans-Appalachian geography that he thought Lake Ontario lay in the latitude of Pennsylvania, and Lake Erie was correspondingly farther south and closer to Virginia. Difficulties in determining longitude also led Spotswood to collapse trans-Appalachian territory west to east. From reports by Indians and his own observations, he concluded that Lakes Erie and Ontario were only five-days' march from the passes over the

Blue Ridge. What benefits Virginia could derive by trade with western Indians were offset, therefore, by the threat posed by French colonies. Thus Spotswood came to see the significance of his 1716 journey in terms of this threat.[22]

· ℔ ·

The following year Spotswood was given an opportunity to articulate his fears of French encirclement at a crucial moment in the evolution of British colonial policy. The outcome, a new, two-pronged program for protecting Virginia, had profound implications for the peopling of the colony's backcountry and the resultant sectional differences. The moment came in December 1717, when the Board of Trade received a memorial (an appeal) from South Carolina's London agent, Richard Berresford, warning that the "French had a design to dispossess us of all our Plantations in the Continent of North America." Motivated by genuine fear of the French—who were responsible, as many South Carolinians believed, for the Yamasee War—Berresford was also influenced by an effort to oust his colony's proprietary government by blaming it for inadequate defenses during the war. Berresford played upon anxieties over French expansion and new trade rights granted to colonizers and companies in Louisiana. Worse, however, were French attempts to "draw over ye Iroquese Indians etc. to their interest" and to attack the Cherokees, whose support had saved South Carolina from Yamasees and Creeks. Berresford called upon the board to "take such measures as may defend our plantations from ye wars already begun in Carolina and ye others that are daily fear'd from ye French and their Indian Allies elsewhere." These dramatic arguments got the attention of the Board of Trade, which quickly passed the memorial on to Spotswood for comment.[23]

Spotswood seized the occasion to expound his new views on colonial defense. Thinking of his recent journey over the mountain, the governor observed that he had for a "long time endeavour'd to informe [him]self of ye scituation of the French to the Westward of Us." He described "that extensive Communication w'ch the French maintain by means of their water Carriage from the River St. Lawrence to the mouth of Mississippi," warning that

> by this Communication and the forts they have already built, the Brittish Plantations are in a manner Surrounded by their Commerce w'th the numerous Nations of Indians seated on both sides of the Lakes; they may not only Engross the whole Skin Trade, but may, when they please, Send out such Bodys of Indians on the back of these Plantations as may greatly distress his Maj'ty's Subjects here, And should they multiply their Settlem'ts along these Lakes, so as to joyn their Dominions of Canada to their new Colony of Louisiana, they might even possess themselves of any of these Plantations they pleased.

Spotswood pointed out that "nature, 'tis true, has formed a Barrier for us by that long Chain of Mountains w'ch run from the back of South Carolina as far as New York, and w'ch are only passable in some few places." But "even that Natural Defence may prove rather destructive to us," he continued, if the passes "are not *possessed* [emphasis added] by us before they are known to them." Spotswood concluded with the recommendation that "we should attempt to make some Settlements on ye Lakes, and at the same time possess our selves of those passes of the great Mountains."[24]

By 1718, therefore, Spotswood had redefined his approach to defending Virginia. Regulating the Indian trade had failed as a result of opposition to the Virginia Indian Company and the decline of commerce with the Indians. Military force proved effective only as a response to specific emergencies, not as a means for the continued security of Virginia frontiers. More and more, Spotswood came to rest the colony's defenses on the Blue Ridge, the high ridge of mountains that he, himself, had crossed. Virginians ought to take possession of the passes but at the same time not limit settlement to the ridge. Ultimately, colonial security depended on breaking the French communication between Canada and Louisiana. This could best be achieved by a salient of English settlement on Lake Erie.

· ⚘ ·

Another 1717 development that preceded the Berresford memorial forced Spotswood and the Council to rethink the role of the Blue Ridge in Virginia's Indian policy. In early April a party of a hundred Catawbas and other Indians of the North Carolina piedmont arrived at Fort Christanna. They came to conclude a treaty with Virginia that would reopen the trade Spotswood had closed during the Tuscarora War. With them were eleven children of various headmen to serve both as hostages for securing the peace and as students at Christanna's Indian school. The Indians had already disarmed themselves and camped outside the walls of the fort on Tuesday, April 9, when Spotswood arrived and found them in a "good Disposition to Continue in Peace." The next day, shortly before dawn, however, a band of Iroquois warriors swept down upon the sleeping, defenseless camp, killing or wounding seven Catawbas before fading back into the woods with five captives, including a headman. Spotswood found it "impossible to express the Rage of these People . . . [who] immediately concluded that this Attack was contrived by the Treachery of the English." The governor "pacifyed" them only with a promise "to obtain Satisfaction for the Injury, and considerable presents."[25]

With the Council's urging, the governor then dispatched Captain Christopher Smith to New York to procure the return of the captives and Iroquois assurances to halt the southern raids in compliance with the peace of the Covenant Chain. The Iroquois indeed promised that "none of their People shall henceforth go out a fighting this way." But so cautious still were members of the Virginia Council that, when they received Smith's report the following August, they passed resolutions defining the governor's Indian defense plan for the last five years of his administration. Concluding that the "said Insult on this Government is a manifest Breach" of the Covenant Chain, the Council proclaimed that the "Peace of this Government cannot be secure unless the said five Nations are confined in their Ra[n]ges to ye other side of the Mountains." Working out a way to keep the Iroquois beyond the Blue Ridge was Spotswood's problem.[26]

So much weight did Spotswood place upon the Council's resolutions that he set out in the fall of 1717 to confer with the governors of Pennsylvania, Maryland, and New York in person. While in Albany he met with Governor Robert Hunter and left a plan to be presented to the Iroquois the following spring, when treaty conferences would resume. Spotswood proposed that thenceforth Iroquois parties heading south through Virginia would stay to the west of the Blue Ridge and cross that barrier only with an official pass from the governor of New York. Meanwhile, Indians resident in Virginia would promise to remain to the east of the ridge.[27]

· ⚷ ·

During the final years of his administration Spotswood and the Council took determined action to effect the new policies of taking possession of the passes over the Blue Ridge and establishing the ridge as a barrier between traveling and resident Indians in Virginia. The issue of the passes came first in a manner that reveals how literally Virginia authorities took the meaning of "possession." In November 1720 the governor described what he called his "Political Creed" to the assembly. "If a Conscientious discharge of our duty engages us Governours to be Specially mindful of Great Britains interest," he reasoned, "yet I cannot See why that may not go hand in hand with the prosperty of these plantations. . . . I look upon Virginia as a Rib taken from Britains Side and believe that while they both proceed as living under the Marriage compact, this Eve must thrive so long as her Adam flourishes." He then directed the Burgesses's attention to the "Stake I have among you," referring, of course, to land and its use in uniting the interests of crown and colonists. Finally, the governor asked the legislators for their "consideration whether the giving Encouragement for Extending your Out Settlments to the high Ridge of Mountains, will not be laying hold of the best Barrier that nature could form, to Secure this Colony from the Incursions of the Indians and the more dangerous Incroachments of the <u>French</u>."[28]

The background to Spotswood's rhetorical flourishes was a long dispute between the governor and the legislature over numerous domestic issues. But on this occasion the Burgesses proclaimed their "Joy not to be Expressed That we are now met to See a late unhappy Division So unexpectedly United." They promised to "Set our selves Earnestly and Sincerely to consult the United Interest of our Royal Sovereign and this Dominion." Learning that there were at least "two Passes in the Great Ridge of Mountains," the Burgesses quickly took up demands that "two Countys of narrow extent should be Laid off leading to those Passes." The result was "an act for erecting the Counties of Spotsylvania and Brunswick" to defend the "frontiers towards the high mountains [that] are exposed to danger from the Indians, and the late settlements of the French to the westward of the said mountains." To encourage settlement, the Burgesses remitted taxes in the new counties for ten years, deferred land payments there, and appropriated money for public buildings. The defensive purposes of settlement, however, were also promoted by further expenditures to arm "each christian titheable" with a musket, bayonet, bullets, and gunpowder. Spotswood chipped in by petitioning the crown to remit quitrents in the new counties and taking forty thousand acres for himself.[29]

The Assembly and governor clearly anticipated that settlement in the new counties would proceed along lines already established at Germanna. Most of the new citizen soldiers taking up Piedmont lands would be "foreign Protestants [who] may not understand English readily." To encourage them the Burgesses provided that "if any such shall entertain a minister of their own, they and their tithables shall be free [from tithes, or taxes for the church] for ten years." The Assembly thereby took a major step toward fostering ethnic and religious diversity on the Virginia frontier.[30]

The Assembly of 1720 was also critical in the development of Spotswood's Indian policy. Earlier that year the Board of Trade had cautioned the governor that the "Indians should not be govern'd with a high hand, but led by gentle means and fair usage, considering the increase of the French power in North America." On November 11 Spotswood met with the Burgesses and asked if, in their opinion, "gentle means" meant waiving as a precondition of negotiation with the Five Nations certain "Preliminary Articles" requiring the Iroquois to remain west of the Blue Ridge unless they had an official pass. The house responded unanimously that negotiations ought not to be undertaken until the Iroquois had accepted these terms. The very next day Spotswood secured a pledge from Indians living in Virginia's Piedmont that "they will not at any time hereafter . . . Cross the great Mountains nor pass to the Northward of Potomack River" if the northern Indians "observe the same Regulation."[31]

On the evening of October 19 nearly a year later, Spotswood received news from the governor of New York that the Iroquois had accepted the preliminary articles and agreed that the Blue Ridge would be a barrier between their traveling parties and settlements of both Indians and whites to the east. The elated Council immediately proposed that Virginia send commissioners to Albany to "renew the Peace or Covenant Chain with the said five Nations" and that the governor head the delegation. In the company of councilman Nathaniel Harrison and William Robinson, a Burgess, Spotswood arrived in Albany the following fall. There, on September 6, 1722, eighteen sachems of the Mohawks, Senecas, Onondagas, and Tuscaroras agreed not to pass "to the East side of the great Ridge of Mountains which extends all along the Frontiers of Virginia."[32]

In what proved to be the last act of his administration—the governor was called home in fall 1722—Spotswood felt that he had secured the safety of Virginia by preventing the kind of bloodshed that had occurred at Fort Christanna in 1717 and that could escalate into a continental Indian war. But more important to the story of settlement in the Shenandoah Valley, the 1722 Treaty of Albany "effectively encourage[d] the people to extend their own settlements without any future apprehensions of danger from Indian enemies." To this observation to the Board of Trade Spotswood could have added that the agreement with the Indians also addressed another apprehension of westward moving Virginians: the threat posed by their own slaves.[33]

The same day—August 10, 1721—that the Council confirmed the preliminary articles as the basis of any agreement with the Iroquois, the governor informed its members that "diverse Negro's . . . on the Frontiers of Rappa[hannock County] have lately run away & suspected to be gone towards ye Great Mountains, where it may be hard to apprehd 'em, & if they shou'd encrease there, it might prove of ill consequence to ye Peace of this Colony, and of great detriment to the Frontier Inhabitants." So troubling was this development that the governor had already written his counterparts in Maryland, Pennsylvania, and New York to "give orders to their Indians to hunt for the said Runaways among the Mountains and had proposed a reward for bringing them in dead or alive." To the Council the recommendation was urgent enough to be put directly to the Five Nations at the Albany conference.[34]

Authorities in Virginia had good reason for concern about the threat of runaway slaves seeking refuge in the mountains. Africans had been present in the colony since the second decade of settlement; their numbers, however, had grown slowly during the seventeenth century, as did the legal and social institutions of slavery. As late as 1690 only 10 percent of the Chesapeake population was black. The boom in tobacco, land, and slaves of the 1697–1702 peace changed this picture. In 1698 the Royal African Company lost its monopoly over the slave trade, and English merchants competed vigorously to meet the rising demand for bound labor in Virginia. By 1720 more than one in four Virginians was a black slave, and nearly two thousand more were entering the colony every year.[35]

Each one of these unwilling immigrants had a reason to hate or attack white Virginians. That is why members of the Virginia Council had acted decisively and cruelly on March 21, 1709, to reports of a "dangerous Conspiracy formed and carried on by great numbers of Negros, and other Slaves for makeing their Escape by force . . . and for the destroying and calling off such of her Majtys Subjects as should oppose their design." The Council required local justices to discipline all conspirators summarily but to hold the leaders for special punishment reserved by the Council. These—Salvadore, an Indian, and a Negro slave Scipio—were executed, and their heads and members severed for display at nine different locations from the Northern Neck to the Southside.[36]

Despite the threat of draconian punishment, a number of slaves "formed a design to rise and cutt off his Majtys Subjects" while Spotswood was in New York signing the Treaty of Albany. Spotswood's successor, Hugh Drysdale, vigorously prosecuted the perpetrators, but the incident must have redoubled the fears of Virginia slave owners. Nor would anxieties for the "Peace of this Colony" have been much quieted by the admission of the Iroquois at Albany that, though they had agreed to return runaway slaves found in Virginia's western mountains, the ones "we promised last year to send home . . . lye very much out of our way." If, however, any "shall happen to fall into our Hands," the Iroquois vowed to "carry them to Colo Masons on the Potowmack River, for the Reward proposed." Thus the problem of slave maroons in western mountains persisted. During the next three years Maryland authorities sent several delegations to the Shawnees living on the upper Potomac River to address the "evil Consequences of the Shuanuo Indians entertaining our Runaway Negro Slaves" and to make a "reasonable Bargain . . . for bringing down those Negroes already amongst them."[37]

As events would demonstrate, the settlement and social construction of the Virginia backcountry was connected to the establishment of maroon colonies. When Spotswood left office in 1722, however, concerns for runaway slaves represented only one of the forces his actions had set in motion toward the occupation of the West by ethnically and religiously diverse, small-holding farm peoples. The major threats posed to the security of Virginia came from the Indians, who traveled incessantly across the colony's frontiers in the conduct of long-distance wars, and from the French, who were slowly developing a communication—a stranglehold from the English perspective—between Canadian and Louisiana colonies. Virginians feared most an alliance between the French and the Indians, while the colony's greatest diplomatic challenge lay in maintaining the Covenant Chain with the Iroquois as a check against French expansion. Military force proved too weak and too expensive to defend the frontiers, and Virginia lacked sufficient trade to use the Indians' growing dependence on European goods as leverage for loyalty and security. And so the Spotswood administration turned to establishing settlement buffers as Virginia's best defense. Because land to the Indians never entailed obedience to the king's bidding, they declined the opportunity to provide a human screen for colonial tobacco planters. Only subject Europeans seemed responsive to this usage. By the last years of his administration, Spotswood had fixed the Blue Ridge as Virginia's defensive barrier. Passes discovered across it proved a problem, addressed by numerous inducements for armed Europeans, including Germans, to settle two new counties laid off to the east of the passes. The Blue Ridge would also serve to separate Virginia and traveling Indians if agreements with each party to remain on separate sides of it held. The Five Nations were further enlisted in efforts to define the Blue Ridge as a barrier and discourage slave uprisings by promising to return runaway slaves encountered in mountain fastnesses.

· ☙ ·

After 1716, while Spotswood developed a strategy of defense for Virginia based on the Blue Ridge as a barrier against invasion by the French and intrusion by the Indians, colonial officials in London became increasingly alarmed about the security risks of all the English mainland colonies. What they knew about the colonies came largely from correspondence with colonial governors—from the experience of Spotswood and his colleagues. Agents of colonial assemblies and merchants trading in the colonies also contributed to what English authorities knew about the colonial world. The colonial administration in Whitehall was not centralized during this period but was spread among various officials, for example, the secretary of state, and numerous boards or commissions. But the Board of Trade was always at the crossroads of decision making.

By the early 1720s the Board of Trade had fashioned working assumptions about the frontiers of Britain's mainland colonies viewed collectively for practically the first time. The board, moreover, had identified various steps necessary to protect the colonial world against the threats of French encirclement and Indian warfare. The process of gathering information and integrating observations on the problems of frontier security culminated in the famous report of 1721. The ideas it laid out about the cultural and strategic geography of North America represented a reconfiguration of the colonial world from a collection of separate but dependent political entities into a coherent region representing the western extension of the British empire. Having been drawn directly from information gleaned from colonial officials, agents, and merchants, the assumptions about empire woven into the report possessed wide currency throughout the British colonial administration. In effecting the settlement of the Virginia backcountry, Alexander Spotswood's successors never referred directly to the report, but their actions reflected its assumptions. Those assumptions, therefore, help explain the social construction of the backcountry, its dispersed settlement patterns, and the evolution of sectional patterns in the historical geography of Virginia.[38]

The political controversies surrounding the Yamasee War in South Carolina prompted the Board of Trade to collect and assimilate the information that led to the report. Hearing of the disastrous Good Friday attack of the Yamasees on April 15, 1715, which took the lives of 160 Carolinians, Secretary of State James Stanhope put the question of the "most proper and speedy method of assisting and supplying" South Carolina to the Board of Trade. After having interrogated various merchants, planters sojourning in London, and their own records, as well as the South Carolina proprietors themselves, the board blamed the exposure and vulnerability of England's southernmost colony on proprietary neglect. South Carolina, the board observed, had become a "frontier, as well against the French and Spaniards, as against numerous nations of Indians," and a victim of a French-Indian alliance. Thus the board played directly into the hands of South Carolina dissidents eager to discredit the proprietors and install royal government in the colony.[39]

Efforts to unseat the proprietors by playing upon fears of the French and Indians were further pursued in London by the agents of the South Carolina legislature, Richard Berresford and Joseph Boone. It was Berresford's memorial of December 1717 that the Board of Trade forwarded to Spotswood and that provoked the Virginia governor's vigorous warnings against the perils of French encirclement and Indian warfare. The appeal also went to William Keith, governor of Pennsylvania, who, in his reply, stressed honest trade as a means of securing the friendship of the Indians. Fairness, however, required overcoming economic competition among New York, Virginia, and South Carolina. Englishmen in the New World, according to Keith, must develop a "publick spirit and just regard to a national interest." In preparing his response, Keith relied heavily upon the thinking of provincial secretary James Logan. Logan took issue with French claims to the North American interior that conflicted with English colonial charters. Among the "methods that may be proposed to prevent the designs of the French," Logan advocated "all reasonable endeavours" to preserve the friendship of the Iroquois, foster cooperation among colonial governors, and take "special care of the commerce with the Indians." Most important for the future of the Virginia backcountry, Logan implored the Board of Trade "to encourage the Government of Virginia to extend their settlements beyond the mountains, over which the present Governour has happily discovered passes."[40]

The Board of Trade's concerns for colonial security only intensified in 1719, with the successful rebellion of the antiproprietary party in South Carolina and the dispatch of John Barnwell to London to consolidate the revolution in the minds of British officials. Barnwell's brief included a paper entitled "A True State of the Case between the Inhabitants of South Carolina, and the Lords Proprietors." It clearly laid out the strategic importance of South Carolina as a colonial frontier, called for the conquest of St. Augustine, and warned that both the recent French capture of Pensacola and the construction of Fort Toulouse on the upper Alabama River prefigured attempts to "surround this settlement from the mountains to the sea." But in his pleas to the board on behalf of his home colony, Barnwell portrayed South Carolina as only one of the victims of encirclement, invasion, and destruction then menacing all of British North America.[41]

Other developments also encouraged the Board of Trade to adopt a continental perspective on American frontiers. After 1717, reports filtered into London of massive efforts by the newly formed Compagnie des Indes to expand French colonies in Louisiana, including the dispatch of eighteen hundred engagés, or settlers. These endeavors were accompanied by the 1718 publication of a new map by cartographer Guillaume de l'Isle entitled "Carte de la Louisiane et du Cours du Mississipi" (figs. 2.1, 2.2). De l'Isle's depiction of North America dwarfed the English colonies on the Atlantic coast by comparison with the vastness of the French interior, extending from the St. Lawrence almost to the Rio Grande and New Mexico. The map appeared at an awkward time for British negotiators who, during the summer of 1719, opened talks in Paris aimed at determining the boundaries of British and French colonies left unfixed by the Peace of Utrecht six years earlier. It was the Board of Trade that bore responsibility for preparing instructions for British commissioners in Paris.[42]

Troubled by these developments and skeptical of the new British affiliation with the French in the War of the Quadruple Alliance, the Board of Trade questioned the governors of Virginia and South Carolina about the strategic importance of the French on the Mississippi and about the advisability of taking St. Augustine from the Spanish. The query gave Alexander Spotswood another opportunity to propound his rapidly developing theories of colonial defense and imperial strategy. "There can be no doubt but that the French Settlement on Mississippi will, (without timely precautions,) greatly effect both the Trade and Safety of these, his Maj'ty's Plantations," Spotswood pointed out. French competition in tobacco and rice production and in the Indian trade would inevitably diminish British commerce. But the real danger lay in the "Communication w'ch the French may maintain between Canada and Mississippi by the conveniency of the Lakes." "They do, in a manner," continued the governor, "surround all the British Plantations . . . [and] by possessing themselves of the Passes of the Great Mountains, w'ch ly between Us and the Lakes, Either by themselves or their Indians, fall upon and over-run w'ch of these Provinces they think fit." The capture of Pensacola by the French provided unequivocal evidence of their "design . . . to extend their Dominions Eastward from Mississippi towards South Carolina." Expanding upon this connection between settlement and defense, Spotswood concluded that "it is certainly [in] the British Interest to put a stop to their Advancing any further that way" by occupying the coast of Florida and, most significantly by "forming a Settlement as near as can be to cramp their's." Fears of the French were seconded by the now-deposed proprietary governor of South Carolina, Robert Johnson, who prophesied that "if there should ever be a warr between the Crowns of France and England this Province would fall an easy prey to them and very probably Virginia New York and other Plantations to which this Collony is a frontier."[43]

Meanwhile, South Carolina's London agents, John Barnwell and Joseph Boone, continued to press the case for frontier security before the Board of Trade. They described the French method of expansion by constructing frontier forts such as Toulouse and proposed that the English counter by fortifying six strategic locations in the southeast. English forts, however, should be more than military outposts. Surrounding lands should be granted free of quitrents to attract traders and planters. The scheme, although never fully enacted, was quickly endorsed by the Board of Trade.[44]

Overleaf

FIG. 2.1. Guillaume de l'Isle, "Carte de la Louisiane et du Cours du Mississipi, 1718." In the midst of prolonged imperial conflict with England, de l'Isle, Premier Géographe du Roi, inflated France's power in the North American interior by enlarging the Mississippi and Ohio Valleys at the expense of the size and prominence of England's seaboard colonies. Maps K. Top 118. By permission of the British Library.

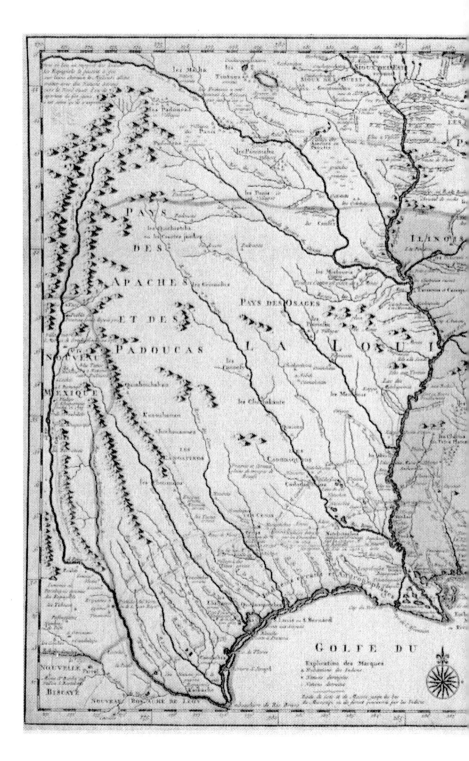

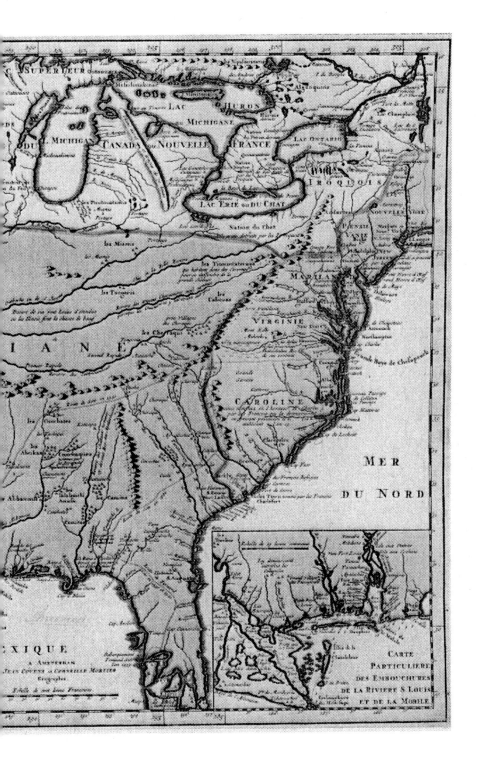

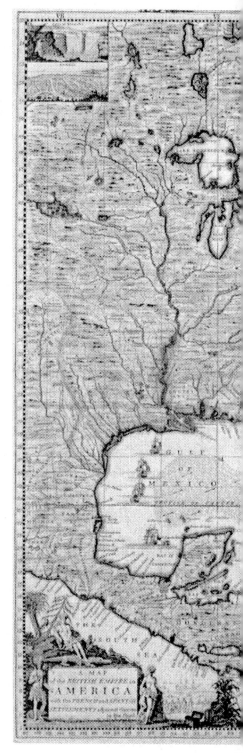

FIG. 2.2. Henry Popple, "America Septentrionalis: A Map of the British Empire in America . . . ," 1733. Here, Popple, son and brother to successive secretaries of the Board of Trade, may have been responding to complaints by colonial authorities about the distortions of de l'Isle's 1718 map. Popple diminished the geographic significance of France's Louisiana colony and expanded British imperium consistent with the policies and actions of the Board of Trade. Maps 1 Tab 45. By permission of the British Library.

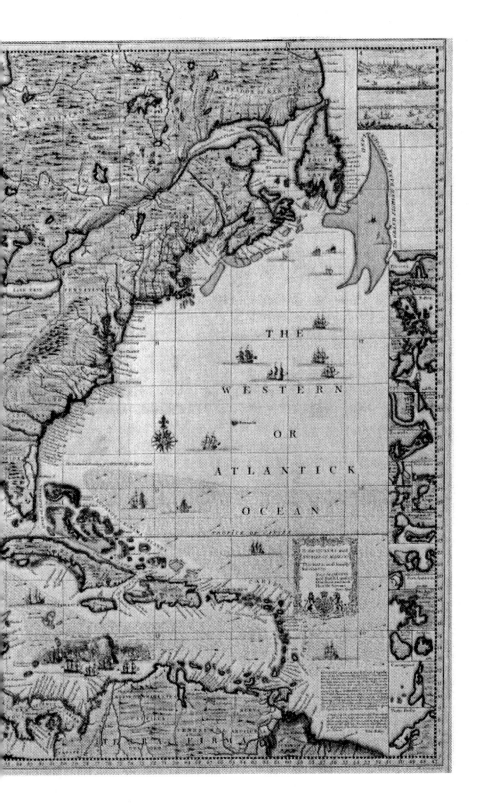

THE

WESTERN

OR

ATLANTICK

OCEAN

Thus, between 1715 and 1720, the members of the Board of Trade acquired substantial information about the condition of Great Britain's mainland colonies. Some of this information was thrust on them by self-interested men, such as the members of South Carolina's antiproprietary party. In other cases the board gathered information to inform various branches of the British government about colonial affairs. However the board came by it, this information must have produced perceptions in the minds of its members that called for action to defend British interests.

The first perception was one of French encirclement. To the east of their mainland colonies, British authorities could take some comfort in the protections provided by the ocean and by English sea power. The Atlantic, however, also opened an avenue of attack, as demonstrated during the War of the Spanish Succession, when Charles Town was twice assaulted by combined French-Spanish forces. To the west were the Appalachian Mountains, which ran like a spine down the interior of North America. Although rarely exceeding four thousand feet, they were regarded as impassable and, as Spotswood pointed out, a "Natural Defence" against both the French and the Indians. But the mountains were a double-edged sword because newly discovered passes exposed English colonies to enemy incursions. Spotswood's misperceptions about the proximity of the Great Lakes and French settlements must have helped place more emphasis on threat than on protection in the minds of British authorities when they considered the mountain barrier. Nonetheless, the sea and the mountains afforded some security in fortifying ports and towns.

Most vulnerable in the geography of North America, therefore, were the northern and southernmost colonies, Nova Scotia and South Carolina. That the former would remain a threat was insured by the capture of Port Royal, the capital of French Acadia, in 1710, and three years later by the Peace of Utrecht. This treaty not only failed to establish English-French borders in North America; it also incorporated five thousand French Catholic Acadians under British control. Despite the obviously biased assertions of the antiproprietary party after the Yamasee War about the imminent peril of the French, few on either side of the Atlantic could deny the significance of French expansion or the vulnerability of South Carolina. Protecting South Carolina became a major concern of British officials; it led to numerous settlement schemes during the 1720s and lay behind the founding of Georgia in the 1730s.

The second perception of North America emerging from the information gathered by the Board of Trade stressed the destabilizing potential of Indian warfare. By 1720 the board had within its collective memory two devastating Indian wars accompanied by apocalyptic reports of colonial annihilation and pan-Indian warfare that could engulf all of British North America. The Tuscarora and Yamasee Wars, in other words, had not been represented to board members as minor scuffles between autonomous colonies and "their" disgruntled Indians. Instead, these were seen as devastating conflicts that could easily escalate into continental wars in which the English would be readily overwhelmed if the French joined the fray. Meanwhile colonial officials, among them Logan and Keith in Pennsylvania and Spotswood in Virginia, as well as various colonial agents, described the Indian trade as the single greatest source of conflict with the Indians and, at the same time, the single most powerful instrument of stabilizing colonial frontiers and securing allies in the struggle with France. In either case, it had been made clear to the board that intercolonial cooperation—not competition—was essential. To make the best use of North America's native inhabitants for the purposes of securing an empire, British authorities had to think continentally.

The third perception before the Board of Trade was one of a colonial population increasingly beset not only by external threats but by internal enemies as well. Colonists had much to fear from an enslaved black population, which, by 1720 in at least one colony, South Carolina, outnumbered white inhabitants. In that year Britain's most exposed frontier experienced its first slave rebellion, and many feared that Spain, in collaboration with Indians, could disrupt the domestic peace of the colony by promising freedom to runaway slaves. Spain did precisely that in 1733 and helped provoke a slave uprising six years later. Alexander Spotswood and Virginia slave owners harbored similar fears, but with a view of the Appalachian Mountains as a haven for runaways. By 1720 South Carolina had already pursued numerous measures checking the importation of more blacks from Africa and encouraging white, Protestant servant immigration. It made good sense for colonial officials to see Virginia's mountains as a locus for that same immigration.[45]

· ⚘ ·

In August and September 1720 the Board of Trade composed several reports on the defense and security of the British mainland colonies dealing primarily with Nova Scotia and South Carolina. The board's work of gathering and sifting information about the colonial world culminated, however, in the report of September 8, 1721. The previous month board members had received orders to prepare a "representation of the state and condition of His Majesty's Colonies on the continent of America, with their opinion what methods may be taken for the[ir] better government and security." The board quickly dug out the draft of an earlier document and, after fourteen additional sessions and much hard work, produced its report on the "respective situations, Governments, strengths and trade" of the North American colonies, to which it "added an account of the French settlements, and of the encroachments they have made in your Majesty's colonies." The board also "offered such considerations, as, in our opinion, may contribute to the improving and enlarging your Majesty's dominions in America."[46]

The report reviewed the government and boundaries of each colony in turn, covering internal politics, intercolonial disputes, taxes, quitrents, trade, population, and defense. Virginia, for instance, tallied fourteen thousand militiamen out of a population of eighty-four thousand white people. Virginians produced "pitch and tar, pipe and hogshd. staves; skins and furrs; and a few druggs," the report continued, "but their dependance is almost wholly on the produce of tobacco." For their "strength and security," Virginians "depend upon their Militia; their plantations being usually at too great a distance from one another to be cover'd by forts or towns." But "for their protection against the Indians who inhabit among them, and that line to ye westward, they have . . . lately proposed to your Majesty a scheme for securing ye passes over the great ridge of mountains . . . that we conceive . . . to be deserving of all reasonable encouragement." Here the board was sticking very close to the script provided by Governor Spotswood.

South Carolina's situation, however, sounded most desperate. It was "exposed in case of a rupture on the one side to the Spaniards, on the other to the French, and surrounded by savages." At the same time that the "frequent massacres committed of late years by the neighbouring Indians at the instigation of the French and Spaniards, has diminished the white men," economic growth had "given occasions to increase ye number of black slaves who have lately attempted and were very near succeeding in a new revolution." The board called for more forts and troops, but most significant for the future of the backcountry, it recommended that measures be adopted for "encouraging the entertainmt. of more white servants for the future."

It was in its treatment of French activities along the Mississippi River, however, that the board's new continental perspective became most apparent. French encirclement imperiled all the colonies: "By one view of the Map of North America [de l'Isle], your Majesty will see the danger your subjects are in, surrounded by the French who have robbed them of great part of the trade they formerly drove with the Indians, have in great measure cut off their prospect of further improvements that way; and in case of a rupture may greatly incommode if not absolutely destroy them by their Indian allies." The board took great pains to describe the routes the French were establishing between Canada and Louisiana and the "encouragement" given "to the discoverers and planters of new tracts of lands." The failure of recent boundary negotiations in Paris was critical to British colonial security. "It is therefore very apparent from these transactions," the board concluded, "that there remains no way to settle our boundaries, but by making ourselves considerable at the two heads of your Majesty's Colonies north and south; and by building of forts, as the French have done, in proper places on the inland frontiers."

Having outlined the conditions and security risks of each colony separately and examined the colonial world as a whole from the perspective of French and Indian threats, the board then offered a series of recommendations "for securing, improving and enlarging your Majesty's Dominions in America . . . 1st. By taking the necessary precautions to prevent the incroachments of the French, or of any other European nation. 2nd. By cultivating a good understanding with the native Indians. And lastly by putting the Government of the Plantations upon a better foot." The board made good use of its new continental perspective, especially in guarding against the French. It urged the need "to begin by fortifying ye two extremeties to the north and south." For the intervening territory, however, "nature has furnished the British Colonies with a barrier which may easily be defended, having cast up a long ridge of mountains between your Majesty's Plantations and the French settlements." Passes "ought to be secured as soon as they shall be discovered," but the board cautioned that "we should not propose them for the boundary of your Majesty's Empire in America. On the contrary it were to be wished that the British settlements might be extended beyond them." Here was the idea, articulated by James Logan and promoted by Alexander Spotswood, that would have significant consequences for the Virginia frontier.

The board next raised the issue of Indian relations to the level of imperial interest. The "security of the British Plantations" was simply a matter of "cultivating a good understanding with the native Indians." Trade was the key: "If fairly carried on, [it] would greatly contribute to the increase of your Majesty's power and interest in America." It would also lead to the extension of British territory, "for on the succesful progress of this trade, the inlargement of your Majesty's Dominions in those parts doth almost intirely depend." The king should build forts on the frontier so that "your Majesty's subjects may be the more easily induced to extend this trade as far westward upon the lakes and rivers behind the mountains" as possible. The Indian trade, too, must be conceived on a continental scale "so that no one colony or sett of people whatsoever may engross the same to the prejudice of their nei'bours." All traders, moreover, "should be instructed to use their endeavors to convince the said Indians, that the Indians have but one King and one interest."

In its observations about colonial government the Board of Trade made several recommendations bearing on the settlement of the Virginia frontier. Evident throughout the report was the board's larger objective of bringing the separate colonies into one accord not just to check the French and better order Indian relations but also to impress upon the colonies a unified obedience to the crown. Having just witnessed the upheavals and divisions that proprietary government could bring to a colony such as South Carolina, the board recommended that "all the Proprietary Governments should be resumed to the Crown" so that "all the British Colonies in America hold immediately of one Lord." It also had concerns about land and land distribution in the colonies that would be reiterated in future years with implications for emerging landscapes in western Virginia. "Exorbitant grants to private persons" were a problem because, by them, "Yr. Majesty is defrauded of your quitrents, ye lands remain uncultivated, and the industry of the fair planter is discouraged." As a remedy, the board called for a strict accounting of quitrents and land patents. More significant for colonial land use were proposals designed to encourage compact settlement and restrict speculation by limiting grants to one thousand acres and voiding them unless two-thirds of their area was cultivated within a term of years.

Two final recommendations were clearly contrived to achieve unity and order in the administration of a British colonial empire. "To render the several provinces on the Continent of America, from Nova Scotia to South Carolina, mutually subservient to each other's support," the board urged the appointment of a lord lieutenant or captain general, "from whom all other Governors of particular provinces should receive their orders." This high official, furthermore, "should constantly be attended by two or more Councillors" from each colony, who would compose a privy council for colonial affairs. Similarly, the colonial administration in London should be centralized, because, as the board pointed out, the "present method of despatching business relating to the Plantations, is lyable to much delay and confusion." To consolidate authority and jurisdiction among the Board of Trade, the Privy Council, the secretary of state, the treasury, the military, and various boards and commissions, the report of 1721 recommended that the chairman of the Board of Trade "be particularly and distinctly charged with your Majesty's immediate orders in the dispatch of all matters relating to the Plantations."

What the Board of Trade brought to colonial administration and ultimately to the colonial world in its 1721 report was an imperial vision, a vision born not of idealism or dreams of imperial grandeur but of necessity. Reconfiguring separate colonies into a coherent, if diverse, whole was a matter of survival for a colonial population whose primary value to Great Britain lay in trade. During the first two decades of the eighteenth century, British authorities came increasingly to understand the profound threat the Louisiana colonies posed to the peace and prosperity necessary to maintain trade. The resumption of a continental war among northern and southern Indians also threatened the English colonies collectively, as groups of Iroquois, Delawares, Shawnees, Catawbas, Cherokees, or Creeks not only traversed the continental interior but also disrupted relations between colonial governments and local Indian tribes. What Englishmen feared most was the growing ability of the French to coordinate Indian alliances and create an overwhelming force that could drive the English off the continent. Although defense in time of peace was a primary concern of the report, it also proposed means of expanding British dominion through settlement initiatives. Designed to counter French expansion in the Mississippi and Ohio River Valleys, western settlements would also forge independent relations with Indians throughout the interior. Faced with such a massive program as checking the French, balancing relations with the Indians, and extending settlement across a mountain range, the members of the Board of Trade had little choice but to look at the colonial world as a single piece and strive to coordinate its various elements.

Even though the report of 1721 advocated a more unified view of the colonial world, it was not a policy paper. In subsequent years the board did not initiate or promote specific measures designed to implement its recommendations. The report never served as a litmus test for proposals by colonizers, merchants, or military officers. No colonial lord lieutenant or captain general was ever appointed, and the London administration remained as decentralized as before. Yet the report was not without influence. With the exception of these two final recommendations, the report had been cobbled together from answers to various queries, other statements by imperial officials, and the depositions of colonial agents and merchants. It was, in essence, a mosaic of working assumptions widely held throughout British colonial officialdom. Because of the way it was drafted and constructed, the report represented a consensus of broadly shared opinions and ideas. It did not have to be implemented as policy because it was already reflected in the actions of numerous colonial officials. Most of what it recommended came to pass because of this consensus.

· ✿ ·

For the story of settlement and landscape in the Shenandoah Valley the most critical assumptions of the report of 1721 had to do with the expansion of Virginia under the auspices of empire. By the third decade of the eighteenth century, large numbers of people were moving vast distances across the earth under those auspices. From the perspective of imperial officials, new immigrants flooding into North America from the north of Ireland and central Germany were ideal instruments of imperial expansion and backcountry settlement. They were Protestant, yeoman, and white.

Throughout the seventeenth and eighteenth centuries Great Britain was locked in a set of imperial struggles with France and Spain. Colonial wars were not only about wealth and trade but also about religion and a prolonged contest between the cultures of Protestantism and Catholicism. Efforts to convert Native Americans in New France, New Spain, New England, and the Chesapeake or Carolina colonies were less an altruistic attempt to save the souls of heathens than to gain the loyalty of the uncommitted in a global conflict, just as twentieth-century superpowers in the midst of a cold war poured money and arms into Third World countries for the allegiance, not the benefit, of their peoples. The dangers of harboring Catholics on an English Protestant frontier were made nowhere more plain than in Nova Scotia. Here, as the report observed, were thousands of people "entirely in the French interest" who, "being influenced by their priests[,] have hitherto unanimously refused to take the oaths of allegiance to your Majesty." Moreover, their "communication and intermarriage with the neighbouring Indians, have gained them to their party." Thus, in the northernmost of Britain's two most critical frontier provinces in North America, there was "all the reason in the world to apprehend that upon any rupture between the two Crowns, they may openly declare in favour of France." Conclusion: "It is absolutely necessary for your Majesty's service, that these French inhabitants should be removed."[47]

That large numbers of people were to be shuffled around the peripheries of empire for the purposes of defense or security was nothing new. In the previous century the Plantation of Ireland had been effected to subdue a Catholic menace on the fringe of the British Isles through induced Protestant settlement. More recently, the depredations of Catholic France in the German Rhineland throughout the wars of the seventeenth century and the violence against Protestants following the revocation of the Edict of Nantes had left a deep distrust of the Roman Church among German and Swiss peoples already on the move for a variety of economic reasons and willing to undertake backcountry settlements under the auspices of the British crown.[48]

The uprooted of Protestant Ireland and Germany possessed other attributes that made their communities natural buffers against Catholic or Native American threats on the frontier. They came from diversified small-farm economies in Europe, and they migrated as families. In the New World their desire for a competence in landholding combined with modest means to generate communities of yeoman freeholders who took up and developed middling-sized tracts of land. They created socially and economically integrated settlements with dense networks of kinship, trade, and religious affiliation. Trained to arms in militia forces they would, in theory, fight to defend their independence. Thus they appeared to conform to the strictures of the report of

1721 against land speculation and its encouragement to the "industry of the fair planter." It was these same expectations about land and labor that both the proprietors of South Carolina and the colony's assembly had put forth in 1716 as a means to settle frontier lands recently abandoned by the Yamasee Indians in two- to four-hundred-acre parcels occupied and developed by newcomers from Great Britain, Ireland, or other countries. This same assembly had also adopted measures encouraging white servant immigration and restricting the importation of black slaves, assuming that its new population of small farmers would depend on family, not slave, labor on the frontier.[49]

The new immigrants to North America in the eighteenth century had the additional appeal of being white. The members of the Board of Trade understood the threat to white Englishmen and women when outnumbered by blacks whom they held in bondage. When first informed of the slave rebellion in South Carolina, the board quickly reported on how the "whole Province was lately in danger of being massacred by their Own Slaves who are too numerous in proportion to ye White Men there." The call in the report of 1721 for the immigration of more white servants was designed to check the emergence of black majorities in the plantation colonies. Alexander Spotswood's report to the Virginia Council about the threat to the "Peace of this Colony" by slaves who had "lately run away & suspected to be gone towards ye Great Mountains" had been made at the same time the Board of Trade was preparing its own report in August 1721.[50]

This incident and others may have been on the minds of the board eleven years later, when it advised the Privy Council that "it has been the *constant sense* [emphasis added] of this Board, that all ye British Colonies, and especially the two frontiers, should be peopled as amply and as soon as possible wh. white inhabitants." During the intervening period the board promoted backcountry settlements of white farmers by remitting quitrents, limiting the size of land grants, and encouraging colonies to offer settlement bounties. The board endorsed numerous proposals for new frontier settlements, such as those by Daniel Hintze in 1729 for a colony of German and Irish Protestants in Nova Scotia or by Jean Pierre Purry for a Swiss-German community, Purrysburg, on the Savannah River in South Carolina. It was the board's "constant sense" that led it to instruct Robert Johnson, returning to South Carolina as the royal governor in 1729, to lay out eleven new townships along the colony's western and southern frontier. "The number of white men in Our said Province," the board commented, "bears so small a proportion to that of ye blacks, which is not only a hindrance to ye peopling and settling the same, but may be also of dangerous consequence from ye attempts of an enemy and even from an insurrection of ye negroes." Thus the board could confidently and knowledgeably advise the secretary of state in 1734 that "nothing can be more conducive to the service of the Crown, and the general interest of Great Britain, than that all your Majesty's Colonies in America and particularly the two frontier provinces of Nova Scotia and South Carolina, should be fully peopled with white inhabitants."[51]

By the early 1720s the groundwork had been laid for the peopling of Virginia west of the Blue Ridge. Acting on his "Political Creed," Alexander Spotswood had linked the interests of Virginia planters—soon to include himself—with the imperial concerns of British authorities in granting land, defending Virginia, and extending the king's dominion. In doing so he had not only established the Blue Ridge as a barrier against both the French and the Indians but also contributed to the continental reconfiguration of North American frontiers through his influence with the Board of Trade. The board understood that the ridge of high mountains served all the colonies as a natural defense and that settlement as the key to imperial interests ought to be pushed beyond the ridge. That eighteenth-century backcountry communities were composed of ethnically diverse, white, Protestant, freehold-farm families owed as much to the different cultures of the new immigrants as to the use to which imperial authorities put those cultures. The settlement of Virginia's Blue Ridge frontier did not occur immediately as a result of Spotswood's program of defense for Virginia or as a direct consequence of the report of 1721. But the working assumptions written into the report through information and proposals provided by Spotswood and others were shared broadly by contemporaries and also by later colonial officials. So it was that William Gooch, working within the framework of these assumptions, would orchestrate the settlement of the Shenandoah Valley and insure the region's sectional distinctiveness.

· �< ·

At the time of his appointment as lieutenant governor of Virginia in 1727, William Gooch had been an officer of the crown for twenty-three years. Commissioned a captain in 1704, he fought at Blenheim and served the duke of Marlborough throughout his campaigns. Although his correspondence never mentioned the report of 1721, it is unlikely that he would have been unfamiliar with the Board of Trade's thinking on the strategic importance of its North American colonies in a global struggle with France, Spain, and at various times and places with Native North Americans as well.

Gooch had inherited a bad situation in the Virginia Piedmont. His immediate predecessor, Hugh Drysdale, had described the problem to the Board of Trade in language resonating with the board's own concerns about land speculation in the report of 1721:

The lands in those counties especially Spotsylvania, are parcelled out and patented in a manner so inconsistent and directly opposite to their Excellcies.' commands, that I am att a loss to reconcile them to the purport and design of their intentions. . . . Hence it is that these lands, which by the Lds. Justices' commands, are limited to bee granted in noe greater quantities, than 1000 acres to any one person, are parcelled and patented out in tracts of 10, 20 and 40,000 acres apeice to a few, and little left to dispose off, besides the most remote, barren, and unprofitable: Hence it is that the intention of the Crown, to make that county of Spotsilvania, a well inhabited fronteer, is frustrated.

Despite a Privy Council limitation of 1,000 acres on land grants for Spotsylvania County, between 1721 and 1730 the Virginia government issued 116 grants averaging more than 2,960 acres each in the portion of Spotsylvania that would become modern Orange County. It was in this context, then, that Gooch had defended the "men of substance" who speculated in large tracts of land and encouraged the "meaner sort of People" under their "Shade & Protection."[52]

The settlement of the Virginia Piedmont in large tracts, which would soon become plantations and support large numbers of slaves, may have encouraged Gooch to look beyond the Blue Ridge to foster the type of small-farm frontier society originally intended for Spotsylvania County. This step would certainly have been consistent with the recommendation in the report of 1721 that "British settlements might be extended beyond the ridge." By the late 1720s, having been in office only a few years, Gooch would have been experiencing other pressures to extend the reach of Virginia settlement.

Like the settlement of Spotsylvania County, Alexander Spotswood's efforts to insulate Virginia from traveling parties of northern and southern Indians appeared not to be working according to plan. During the summer of 1726 the Iroquois killed a Virginian "by mistake" while pursuing "certain Indian enemies." The slain white man lived east of the Blue Ridge, where, according to the Treaty of Albany, northern Indians could travel only with a governor's pass. This treaty, asserted the Council, "will be rendered altogether ineffectual if such excuses as this shall be accepted . . . since these Indians may always find the like pretence for coming into this Government contrary to the express words of the Treaty." By the next year the infiltration across the Blue Ridge had reached such proportions that Robert Carter, president of the Council and acting governor, alerted the Board of Trade to a "threaten'd invasion from the Western Indians. Their pretences at first was to revenge themselves of some of our Tributarys and the Tuscaruros; but having met with some success in that enterprize, they begin to talk more insolently, and to threaten our frontier inhabitants." Then, scarcely a week before he wrote to the Board of Trade endorsing large grants in Spotsylvania County, Gooch warned its members that "as our Frontier Inhabitants lye at the same time exposed to the barbarous Insults of these Indians, and the foreign Nations they call in to their aid, this in all probability will involve us in continual Skirmishes & Alarms." In settling the Blue Ridge backcountry, therefore, Gooch may have been attempting to force the Indians farther west, well beyond the mountains, as a means of preventing the kind of hostilities that had so recently troubled Virginia.[53]

Gooch may also have had difficulties with the Northern Neck Proprietary in mind when he looked to the northwestern part of the colony. The proprietary, established in the seventeenth century by royal charters, encompassed all the land between the Potomac and Rappahannock Rivers. By the early 1720s proprietary rights to dispense lands and collect quitrents had devolved on Thomas, sixth lord Fairfax, who initially showed little interest in his inheritance, partly because a trust agreement diverted what income it produced to his sister. But this arrangement ended in 1728, by which time proprietary boundaries were in dispute. At issue was the western extent of the Potomac. The Rappahannock clearly headed on the east flanks of the Blue Ridge. By claiming that the Potomac began at the confluence of the Shenandoah and another river called the Cohongarooton, William Gooch and the colonial government in Williamsburg limited the western extent of the proprietary to the Blue Ridge. Fairfax and his agent, who was none less than Robert Carter, asserted that the Cohongarooton was in fact the principal branch of the Potomac, which headed deep in the Appalachians, thus extending proprietary claims across the entire lower Shenandoah Valley.[54]

On June 13, 1728, when Gooch and the Council issued a series of grants totaling twenty-six thousand acres on the west slope of the Blue Ridge, Carter protested that the "governor will not pass any patent or patents for any lands lying" within proprietary boundaries. Gooch was quick to respond, citing a 1707 Privy Council instruction that the Virginia governor be "very watchful that his Majesty's lands be not invaded under any pretence of a Grant to any Proprietor." On the governor's mind, as well, could have been the antiproprietary sentiments of the report of 1721 and its injunction that "all the Proprietary Governments should be re-assumed to the Crown." Although the Northern Neck Proprietary bore no governing powers, Gooch would clearly have been inclined to view it as a threat to British imperial interests. Crown grants to western lands would help confirm those interests.[55]

Although the French were an ever-present concern, William Gooch had an especially pressing reason to worry about the mountains of western Virginia in 1729. On June 29 the governor wrote the Board of Trade that "a number of Negroes about fiftenn belonging to a new plantation, on the head of James

River formed a design to withdraw from their master and to fix themselves in the fastnesses of the neighbouring mountains." They took arms and ammunition with them, as well as provisions, cloths, bedding, and tools, to a "very obscure place among the mountains, where they had already begun to clear the ground." Their owners and a party of armed men soon discovered them, however, and after a brief exchange of gunfire, returned them to slavery. "A design," concluded Gooch, "which might have proved as dangerous to this country, as is that of the negroes in the mountains of Jamaica to the inhabitants of that island . . . has happily been defeated." The English colony of Jamaica had suffered a maroon war with escaped slaves living among its northern mountains since the early 1720s. Gooch knew this and no doubt agreed with the "constant sense" of the Board of Trade that colonial frontiers ought to be settled by white inhabitants. He therefore recommended the adoption of "some effectual measures for preventing the like hereafter, it being certain that a very small number of negroes once settled in those parts, would very soon be encreas'd by the accession of other runaways."[56]

One of those "effectual measures" may have come to Gooch's attention shortly after the affair of Virginia's slave maroons. It appeared in the form of a grand vision for a thirteenth English mainland colony covering a huge interior area represented today by the states of West Virginia, Ohio, Indiana, and Illinois and including additional portions of Kentucky and Maryland. Called Georgia and engrossing 120,000 square miles, it was the inspiration of Jacob Stover and Ezekiel Harlan (fig. 2.3). Stover, a native of Zurich, had immigrated to New York with Jost Hite and other German and Swiss refugees to labor in the royal tar works there. When the tar manufactory failed, Stover acquired land in the Oley Valley of Pennsylvania, a reputation as a pioneer of frontier settlements, and a friendship with Harlan. As an Indian interpreter for the Pennsylvania government, Harlan knew the physical and cultural terrain of the backcountry intimately.[57]

Stover had recently made a three-month exploration of the Shenandoah Valley and western lands. There he found "good Pasture Ground fitt for planting of Vineyards on the side of the Mountains and a very good soyle for Hemp, Flax, and all sorts of Grain." With Harlan he would undertake the set-

Overleaf

FIG. 2.3. Jacob Stover, "Draught of a Tract of Land on the N.W. side of Virginia . . . ," [1731]. Stover and his associates, including William Keith, submitted this map to the Board of Trade to support their petition for an interior North American colony named Georgia. CO 700/Virginia 7, Colonial Office Papers, Public Record Office, London.

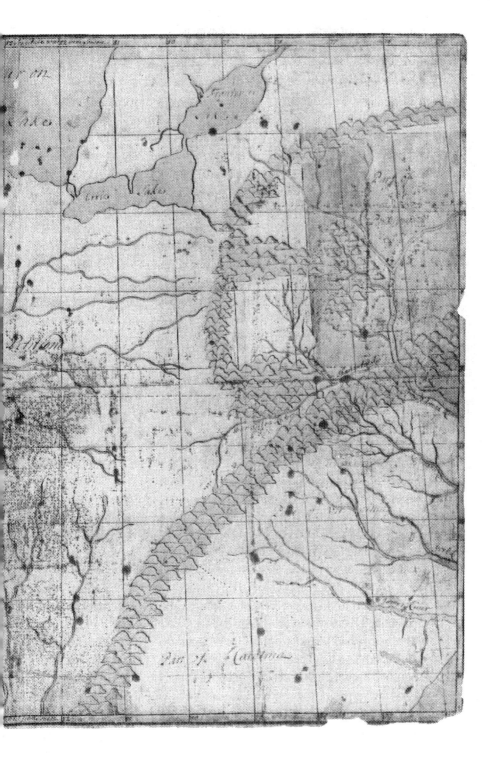

tlement of this vast tract "without any Charge to the Government, notwith-
standing the great difficultys that attend it, which hitherto neither the Inhabitants of Virginia nor any Person have attempted to undertake by reason of
the difficulty of the Passage and the apprehensions of being so farr seperated
from Virginia by the Mountains." That the arguments Stover and Harlan put
forth to justify their undertaking could have been read from the report of 1721
demonstrates the extent to which its assumptions were shared throughout the
colonial world. "If it is neglected to extend the bounds of Great Britain beyond these Mountains to the West," the partners pointed out, "it is probable
that the ffrench in a short time may take possession there of." If Britain—or
rather Stover and Harlan—succeeded, the "French Settlements of Missisipy
and Canada would thereby be prevented to Join together, as there intention
is." "Georgia," aptly named after the British monarch, would moreover be
Protestant, yeoman, and white. Stover promised that the "strength of the Subjects of this Kingdom in America would be considerably encreased by carrying over a great number of Germans and Swiss Protestants." They would
"apply themselves . . . upon such productions as are very much desired in this
Kingdom Vist Hemp, Flax, Silk, Potash, Salt Petre with other valuable Commodities in which the Germans and Swissers are particularly skilled." Independent and self-reliant, the German and Swiss settlers were "alsoe reputed to
be a good Militia."[58]

Stover made these statements in a petition to the Board of Trade early in
1731. During the following year and a half he and additional partners would
pursue their plans before the board, but all eventually came to naught over the
objections of Lord Fairfax and the proprietors of Maryland and Pennsylvania.
"Georgia," however, may have been just what it took to move Gooch to initiate western settlement plans of his own. Precisely when Stover's scheme was
unveiled in Williamsburg is not known, but on June 17, 1730, the Virginia
Council granted 10,000 acres to Stover on the "West side the great Mountains
and on the Second fork of Sherundo River . . . for the Settlement of himself &
divers Germans & Swiss Families his Associates whom he proposes to bring
thither to dwell in two Years space." The Council then attached the unprecedented condition to the grant that "one Family for each Thousand Acres do
come to inhabit there within the time propos'd."[59]

Never before had Virginia authorities required that "families" actually occupy new lands as a qualification for receiving patents. For decades the Board
of Trade had been lobbying the colonial government to enforce requirements
that a minimal portion of every tract be cultivated within three years of patenting. Instructed accordingly, Alexander Spotswood, during his first year as

governor, secured the appropriate legislation from the assembly. And "to the End that boundless desire of takeing up Land Above the Capacity of the taker up to Plant & Cultivate may be restrained," the governor by proclamation required that all grants larger than four hundred acres bear the Council's approval and his signature. Cultivation requirements, however, had been openly flaunted, and, as evidenced in Spotsylvania County, large grants were issued freely during the 1720s. But promoting compact communities of cultivators had been a purpose of the Board of Trade in the report of 1721. The family settlement requirements can thus be seen as a special condition imposed on the backcountry frontier that reflected a long-standing objective of the royal government both in London and Virginia.[60]

Other aspects of the Stover episode demonstrate how his proposals came to serve as a model for backcountry settlement and help explain the social and economic distinctiveness of the frontier. When Stover presented his proposals in London, the Board of Trade turned to William Keith, the then-retired governor of Pennsylvania, for counsel. Board members must have been concerned with Stover's status as an unknown, and in the paternalistic world of British politics, they may have doubted the ability of this commoner to attract the large number of settlers needed for a successful colony. Keith came to Stover's defense, arguing that "Persons of a low Degree in life who are known amongst their equals to be morally Honest and Industrious will sooner persuade a multitude into a Voluntary Expedition of this Nature than those of greater Wealth and Higher Rank who are ever liable to the suspicion and Jealousy of the Vulgar." In effect, Keith simply reversed the social formula with which Gooch had defended large grants in the Virginia Piedmont.[61]

Gooch may never have heard Keith's argument, but subscribe to it he did in establishing buffer settlements of foreign Protestants throughout the Virginia backcountry. On the same day that Stover received his ten thousand acres, the Virginia Council granted thirty thousand acres to John Van Meter under the same family settlement requirements for "divers of his Relations & friends living in the Governmt of New York." Van Meter's brother Isaac acquired another ten thousand acres for "divers other German Families [who] are desirous to settle themselves on the West Side the Great Mountains in this Colony." John and Isaac Van Meter soon sold their land rights to Jost Hite, who, with Robert McKay, also acquired his own one-hundred-thousand-acre grant on October 21, 1731, "upon the above Number of Families [100] coming to dwell there within two Years." By that time Alexander Ross and Morgan Bryan had already obtained their grant of equal size for a hundred "divers other Families of the sd Province" of Pennsylvania.[62]

In all, between 1730 and 1732 Governor William Gooch and the Virginia Council issued nine grants totaling 385,000 acres west of the Blue Ridge to individuals or partnerships. Each grant required settlement by families. With the exception of William Beverley, the Essex County planter, the individuals receiving grants were not "men of substance"; none was from Virginia, nor were they even English. On their social standing alone, they never would have commanded the attention of the Virginia Council. But they were William Keith's "Persons of a low Degree" competent to "persuade a multitude into a Voluntary Expedition" into the Virginia backcountry. Because these men were well connected among recent immigrants to the middle colonies from the north of Ireland and central Germany, this multitude and their self-created, yeoman-farm communities were guaranteed to be ethnically diverse, white, and Protestant. William Gooch and the Virginia Council knew precisely what they were doing in bringing these people to the Virginia backcountry. "For by this means," the governor informed the Board of Trade, "a strong Barrier will be Settled between us and the French; and not only so, but if by encouraging more Foreigners to come Hither, we can once gett the Possession of the Lakes, which are not very far distant, we shall be then able to cutt off all Communication between Cannada and Mississippi, and thereby so much weaken the Power of the French as to have little to fear from that Quarter hereafter."[63]

. ☙ .

Why did a society develop on the Virginia frontier whose social and economic construction profoundly altered the identity of the colony? William Gooch had put the rationale quite succinctly in his statement to the Board of Trade: to serve the interests of Virginia in defending its frontiers and of the empire by extending British dominions. This answer, however, was the product of more than three decades of historical change and response. The expansionist tendencies of Great Britain, France, and Spain, combined with a culture of conflict among Native Americans, had made settling the backcountry beyond the Blue Ridge expedient from the perspective of London and the colonial capitals. From the viewpoint of prospective settlers, land made available by virtue of imperial expediency meant the means of survival and competence for families and communities. That these men and women were white, Protestant, and given to working the land in patterns of diversified grain-livestock agriculture that did not depend heavily on slavery or produce black majorities was fortunate but not fortuitous. These were the people who had long been thought to create ideal settlement buffers. They were also the people who had long been shuffled around the peripheries of European empires wittingly or unwittingly in the service of monarchs. They ended up on the Virginia frontier as the result of a combination of interests. What they did there—the ways of life and livelihood they pursued, the communities and towns they built, the landscapes they created—continued to be the consequence of complex interactions among personal ambitions and the possibilities made manifest by the larger interests of colony and empire.

Chapter 3

Settling the Shenandoah

WINTER WOULD have been settling upon the Shenandoah Valley in late 1731, when Jost Hite and a group of settler families arrived to take up Hite's lands. Legend records that they numbered sixteen. That at least half were the families of Jost and Anna Maria Hite's children lends an epochal quality to the venture—the patriarch and his numerous kin braving the wilderness in search of new lands. Accompanying them were Hite's partner, Robert McKay, and a friend, Peter Stephens. Hite would have to find many more families to fulfill the settlement requirements of his land orders.[1]

How he learned about opportunities to acquire land in western Virginia is not clear (fig. 3.1). As other Pennsylvanians testified, he could have been informed by "Hunters and Traders the common finders of Back Lands that the Lands in the Colony of Virginia were rich and good." According to family tradition, John Van Meter, an Indian trader himself, had found lands he liked in the Appalachian valleys of the Potomac River's South Branch about 1725, while accompanying a party of Delaware Indians raiding the Catawbas. A New Yorker, Van Meter would likely have been in close touch with Delawares who lived along the upper branches of the Delaware River. Although the foray ended in retreat, Van Meter vowed that some day his sons would own some of the fine lands lying to the south. Van Meter might also have been in touch with Hite, whose first years in America had been spent in New York. The two men were certainly acquainted in August 1731, when, several months before Hite received his own one-hundred-thousand-acre land orders, John and Isaac Van Meter sold theirs, for forty thousand acres, to him.[2]

Hite had promised the Virginia Council that "divers others Families to the number of one hundred . . . [were] desirous to remove from thence [Pennsylvania] & seat themselves on the back of the great Mountains." Having formed "Companys of Adventurers" and "made a Stock sufficient to provide & carry out all Necessarys for their Subsistence & defence," the first group of families set out for Virginia. These men, women, and children, numbering perhaps a hundred in all, must have composed a motley company. Many had wagons pulled by horses or perhaps oxen. Where roads were absent, forests were capacious enough to permit the passage of wheeled vehicles. But any order of march would have been impossible to maintain because wagons had to be leveraged over roots and stumps or diverted around dead falls. If the fall rains were heavy, streams would have been difficult to ford and valley slopes negotiable only by unhitching and combining teams. Interspersed among the wagons or stretching out ahead or behind were herds of livestock that included not only horses and cattle but no doubt chickens, pigs, turkeys, and geese. Progress was slow and limited on bad days to only a few miles. The journey from Pennsylvania to Opequon could have consumed two months or more.[3]

The route would have taken Hite and his party westward from Perkiomen Creek, where Hite had been forced hurriedly to sell his homestead in order to "make a Provision for his numerous family." By the time they reached Lancaster County, where only one or two families on average occupied every square mile, these travelers would have realized they were passing the frontier of European settlement. Lancaster had been formed in 1729, and its county town surveyed only the year before Hite's passage—hardly enough time for more than a few structures to be erected. Once the men and women journeying to Virginia crossed the Susquehanna, they would have found conditions much the same as those Jonnhaty and his party encountered a decade later except that settlements were even fewer and the going for wagons and livestock tougher. How they navigated their way to their new home is unknown, but Indian paths may have guided their route. If they utilized the same shallows where Jonnhaty crossed the river at Harris's ferry, Hite and company could have followed the so-called Virginia Road to the Potomac. Or, if passing through Lancaster Town, they would have taken the Monocacy Path. Most likely they crossed the Potomac at fords about ten miles above the mouth of

Overleaf

FIG. 3.1. "A General Map of the known and inhabited Parts of Virginia," [1731]. Virginians knew little about the land west of the Blue Ridge in the early 1730s, when this map was drafted. According to the legend appearing along the upper Potomac, the "Course & Length of the River is not certainly known." CO 700/Virginia 6, Colonial Office Papers, Public Record Office, London.

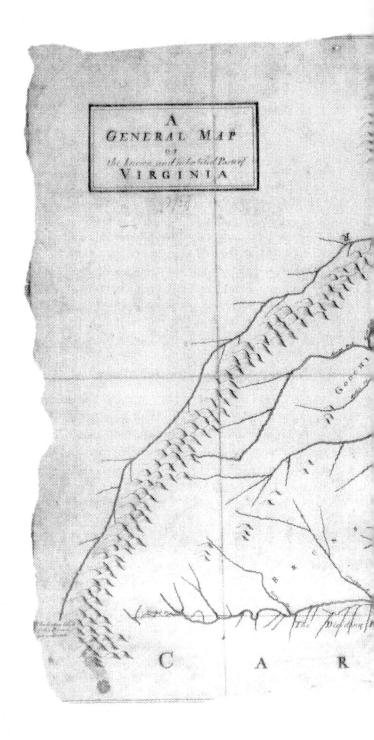

A
GENERAL MAP
OF
the known and inhabited Parts of
VIRGINIA

the Shenandoah River and proceeded southwest toward the Opequon. This route later came to be called the Jost Hite Road, or "Hites Waggon Road."[4]

If Hite blazed this path during the migration of the initial families that accompanied him, then he kept to fairly high ground lying between streams that emptied into the Opequon to the west and the Shenandoah or Potomac to the east. The lands, all limestone, supported a continuous forest dominated by oaks and hickories. After skirting some of the steepest banks along the Opequon, the road crossed the creek and led west, rising out of deeply dissected shale valleys. Approximately at the contact with the western band of limestone land, the road met the Indian path descending from the Potomac near Charles Friend's. However Hite reached this point, he then continued south another six miles or so to where the path crossed the headwater stream of the Opequon. Here he rested, and here the families who followed him were "obliged to live in their Waggons til they could build some small Huts to shelter themselves from the Inclemency of the weather." These men, women, and children probably told the story of their journey and its trials for years to come, but what is important to remember from it is the long stretch of vacant land they traversed before arriving at Hite's stopping place. They may not have seen another European after leaving the Susquehanna River more than a hundred miles behind. Unless they encountered other small groups of migrants or traveling parties of Indians on their way either north or south to forage, hunt, or fight, they had this new land to themselves. No adjacent settlements, existing roads, or nearby towns would influence or shape the way they took up the land. What they did, where they settled, how they devised farms, landholdings, communities, and eventually towns was up to them and their negotiations with land speculators such as Jost Hite, with surveyors, with the land itself, and with previous alterations made to it by Native Americans. Thus, within certain limitations, the landscape settlers created would be an artifact of their own intentions. This chapter explores the provenance of that artifact.[5]

Reading the forest and tracing the course of the Opequon another five miles to the west over well-watered limestone land, Hite knew he had found a promising area capable of yielding prosperous, productive farms. In the years to come he surveyed the 5,018-acre tract that engrossed most of the Opequon's watershed. But neither Hite's sons and daughters nor others among the original families took up lands there. Instead, they dispersed within a radius of about twelve miles from the patriarch. George Bowman and Hite's daughter Mary, for instance, kept moving south along the Indian path and contact zone between shale and limestone soils until they met Cedar Creek, a tributary of the Shenandoah's North Fork. There they carved out a 1,000-acre tract of land straddling the creek and built a house known as Fort Bowman. About halfway between Hite's Fort—as it came to be called—and Bowman's, Jacob Chrissman and Magdalena Hite found good land, which they purchased from Hite in 1740. Peter Stephens and his wife, Maria Christina Rittenhous, took up approximately 670 acres between Hite and Chrissman. Paul Froman and Elizabeth Hite, who did not settle on the shale-limestone contact, were located near a gap in Little North Mountain about eight miles to the southwest. Hite's partner, Robert McKay, initially fixed his home place much farther away, on a small run near the Potomac River, and only later on a tract of bottomland on the Shenandoah's South Fork. The single greatest conclusion to be drawn from how Hite's household and other families acted upon arriving at Opequon is that they scattered. Neither for the sake of protection nor for social and economic convenience did they cling together.[6]

Much the same can be said about those who occupied lands within the more constricted confines of Hite's own Opequon tract (fig. 3.2). Hite received a patent from the colonial government for this land on October 3, 1734. Two and a half years later he signed a deed for 450 acres with Stephen Hotsinpiller. This German blacksmith had arrived in Philadelphia in 1728, and after marrying the daughter of Germanna settler Melchoir Brumback, he moved his growing family to Opequon. Venturing upstream about a mile from Hite, he devised an elongated tract about two thousand feet wide and nearly three miles long across the creek. On a little rise several hundred feet from the water, he began building his farmstead. Although he was the last man to receive a deed from Hite for land in the five-thousand-acre tract, Ulrich Poker had arrived along the Opequon at least as early as Hotsinpiller. On a low terrace one-half mile downstream from his neighbor, this German immigrant settled in the center of another narrow tract, which receded from the creek. Upstream, Robert Allen began his homestead on a similar terrace overlooking the creek. Little is known about Allen's early life, but he was probably born in County Armagh in the north of Ireland. He and his wife, Sarah, left sometime after their eldest son was born and no doubt heard of the opportunities for land at Opequon after arriving in Philadelphia sometime in the late 1720s or early 1730s. Allen purchased 650 acres from Hite in a tract that differed from those of his German neighbors not only in its size but also in its more nearly square shape. So it went, up and down the Opequon, until fifteen families, including Hite and his son John, constituted the community. About half were German and half Scots-Irish, and some probably English or Scottish. Peter Mauk and Abraham Wiseman, both Germans, carved out landholdings that tended to be longer than they were wide as they receded from the creek. Like Robert Allen's land, the properties of many of the immigrants from the north

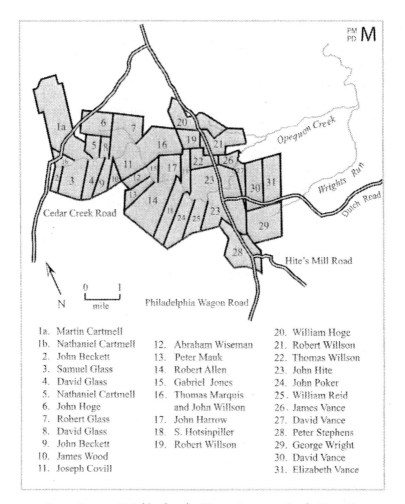

FIG. 3.2. Open-Country Neighborhood at Upper Opequon Creek. Many European settlers in the Shenandoah Valley purchased land from Jost Hite along the upper Opequon Creek. Spreading out, they formed an open-country neighborhood. Based on maps by Geertsema, in O'Dell, *Pioneers of Old Frederick County.*

of Ireland tended to be less elongated. Everybody fixed homesteads on creek terraces in a reckoning of the land closer to the natural environment than to any societal interest or collective worry over defense.[7]

A comparable pattern was emerging simultaneously around the landholding of Alexander Ross some ten miles to the northeast (fig. 3.3). Ross had received his land orders from the Virginia Council a full year before Hite. On November 12, 1735, he obtained a patent for his 2,373-acre tract, and on that same day thirty-four families received thirty-six patents in all under the Council's orders. A total of seventy families, however, had been brought to Virginia by Ross and his partner, Morgan Bryan. With the establishment of a Quaker meeting on Ross's property in 1734, the community these landholders established had an initial social and spiritual focus that Hite's settlers lacked. But they did not cluster around this meeting. Ross sold three tracts from his own land ranging between two and four hundred acres—one to his son and one to the son of Morgan Bryan. Otherwise those who received land under Ross's orders scattered. Unlike Hite's settlers on the Opequon tract, they were not taking up holdings within the confines of any presurveyed boundaries. But they did establish a pattern: a large U with one arm running along the shale-limestone contact to the east of the Opequon Meeting and the other arm extending along the base of Little North Mountain. Through each line of tracts ran a wagon road, which probably followed an Indian path. Ross's tract, his homestead, and the Opequon meeting stood approximately in the open mouth of the U.[8]

· ⚭ ·

The patterns of open-country community emerging at Opequon might have appeared very different if Indians had also been dwelling in the Shenandoah Valley. Their absence may have struck Opequon settlers as providential justification for dispersing in search of the best lands. But interpreting what happened at Opequon can be placed in better perspective by situating the Shenandoah Valley within a much larger region encompassed by the watersheds of the upper Potomac and upper Ohio Rivers immediately to the north. Virtually no one was living in this vast area during the opening decades of the eighteenth century, when the English feared a French communication between Canadian and Louisiana colonies and when the Five Nations of the Iroquois resumed their mourning wars across the continental interior.

Throughout the first half of the seventeenth century the Ohio Country had been inhabited by diverse native peoples, including the Eries, Shawnees, and Monongahelans. They were hunters, gatherers, and farmers who participated in a large trade network, which extended east to the Susquehanna River and reached from Ontario far southward. As the fur trade with Europeans grew, the region became known for an abundance of beaver pelts; so thought the Iroquois as they moved into the area by mid-century, in what came to be called the Beaver Wars. The Eries scattered, some seeking refuge eastward along the Susquehanna, while the Shawnees and others moved south as far as the Creek homelands in the southern uplands or along either the Delaware River far to the east or the Mississippi to the west. Some Shawnees stopped

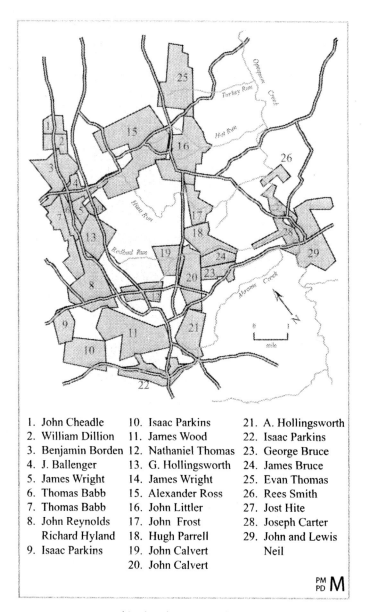

1. John Cheadle	10. Isaac Parkins	21. A. Hollingsworth
2. William Dillion	11. James Wood	22. Isaac Parkins
3. Benjamin Borden	12. Nathaniel Thomas	23. George Bruce
4. J. Ballenger	13. G. Hollingsworth	24. James Bruce
5. James Wright	14. James Wright	25. Evan Thomas
6. Thomas Babb	15. Alexander Ross	26. Rees Smith
7. Thomas Babb	16. John Littler	27. Jost Hite
8. John Reynolds	17. John Frost	28. Joseph Carter
Richard Hyland	18. Hugh Parrell	29. John and Lewis
9. Isaac Parkins	19. John Calvert	Neil
	20. John Calvert	

FIG. 3.3. Open-Country Neighborhood at Hopewell. The neighborhood surrounding the Hopewell Meeting took shape as Quakers acquired property through the land orders granted to Alexander Ross and partners by the governor and Council of Virginia. Based on maps by Geertsema, in O'Dell, *Pioneers of Old Frederick County.*

along the upper Potomac and established settlements such as the one Europeans called King Opessa's Town. These were the towns that so vexed Maryland authorities by proffering haven to black runaways. When he scouted the region in the years before 1710, Swiss colonizer Franz Louis Michel reported that "some Indians" lived there, but Opessa's Town clearly had been abandoned by the 1720s. So the ridges and valleys of the mountains from Virginia to New York and the Appalachian plateau to the west constituted one large unoccupied region by the time English authorities began to conceive of settlements west of the Blue Ridge.[9]

Viewing the upper Potomac and Ohio Rivers as a single region is instructive because at approximately the same time that Europeans began moving—or were moved—into the Shenandoah Valley, Native Americans migrated westward from Pennsylvania into the Ohio Country. Thus, this one large vacant region was reoccupied simultaneously by Native American and European settlers. Both groups came for land and the competency in economic, social, and political affairs of life that independent control over land brought. But the migrations of these diverse peoples were also responses to European imperial interests and attending conflicts. What happened at Opequon as European settlers scattered in pursuit of their own interests also happened in the Ohio Country. The Indians, in the words of one historian, "lived in a world of their own making." So did Europeans. Within two decades or so these groups would both be struggling to defend their independence, and in one of the ironies of history, they struggled against each other.[10]

Although they had earlier hunted the area, the Delawares made the move westward from central Pennsylvania in 1724, establishing the town of Kittanning on a bend of the Allegheny River. The Shawnees followed soon after. By the end of the 1730s Iroquois groups were migrating south and west to new towns in the Ohio Country. At virtually the same moment in autumn 1731, when Hite's party of pioneer families was edging toward Opequon, Pennsylvania traders counted ten Shawnee, Delaware, and Iroquois towns or hamlets along the Allegheny River. The Indians ventured west partly in response to reports that the long-abandoned lands were teeming with game. For Shawnees the move had all the additional attractions of a homecoming. Keeping tabs on the Delawares also made good sense considering the reputation these Indians had in the Susquehanna Country for trading away other Indians' lands.[11]

But forces larger than the attractions of self-betterment lay behind these moves. The Board of Trade's report of 1721 had made it clear that the "security of the British Plantations" depended upon "cultivating a good understanding with the native Indians." Nowhere were these relations more critical than in New York and with the Iroquois, who occupied the geographic and diplomatic divide between the colonies of England and France. English authorities knew that Anglo-American security depended upon keeping bright the Covenant Chain of Iroquois diplomacy. New York governor George Clarke had put it so well in warning William Gooch that "if we lose them and the French gain them what will become of all the Provinces is but too obvious to every one." For New York the 1721 report recommended that "care should be taken to put ye forts already built in ye best condition they are capable of, and to build others in such places where they may best serve to secure and enlarge our trade and interest with ye Indians, and break the designs of ye French." By that year the French had already beaten New York to the falls of Niagara and the best strategic location for a fort and trading post. The English were forced to settle for a position much farther east on Lake Ontario at Oswego.[12]

With the French and the English well established at opposite ends of Iroquoia by the mid 1720s, however, the Five Nations sensed a threat to the neutrality established in the Grand Agreement of 1701 and to their ability to play one imperial opponent off against the other. Their response set up the move by Delawares and Shawnees to the Ohio Country as a vector of the same forces that placed large numbers of German and Scots-Irish settlers in motion to Opequon. With the trade Niagara and Oswego brought to Iroquoia also came alcohol, disease, and disturbances to the balance between French and English influences in Indian society. In 1726 the Iroquois attempted to recruit the Delawares and Shawnees living along the Susquehanna River as allies in an effort to oust the English by force. Turned down, the Iroquois rebuked these Pennsylvania Indians "as women for the future, and nott as men." To the Shawnees they said, "Look back toward Ohio, the place from whence you Came, and Return titherward, for now wee Shall Take pitty on the English and Lett them have all this Land." The next year an Iroquois delegation complained to Pennsylvania governor Patrick Gordon and other Pennsylvania officials that "both the French & the English are raising Fortifications in their Country" and that they feared "some ill Consequences from it." They offered to sell "their" lands on the lower Susquehanna, where the truculent Shawnees and Delawares lived, in exchange for promises that no English settlements would extend upriver. Eager to secure this western borderland, Pennsylvania took the Five Nations up on the offer, negotiating a series of transfers during the next decade that forced the Shawnees and Delawares out to the Ohio Country.[13]

In taking up new lands the Indians, like the Europeans in the Shenandoah Valley, were responding to the pressures of imperial conflict while seeking refuge from the dominion of others over their lives and welfare. Once in these new lands, Indians and Europeans alike possessed a free hand in developing communities according to their own intentions and ambitions apart from the dictates of colonial officials or the influence of preexisting settlements. By the early 1730s the towns in the Ohio Country supported more than two hundred families. These were not the concentrated, fortified, and palisaded settlements that dominated this region and Iroquoia during the Beaver Wars. As noted earlier, the peoples of these towns dispersed along rivers and streams, sometimes clustering cabins and sometimes scattering them singly. Fields for corn and vegetables were spread out along lowlands. Onondaga, for instance, was described as a "strange mixture of cabins, interspersed with great patches of high grass, bushes, and shrubs." According to a modern historian, these towns were all "open, sometimes ramshackle, settlements."[14]

Despite their jumbled appearance Indian towns possessed their own internal order readily apparent to any Indian or European who understood the close association of land, family, kin, ethnicity, and gender. Like Opequon, the Ohio Country was a multiethnic frontier. Individual towns were predominantly Shawnee, Delaware, or Iroquois, but interaction among ethnic or tribal groups was considerable. Each town revealed its own carefully laid out ethnic and kinship geography. Clusters of houses at Kittanning along the Allegheny River, for instance, represented related lineages (fig. 3.4). In the matrilineal societies of the Delawares and Shawnees, men married into the kin groups of their wives and lived in the households of their wives' families. Housing clusters would then have contained women of several generations related by kinship, their in-marrying husbands, and their children, whose family identity would have been determined by their matrilineage, not by paternal descent. "Bushes, and shrubs" may have masked extensive crops and agricultural patterns closely adjusted to matrilineal society. Women working in fields, which they—not their husbands—owned, grew corn, beans, and squash using hoes. Nothing about the landscape they created would have seemed arbitrary to them. Cultivating corn in hills and encouraging beans and squash to encircle the growing stalks gave their fields an unkempt appearance to Europeans, who were accustomed to plow culture and the large open fields it required. Visitors could have easily mistaken a carefully worked Indian crop for scrub. Intermixing crops made a great deal of sense. While minimizing the labor required for preparing soil, the system made good use of the nitrogen-fixing capacity of legumes. Meanwhile, the broad leaves of the squash discouraged the growth of weeds.

Paths winding among cabins and fields connected people and places without regard to notions of private property and public space. Obviously, the new towns along the Allegheny River bore little resemblance to the grids of

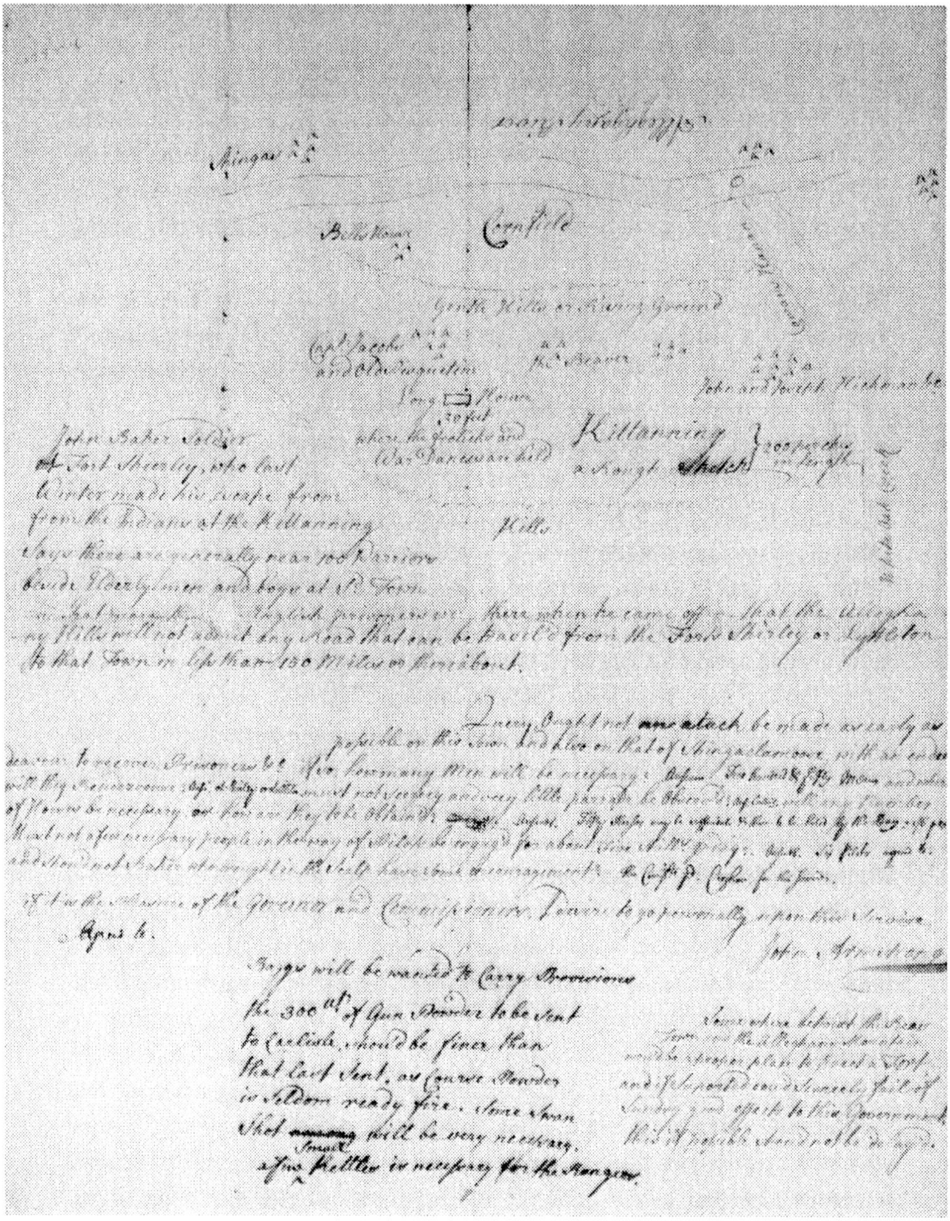

FIG. 3.4. Kittanning, about 1755. This Delaware Indian town appeared spread out along the banks of the Allegheny River when documented by John Armstrong. "Scheme of an Expedition to Kittanning," 1755, Misc. Mss. Collection, American Philosophical Society, Philadelphia.

streets and blocks that were at that same time coming to define Anglo-American towns. Nonetheless, an order regulated how people communicated across the land. At the cultural center of Kittanning, for instance, stood the thirty-foot longhouse where the "frolicks and War Dances" were held. Although it stood outside the circles of house clusters, it occupied the highest ground in the community. In societies that were quickly adopting smaller cabins and abandoning the multifamily longhouses of the Iroquois, this traditional structure provided sacred space for the rituals of those embarking on dangerous undertakings and seeking harmony with guiding spirits. From this central place emanated the routes and ways that everyone in the town needed to connect their working and family lives to the forces that bound them together in civil society. The network would also have facilitated the exchange of goods derived from hunting, gathering, and farming. The survival and well-being of the community depended on the free flow of foodstuffs, tools, weapons, and other items traded as gifts. One group of Indians described this exchange economy to the proprietor and Council of Pennsylvania in 1736, pointing out that in their world "there is never any victuals sold, the Indians give to each other freely what they can spare, but if they come amongst our People [the Pennsylvanians] they can have none without paying."[15]

The response of the proprietor and Council helps us understand Opequon as a world European peoples were making for themselves. Pennsylvania authorities explained to the Indians that "all the White People, tho' they live together as Brethren, have each, nevertheless, distinct Properties & Intrests, & none of us can demand from another Victuals or any thing of the kind without payment. One Man raises Corn & he sells it, Another raises Horses & he sells them, & thus every Man lives by his own Labour & Industry, & no one has a Right to take away from another what he thus earns for himself, & all Victuals cost money." In dispersing, seeking home sites, surveying land, and especially in soliciting patents for their holdings, Opequon settlers were creating a geography of private property suitable for this kind of economic exchange.[16]

· ⚹ ·

Recall that from the Indian perspective, the Opequon settlers "came like Flocks of Birds, and sat down on both Sides" of the Indian path along the Shenandoah Valley. Birds, like humans, take up lands capable of sustaining their species. Adequate living space must contain food, water, cover or protection, and materials for nesting. Birds occupy this space not only by identifying nest sites but also by asserting control over it as their territory. Taken collectively, nest sites and territories compose a habitat. Just as a bird's nest is comparable—and has often been compared—to a human dwelling, so animal territory represents a counterpart to farm tracts (fig. 3.5). For humans, dwellings and properties constitute a community whose habitat is called landscape and whose form we have designated an open-country neighborhood.[17]

The comparison between avian habitats and human settlements can be taken a step further. Birds define their territories by ritually repeating a distinctive song at key points on the perimeter of the area surrounding the nest and essential to its protection. According to the metes and bounds survey system employed throughout the English colonies, property corners were marked by witness trees. In conducting a traverse survey, surveyors would delimit property boundaries by lines sighted between these trees according to compass bearing and length in surveyor's poles of sixteen and one-half feet. When the survey was complete and often for years to come, only these witness trees, not fences, defined property boundaries. Initial settlers fenced cultivated fields only to keep animals out of crops. Although the custom was dying out by the eighteenth century, the property holders of a community from time to time walked what was in essence an open range and collectively stood witness to property corners. Called processioning, this ritual was repeated in four-year intervals as a function of the established church. Like bird song, witness trees and processioning made the entire community cognizant of the divides that distinguished the resources necessary to the survival of one family from those of other families.[18]

Although not always apparent to a casual observer, birds do not occupy the land in a haphazard, random, or arbitrary way. The nest sites of mating pairs, their territories, and their habitats are carefully adjusted to the environment and the means at a species' disposal to procure food, shelter, and protection. Different species seek distinctive locations for nests: tree branches, dense scrub, exposed heights, or sheltered ground cover. Size of territory and preference in microclimate also vary with species. The map of settlement tracts at Opequon bears a striking similarity to maps of avian territories. But the pattern of dispersing, locating dwellings, establishing farms, and surveying properties at Opequon also conformed to a variety of external forces, which have no counterpart in animal life. The emerging landscape of the Opequon settlement in the 1730s and 1740s was a world of the settlers' own making only by degrees. Constraints came in the form of laws or the policies of colonial officials; the interests of land speculators like Hite, Ross, and their partners; and the system or practice of surveying as it had developed in English Virginia up to that time.

Alexander Spotswood's 1710 proclamation "declaring her Majties Pleasure Concerning ye granting of land" provides a good example of the effect colonial policy could have on an emerging settlement landscape. Spotswood's con-

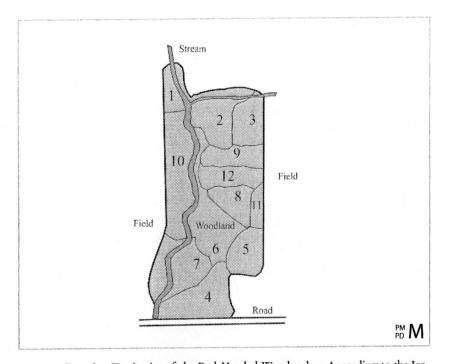

Stream

1

2   3

9

10

12

8   11

Field   Field

Woodland

6   5

7

4

Road

PM
PD   M

FIG. 3.5. Roosting Territories of the Red-Headed Woodpecker. According to the Iroquois, European settlers "came like Flocks of Birds, and sat down on both Sides" of the Indian trail through the Shenandoah Valley. A comparison of this drawing of bird territories to the maps of European settlements suggests that the association of avian and human territories was more than metaphorical. Based on L. Killam, "Territorial Behavior of Wintering Red-Headed Woodpeckers," *Wilson Bulletin* 70 (1958): 347–58.

cern during the first year of his administration was for remedying abuses "to the End that the Industrious Poor of this Colony & others who Shall Come to Dwell here may not want [lack] Land whereon to Imploy their Industry whilst others possess more than they are able to Cultivate." To achieve this end Spotswood stipulated that grants larger than four hundred acres bear his approval, and he required that "every Patentee be Obliged in ye best & most Effectual Manner to Cultivate & Improve Three Acres part of every fifty." Land, in other words, was to be apportioned according to the needs of an average family and would have to be developed, not held for speculation. Patentees, moreover, must "take the land as it Naturally falls" and not monopolize its most valuable resources. Holdings were to be laid out "in Such Manner as the Breadth may bear ye proportion of one Third part at least to the Length" so that "regard be had to the profitable & unprofitable acres." Taking up long narrow tracts of the best bottomlands was forbidden. Through legislation and oversight by the Council, Spotswood strove continuously to implement these provisions, but he never achieved the compliance of Virginians in a program that could otherwise have had a profound effect on the colony's Piedmont landscape after the 1720 land acts.[19]

Although designed to check the abuses of land speculation, Spotswood's proclamations also served the interests of later speculators, such as Jost Hite, Alexander Ross, and others in the Shenandoah Valley. Hite, for instance, wanted to utilize most efficiently all the varied types of land in his five-thousand-acre tract. Unclaimed lands with unwatered, poorer soils would have been difficult to sell. That all the holdings deeded from this tract bordered or crossed the Opequon reflects this interest. The differing configurations of individual holdings and their association with distinctive ethnic groups, however, suggest that the division of the parent tract proceeded according to the wishes of purchasers, not a plan imposed by Hite. Settlers, in other words, were not selecting presurveyed lots from what today would be called a development. Nonetheless, economic interests such as Hite's in the effective settlement of lands could have had a significant influence on the landscape. As proprietor of the Northern Neck, whose jurisdiction eventually included the lands of Hite and his counterparts, Thomas lord Fairfax shared similar interests with Hite and the others. All those, therefore, who dispensed lands wanted compact, contiguous settlement mixing good and poor lands so that no tract would be useless. Their interests, like the proclamations of the governor, influenced the emerging landscape at Opequon.

So too would the practices of surveyors. Of all the influences on an emerging landscape none was potentially greater than the surveying system and the timing of the survey in the land-acquisition process. When survey preceded settlement, surveyors and their instructions shaped the land with a strong guiding hand. A century later, for instance, the United States Rectangular Survey imposed a north-south grid of mile-square parcels on western lands. The placement of roads, dwellings, farmsteads, and public structures conformed to the survey, which is today still the most significant influence on the landscape. East of the Appalachians, however, and particularly in the southern backcountry where Opequon was the earliest settlement, the metes and bounds survey system prevailed. Here survey often followed settlement and represented a codification of the landscape settlers had already negotiated directly with the environment and with one another.[20]

The metes and bounds survey system as it was employed in colonial Virginia had a long history. The need for fixed systems of land measurement increased in late medieval England as conventions of land tenure stabilized and a capitalizing agrarian economy commodified land values. Some ancient property systems used in early modern Ireland, for instance, still employed variable units adjusted in size to the land's capacity to support livestock. Manor lands, likewise, were more often apportioned according to use rather than value. Communal rights guaranteed individual access to arable land, pasture, meadow, woodland, and so forth. Increasing population, the spread of tillage, and the enclosure of the commons for sheepherding necessitated the quantification of the land in aerial units. Inflation during the sixteenth century intensified this trend as more and more landlords insisted on money payments for rents.[21]

Economic pressures, combined with the scientific revolution and the spread of printing, produced standardized practices of land measurement in the seventeenth and eighteenth centuries. Numerous books instructed would-be surveyors to apply the arts of geometry and arithmetic to the land. From the growing science of navigation, surveyors adopted new instruments for determining location, angle measurement, and area. In the seventeenth century platting land by triangulation from a fixed number of interior stations became the most widely used form of surveying in England, where few trees obstructed the surveyor's view. Much more common in North American colonies, where land holdings were large and the woods dense, was the traverse survey. Here the surveyor proceeded around the perimeter of a tract marking boundaries by compass bearing and distance in poles. The traverse survey was first employed in Virginia in 1641. During the remainder of the century the adoption of the 360-degree compass card and the replacement of the simple compass by the circumferentor with sights allowed for greater and greater precision in land measurement.[22]

As surveying techniques improved, so did administrative procedures for regulating surveying practice and incorporating it within the land-distribution system of Virginia. The foundation of the system rested upon the county surveyor. This official was charged with the responsibility to "survey, measure & lay out all or any part or parcell of Land within the said Bounds & Limits" of the county. Each surveyor owed his appointment to the surveyor general of the colony, whose office was a privilege of the trustees of the College of William and Mary. This institution played virtually no role in selecting, training, or certifying surveyors; it only benefited from a portion of their fees.[23]

Anyone acquiring property in seventeenth-century Virginia first obtained a headright. Granted by clerks of county courts, these open proofs of transporting people to the colony conveyed land at the ratio of one transport for fifty acres. In practice, headrights were bought and sold privately, creating a land market. Once obtained, the right could be used in any of the colony's existing counties, where they served as a warrant authorizing a county surveyor to mark off available land identified by the holder. The prospective landowner then entered the completed survey plat and description in the office of the colonial secretary, who issued a patent signed by the governor and bearing the colony's seal. By the second decade of the eighteenth century the treasury right was quickly replacing the headright as a check on the abuses of land speculation. Before 1717, when Governor Alexander Spotswood proclaimed that treasury rights could be purchased from county surveyors, these rights were for sale only by the receiver general of the colony. Otherwise the procedure for acquiring land under the treasury right was much the same as under the headright. In either case land was conveyed by patent in free and common socage, whereby the owner could develop it, profit from it, and divide or convey it at will in exchange for the annual payment of a small quitrent to the king.[24]

At several points in the land-granting process external influences came into play affecting the size and shape of surveys and thus the emerging landscape. Although the headright system had been devised to link land with available labor at a fixed ratio, the system as implemented gave the colonial government little opportunity to limit land speculation and the engrossment of large tracts. Constrained only by their own means, claimants nonetheless had to adjust their prospective boundaries to existing holdings. And surveyors often worked under instructions to close the perimeters of all adjacent tracts. For personal, financial, or political reasons surveyors could affect both the shape of tracts and who received surveys for them. They could, at least in theory, serve as filters selecting out those deemed unsuited for the land-owning classes in Virginia. Since landownership conveyed civil power in Virginia, surveyors could help contour the lay of colonial politics. Locked in conflict with colonial elites in the House of Burgesses and the colonial Council, Alexander Spotswood certainly possessed an interest in cultivating new constituencies. Colonial politics, therefore, may explain the provision in the governor's 1710 proclamation for "preventing any Undue preferrence that may be Given by Surveyors to particular persons" and providing that "all her Majties Subjects may have Equall priviledge of makeing their Entry's."[25]

The shape of tracts, the resources of the land they bounded, and the aggregation of all the surveyed tracts in a region, known as the cadastre, might be conceived as a product of counteracting centrifugal and centripetal forces. Pushing tract boundaries outward and giving them confirmation were the intentions and ambitions of those taking them up. Pressing inward and giving tracts shape—and meaning—were the constraints imposed primarily by colonial law and policy, the interests of speculators, and the practice of surveying.

Any single property line, then, represented a vector resolving these various outward and inward forces. Collectively, the lines defining a tract composed an artifact—a physical object in whose shape can be read all the contending influences of maker, buyer, material, style, cost, and so forth. This artifact considered either individually as a property holding or collectively as a cadastre therefore has provenance, or a set of associations in time, space, and place that render it meaningful for its makers, users, and those who study or appreciate it.

· ☙ ·

The cadastral artifact was probably more expressive of the interests of settlers in the Shenandoah Valley—and freer from the constraints of outside forces—than on any other settlement frontier in the eighteenth-century backcountry. Encoded in the cadastre, in other words, were the values, ideals, ambitions, and self-imposed restraints of the pioneer generation. The property map of Opequon, then, can be read as a text for what men, women, and families did in fashioning their own world largely uninhibited by the forces shaping the process of landscape creation elsewhere. Considering the imperial purpose for which this settlement had been created and the powerful forces unleashed by imperial encounter and conflict among European and Native American nations, this development requires some explanation.

In drafting the orders for Shenandoah Valley lands during the early 1730s, the Virginia governor and Council effectively transferred much of the colony's power over shaping surveys and settlements to men like Hite and Ross. What these men received from the colony was the authority to sell land and oversee the land-granting process from selection to survey. These powers came as land orders, not grants. Colonial officials probably intended that those who received land orders would survey the entire specified acreage in a single large tract. Compact settlements would better serve the interests of defense by creating a denser buffer against enemy intrusion and facilitating the formation of militia forces. The Van Meters would thus stake out tracts of ten thousand and twenty thousand contiguous acres; Hite and Ross, one hundred thousand. All settlers would be located therein. The Council made its intentions plain in its orders. When the men holding land orders had met the family settlement requirements, "patents shall be granted them in Such manner as they shall agree to divide" their total acreage. A few years later and for equally large orders in the upper Valley to the south, William Beverley and Benjamin Borden did precisely this. And this procedure was exactly what Fairfax expected when he later complained that Hite and McKay had "never attempted to make a regular survey of the 140,000 acres [their orders plus the Van Meters's] that so the bounds and courses thereof might be known, but continued to sell what was valuable and suffered the purchasers to make their surveys as they thought most for their interest."[26]

Why did the governor and Council establish a new set of procedures that effectively surrendered the traditional colonial power over distributing western lands? And why did the men who gained this power disperse it further among settlers? Authorities knew very well that no Virginia county extended west of the Blue Ridge. According to the 1720 land act, Spotsylvania County ended at the Shenandoah River. The headright and the treasury right system could not function apart from the apparatus of county government. There were simply no clerks and no surveyors to distribute land rights or conduct surveys. In organizing land for distribution under the unprecedented system of land orders, the executive branch of government may also have been acting with a keen eye to politics. Creating a county in colonial Virginia required an act of legislature. This took time, political influence, and approval by the Privy Council. During the years the 1720 land act was under review in London, Virginia planters, who dominated the legislature, engrossed massive tracts of Piedmont lands. These landholdings would, in years to come, form the basis for a plantation society dependent on tobacco and slavery. This was precisely what the governor and Council did not want to happen west of the Blue Ridge. Land orders and family settlement requirements placed upon "Persons of a low Degree," as William Keith described them, were calculated to create a western buffer of white, Protestant, yeoman farmers in unorganized territory where Virginia planters and speculators would not risk investment in either land or slaves. This is just how Hite, himself, saw the matter when he observed that "in 1730 when the Countrey was unsettled, & a Wilderness was to be explored whose Surface was Rocks & Mountains, & it's Inhabitants Wildbeasts or Hostile Indians, without any necessarys, but what were carried with them at great expence; nothing but a prefference to the choice lands, would tempt men to become adventurers." On another occasion, when Lord Fairfax objected "to the Form of the Surveys alledging that they were not made according to the Law the Breadth being less than one third of the Length," one of Hite's associates responded that this "Indulgence" was "allowed to the first Adventurers who had explored such an almost unknown Wilderness as that was when they obtained their Grant which it was supposed the Council thought a sufficient reason for dispensing with the Rigour of the Law."[27]

Just as the governor and Council deferred to the very men who could, again in William Keith's words, "persuade a multitude into a Voluntary Expedition" of settling the Shenandoah Valley frontier, so these men, to achieve this objective, deferred to the interests of the multitude. The men who held the land orders and bore the responsibility for finding one family for every one thousand acres gave settlers a free hand in selecting dwelling sites and defining property holdings. This freedom was precisely the object of Fairfax's complaint when he protested Hite's practice of selling land "to that person that would give the greatest Price and that too in such Quantities figures and Positions as the several Purchasers thought proper without Regard to form order Custom Usage Equity or Laws of the Colony." To Fairfax's dismay, Hite had "suffered the Purchasers to make their Surveys in what manner they thought best suited their Interest."[28]

That settlers, not speculators, drove the settlement process was attributable, at least in Hite's case, to loose office practices. "Neither of the Original Grantees [Hite and McKay] were men accurate in business," as one settler put it. "No clear Statement of Accounts is to be found in the Possession of either Party." Nor, evidently, were survey warrants. Most settlers appear to have negotiated their own terms with surveyors with little direction from Hite or anyone else. The surveys and the cadastre that resulted appeared just as Fairfax said: "without Regard to form [or] order." In fact, George Hume, the duly appointed surveyor for Spotsylvania County refused to work west of the Shenandoah River, so the governor had to take the extraordinary step of appointing aging Knight of the Golden Horseshoe Robert Brooke as special surveyor for lands on the Shenandoah River. In his complaint against Hite, Fairfax singled out the "surveys made by Robert Brooke . . . for John Vanmeter[,] William Vestal[,] Jost Hite," and others for violations of the legal standards of surveying practice. In a demonstration of how surveyors bent to the will of settlers, Brooke's successor conducted a survey in the early 1750s for Abraham Van Meter and John Keywood. When the surveying party "came to the corner of the line wch was to divide between Keywood and Vanmeter, . . . [the latter] was called on by the surveyor, who said to him, 'as you and Keywood has agreed the matter come and set the compass to run this land' upon wch Vanmetre stepped up, and looking through the sight of the compass turned it a small matter, and raising himself up said 'I believe this will do.'" That settlers set the sights of surveyor's compasses is further substantiated by twenty-nine of the eighty-two surveys Brooke recorded between 1732 and 1734 that violated the one-third breadth-to-length rule of the colony. Brooke continued to survey even after the legislature created Orange County in 1734 and extended it westward across the Shenandoah Valley. Upon the complaint of the duly appointed county surveyor in 1738, the Council finally had to order the secretary of the colony to deny all surveys from Brooke.[29]

The freedom Opequon settlers exercised in selecting settlement sites and properties can, then, be attributed to two related developments. To procure the desired kind of settler—Protestant, white, and yeoman—and the preferred family-farm settlements, the governor and Council delegated their authority to manage the land-granting process to men who, by their associations, could readily effect these purposes. Similarly, these men, in order to recruit sufficient settlers in two years to fulfill the one-family-per-one-thousand-acre stipulation in land orders, allowed settlers the freedom to devise their own tracts of land even if they wittingly or unwittingly violated colonial law or policy.

The isolation of Opequon intensified the exigency of its settlement. To Hite and others the great distances to established communities and markets justified the extraordinary liberty granted settlers in shaping the landscape. The program of induced settlement accomplished just what Virginia and English authorities wanted: two frontiers, one on the edge of a plantation world expanding through the Piedmont and the other as an island of western settlement serving to buffer both the internal insecurity of a slave society and the external threat posed by Indian and French marauders. Between these two frontiers lay forty to fifty miles of unoccupied territory. As late as the 1750s the number of white tithables in Shenandoah Valley counties was more than double the number in counties immediately to the east of the Blue Ridge. Opequon was "so far distant from any Settlment," Hite himself argued that settlers "could scarcely procure any one thing necessary nearer than from Pennsylvania or Fredericksburg (which was near two hundred miles distant) and to which for the greatest and most difficult parts of the Way they were obliged to make roads." In one measure of what isolation meant to Opequon settlers, they may have had to make their own roads, but they could make them anywhere. No contiguous landscape of existing roads, ferries, towns, or markets influenced landscape evolution at Opequon. If isolation was a hardship, it also increased the freedom Opequon settlers possessed to shape the world they were making.[30]

. ☙ .

To examine the world emerging at Opequon is literally to read the minds of the men and women who made it. In establishing farmsteads, surveying property holdings, laying out roads, and planning towns, Opequon settlers were acting on—and acting out—ideas, beliefs, assumptions, and concepts that gave their personal experience meaning. Taken together these habits of the mind can be called *mentality*. Mentalities are rooted in culture and are expressed in the activities and creations of individuals. Artifacts—the objects the people of any culture create—have meaning because they are expressions of their makers and users. Thus landscapes, as aggregates of many different artifacts, compose a text embedded with the mentalities of their creators. As we have seen, the making of a landscape occurs at many different levels, or scales, in any culture. Laws or policies, the ambitions of land speculators or agents, the practices of surveyors all affect what the people settling a new land do. At Opequon these influences had minimal impact on the families moving southward along the great valley of the Appalachians to take advantage of opportunities imperial conflicts among European powers and Indian nations had made possible. The mentalities of these newcomers could come fully into play in complex negotiations between culture and the land itself as modified by previous occupants.

Certainly settlers came with ambitions of acquiring land, bettering their lives, and improving the economic circumstances of their families. In today's world these aspirations and efforts to capture as large a portion of a region's resources as means allow could lead to land wars. Men and women would want to capitalize on their opportunities to build farms, to produce, and to render life more secure. They would scramble and vie with one another in a competition to do best for themselves. They would take risks, invest labor, and if successful, increase their wealth and contribute to the growing corpus of regional wealth. But in a precapitalist society—as Opequon surely was in the 1730s, if only by necessity of being "far distant from any Settlment"—other mentalities would have come to bear upon the settlement process.

In writing about the later settlement of Kentucky, Joseph Doddridge characterized mentality as the "public character of society [which] . . . in the lapse of time . . . becomes a matter of conscience." According to Doddridge, "this observation applies, in full force, to that influence of our early land laws, which allowed four hundred acres, and no more, to a settlement right. Many of our first settlers seemed to regard this amount of the surface of the earth, as the allotment of divine providence for one family, and believed that any attempt to get more would be sinful." Providence aside, many immigrants who took up land at Opequon had left economies of scarcity in Europe. Here the ambitions of any single individual to amass wealth or natural resources could threaten the lives and livelihoods of everyone in a community. Economies in which necessities were scarce worked as a zero-sum equation in which the amount of total wealth available for the sustenance of the community was viewed as a constant. For one individual or family to capture more than an equitable share of it diminished the resources available for the sustenance of others. All had rights to draw from the aquifer of wealth, but if someone tapped it too deeply, the wells of others might run dry. Ambition was necessarily suspect. Doddridge concluded his discussion with the example of his

father, who, "like many others, believed that having secured his legal allotment, the rest of the country belonged of right, to those who choose to settle
in it."[31]

The history of Kentucky settlement, the furious scramble for land, the engrossment of large tracts by speculators, the shingled, overlapping surveys,
the decades of legal controversies—to say nothing of the frustration, anger,
and occasional violence of the settlers—do not gainsay the authenticity of
Doddridge's testimony. Moreover, the chaos of settlement in Kentucky was
not presaged by developments at Opequon. Orderly settlement at Opequon is
not evidence in itself of any sway by the principles of Doddridge's father
over its landscape, but the history of landownership and land division there
bears out the idea that most settlers aimed at acquiring sufficient land to provide for the welfare of the family from year to year and for patrimonies for the
next generation. They wanted a competence. Only a few bought and sold
properties quickly for profit. And the cases of landowners subdividing and
selling portions of their lands were far fewer than those in which parents be-
queathed their holdings intact to children. Few landowners failed to take advantage of commercial opportunities to profit from surplus crops and livestock when markets did penetrate the backcountry. But responding to the
market was not incompatible with the aims and ambitions of achieving competence. Indeed, trade, whether it was in barter with neighbors or for cash
with a merchant, was just as much a means of sustaining the family as it was to
amass wealth.[32]

Historians have exerted considerable energy in debating whether men and
women living and working before or apart from the Industrial Revolution participated in a moral economy of mutual commitment to preserving the common wealth of a community or in a competitive economy of private welfare
advanced by expending and expanding a community's wealth. The settlement
of Opequon occurred at a time and in a place in which values and necessity
combined to constrain acquisitiveness and ambition. There, the primacy of
competency over competition in the mentality of settlers would have had a
significant impact on the landscape they created.[33]

How individuals acted in moving to what they called a "Wilderness . . .
whose Surface was Rocks & Mountains" and transforming it into a landscape
of farms and fields, roads and fences, crossroads and towns was a product of
complex cultural forces. Settlers' perspectives on the world they were making
and their role in it were no doubt conditioned by their knowledge of it. What
this generation knew about nature and human obligations for preserving or
developing it was in large measure conditioned by the Bible and an understanding of Scripture gained through hearing sermons or reading sermon lit-

erature. For many men and women who took up land at Opequon, the Bible was the single most important intellectual force giving shape to their mental universe. They were, after all, predominantly Protestant by imperial intent and thereby took the Old and New Testaments as the word of God received in guidance for human action. Moreover, the large majority of settlers emanated from the reformed tradition of the German and Scottish churches. Having rejected the strictures of priests and denied the power of sacraments over daily life, they had also disavowed the Anglican Book of Common Prayer and the social authority it bestowed on an upper class of clerics and aristocrats. They turned to the Scriptures and to each other in the communion of the congregation under ministerial leadership for advice on how to harmonize action and belief.

Many Protestant settlers came to Opequon armed with an English translation of the Bible in which the Latin text had been transformed into an instrument of extraordinary grace, beauty, and power. In the potency of the language of King James, people would find authority over the world around them. In Genesis, for instance, they learned to "be fruitful, and multiply, and replenish the earth, and subdue it: and have dominion over the fish of the sea, and over the fowl of the air, and over every living thing that moveth upon the earth." This was not a passage to breed doubt about expropriating property from wilderness. Nor would it discourage the clearing of forests or the breaking of new earth under the plow. Seeing their arrival in a new land through the lens of Genesis, settlers would have dispersed and occupied it as an expression of the dominion granted them by providence.[34]

Concepts of private property also populated the mental world of backcountry settlers. The unusual procedure of issuing land orders to men like Hite and Ross was, for the governor and Council, a means of bringing land west of the Blue Ridge under patent without creating either new counties or a plantation society. To settlers, a patent conferred the power of private property and the security a landholding meant for the survival and sustenance of the family. Settlers could sell the land they patented, give it away, rent or lease it, and mortgage or bequeath it. They could do all this only in the name of the king. The term *patent* was derived from the Latin *patente,* meaning open. Letters patent were literally open letters: public declarations used by the crown to confer a right, convey a title, award property, or authorize an action. In 1578, for instance, Queen Elizabeth granted Humphrey Gilbert a patent to "discover . . . such remote, barbarous, and heathen lands, countries, and territories not possessed by any Christian prince or people nor inhabited by Christian people and the same to have, holde, occupy and enjoy." The same patent was later transferred to Gilbert's half brother, Walter Raleigh, and used to found the Roanoke Colony. The patent represented a text that extended the power of the English monarch over new territory and legitimated English colonization of foreign lands. A symbol such as a cross or a crown could be erected on newly claimed land to perpetuate the dominion of the sovereign. Fulfilling the intention of a letter patent, however, implied settlement. In the colony, dominion required that land be occupied, converted into property holdings, cleared of forests, fenced, built upon, planted, and rendered productive.[35]

A regal patent therefore conveyed more than private rights to property. It conferred upon the holder the sovereign purpose of developing land to extend the dominion of the crown. In instructing colonial governors to enforce upon settlers the requirement to cultivate and improve three out of every fifty patented acres, the Privy Council was not simply limiting land speculation; it was also asserting the authority of the crown over royal domain. This is why the Virginia Council's orders to Hite and Ross and others like them provided for patenting land outside the jurisdiction of any extant Virginia county. The Opequon settlement existed to fulfill the injunction of the report of 1721 that "British settlements might be extended beyond" the Blue Ridge.[36]

Witness trees or other markers—each very carefully described in a patent—represented not only the corner of an individual's property but also, in some measure, the authority of the crown. Thus, when the surveyor had finished fixing the boundary between Abraham Van Meter and John Keywood, he "directed the parties to set a stone in the ground at the stake" where there was no tree to mark. Van Meter then said to Keywood, "When I have time we will fix a stone here." As the chain carrier, John Dixon, related the story: "Some time after Vanmetre came to Keywood's and . . . [they] went to the stake and set a stone at it in the ground as their boundary." In this symbolic act Van Meter and Keywood performed an important ritual signifying the appropriation of the land as well as the extension of English authority over it in a permanent monument for all to see. That the surveyor directed this action be accomplished and the adjoining landowners so readily complied suggest that its significance was well understood within the community.[37]

Opequon settlers would also have subscribed to other widely held ideas about property. In arguing for a preemptive right for land in Pennsylvania, William Penn's lawyers contended that "in new-settled Colonies Possession and Improvement is the best Title any man can have." Not only did improving land express the power of the letter patent to extend the authority of crown over colony, it also established a settler's use right to the land. "*As much Land as a Man Tills, Plants, Improves, Cultivates, and can use the Product of, so much is his Property,*" John Locke asserted. "He by his Labour does, as it were, inclose it from the Common." Few of those who settled Opequon would have read Locke, but the idea of a use right to land attaching to its first cultivator was hardly new with this philosopher, and by virtue of popularizers his ideas enjoyed wide currency in the eighteenth-century Anglo-American world. As we shall see, many Opequon settlers selected and began cultivating land before taking any steps to patent it or even to contact the men empowered by land orders to secure patents; this suggests that they believed that investing labor in the wilderness transformed waste land into personal property.[38]

. ⚘ .

Professing use rights to land had the added benefit for Anglo-Americans of dispossessing Native Americans of their rights. What European settlers encountered in the Shenandoah Valley was hardly wilderness, if wilderness is land devoid of human improvement. The "old fields" found on the banks of streams and rivers were obvious indicators that a settled, agricultural people had once occupied the land. But to most Europeans, Indians were hunters and gatherers who cultivated gardens to supplement an extensive subsistence economy, which depended upon vast amounts of land to support comparatively few people. Cultural preconceptions about who was first on the land and what was natural were so strong that one description of pioneer settlement claimed that "when the country was first *discovered* [emphasis added], there was considerable openings of the land, or natural prairies, which are called 'the Indian old fields' to this day." The far more intensive European forms of agriculture, settlers claimed, made much better use of land than hunting and gathering did and fulfilled the biblical injunction to make the earth blossom. Improving the land in farms conferred a use right that superseded the "inferior" rights of Indians. Moreover, Indians claimed, used, and defended land in common. From the European perspective, cultivating land presupposed a higher form of ownership as private property. "It cannot be supposed," Locke observed, that God "meant it should always remain common and uncultivated." Possession was the product of investing labor in the land to render it productive. Harvesting its natural resources conveyed no title to it, and colonial laws did not even recognize property rights in game. Settlers, for instance, freely hunted animals across property lines. In collecting the settlement accounts of pioneers, Samuel Kercheval reflected many of their opinions. Indians had a "rightful and just possession of this fine country," he remarked. But "when God created this globe, He probably intended it should sustain the greatest possible number of His creatures. And as the human family, in a state of civil life, increases with vastly more rapidity than a people in a state of nature or savage life, the law of force has been generally resorted to, and the weaker compelled to give way to the stronger."[39]

Quakers, for one, did not believe that force voided the prior rights of Indians. In the Quaker colony of Pennsylvania, William Penn established the policy of purchasing land from Native Americans prior to settlement. In addition to ejecting white squatters from Indian land, Penn prohibited settlers from purchasing it without permission from the proprietary. Quakers settling with Alexander Ross formed the Hopewell Meeting under a special injunction to pay both the Indians and the colonial government for their lands. Fellow Quaker and traveling minister Thomas Chalkley, writing to members of the meeting in 1738, pointed out that "as Nature hath given them [Indians], and their Fore-fathers, the Possession of this Continent of *America* (or this Wilderness) they have a natural Right thereto . . . and no People, according to the Law of Nature and Justice, and our own Principle, which is according to the glorious Gospel of our dear and holy Lord Jesus Christ, ought to take away, or settle, on other Mens Lands or Rights, without Consent, or purchasing the same." But Hopewell settlers never could find a willing seller because native lands were "considered the common hunting ground of various tribes, and not claimed by any particular nation who had authority to sell."[40]

Quakers and other settlers, however, had no difficulty in finding the remnants of previous Indian occupations of the region they were transforming from "wilderness" into private property. The terrain of Indian improvement, like settler mentality, was therefore a factor in negotiations between the new occupiers of the land and the land itself. Bringing mind and environment together, these negotiations produced a landscape. Because settlers often sought out "old field" clearings for their own settlements, Kercheval's accounts of the pioneers recorded many sites of deserted Indian towns. On the Potomac River within a few miles of where Hite crossed it, one settler built his home in the middle of what was a palisaded Indian settlement. A century later Kercheval described it as a "circular wall . . . made of earth . . . plainly to be seen." Evidence of at least four other Indian villages survived farther south along both branches of the Shenandoah River and at its forks. Even where new growth obscured old fields, settlers found, in one instance, "many pipes, tomahawks, axes, hommony pestles, &c.," and, in another, the "numerous fragments of their pots, cups, arrow points, and other implements for domestic use."[41]

Other evidence of Indian life also reminded European settlers that their "wilderness" was hardly pristine. Indian mounds or graves were numerous, and many were quite large. On the west side on the Shenandoah's South Fork, for instance, there were "three large Indian graves, ranged nearly side by side," as Kercheval recalled. They were "thirty or forty feet in length, twelve or fourteen feet wide, and five or six feet high. Around them, in circular form, are a number of single graves." Kercheval reported at least eight other locations of mounds and graves. A burned-over landscape left by Indian hunters would have had an even more dramatic impact on settlers. While surveying the Virginia–North Carolina boundary in 1728, William Byrd crossed the "route the Northern Savages take when they go out to War with the Cataubas and other Southern Nations." He observed that "on their way, the Fires they make in their camps are left burning, which . . . soon put the adjacent Woods into a flame." What Byrd attributed to accident or negligence was no doubt an intentional strategy of clearing the underbrush to ease travel and encourage game.[42]

Features such as old fields, mounds, graves, and fire-cleared forests reflected a long history of Native American cultural response to environmental change and technological development. The old field village sites can be traced to hamlets of three or four clustered households, which appeared for the first time in the Shenandoah Valley during the Early Woodland Period beginning about 1200 B.C. By this time humans had already occupied the region for more than eight thousand years and had adapted to a gradually warming climate and an environment rapidly diversifying in plants, animals, and other natural resources. As technologies for food procurement, processing, and storage developed, populations grew larger and more secure. Pottery found in Early Woodland hamlets was evidence of greater sedentism and more efficient use of food resources.[43]

Cultural and environmental diversification continued throughout the remainder of the Woodland Period, which lasted until the arrival of Europeans. Hamlets gave way to villages, which divided and multiplied as subsistence demands increased and societies grew more complex. The arrival of corn, bean, and squash agriculture about A.D. 900 constituted a major cultural horizon marked by the rapid intensification of all the trends of the preceding nine thousand years: population growth, subsistence diversification, social stratification, sedentism, and village life. Some of these developments were reversed, however, by the so-called Little Ice Age, from the fourteenth to the eighteenth century. This cooler, dryer period reduced agricultural yields and, in turn, encouraged hunting, territorialism, and more intergroup conflict. Native Americans erected protective palisades around villages, like the one on the Potomac River, at this time. Iroquois expansion and competition for beaver, however, led eventually to the abandonment of the Shenandoah Valley by native peoples in the mid-seventeenth century. What European settlers inherited, then, was a landscape reflecting nearly twelve millennia of human change and development.[44]

· ⌘ ·

Arriving at Opequon and scattering in search of the best farmstead sites, Europeans read the land for all it could tell them about its potential. Archaeological evidence suggests that either they scouted the environment with an eye similar to the Indians' or they consciously took advantage of how Native Americans had previously modified the environment. More than a third of those families that settled along the upper Opequon on or near Jost Hite's five-thousand-acre tract occupied sites previously inhabited by Indians and containing prehistoric artifacts. Both Indians and Europeans located their habitations on terraces with good access to the Opequon or around springs feeding its tributaries. Whether or not Indian fields survived at these sites and eased the settlers' burden of clearing the forest is unknown. Regardless, this evidence suggests that settlers had definite ideas about what they were looking for in a home site.[45] But they left no record of their environmental perceptions except those encoded in the land cadastre itself. Various explorers and travelers, however, provided detailed accounts of environments in the Shenandoah Valley and its associated regions from Pennsylvania to the Carolinas. Although explorer accounts usually predate the settlement of the Valley, visitors from other parts of the Americas and from Europe came later to see what the settlers had done and to study the society and landscape they created. Because the mindset, or mentality, of those Europeans who first encountered the land and negotiated its settlement can be viewed through these accounts, they provide a primary means of understanding complex relationships between culture and environment.

Some travelers took detailed notes to help themselves or their readers plan a future move to America. Others were speculating in land or looking for a good place to settle. In any case, most judged land quality by its vegetation cover. Prior to any quantitative measures of fertility or scientific knowledge about the relation between soil characteristics and agricultural productivity, most travelers associated good soils with hardwood forests, primarily oak-hickory, and poor soils with pine woods. Lands that did not support hardwoods and particularly those covered with brush or scrub were considered infertile or barren. Open areas of grassland were especially interesting because they were neither forested nor barren. With their eye fixed on the land as an investment or as the foundation of new societies, travelers carefully documented various forest environments and commented on why open or barren areas were unforested.[46]

Early accounts of the vegetation cover of the Shenandoah Valley give the clear impression of a mosaic of forest and open land. No grassland prairie blanketed the Valley as Kercheval and later historians would claim. In distinguishing between "land that is dry and barren" and "good land, where are great forest trees of oak," Swiss merchant Franz Louis Michel was also describing the mixed vegetation of glades and woodland. Similarly, the French Huguenot refugee Durand of Dauphiné, visiting Virginia in 1686, found the interior "entirely covered with trees"; but "there are also great areas, twenty or twenty-five leagues from the sea; these are the fine meadows where . . . the savages had their plantations." Along the Monongahela River in 1751, explorer and trader Christopher Gist depicted a similar environment, consisting of "level farming land, with fine Meadows, the Timber white Oak and Hiccory." Arriving in the Shenandoah Valley in 1759, traveler Andrew Burnaby encountered "majestic woods; the whole interspersed with an infinite variety of flowering shrubs."[47]

Hickories and oaks dominated the forests of the eighteenth-century Shenandoah Valley, but pines and other conifers figured prominently. In 1782, for instance, the Marquis de Chastellux commented on the "strong robust oaks and immense pines" he encountered near Natural Bridge. The naturalist John Bartram, traveling between Winchester and Stephensburg in 1759, "rode over very stoney ground producing great red ceder pines." Near Woodstock in the early 1770s, Presbyterian minister Philip Fithian observed that "the Valley here is narrow; the Soil sandy; The Timber mostly Pine." At the Stone Meeting House north of Staunton in Augusta County, Fithian also found that "this Neighberhood is covered with Pine." Several travelers mentioned dogwoods in their accounts. The Methodist missionary Thomas Coke, who visited southwest Virginia in spring 1791, observed that "the oaks have spread out their leaves, and the dogwood, whose bark is very medicinal, and whose innumerable white flowers form one of the finest ornaments of the forest, is in full bloom."[48]

The witness markers used to designate property corners for 999 land grants issued in the lower Shenandoah Valley before 1800 confirm both the forested nature of the land and the dominance of oaks and hickories in the forest. Throughout the eighteenth century the proportion of markers represented by trees remained at 90 percent, with no significant increase or decrease in the use of stones, stakes, posts, or poles where trees were presumably lacking. At the same time, the most commonly marked species was white oak, followed by pine, hickory, red oak, black oak, and chestnut oak. If the frequency with which tree species were designated as witness markers reflected the forest composition, then European settlers encountered a forest of 71 percent oak, 14 percent hickory, 6 percent pine, and 3 percent walnut.[49]

Travel accounts for areas adjacent to the Shenandoah Valley fill out the picture of the great oak-hickory and pine forests that enshrouded the land. In his journeys throughout the middle settlements of North America in 1759, Andrew Burnaby mentioned more than twenty-six species of forest trees, including hickory, maple, cedar, sassafras, dogwood, locust, redbud, tulip tree, catalpa, chinquapin, persimmon, and chestnut. English traveler John F. D. Smyth visited North Carolina in the 1780s and in the vicinity of Halifax observed that the "timber is of an immense bulk on the low grounds, and consists of white and yellow poplars, black walnut, hornbeam, red bud, sweet gum, dog wood, sycamores, oaks, ash, beech, elm, &c. On the rich high land, it consists of hickory, sassafras, oaks &c. and on the inferior high land, of lofty pines, of a great height, mixed with scrubby oaks, black-gum, and maple." He added that these "trees are almost the same in every respect with those produced in Virginia." The scale of American forests also awed Nicholas Cresswell. While traveling in the Appalachian highlands along the Youghiogheny River in 1775, he found himself in the deep shade of "Walnut and Cherry Trees [that] grow to an amazing size. I have seen several three foot diameter and 40 foot before they come to a limb," he added.[50]

Most travelers paid close attention to variations in the forest affected by elevation, latitude, and soils, and they generally regarded bottomlands as the richest environments. While in Maryland during the 1790s, Isaac Weld commented that "in the neighbourhood of the creeks and between the hills are patches of rich black earth, called bottoms, the trees upon which grow to a large size." In Pittsylvania County, Virginia, John Smyth found "the growth of the timber on the low land is very large, but not equal to that on the low grounds of the Roanoak." And James Kirke Paulding found the banks of the Shenandoah River "skirted with lofty elms" in 1816.[51]

In contrast to the luxuriant hardwoods of the bottomlands, travelers generally depicted the Blue Ridge as covered in scrub. Crossing the ridge in 1774 Nicholas Cresswell, for instance, described a "high barren mountain, producing nothing but pines." The pattern of bleak uplands and rich, fertile lowlands extended westward across the Appalachians. According to seventeenth-century explorer John Lederer, "the Apalataean Mountains . . . are barren Rocks, and therefore deserted by all living creatures but Bears, who cave in the hollow Cliffs." In western Augusta County, Cresswell found "the mountains are barren and rocky, but the Valleys tho' very narrow are in general rich." While on his way through the Appalachian Mountains to Tennessee, John Smyth observed a slightly different pattern, in which "excellent strong rich land, of a deep red, or a dark reddish brown colour, with very large tall timber" occupied the summit of one peak, but the western slopes were "almost bare of soil; the trees and all the vegetation poor, scanty, and miserable." Variations in vegetation cover were also discernable as travelers moved north and south along the Shenandoah Valley or the Blue Ridge. As John Bartram observed, "all ye way along this mountain thence southward every 100 miles produces one or more different plants."[52]

Travelers usually reserved the term *barrens* for particularly poor land. Jacques Pierre Brissot de Warville employed this word to describe the "very center of the valley [where] there are leagues of land covered with rock and not fit for farming called the Barrens." Maps sometimes referred to this shale area as "Slate Outcrop Piney or Barren Hills." Nonetheless, *barrens* was not a term used to describe unforested land. In fact, barren land was customarily associated with pine forests. Heading southwest from present-day Strasburg in the early 1750s, Moravian travelers observed that "the country was pretty barren, overgrown with pine trees." Andrew Burnaby remarked that "the soil of Virginia is in general good. There are barrens where the lands produce nothing but pine trees." And in South Carolina, John Smyth found that the "high or barren land is divided into oak and pine barrens; of which the oak is always the sign of the more fertile soil, for the pine barrens are only pine or fir-trees growing, scattered promiscuously, in a bed of loose, deep sand, which scarcely produces a single blade of verdure."[53]

Natural openings were as significant as forests to European settlers in the Shenandoah Valley. The earliest explorers in Virginia consistently noted these clearings. John Lederer had called them "savanae" in 1670. Thomas Batts and Robert Fallam, who followed Lederer into Appalachian Virginia the next year, encountered "curious meadows on each" side of a river they crossed west of Roanoke Gap. "Going forward," they wrote, "we found rich ground but having curious rising hills and brave meadows with grass about a man's hight." In 1775, while traveling through what is now southwestern Pennsylvania, Nicholas Cresswell "dined at the Great Meadows, a large marshy place clear of trees," and that same year Philip Fithian found "large Plains, or as the Inhabitants call them, Glades, quite bare of Timber" along the Susquehanna River. Also in Pennsylvania, John Smyth "descended . . . [Wart] mountain on the north-west side, and staid all night at the border of a beautiful small savannah or meadow, a little way from the base of the mountain."[54]

Few travelers or explorers estimated the dimensions of forest openings, but no traveler gave the impression that they were of any great size—certainly none was as large as a prairie. In North Carolina, Smyth observed "in different places in the woods, some considerable glades, savannahs, or meadows. These are natural openings, of a few acres in extent, quite destitute of timber, not a tree, nor even the vestige of one, to be perceived in them; but the ground therein is always covered with abundance of excellent long grass." Philip Fithian, while traveling through Penns Valley in Pennsylvania, also found "large open Plains, cleared either by the Indians, or by accidental Fire, hundreds of Acres covered with fine grass."[55]

Travelers and explorers generally did not regard open lands as barren despite the absence of trees. In their minds these areas would have been capable of producing forests. The problem then became explaining why trees were lacking. Some travelers connected natural meadows to wetland environments. "Such meadows are generally to be found near the head spring, or source of small branches of running water," John Smyth said. Others commented on natural meadows along the Shenandoah River. According to the duc de La Rochefoucauld-Liancourt, "the banks of it are, in some instances, covered with fine natural grass." Along tributary streams flowing down from the Blue Ridge, James Kirke Paulding found that the "sides of these are sometimes skirted with narrow strips of meadow."[56]

Some travelers and explorers speculated that periodic flooding had produced these meadows and savannas. Savannas, according to John Lederer, "all the Winter, Spring, and part of the Summer, lie under snow or water." Knight of the Golden Horseshoe John Fontaine described a savanna on the Meherrin River near Fort Christanna: "We see this day several fine tracts of land and plains called Savannas which lie along by the river side, much like unto our low meadow lands in England. There is neither tree nor shrub that grows upon those plains, nothing but good grass, which for want of being mowed or eat down by the cattle grows rank and coarse. Those places are not miry, but good and firm ground. Those plains are subject to inundations after great rains and when the rivers overflow, but there is seldom above 6 or 8 inches water over them."[57]

Several travelers suggested that, in addition to rains or snow, stream damming caused flooding. Beavers certainly flooded lowlands and destroyed forests, but perhaps the most intriguing explanation for natural meadows attributed stream damming to deposits of calcareous earth, or marl. Marl forms as a calcium carbonate precipitate on rocks or even sticks and twigs along streams in limestone land. Accretions can create natural dams. John Bartram noticed this phenomenon when he visited the Shenandoah Valley in 1759. After crossing the Opequon Creek on his way to Winchester, he observed "ye effects of ye incrusting limestone waters which is of that nature that where it runs it incrusts round brush or leaves or stones or any thing in its course frequently stopping its course & overflowing ye adjacent low grounds." The Philadelphia naturalist Benjamin Smith Barton observed a similar occurrence in 1802 near Warm Springs, Virginia, where the water "had deposited a considerable quantity of calcareous earth. In some places, the earth is so abundant, that it has formed little dams, as it were, quite across the stream." Francis Asbury, the Methodist circuit-riding preacher, provided another explanation for the connection between rivers and clearings: "It is amazing to behold how the ice, coming down the Potomac, has swept the banks, cutting through large trees, removing rocks of incredible size, and smoothing the river banks, as though many hundreds of men had been employed for that purpose."[58]

Animals attracted to salt springs along rivers and streams may have also played a role in creating and maintaining forest openings. At the "largest Lick I ever saw," Nicholas Cresswell encountered a herd of more than two hundred buffalo in 1775. "I suppose here is 50 acres of land trodden by Buffaloes, but there is not a blade of grass upon it." At approximately the same time Philip Fithian was visiting in Augusta County, where "Pastures take their Name from the killing in this, several Buffaloe-Calves—in the other a Drove of Buffaloe Cows—& in the last some Bulls. But they are properly called Pastures for each are fertile."[59]

Several travelers reported that severe storms may have cleared large areas in the forests. In the Appalachian Mountains of Virginia in 1775, Cresswell crossed an area called the Fallen Timbers. "The Trees are either torn up by the roots or broke off near the ground," he wrote. "Some Oaks 2 foot diameter are broke off and the tops carried to a considerable distance. Scarcely one tree left standing. I am told it continues 100 Miles in a west course and about a mile broad." Other observers attributed clearings to extraordinary natural events. Regarding the "hundreds of Acres covered with fine grass" he encountered in Pennsylvania, Fithian conjectured "that hot blasting Fumes which rise from Veins of Brimstone have destroyed the Timber, as they have, in places, found pure unmixed Brimstone, that will burn quite away without leaving any Dross." John Bartram also found evidence of natural brimstone during his travels, but it was his fellow scientist Benjamin Smith Barton who documented an active volcano in the Shenandoah Valley. "About 45 years ago," he noted, "a hill or volcano, distant about 35 miles from Winchester, in Virginia, and near the Patomak, had emitted fire and ashes, for a considerable distance."[60]

Periodic fire could maintain grassland or scrubland, but crown burns were probably not common enough to clear extensive forests. As Isaac Weld explained, "there is but very little brushwood in the woods of America, so that these fires chiefly run along the ground; the trees, however, are often scorched, but it is very rare for any of them to be entirely consumed." Most fires only reduced the forest understory and ground cover. They could have been touched off by lightning, for as Johann David Schoepf observed, the "oppressive heat [of Virginia] is accompanied by frequent sudden changes almost every day, and dreadful thunder-storms." More commonly, however, travelers and explorers attributed fires to Indians. In commenting that "all the country [of Virginia in 1724] is but one continued forest," Hugh Jones described "patches of some hundred acres here and there cleared; either being formerly seated by Indians, or the trees being burnt in fire-hunting." Among the Oenock, John Lederer likewise found the "country here, by the industry of these Indians, is very open, and clear of wood."[61]

Travelers' complaints about thickets shed some light on why Indians burned the forest. In one instance, Lederer found that "the ground is overgrown with underwood in many places, and that so perplext and interwoven with Vines, that who travels here, must sometimes cut through his way." While journeying toward the Blue Ridge in 1716, John Fontaine encountered thickets "so well laced together that in getting through it tore off a great deal of our baggage and our clothes all to rags." A little farther, he discovered that the "sides of the mountains are so full of vines and briars that we were forced to clear most of the way before us." In North Carolina somewhat later, John Smyth "met with an impenetrable thicket of young hiccory saplings, growing so near to each other, and their branches so perfectly interwoven, and entangled together, that it totally obstructed my farther progress."[62]

Many thickets developed as clearings and old fields reverted to woodland. While exploring western Virginia in 1671, Thomas Batts and Robert Fallam came upon "a piece of very rich ground where on the Moketans had formerly lived, and grown up with weeds and small prickly Locusts and Thistles to a very great height that it was almost impossible to pass." In the same area where he described grasslands of several hundred acres, Philip Fithian also encountered glades "covered with Shrubs, Ground-Oak, Hazles, &c." And farther south in North Carolina, John Smyth found that persimmon trees "grow chiefly in or near about the edges of glades, savannahs, and in old fields." According to Andrew Burnaby, abandoned tobacco lands in Virginia became "beautifully covered with Virginian pines." Isaac Weld concurred: "In some parts of Virginia," he wrote, "the lands left waste in this manner throw up, in a very short time, a spontaneous growth of pines and cedars."[63]

Many travelers and explorers, however, described the forest understory as open and their way unimpeded. Journeying from Winchester to present-day White Post in the Shenandoah Valley, Ferdinand M. Bayard passed through "forests whose hardy and tall trees did not permit bois-du-chien (dogwood) or bramble to overgrow the open spaces between the trees. A deep green turf covered those spaces and invited the tired traveler to rest." Other travelers also found grass growing under the cover of trees. On his journey toward the Blue Ridge, John Fontaine discovered "the largest timber that ever I see, the finest and deepest mold, and good grass upon it." A forest floor of grass may have been the product of the "rich, brown, loamy" soil Weld described as common throughout the Great Valley from North Carolina to Pennsylvania. In Frederick County, Virginia, Cresswell commented that "when there is a plentiful Mast (what they call Mast are acorns, Walnuts, Chestnuts, and all wild fruits) the Hogs will get fat in the woods with little, or no corn."[64]

Although many of these observations were made at places or times far removed from the Shenandoah Valley in its settlement period, they do, as an ensemble, create a varied portrait of a rich and complex environment. Taken together they also lay out how Europeans evaluated the land according to the purposes for which they took it up. What newcomers chose to comment on, in other words, reflected what they were looking for. They found and depicted an environment dominated by hardwoods. An oak-hickory forest marked the best lands, and chestnuts the higher elevations. Pines and conifers populated poorer, shale soils or exposed uplands. The forest cover was not, however, continuous. A mosaic of different forest types with significant areas of open land defined this landscape. Whatever the cause of these openings, they were significant and attractive to Europeans for the labor saved in forest clearance. Much open land appeared on the banks of water courses. Locating dwellings and farmsteads on bottomland terraces probably had as much to do with the distribution of natural meadows as with access to water. Glades and grasslands were also found in upland locations, but they are more difficult to explain there. Some could have been Indian old fields. Once cleared, fire could have maintained them, but most Indian burning was intended only to eliminate thickets on the forest floor. Ease of travel and improved hunting may explain why Europeans settled along the old Indian path, where frequent campfires produced regular burnings.

· ✑ ·

When Jost Hite referred to the Opequon area as "unsettled & a Wilderness" he was not describing chaos or denying a natural order. He and fellow settlers would have closely observed signs of where to settle, where to mark property boundaries, and where to create communities. Hite also added that the region had previously been inhabited by "Hostile Indians." How settlers behaved on the land—how they attached their culture to it—was affected by how the Indians had already altered it. Europeans may have failed to recognize the imprint of Indian culture or dismissed it as the work of savage hands, but their wilderness was neither untouched nor pristine. Hite made these observations about wilderness and Indians in the course of a legal argument that itself provides a rich source of information about the actions and ambitions of settlers.[65]

Hite's case had its origins in a dispute between Fairfax as proprietor of the Northern Neck and the colonial government of Virginia over who had the power to grant land and collect quitrents in the area of the Opequon settlement. In an opening move Fairfax secured an order from the Privy Council in 1733 to halt all land granting in the disputed territory until the issue could be resolved. He then sailed to Virginia to protect his interests. Surveys of the Potomac to determine its proper headwaters were conducted in 1736 by commissioners representing both Fairfax and the colony. The matter was then remanded to London. Before returning to England to lobby the Privy Council personally, Fairfax traveled to the Shenandoah Valley, where he met with Opequon settlers in the homes of Jost Hite, Peter Wolf, and Thomas Branson. He reassured the men and women who had come to Virginia under the auspices of colonial land orders that "he would not hurt them," that he only "wanted to have the Country settled." He did not want "any poor man to quit the Place for want of Land." But he warned Hite that if he won the dispute with the colony he would require "fair and regular surveys." Win he did in 1745, when the Privy Council recognized the proprietary's and not the colony's claim to northwestern Virginia. But the Council cautioned Fairfax that "all the Grantees of Lands under the Crown within the Boundaries aforementioned shall quietly enjoy their Lands according to their respective Grants."[66]

Fairfax returned to Virginia in 1747 and kept his word to both Hite and the settlers. It was at this point that Fairfax objected to Hite's sales to people who "would give the greatest Price" for land in "Quantities figures and Positions . . . without Regard to form order Custom Usage Equity or Laws of the Colony." To Hite's settlers who had engrossed watercourses in violation of the colony's length to breadth requirements but who were willing to resurvey their lands properly, Fairfax issued new grants. Other settlers, who despaired of obtaining a title to their land through Hite, also sought a Fairfax grant. These were the landholders that Hite then named along with Fairfax in his 1749 chancery suit to recover title to proprietary lands. At stake were the holdings of fifty-four families, who, when the suit turned against them, had to document their steps in settling at Opequon. Thus ordinary people explained how they had learned of available land in Virginia, and they recorded their various motives in deciding to take advantage of opportunities at the Opequon settlement. They described their move there, the actions they took in identifying and securing land, the influences on those actions, and numerous other insights into the land-selection process.[67]

Most of those deposed in the case had come to the Opequon settlement from Pennsylvania, New Jersey, and New York. How they heard of opportunities to acquire land in Virginia composed a crucial part of their settlement stories. For many, the news came by word of mouth, or as New Yorker Joseph Langdon put it, "by the common fame of the goodness and Cheapness of the Land." Enticed by "his Majesty's Encouragements offered to Settle there," Langdon also knew of the imperial purpose behind the new settlement. Men such as Henry Funk were among those who spread the word about the Opequon settlement. As a young man in the late 1730s or early 1740s, Funk journeyed from Opequon to Philadelphia. "And from his returning Home Again through the then province of Pensilvania," as he put it, he "cal'd upon some of his friends," who asked him "whether there was more Land for Sale with him Meaning of Mr. Joist Hites Land." Funk departed with a promise to find out and send word back to Pennsylvania.[68]

Hite and others with Opequon land orders had to rely on more than hearsay to attract families to Virginia and fulfill their settlement requirements. In an attempt to recruit settlers, Hite dispatched his close associate Peter Stephens in the late 1730s to the "Town of Lancaster and other places in Pennsylvania" to post "Advertisements . . . for the purpose of publishing the Sale of their Granted Lands at the rate of Three pounds for an hundred Acres." Stephens took the added precaution of copying circulars "in the German language[,] which they also set up." Stephens's efforts paid off, because "shortly after the setting up the said Advertisements a great number of people came from Pennsylvania and other places in order to purchase of the said Lands." Advertisements had a far-reaching effect. At least one resident of far away Albany, New York, Andrew Falkenburg, migrated to Virginia on the strength of them. Hite, himself, on occasion traveled to Pennsylvania, where he met prospective settlers in their homes. In one instance, John Baughman (Bowman) of Lancaster County purchased more than fifteen hundred acres from Hite before moving to Opequon.[69]

Getting to Opequon was, of course, another story. Settlers were well aware of the dangers of establishing a settlement in the Virginia backcountry, as one put it, "beyond the mountains . . . against the inclinations of those natives dispersed through the woods in hunting parties," so they formed "Companys of Adventurers" to provide for the common store and defense. Some no doubt packed their belongings on horses, but many took wagons and were "obliged to make roads." The need for collective efforts diminished with time, and more men such as George Wright "came into this Colony . . . from Pensilvania with his family." Others, however, preceded their families. William Rogers, for instance, came to Opequon alone "to seek Land in order to make a Settlement for himself and family." Only later did he "set off from his new design to go for them." Philip Windle, the man who found Hite sitting in his doorway, brought sons Christopher, Augustine, and Valentine with him on a search for their patrimony lands.[70]

Settlers' stories betray considerable confusion about how to secure land at Opequon. Hite and the others might have succeeded well in advertising their lands but not in getting a message out to new arrivals about procedures for claiming, surveying, or patenting them. William Rogers, for instance, admitted that "when he came up from Pensylvania he was an intire Stranger to the methods that he found since used to wit of getting Orders of Council to take up tracts of Land." He "asked no Questions." Making first a "search to find such as he might think would do for him," he soon "pitched upon land he liked" and selected 216 acres tucked in a bend in the North Fork of the Shenandoah River. Informed that it was land belonging to Lord Fairfax, he "improved as such by which it might remain in his name." Only on his way home to Pennsylvania for his family did he encounter Hite. "Happening to call at Mr. Hites . . . and being asked sundry Questions concerning his Business . . . he freely told his Business and how he had proceeded and where his design lay &c." Eager to thwart Fairfax's claims, Hite then "told him the Land was his and not his Lordships." Persuading Rogers to "desist from his purpose," Hite offered the land to him at £3 per hundred acres. To settle the matter, Rogers agreed to pay Hite ready money, if Hite would "make him a title . . . or give him good Bonds."[71]

What progress Joseph Langdon made in securing land was as muddled and haphazard as Rogers's. Arriving at Opequon "he did make Search for Land and did find some to his liking" in a bend of the Shenandoah's North Fork a few miles south of Rogers's holding, but "before he did settle the same [he] did hear of the orders to Hite." Off he went "to mr Hite and told him the affair and where the Land lay." To Langdon's surprise, Hite "intirely denied to have any claim to it and would have nothing to do with it." So Langdon went to Hite's partner, Robert McKay, who "would sell him the Land." The only guarantee Langdon received, however, was an order by McKay to his son that if he "should die before a Deed could be made to see that . . . [Langdon] should not be hurt nor disturbed." As to the usual price of £3 per hundred acres, McKay responded that Langdon, not being among the first settlers, "must give a small matter more." About all this confusion Langdon lamented that "when he came [to Opequon] he was intirely ignorant of the new methods men had taken to make themselves Estates at the Expence of other poor men to wit by obtaining orders of Council for a great Quantity & selling it to those that came for relief at such prices as they could get."[72]

Some land seekers went to Hite first. Hearing Hite "had many thousands of acres of Land to dispose of," Pennsylvanian William Ewing set off for Opequon "to take up Land and settle." Arriving in April 1737 he "applied" to Hite and "agreed with him for about twelve hundred and ten acres at the rate of five pounds for every hundred [acres] which had been before surveyed." The land Hite assigned Ewing lay in a 2,050-acre tract Hite had patented in December 1734. When Hite never performed on the bonds he exchanged with Ewing for the sale, Ewing went to Fairfax, who granted him only 625 acres at the same location. Similarly, George Wright had heard that Hite had "large Quantities of Land to dispose of." He, too, "applied" to Hite and "accordingly agreed with him for six hundred acres for fifty pounds" or more than £8 per hundred acres. After arriving in Virginia from New York, Andrew Falkenburg worked for Hite and his partners carrying the chain in surveying crews. From time to time he made "improvements" on other people's land and eventually improved a tract of his own along a tributary of the Shenandoah River. Observing that "every Settlement that wass maid On the Granted lands Saved them One thousand Acres," Hite and McKay eventually employed Falkenburg "to Show thair Lands to farmers in Order that they might get the Lands Settled Least thair Grants Shou'd Elapse."[73]

Like Falkenburg, Jacob Funk scouted settlers for Hite and McKay. Funk lived along the North Fork of the Shenandoah River, where he operated a mill near the future site of the town of Strasburg. He helped Philip Windle find the patrimony land for his sons. That day in the doorway after Hite had asked Windle where he came from and where he and his sons were going, Windle replied that they were "going up as far as Old Jacob Funks and was hunting for Land." Hite responded that he had "Land to Sell near the said Jacob Funks and if they Wou'd Stay a few days at the said Jacob Funks to rest their Horses that the said Windles might get some body to go with them and look some land where they did like." This conversation took several hours, and in the end it was Funk who went with them "to look out land and Came to the tract of Land calld. the North Mountain tract which they liked very well." They returned to Funk's house that night, but the next day the father and three sons "moved with their waggon and Baggage to the above said tract of Land and Erected a Cabin." Their first thought was to establish a use right to the land; only later did they seek to purchase it.[74]

Windle and his sons were not the first to arrive on the North Mountain tract. Other men, such as Ulrich Stoner, Thomas Little, and George Seller, had come before them. The land that John Baughman had purchased from Hite also lay in this tract. The entire tract enveloped 4,600 acres, which Hite had surveyed with Robert Brooke in November 1734 (fig. 3.6). But he had not received a patent for it before Fairfax's moratorium on land granting took effect at Opequon. Like his larger tract along the Opequon Creek, Hite had not surveyed division lines before he allowed families to self-select their settlements. The North Mountain tract therefore provides a microcosm of the landscape development that took place throughout the Shenandoah Valley. As an emerging open-country neighborhood removed by several miles from other settlements, it was, in a sense, the human counterpart to the habitat birds create in establishing nests and adjoining territories.[75]

In devising the North Mountain tract, Jost Hite made a set of environmental decisions similar to those defining his Opequon Creek tract. The latter engrossed limestone lands throughout the creek's western watershed adjacent to the shale-limestone contact. The western boundary of the North Mountain tract similarly ran along a fault separating shale lands to the west from limestone lands within the tract. Several streams, including Toms Brook and Pughs Run, watered these lands. If Hite was reading the forest for clues about the land, he would have noted the overwhelming dominance of oaks and hickories in the same frequencies found on the best lands throughout the Shenandoah Valley. As elsewhere, walnuts denoted bottomland, and a conifer marked a little patch of what the surveyors called "piney Land." In only one location, perhaps a small glade or Indian old field, did surveyors employ a stake. What Hite got at North Mountain was a tract that captured the same environmental diversity as elsewhere along the shale-limestone contact and the same well-watered limestone land that characterized his home property along the Opequon.[76]

The fall following the arrival of the Windles at North Mountain, Jost Hite showed up with surveyor James Wood and another Opequon settler, Jacob Nisewanger. The men proceeded "to Lay Off the said North Mountain tract into Lotts." North Mountain settlers Valentine Windle, George Seller, and Thomas Little not only observed the proceedings but also "helped to Carry the Chain." Little's wife, Mary, later stated that she "perfectly well remembers the Surveyor running the division line between a lott laid off for her Husband and a lott laid off for George Seller that the Surveyor after laying the said Lotts Shew'd her several platts, and said, see here pointing on the platt, this is your Husbands Land, pointing to another platt, this is your neighbour George Seller's land, and then to another saying this is your Neighbour Ulrich Stoners land."[77]

Paying for the land was another matter. Philip Windle and his sons conceived a particularly creative solution to this problem. The father had agreed to pay £3 for every one hundred acres of the North Mountain land acquired for his sons. When Windle asked Hite "how soon it was to be paid," Hite responded that "he would get the Land Surveyd & Make them deeds for the

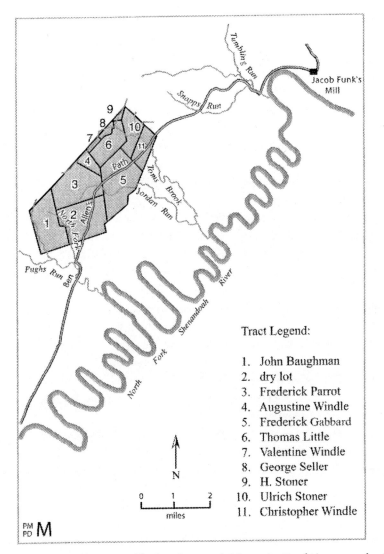

FIG. 3.6. Open-Country Neighborhood at North Mountain. By their own reckoning European settlers divided Jost Hite's forty-six-hundred-acre North Mountain tract into parcels that provided access to a variety of natural resources. The result was a vernacular landscape. Based on maps by Geertsema, in O'Dell, *Pioneers of Old Frederick County.*

same as Soon as he cou'd and then they Shou'd Pay him for it." Hite was overly optimistic, because land patenting in the North Mountain tract would soon fall subject to the moratorium on distributing all land west of the Blue Ridge. But at the time, Hite was building a mill and had "Broke down his waggon wheels," presumably hauling heavy stone. When he encountered Windle near the Anglican chapel in the town developing around Funk's mill, he "ask'd him for four of his Waggon wheels . . . in part pay towards the said Land at the Rate of 10s each wheel." Windle agreed and eventually traded four more wheels to Hite in exchange for North Mountain lands.[78]

The settlement narrative of Frederick Gabbard demonstrates how eagerly newcomers at Opequon sought land and how desperate they became when hopes were thwarted. Gabbard and his family arrived at Opequon from Pennsylvania in spring 1738 and found Jacob Funk. Gabbard asked if Funk "knew of Any Land to be Sold"? To Funk's reply that there was "none for Sale at this time," Gabbard lamented that "he did not know what he shou'd do, if he could Get no Land." Funk volunteered that "he would let him have some Ground to make a Spring Crop," and Gabbard "went to work on it Seven or Eight days." Then John Parrot came down from the North Mountain tract and told Gabbard that he "knew a tract of Land for him [there] which was called the bear Spring tract." The land had already been surveyed, so Gabbard went home with Parrot to view it. The following day Gabbard went to see Hite and make arrangements to pay for the land. Gabbard then set off with his wagon, team, and family to take possession of his new holding. Parrot figured in another North Mountain land transaction. On May 31, 1739, several years after the North Mountain survey, Frederick Parrot, possibly John's brother, purchased part of a 950-acre lot from Hite. Eight years later Rinehart Borden purchased 200 acres from Parrot. Then, in 1750, Parrot sold a tract to Borden described as "John Parrotts plantation."[79]

The ensemble of surveys, dwelling sites, farmsteads, buildings, fences, and roads articulated at North Mountain in a wooded, well-watered environment of good soils composed what can be called a vernacular landscape. It was vernacular because the people who occupied it fashioned it largely free of influences apart from their own expectations and ambitions. The boundaries of the entire tract as surveyed by Jost Hite and Robert Brooke in 1734 constrained their actions, but settlers—at least the earliest settlers—otherwise had a free hand in the self-definition of their territory and nest site. Later settlers had to conform to the possibilities remaining to them. The Windle brothers, for instance, lodged their tracts within the open spaces surrounding the holdings of earlier arrivals, the Little, Stoner, and Seller families. Only after the arrival of the Windles were interior boundary lines surveyed and then with the assistance and, no doubt, the direction of the settlers themselves. By the time Frederick Gabbard arrived at North Mountain, the remaining land constituted a single, defined lot, which he accepted wholesale. The only cultural feature that may have affected the location of lots and dwellings was a path, "Ben Allen's path," which James Wood indicated on Christopher

Windle's holding at the northeast corner of the North Mountain tract. During the early 1730s Allen had acquired land about twenty miles farther south in the Shenandoah Valley, where Mill Creek emptied into the Shenandoah River. By 1743 he was operating a mill there. Whether or not Allen's Path followed an earlier Indian route is unknown, but it did connect the North Mountain tract to Jacob Funk's and was the route that Parrot, Gabbard, and the Windles would have taken to their new homes.[80]

The landscape that emerged at North Mountain was, therefore, a product of negotiation—negotiation among settlers, Jost Hite as land speculator, surveyors Robert Brooke and James Wood, and the land itself. The settlers were the most active agents in this negotiation. Hite established the physical limits of the emerging open-country neighborhood, and as the Windles' case suggests, he might have screened potential residents. Hite's financial interests, however, clearly lay in settling the land as quickly as possible. He would more likely have encouraged all comers rather than discourage the unworthy. That surveyors were not merely servants to the interests of settlers was indicated by an incident involving Augustine Windle. His father had contracted with Jost Hite on his behalf for 250 acres of the North Mountain land. Then James Wood, "by direction and in the presence of said Hite made a Survey" for Windle. "But," complained Windle, "instead of 250 acres only 135 Acres were laid off." It was at this point that Hite received the wagon wheels for this land. What Windle acquired in exchange was a small but extremely valuable tract straddling the headwaters of Toms Brook near the North Mountain fault and shale contact.[81]

The resolution of interests represented by Hite, Brooke, Wood, and the North Mountain settlers produced eleven tracts from the 4,600 acres. These ranged from 30 to 944 acres and averaged 426 acres—very close to the 402-acre average for all of the lands patented at Opequon before 1735. The smallest tracts, such as Valentine Windle's, captured rich bottomland soils along the western perimeter of the North Mountain survey, where habitat diversity would have been greatest due to the shale-limestone contact. The largest lots lay in the more arid southern half of the North Mountain tract, where one was labeled "A Dry lott" by surveyor James Wood. Thus, the negotiations among various interests produced a pattern of smaller lots on better land and larger lots on poorer land. All of the lots shared other characteristics. Each had water, and even the dry lot contained a spring. Amidst a topography of rounded knolls and broadly rolling valleys, every tract possessed a variety of upland and lowland environments. Consequently, most tracts were irregular. Only Valentine Windle's was rectangular. Some tracts had as many as nine sides, and in many, no sides were parallel. Bottomland holdings often exceeded the colony's three-to-one ratio for length to breadth. That no axial division lines transected the entire North Mountain tract strongly suggests that surveyors, wherever possible, were following the wishes of settlers in the partition of the community.[82]

Relationships among the configuration of lots, topography, and natural resources can be discerned. Five of the eleven lots had boundaries that paralleled streams. Several were rectilinear, with division lines crossing streams approximately at right angles. What this pattern suggests is that settlers entering the country were attending to two characteristics of the land: water and soil. They read the land for its quality according to forest cover, and they selected limestone soils. Some settlers, where holdings were small, captured bottomlands almost exclusively. Others preferred a variety of upland and lowland topographies. The artifacts settlers created in devising a property holding for a farm were, therefore, shaped principally by the drainage pattern of streams and creeks. The message Europeans etched upon the land expressed the desire for good, arable bottomlands in many places free of forests and for adjoining uplands, where meadows and pastures could be established. Rarely did settlers utilize a watercourse as a property boundary.

· ✛ ·

The settlement decisions made at the North Mountain tract were repeated in hundreds of instances of land surveying and patenting throughout the Opequon settlement during the 1730s. Each property line represented a vector resolving the forces of settlers, surveyors, and speculators interacting with the environment. The least common settler experience was that of the anxious Frederick Gabbard, who was happy to get the last remaining lot in the North Mountain tract. More usual was the situation of Christopher, Valentine, or Augustine Windle, who devised their own tracts in negotiation with neighbors but within predefined boundaries. More to the point of this chapter were the cases of William Rogers or Joseph Langdon. They, like many others, arrived at Opequon unaware of the role that Jost Hite, Alexander Ross, or other speculators played in the land-acquisition process. They first found land that suited them and only then negotiated its survey and purchase. Patterns in the landscape they created suggest that newcomers kept an eye on watercourses as the guide to the land they wanted and an eye on vegetation or forest cover as the key to land quality.

Three patterns in the earliest cadastre at Opequon articulate settler interest in the land. All three testify to Fairfax's complaints about the self-interestedness of settlers and the violations of survey standards or statutes. These patterns also took into account the subtle environmental differences between limestone and shale land without exclusive attempts to engross one or avoid the other. Many tracts were isolated or set off in open territory with only one or two other tracts. In most cases, these tracts enveloped the headwaters of short streams emptying into the Shenandoah River from adjacent limestone lands. Tracts were more often grouped in either linear or clustered patterns.

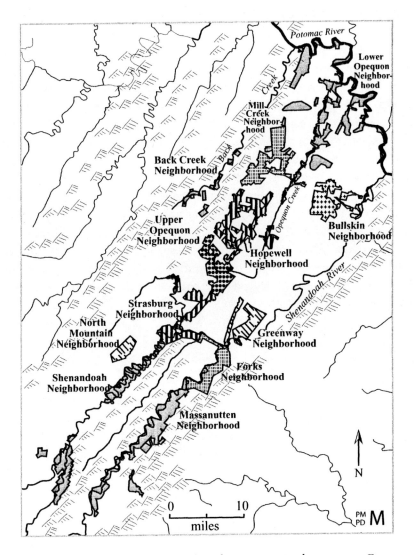

FIG. 3.7. Open-Country Neighborhoods at the Opequon Settlement, 1735. European settlers at Opequon organized their dispersed settlements into distinct open-country neighborhoods, often along streams or creeks and on the best-watered, most fertile land.

Based on maps by Geertsema, in O'Dell, *Pioneers of Old Frederick County*.

Linear configurations appeared along either roads or watercourses. The prominent string of landholdings extending along the shale-limestone contact and the old Indian path from a location near the Hopewell Meeting south for twenty miles to Cedar Creek demonstrates how early communication routes structured settlements. Settlements on streams or rivers, such as those along Crooked Run or along the North and South Forks of the Shenandoah, provide examples of how watercourses gave linear shape to the emerging landscape.

Elsewhere throughout Opequon, settlers clustered in patterns similar to the ones that developed at North Mountain or within Hite's Opequon tract (fig. 3.7). Larger settlements appeared where settlers freely combined into open-country neighborhoods, usually around the watersheds of major streams and creeks. In addition to North Mountain, Opequon Creek, and Hopewell, these communities took shape most notably along Mill and Middle Creeks, which emptied into the lower Opequon, around the headwaters of the Shenandoah River tributary known as Bullskin Run, and on the lands drained by Bordens Marsh Run and Willow Brook. As already demonstrated at Opequon, however, clustering meant no more than joining tracts of land. Whether in isolated tracts or in linear or clustered arrangements, settlers fixed themselves on the land according to the environmental opportunities and natural resources within each property holding. Forces of dispersal, not concentration, governed the emerging landscape. Settlers traded goods and services with neighbors, but they, at least initially, did not focus these activities in towns. Opequon was a settlement without a center.

Chapter 4

Bounding the Land

I F THE FIRST PHASE of landscape evolution in the Shenandoah Valley began with Native American alterations to the land and the adjustments made by Europeans dispersing across it in the 1730s, then bounding the land brought this initial phase of landscape evolution to a close. Dispersal occurred in the conspicuous and conscious absence of any meaningful or overt controls over the land-selection process beyond individual choice, so dispersed settlement was a vernacular artifact of the values and interests of those who first took up the land. That the land was there for the taking, however, was a matter of imperial interest—the expression of the power held by those responsible for the security and expansion of English dominion in the New World. A coincidence of interest between settlers and imperial authorities, therefore, was responsible for the movement of Europeans, most of whom were not English, into the Shenandoah Valley.

Bounding the land would result from a similar coincidence of interests. Bounding meant the creation of a county and the establishment of county boundaries around and defining a settlement, which, in the case of Opequon, developed outside any existing Virginia county. Bounding the land also entailed the establishment of a county court. Courts would conduct the county's economic and legal business in the county town. Here people would gather on court days, and here merchants, artisans, and innkeepers would set up their businesses. Thus, town founding signified the centering of the land and the beginning of the second phase of landscape evolution. The men and women of the Opequon settlement wanted and needed the courts and the focused economy of town life. For the sake of securing the colony, imperial authorities in Williamsburg sought these institutions as well. Revealing the motive forces behind landscape change therefore requires a perspective that incorporates the individual and collective interests of settlers within the larger, geopolitical and strategic influences that defined frontiers and made their settlement an expression of imperial interests.

The interests of settlers and the interests of empire met in the transformation of what Europeans called wilderness or waste land into private property and domain. Waste land was not waste because it was barren, but because it was unorganized—it was not constituted as property. Domain existed as the extension of sovereignty over territory, and it rested upon the authority of the king to grant land or, in other words, to fabricate property as the creation of the state and place it in the hands of the king's subjects. To the subjects of the king, however, the ownership of land meant independence, not from the king, but from the subject relations of feudal society as tenants or laborers. Settlement at Opequon began with the administrative procedures that made land patenting possible. The exercise of royal authority, however, depended on the formation of counties and county governments. As the institutional center of county government, the county court became the agent for the transformation of wilderness into domain as private property. It functioned as the court of record for property ownership and conveyance as well as a civil court for resolving disputes over property and a criminal court for punishing crimes against property. The court also served the interests of settlers by securing property, which to them meant competence in the affairs of life. By issuing road orders the court also defined the rights and ways that allowed people to move across the landscape of private property, thereby giving meaning to individual ownership of property by creating the potential for economic development as well as enabling the process of community formation. The militia was also a creature of the county. Militia officers swore their commissions before the court and the able-bodied men of the county mustered in county units for the protection of their own property and the colony's interests alike.

So the process of bounding the land evolved in negotiation between the inhabitants of Opequon and colonial officials. The two parties shared interests, but the colonial government of Virginia proceeded slowly, cautiously, and deliberately in erecting counties and courts. Neither the governor nor the Council had confidence that the people of the frontier—so different in ethnic background, religion, economy, and outlook from themselves—were capable of managing their own affairs under the powers of the county. Colonial officials controlled the timing of county formation and the establishment of courts not in response to the wishes of frontier settlers but in the interests that those settlers served on the frontier: the security of colony and crown.

As county boundaries came to define the Opequon settlement and county courts acted to secure property, the otherwise vernacular landscape of dispersal grew into a landscape expression of official culture. Bounding the land, in other words, marked a transition from the vernacular to the official. A careful examination of the forces impelling this transition might best begin with a detailed look at the vernacular landscape—the dwellings, farms, roads, places, and connections between places—contrived in the process of settlement dispersal.

· ⚘ ·

Once again, materials gathered in the resolution of the Hite-Fairfax lawsuit provide detailed insights into this landscape as it emerged at Opequon during the early years of settlement. The decision handed down by Virginia's high court of chancery in Richmond on May 8, 1786, awarded to the heirs of Jost Hite all those lands Hite had claimed under the one-hundred-thousand-acre order the Council had granted him in 1731. Some of Hite's settlers had received patents for their land prior to December 1735 and others had not, because of the moratorium on land granting imposed on Virginia's Northern Neck until conflicts over rights to the region had been resolved. Many of the disappointed had subsequently gone to Fairfax for new surveys and proprietary grants. Hite was suing for these lands, and the 1786 decision awarded them to his heirs unless the people on these lands possessed purchase bonds or contracts with Hite.[1]

The plaintiffs, according to the decision, were "also intitled to the profits of the said lands" from January 1, 1750, "after making thereout a reasonable allowance for lasting improvements." Thus, from July to August 1786, Jonathan Clark conducted surveys of the disputed properties, scrupulously recording detailed information on the age, construction, size, and other features of dwellings, barns, and outbuildings. He also assessed improvements to the land itself, including orchards, cleared fields, and planted meadows. Clark happened to be Isaac Hite's son-in-law, and Isaac Hite, grandson of Jost Hite, was chief among the patriarch's heirs pursuing his case and land claims. Clark possessed the added distinction of being older brother to both George Rodgers Clark, famed as Virginia's conqueror of western lands during the Revolution, and William Clark, co-commander with Meriwether Lewis in the celebrated expedition bearing the two men's names. The elder Clark began his work in the Shenandoah Valley with the North Mountain tract.[2]

In late July 1786, he visited thirty-three parcels of land carved out of the original eleven surveyed almost half a century earlier by James Wood. What he saw, however, was very different from the landscape Wood and North Mountain settlers had created fifty years before. Gone were the carefully adjusted boundaries negotiated among surveyor, settler, and environment; in their place was a new and far more official landscape—official insofar as it reflected the interests of Lord Fairfax. The irregular holdings, with few parallel sides or right angles contrived to capture settler desires for a maximum of well-watered bottomland and a variety of upland and lowland conditions, had all given way to a neat, rectangular, gridlike pattern of tracts roughly oriented with the strike of the Shenandoah Valley and joined in such a way that each had more or less equal access to water. Whereas the earlier surveys represented the mind of North Mountain's first settlers articulated as a vernacular expression on the land, the later surveys Clark confronted were the work of Fairfax, who, as proprietor to the land, imposed a rational system designed to maximize its utility for all comers.[3]

Fairfax had returned to Virginia in 1747, intent on assuming an active role as proprietor to his newly confirmed western lands. This meant settling the land as effectively and efficiently as possible and rendering it productive for all settlers, who would then pay a quitrent to him. He was appalled by what Hite had allowed to happen on the land. "So Flourishing a Country . . . by unequal & Irregular Surveys," he complained, was "rendered almost wholly useless." Hite, "by selling the Waters and Springs together with the best Land . . . , [had left] great Tracts useless and untenantable." Fairfax swore that "from the first time he saw the Surveys . . . he had it principally in view to alter at least their Situation in such sort as to render the Waters & Springs as universally necessary and convenient as the nature of the Place would admit." Between 1750 and 1752 the first North Mountain settlers, including Mary Little, George Seller, Ulrich Stoner, Rinehart Borden, and Augustine, Valentine, and Christopher Windle, had all accepted new surveys of their original claims and received grants from Fairfax (fig. 4.1). Others, such as Benjamin Layman, Jacob Rife, and Peter Mauk, acquired land from Fairfax under the new scheme in the 1760s or later. All had little choice but to accept the official landscape imposed by Fairfax.[4]

The landscape Jonathan Clark saw in the 1780s had of course been altered by two to three generations of settlers since its initial occupation, but it still harbored remnants of the settlement era. Clark described many houses and farm buildings as "old" or "much worn." The landscape they created would have been altered less than landscapes in uncontested areas, and they reflected more closely an original state if, as could reasonably be expected, the cloud placed over land titles by the Hite-Fairfax suit discouraged improvement.

"Old" houses tended to be small and roughly square. A "much worn" log dwelling, twenty by eighteen feet, stood on Thomas Little's land. On George Seller's home place, an "old logg House 22 × 16" survived. Perhaps the best evidence in the Clark surveys of an original structure appeared in his eval-

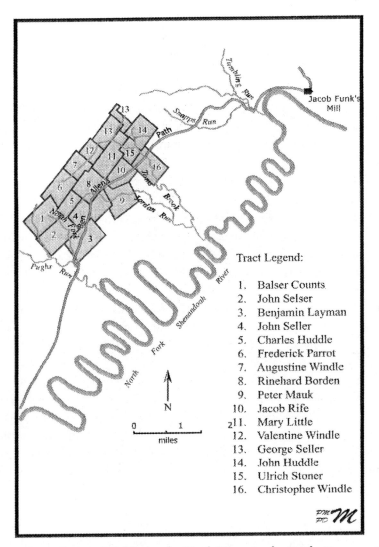

Tract Legend:

1. Balser Counts
2. John Selser
3. Benjamin Layman
4. John Seller
5. Charles Huddle
6. Frederick Parrot
7. Augustine Windle
8. Rinehard Borden
9. Peter Mauk
10. Jacob Rife
11. Mary Little
12. Valentine Windle
13. George Seller
14. John Huddle
15. Ulrich Stoner
16. Christopher Windle

FIG. 4.1. Open-Country Neighborhood at North Mountain after Fairfax Resurvey. Objecting to the way settlers engrossed the most fertile and best-watered lands, Lord Fairfax required extensive resurveying after his return to Virginia in the late 1740s, causing an official landscape to replace the vernacular landscape settlers had created earlier. Based on maps by Geertsema, in O'Dell, *Pioneers of Old Frederick County.*

uation of Valentine Windle's property. Valentine, his father, and brothers had built a "cabin" as their first act in claiming North Mountain lands. When Clark appeared, notebook in hand, the aged Valentine was still living in an "old and indifferent" log house forty by eighteen feet. On his brother Augustine's property stood an "old logg'd House 24 by 16." Jacob Parrot's farmstead contained "one old Logg Cabbin 22 × 18," and Ulrich Stoner's, a "Logg dwelling House 1 ½ Story 30 by 20 feet, half worn, Stone Chimney in the Middle."[5]

The oldest houses Clark described on the properties of the original landholders at North Mountain exhibited many common characteristics. They were all log and approximately square or rectangular. Dimensions varied from twenty to twenty-two feet on the long, or eave, side and sixteen to eighteen feet on the gable ends. Several dwellings had evidently been enlarged. Valentine Windle's rectangular house, which had two stone chimneys, undoubtedly on opposite ends, was probably constructed of two log cribs joined or separated by sufficient space for an intervening hallway, or "dogtrot." Constructing a new log structure adjacent to an existing one was a common manner of expanding structures. Much the same was probably true for Ulrich Stoner's house, where an original end chimney on one log crib was captured within a log addition, leaving the chimney in the middle of a structure sometimes called a saddlebag house.

Although most of the earliest settlers at North Mountain were German, the dwellings they constructed gave little direct evidence of Germanic origins. Joining log walls with corner notching was certainly in the vocabulary of construction technologies available in contemporaneous provinces of Germany but was probably not common in the area of the central Rhineland where many of the Opequon settlers originated. The European origins of American log construction is a much debated topic even today, but suffice it to say that interethnic familiarity with log architecture would most likely have been the result of the time Germans, Scots-Irish, and Anglo-Americans spent together in Pennsylvania and surrounding colonies. Clark's surveys also indicated that North Mountain Germans were not building dwellings based on the continental designs of the *Flürkuchenhaus*, or *Ernhaus*. These asymmetrical structures were defined by a massive central chimney surrounded by three to four rooms, usually on two stories. No North Mountain structures compared to these large and roughly square dwellings, which averaged twenty-eight to thirty by thirty-two to thirty-six feet. *Flürkuchenhauses*, however, were found at the Massanutten Settlement, which Jacob Stover established on the South Fork of the Shenandoah River, and also on the Opequon tract, where Jost Hite's dwelling conformed to this house type, as did Stephen Hotsinpiller's and probably others.[6]

Most of the oldest dwellings at North Mountain were consistent with the single-pen log structures built throughout the upland South at least from the settlement period—in some areas lasting to the end of the eighteenth century—to the middle of the nineteenth century. These structures were generally square to rectangular in plan with a pitched roof, gable-end chimney, and dimensions of sixteen to eighteen feet by twenty to twenty-two feet. A single door and window composed the long façade. Most were constructed with V or half-dovetail notching. Round logs were squared when intended for clapboarding. The Scots-Irish who settled around Hite at his Opequon tract commonly constructed this type of dwelling. Similar structures also appeared in stone, which indicates that consistent size was not a consequence of log construction or the length of available timber. Consistency, instead, suggests association with a well-established house type: the small, single-unit, direct-entry dwellings identified by geographer Alan Gailey as one of the most common houses in the north of Ireland in the eighteenth and nineteenth centuries, especially during the Great Famine of the 1840s (fig. 4.2). Although larger houses were often constructed in Ireland by stringing single units end to end in much the same manner as Windle and Stoner expanded their dwellings, smaller structures represented a response to economic stress through, in Gailey's words, the "simple reduction of the house to the kitchen unit alone." Under the comparable pressure of settling a frontier and investing available labor and resources in farm building, the Scots-Irish appear to have responded in a similar manner. What survived at Opequon in the ethnic architectural experience of the Scots-Irish was not a particular form or plan as a mental template of a proper house, but a flexible approach to house construction and a modular way of thinking that were highly sensitive to the economic and material conditions of the eighteenth-century frontier. Because houses were readily expanded or contracted in response to economic or environmental demands, small, single-unit structures prevailed during the frontier period.[7]

Among Germans at North Mountain a similar approach to housing prevailed. Scaling dwellings to physical situations, employing a variety of construction technologies, and altering or expanding structures with changing conditions all gave meaning to the dwellings revealed in Jonathan Clark's survey. Single-pen or single-unit house construction also reflected an architectural vocabulary widely shared among all ethnic groups as a response to the demands of establishing a farm under arduous conditions.

Clark recorded a variety of outbuildings on the properties of original settlers at North Mountain. There were several stables and spring houses, a bark mill, a house for drying leather, and an oil mill, but barns were the most common farm structure. Valentine Windle, for instance, possessed an "old round

FIG. 4.2. Stone Cabin in County Fermanagh, Northern Ireland. This single-unit, direct-entry house reflects a type of dwelling common in eighteenth- and nineteenth-century Ireland, when economic stresses forced the reduction of living space to a single room. At the same time on the American frontier, the strains of farm building encouraged the construction of similar structures in both stone and log. The famous frontier cabin was the result. Photo and survey: Philip Mowat.

logg Barn 40 by 25 feet," while his brother Augustine apparently still used an "old Logg'd Barn 44 by 24." The Windles' barns were fairly typical of the "old" barns at North Mountain. With dimensions averaging forty to forty-six feet long by eighteen to twenty-six feet wide, most of these structures were probably double-crib arrangements with rectangular pens separated by a bay large enough to accommodate a threshing floor or a wagon. That barns considerably exceeded the size of houses further indicates that the stresses of developing new land, which restricted house size, at the same time encouraged a greater investment in agricultural infrastructure.[8]

Two types of barns were common in early southeastern Pennsylvania, the source area for many Opequon settlers. The *Grundscheier*, or ground barn, was a small stone or double-crib log structure with a single story. Much larger and more complex was a two-level barn with an overhanging forebay. It proved more difficult to build and less adaptable for log construction, but it served as the prototype for the famous Pennsylvania bank barn, which, during the course of the eighteenth century, would become the key support structure for commercial grain-livestock agriculture. The Clark surveys suggest that at North Mountain ground barns prevailed in the settlement era and served multiple purposes, from the storage of feed and grain to the stabling of animals (fig. 4.3). Many would have been roofed with a traditional covering of thatch. Three "old" or "half worn" thatch-covered barns survived to be surveyed by Jonathan Clark. Most of the barns Clark described as "new" were shingled.[9]

Passing through the North Mountain settlement, Clark encountered a landscape still largely wooded. Of a total forty-six hundred acres, only slightly more than thirteen hundred, or 29 percent, were cleared or cultivated. About half the households had small orchards averaging about seventy trees, and two-thirds had improved some meadowland. Half a century earlier, of course, the extent of land cleared for crops or developed for apples or hay would have been far less. A visitor among early settlers at North Mountain would have found only isolated openings in the forest cover, some natural meadow usually along stream bottoms, and occasional patches of field crops or pasture. Shelter could be had only in small log cabins, rarely enclosing more than four hundred square feet. Animals had greater space in barns, which were often double the size of houses, but shared it with stored crops, tools, and perhaps a wagon or dairy.[10]

What is notable about this early landscape is what it was not. Absent, of course, were the grand houses of a gentry class of tobacco planters. Missing, too, was any significant disparity between the houses of the great and the small. Cramped though they were and simple in both construction and plan, the cabins of the Littles, Windles, Sellers, Stoners, and others were all much the same in size and social significance. These were the dwellings of families neither rich nor poor but all owners of their own land—or desirous of owning it when the case between Hite and Fairfax was resolved. They were not tenants, nor would they be, regardless of the outcome of this dispute. Fairfax had made his hopes for quitrent-paying landowners clear during his first visit to the Shenandoah Valley. He wanted the land settled by smallholders, not the planter gentry. Settlers could reasonably expect that whatever they invested in improving their land would be theirs to enjoy or bequeath. Similarly, there was no large population of African American slaves as in the plantation landscapes in Virginia's Piedmont and Tidewater to the east of the Blue Ridge. No rude cabins back of the big house would remind the visitor of a class of people with no hope of benefiting from their own labor. Slaves and slavery would become a part of life and economic endeavor at Opequon, and by Clark's time upwards of one in five residents of the lower Shenandoah Valley was black and a slave—his own father-in-law owned twenty-eight slaves. But for the time described by Clark's "old" buildings—for the social meaning encoded in these structures and in the text of the landscape they created—slavery and the great inequalities of power and wealth it implied had little significance.[11]

FIG. 4.3. Ground Barn, Frederick County, Virginia. Double-crib, log, ground barns similar to this one served as the principal agricultural structure for early settlers at Opequon. Photo: Ben Ritter.

The landscape of early settlement still evident in Clark's surveys of North Mountain prevailed throughout the Opequon settlement. During the warm days of July and August 1786, Clark visited and appraised 218 land holdings describing a total of fifty-six "old" dwellings. He characterized the greatest number of them as *cabins*. The term had no precise meaning in the eighteenth century, but it was employed to describe the rudest structures on the frontier and elsewhere. Although not all log buildings were cabins, one writer distinguished round-log cabins with roofs of clapboards and weight poles from houses of hewn logs and shingled roofs. All of Clark's cabins were small, ranging between 200 and 480 square feet. Even though a third or more of the old buildings had dimensions sufficient to accommodate two rooms, only one exhibited the size and shape of a *Flürkuchenhaus*. Less than a fifth extended upwards a half story, and only one possessed a second story.[12]

Clark's assessments of barns and other farm buildings throughout the remnants of the early Opequon settlement bear out the representativeness of the North Mountain landscape. About a third of the old barns fell within the same range of dimensions evident on this sample tract. Three barns outside of North Mountain were quite large, measuring sixty feet by twenty-two or twenty-four feet, and a class of small barns, thirty to thirty-six feet long by eighteen to twenty feet wide, had no counterpart at North Mountain. When described, roofs at North Mountain and elsewhere were most commonly covered in thatch. Construction was consistently of log, with the exception of three framed barns. The surviving skeletons of two log structures with dimensions indicating either a large house or small barn give a good description of double-crib construction. One had "two very old round log pens with a 12 foot passage, Cabbin roof—worn out 36 x 20" and the other, "two old pens & 12 foot passage the whole under Cabbin roof, 40 by 18, no floor or doors." The pens, or rooms, were small, measuring twelve by twenty feet in the first example and fourteen by eighteen in the second. The twelve feet remaining between the pens, as a characteristic road width, could readily accommodate a wagon but also represented an average width for a hall in a center-passage dwelling. In a cabin roof, log purlins spanned the distance between gable ends and supported a covering of slats and riven clapboards held down by the weight of log poles.[13]

Farmsteads throughout the Opequon settlement contained a variety of outbuildings. Most numerous and distinctive among those Clark called "old" were kitchens. Confining the heat and odors of cooking to a detached kitchen became more common throughout the eighteenth century and constituted the architectural norm in the next century. Smaller than a cabin, the most common kitchen measured sixteen by sixteen or eighteen feet. Stables appeared less frequently than kitchens, and only six were old by Clark's day. Whereas practically every farmstead possessed a barn, only a few had these structures designated specifically for animals. Stables varied from as small as sixteen by eighteen feet to as large as forty-four by twelve feet, but in almost all cases barns outsized them. Other old outbuildings cataloged by Clark as possible survivals of the settlement landscape included smaller numbers of spring houses, dairies, corn houses, henhouses, and a still house.

· ⚜ ·

What can be inferred about the settlement landscape from Clark's account of improvements to land at North Mountain seems to apply throughout the early Opequon community. In addition to land cleared for cultivation, orchards, or meadows, mills constituted a critical element of this landscape. Well before the days when great merchant mills ground vast quantities of some of the world's finest flour from Shenandoah Valley grains, smaller mills played a vital role in the economic life of the settlement community. Cracking grain and grinding meal fine enough for bread flour could be done by hand, but the labor was intensive and the regular needs of a single family could occupy a person for the better part of each day. Thus employing waterpower to grind grain mechanically represented a labor savings critical to the survival of a household, especially at times when the demands of frontier farming required the efforts of every hand. Constructing a proper horizontal-shaft water mill with a twenty-foot wheel and a headrace of a mile or more, as required by the gentle gradients of Shenandoah Valley streams, was an undertaking that could demand years to complete. A tub mill with a turbinlike set of blades on a vertical shaft with only enough fall for water to tumble a few feet into a tub around the wheel could very effectively grind sufficient grain for a small community.

Christopher Windle might have employed such an arrangement at North Mountain, which Clark described years later as a "very old Mill unfit for use, dam broke." Otherwise "old" mills were noticeably absent from Clark's accounts. In the surveys he conducted between 1732 and 1734, however, Robert Brooke documented the early importance of mills. Alexander Ross's partner, Morgan Bryan, had constructed a mill when Brooke surveyed his holding a few miles from the Potomac River on December 23, 1734. Eight months earlier Brooke had documented the "Small Grist Mill" John Smith built twenty miles to the south on a tributary to the Opequon appropriately named Mill Run (fig. 4.4). Smith's mill was significant for the added reason that it stood precisely where the Philadelphia Wagon Road crossed Mill Run.[14]

The proximity of roads and mills was no accident. So important was this association to the emergence of an economically effective landscape that the

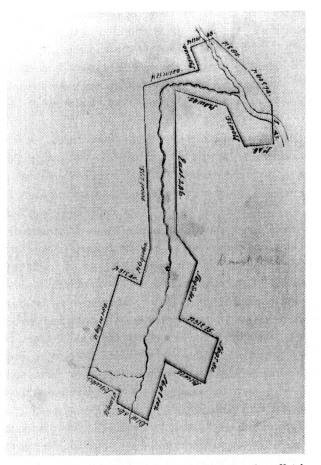

FIG. 4.4. Survey by Robert Brooke for John Smith, 1734. Brooke, official surveyor for "Lands on Sherrando River," laid off this plot for Smith on March 25, 1734. Smith's tract, which included a grist mill on a tributary to the Opequon Creek, engrossed the best bottomland in the area. Robert Brooke Survey Book, 1732–1734, p. 11, Thornton Tayloe Perry Collection, Virginia Historical Society, Richmond.

Virginia House of Burgesses required millers to construct their dams wide enough for a roadway. As early as 1667 the Assembly declared that "it would conduce much to the convenience of this country, both for the grinding of corne and of neerer roads[,] if mills were erected at convenient places." By 1714 mill dams were required to be a road width of ten feet, a stipulation later increased to twelve feet. Making the landscape work for the first generation of Opequon settlers required that roads or paths connect farmsteads where goods were produced to farmsteads where they could be traded and to mills where grains could be ground for home use or exchange with neighbors. In the absence of towns, the triangular relationships between farms, mills, and roads not only formed the cultural core of the landscape, but in a subsistence economy, this landscape formed the very premise of household self-sufficiency or competence. That this system worked well helps to explain the absence of towns as economic centers in the early landscape of the Opequon community.[15]

If a vernacular landscape expresses the immediate needs, desires, or ambitions of its occupants, then early roads at settlement communities such as Opequon were decidedly vernacular. This point is worth making because modern roads, insofar as government agencies design and align them, exemplify what is official in the landscape. That today's roadways often fail to articulate the interests of those living along them is demonstrated by the numerous protests road plans provoke from landowners or advocates of environmental protection and historic preservation. In the eighteenth century, however, roads were laid out, constructed, and maintained by the people who used them and lived along them. Procedures were well established in the county courts for creating roads. The people who needed a road between specific locations initiated the process with a petition to the court. If the court found merit in the proposal and encountered no opposition, the justices would appoint representatives among the petitioners to "view, mark, and lay off" a new right of way, thereby assuring that the route would meet the interests of its primary users. Within the next month or so the viewers would gather, designate the roadway, often by blazing trees with a distinctive mark, and return a description of their work to the court. Barring objection, the court would then appoint a road overseer from among the viewers with the legal power to order the tithables, or taxpayers, along the new route to turn out, construct the road, and then maintain it, all under pain of fine.

Roads were only routes, or rights of way. They did not become the property of the county, but they were public. The designation of a public road assured anyone the right to travel across private property. Roadways, in fact, tended not to follow property boundaries—a practice that might be expected if desires to minimize their impact on private property prevailed. Instead, roads regularly crossed land holdings in a pattern imposed by terrain and expressive of property owners' interests. Thus road placement, like every element of the landscape, represented a negotiation among settlers, authorities, the environment, and the cultural landscape settlers had inherited from Native Americans. Because members of the court, who were property holders themselves, usually shared the interests of all landowners, the official voice in these negotiations was mute. As Indians had made clear in complaints about the unjust appropriation of their lands, settlers often fixed their homesteads along established Indian routes. Otherwise, the lay of the land itself contributed to the placement of roads. With minimal labor invested in their construction, roads, consisting of ungraded, unditched, and unpaved tracks, usually avoided bottomlands, even when level, in preference for dryer, better-drained uplands and ridges. Where property boundaries followed streams, as they often did, roads, in the efforts of overseers to seek high ground, usually crossed streams and therefore traversed property holdings. Other reasons, however, explain why roads and the public they served were poor respecters of the privacy of property holders.

Roads not only crossed property boundaries but often passed immediately in front of houses or between houses and barns on early farmsteads. Regardless of whether families located houses on existing roads or arranged to have roads run by their houses, rural dwellings often bore the same immediate relationship to roads that townhouses had to streets. Visitors could pass directly from public space into the privacy of the home. Householders sitting in their doorways, as Jost Hite was on the day Philip Windle encountered him, were subject to whatever inquiry, news, or intrusion the traveler brought. A close reading of this landscape of roads and houses suggests that this kind of interaction is just what people wanted. Like the pattern of mills and roads, public and private space on farmsteads were not mixed by chance. Because the operations of mills were regulated by the county courts—millers could only charge a fixed toll and could refuse no customer the essential service of grinding grain—mills were themselves public places. This landscape therefore expressed the needs of its inhabitants to connect with one another. Interaction made possible the exchange of goods and information everyone needed for survival and economic competence, and it occurred in the public space of the mill, the doorway, or the road.[16]

The association between John Smith's mill and the road to Philadelphia was replicated again and again in the Shenandoah Valley as the landscape changed and developed during the course of the eighteenth century (fig. 4.5). The pattern became codified in the public landscape of Opequon, but at the same time it remained intricately entwined with the private landscape of property holdings and farmsteads. For the settlement generation during the first years, the establishment of mills and roads was strictly a vernacular process—no county court existed to endorse a route as a public road. An informal pattern of roads and paths thus emerged according to needs and circumstances. Evidence of this pattern appeared in Robert Brooke's surveys, and foremost among the roads Brooke documented was the wagon road used by Jost Hite. Several surveys in the northeastern portion of the Shenandoah Valley depicted the course of this route as it wound from a ford across the Potomac southeastward toward Hite's homestead. For most of its course the road kept to the high ground along the divide between the drainages of the Shenandoah River and Opequon Creek. Where it crossed the holding of Benjamin Burden, Andrew Hampton, and David Griffith, Brooke sketched it as a double dotted line and labeled it "Hites Waggon Road." From this location the road continued southwest, crossing the Opequon Creek twice—the second time at Hite's homestead. At this point it had already merged with several roads or paths extending from Pennsylvania, including the one passing by John Smith's mill and the route along the old Indian path west of the Opequon Creek. The road appeared again on Brooke's surveys of several tracts about eight miles south of Hite, where his grandson Isaac would one day settle.[17]

Brooke also noted paths in his survey. Paths accommodated foot travel or packhorses but were not maintained for wagons. One path crossed the survey for Borden, Hampton, and Griffith and led from Hite's wagon road to the land holding of Lewis Thomas, about two miles to the south. Paths often connected individual holdings or groups of adjoining properties to wagon roads, for example, the path that Brooke described as leading "from John Littlers to Abraham Hollensworths," where it joined Hite's road. In all, four paths appeared in Brooke's surveys.[18]

During the first decade of European occupation at Opequon a regional orientation began to emerge in the pattern of roads and paths that knit the settlement together. Hite's road, the road by John Smith's mill, and the road along the Indian path provided a distinctive north-south alignment to the settlement. None of these routes crossed the Blue Ridge; all led directly toward Pennsylvania, across the Potomac River. Complementing this linear arrangement was a developing complex of roads and paths clustering around key locations on the landscape. Not surprisingly, one such place was Jost Hite's homestead. Anyone seeking a patent for land had to find him there. Travelers were apparently numerous enough for Hite to open his house as a tavern. When Lord Fairfax wanted to reassure settlers about the security of their claims under his proprietorship, he met with this anxious group at Hite's house. By 1737 Hite was operating a mill along the Opequon, and he, with more than forty neighbors, petitioned that they "lay under great illconveniency for want of a Road" to a nearby gap over the Blue Ridge. This was the first effort to connect the Opequon settlement to the plantations and ports of Virginia's Tidewater. Later, another route would link Hite and his neighbors to a new community developing at the forks of the Shenandoah River, around Thomas Chester's settlement.[19]

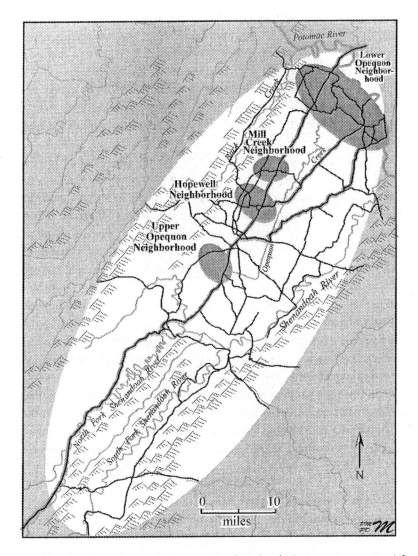

FIG. 4.5. Roads at the Opequon Settlement. Roads and paths knit open-country neighborhoods together for purposes of trade and social interaction. Long-distance routes
connected the Opequon settlement to centers of commerce in Pennsylvania and later to
eastern Virginia. The oldest roads at Opequon (shaded) led northward, and clusters of
roads marked the earliest open-country neighborhoods at Hopewell, Mill Creek, and
Upper and Lower Opequon. Based on maps by Geertsema, in O'Dell, *Pioneers of Old Frederick County.*

Meanwhile, Alexander Ross's settlement was emerging as another cross-roads. One branch of the Indian trail, soon to become a public road, traversed the property of his neighbor and fellow Quaker, John Littler. The road to Pennsylvania by John Smith's mill also traversed Ross's land where the Hopewell Meeting House stood and continued westward, where it joined another Indian path at the foot of the Allegheny Mountains. Additional roads from Ross's would eventually link the meetinghouse to other routes leading east across the Blue Ridge.[20]

Emerging across the landscape of the Opequon settlement during its first decade, therefore, was a pattern of transportation and communication characterized by long distance routes to Pennsylvania and a nascent connection east across the Blue Ridge to plantation centers in Tidewater Virginia. Crossroad communities developed around the settlements of men who held power to dispense land or the resources to establish mills and ordinaries. What this road system made possible was a landscape that functioned to sustain the competency of independent households. Here paths—the least imposing routes—were perhaps the most important. Although only a few appeared in Brooke's surveys and many escaped notice until designated as public roads, paths linked land holdings to other land holdings and to wagon roads, which led in turn to mills and taverns or other places where people gathered. This informal system of roads and paths was the key to population dispersal. The scattered settlement of Opequon worked because its people could move freely across the land in routes of their own creation. The establishment of a county and the appointment of a court would allow landholders to secure the pattern they had imposed upon the land. These official acts were a vital concern to everyone.

· ৻ৢ৳ ·

At about the same time that Hite, Ross, and their partners were submitting surveys to the Council in Williamsburg to obtain patents for themselves and their settlers, the people of the Shenandoah Valley began to petition the same Council for the protections to property that a county court could provide. At a meeting of the colonial Council on June 12, 1734, Hite "made proof of the Seating of Lands convey'd to him by John & Isaac Vanmader on the western Side Sherrando River by bringing there on to Dwell one Family for Each 1000 acres and also part of the Land granted him & Robert Mackay and others thereunto adjoining." The Council then ordered that "Patents be granted to the Several Masters of Familys residing there for the Quantitys of Land surveyed for them." Although the conflict with Lord Fairfax would prevent all of these families from receiving patents, a total of ninety-four were living on the land. Ross and Morgan Bryan, too, were collecting surveys and preparing to submit them to the Council. On April 23, 1735, they "made due proof of their bringing upon & Setling Seventy Families on the Lands granted them." Thus, within three years of the arrival of the first wave of Europeans in the Shenandoah Valley, about eight hundred people constituted the Opequon settlement.[21]

Even before Ross appeared before the Council, a number of the "Inhabitants on the North West side the Blew Ridge of Mountains" petitioned this body for the appointment of magistrates to "determine Differences and punish Offenders," because Opequon was "far remote" from the established counties of the colony. On April 23, 1734, the Council had consequently designated Opequon landowners Jost Hite, Morgan Morgan, John Smith, Benjamin Borden, and George Hobson as justices of the peace in Spotsylvania County. Hite, Morgan, and Hobson would still be justices eight years later, when Jonnhaty and his party of Oneidas and Onondagas appeared in the Shenandoah Valley. Spotsylvania County extended no farther west than the Shenandoah River, so the justices were relieved of any obligation to attend regular court sessions; the five new members were to perform only the limited functions of the justice of the peace within their neighborhoods. The conservatism of the Council in limiting the powers of local government on a western frontier of foreign Protestants was further indicated by the provision that these conditions would prevail until "there be a sufficient Number of Inhabitants on the North West side of the said Mountains to make a County of itself." But as events proved, it was not local population growth, but large-scale imperial conflicts, that would lead the Council to establish county government in the Shenandoah Valley.[22]

The problem of the Opequon settlement lying outside any county, however, would be resolved sooner. On September 7, 1734, the attorney general of Virginia presented a bill to the House of Burgesses calling for the division of Spotsylvania County. Named Orange County, the new jurisdiction extended west to the "utmost limits of Virginia." By the first week of October, the Burgesses, Council, and governor had all agreed to the act. When the court of Orange County first met the next January, all previously appointed justices from the Opequon settlement sat on the new commission of the peace.[23]

Authorities in Williamsburg might have thought they had done all they could to bring order and security to the frontier by equipping settlers with the administrative and legal means needed to settle their differences and punish lawbreakers. For a short while after the formation of Orange County, moreover, a diplomatic solution seemed possible to the Indian warfare that so disrupted the Anglo-American frontier. At about the same time the first court of the new county convened, the Six Nations, recently devastated by smallpox epidemics, had appealed to the English governor of New York for aid in negotiating peace with the southern Indians. For the next few years much of the time of several colonial governors, including William Gooch, would be consumed in diplomatic efforts to end the wars of the Iroquois, Catawbas, and Cherokees. These attempts would fail, but ironically, they furthered the efforts of Virginia's frontier settlers to establish separate counties in the Shenandoah Valley.[24]

Immediate hopes for peace were dashed on April 22, 1736, when the Virginia Council received reports that the "Northern Indians in great Numbers have lately pass'd through the Frontiers of this Colony under pretence of going to War with the Cattawbaws & by their Insolent behaviour given great Disturbance to the Inhabitants." Early the next month the Council ordered that the "Southern & Northern Indians be severally Invited to meet here next April for setling a peace between those Nations as the best way for securing the quiet of Our Frontier Inhabitants." Through the intercession of Pennsylvania and the diplomacy of Pennsylvania interpreter Conrad Weiser, Virginia authorities soon learned that, although the Six Nations insisted on Albany, not Williamsburg, for negotiations, they promised a cease-fire in the southern wars. Nonetheless, a messenger sent to the Carolinas soon returned with the discouraging news that continued raiding by the Iroquois had taken nearly a dozen lives among the Catawbas and that the latter "are so exasperated that they will hearken to no terms of Accomodation, at least till they have their Revenge." Having fallen "into a friendly Conversation with a party of the Six Nations," however, the Cherokees had already sent a peace delegation to Iroquoia. In further negotiations through the governments of Pennsylvania and New York, a date of August 8, 1738, was finally set for the Albany talks to begin.[25]

The year 1738 was one of great frustration for the advocates of peace. The southern tribes had killed a Cayuga Indian, and Iroquois parties were seeking revenge by early spring. Then, during the first week of April, William Gooch received word that two white men on the frontier had been killed by Indians. A petition soon followed from the "Inhabitants on Sherrando River" complaining that the "Northern Indians frequently passing through their plantations Commit frequent Outrages and have lately killed one of their men." The governor and Council quickly dispatched thirty muskets, eight pairs of pistols, powder, and ball from the magazine in Williamsburg to John Lewis, who was appointed captain over the inhabitants of Beverley Manor, near the place of the killings. Although Lewis had been ordered not "on any pretence whatsoever [to] offer any Violence" to Indians unless attacked, the cease-fire on the frontier hardly seemed effective as the Albany peace conference approached. What happened next rendered the parley moot. During the last week of June,

Williamsburg was stunned by the news that even more whites "who were settled far back on the Frontiers" had been killed by the Indians. No one knew
whom to blame. Early reports condemned the "Alleganey Indians." Seemingly more credible sources, however, suggested that a "treacherous" attack
by the Iroquois had again "so exasperated" Catawba warriors that they "pursued their northern enemies as far as the river Cahongarooton [Potomac] and
gave them a notable defeat." Iroquois survivors then "fell upon three families
of the English inhabitants on the back of the mountains and barbarously massacred eleven of them." Gooch immediately dispatched messengers to the
northern towns to "demand the murderers," but the Six Nations condemned
the "French Indians from Lake Erie" for the affair. Not until a full year later
did the Virginia governor receive a letter from the Catawbas reporting that
"they had found out some of their Nation murdered the English on Cohoa-
garooton last year And that they had put them all to death for it." Meanwhile,
uncertain Virginia authorities did what best they could to safeguard their
frontiers.[26]

On November 1, 1738, William Gooch stood before the assembled members of the Virginia House of Burgesses and Council. He reviewed his attempts "to negotiate a Peace between the Northern *Indians,* under the Government of *New-York,* and the *Cattabaws* and *Cherikees,*" admitting that
"whilst they are at War . . . [the frontiers] would be exposed to the Ravages of
both Parties." But the "late Incursions of the *Indians* and the Murders they
have perpetrated on the Inhabitants beyond the great Ridge of Mountains"
left him with "no Hopes of Success." Turning to the Assembly, he asserted
that the "Safety of That Frontier must depend on your Councils and Assistance." In response to the governor's call for action the legislature took up
and passed three measures during the next weeks reflecting separate approaches to the problem of frontier security: military, domestic, and political.
On November 8 the House began consideration of an act "for making more
effectual provisions against Invasions and Insurrections." Originally passed in
1727, because the "frontiers of this dominion, being of great extent, are exposed to the invasions of foreign enemies, by sea, and incursions of *Indians* at
land," the legislature endorsed it again. To centralize military command in
time of emergency, the act empowered the governor to raise "such a number
of forces, out of the militia of this colony, as shall be thought needful for re-
pelling the invasion, or suppressing the insurrection." The governor's powers
were complete with authority to impress men, provisions, and supplies into
the service of a colonial army.[27]

As a domestic strategy of defense, the Assembly sought to occupy Virginia's frontiers more effectively. Originally entitled "A Bill, for the Encour-

agement of certain Foreign Protestants," an "Act, to encourage Settlements on the *Southern* Boundary of this Colony" recognized that because "lands lying upon Roanoke river . . . are for the most part unseated and uncultivated . . . settling that part of the country, will add to the strength and security of the colony." Accordingly, the measure exempted settlers from "paiment of public, county, and parish levies" and allowed newcomers unlikely to produce any tobacco to pay fees for public services, such as recording a deed or serving a writ, "in current money." The measure also eased procedures for the naturalization of "any alien settling there," allowing the governor to grant letters of naturalization on certification by the clerk of any county that an immigrant had "taken the oaths appointed by act of parliament." Naturalization had long been a keen interest of German, Swiss, and other immigrants who were not subjects of the English crown by birth. In his petitions for a huge new colony along the Mississippi and Ohio Rivers, Jacob Stover, for instance, had pointed out that "naturalization for this People as Forreigners is most humbly desir'd, that they may be qualified to Serve Offices and to have a lawfull right to their Lands."[28]

Most significant for the story of landscape change in the Shenandoah Valley, however, was the chain of political events set in motion by a November 8 resolution in the House of Burgesses "that Provision be made, for the Security and Encouragement of the Inhabitants beyond the great Ridge of Mountains." Three days later the committee charged with the task of responding to the resolution proposed "that all that Part of the said County of *Orange*, which lies to the Westward of the Top of the Blue Ridge of Mountains, be separated from the rest of the said County, and erected into Two distinct Counties." The resulting bill made clear that the "strength of this colony, and it's security . . . are like to be much increased and augmented" by "giving encouragement to such as shall think fit to settle" upon the "rivers of Sherrando, Cohongoruton, and Opeckon." In addition to bounding these settlements in new counties, the legislature offered all the encouragements granted settlers along the Roanoke River. Proclaiming that "enlarging the frontier Settlements and Strengthening them by proper encouragements for Cohabitation hath always proved the most effectual Method Securing the Country against the Indians," the governor signed this act and the previous two into law on December 21, 1738.[29]

In a significant ploy for the perpetuation of royal power in new territory, the two counties were to be named Frederick and Augusta, after the Prince and Princess of Wales. Protecting that power in new settlements dominated by non-English peoples, however, was a problem for Williamsburg authorities. Governor Gooch, for instance, had recommended in 1733 that Stover's

Georgia colony not be independent but be incorporated into Virginia. Among the "inconveniencies" of "erecting new provinces," Gooch singled out the "difficulty of bringing foreigners to the knowledge [and] under the subjection of the English laws, where they are left to themselves, and not incorporated with an English Government." But the incidents of 1738 had demonstrated to the governor the value of local governments, even among foreigners. No viable militia unit or office corps existed west of the Blue Ridge to which the governor could send arms and ammunition. He had had to commission an irregular force under John Lewis, an Irish immigrant largely unknown in Williamsburg. To complicate matters, the militia was an arm of county government, and the establishment of a county took an act of legislature. This was not an easy accomplishment in colonial Virginia, where the Assembly convened irregularly and only for brief periods. Williamsburg was in a bind.[30]

Gooch explained how the legislation for the new counties provided a way out: "Because most of the People likely to settle there are illeterate and many of them not yet understanding the English Language, it is left to the Governor and Council to fix the time, when Justices and other officers are to be established." By legislating the new counties into existence but requiring that they "remain part of the county of Orange . . . until it shall be made appear to the governor and council . . . that there is a sufficient number of inhabitants for appointing justices of the peace, and other officers, and erecting courts," Williamsburg authorities, on the one hand, bought time in light of doubts about the governing capacity of non-English subjects while, on the other, they acquired the power to bring county courts quickly into session by executive action in an emergency. In June 1739, twice in May 1740, and again in April 1741 residents of the Shenandoah Valley petitioned the governor and Council that the "County of Frederica May immediatly take Place," complaining that the "difficulty of obtaining Justice" in the distant court of Orange County allowed crimes and "persons of a Scandalous Life" to go unpunished. Each time the Council deferred consideration of these petitions. Events would make clear that the conditions under which the new counties were to be established would be determined by the defense of the colony and not the interests or numbers of frontier inhabitants.[31]

By the end of 1738, the volatile situation created by the movement of Europeans into the Shenandoah Valley was evident to colonial authorities. Tensions between Indians and settlers had resulted in the deaths of more than a dozen whites and an unrecorded number of Native Americans. Virginia legislators had strengthened the militia organization of the colony, armed western settlers, and redoubled efforts to occupy western lands in the name of the English king through settlement inducements and county organization. "If

Spring tempts them [Indians] to renew their Hostilitys," William Gooch warned, "'tis not to be imagined that People who have now Arms in their hands, will suffer the Heathens to insult them with Impunity." The governor admitted that he knew "not in what state they [Cherokees and Catawbas] are in with the Northern Nations," but he had disturbing news about the Iroquois. In February 1739 he wrote to the Board of Trade that they were now "pretending to be Lords Paramount of the Lands on the western side of those Mountains [Blue Ridge], insist upon it as agreed by the Treaty [of Albany, 1722] that as they were not to Pass to the Eastward, the English were not to get to the Westward." The need for negotiation was greater than ever before.[32]

. ⚜ .

Additional pressures to end the Indian wars in the backcountry and reach an understanding with the Indians came from other colonies and from Europe. Toward the end of 1738, George Clarke, governor of New York, drew increasing fire from London for failure to regulate Indian affairs and prevent fiascoes like the one in Virginia. "We cannot help observing," the Board of Trade wrote, "that it seems very extraordinary to us, that these five Nations who are protected by the British Government should employ their force to destroy other Nations of Indians under the same protection which is effectively doing the work of our common Enemy," the French. "We must therefore recommend it to you in the strongest terms," the board continued, "to employ all your credit and Authority . . . to facilitate a lasting friendship . . . between the said five Nations and the Cherokee and Catabaw Indians." Meanwhile, Clarke was growing increasingly worried about losing the Iroquois altogether. Mindful of French claims to all the lands within the St. Lawrence River watershed, the New York governor warned his London superiors early the following year that "if these pretentions had any foundation the greatest part of the Six Nations would be theirs, they would come close to Virginia and other Colonies and confine the English Dominions to the limitts of our present settlements." To make matters worse, England declared war on Spain in June 1739, when Robert Jenkins's complaints to Parliament about the loss of his ear in a scrape with Spaniards off the coast of Florida brought to a head longstanding commercial disputes between the two nations and aggravated tensions over the control of Georgia. The so-called War of Jenkins's Ear was soon absorbed in a larger European conflict over the Austrian succession, in which war between England and France loomed imminent.[33]

Prospects for negotiation appeared bright at first. In an opening move George Clarke wrote William Gooch requesting that the Virginia governor secure a commitment from the southern Indians to send deputies to Albany to confer with the Six Nations; but no Cherokees or Catawbas appeared. Clarke, pressured by reports of a combined French and Indian force marching south to attack the southern Indians, proceeded unilaterally, meeting successfully with Iroquois headmen in August 1740. That fall the governor and Council of Virginia dispatched Robert Munford to the Catawbas and Cherokees "with the Peace concluded by the Governor of New York in their behalf with the Six Nations . . . and to Desire them to Send their Deputies at the time appointed in the Year 1742 To Albany to meet the Sachims of the Said Six Nations, and there to confirm the Peace." Again the deputies failed to appear but both southern tribes agreed to the peace proposal and sent beads, pipes, tobacco, and wampum instead. On June 15, 1742, George Clarke could announce to the headmen of the Six Nations that their southern adversaries had ratified the peace.[34]

It was precisely at this time, of course, that authorities in Maryland were ferreting out a conspiracy of "several Nations of Our own Indians to rise and cut off the English, . . . assisted with 500 of the Shawan & Northern Indians." The grim news that Maryland spread in July 1742 must have come as a deep shock to leaders in neighboring governments who thought peace on the frontier was at hand. Although the French connection behind English fears never materialized, a group of Senecas and Onondagas did meet with the governor of New France that same July. They reported on the still-intended meeting with the southern Indians, scheduled for the following spring. But the Frenchman knew about the peace accords and cautioned the Iroquois that all of Canada's Indian allies were still at war and would be insulted by a separate peace. Whether or not this episode sparked Jonnhaty's raid against the Catawbas is not clear, but the Iroquois leader and his followers departed soon thereafter. The disastrous conclusion of this venture in the fight with John McDowell and his men the following December would also have spelled doom for years of diplomatic efforts by the Virginia government. The actions of William Gooch and other Virginia leaders in the aftermath of this tragedy can be explained in part by their profound frustration.[35]

The governor and Council of Virginia at first had only the reports of the Augusta County skirmish from James Patton to work with. Patton clearly blamed the Indians for the violence. Promising to give the Six Nations "speedy Information of our Resentment," Gooch conveyed Patton's view on events to New York governor George Clarke in the January 1743 letter that took three months to arrive. Meanwhile, Gooch reiterated this view in his report on the unfortunate affair to the Board of Trade. He condemned the attack as "Barbarous and Absurd" and bemoaned that "nothing less than Blood or Money will satisfie them." In the meantime, he promised to "take all possible

Care to prevent more mischief." In Pennsylvania, the governor and Council had heard the Indian side of events from the trader Thomas McKee. Fearing a complete breakdown of peaceful relations with the Indians, Pennsylvania authorities dispatched Conrad Weiser to the Indian town Shamokin on the Susquehanna River with assurances for the "continuance of our friendship." Soon thereafter Governor Thomas informed Gooch of the "manner in which the Indians represent this Action." In Gooch's response, read on April 5, Pennsylvania authorities could sense the frame of mind still pervading Virginia. "Indians are said to have been the Occasion of the late Skirmish," asserted the Virginia governor, who also included copies of Patton's two letters as proof. By this time the Pennsylvania government had in hand Weiser's findings that the Indians "had actually charged the Virginians with being the Agressors, and firing upon them as they were beginning their March with their Bundles upon their Backs." Little good this view did in Virginia, however.[36]

It was in this atmosphere of fear and confusion, when high officials talked of revenge and prepared for defense in a long-anticipated Indian war, that the Council took up the petition calling for Frederick County to "imediately take place." On April 23, 1743, during its first full session since the outbreak of violence in the Shenandoah Valley, the Council ordered that the court of Frederick County convene for its initial meeting the following October. On the commission of the peace were six justices who had previously sat on the Orange County Court, including veterans Morgan Morgan and Benjamin Borden. Nine new justices made the court representative of a powerful group of Opequon landowners. Among the justices was James Wood, previous surveyor for Orange County west of the Shenandoah River. Wood had received other honors, including appointment as collector of the colony's duty on skins and furs, as justice to the Orange County Court, and as colonel in the Orange militia. He would serve as county surveyor for Frederick and its first clerk of court. Thomas Rutherford would become its first sheriff. Thomas Chester represented the settlement at the forks of the Shenandoah River. Among other early settlers on the court were David Vance from Hite's Opequon tract, Thomas Little from North Mountain, and Lewis Neil, who, with his brother John, owned extensive lands and operated a mill along the Opequon Creek where it crossed Jost Hite's road.[37]

In all, the justices were a diverse lot. Each was an immigrant to Virginia, most from across the Atlantic. Some were from England; others hailed from Wales, Scotland, or Ireland, and at least one was a French Huguenot. Noticeably absent were Germans or recently naturalized subjects of the British king. These justices, then, were English speakers who would meet together monthly and manage the legal and administrative business of the new county. They would resolve civil differences among its peoples and sit in judgment on them in criminal cases. They would secure property by registering deeds and wills, designate public roads, and provide for the common defense. The time had clearly come when concern for the "strength of this colony, and it's security upon the frontiers" outweighed anxieties about frontier peoples wielding the instruments of English government.[38]

. ☙ .

Responsibility for the skirmish between Jonnhaty and McDowell and the merit of Iroquois land claims in the Shenandoah Valley were yet to be determined. The course of events as all sides sought a peaceful solution would, as in the past, have a profound impact on the history and landscape of the Opequon settlement. By the time the Frederick County Court first met, significant progress had been made in calming passions and placing differences on a path of negotiation. The initial problem had been convincing the Virginia government of the justice of the Indian side of the story. Chief executives in Pennsylvania and New York realized what hung in the balance much earlier than Gooch did. Their intercession was critical. Although George Clarke of New York initially sided with his counterpart in Virginia, his own investigations soon persuaded him otherwise. From the sachems of the Six Nations, New York's Commissioners of Indian Affairs learned that "on the contrary[,] our men say That they have been very hardly used by our Brethren of Virginia" and that the sachems themselves had "used all our skill and authority that none should go a fighting." In late May 1743 these commissioners reported that the "Sachims are inclined to make up the breach and to come to Albany for that purpose at any time that shall be fixed upon . . . but desire earnestly that the Governor of Virginia may be present." Clarke had earlier written Gooch to point out that a breach with the Iroquois would open the way for the French to drive English planters "into the shelter of towns or under the cover of forts." He urged the Virginia governor to "listen to overtures of Reconciliation [rather] than to the sanguine impulses of revenge." Following the recommendation of his commissioners, Clarke wrote Gooch in June: "I realy think your sending some prudent person with one or two of each Indian nation depending on Virginia, Carolina & Georgia to Albany, there to treat with the Six Nations, will have a very happy effect not only in healing this breach, but for preventing the like for the future."[39]

Similar developments were also moving Pennsylvania authorities toward assuming leadership in the effort of negotiation and reconciliation. In February, Gooch had written Governor Thomas requesting Pennsylvania's mediation and expressing an "inclination to make up the matter of the Late Skirmish in an Amicable Way." Thomas then dispatched Conrad Weiser a second time to Shamokin, where Shikellamy again stressed the "unjust Treatment our Warriours met with in Virginia." This Iroquois headman offered to "come to an Amicable Accomodation with the Governor of Virginia if he will come to reasonable Terms." Toward the end of this council, Weiser asked his friend what prevented the Six Nations from traveling south to resolve land claims. Shikellamy's answer would open the door to reconciliation—but on Indian, not English, terms. How could the Indians "come down with a Hatchet Struck in their Head," Shikellamy queried. "The Governor of Virginia must wash off the Blood first, and take the Hatchet out of their Head and Dress the Wound (according to Custom he that Struck first must do it)." Only then would the Six Nations "speak to him & be reconciled to him, and bury that affair in the ground that it never may be seen nor heard of any more so long as the World stands." Otherwise, the Iroquois headman "believed there would be a War."[40]

To Shikellamy the proposed negotiations must constitute a traditional Iroquois condolence ritual. On the loss of a relative, clan members mourned deeply and withdrew from the daily affairs of the tribe to direct their despair into various rituals. Kin groups were expected to "cover" the grief of the survivors with funeral rites, feasts, and gifts. In cases of murder, condolence rituals assumed heightened importance. Unless the murderer's clan members performed them properly and promptly, and their gifts were sufficient to overcome the suffering of the bereaved, the victim's relatives were obligated to exact revenge. Retribution in the absence of condolence could easily lead to feuding and disruption for the whole tribe. What Shikellamy was telling Weiser was that the families of the men killed in Virginia were grieving—they were suffering as if the killers had sunk a hatchet into their heads. As the leader of his society, the governor of Virginia had to relieve their anguish by symbolically removing the hatchet and bestowing gifts of condolence upon them. This was the context in which all diplomacy had to be conducted.[41]

Shikellamy traveled back to Philadelphia and met with the governor and Council on April 23, the day that the Virginia Council commissioned the Frederick County Court. The message for Pennsylvania authorities was the same message Shikellamy had given Weiser. The governor responded that he would not abandon "mediation till every thing concerning your Uncles [the Iroquois] & the Virginians be brought to a good Understanding." Two days later Thomas sent Weiser's report to Gooch and instructed the Virginia governor on the diplomacy of condolence. The "six Nations insist upon the Virginians having been the Agressors," Thomas confirmed, adding that "from all the Circumstances I have been able to Collect, I am of that Opinion." "Nothing now remains," he continued, "but to take the Hatchet out of their Heads—that is, I suppose, to send Commissioners to Albany to declare your Concern for the rashness of your remote Inhabitants, and at the same time to make them a present."[42]

Responding on May 5, 1743, William Gooch conceded: "Had I known of the good Understanding, and how firmly the ffriendship between Your Province and the Indians is establish'd, I should not have Troubled the Governor of New York on this Subject." Henceforth Pennsylvania would take the lead in mediating the dispute, and negotiations would eventually be held in that state instead of the traditional council location at Albany. More significant for what was to follow, the Virginia governor admitted that "if what the six Nations insist upon be true, that we were the aggressors, the matter has been greatly misrepresented to me, and I should be much concerned." Despite this tone of accommodation, Gooch evidently did not comprehend what the Iroquois expected of him to cover their grief. "A journey to Albany at this Season, to take the Hatchet out of their Heads, is a Concession we would willingly avoid," he quipped. But as a "token of our sincere Disposition to preserve Peace and friendship," he did offer a present of £100. After receiving this information the Pennsylvania governor dispatched Conrad Weiser a third time to the Iroquois to fix a time and place for negotiations.[43]

On June 21 the Pennsylvania interpreter arrived in Onondaga, where, at the outset of discussions, Jonnhaty, "a very thoughtful and honest Man," related the story of what happened in Virginia once again. Weiser's presence was a sign to everyone of the desire for reconciliation on the part of the English colonial governments, but there was a problem: The governor of Virginia had to personally remove the hatchet from the heads of the bereaved. The Indians then did something that Europeans would have thought most unusual: They designated the Onondaga headman Canasetego to "speak in behalf of the Government of Virginia," that is, to assume the person of William Gooch in the diplomacy of condolence. The governor of Virginia in the form of Canasetego first presented a belt of Wampum to the "ffamilys in Mourning . . . to condole with them and moderate their Grief," proclaiming that he "came here to your fire to fetch home the Hatchet." To the other headmen at the council fire he offered a second wampum belt, "to take away the Bitterness of your Spirit, and to purge You from the abundance and overflow of your Gall." The present of £100 in goods lodged with the governor of Pennsylvania was described "as a token of my own and my People's sincere Disposition to Preserve Peace and ffriendship with you." And finally, a request was made to "let the place and Time be appointed" the following spring for a council to resolve the dispute over land claims. To all these professions, the Indians gave the "usual Cry, by every Nation in Particular . . . by way of thanksgiving & Joy."[44]

In turn the Iroquois headmen responded, "We thank You . . . for removing your Hatchet and for burying it under a heavy Stone." These leaders then presented a belt of wampum to the Virginia government to "serve to remove our Hatchet from You and not only bury it, but we will fling it into the Bottomless Pitt, into the Ocean, there shall be no more Use made of it." "You have taken away the bitterness of our Spirit," they continued, "and purged us from the abundance and overflow of our Gall." In nine moons' time they would "come down within the Borders of Pennsylvania" to discuss the matter of land claims. One final issue, however, so troubled the Iroquois leaders that they asked Weiser to "take Notice of what should be said to put it down in Writing immediately." The headman Zillawoolie then observed that the Six Nations were "ingaged in a Warr with the Catabaws which will last to the End of the World, for they molest Us and speak Contemptuously of Us, which our Warriours will not bear, and they will soon go to War against them again; it will be in vain for Us to diswade them from it." All the recent efforts toward peace with the English colonies were threatened by the ease with which hostilities could again break out as Iroquois war parties traveled south through Virginia's western settlements. The Indians promised to be on "good Behaviour every where amongst our Brethren the English," but added that "we desire you, by this String of Wampum, to publish it amongst your back Inhabitants to be of good behaviour to our Warriors, and look upon them as their Brethren, that we may never have such a Dangerous Breach hereafter." Zillawoolie then got to the heart of the matter by repeating the story of the Indian road, which had played such a prominent role in the emerging landscape at Opequon. "Some Years ago we made a new Road on the outside of your Inhabitants, tho' they had seated themselves down upon our Land, now your People seated themselves down again upon the new Road and shut it up, and there is no more room for a new Road because of the Terrible Mountains full of Stones and no game there, so that the Road cannot be removed." The question of this road would have to be resolved in the deliberations of the next spring.[45]

· ☽ ·

Slowly the moons ticked time away until spring 1744, when negotiations were to begin at the Pennsylvania town of Lancaster. There the representatives of the Oneidas, Onondagas, Cayugas, Senecas, and Tuscaroras would treat with delegations from Maryland and Virginia on the issue of land claims. Pennsylvania governor Thomas and interpreter Weiser would mediate the discussions. Heading the Virginians was Thomas Lee. This prominent member of the Virginia Council lived at Stratford Hall in Westmoreland County and was a noted Northern Neck expansionist. He had served as land agent for the Northern Neck Proprietary and performed a stint in the House of Burgesses before elevation to the Council. Joining him was William Beverley, who had long been involved in western land speculations. Their interest in resolving Iroquois claims to Virginia lands west of the Blue Ridge would prove to be not wholly disinterested.

On June 22, 1744, a party of 252 Indians from the Six Nations arrived in Lancaster. At their head was Canasetego. In his opening speech three days later, the Pennsylvania governor referred to the skirmish on the Virginia frontier that had brought all the parties together and to the condolence rituals Conrad Weiser had orchestrated on behalf of Virginia the previous summer. "Who were the Agressors," he observed, "is not at this time to be discussed—both Parties having agreed to bury that affair in oblivion." The present meetings were "for accomodating all Differences, and for setling a firm Peace, Union, and Friendship as well between the Government of Virginia as that of Maryland and the Indians of the Six Nations." But George Thomas then turned to the representatives of Maryland and Virginia saying, "but I hope, Honourable Gentlemen Commissioners, it will not be taken amiss if I go a little further, and Briefly represent to you how especially necessary it is at this Juncture, for His Majesty's Service and the Good of all His Colonies in this Part of His Dominions, that Peace and Friendship be established between Your Government and the Indians of the Six Nations." Two weeks earlier, on June 11, 1744, Thomas had learned that England was once again at war with France. This European conflict over the distant affair of succession to the Austrian throne would have a profound effect on the North American colonies, as Thomas made clear: "These Indians by their Situation are a Frontier to some of them, and from thence, If Friends, are Capable of Defending their Settlements; If Enemies, of making Cruel Ravages upon them; If Neuters, they may deny the French a Passage through their Country, and give us timely Notice of their Designs. These are but some of the Motives for cultivating a good Understanding with them, but from hence the Disadvantages of a Rupture are abundantly evident." Make peace, in other words, or face dire consequences.[46]

Once again the security and strategic interests of the British empire coincided with the material interests of British colonials in land. This time, however, men with their eye on the land had far grander plans than those the Hites, Rosses, or hundreds of immigrant farmers held in seeking a competency for their families. A promise of £300 rather quickly resolved the issue of Iroquois land claims in Maryland. The matter of Virginia lands was more complicated, but on July 2 the Iroquois signed a deed recognizing the "King's Right to all the Lands that are or shall be by his Majesty's Appointment in the Colony of Virginia." They received £200 in goods and gold in exchange. The Indians no doubt thought that they were finally receiving compensation for lands in the Shenandoah Valley, but they were in fact trading away a far larger territory. In the Virginia charter the king had "appointed" Virginians with a four-hundred-mile-wide swath of land reaching from the Atlantic to the Pacific Ocean. Thomas Lee knew that however vague, unknown, or disputed these boundaries were, they included the area known as the Ohio Country. It was here, of course, that numerous Shawnees, Delawares, and other Indians had settled since the 1720s. The Iroquois cession could be interpreted as vacating the land claims of the Ohio Indians. What Lee should have suspected, however, was that from the Indian point of view, any ability the Iroquois had to sell the homelands of the Ohio Indians depended only upon the dubious claim of the Six Nations to sovereignty over their neighbors in the Covenant Chain. The significance for the Opequon settlement of what happened at Lancaster would soon become painfully clear.[47]

For the moment, however, the Iroquois had a more pressing concern. "The Affair of the Road," they asserted, "must be looked upon as a Preliminary to be Settled before the Grant of Lands." "After we left Albany," they again explained, "we brought Our Road a great deal more to the West that we might comply with Your Proposal, but tho' it was of your own making your People never observed it, but came and lived on Our side of the Hill [Blue Ridge]." To the Indians the issue concerned their right to travel through Virginia's western settlements. Not to be daunted in pursuit of a peaceful understanding with the Six Nations in light of the French threat, Virginia replied that "if you desire a Road, we will agree to one on the Terms of the Treaty you made with Colonel Spotswood." A separate agreement clarified the direction and use of the "new Road, to the Catawbas." It would follow the "present Waggon Road from Cohongoronto above Sherrando River, through the Counties of Frederick and Augusta" and pass by the houses of James Wood, Jost Hite, Jacob Funk, Benjamin Allen, and ten others to the last Virginia settlements on the New River. Warriors from the Six Nations using the road had to carry a pass from the governor of New York, which "shall be also from Time to Time signed, by every Justice, to whom they shall produce it in their Journey through Virginia." The Indians were not to "permit any Frenchman to go with them" or to "take or kill, any Thing belonging to any of the People of Virginia," but "when they are in Want of provisions, they shall apply to the first Justice of the Peace, Captain, or other superiour Officer who shall happen to live on, or nigh the said Road . . . [who] shall supply them with sufficient Provisions, to serve them to the next Justice or Officer, and so on, throughout their Journey through Virginia."[48]

· ☙ ·

The Lancaster Treaty, therefore, brought to a close a chain of events touched off by Jonnhaty and his trip along the road two years earlier, which had ended so disastrously in the woodlands of the upper Shenandoah Valley. That what happened was a disaster owed, first, to the "right of conquest" the Iroquois asserted to western lands in Maryland and Virginia and, second, to the fears engendered in the inhabitants of these two colonies by the exposure of a conspiracy to attack frontier settlements in the defense of these rights. To Indians, the settlers were trespassers on their lands. To whites, the Indian presence was proof enough of the conspiracy. The significance attached to the skirmish in the Shenandoah Valley by contemporaries both Indian and white, however, can be traced to developments stretching back to the beginning of the eighteenth century, when the French planted a Mississippi colony with a "communication" to Canada that threatened English mainland settlements and when the Iroquois launched wars against the southern Indians that disrupted English frontiers. Spotswood's attempt to establish the Blue Ridge as a barrier against both the French threat and Indian intrusions served primarily to intensify anxieties about the French and to promote misunderstandings with the Indians. In the meantime, the Board of Trade's report of 1721 fixed in the minds of imperial authorities the advantages of settling white, Protestant, yeoman farmers on colonial frontiers beyond the Blue Ridge. This Virginia governor William Gooch achieved within a decade, thereby assuring continued conflict with Native Americans. Concern with what Gooch called the "preservation of the Lives of our Fellow-Subjects in that scattered Settlement" required a series of political measures to bound their settlement, first in the county acts of 1738 and then in the establishment of local government in Frederick County five years later. The creation of counties and county governments was part of the same process that led to the Lancaster Treaty, thus closing the cycle.[49]

In this process the Native American imprint on the Shenandoah Valley began to give way to an increasingly Europeanized landscape (fig. 4.6). A mosaic of oak-hickory woodlands and open grasslands characterized the environment Indians encountered in their travels along the Valley. Fires they set or fields they cleared would have contributed to the savanna-like quality of this landscape and its spacious forest understory. At least one of the Indian roads followed the boundary between shale and limestone lands, where the variety of plant and animal life would have been greatest. European settlers made use of this landscape by settling along the Indian road and fixing the sites of their dwellings and farms in open, bottomland areas. The most salient feature of early settlement was dispersal—Europeans simply scattered in search of the best lands. Dispersed settlement represented an accommodation between the interests of settlers in procuring the resources necessary for economic independence and the interests of colonial authorities in the rapid deployment of people on the land as a strategic means of defense and imperial expansion.

Dispersal, however, brought problems. Property beyond the bounds of an existing county could not be secured. Justices attached to neighboring counties were appointed, and the boundaries of new counties were extended westward to include the Shenandoah Valley. Doubts about the capacity of non-English peoples to wield the instruments of English law and governance, however, delayed the establishment of local political institutions. Scattered settlements were vulnerable, and vulnerability was nowhere more evident than in conflicts with Indians. Hostilities led the legislature to establish separate counties in the Shenandoah Valley in 1738 and appoint the first court in one of those counties five years later. Ordering the backcountry by placing bounds around the Opequon settlement was, therefore, a security measure.

In the minds of colonial officials the Lancaster Treaty represented one more step in the process of securing the backcountry and protecting the Virginia colony. As the governor told the House of Burgesses in September 1744: "I have, with the Advice of the Council, concluded a Treaty of Peace and Friendship with the Northern Indians; and procured for our Inhabitants, seated to the Westward of the Mountains, a quiet Possession of all the Lands to which those Nations claimed a Right." At the same time, the treaty guaranteed the Indians of the Six Nations a right of passage through the new Shenandoah Valley counties with privileges of obtaining provisions from colonial officials along the way. The Lancaster Treaty was not just a culmination of tendencies that had been at work since the early eighteenth century to create, order, and bound European settlement west of the Blue Ridge. It was also a point of departure for new or related forces that would intensify conflict among European imperial powers, produce further hostility between English colonists and Native Americans, and yield unexpected consequences for the landscapes of the new western settlements.[50]

Most immediately, the Treaty of Lancaster touched off a flurry of land speculation among Virginians that in turn brought the Shenandoah Valley settlements into new relations with Native Americans and with the French. A new stage of landscape change would result. In 1743, before the outbreak of hostilities in which he would play a part, James Patton applied to the Virginia

Council for a grant of one hundred thousand acres along the New River. The Council turned him down with a promise that, if war developed with France, he could have the lands. On April 26, 1745, Patton received his grant in the midst of the war. That day the Council distributed a total of three hundred thousand acres of far western lands to several groups of speculators, including the Greenbrier Company, directed by Council president John Robinson.[51]

During the next decade 3,330,000 acres passed through the Council into the hands of land-hungry Virginia speculators. Among the members of the Greenbrier Company and a leading investor in schemes of western development was William Beverley. But it was Thomas Lee who would take the steps leading to new and unprecedented outbreaks of violence with both the French and the Indians. In the years immediately following the Treaty of Lancaster, he led the formation of the Ohio Company. On October 20, 1747, Lee and eleven others petitioned the Virginia Council for 200,000 acres to be laid out in the Indian lands of the Ohio Country. He and his collaborators had ambitious designs for what were also the homelands of the Shawnees, Delawares, and others who had moved to the upper Ohio basin beginning in the 1720s. These were the lands ceded, at least in theory, by the Iroquois at Lancaster in 1744. The move was so grand, so audacious, and so filled with ill portent that William Gooch, in his last years as governor, sent the proposal to London for approval. The response he received would have an immeasurable impact on the settlements he seeded at the outset of his administration twenty years earlier.[52]

Overleaf

FIG. 4.6. Peter Jefferson, Robert Brooke, and others, "A Map of the Northern Neck in Virginia," 1746. Geographical knowledge of backcountry Virginia had increased considerably by the time Jefferson and Brooke completed this map. It locates the headspring of the Potomac River, identifies geographical features, and locates settler families. CO 700/Virginia 11, Colonial Office Papers, Public Record Office, London.

A MAP OF THE
NORTHERN NECK
IN VIRGINIA

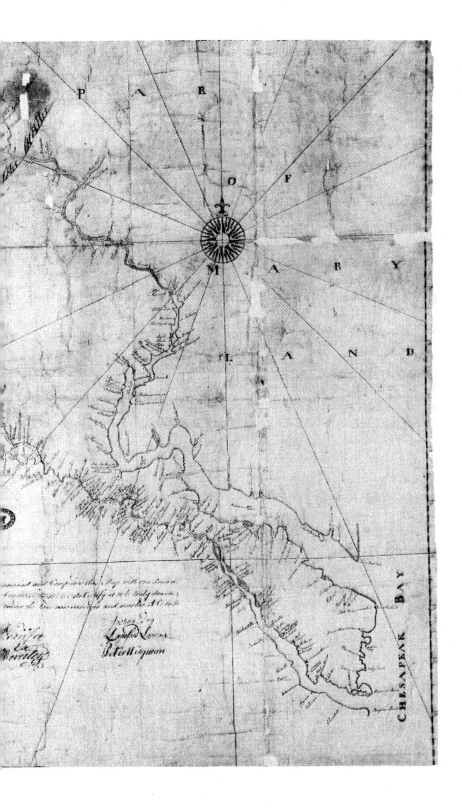

Chapter 5

Centering the County

COGNIZANT THAT England was at war and that their region was alarmingly exposed to the ravages of England's North American enemies, thirteen men met in Frederick County on November 11, 1743, to take the necessary oaths and qualify as justices in the newly convened county court. Each man had been named in the commission of the peace for the county issued by Virginia's governor, William Gooch. Because the county had no town or other central place, the site of their meeting remains a mystery, but tradition holds that the justices gathered at the home of surveyor James Wood. Their first act as a court was to endorse a commission from the colonial secretary, Thomas Nelson, appointing Wood as clerk. Other business passed under the new justices' purview that day: Thomas Rutherford was sworn as sheriff, George Hume became the new county surveyor, several lawyers took the oath of an attorney, and various wills were probated and deeds recorded. As gentlemen justices, not professional jurists, the new magistrates ordered their clerk to "fetch the Law books from Mr Parks," the colony's official printer in Williamsburg, for their guidance. And they directed the sheriff to build a "Twelve foot Square, Log-house logg'd above & below to Secure his Prisoners." In the months to come the justices would conduct the routine business of a county court seemingly without attention to the conflict raging in distant parts of North America. But first among the justices' duties was the creation of an ordered political world that could contain hostilities if they came to Virginia.[1]

It was fundamental for maintaining civil order amid strife not only to establish the political institutions that bound a people together but also to create the familiar landscape in which these institutions could function effectively. Centering this landscape on a county town would focus public attention on the power of the court and provide the court with a site from which to exert its influence. It would also initiate the second phase of landscape evolution in the Shenandoah Valley. Thus, when the court met the following March, one year after England had declared war on France, James Wood announced that he had surveyed twenty-six lots and two streets on the easternmost corner of his own property (fig. 5.1). Although most of the lots lined a primary north-south street in a rudimentary grid, additional lots at the cross street composed a civic square for public buildings.[2]

The site Wood selected for "Frederick Town" was a comment on the power of the court in creating the landscape. In the absence of Wood's survey, a town would most likely never have appeared at this location. It stood between the open-country neighborhoods developing around Jost Hite's and Alexander Ross's homesteads. One-half mile of unpatented land separated it from the Philadelphia Wagon Road, which joined these neighborhoods to Pennsylvania. Wood's site was heavily forested, and as one visitor commented at the time of the American Revolution, it was also "low & disagreeable." Fifteen years later, another traveler could not "conceive the motives that led to the construction of a town on this spot, where only as much water is found as is required for the use of the houses." In May 1744 the court turned the Philadelphia Wagon Road westward to connect to the town's main street, but not for another two years did the justices order Isaac Parkins, who operated a nearby mill, to "cause the Stumps and Grubbs in the Main Street of the said Town to be Cut up & the Holes filled from side to side." Many lots remained uncleared at this time.[3]

Conveyance of the town lots proceeded slowly, perhaps because Wood had not yet received a patent for them. At best, lot holders enjoyed only the security of a bond from the county court to insure purchase. But the bonds did require that each lot holder "shall within two years from the day of the sale of the said lots, build or cause to be built on each lot one house either framed work or squared logs, dovetailed, at least of the dimensions of 20 feet by 16 feet." Within a year of the survey, eight men from surrounding open-country neighborhoods held bonds: Jonathan Frost and James Bruce, who lived near Hopewell; Peter Stephens, the associate and neighbor of Jost Hite; and Andrew Campbell, a member of the court who operated an ordinary on the wagon road about twenty-five miles north of Frederick Town. Isaac Parkins, lawyer James Porteus, sheriff Rutherford, and the hatter, William Dobbins, had also invested in town lots. Each with a stake in the countryside surrounding the town, these men did not constitute an urban population distinct from the peoples of the countryside.[4]

What set the fledgling town off from its surroundings was not its people or their economic activities but the landscape of political authority the county

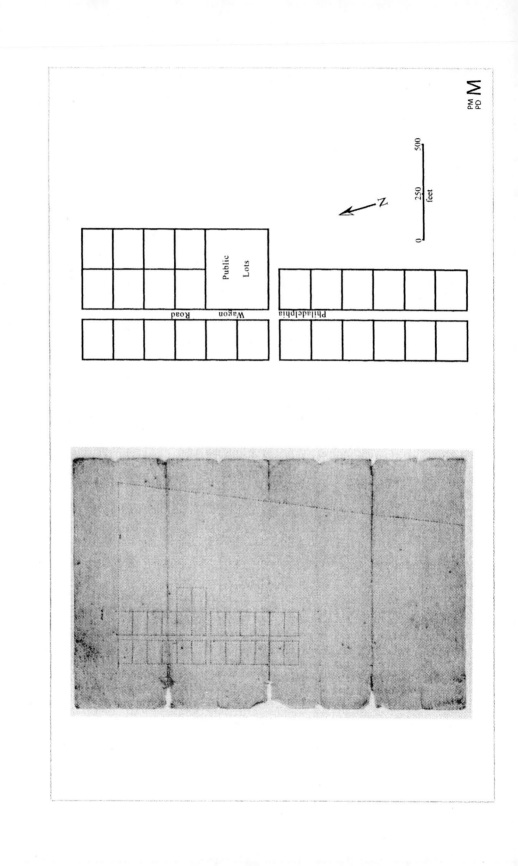

court created on the public lots. The courthouse dominated this landscape. Construction began a few months after Wood had conducted his survey of the town lots. Miller Isaac Parkins supplied 526 feet of plank for the project, local builder and merchant entrepreneur John Hardin undertook the carpentry work, and stonemason Duncan O'Gullion "agreed to finish the Walls of ye Court house as high as the Plate." By November the building was under roof. No description of the building survives, but it did boast a fireplace, twelve chairs for the justices, and usage rough enough to require mending the seats within a year or so of opening. Clerk James Wood worked from a railed table separated from the justices' bench by a lawyers' bar and witness box.[5]

The various instruments of punishment that surrounded the courthouse were essential to the operations of the court. They were visible reminders to the people of the court's power to discipline the unruly and shape society according to the dictates of the common law. At their second session the justices ordered two of their own number, John Bruce and William McMachen, to "agree with Workmen for Erecting a Pillory Stocks & Whipping post." Offenders committed to the pillory or stocks were subject not only to public humiliation for their crimes but often to physical abuse from outraged members of the community, as well. Whipping was a punishment usually reserved for slaves by the laws of the colony. In 1746 two of the justices undertook the construction of a ducking stool, "according to the Moddal of that at Fredericksburgh." When completed it had a stone pit "7 foot Deep & 6 foot Square in the Clear" filled with water, into which a plunge could correct the ways of recalcitrant scolds or obstinate cheats.[6] The prison took longer to build; almost five years were required to complete a structure with a dungeon stout enough for the sheriff's prisoners.[7]

At least as significant to the people of Opequon as the courthouse was the clerk's office. There the records of court proceedings were secured, but deeds and wills that guaranteed the people's rights of ownership to private property were even more important. Once an individual received a patent or grant for a parcel of land, that land was conveyed only by deed or will. Upon presenta-

Facing page

FIG. 5.1. James Wood's Survey of Frederick Town. Wood, clerk of the Frederick County Court, laid off Frederick Town as the county seat in early 1744. On the left is his sketch of the town lots; on the right, his original grid plan redrawn. Wood's sketch: Winchester Preliminary Drawing of Proposed Town by James Wood Sr., James Wood Collection, 711THL, Archives Room, Handley Regional Library, Winchester. Plan: Based on Garland R. Quarles, *Winchester, Virginia: Streets-Churches-Schools* (Winchester, Va.: Winchester–Frederick County Historical Society, 1996), 40.

tion of these documents to the court, the justices ordered that they be copied in the great, leather-bound books kept by the clerk. Any dispute over property could be referred to these books, and landowners knew that the security of their holdings lay with the clerk's ability to maintain and protect accurate records. In the clerk's office, then, lay the physical evidence of the people's ambitions and aspirations for competency in the affairs of life. If logs were good enough for the first prison, only stone could serve the needs of the clerk. By November 1744 much of the work on the "Stone office" was complete, and within a year the court had obtained a substantial cupboard or "press . . . to hold ye Records." Soon the office must have acquired a working atmosphere. In addition to minute, order, deed, and will books lying in the press were the law books James Wood had fetched from the public printer in Williamsburg. The court also owned sixteen copies of "Webs Justices." As gentlemen the justices were expected to be capable of applying the principles of the common law through the exercise of reason and fairness, but the procedures of the law were cumbersome and complex. The copies of George Webb's *The Office and Authority of a Justice of Peace*, available to each member of the court, would have guided their collective actions. Extra copies were, no doubt, kept in the clerk's office as well.[8]

By the mid-1740s a courthouse, prison, office, stocks, pillory, whipping post, and ducking stool defined the public square of the county town for the people of Opequon. What was missing was an Anglican church. The construction of a place of worship for the established church of colonial Virginia was the responsibility of the vestry, the governing body of the parish. After an initial local election, vestrymen selected their own members. Not only did vestries possess responsibility for hiring ministers, building and maintaining church buildings, and governing the affairs of the church; this nonrepresentative body also wielded real civil powers. To relieve the poor and destitute in the county, the vestry could impose a levy or tithe upon the people. The same act that established Frederick County in 1738 also created the parish of Frederick. Six months after its first meeting, the Frederick County Court wrote to the governor for "a Power to Choose a Vestry" for the parish.[9]

That neither the date nor the results of the vestry election has survived is evidence enough of the fragility of central authority at the Opequon settlement. The vestry's failure to construct a substantial parish church in the town for almost twenty years is further indication of the weak role the town played in the settlement geography. Consistent with the dispersal of households throughout a large area, the vestry preferred instead to construct several chapels of ease. Chapels were smaller and more modest structures, in which lay readers conducted services in the absence of a minister, and no minister served the parish consistently until the early 1760s. A chapel built upon the South Fork of the Shenandoah River in the 1750s provides a good example of these structures. At twenty-two by thirty feet, this squared and dovetailed log structure with a shingle roof would have looked like a dwelling were it not for the extra two or three feet of height added to the walls. Two sash windows on the long—or eave—sides lit the interior, and a door centered between the windows on one side rendered the front façade consistent with the common appearance of eighteenth-century vernacular structures. A plank floor supported benches for the communicants, a clerk's desk, and a pulpit with a reading desk and sounding board. Sometime before August 1741 the vestry of Orange County built the first Anglican chapel at Opequon, along the Philadelphia road on the property of Morgan Morgan. By mid-1745 chapels were under construction in the northern part of Opequon near the Potomac River, to the east not far from the Shenandoah River, and in the south along Crooked Run. By the early 1750s, however, the chapels were "decayed, and ruinous, for want of covering, and weather boarding," and the House of Burgesses had to dissolve the vestry because its members had converted £1,570 "to their own use" instead of "building and adorning churches." A rudimentary parish church was also rising in Frederick Town, but the vestry spent no more on it than on the chapels. Not until 1762 would a new vestry contract for a conspicuous thirty-two by fifty-six foot stone edifice surmounted by a sixty-foot steeple.[10]

While the vestry dallied with the construction of chapels, Quakers, Presbyterians, and other non-Anglicans were busy building meetinghouses throughout the Opequon settlement. Within a few years of moving to Virginia, Scots-Irish settlers at the open-country neighborhood on Hite's Opequon tract had built a Presbyterian meetinghouse on the nearby lands of William Hoge, and members of the Society of Friends were working on a stone meetinghouse on the lands of Alexander Ross. In 1736 Opequon Presbyterians petitioned the court of Orange County "that meeting places might be erected" because "the Rev. Mr. William W[illia]ms, minister of the Gospel, hath promised to supply us in the administration of his office." The next year Governor William Gooch wrote to the justices of the county that Williams "hath applyed to me signifying his intention to set up a Presbiterian Meeting house amongst the inhabitants on Sherrando." The governor asked the court to administer the required tests and oaths to Williams and determine the location of the meetinghouse, "after which he is not to be molested in the exercise of his ministry so long as he behaves himself loially to the King and peaceably towards the Government."[11]

Cognizant that peopling the Virginia backcountry with non-English immigrants required religious toleration, Gooch had also answered a plea from the

Presbyterian synod of Philadelphia for his "favor in allowing them the liberty of their consciences," with the assurance that he was "always inclined to favor the people who have lately removed from other provinces to settle on the western side of our great mountains." "So, you may be assured," he continued, "that no interruption shall be given to any minister of your profession who shall come among them, so as they conform themselves to the rules prescribed by the Act of Toleration in England, by taking oaths enjoined thereby, and registering the place of their meeting, and behave themselves peaceably." These places were dispersed throughout the Opequon settlement, and neither Presbyterians nor Quakers nor any other dissenting denomination would build a meetinghouse in the county town for several decades after its founding.[12]

The dispersal of places of worship throughout the open-country neighborhoods of the Opequon settlement was indicative of decentralized authority in the new county. The court and its institutions dominated the county town, but James Wood had not laid it out in a manner that focused attention on its public structures. The baroque plan of Annapolis, Maryland's capital, directed attention from practically anywhere in the city to a capitol building and a church situated within circles from which the primary roads of the town radiated (fig. 5.2). The Duke of Gloucester Street in Williamsburg led from the College of William and Mary, Bruton Parish Church, the county courthouse, the armory, and a spacious mall in front of the governor's palace directly to Virginia's capitol building (fig. 5.3). Although backcountry towns would never be conceived on such grand terms, lots in county seats in Pennsylvania and later Virginia were sometimes arrayed so that a public square stood prominently across the intersection of primary streets. Public structures and the instruments of court authority, however, would readily escape the gaze of anyone traveling along the streets of Frederick Town, where the public lots were lodged between streets without a prominent public square and vistas approaching it.[13]

The behavior of citizens and the justices themselves also bespoke the attenuated authority of central political institutions. During the court's first six months an average of five and never more than eight of the thirteen justices attended court sessions, and only three of the original justices still sat on the bench ten years later. Moreover, the first grand jury of the county, meeting in May 1744, indicted one constable for "being a Disturber of the Publick Peas" and clerk of the court James Wood for "getting Drunk & Swearing two Oaths." Justice Andrew Campbell was also charged with the same offense as Wood's. The following year, "Swearing at the Barr" brought a five shilling fine to attorney James Porteus, while another lawyer, John Quin, "indeciently behaved himself at the Barr" and received the same punishment. The court also fined Rev. William Williams twenty-six shillings for behaving "indeciently before the Court" and a hefty £4 for performing marriages, the exclusive prerogative of the Anglican clergy. Public disregard for the sanctity of their proceedings forced the justices to forbid "Paceing or Raceing thro' the Public Street by the Court house" during court sessions.[14]

· ⚜ ·

Did the establishment of a county town quicken economic activity of the region and begin to focus trade on a central place? The exchange economy that characterized rural life at the Opequon settlement complicates the answer to this question. Court sessions clearly brought life to the town economy. Lacking a corporate charter, the town could not conduct a public market for trade in bread, meat, and other foodstuffs, but the court did order clerk James Wood to write to "Robert Jackson Merchant in Fredericksburgh to procure from England Standard Weights & Measures according to An Act of Assembly." These standards would prove useful in cases of dishonest tradesmen. Court sessions stimulated trade in other ways. By the act establishing Frederick County, the court convened on the second Friday of each month. Many sessions continued until Monday, with Sunday idle. Justices, lawyers, and anyone with business before the court who lived a day or more's journey away had to find lodging, so the court did a brisk business in issuing ordinary, or tavern, licenses. During its first session eleven Opequon residents received the court's approval to sell alcohol at private houses, and at least three of these licenses went to men holding bonds for town lots: Andrew Campbell, John Hopes, and Thomas Rutherford. Although Campbell's tavern was most likely twenty-five miles away on his home tract, John Hopes built a tavern in town. David Vance, a justice living along the upper Opequon about six miles south of town, stayed with him numerous times on evenings after the court had adjourned. James Wood, whose house was a mile from the courthouse, likewise lodged with Hopes during the occasional court session. Peddlers from as far away as Pennsylvania or eastern Virginia not only received their licenses from the court but also made a point of passing court days in county towns, when an influx of people made for good business. Like justices and peddlers, travelers often stayed at ordinaries. As a youth of sixteen, George Washington crossed the Blue Ridge for the first time with a surveying party in March 1748 and stopped in Frederick Town. After a "Review of the Town" he returned to his "Lodgings[,] where we had a good Dinner prepare'd for us Wine & Rum Punch in Plenty & and a good Feather Bed with clean Sheets which was a very agreeable regale."[15]

Much of the economic life of the town centered on its stores. James Wood, for instance, built a substantial "shop" on one of his town lots. Constructed of

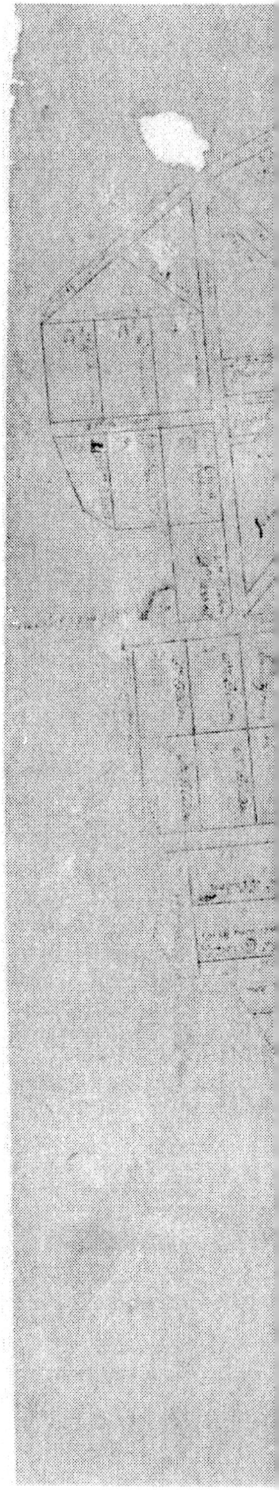

FIG. 5.2. James Stoddert, "A Ground platt of the Citty and port of Anapolis," 1718. Maryland Governor Francis Nicholson planned the new capital of Maryland in 1696 with streets radiating from the state house and church. The vistas provided by these streets focused public attention on the governing institutions of the colony. James Stoddert, "A Ground platt of the Citty and port of Anapolis," 1718, MSA SC 1427-1-6, B5/01/0, Special Collections, Maryland State Archives, Annapolis.

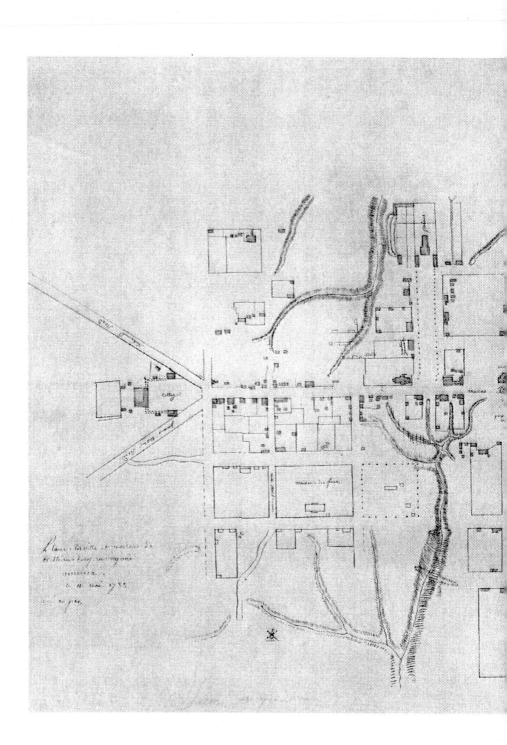

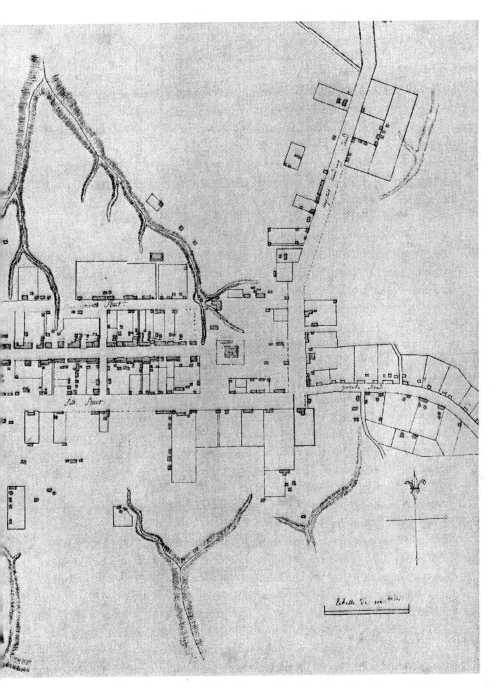

FIG. 5.3. Frenchman's Map of Williamsburg, 1782. An unknown officer, probably attached to Rochambeau's army during the Yorktown campaign, drafted this plan of Williamsburg. The Duke of Gloucester Street and a broad mall afforded vistas to important public buildings, including the capitol, the governor's palace, Bruton Parish Church, and the College of William and Mary. Swem Library, College of William and Mary.

stone, it had plastered walls, sash windows, and a second story or loft reached by a set of stairs. No merchant himself, Wood rented the shop to others. On January 22, 1746, Benjamin Perreyra agreed to take it for £5 per year. Perreyra was a merchant in that he bought goods to sell again, or more accurately, he acquired goods on credit and exchanged them on credit with people throughout the "dispersed general store" of the Opequon settlement. Although country produce lined his shelves, much of his stock in trade came from merchants like John Carlyle in eastern Virginia or others in Pennsylvania. What could be acquired in his shop belies images of material backwardness on the frontier. Richard Robins, for instance, obtained four and one-half yards of broadcloth, two and one-half yards of blue broadcloth, and a half pound of soap on December 18, 1746. Other customers acquired claret, snuff, sugar, silk, shalloon, and buckram at about the same time.[16]

Although Perreyra conducted his business in the county town, nothing in the nature of the exchanges that took place in his shop required a town location or implied any centralizing influences in the regional economy. His business, in fact, was well suited to settlement dispersal at Opequon, as evidenced in his dealings with Lyman Lipman. Lipman was a peddler whose license fees Perreyra paid. Lipman acquired calico, linen, silk, and cambric from Perreyra and then traveled throughout the Opequon settlement, often exchanging goods for notes of hand, which he then assigned to Perreyra in the settlement of accounts. Lipman's connection with Ulrich Poker, a German settler living in the open-country neighborhood along the upper Opequon, shows how trade could be conducted across large distances. Poker was himself carrying skins north to Pennsylvania, where he exchanged them for saddles carried back to Opequon. On one occasion Lipman acquired a woman's saddle and a woman's gown from Poker in exchange for a handkerchief and a debt of £4 10s. 6d. Complicating matters but also demonstrating how trade that Benjamin Perreyra initiated at his shop in Frederick Town diffused throughout Opequon, Lipman exchanged goods with another peddler, Richard Cronk. From late 1746 to mid-1747 Cronk acquired various textiles, chocolate, beeswax, sugar, paper, knives, shoes, needles, and brandy from Lipman in exchange for skins that Cronk, like Poker, had acquired from hunters at Opequon.[17]

The far-flung activities of Wood's next shop tenant also show how trade in town could be dispersed throughout the Opequon settlement. Peter Tostee rented Wood's shop beginning in November 1748, but at the same time he was also operating another store about thirty-five miles west on the South Branch of the Potomac. Tostee had been trading in the region long before the founding of the town, and he assigned the Frederick Town store duties to shopkeeper Thomas How. Tostee himself might have remained along the upper

Potomac. Besides John Hopes's tavern and the shops managed by Benjamin Perreyra and Peter Tostee, little else seemed to be happening in Frederick Town during its first years. William Dobbins lived there and probably made hats in the twenty-four-foot square house that stonemason Duncan O'Gullion had built for him. James Wood and members of Jost Hite's family acquired hats from Dobbins. Other men, such as John Frost or James Bruce, who secured the first town lots had farms and households a few miles away or as far as a full day's journey. One lot holder, Isaac Parkins, operated a mill about two miles south of the town. Thus, a traveler visiting Frederick Town in the 1740s would have encountered only a scattering of stone and log buildings, the public structures on the public lots, streets obstructed by stumps, and many uncleared private lots. Moravian missionaries passing through town in 1753 counted about sixty "rather poorly built" houses, suggesting a population of only several hundred people.[18]

. ⚘ .

The town began to change in the early 1750s, partly owing to the influence of Lord Fairfax (fig. 5.4). After spending several years in England successfully defending his claims to land west of the Blue Ridge for the Northern Neck Proprietary, Fairfax returned to Virginia in 1747, residing initially with his cousin William Fairfax at Belvoir near the Potomac River. Two years later he relocated to the Shenandoah Valley and built a home he called Greenway Court a few miles west of the Shenandoah River. There he opened an office and began to administer the affairs of the proprietary. Fairfax soon gained appointment to the county court and took an evident interest in the courthouse town emerging on James Wood's lands. Probably through Fairfax's influence, the Virginia Assembly adopted an "Act for establishing the town of Winchester." The new law acknowledged that James Wood's town had attracted "divers persons, who have since settled and built, and continue building and settling." It then called for the survey of fifty-four additional lots; twenty-four on James Wood's land "in one or two streets, . . . to run parallel with the street already laid off." The "remaining thirty lots, to be laid off at the north end . . . with a commodious street or streets, in such manner as the proprietor thereof, the right honorable Thomas Lord Fairfax, shall think fit." Fairfax also saw fit to survey eighty, five-acre outlots adjoining the town to the north and east, each lot linked by deed to a town lot (fig. 5.5). Outlots for gardens and livestock were uncommon on the American landscape but did appear in English towns in the north of Ireland, where the self-sufficiency of the residents was essential for defense against an often hostile indigenous population. Significantly, Fairfax adopted this same form for the town he was now helping to

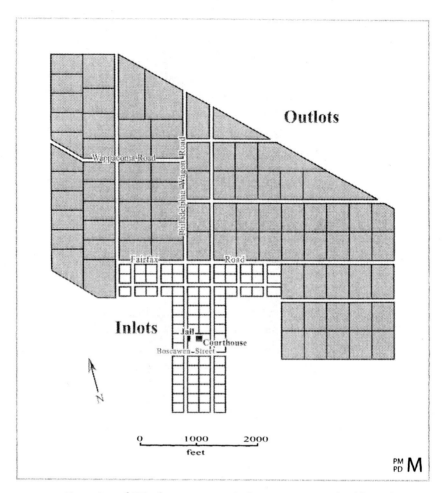

FIG. 5.4. Expansion of Winchester, 1752. Winchester grew considerably in the early 1750s owing to lot additions by James Wood and Lord Fairfax from their private lands. To each town lot Fairfax attached a five-acre outlot, creating a commons where inhabitants could graze livestock and cultivate gardens to enhance the self-sufficiency of the town. Based on Quarles, *Winchester, Virginia,* 43, 45.

govern on the perilous Virginia frontier. Adding to the martial symbolism of the new plan was the name *Winchester,* adopted for the first time in the town act; Fairfax had served under Charles marquis of Winchester while a cornet in the Royal Regiment of Horse Guards.[19]

According to the act, the people of Winchester would benefit from "the same privileges, which the freeholders of other towns . . . enjoy." These, however, included only the right to hold two fairs a year on the third Wednesday in June and October "to continue for the space of two days, for the sale and vending all manner of cattle, victuals, provisions, goods, wares, and merchandizes, whatsoever." The town would not have a weekly market, nor would it enjoy self-government as a corporation under a mayor and council with the power to pass ordinances for the regulation of town affairs. Even seemingly minor measures such as keeping hogs from running wild in the streets would require action by the colonial legislature. Thus, although the 1752 act acknowledged the expansion of Winchester, it failed either to grant it autonomy as a settlement distinct from the surrounding countryside or to recognize any critical economic function apart from the exchange economy embracing the entire Opequon settlement.[20]

. ⚘ .

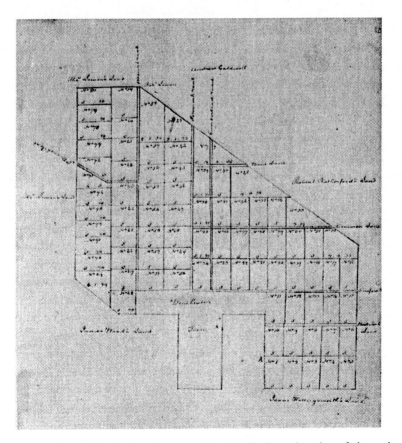

FIG. 5.5. Lord Fairfax's Outlots. Surveyor John Baylis drew this plan of the outlots Fairfax added to the town of Winchester in 1752. Frederick County Clerk's Office.

Economic life at Opequon resided in the countryside. Production, services, marketing, and exchange proceeded actively within the dispersed open-country communities spread out along the creeks and drainages of the Shenandoah Valley. Dispersal, in other words, did not impede the economic function of the settlement. Dispersed economies and the absence of towns were nothing new to Virginia. The system of tobacco marketing had discouraged town formation throughout the Chesapeake. Planters marketed their crop directly in London or at out-ports such as Bristol or Whitehaven without the services of local merchants, whose activities might have provided the nucleus for town development. Chesapeake planters were, therefore, unlike English farmers, whose economy depended on corn exchanges emerging in English towns in the seventeenth and eighteenth centuries. Relying on plantation slaves for blacksmithing, shoemaking, weaving, or tailoring also discouraged the formation of towns as centers of artisan services. This situation changed somewhat in the eighteenth century, as factors of Scottish merchant firms established stores in Chesapeake communities and began buying tobacco directly from planters, especially small planters. Trading activities also developed around the tobacco warehouses called for by Virginia's Tobacco Inspection Act of 1730. But even by the time of the American Revolution, the Chesapeake was noticeably townless, a condition that traveler Andrew Burnaby attributed to "the cheapness of land, and the commodiousness of navigation: for every person may with ease procure a small plantation, can ship his tobacco at his own door, and live independent." A few years later German visitor Johann David Schoepf observed that "in all Virginia there is no commercial town which in the extent of its business may be compared with Philadelphia, New York, Boston, Baltimore, or Charleston; the natural situation and activities of those provinces bring together in their chief towns almost the whole trade of the interior, whereas in Virginia this is greatly distributed, owing to the numerous navigable streams penetrating the country."[21]

The conditions that inhibited the growth of towns in the Chesapeake could hardly have prevailed in the backcountry. Westerners grew some tobacco, but great distances to markets and warehouses discouraged its production. None of the Chesapeake rivers was navigable as far west as the Shenandoah Valley, and slavery as practiced in the Chesapeake was uncommon. Certainly no backcountry farmer was self-sufficient in artisan services. Nor can the absence of towns in the backcountry be attributed to the subsistence nature of the economy. Because the land was undeveloped, a large percentage of production went to meet the needs of families, but to insure self-sufficiency much of what was produced was exchanged. Exchange, however, did not entail the existence of a market economy or require the establishment of towns as market places. Indeed, the distinction between market and subsistence production cannot be applied to the Opequon settlement, where an exchange economy allowed the flow of goods and services to overspread a large region without encouraging the growth of towns or markets. Men and women produced a wide variety of goods and diverse services, which entered into a system of exchange that worked well across extended space to give households a competence in economic affairs without the need to cluster production, distribution, and consumption in towns.

· ⚐ ·

First generation settlers at Opequon directed most of their labor toward farm building—toward rendering the land productive. This was certainly the case with James Wood. Although he derived a substantial income as clerk of court, Wood also supported his family by farming. What he did to develop his land was broadly typical of the activities of most Opequon households (fig. 5.6). Key to success were exchanges for goods and services with neighbors. Wood's actions demonstrate that farm building was not an activity that took place within the vacuum of one household. Success could be achieved only to the extent to which one household could draw upon its credit with other households (fig. 5.7). The development of the land at Opequon—the creation of a distinctive landscape—was therefore a collective enterprise expressing as a whole the drive for competence by each individual farm family.

In the mid-1730s Wood married Mary Rutherford, the daughter of the first sheriff of Frederick County, and built a house near some powerful springs on his property. That he paid Timothy Holdway three times what the vestry of Frederick Parish would later spend on constructing chapels indicates that this house was much more than a simple log dwelling. The ladder Holdway made suggests that the house had two stories or at least a loft. For this new household Wood also acquired a chest, bedstead, bread tray, washing tub, pail, and wheelbarrow from Holdway. The cow and calf he obtained the same year from John Littler, who lived near the Hopewell Meeting House, might also explain the use to which Wood put the coolers and piggin Holdway made for him. Both items were used for dairying. Wood's family was growing during these years; he and Mary produced three boys and two girls between 1739 and 1747. Wood was able to meet the needs of this burgeoning family from his income as surveyor—he submitted twenty-one surveys in 1741—as his accounts with the firm of Harmer and King reflect. From these merchants he acquired seven and one-half yards of striped holland fabric, other textiles, a copper sauce pan, and a pair of scissors. From Robert McKay he obtained kersey, metal buttons, steel buckles, cambric cloth, and knee buckles. He also hired

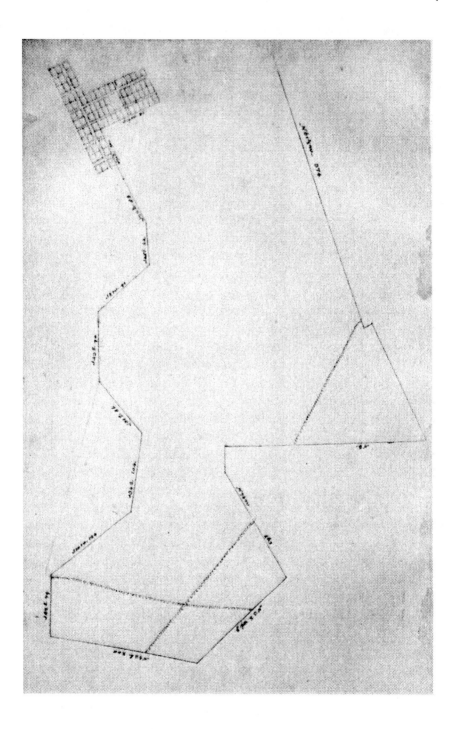

Facing page

FIG. 5.6. James Wood's Home Tract. Wood developed portions of this tract of land for farming throughout the 1740s. The undated survey, probably by James Wood, also depicts the lots and streets of Winchester after the expansion of 1752. Frederick County Clerk's Office.

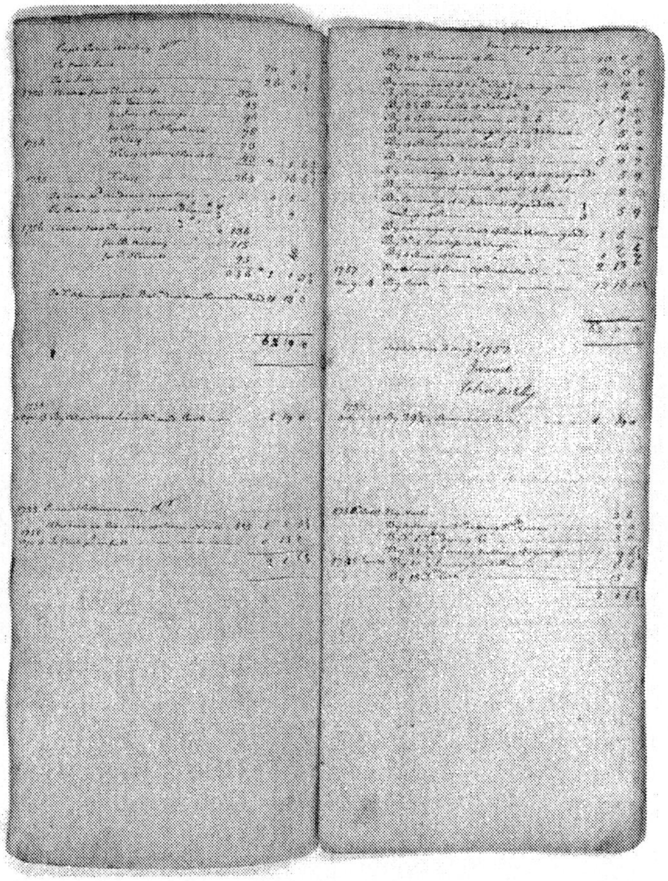

FIG. 5.7. James Wood's Account Book. As Frederick County Court clerk, Wood kept this account book from 1744 to 1759, when he died. In it he documented both the public business of the court and such private affairs as the expenses of establishing a farm. His account with wagoner John Ashby reveals that Ashby received various services from the court and cash from Wood in exchange for cash, carriage, and bulk items like salt, rum, sugar, and corn as back cargoes. James Wood Account Book, p. 137, Account Books, James Wood Collection, 711THL, Archives Room, Handley Regional Library.

the time of several servants and purchased a slave woman, probably for domestic duties.[22]

Wood began to pick up the pace of farm building in the early 1740s, at about the time the county court first met. In 1741 he purchased a wagon, an essential means of transportation for anyone growing grains. The following year he began the construction of fences more likely to keep cattle out of planted fields than to confine them in pastures. The year 1745 saw Wood plant grains on his land and purchase wheat at the rate of about two bushels per month while his own crop ripened. On August 26 a hired hand, William Wilson, "began to Sowe Wheat." Wilson completed the task the following Thursday. Wood also acquired a plow and wheat fan from blacksmith James Carter. Two years later Carter made a harrow and two more plows, as well as a cradle and sneed for Wood. In the meantime Wood began to sow oats. Wheat and oat production required a barn, in which harvested grain could be stored and threshed. On June 6, 1746, William Hand, a carpenter, began work on a framed barn forty-eight by twenty feet, covered on the roof and walls with clapboard. The structure contained a stable and folding doors to a threshing floor. Hand finished the work by August.[23]

As these activities were going on, Wood was gradually increasing the size of his livestock herd. Two days after finishing his barn, he made an agreement with John O'Neal to clear eighteen acres of his land on North Mountain about four miles to the west. O'Neal was to live on the land for two years and care for the four mares, one colt, and forty cows and calves Wood was entrusting to him in return for one-half the increase of the herd. Wood was also developing his home place for livestock, dairying, and meat production. The bottomland along the stream through his property was probably a natural meadow, but Wood improved it in April 1748 by planting twenty-one quarts of timothy grass he acquired from Jacob Nisewanger, who farmed at the open-country neighborhood around Jost Hite's holding. During the early 1740s Wood had been purchasing butter at the rate of two to three pounds a month from Quaker farmer Joseph Lupton. At about the same time in late 1744 that he settled "in full of all Accounts" with Lupton, he acquired three cows with calves from William Burk, who lived a considerable distance away along the South Fork of the Shenandoah River. During the years following, Wood built a meat house for smoking and storing meat and a dairy, which by 1751 had a wooden floor and plaster walls.[24]

Farm building required considerable labor, and Wood relied on both indentured servants and slaves. But interestingly, all Wood's slaves were female. By 1742 he owned the time of one servant woman and the lives of a slave woman and her child. During the next five years he acquired the six and one-half years Alice Aspinal had left to serve on her indenture and a twenty-one-year-old black slave named Sat, with two mulatto girls: Jude, two months old, and Hannah, seven months. For farm work Wood appeared to prefer engaging the time of free laborers. In 1746, for instance, he hired William Wilson for several months, paying him a total of £5 4s. 11d. James Coulter worked for Wood from mid-1751 to mid-1753, receiving £7 10s. every three months. What is significant here is Wood's relative lack of reliance on the labor of others, whether free, slave, or indentured, in the intensive work of farm building. Could building a farm in the Virginia backcountry be accomplished by the labor of one man and occasional helping hands? This possibility suggests that developing the land at Opequon—transforming nature into landscape—was work well within the capacity of the families that settled there. The exchange of labor might be necessary from time to time, but, unlike the tobacco economy of the Chesapeake and its associated landscape, the improvement of backcountry lands for agriculture and householding did not require extensive inputs from bound labor, either white or black.[25]

Just as Wood did not invest heavily in a labor force to develop and work his lands, so his accounts give no evidence that he produced large surpluses of crops or livestock for sale. Nonetheless his labors as clerk of the Frederick County Court brought him a considerable income, some of which he spent in the shop he rented out in town. Wood's acquisitions from the stock of Benjamin Perreyra and later of Peter Tostee indicate a significant emphasis on domestic consumption over the needs of farm production. Wood kept accounts with Perreyra from November 1745 to March 1747 and with Peter Tostee from July 1747 to February 1748. During this period Wood obtained only four sickles and one scythe for the farm; the absence of hoes, rakes, shovels, axes, rope, harness, or other farm equipment is significant. Wood expended his credit, instead, on the home. His largest household acquisitions were textiles, including fustian, cambric, linen, osnaburg, broadcloth, flannel, buckram, silk, and holland. Dry goods, such as bobbins, needles, thimbles, ribbon, buttons, thread, and lace, also came from the stores in town, as did scissors, a looking glass, and four small knives. Although store accounts appear in Wood's name, the shopping may well have been the domain of his wife, Mary, with the assistance of servant Alice Aspinal or the slave woman Sat.[26]

If shops in town met many of James and Mary Wood's needs for their growing family, what Wood required for the farm and for rendering the land productive he acquired within the exchange economy that stretched across the entire Opequon settlement (fig. 5.8). As has already been pointed out, livestock came from various individuals, including John Littler, Hugh Parrell, and William Buck; blacksmith James Carter supplied plows and harrows; Jacob

Nisewanger furnished grass seed; labor came largely by the job from workmen such as William Wilson, or from Nicholas Fry for farm gates, John Howard for flooring the dairy, William Hand for building the barn, or James,
George, and Jonathan Bruce for putting up the meat house. The full extent of
Wood's exchanges with Joseph Lupton reveals the nature of economic activity in a landscape of settlement dispersal. Lupton not only produced surplus
butter and cheese but also wove cloth at his farm a few miles to the north of
Wood on Apple Pie Ridge. In balancing accounts with him on May 24, 1742,
Wood gave him a "small piece of Gold" and "one pound & a half of woll."
Although Wood henceforth supplied his own dairy needs, Lupton continued
to weave for the Wood family—nineteen and one-half yards of linsey in
1749—in exchange for gunpowder, lead, and cash.[27]

Wood conducted numerous other exchanges with settlers throughout Opequon for various goods and services necessary on the farm. On April 13, 1742,
for instance, he settled with William Glover for what he owed on a draw knife
and hammer acquired earlier from Glover's father, Edward. William lived
about four miles south of Wood on Buffalo Lick, a tributary of the Opequon
Creek. The farmstead of James Carter, the blacksmith, lay a few miles farther
east along the creek. Wood also did business with William Gilliam, a
wheelwright who dwelt several miles away along the original trace of the
Philadelphia Wagon Road.[28]

The people upon whom James Wood depended to clothe his family were
also spread throughout the Opequon settlement. In August 1742, for instance,
Wood acquired women's and children's shoes, children's stockings, and men's
worsted stockings from William Jolliffe, a neighbor of Alexander Ross living
more than five miles from Wood. The following year Jonathan McMachen
supplied shoes for Mary Wood and children Elizabeth, James, and Mary.
McMachen, the son of justice of the peace William McMachen, lived on land
acquired from his father about halfway between Wood's farm and William
Jolliffe's land. A few years later tailor Reuben Paxton made a linen jacket, four
pairs of breeches, a coat, and three loose-fitting shirts called banyans for
Wood. Where Paxton lived at this time is uncertain, but he later acquired land
along the Opequon not far from the Potomac River.[29]

The exchange relationships James Wood established often overreached the
Opequon settlement. For some goods Wood turned to Pennsylvania or Tidewater Virginia. In April 1748, for instance, he acquired various items from Joseph Simons of Lancaster, Pennsylvania, valued at £3 19s., including a ream
of writing paper, two pounds of chocolate, one pound each of coffee and tea,
and a loaf of sugar. Four years later Wood paid neighbor and wagoner Samuel
Pritchard £2 3s. 11¼ d. for carting various "Sundries from philadelphia" to his

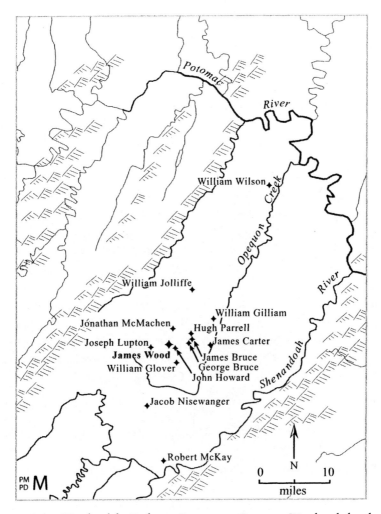

FIG. 5.8. James Wood and the Exchange Economy at Opequon. Wood traded under accounts with numerous individuals broadly dispersed throughout the Opequon settlement. In this manner he, like everyone there, secured what was needed to sustain a family and build a farm. Based on Ended Causes, 1743–1909, Frederick County Court Papers, Library of Virginia.

home at Opequon. The frequency of Wood's dealings at such great distances was far less than for his exchanges locally, but they indicated the vast geographical space over which an exchange economy could function. Wood's economic relations with merchants in eastern Virginia appear to have been limited to exchanges involving tobacco. In one example, a Mr. Thomas received £5 from Wood for wagoning four hogsheads of tobacco, probably to the warehouse at Falmouth, and returning with two bags of salt and one barrel of corn. Wood's accounts bear no evidence that he was producing tobacco at his farm, but as county clerk he regularly accepted the "weed" in payment of court fees.[30]

To build a farm and establish a household, James and Mary Wood relied upon many people. The Woods produced some of their own foodstuffs but often acquired items such as butter and cheese from neighbors. For blacksmithing, tailoring, shoemaking, and other needs they turned to people dispersed throughout the open-country neighborhoods at Hopewell and Hite's Opequon tract. Acquiring competency over economic affairs was for James and Mary Wood a process of exchanging goods and services with men and women of surrounding households who were themselves involved in exchanges with other near and distant neighbors. Wood was also the clerk of the new county of Frederick and an experienced surveyor. He laid off the county town, arranged for the sale of lots, built a shop in town, and rented it to several men who traded merchant goods to him and others at the Opequon settlement. But the network of exchange relations that made building a farm and setting up a household possible for James and Mary Wood had been established long before the creation of Frederick Town. Even as the town took form, the Wood household was by no means dependent upon the economic centrality it provided. The Woods, in other words, did not need the town James Wood had founded.

. ⚭ .

What the Woods and their children, servants, and slaves did to improve the land and build a home was repeated hundreds of times by households throughout the Opequon settlement. The pattern of these efforts indicates that the economic life of the Wood household cannot be interpreted apart from that of households in widely scattered places as far away as Lancaster, Philadelphia, or Falmouth. This life was deeply imbedded in an extensive network of exchange spread across the space of the Opequon settlement and beyond (fig. 5.9). In taking up the land, settlers had been largely free to define—not simply select—tracts according to self-determined criteria. The labor and values they invested in the land reflected what they wanted to receive from it. The result was a vernacular landscape in which the objectives of economic competence had been encoded. In the pursuit of self-control over their economic affairs, however, families did not act individually or autonomously; competence required intensive interaction with neighbors. In the resulting exchange economy the production and consumption of goods and services depended upon sustained economic relations among producers and consumers. This economy cannot be characterized as either commercial or subsistence;

only in the huge volume of goods and services exchanged can a market be said to have existed. The objective of market engagement, however, was economic competence, not profit or capital accumulation. Supply, demand, and markets did not set prices. The costs and availability of goods reflected a consensus of neighbors. Money was not the medium of exchange. Gold and silver as bul-

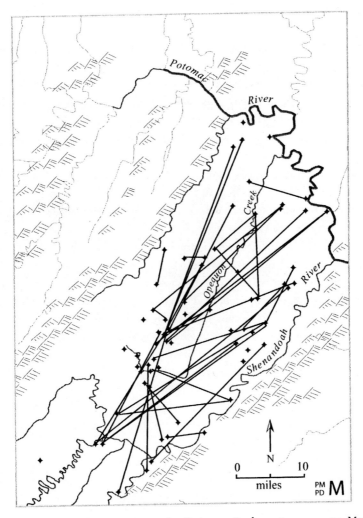

FIG. 5.9. The Exchange Economy at the Opequon Settlement, 1744–1754. Men and women traded goods and services across long distances at the Opequon Settlement. Keeping track of debits and credits in book accounts, they were able to sustain vigorous economic activity in the absence of market towns. Stars mark the location of trading partners. Based on Ended Causes, 1743–1909, Frederick County Court Papers, Library of Virginia.

lion or coinage changed hands just as goods or services did and had value only in the balancing of accounts.

Farm and household organized production at Opequon, and a walk through the community in the 1740s would have revealed small fields of corn, wheat, rye, oats, and barley. Occasional tobacco patches could be seen, or the lanky growth of hemp and flax plants for cloth. As the primary draft animals, horses plowed the land and hauled its produce. Other livestock—cattle, sheep, or swine—provided for a wide variety of farm needs. What Opequon settlers produced appeared in the accounts they kept as a record of exchange. Exchanges sometimes went awry, and debts led to suits in the county court. When sworn as an accurate statement of debits and credits before a justice of the peace, account statements could be presented as evidence. Where they have survived as court documents, they reveal the extent and complexity of the exchange economy at Opequon.

Corn was almost ubiquitous in accounts because its high yields and low labor requirements made it ideal as a subsistence crop. This grain, for example, figured prominently in the exchanges conducted by John Crowson and miller Thomas Chester in 1744. The four barrels and two pecks of corn that Crowson received from Chester was valued at £2, considerably more than any other single entry in the accounts of these two men. Chester, however, also supplied Crowson with a bushel of wheat, twelve and a quarter bushels of rye, 34 pounds of beef, and 198 pounds of pork. That Crowson's contribution to the relationship was for "work done to ye mill trunk" valued at 3s. 9d. explains why the exchange ended in court. The close integration of corn into household subsistence was also evident in dealings between John Beckett and John Davison. Between December 1749 and September 1750, Davison received various quantities of cheese, butter, bacon, hog fat, and liquor from Beckett. In return, Davison supplied several bushels of corn and wheat, while also "making 2 Bushills of Ry into malt" for his trading partner. Beckett's brother-in-law, James Vance, also grew "Ingin Corn" and a mix of crops that included wheat, rye, barley, oats, hay, flax, and hemp. Combined with the three mares, one colt, one horse, twelve sheep, five steers, seven cows, five calves, and two heifers valued in his inventory, these grains indicate the diverse uses to which Vance put his land for the subsistence of his family. Corn, however, also appeared in accounts as a means of paying rent or providing freedom dues for a servant. Some men, for example, William Branson, paid off store accounts with corn. In exchange for such goods as linen, shalloon, powder, shot, gun flints, a knife, a silk cape, stockings, handkerchiefs, sugar, allspice, indigo, a pair of scissors, a buckle, a candlestick, and a blanket from storekeeper Lawrence Stephens, Branson tendered not only corn but also deerskins and cash.[31]

Wheat, like corn, appeared commonly in exchanges among households at Opequon. This premier grain would, by the late 1760s, become the primary staple export crop of the Shenandoah Valley and the source of commercial profit for its producers, but in the 1740s wheat appeared in accounts as only one element of mixed agriculture. Consider blacksmith John Shearer, who debited James Davis for a variety of services performed between October 1745 and August 1746, including "Sharpening Plow Irons and Mending a Pitch fork," repairing clevises, shoeing horses, sharpening colters, and fixing a "Claper in a bell." Shearer also supplied Davis with several bushels of wheat and a bushel of corn. In return Davis gave Shearer one and one-half bushels of wheat, a pair of shoes, and a quart of whiskey. Wheat passed back and forth between the two men but only as a part of a larger pattern of exchange. Wheat entered into the exchange economy at Opequon in other ways as well. Attorney Richard Rogers accepted several bushels of wheat and Indian corn for drafting a mortgage, a bill of sale, a deed, and performing other legal services for Edward Rogers. Interestingly, the lawyer also charged his client for a borrowed runlet—or small barrel—and for knitting three pairs of socks for him.[32]

Accompanying wheat and corn in accounts were small amounts of oats, barley, and rye. David Jaycox, for example, was indebted to Jonathan Jaycox for wheat, rye, corn, and oats in quantities ranging from one to four bushels exchanged at various times from 1744 to 1746. William Perkins partially offset the nails, cloth, rum, molasses, and a bearskin he acquired for merchant William Ramsay with one and one-half bushels of oats in 1744. Ramsay would soon join the founders of Alexandria, a port town destined to play a prominent role in the marketing of Shenandoah Valley flour. Rye could be put to various uses in the Valley's exchange economy. From Lawrence Stephens's brother, Lewis, for instance, Edward Rogers received a breasted saddle in June 1743 in exchange for eight bushels of rye, probably used for flour. Rye, however, could also be distilled into whiskey. In debt to Christopher Holmes, John Hardin signed a note on January 5, 1747, to pay his neighbor one hundred bushels of rye to be delivered by the end of March—half to Isaac Parkins's flour mill and half to either Johnston's or Alfhood's still. Barley appeared infrequently in accounts, but it, like rye, had an auxiliary use when malted for brewing beer.[33]

It is safe to assume that every farmer at Opequon grew edible grains such as corn or wheat, and many also produced rye, oats, and barley. The same cannot be said for tobacco. Although the Shenandoah Valley would later become famous for its wheat crops, the region was never known as a tobacco-producing area. Tobacco was simply not a part of the traditional farming cultures of immigrants from Germany or Ireland. Growing the extremely labor-intensive crop in large quantities with slaves would also have struck these newcomers to Virginia as strange. Tobacco differed from grains in other ways as well. Its export to Europe was regulated by legislation and channeled through public warehouses, where it was inspected and tobacco certificates issued. Not only did these certificates circulate as money, but tobacco was also employed as a standard of value for other commodities. Tobacco, moreover, could be used to pay public levies and fees. In the Shenandoah Valley, however, tobacco producers had to transport their crop over the Blue Ridge to warehouses at Hunting Creek (later Alexandria), Falmouth, or Fredericksburg. To some degree, therefore, growing tobacco in the Shenandoah Valley signified the presence of settlers from eastern Virginia and their plantation culture.

Tobacco also had value in the local exchange economy. Although James Wood accepted many commodities in trade for his fees as county court clerk, tobacco's significance among these items was indicated by the twenty tobacco hogsheads he had cooper Stephen Sebastian make for him in 1750. Because Opequon settlers smoked tobacco in pipes or took it as snuff, the weed sometimes appeared in exchanges between farmers. Jonathan Heath and Philip Babb, for example, must have been close friends or associates. In the 1750s they lived several miles apart on good limestone farmland within a few hours' ride north of the new county town James Wood had surveyed. Not only was Heath a lathe worker who gave Babb a turned cane, two high bedsteads, and two low bedsteads between 1750 and 1751, but he also supplied his neighbor with tobacco and some spare cash during these years. Babb, in turn, cut some stones for Heath and provided him with butter, duck eggs, or hens' eggs on various occasions (fig. 5.10). Regarding tobacco much like money, men signed notes of hand to pay a neighbor a particular sum in the crop by a certain day. Although notes could be drafted informally between parties involved in an exchange, they were enforceable by the county court when sworn like an account before a justice of the peace. John Self, for example, signed a note to John Hardin for 1,168 pounds of tobacco "to be paid on ye River of Shanandor at the plantation where he now Lives." Similarly, in a note dated January 31, 1744, Robert Edge promised "to pay ore caws to be payd" a total of 1,058 pounds to Hardin.[34]

Hardin's own career, always closely associated with tobacco, was documented in numerous public records and suit papers. In November 1740 Hardin purchased 380 acres on a branch of Redbud Run near the Heath household and the Hopewell Meeting House. He was apparently living there when he completed the carpentry work on the county courthouse in 1745 and purchased a stock of horses, mares, cattle, sheep, hogs, and poultry from John

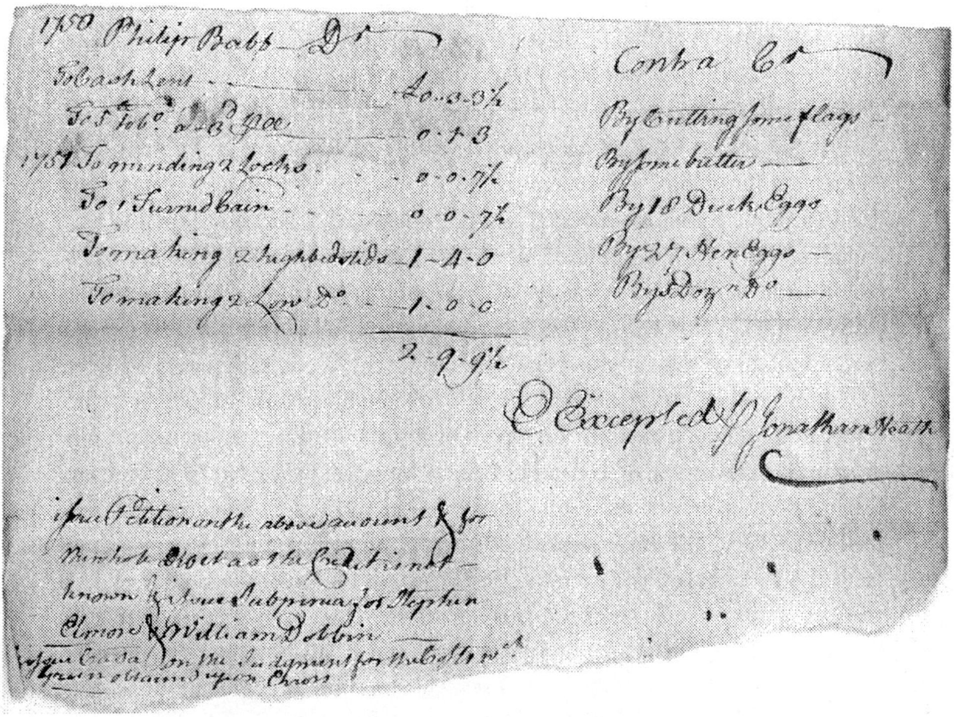

FIG. 5.10. Account of Philip Babb with Jonathan Heath, 1750–1751. Living a few miles apart, Babb and Heath engaged in an exchange of artisan services and agricultural commodities. This trade defined everyday life at the Opequon settlement. Account of Philip Babb with Jonathan Heath, 1750–51, *Heath v Babb*, Dec. 1752, Ended Causes, 1743–1909, Frederick County Court Papers, Library of Virginia.

Hammond. Later that year, however, stonemason Duncan O'Gullion described him as "Martchant Neare to Shanodo." Hardin indeed dealt in merchant goods, and on one occasion in 1748 he sold Jacob Hammon a variety of items including linen, osnaburg, buckles, gloves, paper, a penknife, and other dry goods totaling £2 11s. 4½d. Hardin at times handled considerable quantities of tobacco. On March 18, 1745, John Huston signed a note of hand to pay Hardin 1,093 pounds of tobacco for a debt that included Hardin's charge of £1 10s. for hauling the tobacco to market. But tobacco production alone was insufficient to keep an entrepreneur like Hardin busy, as a note Edward Nelson assigned to him on September 7, 1746, for one hundred bushels of rye indicates. This could have been the rye that four months later Hardin promised to pay to Christopher Holmes. Hardin's activities confirm that commercial tobacco was raised west of the Blue Ridge as early as the 1740s. Some of this tobacco was for local consumption, but its range of exchange was not local. Some Shenandoah Valley farmers grew tobacco for the same reasons planters grew it elsewhere in Virginia: for trade in the Atlantic economy.[35]

Flax, too, was an agricultural product that had an exchange value inside and outside the region because, when processed, it could be spun into linen yarn and woven into cloth. The extent of flax production is difficult to gauge, but flax was rarely found in conjunction with tobacco. If tobacco production was an indicator of cultural connections to Tidewater Virginia, then flax and linen would have signified associations with the small-farm agricultural traditions many settlers brought with them from Ireland and Germany, where the man-ufacture of linen was an important economic activity. In both places weavers sold their product on commercial markets to linen merchants, or mercers, who traded the fabric throughout Europe. During the century of Protestant mi-gration from the north of Ireland to British America, the export of linen from Ireland grew from one million to forty million yards. At Opequon, flax, flax seed, linen yarn, and cloth were all exchanged among farmers. In one account from the early 1740s, for example, John Russell received one bushel of flax seed from John McCormick. Mixed into this exchange, however, were two handkerchiefs, a half bushel of Indian corn, and English millet. McCormick, moreover, made a pair of shoes and several shirts for Russell and on several occasions paid his debts. In return, Russell worked for McCormick, threshing wheat and mowing hay. Not only did Russell acquire flax seed from McCor-mick, but he broke, or scutched, flax for him—thirty-three pounds on one oc-casion and one hundred on another. As part of the exchange McCormick wove linen for Russell and, in one instance, debited him eighteen shillings for thirty-six yards of cloth (fig. 5.11). Much linen cloth was also traded outside the region as early as the late 1730s. In 1739 Governor William Gooch wrote the Board of Trade that "our new Inhabitants on the other side of the Moun-tains, make very good Linnen which they sell up and down the country."[36]

The production of linen cloth from raw flax was a laborious and time-con-suming process requiring many steps. After cutting, the flax stalks were retted, to weaken the tough outer sheath housing the fibers. Retting could be accom-plished by laying cut flax in the weather over a winter or in a shorter period of time by sinking it in a pond. When dried, the retted sheaths were removed by crushing them in a flax break and chopping them with a scutching knife. Hackling cleaned and straightened the remaining fibers for spinning into linen yarn, which was followed by weaving. The cloth had to be beetled, or wetted and pounded, to consolidate the fibers and, if desired, bleached in the open sun. Brown linen could be used or exchanged, but white linen was more val-uable. Evidence for linen production survived in the flax breaks, scutching

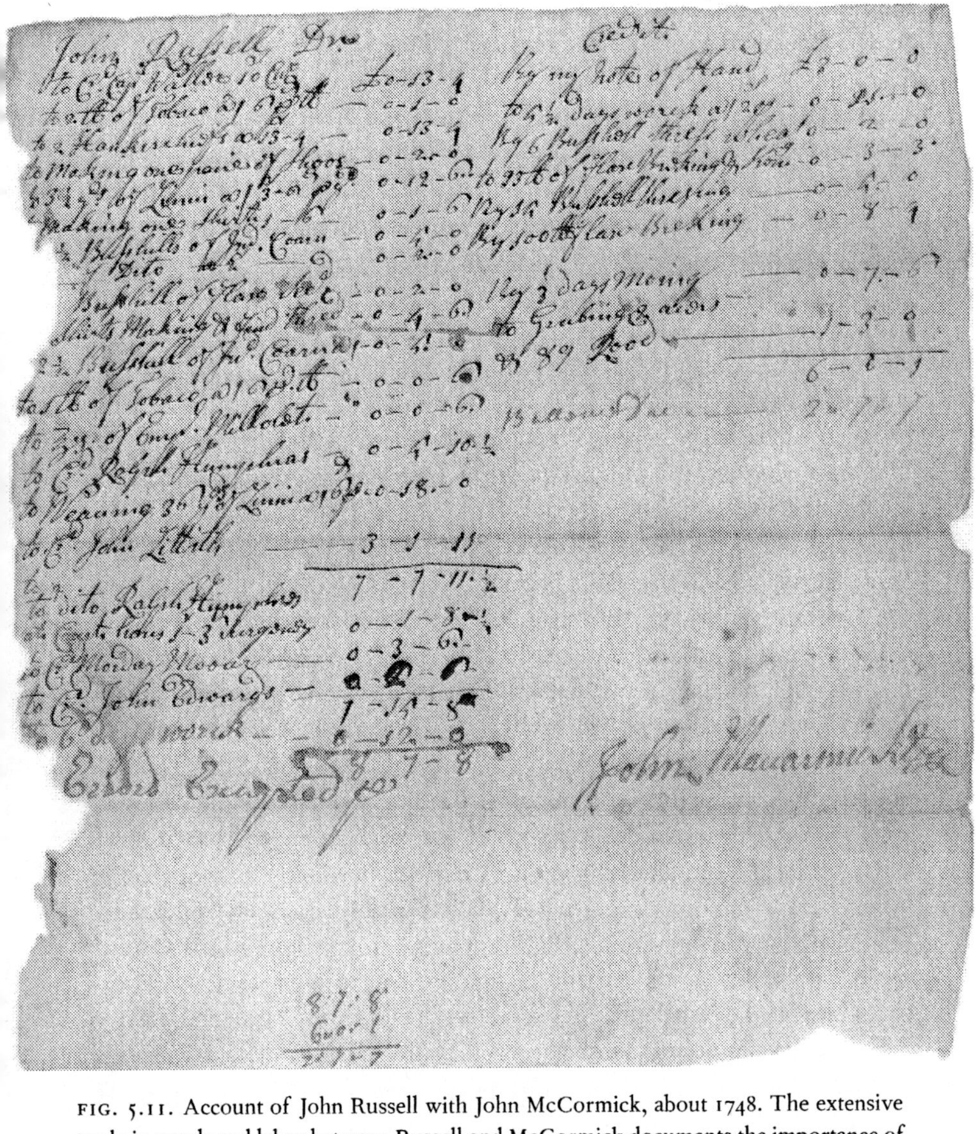

FIG. 5.11. Account of John Russell with John McCormick, about 1748. The extensive trade in goods and labor between Russell and McCormick documents the importance of flax cultivation and linen production in the exchange economy at the Opequon settlement. Account of John Russell with John McCormick, n.d., *McCormick v Russell*, Aug. 1748, Ended Causes, 1743–1909, Frederick County Court Papers, Library of Virginia.

knives, spinning wheels, looms, as well as the raw material or finished cloth settlers owned. Sixteen probate inventories taken between the 1740s and the 1790s among twenty-five of Hite's Scots-Irish settlers along the upper Opequon revealed some traces of linen production. Each of the sixteen families possessed a spinning wheel to produce yarn and many owned hackles or flax breaks. Only seven, however, had a loom. Thus, spinning households were supplying yarn to weaving households at a ratio of about two or three to one. Linen appeared in four estates in quantities that suggest the kind of trade described by Governor Gooch. When he died, James Colvill possessed fifty-one yards of "tow" linen, a low-grade cloth made from the remnants of scutching, but Robert Glass had thirty-eight yards of eight hundred linen, a much finer cloth.[37]

Linen entered the exchange economy at Opequon under several guises. Like most items of farm production, it was traded among farmers. Consider, for instance, the Reilys: In the 1740s Patrick Reily lived in the open-country neighborhood along Mill Creek at its crossing with the Philadelphia Wagon Road; Ferrol and Terrance Reily occupied land purchased from Morgan Morgan about five miles away, on a road that looped west and south toward Frederick Town. In 1745 and 1746 Ferrol and Terrance worked for Patrick, splitting rails and making fences, harvesting, cutting wood for a still—Patrick operated an ordinary—and performing other farm tasks. They also gave Patrick two yards of ten hundred linen. In another exchange among neighboring households John Smith Jr., whose father operated the mill at the crossing of Turkey Run and the wagon road, offset part of his obligation to William Green with three and one-half yards of checked linen and thirty-six feet of walnut boards. On his part Green had "Paid Patrick Reics [Rees] Children for bringing Your mares to You," "Paid Catherine Rogers for you for Cakes," "Paid Ulrick Bucher [Poker] for Liquor for You to take Home," and exchanged a saddle, a gelding, and some cash. In all these accounts, linen in fairly small quantities was traded back and forth among households as part of a larger pattern of domestic exchange. Linen served other purposes in this pattern as well. Robert Eadmeston, for example, compensated Mary Ross for "7 months Commendation [accommodation]" by "waving [weaving] 25 yard of Cloth" on one occasion, ten yards on another, and by making a ladder (fig. 5.12). Stonemason Duncan O'Gullion paid workman George Brown three and one-half yards of linen, four and one-half yards of cotton, a pair of shoes, and one bottle of liquor for a black horse and a total of sixteen days of work and board. James Jackson, who also worked for O'Gullion, received seven yards of brown linen in partial payment for eighty-three days of work. Similarly, George Keith Gibbons was a carpenter who performed various services for John Collings, including laying three hundred feet of both sub- and finished flooring, "Cuting out door and facing and hanging an old door," "running up a pair of stares," and "makeing a Log sled." In return he received a horse, "3 yards of Lining," a grindstone, and other goods or services.[38]

Linen figured as well in the activities of merchants, and both Peter Tostee and Benjamin Perreyra stocked the fabric in their stores. Throughout 1747–1748 peddler Lyman Lipman received various textiles from Perreyra, including seven yards of linen. During the next two years Perreyra's successor, Peter Tostee, supplied linen in lengths between one and six yards to Robert Lemon, James McCoy, James Lemon, George Brown, Murty Hanly, Robert Hutchins, John Lane, and William Bennet, among others. Not all merchants trading in linen were local. Opequon settler John Frost was in Falmouth on November 30, 1743, when he acquired seven yards of "fine Brod. Linn." from Andrew

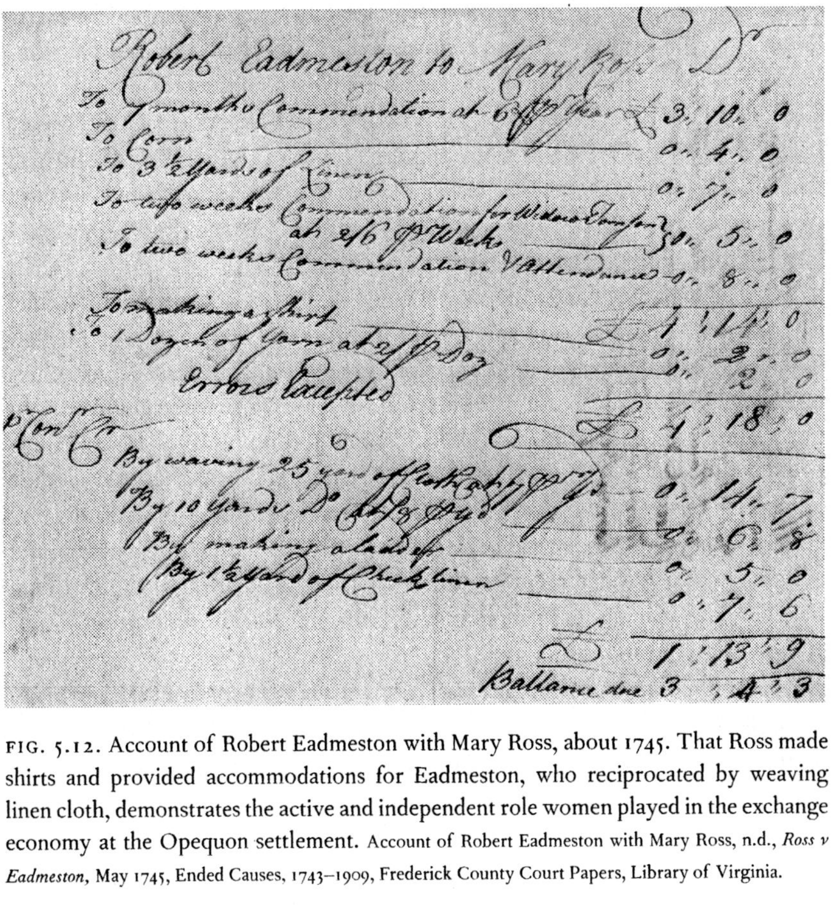

FIG. 5.12. Account of Robert Eadmeston with Mary Ross, about 1745. That Ross made shirts and provided accommodations for Eadmeston, who reciprocated by weaving linen cloth, demonstrates the active and independent role women played in the exchange economy at the Opequon settlement. Account of Robert Eadmeston with Mary Ross, n.d., *Ross v Eadmeston*, May 1745, Ended Causes, 1743–1909, Frederick County Court Papers, Library of Virginia.

Ross, along with osnaburg, shalloon, plaid, one dozen table knives, six pounds of sugar, and one felt hat.[39]

Like only a few other commodities, linen was both traded in the exchange economy and used as a standard for exchange. Values for various goods were often expressed in linen. The £3 10s. debt that Richard Mercer owed Abraham Hollingsworth in October 1744, for example, was to be settled in "rie at two shillings pr bushell til it Coms to that . . . to be deliverd at Isaek Parkens mill and the Quntity of twenty five yeards of safreen nine hunder Lining . . . yeard wide." In September 1747 Moses Downor found himself in debt to Epharim McDowell for one cow valued at £2 5s. or twenty yards of ten hundred linen. In another case coming to court exactly two years later, Phillip Babb sued John Lemon for £17 16s. 3d. Pennsylvania money "or the valey of it in Lenon Cloth good Merchant yard wid eight hundert Lenon." Debts sealed by a note of hand often stipulated payment in linen rather than money. A great deal of both debt and linen passed through the hands of tavern keeper John Nealand. On January 13, 1742, he signed a note to pay Jost Hite "twenty Yards of a Good wite ten hundred Linning" before April 1. Eight months later he committed himself to send Hite forty yards of linen by October and another forty yards by Christmas. Within two years he promised Hite's son Isaac "fourty five Yeards of a good Brown ten hundred Linnen." Quantities of linen in notes could be quite large. In February 1744, Thomas Rennick, for instance, promised to pay Waller Drenen "Eighty yards of ten Hudred Linen yard brod" by the following November.[40]

None of these exchanges, however, suggests that a market existed for linen at Opequon analogous to what settlers would have known earlier in their homelands. No Opequon settler appeared to be producing linen in quantities large enough to live off the income from its sale. No one seemed to be acquiring linen to sell again. Even John Nealand did no more than cycle linen through the exchange economy. Notes of hand for linen circulated as they were assigned from party to party. Linen may have had a universally recognized value, and linen was traded vigorously back and forth within and without the Opequon settlement, but its worth still lay in exchange within a system of debits and credits that bound producers and consumers together in an economic community.

Hemp, like flax, could be put to various uses. Coarser and darker, hemp fiber was not suitable for fine fabrics, only burlap and canvas. With a woolen weft, it was occasionally woven into linsey-woolsey, but its primary use was for cordage. Recognizing hemp's value for naval stores, Parliament and colonial governments encouraged its production. Although the Virginia government had been promoting hemp as an economic base for western settlement since 1722, and although the House of Burgesses in 1745 supplemented an existing bounty of four shillings per hundredweight with an additional two shillings for hemp exported to England, very little evidence exists for its production in Frederick County during the 1740s. James Vance grew hemp, but otherwise accounts and probate records were silent on this score. Significantly, Virginia's Burgesses considered but did not pass a measure calling for the establishment of a public warehouse and hemp inspection station in Frederick County in 1748. Not for two decades would the crop have any commercial significance in the lower Shenandoah Valley, and, inferior to flax for textiles, it apparently possessed little exchange value.[41]

Anyone traveling from farm to farm along the primitive roads of the Opequon settlement would have encountered numerous livestock. Cows, horses, pigs, and sheep were everywhere, because each provided the basic needs of farm life. Cattle gave meat, leather, and dairy products; horses, motive power for agriculture and transportation; pigs, a wide range of foodstuffs; and sheep, meat, and wool. Geese and turkeys were domesticated for food and feathers. A milk cow was especially useful on a frontier farm; a single cow could provide many of the food needs of a small family. The value of cattle in the exchange economy was demonstrated by Edward Rogers when he paid off part of his debt to Duncan O'Gullion with a steer and one-half bushel of onions. Cattle appeared in almost 90 percent of the probate inventories of Scots-Irish settlers on the upper Opequon Creek, with horses, swine, and sheep in comparable frequencies. Another reason why travelers would have encountered livestock everywhere is that animals foraged on an extended commons of unfenced land extending across property boundaries. Virginia law in the 1740s required farmers to fence livestock out of tilled fields, not to confine their animals within enclosed pastures. John Buller learned this lesson when he killed a mare belonging to Opequon Creek neighbor Joseph Colvill "under pretence that [it] . . . broke into ye enclosures." Colvill argued that "in fact, the said Defendant had no Lawful fence to keep his or any other Creature out." Virginia courts usually acted in these cases to protect the property of livestock owners.[42]

Highly mobile themselves, animals readily entered into the fluid economy of debit and credit. When Richard Poulston found himself in debt to Richard Snowden in May 1743, he wrote that "as I know the Money [is] Due I am realy Sorry I gave you that trouble." But as Poulston explained, "tho' as I have not the Money at present and it is hard to get in this part of the world I hope You'll take Cattle horses or hogs for the Debt." Not only could livestock be driven by settler families removing to the Opequon settlement from Pennsylvania or over the Blue Ridge from eastern Virginia, but all animals, even turkeys, could be herded to livestock markets on the Atlantic seaboard. One drover, James

Rutledge, was apparently on his way north when he stopped at Robert Willson's farm on the upper Opequon and not only bought three cows for a total of £5 5s. but also pastured 150 head for five nights for the sizeable sum of £9 7s. 6d. That Shenandoah Valley beef cattle were often destined for Philadelphia markets was painfully apparent to George Washington, who, as commander of the Virginia Regiment during the Seven Years' War, found himself short on provisions and complained that the "pensylvania butchers are buying quantities of Beef *here,* which should be put a stop to, if we are to march towards the Ohio." Ordinary keeper and justice of the peace Andrew Campbell, in partnership with merchant Hugh Parker, exported cattle to Pennsylvania for credit in beef, hides, tallow, hearts, and tongues with Philadelphia merchants while paying Terrance Reily three shillings a day for work with the herd.[43]

Cattle entered the local exchange economy at Opequon in many ways. A cooper, John Burris, also frequented Andrew Campbell's tavern, where, in exchange for rum, beer, planter's punch, and other refreshments, he provided some cash and a cow worth more than £2. In another example, Absalom Haworth, a cordwainer, found himself in debt to "farmer" Mathias Elmore for £15, "to be paid in Money or in Creatures Either horse kind or Cow kind." Merchants like Peter Tostee often dealt in cattle. In partial exchange for rum, sugar, calico, shalloon, osnaburg, ribbon, stockings, hats, snuff, wine, broadcloth, and a knife, Tostee accepted a horse, two steers, several cows, and some cattle from justice of the peace Solomon Hedges, who lived in the northernmost part of Opequon along the Potomac and was often in Frederick Town for court days. Richard Morgan, who lived not far from Hedges, was also a debtor of Tostee's and a creditor for a cow, some cash, and one hundred pounds of iron in 1750.[44]

Horses, like cattle, were not only essential to the system of mixed farming practiced west of the Blue Ridge but also a vital component of the exchange economy, which made this system work. Oxen, so widely used in eastern Virginia for hauling and other plantation duties, by contrast, appeared only rarely in the West. In 1743 Jonathan Littler sold Edward Mercer, a distant neighbor, a horse for £7 in partial exchange for twenty-two gallons of brandy. William Howell was out about the same amount to Samuel Earle for a horse in exchange for carpentry work. John Wilcocks dug a well for Gersham Keys for a horse, Joseph West built a chimney for John Nealand for a horse, and Duncan O'Gullion received a horse from his workman George Brown. The keeping, care, and use of horses also generated numerous exchanges throughout the Opequon settlement. Blacksmith William Mitchell, for example, not only credited Enoch Anderson 4s. 6d. for shoeing his horse, but almost four times that amount for "Keeping" it. "Breaking of a Young Mare" for saddle or harness was the source of the 5s. 9d. credit Bryan Roark received from Hugh Ferguson in August 1745. Edward Nelson not only hired out his horse to John Nealand "to go on the Ridge 6 Days" but also debited Nealand 5s. 9d. for "taking up Your mare." A horse lost on the open range no doubt provided the one shilling credit Ralph Falkner received from Neal Thomas for "finding Your horse." Supplying fodder and stabling for horses was one of the many functions of ordinary keepers like Thomas Doster, who debited tailor Reuben Paxton for "Muggs of Beer," "Gills of Liquor," and "Bowls of Punch," as well as for "Keeping thy Horses."[45]

Sheep and swine appeared commonly in probate inventories, but because their value was primarily for household use, these animals did not enter as often as cattle and horses into the exchange economy. Farmers, however, did trade them back and forth, and on one occasion tavern keeper Robert Lemon credited William Senter for "1 fatt Sheep" against beer, liquor, and other goods. Woolen yarn and cloth, unlike linen, appeared infrequently in accounts, but in one instance Samuel Walker credited Barnet Lynsey for a bull and one pound of wool against debts for liquor, corn, wheat, and rye. Wool cards, used for combing raw wool before spinning, appeared occasionally in merchant accounts. Mutton also figured in exchanges among farmers, merchants, artisans, and others. William Senter was credited for sheep and mutton by tavern keeper Robert Lemon. In another case, Stepto Clark received mutton from merchant Peter Tostee on credit, which he paid off in part with work.[46]

Swine or hogs supplied the dispersed general store at Opequon with meat. Left to roam the range between farmsteads, they could become quite wild before being captured and slaughtered, most typically in December as food for the winter. The exchange of various commodities between Jeremiah Cloud and James Willson in November 1748 is characteristic of the way that trade in swine was embedded within reciprocal relationships among farm households. Along with a cowhide, a bridle, and a complete wagon outfit, including four horses, a mare, a wagon, gears, and two bells, Willson received a hog from Jeremiah Cloud. In return, he not only earned £10 in credit for driving a wagon for Cloud, but he gave his trading partner a horse and half a barrel of corn. Cattle herder James Rutledge, on the other hand, agreed to pay Thomas Rennick £10 for ten hogs.[47]

As an extractive industry, procuring skins and furs was different from all other productive efforts of household and farm in the Shenandoah Valley. The skin and fur trade with Native Americans had contributed significantly to the economy of seventeenth-century Virginia, but it was never as central to the economic life of the colony as it was in South Carolina or New York. After 1720 the trade dwindled into insignificance as a source of economic growth, but it did supplement the economies of settlements west of the Blue Ridge, where, as John Bartram pointed out, hunters led a "lazy life." The commerce in skins and furs nonetheless remained a source of controversy, and the most important issue in the Shenandoah Valley trade was who profited from it. As William Gooch complained to the Board of Trade in 1739, "Pedlars import Rumm and other Spirituous Liquors . . . , and with such like trifling Commodities, brought hither by Land, they purchase Skinns at the People's Houses, and without paying any duty for them carry them to Philadelphia, and other Towns, where they are manufactured into Gloves and Stockins and sold in the Plantations."[48]

During the 1730s Pennsylvania traders began to follow Native Americans into the Ohio Valley. Some traders went south to the Opequon settlement for deerskins and furs from beavers or raccoons. Indians traveling the Valley might have provided some of the stock in trade, but most of it came through the hands of white settlers. As in Pennsylvania and the Ohio Country, the trade in Virginia depended on the flow of alcohol. Worried about the disruptive effects of ardent spirits on both Indian societies and frontier communities—but concerned more about revenues from the trade in liquor, skins, and furs—the Virginia Council in 1735 ordered Henry Lee, collector of duties on liquor for the Potomac River area, to "appoint a fitt person resideing in the County of Prince William to receive the Duties of Liquors coming from Maryland to that part of the Country and to Seize such as shall be Clandestinely Imported without paying such Duty." Going a step further the next year, the Council asked the attorney general "to consider in what manner the Importation of Rum & other Liquors by land from Pensylvania may be best prevented . . . & to bring Suit against such as Export Skins & Furrs out of this Colony by Land without paying the Duties laid thereon." Not satisfied that the trade was yet under Virginia's control, the House of Burgesses in 1738 passed an "Act for licensing Pedlars; and preventing frauds in the duties upon Skins and Furs." The measure called on county courts to license peddlers, on peddlers to sign bonds insuring the payment of export duties, and on the governor to appoint collectors, "who shall reside near the frontiers of this colony." James Wood, already surveyor for Orange County, became the first collector.[49]

Wood worked vigorously in his position, regularly collecting duties from such prominent Opequon settlers as John Hite, Peter Tostee, Benjamin Perreyra, Samuel Divinny, Thomas Cresap, Henry Brinker, Stephen Hotsinpiller, and Lewis Stephens. And on at least one occasion, justice of the peace Andrew Campbell seized skins being smuggled out of Virginia. The trade in skins and furs also figured prominently in the local exchange economy at Opequon. Hunters and trappers as well as farmers who hunted or trapped on the side exchanged their skins and furs with other settlers. Some settlers collected these commodities for exchange with peddlers or for direct export. At least one Virginia merchant, Charles Dick, dealt in Valley furs, asking Daniel Hart to "purchase me some Deer skins from your Merchts. there or anybody else" for delivery to Falmouth. Otherwise most of the men who paid duties to Wood kept accounts with people who supplied them with skins and furs. Andrew Campbell exchanged breakfast, dinner, punch, rum, and a mug of beer at his tavern for sixteen deerskins from Peter Bradford. Campbell probably relied on the skin and fur trade to stock his cellars with Pennsylvania liquor. On another occasion Campbell acquired deerskins from Peter Tostee, who was in turn receiving skins for credit in his store. In one instance, James McCoy and James McKee signed a note in 1746 agreeing to provide Tostee with £3 10s. 9d. "in good Merchentable Dear Skins." That year Tostee paid Wood £1 10s. 5¼d. in duties for the equivalent of nearly five hundred skins. That Wood also debited him for the duty on fifty-two and a half gallons of rum suggests that Tostee, like Campbell, was engaged as deeply in the liquor and skin trade in Pennsylvania as he was in the local exchange economy. This merchant trader continued to pay duties on both skins and alcohol for the next two years. Skins and furs also entered into exchanges among farmers. In the case of Hugh Ferguson and Bryan Roark, Ferguson found himself in debt to Roark not only for breaking the mare but also for five buckskins, a heifer, and a hat, as well as for "going to Hunting Creek" for a note of hand to lawyer James Porteus and for "Driving of a Bull from the Widow Bordens to yr house."[50]

Artisans, like hunters and trappers, produced goods for exchange. The large number of identifiable artisans and the wide variety of their skilled trades at Opequon suggest that the economy of this frontier settlement diversified quickly during its first two decades. Diversification was, in fact, fundamental to the functioning of an exchange economy. At least twenty-six different trades were represented by artisans dispersed throughout the settlement. Carpenters, joiners, masons, painters, gardeners, bricklayers, builders, fullers, and dyers supplied their skills to the regional economy. Other artisans produced shoes, cloth, hats, saddles, watches, guns, barrels, wheels, chairs, locks, tinware, turned objects, and cabinet goods. Artisans' accounts, however, rarely isolated skilled services or manufactured goods from the many other items commonly exchanged among households. Few, if any, artisans, in other words, attempted to derive their living exclusively from their trade. In their accounts, therefore, labor was valued far more frequently than the products of labor. In his exchange with Samuel Earl in 1750, for example, William Howell received a horse in trade for a saddle, bridle, and "Carpenders work," and William Goodchild received malt, wheat, brandy, beer, mutton, cash, and buttons from Robert Pearis in 1752 in exchange for "Makeing a Coat & Jacoat and for haircloaths for Ditto" and "Makeing a Sute of Black Bombofine & hair Cloaths for ye Coat." What these accounts suggest is that artisans used their labor to complement farm production for credit with their neighbors. They were not manufacturing goods for sale in a market economy. Instead, they traded their skills for other labor, goods, or services in the exchange economy of the community.[51]

Labor took many forms. Free men and women often worked for wages by the day, but many toiled for terms up to a year. Some individuals bound themselves as indentured servants, to labor for the number of years required to pay off a debt, and African American slaves passed a lifetime in unrequited labor. Farmers often worked for each other according to the demands of the agricultural cycle, as the following examples describe. Amid their wide-ranging exchange of goods, such as Indian corn, flax seed, millet, tobacco, or linen, and tasks, including shoemaking, breaking flax, weaving, tailoring, or threshing, John McCormick performed "6 days worck" for John Russell, while Russell in return passed "5½ days worck[ing]" for McCormick. In their accounts artisans often recorded stints of labor by their workmen. George Brown, from whom Duncan O'Gullion had received the horse, twice worked for this builder in 1748 for periods of eight days. On nineteen different occasions in 1752 James Jackson labored for O'Gullion for periods from two to twelve days at 1s. 6d. per day. Jackson also debited his employer for his "wifes Account against you for Sundry Services done." O'Gullion compensated Jackson by providing shoes, linen, "Punch at James Lemons," and "Several Mugs of Beer from Andrew Caldwell." On another occasion Roger Burkam hired his son Charles to O'Gullion for seven months. The terms for which individuals exchanged labor could be quite long. Barnett Warde, for instance, worked for William Randles in three-week to three-month stretches during the late 1740s, receiving bolts of linen in return. Both Benjamin Perreyra and Peter Tostee hired labor by the term. Mary Bailey performed housekeeping and other chores for Perreyra, receiving twelve shillings a month and "15[s.] for washing for you." During spring 1749 John Wolcock worked at Tostee's "mill Seat" and kept a record week by week for several months working two to six days a week.[52]

Labor by the day or the term was usually negotiated informally by both parties, but an indenture was a legally enforceable contract in which debtors agreed to work for a fixed period in exchange for the retirement of their debt, and for food, clothing, shelter, and sometimes for training in a skilled trade or rudimentary education in reading, writing, and figuring. A creditor could sell or exchange an indenture requiring a servant, as the laboring party to the agreement was called, to move from master to master. Indentures were usually recorded as a deed in county court records, but information about indentured service was more often deposited in court documents when one party violated the contract. Servants sometimes had to sue masters for their freedom on the completion of their service. In 1746, for instance, Rose Bignal petitioned the Frederick County Court for her freedom, recounting how she "was imported without Indentures from London into this Colony and Sold as a Servant for five Years to one John Timmons & by him to one John Dawkins who afterwards Sold her to one Thomas Williams, That Your Petitioners time expired the tenth day of Last March past, that the said Williams detains her as a Servant altho' She is free." Masters, in turn, petitioned the court to extend the time of runaways to cover the costs of recovery and days lost. In one case, servant John Casey was charged with "11 Weeks Run away time Wanting two Days Expenses in Retaking you the first time the Same in Retaking & bring[ing] you from Pensilvania." Violence between master and servant or among servants could also inscribe this otherwise invisible servant population into the historical record. In one case Isabella Rob complained to the Frederick County Court that her master, Richard Rogers, "beat & used her in a Barbarous Manner." Not surprisingly, Rob absented herself from Rogers's service for up to nine days on four separate occasions between October 1745 and January 1746.[53]

Although servants constituted an often troublesome population, their skills helped run the exchange economy. Masters traded their labor much as they would flour, horses, linen, or any other good, as Thomas Gray did when he debited Frederick Gabbard three pounds for "30 Days work of Patterick Morain My Servt. a Mason." Servants were traded from master to master. Not only did Neale O'Gullion, Duncan O'Gullion's brother, consume punch, rum, and various meals during overnight stays at the tavern of Henry Porter, but he also acquired a "Sarvant Woman" for £12 from the tavern keeper, whom he paid in part with 615 pounds of beef. Servants were also used to pay debts, as in the case of Thomas Rutherford, who signed a note on January 3, 1746, to supply Jacob Penington with "one likely Helthy Servant man whose time of Servis is to be for Seven years."[54]

Slaves, like servants, are difficult to document in the exchange economy at Opequon. In 1754 a census of Frederick County tithables indicated that about six hundred eighty slaves resided among a white population of approximately eighty-seven hundred. Many bondsmen and women no doubt labored on Shenandoah River quarters belonging to Tidewater planters like Carter Burwell. Life for these slaves would not have been much different from what it was for blacks growing tobacco elsewhere in Virginia. Valley slaves would, however, have suffered isolation from networks of kin and community that were just beginning to ameliorate the harsh conditions of slave life and labor in eastern Virginia. Slavery among the small farmers engaged in mixed agriculture elsewhere at Opequon took on a distinctive cast. Slave sales were very rare, and only one case argued in the county court from 1743 to 1753 involved the sale of a slave. In this instance, Isaac Baker accused John Nealand of disguising an older black man as a youth of eighteen or nineteen with his face "Close Shaved and his Skin . . . made to seem very Smooth by blacking and Greece." That Nealand could perpetrate such a hoax suggests that slave sales were unusual and buyers unfamiliar with human merchandise. The case of Dorothy Cartmell gives further indication that, although a society with slaves existed west of the Blue Ridge, slavery was not the norm. A widow in 1746, Cartmell was charged with concealing a slave woman, Peg, from the county court justice, William McMachen, during the annual enumeration of tithables in Frederick County. Through her will Cartmell later freed Peg in a private act of manumission, which Virginia law did not allow. The illegal concealment and liberation of Peg betrays an indifference or hostility toward slavery and the discipline required to maintain the institution in a small-farm society whose labor demands could be met in many different ways.[55]

In the exchange economy of farm households at Opequon, slave labor rarely entered into the mix of goods and services traded back and forth. Duncan O'Gullion did hire out his "Mullatto Servant Girl" to tavern keeper James Lemon and complain when Lemon refused to return her; but even in this case the free or slave status of the girl was not clear. Slave owners at Opequon adapted the institution of slavery to their economic world instead of adopting a plantation society of tobacco production. William Picket, for instance, hired his "negro woman" to Ralph Humphreys for a year on condition that Humphreys "learn her to Spin upon a Linnen wheel and to find her a wheel of 20s price." Humphreys failed in his part of the bargain, and Picket sued for £5 in damages. The incident illustrates several facets of slavery in the early Shenandoah Valley. First, slave hiring was practiced as early as the 1740s. Slaves could be engaged on short or long terms as one man's wheat became ripe, as a fence needed building, or a crop of corn harvested. Thus, a slave owner who lacked sufficient work during a slack time in the cycle of his crops could still derive income from investment in a slave. Slaves from several farms could be assembled as a harvest team to take in the crops at each farm in turn. For some free men the ownership of a slave represented a capital investment. At Opequon in the 1740s, however, the full development of slave hiring as a means of adapting slavery to the diverse labor needs of a mixed-farm economy was far in the future, but the actions of Picket and Humphreys reveal an eagerness on the part of slave owners to teach slaves those skills essential to household competence. Slaves thus assumed value as individuals, and slave owners acted to protect this value. Charles Buck, for instance, kept an injured slave boy with doctor Daniel Hart for several months and paid a large sum for dressings and salves.[56]

Women as well as men entered fully into the exchanges that brought competence to households. Gender distinctions were nonetheless significant in the application of the common law and the dependent status it imposed upon women as *feme covert*. For the decade following 1743 fewer than one in fifty cases heard by the county court involved women because under the *feme covert* doctrine men were legally responsible for the actions of their wives. Outside of marriage, however, single women could own property and seek its protection in the courts, but strong social pressures encouraged single women to assume dependent status in the households of fathers or other male relatives. Within their own households married women could nonetheless act independently to obligate their husbands before the law. Alice Anderson, for instance, signed a note in which she did "hereby Promise in behalf of my Husband John Anderson that he shall Pay unto Messrs. Ralph Falkner [and] John Muschett, Merchts in Powtaba in Maryland" the sum of £1 18s. 10½d. in six weeks' time. In a similar instance, William Picket sued William Johnson in 1748 on a note Ann Johnson signed to Picket for two thousand pounds of tobacco.[57]

Women also acted before the law on their own behalf. Ann Lilburn's husband, John, had been dead for six years when she sued James McCracken in debt for twelve bushels of Indian corn, ten bushels of barley, one bushel of malt, and £1 10s. that Lilburn had paid Rev. William Williams for McCracken. Women likewise kept their own accounts. Gilbert Parker, for example, acquired a debt "to Margaret Ramsey before marriage" worth £6 11s. in onions, malt, honey, a cloak, a cow, a calf, a yearling, and several debts that Margaret had settled for him. Other men appeared in the accounts of women. Mary Ross kept her own accounts in her dealings with Robert Eadmeston, and John Stewart found himself in debt to Sarah Williamson for "Cash Lent You at Times," "one Lindsey Woolsey Jacket & Britches," "one Holland Shirt," "Triming for Your Coat," and "one Silk Handkerchief." In another case Sarah Shepherd sued John Burris for "ye Sum of forty Seven Shillings four pence maryland money or Linnen at market price as also a Shirt Cloth for ye interest." Women also traded with merchants. In 1743 Rachel Hood acquired a blanket, several rugs, various textiles, petticoats, garters, buckles, a pair of shoes, and a dozen pipes from William Griffiths. During October 1750 Sarah Davis obtained ivory and horn combs from Peter Tostee, as well as thimbles, razors, broadcloth, soap, buttons, and mohair.[58]

Thus the exchange economy at Opequon was not strictly a man's world. Women were actively engaged in it, although their infrequent appearance in debt suits underscores their role as *feme covert*. Nonetheless, the flow of goods and services in this economy was fluid across gender lines. When women engaged in exchanges, they did so on the same basis as men. Women purchased items such as petticoats or combs more often than men did, and they made shirts for men or trimmed their coats, but these activities say more about the gendered division of labor than about gender divisions in the exchange economy. What is significant in these exchanges is that, although what women exchanged reflected women's work, women could enter into the exchange economy on the basis of this work and its products much the same way men did.

· ⚘ ·

Production and the wide variety of goods produced in the economy of the early Shenandoah Valley cannot be separated from exchange because we know about what was produced only insofar as it was exchanged. Exchange was essential to survival. No farm family was independent. Competence required households to trade for essential goods and services. Only through exchanging labor, surplus farm production, or goods such as skins, furs, or textiles could a family provide for its livelihood from year to year and for its stability on the land from generation to generation. Production and exchange were bound together in this formula.

It was through the medium of debits and credits that goods and services flowed among producers and consumers in an exchange economy. An exchange economy is not a barter economy premised upon direct trade of one good for another or upon compensating labor with farm produce. Barter economies work poorly over long periods of time because they frustrate capital accumulation and they break down across extended space when exchange requires face-to-face transfers. They are, therefore, poorly adapted for sprawling but rapidly developing cultural frontiers, such as that at Opequon. Both exchange and barter economies, however, facilitate economic activity among producers and consumers in the absence of merchants, traders, and other middlemen. Nor are exchange economies necessarily cash economies, although many exchanges involve cash. As an anonymous medium of exchange, money enables the flow of goods and services among strangers across distance and time. Goods produced in one place can be accepted anywhere, and value can accrue from year to year. These are considerable advantages to anyone struggling to establish a frontier farm. The goods and services flowing through an exchange economy are indeed equated in currency—so much for a bushel of corn, a yard of linen, a day's work, and so forth. Nonetheless, this economy does not depend upon money changing hands. Coinage or bullion are passed along much like any other good or service, but an exchange economy can function well without gold or silver.

Book accounts, not barter or money, made exchange economies work. Methods for keeping accounts in double- or single-entry systems of recording both debits and credits were well-developed throughout the Atlantic world by the beginning of the eighteenth century. For each customer merchants noted debits and credits on facing pages of account books: debits, or those actions to which the customer was in debt to a merchant, on the left-hand page; and credits, or those actions by which the customer was a creditor of the merchant, on the right. Daily transactions were noted, customer by customer, in a daybook or journal and later transferred to account books. When a customer acquired "sundries" in a single-entry system, the merchant would debit the customer as receiver of the goods. The reverse took place when the customer reciprocated with so many pounds of flax seed, bushels of corn, or days of labor: The customer became the creditor. The more sophisticated system was called double-entry bookkeeping not simply because it distinguished debits from credits but because every transaction required two entries in the account book, just as in any exchange there is a creditor and a debtor, a giver and a receiver of goods. Merchants represented themselves in various "real" accounts usually by commodities—a cash account, a sundries account, a skin and fur account—or in "nominal" accounts, such as expenses, revenues, or profit and loss. The linen account thus became the creditor for bolts of cloth given to customers; the wheat account, debtor for bushels of wheat brought in. One transaction required a debit or credit to the customer and an offsetting credit or debit in the merchant's own accounts. In either system, the value of all commodities was carefully equated in pounds, shillings, and pence. Although merchants would credit customers from time to time for cash, money served as only one means among many by which merchants and customers would strive to balance debits and credits.[59]

Surviving accounts from the Opequon settlement in the 1740s and early 1750s reveal that merchants—those whose profession it was to buy to sell again—traded within the regional exchange economy, but most trade at Opequon went on among farm households or with the weaver down the road or the blacksmith on the other side of the creek. The logic of double-entry bookkeeping sustained this economic world, but in practice most people kept track of exchanges through the single entry of debits and credits in personal accounts alone. People kept book with each other, marking down a cow and calf, so many bushels of corn, several days' work, or a few shillings here and there received as credit or given as debit. Goods and services were all expressed in currency equivalents from a common store of knowledge about the relative worth of things. Exchanges could be maintained from year to year and tracked across miles of open space. The salient feature of the Opequon settlement was space, or, more accurately, dispersal. Families had spread out upon the countryside in the search for good land. Colonial policies and the practices of those with land to dispense allowed for the scattering of households in the private capture of natural resources as a means of fostering settlement and securing western frontiers.

Dispersed conditions persisted, and no town developed for more than a decade after settlement had begun at Opequon. The governor and Council did not require that a town be surveyed as a condition of land orders issued in the 1730s or as a response to crises with the Indians throughout that decade. Chartering towns was regarded as the purview of the legislature, and years earlier the House of Burgesses had passed legislation encouraging town formation, but these measures had been disallowed by the crown as infringing upon the royal prerogative and the authority of Parliament. The towns that the Burgesses did encourage were intended for commerce, not defense. Nor did the economic forces at work throughout the Opequon settlement call a town into being. No landowner before James Wood took the initiative to survey streets and lots or encourage the erection of stores, shops, taverns, and houses. Compact settlement, moreover, failed to accrue around significant locations in the cultural geography of Opequon. Jost Hite's or Alexander Ross's farmsteads could have become economic centers or central places. People gathered at them to buy or sell land and to grind grain at a mill or drink beer and whiskey at a tavern. A town could have served the frontier community as a collecting point, where goods or commodities produced on farms—wheat, rye, corn, livestock, or even linens—were gathered by merchants for export from the region. Or it could have been the location to which farm families were willing to journey to acquire imported goods otherwise unavailable at Opequon. Such a town would have reordered the road network from a trellis branching off major arteries into a hub-and-spoke arrangement. These developments would come to pass with the establishment of a county town in the 1740s, but the town-country world of the Shenandoah Valley would never function according to this classic configuration of a central-place economy. [60]

What allowed for dispersal and vigorous economic activity at Opequon in the absence of a town was the exchange economy. The system of book accounts as a medium of exchange enabled men and women to trade goods, services, and labor back and forth across distances of thirty-five to forty miles or more. This is not to say that barter would prevent exchange across the dispersed geography of Opequon, but barter was inefficient, and money for a cash economy was too scarce to become a medium of exchange instead of an object of exchange. To say that book accounts allowed men, women, and families to work toward and achieve economic competence is simply to point out that the settlement economy during Opequon's first decades was not in an undeveloped or developing state awaiting commercialization and centralization. The exchange economy worked perfectly well to accommodate the needs of the settlers; how it worked, however, was complicated.

Many simple exchanges operated directly between two households. In examples already cited, Edward Mercer and John Littler exchanged a horse and brandy in 1743. The two lived about twenty-five miles apart: Littler near the Hopewell Meeting House and Mercer to the northwest along Rocky Marsh Run, a small tributary to the Potomac. About ten miles separated Lewis Stephens and Edward Rogers, who traded a saddle and eight bushels of rye that same year. Both Littler and Stephens kept accounts of these transactions and used these accounts as court evidence when not fully compensated for their part of the exchange. How important the system of book accounts was for exchange and economic activity is shown by the accounts Mary and George Hoge—stepmother and son—kept with each other. During the year after his father's death in 1749, George helped the new widow with a number of chores at the family home a few miles from Jost Hite's farmstead. The stepson worked a day at harvest, spent another day "halling in grain . . . with my own horses," and plowed a one-acre field in which he also sowed flax. From his stepmother he received three bushels of corn on one occasion and fifteen on another, cider at the sale of his father's estate, and a considerable quantity of hay. Mary also debited George for "Wintering two Sows With Corn" and for "Cash paid the Widow Minor" for him. George and Mary Hoge lived only a few miles apart, but regardless of the affection they may or may not have shared, lending a hand with some plowing, hauling, or herding and helping out with corn, cider, or hay here and there was not simply a family affair (fig. 5.13). Accounts were strictly kept, and arrears were disputed in court.[61]

Keeping accounts, therefore, structured space at Opequon just as it ordered social relations. In this sense, the system of book accounts and the exchange economy it sustained represented a Newtonian world that operated according to natural law comprehensible through reason and observation. Double-entry bookkeeping and its single-entry derivative, in fact, evolved as part of the same set of complex intellectual developments that produced a vision of nature and the universe moving to the physical principles and mathematical laws

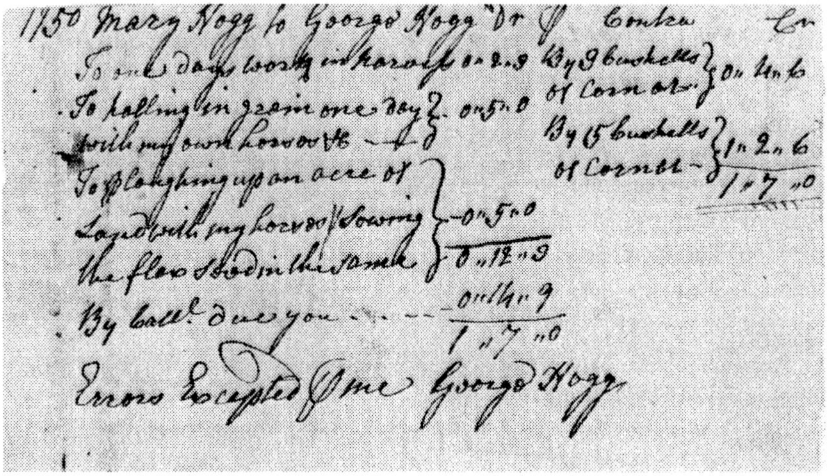

1750 Mary Hogg to George Hogg Dr ℘ Contra Cr

To one days work in harvest	0..2..3	By 9 bushells of Corn at	0..4..6
To falling in grain one day with my own horses &c	0..5..0	By 15 bushells of Corn at	1..2..6
To plowing up an acre of Land with my horses & sowing the flax seed in the same	0..5..0		1..7..0
	0..12..3		
By ball. due you	0..14..9		
	1..7..0		

Errors Excepted ℘ me George Hogg

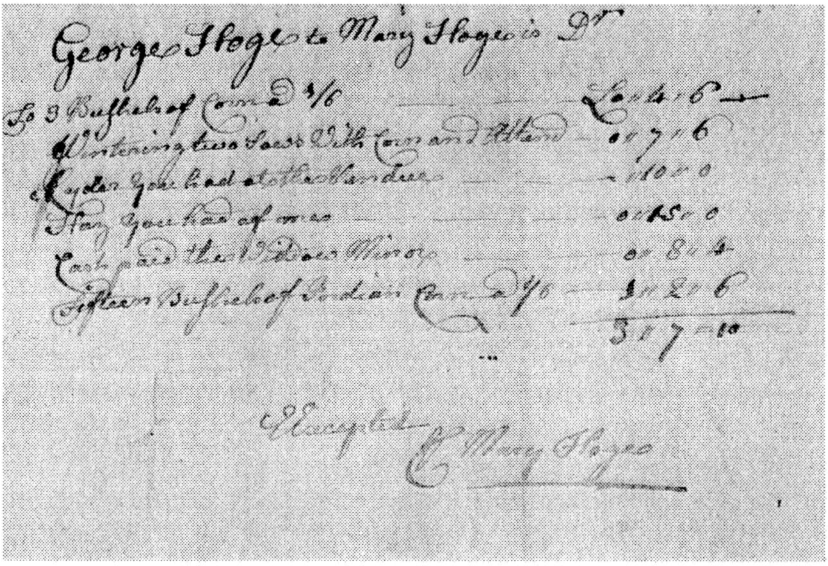

George Hoge to Mary Hoge is Dr

To 9 Bushels of Corn @ 3/6	£0..4..6
Wintering two Sows with Corn and Attend	0..7..6
Rydes you had at the Vendue	0..10..0
Hay you had of me	0..15..0
Cash paid the Widow Minor	0..8..4
Fifteen Bushels of Indian Corn @ 1/6	1..2..6
	3..7..10

Excepted ℘ Mary Hoge

FIG. 5.13. Accounts of Mary Hoge and George Hoge, 1750. These accounts of stepmother and stepson demonstrate that family affairs were carefully documented in the exchange economy at the Opequon settlement. Account of Mary Hoge with George Hoge, 1750, and Account of George Hoge with Mary Hoge, 1750, *Hoge v Hoge,* Aug. 1751, Ended Causes, 1743–1909, Frederick County Court Papers, Library of Virginia.

Isaac Newton described. In Newton's universe, time and space were static. Heavenly bodies transected space in motion so constant that it could be measured as time. Similarly, at Opequon, the system of reckoning debits and credits allowed men and women to track exchanges across great distances and through considerable periods of time. The value of a cow and calf acquired in the spring could be offset with wheat after the July harvest, or flour after threshing and grinding in the fall. Linen woven over the winter could be offered in trade for blacksmithing carried out the season or the year before. Moreover, the complex spatial pattern of these exchanges, which crisscrossed the landscape in dense webs of interconnection, were all recorded as lists of debits and credits, often in account books, but just as frequently scribbled on loose scraps of paper. Intricate as it was, to the men and women of Opequon it all made perfect sense.[62]

In the world of the exchange economy the Newtonian concepts of order in nature and the harmony of the spheres were expressed in the idea of balance. Both nature and the economy operated like clockwork mechanisms. Where an escapement device in a clock employs the regularity of a pendulum to measure out the impetus of springs or weights to the gear train and eventually the hands, the periodic reckoning of debits and credits and the striking of a balance between them in book accounts allowed for orderly economic exchanges to progress through time. Partners in an exchange would periodically balance accounts by summing debits and credits and calculating what amount—that is, the balance—added to either column would bring the account into equilibrium. The object of the exercise was to render debits equal to credits. The balance could then be forwarded to the next blank page in the account book, allowing the exchange to continue indefinitely. In many cases, the final reckoning of accounts was made only from the estate of a deceased trading partner. If the balance grew too large from the creditor's perspective, or if the debtor absconded or became insolvent, the account could become the basis of a suit in law. Going to court, however, represented not the failure of the system, but the mechanism for its continuance, predictability, and reliability.

The exchange between James Wood and Peter Tostee demonstrates how keeping accounts ordered time in the economy at Opequon. In 1747 Wood received "Sundry Articles of Shop Account" from Tostee, while Tostee was debtor to Wood for a marriage license, an ordinary license, and various duties on liquor, skins, and furs. To balance the exchange Wood added £18 9½d. to the credit side of Tostee's account and carried this balance from page eight in his account book to page sixteen, or literally from 1747 to 1748. The two then exchanged the "Sundry Articles" Wood received for the "Rent of my house from Novr. Court 1747 to Nov. 1748" and for various duties on liquor, skins, and furs. Tostee was again in arrears for £9 8s. 6½d., a sum carried to page thirty-seven in Wood's book and the next year, when it became Tostee's initial debit. And so it went into the following year. Similarly, balancing and forwarding accounts among farm households allowed families to continue economic relations in time even though the horse, or bushel of wheat, or gallon of liquor one household received would not be offset by corn, a day's work, or a horse shod for a year or more.[63]

Notes of hand were also a means of regulating time in the Newtonian world of the exchange economy by allowing transactions to progress at specified intervals. On August 29, 1747, for example, Richard Abell promised to pay Michael Campbell "for vely Resevid [value received]" the "Just and full sum of fifty eight yeards of ten Hundred Lin. yeard wid" by September 1, 1748, almost exactly one year later. Campbell then entered the note as a debit of £8 7s. (the value of the linen) in his account with Abell, along with various quantities of bacon, pork, wheat, flour, buckwheat, oats, and liquor he had given him. Campbell also debited Abell for a second note of hand for twelve shillings, which Abell had signed the year before to Robert Hamilton. Because notes of hand were negotiable, that is, assignable from one party to another, Hamilton could use Abell's obligation to him to help satisfy his own debt to Campbell. Campbell dutifully gave Hamilton credit for the note and added the twelve shillings on the debit side of Abell's account.[64]

As exchanges among Campbell, Abell, and Hamilton demonstrate, every debt had to be compensated by an equal and opposite credit, even in cases in which the account keeper was not party to the original transaction. In this way notes not only ordered exchanges in time but also managed them in space. In 1748, in another example, Daniel O'Neill acquired a horse from Matthew Smith, who then assigned O'Neill's note for the horse to Stephen Hotsinpiller. Thus O'Neill owed Hotsinpiller for a horse he bought from Smith. Orders written by one person on their account with another on behalf of a third party were another means of extending exchange across space. On February 2, 1748, William Mitchell wrote to Richard Morgan, "Sir[,] Please let John Nealands have Credit with you for three pounds Ten shillings Pensylvania Currancy and I shall see you paid by our next March Court." Here Mitchell would have credited his account with Nealand for £3 10s. and debited Mitchell the same amount for a debt that Morgan owed Nealand. Thus Mitchell became a kind of banker—in the absence of both banks and currency—underwriting an exchange between Mitchell and Nealand.[65]

The tangible instrument of a note changing hands, however, was not necessary for complex transactions involving several households. The system of book accounts could facilitate exchanges among people removed by space and time from the keeper of accounts. Exchanges between two parties, in other words, could be organized in the accounts of a third party by the meticulous entry of debits and credits. In one example Thomas Balch broke a horse for John Arnold in 1751. In return, Arnold wove a "Piece of Cloth for John Nee-lans [Nealand] on Your [Balch's] Acct." Thus Nealand's accounts organized trade between Balch and Arnold. On another occasion, in 1746, John Smith Jr.'s mare ran away and Patrick Rees's children found and returned the animal, a favor that Smith valued at 1s. 6d. What transpired between Smith and Rees, however, appeared in the accounts of William Green as a debit to Smith when Green credited Rees's children for retrieving the lost mare. On another occasion Green credited Catherine Rogers for the cakes Rogers had baked for Smith, and he gave the 8s. 3d. in credit to Ulrich Poker for the liquor this German settler had traded with Smith. Smith, too, received credit in Green's books for £1 19s. 8½d., which miller Isaac Parkins owed Smith, probably for wheat he had delivered to Parkins's mill. Smith's exchanges with Rees, Rogers, Poker, and Parkins, in other words, were all made possible by debits and credits entered in Green's accounts. Dispersed throughout the Opequon settlement at distances as great as forty-five miles, these people were not close neighbors.[66]

While keeping accounts at Opequon organized the economy in time and place in the absence of—and without a need for—towns as collection points in the exchange of goods and services, the same system of reckoning economic relations connected Opequon across great distances to major entrepôts and Atlantic ports. The frequency of outside contacts was far less than the pace of exchange within the Opequon settlement, and about one in ten surviving accounts mentioned Pennsylvania or markets in eastern Virginia. But reckoning debits by credits and balancing accounts nonetheless rendered Opequon an economic extension of Pennsylvania. The case of Thomas and Ellenor Hart is instructive. In October 1734 they sold their 137-acre farm in Warminster Township, Bucks County, Pennsylvania, and headed southwest. Six months later they agreed to purchase one thousand acres from Jost Hite on Elk Branch and the wagon road to Pennsylvania. Hart, however, kept his ties to his home colony. In 1743 he found himself in debt to Lancaster County storekeeper John Carson for £137, a sum large enough to suggest that Hart was buying in Pennsylvania to sell again in the Shenandoah Valley. That same year Hart signed a note for £12 16s. 6d. to Philadelphia merchant Joseph Shippen Jr. That Hart finally paid off the note two years later through Thomas Rutherford, who was traveling through Pennsylvania, suggests that the people of Opequon often did business for one another when traveling.[67]

At Opequon, however, Hart's situation was considerably different from that of merchants in Pennsylvania market towns or the colonial capital. His home, although located on the Philadelphia road, was remote and separated from other early land holdings by no less than seven miles. And with at least one other Opequon settler, Samuel Dark, he traded not in merchant goods but in subsistence items such as beef, bacon, flax seed, and gunpowder, or services such as hiring a wagon, gelding a horse, or "taking a Calf from a Cow." Whatever goods Hart acquired from Carson and Shippen no doubt passed into the exchange economy at Opequon, but Hart's long-distance trade in Pennsylvania reflected no centralizing tendencies in the Opequon economy.

Charles Seller also traded in Philadelphia. The Seller family had taken up land in the North Mountain tract. During five trips to Philadelphia between 1736 and 1738, Charles acquired blankets, muslin, silk, lace, combs, pins, paper, ink pots, wool cards, gunpowder, lead, and spurs from merchant Edward Shippen to exchange with the people of his open-country neighborhood at North Mountain. James Wood also kept accounts with Shippen, and on one occasion he credited Shippen for the 17s. 5¾d. he "paid Charles Kellar [Seller] as Security for you." Several people at Opequon traded with John Harris, who operated the ferry over the Susquehanna River where Jonnhaty crossed on his way south during fall 1742. Three years earlier Joseph Cloud, whose family lived near the forks of the Shenandoah River, had promised Harris the "sum of to pound at or upon the first day of agust next." And three years after Jonnhaty's passage, John Ellis, a neighbor of Morgan Bryan in the northern part of the Opequon settlement, signed a similar note to Harris for £2 4s. 7d. It was during this time that Ulrich Poker was making trips to Pennsylvania carrying deerskins north for Thomas Williams and bringing back both men's and women's saddles. As previously mentioned, Poker traded one of these saddles to peddler Lyman Lipman in 1747.[68]

Trade eastward from Opequon across the Blue Ridge flowed chiefly to Fredericksburg and Falmouth, two fall-line towns that had emerged as the most significant deepwater ports for the Shenandoah Valley in the late 1730s. Known solely as a tobacco warehouse on Hunting Creek in the 1740s, Alexandria only later became the primary market for Shenandoah Valley flour. Nonetheless, Scottish merchant John Carlyle was dealing in tobacco there by 1745. In its dependence upon tobacco, the fall-line trade differed from the exchanges that took place between Opequon and Pennsylvania. In one example in the late 1740s and early 1750s, John Wood, a carpenter in Frederick County, acquired a plane iron, gunpowder, pepper, broadcloth, linen, other textiles, buttons, thread, a hat, socks, cinnamon, rum, salt, and sugar from Andrew Cochrane, and Daniel and Alex Campbell, among other Falmouth merchants.

Cochrane and the Campbells were members of Glasgow merchant families represented in Falmouth by factors. Wood's credit with these men came from numbered hogsheads at the Falmouth tobacco warehouse. Similarly, Thomas Rutherford acquired sugar, gloves, sheeting, linen, rum, and "Smiths work" from William Ramsay with credit for "1 Hhd. tobo. at Huntg Crck" in 1749. Ramsay and Carlyle were partners. Benjamin Borden Jr., in a third example, found his debt to Robert Shedden for a large variety of hardwares and dry goods acquired from May 1742 to November 1743 only partially offset by tobacco in the Falmouth warehouse. Shedden was a factor for Robert and Thomas Dunlop, "Marchts. in Glasgow."[69]

The activities of Robert Shedden demonstrate how goods moved across the considerable distance between the Shenandoah Valley and the port of Falmouth. The eight bushels of wheat, sixty pounds of cheese, and thirty pounds of butter that John Bazier brought for exchange in Shedden's Falmouth store provide a good indication of what Shenandoah Valley farm households were producing for the long-distance trade. Peddler Richard Cronk also dealt with Shedden. Three months after having received his peddler's license from the Frederick County Court in mid-April 1744, Cronk obtained a sizeable stock in trade, which Shedden secured with a note for £51 8s. 6d. Cronk was also in debt for £16 1s. 9d. to Daniel Campbell. Why Cronk might have failed to meet his obligations to Shedden and Campbell is partly explained by Cronk's dealings with Frederick County settler Robert Lowther. In August 1744 Lowther acquired a gown, linen, powder, lead, other textiles, and liquor from Cronk, who had just obtained forty-two gallons of ardent spirits from Opequon miller and distiller John Neil. In exchange Lowther gave Cronk deerskins, 4d. in cash, 2s. 6d. "due to me upon the acct of Jonathn Coburn," and "my right of a Certain place on pattisons Creek whereon I intended to Live and the Labor which I had done thereon." Lowther's eventual default on the balance due Cronk helped force the peddler into litigation with Falmouth creditors. Although Cronk's affairs went poorly and he spent much time in court, his activities demonstrate how an exchange economy could tie Opequon households to entrepôts in eastern Virginia and how goods could be distributed without a central place for exchange at Opequon.[70]

The exchange economy generated no centralizing forces on the regional landscape. Economic exchange, like the Newtonian world, was essentially static. The balanced entry of debits and credits—sometimes extended over great space—and the periodic rendering of accounts—sometimes stretching across long spans of time—permitted individuals to view the intricate web of relations composing their community as suspended in equilibrium. Change or growth was not intrinsic to the system. Consider profit and its accumulation, widely regarded as a motive force of economic change. Double-entry book-keeping allowed for the calculation of profit or loss, but the maintenance of the necessary real and nominal accounts was rare, and the single entry of debits and credits neither segregated nor aggregated income and expenditures. The sum of balances due as the total excess of debits over credits could reflect profit, but no accounts yielded any evidence of such a calculation. James Wood certainly did not attempt it in his account book. Moreover, no one appeared to reckon all their accounts at the same time or even at regular intervals.[71]

If economic growth or its geographic concentration reflects the aggregation of profits over time, then keeping accounts at Opequon and the exchange economy it sustained did not nurture a world view in which production and trade generated new wealth. Total wealth in the economy was instead regarded as a constant. For one individual or family to amass great wealth by maximizing profits would leave less wealth for others in the community, threatening them with incompetence and dependence, if not suffering and starvation. Distinctions of wealth certainly existed in exchange economies, but affluence derived less from money than from the extent of credit relations and the degree to which obligations could be translated into political influence or conspicuous display in a house, personal dress, or refined entertainment. Profits, moreover, as the fixed sum of debts due meant little in this world in which relations of debit and credit were so elastic. Entrepreneurs were regarded with deep suspicion, and few people would have seen much advantage in concentrating economic activities in any one particular place. Peter Tostee could operate stores just as effectively on the South Branch of the Potomac as in the county town, and Richard Cronk could roam the countryside conducting much the same type of trade as merchants like Tostee did in stores.

This is not to say that the fledgling town taking shape along the wagon road in Frederick County was insignificant. With the platting of its grid and the erection of a courthouse, jail, whipping post, stocks, pillory, and dunking stool, it began to take on the features of an English shire town. Men and women in households scattered across the Opequon settlement would have looked to this town often in their lives. Many journeyed there to prosecute or defend themselves in a suit for debt or to register a deed, serve on a jury, or present a charge on the county levy. While in town these men and women no doubt did business with Benjamin Perreyra or Peter Tostee, got a hat from William Dobbins, or refreshed themselves at John Hopes's tavern. The power of the court, in turn, extended from the town deep into the countryside through orders to build roads, licenses to operate ferries, or writs served for one purpose or another on various people. The importance of the court in protecting property or regulating criminal and civil strife cannot be underestimated. Registering a deed guaranteed that the power of the state and the common law could be brought to bear in defense of a property owner's interests.

Yet what Perreyra, Tostee, Dobbins, and Hopes did in town could just as readily be pursued in the countryside, as the activities of numerous individuals demonstrated. The lifeblood of the economy flowed through the thousands of exchanges that went on across the landscape as families sought from neighbors what they needed to live competently. Thus Frederick Town, later Winchester, was poorly integrated into the countryside. Or, perhaps more accurately, the town functioned simply as an extension of the countryside. Within two decades of settlement at Opequon, a town and country landscape had not yet taken shape. The forces that would call this landscape into being have to be sought, not in the exchange economy that created the countryside or in the drive for competence that shaped its landscape, but in the large-scale movements of empires and the strategic interests of global conflict. It was these movements, after all, that had created Opequon in the first place.

Chapter 6

From Strategic Place to Central Place

IN THE FALL OF 1753 Winchester was only seven years old. Its charter, issued the year before, had given the fledgling community its name. This legislative act had also called for the original grid of two cross streets and twenty-six lots to be expanded by fifty-four new lots on streets laid off to the east and north of the main street, which connected to the Philadelphia Wagon Road. Each of the eighty half-acre town lots was linked to a five-acre outlot, where self-sufficient townspeople could cultivate gardens and keep livestock. Lord Fairfax, proprietor of the Northern Neck and now proprietor of the town, issued patents for all the lots, dispelling any cloud on their title.[1]

Thus the legal and spatial order of European settlement began to impress itself upon the land. Life in the town assumed the rhythms of an agricultural world, even if the town economy was undeveloped and poorly integrated with the ways in which people made a living in the countryside. Several hundred men, women, and children lived in the "poorly built" houses Moravian visitors had described. Many of these dwellings were log—a crib enclosing a room or two. Some were stone. The county court met regularly in a courthouse strategically located near the town's central crossroads. Adjoining the courthouse stood the jail, the instruments of eighteenth-century punishment, an unfinished Anglican church, several taverns, and the shops of artisans and merchants. On an average day, little would appear to be happening in this town. Opequon farmers David Vance, Jost Hite, or John Littler might be stopping in Peter Tostee's store or John Hopes's tavern. William Dobbins might be working away on a hat for James Wood. A stone chimney might be rising under the hand of mason Duncan O'Gullion. Perhaps Isaac Parkins was still pulling up stumps from the street. But the unhurried, desultory life of the town was about to change abruptly and dramatically.[2]

Herald of change, Andrew Montour appeared in Winchester about three o'clock on Monday afternoon, September 10, 1753. He was one of those men frequently found on the early American frontier who moved easily between the worlds of Native Americans and European settlers. His French-Canadian mother had often lived among the Iroquois, and his father was a Seneca. Montour possessed a "countenance . . . decidedly European" and could be seen wearing a broadcloth coat, a scarlet waistcoat, breeches, shoes, stockings, and a hat. But he painted his face like his father's people and hung his ears with brass pendants. The government of Pennsylvania employed him as an interpreter with the Indians because he could broker relations among peoples of vastly different cultures. More than a year earlier at Logstown, near the forks of the Ohio, Montour had helped Virginia and Pennsylvania negotiate a treaty with the Ohio Iroquois confirming the land cessions made at Lancaster eight years earlier. He came now in the company of ninety-eight Delawares, Shawnees, Wyandots, and Twightwees, including women and children.[3]

The mass of visitors was four miles away and would be arriving shortly. They came on the invitation of Virginia governor Robert Dinwiddie to resolve certain issues left hanging at Logstown, such as the construction of a "strong house," or fort, in the Ohio Country, and to answer the governor's plea to assist Virginia in ousting the French from this region and opening parts of it to Virginia settlers. For their part, the Indians also wanted to be rid of the French, but they desired assurances that Anglo-American settlers would stay away as well. Awaiting them—for more than three weeks—was William Fairfax, the governor's commissioner for the negotiations. At Montour's arrival, Fairfax's son, George William, commander of the county militia, hastily assembled fifty of his men, who, "after being Exercis'd, were drawn up in a Line at the North end of the Town." Lord Fairfax, also in town for the negotiations, soon headed off to greet the Indians with such commissioners as James Wood, William Cocks, in whose tavern some of the negotiations were to be held, and John Carlyle, the Alexandria trader who was also son-in-law to William Fairfax. The commission, reading like a who's who of the frontier, included the experienced traders, negotiators, and diplomats George Groghan, William Trent, and Christopher Gist.[4]

At about six that evening the converging parties met on the wagon road north of town. The Indian greeting of a musket volley was followed by the European custom of shaking hands all around. Together Indians and whites walked to Winchester, where the militia received them with another volley and the visitors were ushered to quarters in a "shell of a Building formerly design'd for a Church, & which was rough Floor'd on that Occasion." Speaking for the governor of Virginia, William Fairfax welcomed the guests and, with all the niceties of frontier diplomacy, offered condolences for their recent losses at the hands of the French. Through Montour's translation, Scarouady, also known as Monacatoocha, an Oneida headman and leader of the Mingo Iroquois of the Ohio Country, returned the welcome and expressed the hope that Fairfax would "open His Heart, & express his Mind freely" in the negotiations to follow. The Englishmen then "drank a good Health, to the Six Nations & their Allies," and the Indians, in turn, toasted "prosperity to . . . the King of Great Britain, & the English Nation." Bidding "each Other a good Night," the hosts departed and the visitors settled down to a smoke and dinner.[5]

The negotiations at the courthouse with private sessions at Cocks's tavern concluded on Monday, September 17. In the end, neither side received the desired assurances. As William Fairfax would write to Governor Dinwiddie, the "Indians did not possitively, in Answer to my speechs, give a Concession to the Lands on Ohio." The native headmen had warned the Virginia commissioners "not to let suffer Your People to settle on Our Lands at this troublesome Time." Only when they could successfully "drive the French away quite out of Our Country" would the Indians "consider what to say to you about the Lands." All trade, moreover, would have to come through their hands, and they would deal only with Montour, Trent, and Gist. Alcohol would be forbidden. "On the full Moon in May next" both sides promised to meet again.[6]

The Indians clearly saw themselves as independent sovereigns in the Ohio Country, but their commitment to meet again at Winchester emphasizes the geographical significance of their encounter with the Virginia commissioners. In 1752 they had refused to go to this frontier settlement, asserting that "we expect you will send our Father's [Governor Dinwiddie's] Speeches to us here" at Logstown. Undaunted, Dinwiddie wrote to Thomas Cresap and William Trent the following winter that he had sent word to "Onondagoa to get some of their Chiefs to meet and receive the Pres'ts in May next at Winchester." By September 1753 Winchester had become a strategic place in the landscape of Anglo-Indian affairs, and the Indians came. Knowing that the growing conflict in the Ohio Valley required dramatic action, Dinwiddie called for all Native American groups bordering the British colonies from New York to Georgia to attend the spring 1754 meeting in Winchester and sign a "proper Treaty," which, as he declared to the Board of Trade, would be a "very great national Service." But Dinwiddie waited alone in Winchester for sixteen days the following May while the Indians, as he put it, "c'd not properly leave their people" because the "French had invaded and taken Possession of their Lands." In an act of duplicity escaping Dinwiddie, Virginia forces had also invaded the Ohio Country and engaged the French in an action widely regarded as the opening volley of the Seven Years' War. The third of the projected Winchester meetings was to be held in April 1755 for a treaty between the still-warring Catawbas and the Six Nations. The ill-fated British General Edward Braddock, bound for Fort Duquesne, showed up, but there were no Indians.[7]

Although war preempted negotiations at Winchester, Governor Dinwiddie had succeeded in establishing the town as a center for frontier diplomacy. Later he would work with George Washington, colonel of the Virginia Regiment, to fortify the town and locate the regiment's headquarters there. Thus, before Winchester would serve as a market town, it was a garrison town. It was as a strategic place that Winchester began to function as a town—that town life grew distinct from country life and a town economy emerged. The town population grew under the protection of the garrison, but, more importantly, the inputs to the regional economy due to regimental spending and then to the expenditures of the British army headquartered at Fort Pitt transformed the town into a magnet for the merchant trade and thereby linked its commerce firmly to the Atlantic economy. As the second phase of landscape evolution drew to a close, the long, slow transition from an exchange economy to a commercial economy began. In this manner Dinwiddie extended the process initiated by his predecessors, in which the spatial ordering of the backcountry from settlement, to county formation, and to town founding would proceed in response to imperial conflicts with Native American and other European powers. This larger story—an imperial story—can be picked up again at the time when the court of Frederick County first met, the town of Winchester was surveyed, and England declared war on France in an earlier conflict.

· ⚶ ·

The founding of town and county in the Shenandoah Valley occurred just as the focus of English ambitions and anxieties shifted to the Ohio Country. In April 1745, when the Virginia Council approved James Patton's request for two hundred thousand acres on the New River—where he would "settle one family for each 1,000 acres"—Williamsburg made it clear that it was granting land as one way of fighting the French. The War of the Austrian Succession—King George's War in the colonies—ended in 1748, but in an atmosphere of continuing tension with the French and the Ohio Indians, the Council in 1754 opened millions of acres mostly west of the Allegheny Front to Virginia settlers. Most significant for the story of town formation in the Shenandoah Valley was the famous grant to the Ohio Company.[8]

The exact origins of the Ohio Company are not known, but the speculative interests of its founders were clearly clothed in the imperial purposes for which it received the king's endorsement. Recall that in October 1747, well before the end of the war with France, Thomas Lee and eleven others had petitioned the governor and Council for two hundred thousand acres of western lands. Lee was president of the Council, but more important, he had represented Virginia at the Lancaster Treaty and the cession of western lands by the Six Nations. To the king, Lee and company represented their cause as one that would "enlarge our commerce, . . . and extend your majesties empire in America." In 1749 the company received all the Ohio land it wanted with more to come if it built a fort and settled one hundred families in seven years.[9]

Never effectively occupying its lands, the Ohio Company proved more successful as a trading company. Within days of receiving news of the crown's pending approval of the company's proposal, its members ordered trade goods valued at £2,000 from London and appointed Hugh Parker as "their Factor at the Ohio," with instructions to "cause the necessary Roads to be made and the Houses to be built for carrying on the said Trade to the best advantage." Joined by experienced frontier trader Thomas Cresap, Parker purchased land along the upper Potomac and, during the winter of 1749–1750, constructed the "New Store" at the mouth of Wills Creek, "the most convenient place to settle the Factory and begin the Trade." The company opened its books there the following summer. From a forward store at Rock Creek it shipped goods by a road to Conococheague Creek, then by water to Wills Creek. By August 1752 the company had erected a second store on Redstone Creek and blazed a path to the Monongahela, where Saltzburg, a town of two hundred one-acre lots, was planned for Swiss-German immigrants. Despite royal instructions, the fort at the forks of the Ohio never entered into the company's plans, and it began to rise only in 1754, under the governor's order to Virginia militia forces.[10]

By the early 1750s, then, the Ohio Company had succeeded in establishing trade links to the Ohio Valley and initiating exchanges with Native Americans and European settlers, importing textiles and manufactured goods, and exporting skins and furs. By developing trade in advance of settlement, the Ohio Company penetrated the North American interior, establishing commercial hubs at Wills and Redstone Creeks and a possible third, on the Monongahela River. Enduring settlements at Cumberland (Md.), Brownsville (Pa.), and Pittsburgh eventually emerged at these sites, and in time, early trade routes became major commercial arteries, such as the National Road. This new geography would have a profound impact on existing settlement patterns in the Shenandoah Valley. Noting that "the Trade in Beeves Butter and Cheese which the Inhabitants to the Westward of the great Mountains have generally for want of good Roads carried on at Philadelphia," the Virginia Assembly appropriated funds for "clearing Roads over the Great Mountains," thus establishing commercial ties with eastern Virginia. But it was the war provoked by the company's Ohio land claims that would realign the settlement geography of the backcountry and focus it increasingly on the town of Winchester as its most important strategic place.[11]

Late in 1747 the Ohio tribes dispatched a delegation to Philadelphia announcing a new Indian alliance against the French, the establishment of council fires at Logstown on the Ohio River below the forks, and their desire for aid in ousting French intruders from Indian lands. Less than a year later at Logstown, Pennsylvanians guaranteed the Indians their continued friendship. But soon after the 1748 Treaty of Aix-la-Chapelle, which ended the War of the Austrian Succession, the French governor-general proclaimed that, "though at peace [,] every attempt of the English to settle" west of the Alleghenies must be stopped. The following summer Captain Pierre-Joseph Céloron de Blainville marched south to bury lead plates along the Ohio, proclaiming French dominion and seeding both fear and anger among the Indians. Shawnees and Delawares, however, responded to the encroachments of the Ohio Company with equal displeasure, which Pennsylvania trader George Groghan credited to the "alarm that Mr. Cresap & Mr. Parker Spread amongst ye Ingans." Two expeditions by Christopher Gist into the Ohio Country on behalf of the company between 1750 and 1752 did nothing to calm Indian fears, nor did the Ohio Iroquois's confirmation of the Lancaster Treaty land cessions. The Ohio Indians would likely have maintained a neutrality from which they could play imperial powers off against each other much as the Iroquois had done since the early 1700s, but they were caught in a vise. Between 1752 and 1754 both the French and the English sent troops to the Ohio forks, which led directly to the Seven Years' War (fig. 6.1). These were the developments, then, that intensified forces of geographical centrality in the Shenandoah Valley and stimulated the process of town formation.[12]

· ☙ ·

At this point a remarkable young man stepped into history. His impact on the founding of a new nation out of English colonies in the New World would be incalculable, but more immediately, the events in which he was involved and his influence upon them would play a major role in shaping the landscape of the Shenandoah Valley. George Washington was a youth of sixteen when he first crossed the Blue Ridge with a Fairfax surveying party and visited Winchester for a "very agreeable regale." So taken was he with the country he later described as the "finest part of Virginia; plenteously filled with all kinds of Provision," and so convinced that his own path to reputation and fortune lay in the West, that in the four years following this jaunt Washington qual-

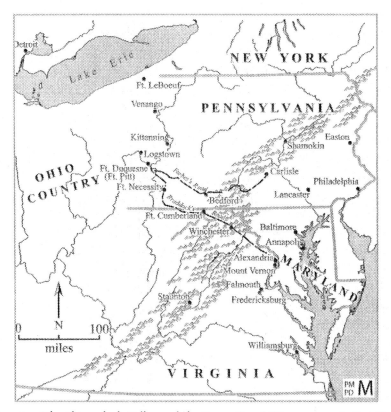

FIG. 6.1. The Shenandoah Valley and the Seven Years' War, 1753–1758. Key North American locations in a global war that profoundly affected the Shenandoah Valley covered the vast region from Virginia north to the Great Lakes and east to the Delaware River.

ified as a surveyor and returned to western Virginia on numerous surveying expeditions. Bragging that a "Dubbleloon is my constant gain every Day that the Weather will permit my going out" to survey, Washington prospered and invested his earnings in land. By the time he was twenty, he owned 2,315 acres of prime farmland in the lower Shenandoah Valley.[13]

In 1752 Washington left surveying to build a military career. He soon received an appointment from Governor Dinwiddie as an adjutant for the militia responsible for training officers in several southern Virginia counties. Meanwhile, he was closely following events in the Ohio Valley, and late in 1753 he learned that the governor was about to warn the French to leave the region. He wanted to be the bearer of that warning. With the governor's approval, the ambitious young man set out for the West and assumed his role in the dramatic imperial struggles taking place there. He proved to be no more successful in ordering the French out of the Ohio Valley than Edward Braddock would be in driving them out by force of arms. But Washington's heroism in saving the tattered remnants of Braddock's army after its disastrous defeat on the banks of the Monongahela River in July 1755 earned him the governor's appointment as colonel of the Virginia Regiment the following August. The twenty-two year old was charged with defending the frontiers of Virginia from the combined forces of the French and the Ohio Indians.[14]

Dinwiddie's orders to Washington—"As Winchester is the nighest Place of rendezvous to the Country which is exposed to the Enemy, You are hereby required to make that Your head Quarters"—made it clear that Winchester lay at the nexus of the backcountry conflict. The young officer reached the town on September 15, 1755, but finding no troops to command, he set off to review fortifications to the south and report to the governor on their status. But news soon reached him from his second in command, Adam Stephen, that "matters [around Winchester] are in the most deplorable Situation." About one hundred fifty Indians had invaded the country, spreading "desolation and murders heightened with all Barbarous Circumstances, and unheard of Instances of Cruelty." Stephen's warning that "unless Relief is Sent to the Back inhabitants None will Stay on this Side . . . [of] Winchester" brought Washington flying back to the town, where he witnessed the "greatest hurry and confusion" among the "back Inhabitants flocking in, and those of the Town removing out, which I have prevented as far as it was in my power."[15]

This was the chaos of frontier warfare. There were no defined battlefields, no trained troops to form up and march about, no centers of command or supply, no place to fall back to, no objective on which to advance. On the evening of his return, for example, there "arrivd an express just spent with fatigue and fear, reporting that a Party of Indians were seen at [a nearby plantation] . . . abt 12 Miles off, and that the Inhabitants were flying in the most promiscuous manner from their dwellings." The young commander leapt into action, ordering the "Town Guards" reinforced, Isaac Parkins's militia company readied, some fresh recruits armed, scouts dispatched "to see if they coud discover the Numbers & Motion of the Indian's," and all preparations made for a morning foray to meet the enemy. Early the next day, however, "arriv'd a Second Express ten times more terrified than the former; with information that the Indians had got within four Miles of the Town and were killing and destroying all before them." Washington quickly collected a force of forty-one men and marched out, only to find that three drunken soldiers "firing their Pistols, and uttering the most unheard off Imprecation's" had caused the alarm. Feeling no doubt relieved and chagrined, the young commander must have seen that this was no way to fight a war.[16]

The people Washington defended were part of the problem. To this young commander and the colonial authorities who stood behind him, the war was an imperial venture to oust the French from the Ohio Valley. The men and women who had been engaged for upwards of twenty years improving the land and building their homes, however, saw this as a distant concern. At the very least war could threaten their competency and at worst destroy the world they had worked so hard to build. The immediate danger of Indian raids aside, the impressment of vital supplies or the absence of a man on militia duty at harvest time could imperil a family's ability to survive a hard winter. In October 1755, for instance, Washington wanted to take the offensive "immediately at the head of some Militia to put a stop to the Ravages of the Enemy," but fewer than twenty-five militiamen turned out, "choosing as they say to die with their Wives and Family's." The priorities and values of one "Noble Captain" rang loud and clear when he proclaimed that "his Wife, Family, and Corn was at stake, so were those of his Soldrs therefore it was not possible for him to come." Frustrated, an uncomprehending Washington complained that the "timidity of the Inhabitants of this Country is to be equalled by nothing but their perverseness."[17]

During the ensuing months Washington struggled, often against insurmountable obstacles, to bring order and system to frontier defense. The ranks of the Virginia Regiment had to be brought up to strength, and its commander dispatched recruiters to attract young men to the service. He called for a revised colonial militia law giving him power to discipline raw and recalcitrant recruits. Recognizing that "without Indians to oppose Indians, we may expect but small success," Washington pressured the governor to ally southern Indians such as the Cherokees to the English cause. The young officer, endeavoring to deploy what troops were under his command as effectively as possible, ordered his rangers to repair to strategic locations and build a "Quadrangular Fort of Ninety feet, with Bastions."[18]

Because his thinking reflected sound military practice, Washington got his way in most things. In April 1757 the Burgesses set the complement of the Virginia Regiment at 1,000 men in ten companies. Although he could report 950 troops on duty the following summer, Washington struggled throughout the war to fill the regiment's ranks. In October 1755 the Assembly amended the militia law to impose the death penalty for mutiny, desertion, defying orders, or striking a superior. Despite deficiencies in the law, an optimistic Washington could advise his second in command that "we now have it in our Power to enforce obedience." Alliances with Indians soon followed. By June 1756 Governor Dinwiddie had secured the support of Catawbas and Cherokees, and the next spring Virginia officers were leading raiding parties of fifteen to twenty

Indians. Four hundred Indian allies camped in Winchester a year later on their way to fight in the Ohio Country.[19]

Throughout his command Washington wished most of all to take the offensive and bring the Virginia Regiment to bear on Ohio Indian villages and the French "intruder's" fortifications. The Virginia burgesses and governor, however, had other notions about how best to secure the settled plantation areas of the colony. When Washington visited Williamsburg to confer with the governor in late March 1756, he learned that the "sentiments of the House of Burgesses . . . [favored] a chain of Forts . . . erected upon our Frontiers for the defence of the people." "This expedient, in my opinion," Washington responded, "will never, without an inconceivable number of men, answer their expectations." The cost of constructing these forts fifteen to eighteen miles apart—a day's march—and garrisoning them with eighty to a hundred men would be too great. From a strategic perspective, moreover, "our Frontiers are so extensive, that were the Enemy to attack us on the one side; before the Troops on the other could get to their assistance, they might over-run and destroy half the Country." Nonetheless, the House of Burgesses approved the chain of forts scheme that March.[20]

Recognizing that a campaign in the Ohio Country now lay beyond the means and the will of the colony and that a series of small fortifications could never by themselves answer Virginia's defense needs, Washington began to argue that "it is absolutely necessary to have a large Magazine, to supply the different Forts with Stores." The location for this stronghold should be Winchester (fig. 6.2). In lobbying vigorously for a regimental garrison at Winchester and characterizing it, "though trifling in itself, [as] a place of the utmost importance to the Country in general," Washington understood that the town developed during the critical period of the 1750s as a strategic place before it became a central place. "It commands the communication from East to West, as well as from North to South," he continued in communiqués to the governor and the speaker of the House of Burgesses. "For at this place do almost all the Roads centre; and secures the Great Roads of one half of our Frontiers, to the Markets of the neighbouring Colonies as well as those on Rappahannock and Potomack." Communications as well as transportation defined Winchester's "centrical situation," as "it is also conveniently situated for procuring the earliest intelligence when the Enemy is about." It was a place of refuge, for the "People, so soon as they are alarmed, immediately fly inwards" and the "men would . . . immediately lodge their families here." Moreover, it "lies convenient to the Inhabitants, for raising the Militia," Washington concluded.[21]

On May 3, Governor Dinwiddie presented Washington's argument to the House of Burgesses, which was about to send the legislation calling for the

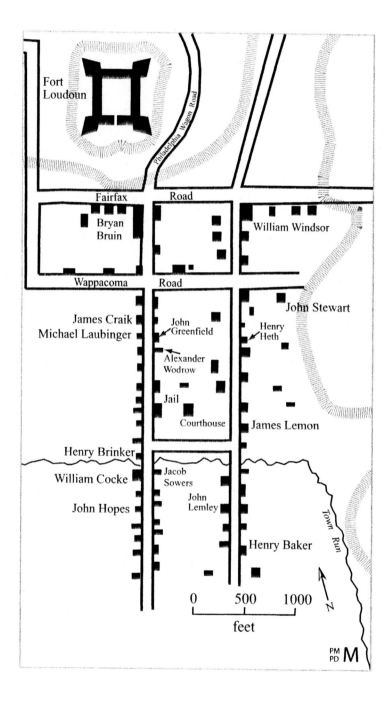

Fort
Loudoun

Philadelphia Wagon Road

Fairfax   Road

Bryan
Bruin   William Windsor

Wappacoma   Road

James Craik   John Stewart
Michael Laubinger   John
                         Greenfield   Henry
                                                 Heth
                         Alexander
                         Wodrow

                         Jail

                         Courthouse   James Lemon

Henry Brinker

William Cocke   Jacob
                        Sowers

John Hopes   John
                        Lemley

                                        Henry Baker

                                                 Town Run

0   500   1000
                              N
        feet

PM
PD M

chain of forts to the Council. Resolving that "a strong Fort be with all Expedition and Dispatch erected at *Winchester,*" the House immediately appropriated £1,000 for its construction. That same day the governor wrote to his commander: "I approve, for the Reasons You assign, the fortifying of Winchester." Three weeks later work on the fort was under way, and in June Washington could report to William Fairfax that "our Soldiers labour on the public works with great spirit and constancy, from Monday morning 'till Sunday night."[22]

Fort Loudoun was by all measures a massive undertaking (fig. 6.3); nothing on the Virginia frontier matched it in size or effort. Situated on a hill to the north of Winchester so as to put a bend in the Philadelphia Wagon Road, the fort commanded a field of fire directly down the town's main street. In design it resembled Washington's quadrangular forts put up by the rangers, but it was much larger, with 240-foot curtain walls connecting four bastions in a square. Constructed of logs with earthen infill and surrounded by a ditch, it safeguarded a barracks for 450 men. As Washington himself said, it was truly a "public works" because its construction and garrisoning had a massive impact on the economy of the town and surrounding countryside. Not only did building it channel considerable sums of money into the hands of local artisans, but provisioning the soldiers who occupied it also stimulated the local economy.[23]

By June 1, 1756, Washington had formed a company of artificers under Captain William Peachy with a complement of more than a hundred men to work on the fort. They received sixpence "extraordinary" pay a day and, "as an encouragement to them to behave well, and to attend diligently to their Duty, . . . so long as they deserve it, four gallons of rum, made into punch, every day." From the garrison, moreover, Peachy could "draw out as many men daily . . . as can be employed to advantage." This entire force, however, could hardly keep up with the work, and in late July Washington issued the following call: "As this public work is intended for the general good of the Country, it is hoped no other arguments need to be used to induce the towns-

Facing page

FIG. 6.2. Winchester during the Seven Years' War. Fort Loudoun, George Washington's headquarters and garrison for the Virginia Regiment, dominated Winchester and the surrounding countryside from a hill to the north of the town. Artisans and merchants lived and worked in a variety of structures lining adjacent streets. Based on Andreas Wiederholdt, Map of Winchester, 1777, Dewey manuscript 973.3 R723.3, Rare Book and Manuscript Library, University of Pennsylvania.

people to contribute their assistance, than the singular advantages which must inevitably arise to this place in particular, both now and hereafter."[24]

Men working for the Virginia Regiment earned good wages. Even before construction on Fort Loudoun began, Washington ordered "carpenters and all the Soldiers off Duty, [to] set to work to-morrow morning by day-break, on the Breast-Work begun at the Court-House." A few days later civilian contractor Daniel Hiver was paid more than £6 10s. for overseeing the effort. Within a week or so of receiving Governor Dinwiddie's order to proceed with Fort Loudoun, Washington had engaged seventy carpenters from the militia to work at the sixpence extra per day. Three days later the commander wrote to Adam Stephen to send down "all the men that are really skilled in masonry." Experienced masons received five shillings a day plus their diet. Smiths, too, were needed not only for fashioning hardware on the fort but also for repairing arms. With regular employment and five shillings a day, smiths such as Joshua Baker could earn more than £100 in eight months. From August to December 1757 John Trigg collected £121 18s. 7½d., and between October 1755 and June of the following year, nine blacksmiths received similar payments from the Virginia regiment. Some, such as John Harrow, had been a part of the Opequon settlement for decades, while Joshua Baker and William Mungar were newcomers who stayed and prospered in the community. In addition to paying wages, the Virginia Regiment also purchased materials, compensating Alex Kennedy £24 for a ton of iron in December 1755 and Isaac Riddle and John Vauts £44 10s. for plank two years later.[25]

· ✤ ·

Legislation calling for the construction of forts along the Virginia frontier stipulated that labor, services, and all goods be compensated in treasury notes. These would "pass as a lawful tender in payment of any debt, duty, or demand whatsoever." What these notes accomplished, in effect, was to release a great flow of money into the exchange economy at Opequon, an economy that had worked perfectly well for decades with very little cash. This infusion then began to alter the shape of the community and the exchange economy that underlay it. Because accounts were kept over long periods of time and settled ir-

Facing page

FIG. 6.3. Fort Loudoun, drawn by George Washington. Trained as a surveyor, George Washington made meticulous drawings for Fort Loudoun in Winchester. The construction of a fort of this size and complexity contributed significantly to economic growth in the town. Plan of Fort Loudoun, [1756], Library of Congress, Washington, D.C.

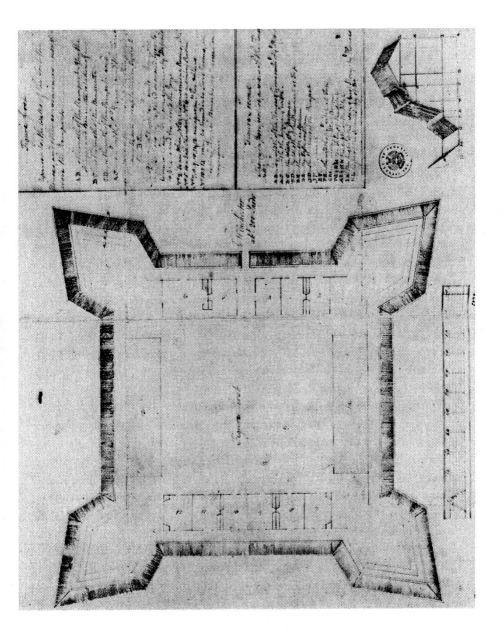

regularly, trade depended on trust within a community of people who knew about each other's assets and ability to repay debts. Strangers in such a world created problems, which could only be alleviated by the anonymity of money. Cash, therefore, did speed the rate of exchange, but there is no evidence that people at Opequon hoarded it as accumulated wealth, which was still best expressed as accrued obligations and the various forms of property into which debts could be converted. Whatever appearance wealth took, however, it could now be acquired more rapidly by laboring at Fort Loudoun or trading with the regiment. New money and more money also affected the geography of settlement. Winchester became the locus of exchange for merchants who depended for trade on the accumulation of money. Since the founding of the town, men such as Benjamin Perreyra and Peter Tostee had traded a wide variety of services and goods, including cash, for what were often simply called sundries—dry goods and hardware, or textiles, ceramics, and tools. Many of these items were imported from Europe and brought to the Virginia backcountry through Philadelphia or the growing river ports of Alexandria, Fredericksburg, and Falmouth. Merchants acquired their stock in trade there as debits, but in the long-distance economy, credits in a bushel of wheat or a day's labor were hard to convey in return. Here money was at a premium. To balance their own accounts, merchants accumulated money as it was traded in the exchange economy. And where it was traded most rapidly was, of course, Winchester. Simply put, money made the town grow.[26]

How much new money flowed into the exchange economy at Opequon? We know something about how much a day's work was traditionally worth from debt suits in the county court. Recall that John Russell and John McCormick worked for each other in the 1740s at two shillings a day credited in their accounts. Mathias Ardis received the same rate from Isaac Hite in March 1747. For stints of farm work ranging from one-half to six and one-half days, Ardis was credited two shillings a day but received bread and butter, meat, corn, liquor, nails, flax seed, salt, wheat, a cow and calf, and one mare in return. Skilled labor brought better returns. Crediting George Brown at the rate of three shillings a day, the mason Duncan O'Gullion actually compensated his workman with items such as three and one-half yards of linen, four and one-half yards of cotton, a pair of shoes, and a bottle of liquor. Even when he worked on his own account "Stoning One Cellar" and pointing a foundation for Benjamin Perreyra, Brown received the same daily rate. Three shillings for a day's work was about as good as it got. Carpenters received 2s. 7½d. per day; harvest work was compensated at rates varying from 1s. 6d. to 2s. 6d. per day, and general farm labor brought as little as 6s. ¼d. daily. By these measures even the sixpence extra pay a common soldier received for working on Fort Loudoun was considerable, and artisans collected two to three times what the exchange economy could afford them. Moreover, the regiment paid in money, not in credits redeemable in the indefinite future.[27]

. ⚓ .

Money flowed into Opequon settlement from the Virginia Regiment through many channels other than payments to workers or artisans. Meeting soldiers' needs, both official and unofficial, generated considerable economic activity. The number of men stationed at Fort Loudoun is difficult to determine—as it was for their officers—but Captain William Peachy's artificers numbered 127 by July 1756, when work on the fort picked up. But the next month Washington reported that his strength in Winchester including "Drafts" had reached 160, and in his official return for January 1, 1757, the young officer indicated that there were 141 men under his command in the town. Thus the complement of the Virginia Regiment at Fort Loudoun throughout the conflict can safely be placed somewhere between one hundred and two hundred men. At times there would have been more, because in June 1757 Washington wrote the governor that they were "indefatigably assiduous in forwarding the workmen: *All* work from day-light to day-light, sundays not excepted; and but one hour in the day allowed for eating, &c. But it is impossible that so small a number of men as we had and now have at work, can be imagined sufficient to complete such a vastly heavy piece of work, in a much greater time than you mention. Nay, 300 men could hardly finish it by next October."[28]

Feeding and provisioning several hundred men was a sizeable task. In a measure of their needs George Washington in June 1757 instructed the commander of one of the outlying forts to "take care that *only* one pound of Flour, and the like quantity of Meat be delivered to each man per day." At that rate, feeding the troops at Fort Loudoun would require upwards of five thousand pounds of these basic foodstuffs every month. Most of the provisions for the regiment came through the office of the regimental commissary and were gathered throughout Virginia. Early in the conflict John Carlyle served as commissary. He was followed first by Charles Dick and then by Thomas Walker. The commissary system was later abandoned in favor of contracting with merchants to supply troops by region. In October 1757, for instance, Alexandria merchant William Ramsay agreed to secure provisions for the regiment at the rate of sixpence per day for each person, including washerwomen. Other examples give a sense of the scale at which the Virginia Regiment drew provisions from the countryside and replaced grain and livestock in the field with money in the farmer's hand. Late in September 1755 Washington purchased 650 "fine Beeves" in Hampshire and Augusta Counties to be delivered at Fort Cumberland by November 1, giving ten shillings per hundredweight. Later that year the commander ordered Thomas Walker to "set up Advertisements, at all the most public places convenient to the Fort, for the Inhabitants to bring in all the Pork they can spare, and that they will be allowed the market price; and ready money for any Quantity." From November 1755 to March 1757 one Augusta County commissary paid out more than £261 for 8,598 pounds of beef, sixty-two beef cattle, 2,518 pounds of pork, 4,817 pounds of flour, and smaller quantities of beans, potatoes, and salt.[29]

Local households profited from the needs of the Virginia Regiment in other ways as well. On June 26, 1756, for instance, Samuel Pritchard, who lived along the drains of Opequon Creek about six miles south of Winchester, received £14 6s. on "his Acct of Hay & Oats for the Troop." Winchester tavern keeper Henry Heth provided pasturage for horses in 1756. More money, however, was to be made by hiring horses to the regiment, as Heth did in May 1758 for the purpose of carrying a dispatch. Other well-known men and women at Opequon received considerable sums for horse hire: David Glass and Nathaniel Cartmell were compensated £3 15s. each in 1757, and Lewis Stephens, William Castleman, Isaac Hollingsworth, and Margaret Rodgers collected between 10s. and £2 for the services of their horses. Others provided the regiment with clothing, and Godfrey Humbert was wealthier by ten shillings for "making a Coffin for a Soldier." James Allen supplied a military chest for £2 7s. 3d. In January 1756 George Washington wrote commissary officer Thomas Walker that provisions were to be drawn for three washerwomen for each company in the regiment "on condition of their behaving well, and washing for the men." The commander allowed for twelve women at Fort Loudoun "to wash and cook for the men." Guides and scouts could earn a tidy income from the regiment. On May 3, 1756, James Mason and Patrick Flarity received £2 for directing John Mercer's company from Falmouth to Winchester, and one year later John Hagar was reimbursed more than £1 10s. for "intelligence of the Road to Logstown and of the Strength and Situation of the Indians thereabouts."[30]

Caring for the sick and injured was one of the most lucrative services townspeople could provide the regiment. James Craik, who entered service as a surgeon in March 1754 and remained Washington's personal physician throughout his life, in one instance alone received more than £77 pay. Local women serving as nurses, such as Mary Wilson, collected as much as £7 at a time. In June 1758, just as the hospital moved to a room in the Fort Loudoun barracks, the regiment paid a total of £18 12s. 6d. to John Greenfield, Alexander Wodrow, and Bryan Bruin for the previous use of their buildings as hospitals. These three proved critical in the development of a merchant economy in Winchester.[31]

· ⟨⟩ ·

An immigrant from Scotland, John Greenfield arrived in Winchester as early as 1754 and within three years was known as a "Merchant Taylor." Greenfield collected considerable sums from the regiment for making match coats and supplying buckskins for moccasins to allied Indians visiting the garrison. Meanwhile, he acquired at least two town lots with structures sufficient for a hospital. In 1754, "Merchant" Greenfield sold a lot to Charles Smith, a lieutenant in the Virginia Regiment. Greenfield, a rising entrepreneur and a captain in the militia, later became a justice on the county court. He died in Winchester in 1769. Alexander Wodrow was already a merchant in Falmouth when he purchased a Winchester lot in 1754. The Virginia Regiment came to town the next year, and Wodrow served it as a sutler. In July 1756 he received the appointment of "Grand Settler" at Fort Cumberland, with the commendation of its officers that he was a "very proper person . . . [who] behaved with the greatest exactness and conformity to the rules and orders of the Garrison—and with much modesty and gentility." During the ensuing years, Wodrow acquired several additional lots, on one occasion joining with James Craik and Charles Smith in purchasing one-half of a prime lot on the wagon road through town. Wodrow was a member of the Masons with George Washington and voted for the aspiring young commander when he ran successfully for the House of Burgesses in 1758.[32]

Bryan Bruin arrived in Winchester after Greenfield and Wodrow but moved quickly to become one of the town's leading merchants. By 1758 he was keeping an ordinary on a lot he bought from Greenfield near Fort Loudoun. Within a few years, however, deeds to town lots and tracts in the surrounding countryside, which he acquired in great numbers, described him as a merchant. His stock of goods came on credit from the Philadelphia merchant firm of Jones and Wister. Taking advantage of the trade boom of the Seven Years' War, Owen Jones and Daniel Wister had moved aggressively on a working capital of £4,340 to secure goods, also on credit, from twenty-three firms in six English cities totaling £94,147. With equal zeal Jones and Wister pressed these goods on numerous merchants, like Bruin, who were trading throughout the Pennsylvania and Virginia backcountries. When an economic downturn in 1761 forced Jones and Wister to call in their debts, Bruin was able to use his extensive land holdings as collateral for mortgages and thereby maintain his solvency. Although he spent much of his time in court, Bruin's career demonstrates how ambitious men could parlay renting a tavern to the Virginia Regiment for a hospital into one of Winchester's foremost mercantile enterprises.[33]

Tavern keeping thus proved to be one of the major routes through which the funds of the Virginia Regiment flowed into Winchester and the surrounding community of Opequon. From its beginning, of course, the town had attracted establishments where people could quench their thirsts and visitors could find lodging, meals, and stabling. Soon after James Wood had surveyed the town in 1744 John Hopes acquired lot number ten as well as a license from the county court to sell liquor. Although many ordinaries were dispersed throughout the Opequon countryside, the business generated by monthly meetings of the court made the town especially attractive. Between its founding in 1743 and the end of the 1750s, the court issued at least sixty-five ordinary licenses, twenty-four going to tavern keepers in Winchester. For many of these men and women, running a tavern was part of a larger mercantile enterprise and store operation—they mixed drink with other forms of trade. And they found numerous ways to tap into the coffers of the Virginia Regiment.[34]

Shortly after taking command of the Virginia Regiment in 1755, George Washington ordered that the "Court-House must be used for Barracks." The court, therefore, sought other quarters for its sessions compensating James Lemon and Henry Brinker £2 for each use of their taverns. When Lemon died the next year, he held £774 18s. 3d. in credit for charges at his establishment, which no doubt included other services provided to the regiment and its soldiers. Visits by these men to taverns and, worse, unlicensed gin-shops, soon became one of Washington's greatest problems. In mid-July 1756, just as work on Fort Loudoun reached its peak, the young commander warned "all the towns people, that they must not allow the Soldiers to be drunk in their Houses, or sell them any liquor, without an order from a commissioned officer; or else they may depend Colonel Washington will prosecute them as the act of Assembly directs. This caution must be particularly given to the Dutch Baker's, John Stewart, and Jacob Sowers." Stewart and Sowers at least held tavern licenses, but Henry Baker possessed only a half lot in town, the deed for which he signed in German. Washington's order did little to keep soldiers from spending their pay on drink, and two weeks later the colonel appeared in court accusing Stewart of "entertaining Soldiers contrary to Orders." He also requested that John Lesley's ordinary license not be renewed. Both actions failed, and three days later Winchester troops received orders that "as many men as the Tents will contain, do immediately encamp" away from the taverns. Only Henry Brinker, Henry Heth, and James Lemon could cater to soldiers, and they were "charged not to sell more than a reasonable quantity of liquor, and at reasonable rates to each man per day." Buying drink at other taverns could bring a soldier fifty lashes. What was a nemesis to Washington was, however, obviously a bonanza to anyone in town with alcohol to sell. A month and a half later the regiment's colonel was still condemning the "paltry tippling houses and Ginned-shops" as a "great nuisance" and chastising the soldiers who "so long as their pay holds good, [were] incessantly drunk, and unfit for Service." Clearly, the regimental payroll was passing right through the troops into the hands of tavern keepers.[35]

The next year the situation got measurably worse. Late in September 1757, while Washington was away attending William Fairfax's funeral, the quarter-master absconded, and a subsequent inquiry revealed a ring of embezzlers in Winchester. Apparently, inhabitants of the town were receiving regimental supplies and provisions from soldiers on credit for drink. Not surprisingly, many involved were tavern keepers. To complicate matters, the only constable in town declined to serve search warrants on those implicated in the scandal. Other leading citizens refused deputization until Alexander Wodrow stepped forward and, with "indefatigable assiduity," searched houses all one night to bring the accused before a three-judge panel the next morning. In all, the booty included twelve canteens, eleven bayonets, eight knapsacks, three gun locks, a musket, a cutlass and numerous cartridge boxes, blankets, coats, jackets, hats, breeches, shoes, and various tools—all regimental property.[36]

Among the accused were tavern keepers William Windsor, Michael Laubinger, and John Lesley, but Washington blamed the sordid affair more broadly on the "credit which the tippling-house-keepers (with which Winchester abounds) gave to many of the Soldiers." Subsequent inaction by the county court prompted the outraged commander to request that the colony's attorney general prosecute the uncooperative magistrates. "Were it not too tedious, I cou'd give your Honor such instances of the villainous Behaviour of those Tipling-house-keeper's as wou'd astonish any person," railed the colonel. "These are the people of a country whose bowels are at this juncture torn by the most horrid devastations of the most cruel and barbarous enemy."[37]

What was obvious villainy to Washington, however, had been normal behavior in the regional exchange economy for decades before his arrival. Washington was perfectly correct in asserting that it was "impossible to maintain that discipline and do that Service with a Garrison thus corrupted." But the young commander of the Virginia Regiment was wrong in claiming that the tavern keepers were a "sett of people, whose conduct looks like the effect of a combination to obstruct the Service, and frustrate the methods pointed out for their own preservation." What soldiers traded for alcohol had always been accepted simply as the means of exchange: goods and services calculated as debits and credits. As early as 1746 the peddler Samuel Divinny had received brandy, punch, cider, food, and lodging from John Hopes, furnishing in return various goods, such as blankets, a hat, and six yards of linen—themselves, no doubt, wrangled from country people at Opequon. In other familiar cases, mason George Brown traded twenty bushels of "slime," or mortar, with tavern keeper Henry Brinker for liquor and punch, and Brown's sometime employer Duncan O'Gullion built a "chimnee above the joyest" for James Lemon in return for punch, beer, brandy, wine, and a room for himself and his cousin. Accepting goods of any sort from soldiers in exchange for "entertainment" at a tavern would hardly have seemed unusual. And when soldiers had cash to pay, the allure of money might have been too much for even the most scrupulous.[38]

Tavern keepers who abided by Washington's orders also prospered. Washington's success at the Frederick County polls in 1758 was attended by the usual practice of treating the voters for the thirsty work of casting ballots *vive voce*. To Henry Brinker, Henry Heth, Alexander Wodrow, and others the ambitious politician, now twenty-seven years old, turned over more than £37 for rum, brandy, punch, cider, and thirty gallons of beer. In addition to seeing the launch of Washington's political career, the year 1758 was a turning point in the future president's life; he resigned command of the Virginia Regiment and embraced the happy prospects of domestic life at Mount Vernon and marriage to Martha Dandridge Custis.[39]

· ⚶ ·

That same year, 1758, was also critical for political developments shaping the landscape of town and country in the Shenandoah Valley. Fort Loudoun was finished—at least as finished as it would ever be. But more important was the conclusion of the Ohio phase of the Seven Years' War. Resolution of the issues that had generated conflict throughout the backcountries of Pennsylvania and Virginia emanated, in part, from the desires of Pennsylvania Quakers for peace and, in part, from growing pressures within Indian society. While British forces under General John Forbes were gathering for what promised to be the final western campaign, the French were becoming less attractive allies to the Shawnees, Delawares, Mingos, and others of the Ohio Country. British successes in Canada, especially at Louisbourg, in Nova Scotia, had halted the interior flow of French trade goods upon which the Indians depended. Many of the Ohio Indians, moreover, began to chafe under French dominion at Duquesne. Early in 1758 shortages at the garrison forced the French to deny food and liquor to a party of Miamis, who then raided the fort's livestock and drew fire from the soldiers. Besides, natives of the Ohio region had gone to war to rid their homelands of foreign intruders. Offers of French aid had been accepted to oust British colonials, whose settlement frontier was presenting the greatest threat. But the French presence had grown as onerous as a British one promised to be. More and more, Indians began to look favorably upon a negotiated settlement. Thus Delaware headmen Tamaqua and his brother Pisquetomen were reassured in mid-1758 at Philadelphia by Pennsylvania overtures to peace. Any cease-fire, the Indians made clear, was premised upon their control of the Ohio Country. Asserting that the "land is ours," they asked, "Why do not you and the *French* fight on the sea? You come here only to cheat the poor *Indians*, and take their land from them."[40]

At Easton, Pennsylvania, in October 1758, representatives of the colonial governments of Pennsylvania and New Jersey met with delegations of headmen from each of the Six Nations, the Delawares, and numerous smaller tribes to forge a treaty. All present agreed that British settlement would halt at the Allegheny Mountains until further land cessions could be negotiated with the Indians. Disputed land between the Susquehanna River and the mountains taken under questionable circumstances through a previous treaty would be returned to the Indians. And a just and equitable trade would be established with the native peoples of the Ohio Country. As a result of the Easton Treaty, the Ohio Indians withdrew from Fort Duquesne, and General Forbes occupied it without opposition in late November 1758. This action brought a temporary halt to conflict over the Ohio Valley. It also installed a significant British force at Duquesne, renamed Fort Pitt, and a series of other western forts ostensibly to prevent white settlement in the West but also to establish British dominion over territory disputed with France and occupied by Indians. Peace for settlers in the Shenandoah Valley and the adjoining mountains, however, was neither complete nor permanent. Fighting soon broke out with the southern Indians, primarily the previously allied Cherokees, over tensions between war parties and settlers in the Valley. Two years later western Indians, not consulted at Easton or considered in the concluding arrangements of the Seven Years' War and angered by both British arrogance and dishonest traders, joined forces in initially successful attacks on British posts throughout the West and on white settlements in Pennsylvania and Virginia. British forces finally regained control of the West in 1764, bringing what was called Pontiac's War to a close and affirming British sovereignty over the interior of North America as determined by the 1763 Peace of Paris.

The significance of these developments for economic life and landscape in the Shenandoah Valley was made evident by the young English cleric and traveler Andrew Burnaby. Son of a clergyman, Burnaby took a Cambridge master's degree and departed for the British colonies. He arrived in Virginia in

July 1759, and after an extended stay in Williamsburg, he set out to see the colony. At Fredericksburg he found a town established "for the sake of carrying on a trade with the back-settlers; and is at present by far the most flourishing one in these parts." After brief visits in Dumfries and Colchester, "two small towns lately built for the sake of the back trade," he stopped at Washington's Mount Vernon, "beautifully situated upon a high hill on the banks of the Potomac; and commands a noble prospect of water, of cliffs, of woods, and plantations." Concluding a side trip to Alexandria, "a small trading place in one of the finest situations imaginable," he wintered in the colonial capital. When spring came, he headed west and crossed the Blue Ridge, "inexpressibly delighted with the scene which opened before me. Immediately under the mountain, which was covered with chamœdaphnes in full bloom, was a most beautiful river [Shenandoah]: beyond this an extensive plain, diversified with every pleasing object that nature can exhibit." The people who inhabited this plain, however, composed his real subject of interest: "The low grounds upon the banks of this river are very rich and fertile; they are chiefly settled by Germans, who gain a comfortable livelihood by raising stock for the troops, and sending butter down into the lower parts of the country." Continuing across the Valley, Burnaby came to Winchester, "a small town of about two hundred houses." Small yes, but three times the size of the town Moravians had described less than a decade earlier, on the eve of the Seven Years' War. "Its late rapid increase, and present flourishing condition" Burnaby attributed to its being the "place of general rendezvous of the Virginian troops."[41]

Was Winchester flourishing? The economic impact of the Virginia Regiment and the construction of Fort Loudoun would certainly suggest so. So would a number of other developments. Not surprisingly, the population of Frederick County fell during the war years but rebounded in 1759, and in the year of Burnaby's visit, it exceeded 1754 levels. Commodity prices, too, were high, having been forced up by the regimental commissary. In the first month of his command, Washington had to expend as much as eleven shillings per hundredweight for beef, but one year later beef brought almost double that amount. December, the traditional month for slaughtering hogs, found Thomas Walker unable to attract any pork at fifteen shillings per hundredweight. By October 1757 the regiment was paying local farmers twenty-five shillings for one hundred pounds of pork. The price of corn rose from less than eight shillings a barrel to as much as twenty-five or more during the war years. Wheat prices increased as well. The value of estates in probate was also a measure of wealth. Their median value doubled during the four years of war following 1754 compared to the four years before. This figure increased again in the years following the end of fighting in the West. Part of this upsurge can be attributed to inflation and the paper money issued by the Virginia legislature. But the sterling exchange value of Virginia notes rose by only 12 percent, leaving more than a third of the percentage increase in Frederick County estates accountable to the accumulation of wealth. Land was not assessed in estate inventories, but increases in land values would likewise augment the wealth of the community. The vast majority of tracts purchased in the seven years prior to 1757 sold in the following seven years at considerably higher prices. Productivity as measured by the ownership of livestock, nonessential furniture, or multiple means of production also increased during the war years.[42]

The war and postwar years were indeed flush times in Winchester and the surrounding Valley. At about the same time Andrew Burnaby visited Mount Vernon, George Mercer wrote to its proprietor that "if you have Wheat Rye Corn or Oats, Cattle, Sheep or Hogs to dispose of there is a Ready & great Market for Them here." Mercer was deputy quartermaster general in Maryland and Virginia for the British army. As one measure of the optimism of good times, Winchester expanded. When the delegation of Ohio Indians arrived for the 1753 parlay, the settlement could boast eighty town lots. When Andrew Burnaby visited, the number of lots had grown by more than a factor of six (fig. 6.4). During fall 1758, as Washington and Forbes advanced on Duquesne, the Virginia Burgesses heard and approved a petition from James Wood "for enlarging the Town of *Winchester* by adding 156 Lots already laid off adjoining thereto." At the same time, Lord Fairfax was working on an addition of 205 lots, which gained legislative endorsement the following spring. Smaller subdivisions as far as a mile away from the center of town brought the total number of lots to more than five hundred. Twenty-five streets now connected these lots, and they began to assume names symbolic of the town and its history.[43]

Most North American towns used the traditional English system of street naming, which included Main, Church, Mill, Cross, and Court Streets. Some towns employed references to royalty in King, Queen, Duke, Prince, or Princess Streets. Philadelphia street names were also popular. Hence Market, Water, Walnut, Chestnut, High, and Front Streets appeared in many Pennsylvania towns. Street names also honored town founders. Although Winchester lacked a Wood Street, the name *Cameron*, for Lord Fairfax sixth baron of Cameron, began to be used for one of the earliest streets in 1758. Other streets reflected the interests of either Fairfax or Wood. Fairfax labeled most of the streets in his additions after well-known locations in London, themselves often named for famous Englishmen. Hence the eastern and northern districts of the town were graced by references to Abchurch, Philpot, Clif-

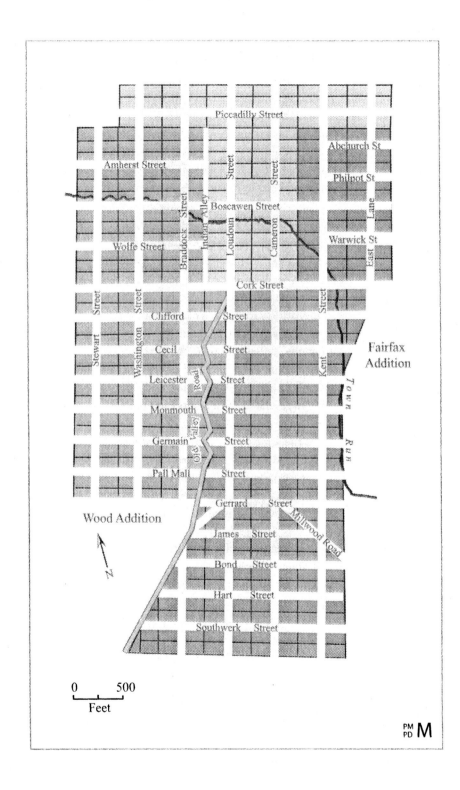

ford, Warwick, Leicester, Piccadilly, and Cork. Wood chose the names of British and American leaders in the Seven Years' War for his streets; Washington Street in Winchester may be the earliest public monument in America to the great man. Joining Washington were other martial worthies, such as Amherst, Loudoun, Boscawen, and Wolfe. Much—perhaps too much—can be made of these names, but they certainly reflected the international role that Winchester played in a global conflict. The names Wood chose for streets also symbolized the strategic military importance of this place situated in the interior of a contested continent. That Fairfax alluded to locations in London for his street names may have reflected a desire to render the little frontier settlement more cosmopolitan and commercially significant than it really was. For Fairfax, Winchester was, perhaps, as much a central place as for Wood it was a strategic one.[44]

· ⚘ ·

The same optimism expressed by enlarging Winchester and giving its streets splendid names appeared throughout the Shenandoah Valley in the formation of new towns during or shortly after the Seven Years' War (fig. 6.5). The site of Staunton had been selected on the land of William Beverley in 1746 as the seat of Augusta County. Named for the wife of the then-governor, William Gooch, the town received a charter similar to Winchester's in 1762. Within a few years five merchants traded there. The first war-baby town, however, was Stephensburg. In the pivotal year of 1758, Lewis Stephens surveyed forty acres he owned eight miles south of Winchester into eighty half-acre lots. As in Winchester, each town lot was linked to an outlot, for the self-sufficiency of residents in time of war. Stephens wrote his first deed on August 6, 1759, and within four years he had recorded forty-eight more in the Frederick County courthouse. These sales were worth more than £500 to him, but if he saw any of this sum in money it no doubt came from the funds released into the local economy by the Virginia Regiment. Nonetheless, Stephensburg lots sold for about half the value of lots in Winchester. The placement of this growing town began, however, to establish a geographic pattern. Many new towns would emerge at six- to twelve-mile intervals in a line along the Philadelphia

Facing page

FIG. 6.4. Expansion of Winchester, 1758–1759. Winchester expanded considerably during the 1750s owing to economic activity generated by the Seven Years' War. With additions by James Wood in 1758 and by Lord Fairfax the following year, the total number of lots in the town soon exceeded five hundred. Based on Quarles, *Winchester, Virginia*, 47, 50–51.

Wagon Road. Communication up and down the Valley's primary artery was obviously a determining factor in the placement of towns, but their spacing was governed by the distances farm families were willing to travel to secondary and primary markets.[45]

Strasburg, the next Valley town to appear, continued this pattern. Chartered in November 1761 by Peter Stover, this fledgling community on the wagon road where it turned around a large bend in the Shenandoah River about ten miles south of Stephensburg, took its name from Stover's European birthplace. The brother of the great but unsuccessful colonizer Jacob Stover, Peter had earlier purchased the land where Jacob Funk had his mill and directed land seekers such as Philip Windle to the North Mountain community. During six months beginning in July 1762, Stover sold thirty-two lots for sums ranging between £6 and £30. At the same time, and at a predictable distance of twelve miles farther south, Woodstock began to take shape. Like Stephens and Stover, its founder, Jacob Miller, was German. By September 1762 this ambitious man had recorded forty deeds for lots in his town.[46]

Two more towns, both located at fords across the Potomac River, were chartered a few months later in the midst of tensions over the Cherokee War and Pontiac's War. Romney was Lord Fairfax's town of fifty acres laid off in half-acre lots as the seat of Hampshire County, about thirty-five miles west of Winchester. Shepherdstown was named for Thomas Shepherd, son of the man who first settled at the site of "Pack Horse Ford," where the Philadelphia Wagon Road crossed the Potomac River. During the fall of 1762 Shepherd received permission from the Virginia legislature to operate a ferry at the ford and to survey a town on the Virginia landing. In less than two years he had recorded deeds for thirty-eight lots.[47]

Thus, in the four years after the conclusion of the western phase of the Seven Years' War, five new towns appeared in the lower Shenandoah Valley and hundreds of lots were sold for a total of several thousand pounds. Staunton, moreover, received a charter comparable to Winchester's. All but one of these towns lay along the wagon road connecting the Shenandoah Valley to Philadelphia. The pattern of these towns, about a day's wagon journey apart, was already emerging. Unlike the earlier attempts at legislating town founding in Virginia, neither these Valley towns nor their location was dictated by the House of Burgesses. Expressions of individual initiative, they took shape as ambitious men surveyed their own land into lots and began issuing deeds to country people wanting to invest in them. Many of these towns developed around preexisting economic activities: a grist mill, a saw mill, a ferry, or a tavern. New towns soon became magnets for merchants' and artisans' activities, as well.

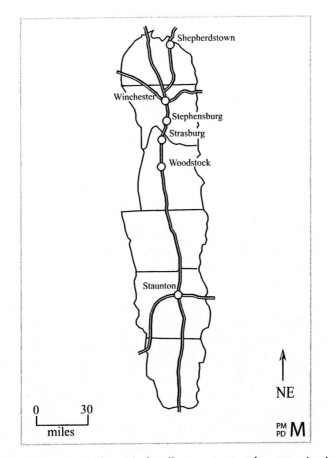

FIG. 6.5. New Towns in the Shenandoah Valley, 1750–1765. The economic stimulus of the Seven Years' War promoted town founding in the Shenandoah Valley. Most new towns were arrayed about a day's journey apart along the Philadelphia Wagon Road in the more populous lower valley. Based on Mitchell, *Commercialism and Frontier*, 192, fig. 25.

How much of this urban ferment can be credited to the Seven Years' War? Did rural settlers flock to towns for collective security? In the midst of the conflict, the founders of Stephensburg discovered that "by living at a Distance from one another" they were "unable to defend themselves from the sudden Attacks of the Enemy." "To obviate which Inconveniences as much as possible" they notified the Virginia Assembly that they were "desirous of collecting themselves into a Body and settling together in a Town." Clearly, the population of Winchester also grew as families sought shelter under Fort Loudoun's guns. But only Winchester boasted fortifications, and the legislature's chain of forts had virtually no effect on the geography of town founding. Much of the money that changed hands over lots, however, must have come from the Virginia Regiment. Even in the regional exchange economy, in which recording debits and credits in book accounts facilitated the flow of goods and services, cash must have had a quickening effect and for some people created surplus resources ripe for investment. Artisans, laborers, and officers of the regiment dominated the group of new lot purchasers in the additions that enlarged Winchester. Money, new towns, and especially the regiment's headquarters town, however, attracted merchants and the commerce they generated. For merchants, cash meant credit with suppliers in eastern ports and the means of making back payments in an Atlantic economy.[48]

. ☊ .

After the Treaty of Easton and the arrival of John Forbes on the Ohio, the enforcement of treaty provisions limiting Anglo-American settlement and fostering an honest Indian trade fell to the British army. Forbes died in March 1759, and command of the Royal American Regiment at Fort Pitt fell to Colonel Henry Bouquet. During the ensuing four years Bouquet led a two-hundred-man garrison there and oversaw the reoccupation or construction of thirteen forts extending from Raystown (now Bedford), Pennsylvania, eastward on the Forbes Road and westward to Green Bay, on Lake Michigan. Provisioning this army, which at times numbered more than four thousand regimentals and provincials, fell to quartermasters and contractors working in western Pennsylvania and Virginia.[49]

On January 4, 1759—less than six weeks after the fall of Fort Duquesne—John St. Clair, deputy quartermaster general for British forces there, sent a circular letter to a number of commissaries and contractors in Pennsylvania and Virginia, including Thomas Rutherford, of the "Winchester District." Rutherford, a "person of Weight," according to St. Clair, was deputy commissary general of Virginia and an agent for military contractors Adam Hoops and the familiar Thomas Walker. St. Clair explained to Rutherford how the "necessity of supporting our Post at Fort de Quene, now Pittsburgh, on which the Safety and Protection of the frontiers of these Colonies depends, has made the General come to a Resolution to reinforce the Garrison, with much Larger number of Troops than was at first intended." Thus, the "demand for Provisions is so far increased, as to require an immediate Supply." Rutherford was asked to post an "Advertisement . . . throughout your County, in the most publick Manner you can, that all the Country people may be acquainted with the Terms proposed." Those who delivered flour to Fort Pitt within six weeks "shall receive Four Pounds Pensylvania Currency p Hundred Wt." Although not in the timely way for which St. Clair hoped, the advertisement had its effect. By the end of July—the season for harvesting winter wheat—Rutherford was writing Bouquet that he was about to dispatch twenty thousand pounds of flour and five hundred bushels of oats to Pittsburgh and that up to five hundred horses "can be purchased here in three weeks." The Virginia backcountry indeed seemed to be a land of plenty. And Rutherford's flour alone would pour £800 back into its economy. By the end of the following month, George Mercer could inform Bouquet that "there was a very great Crop of Oats & Rye made in these Parts this Season. Not less than 20 or 30,000 Bushels might be spared." Of pork, "any Quantity of it may be bought imediately, but tis impossible to say yet for what." Mercer significantly added: "We must settle the Market ourselves in a great Measure."[50]

Mercer soon realized, however, that he faced a serious problem in settling the market, that is, imposing consistent and uniform prices on goods usually exchanged at highly variable rates. Farmers at Opequon produced for the internal needs of the exchange economy, not for the external demands of a market economy. The timing of demand in the market created by the British army did not coincide with the deeply rooted rhythms of agricultural life at Opequon. The quartermaster needed flour, oats, meat, and other provisions in the early fall to insure an ample supply for winter. As Mercer explained the problem to Bouquet, "this Season of the Year, being the Time the Planters here, employ, in making and securing Hay, laying down new Meadows &c, nothing but extraordinary Encouragement (of Money) can induce Them to go out of their comon Road." The remedy, according to Mercer, was indeed money: "They never thresh their Oats till October or Novr, nor will any Thing but the ready Cash, and a good Price bribe Them to it now." Bullion, moreover, would be far more effective than paper money. "The old Misers take more Delight in telling over the Pieces of Gold or Silver, than twice the Quantity of Paper," the Virginia quartermaster continued. "I am convinced £100 in either of these Articles would induce Them to do more than £1000 in Paper." The flow of gold and silver—what Mercer called money or ready cash—began to work major changes in life at Opequon. The interplay between an exchange economy and a market economy would define economic relations in the Shenandoah Valley for the remainder of the century, and changes in these relations would help account for the vitality of an emerging town and country landscape.[51]

· ✿ ·

But why would men and women at Opequon want ready cash if their economy and their livelihoods worked perfectly well without it? One explanation can be traced to their experience in provisioning Edward Braddock's army for its fateful march to the Ohio Country in 1755. By the time of the disaster on the Monongahela, the general held £10,000 in unpaid bills to people in Virginia and Pennsylvania who had provided cattle, flour, produce, forage, teams, and wagons for the expedition. Not until October 1756 did Braddock's successor, William Shirley, order commissary officer Robert Leake to initiate payment. But Leake designated Lancaster, Pennsylvania, as the only place where claims could be presented. For most Virginia families, the costs of the two-hundred-fifty-mile round trip exceeded what they expected in compensation. Their frustration is what Mercer remembered when he wrote to the British commander in September 1759: "Were I once to send a Farmer off with[ou]t his Cash it would ruin the Public Credit, which is only now beginning to be thought something of." "So often," he continued, "has the Public Faith been broke, that they will always take Evidences to a Bargain, and tell Me they will not deal with Me for a Penny, unless I engage to pay Them myself."[52]

Hard money held other allurements to people at Opequon. It did not spoil or go bad like farm products did. It did not dry out or grow moldy. Insects could not eat it. Its quality, hence its value, was not subject to the eye or whim of someone else. More important, it could be carried easily and was good anywhere. It was far handier for toting to Fredericksburg, Falmouth, Alexandria, or Philadelphia than bushels of wheat, barrels of flour, or bolts of cloth. For this reason alone, money became essential to the merchant trade, and it was this trade that made the new economy of towns like Winchester work. But for the moment, in the late summer and fall of 1759, it also made the farmers of Opequon work—and work hard.

How much cash flowed into the economy at Opequon through the coffers of Fort Pitt is difficult to determine. Many people had their hands on it. In addition to Mercer as deputy quartermaster general and contractors Rutherford and Walker, there was also Richard Graham, a salt contractor, and William Ramsay, who dealt in flour. All apparently made disbursements for the commodities they collected and shipped to Fort Pitt. In October 1759 Walker wrote to the British commander that "Money" amounting to £3,244 8s. 10½d. "will in four or five days be all Payed and a Considerable Sum will remain due." At about the same time Mercer complained to Bouquet that he would "want more Money to answer my Engagements here, beside the Sum [£811 11s. 10½d.] you sent Me last with the Money for Messrs Ramsay's [£2,110 2s. 10¾d.] & Graham's [£973 18s. 3d.] Contracts." Late that fall Henry Bouquet himself traveled to Winchester to expedite payments for provisions, and by December 20 he had finished settling accounts in Virginia "except a few, who have yet their Horses in the Service." The following March this officer reported overall payments to Mercer, Walker, and Rutherford of £15,057 16s., bringing the total the British army spent in Virginia to an excess of £18,000.[53]

The lure of ready cash apparently had the effect Mercer promised, and huge quantities of provisions began to flow from the Virginia backcountry to the Ohio Country in fall 1759. The first packhorse convoy got under way from Winchester at the end of September, with a "good deal of forrage, Sheep, Cattle &a." Mercer was soon promising Bouquet that seventy to eighty thousand pounds of flour would be sent out "the soonest it coud possibly be ground," and the next month Walker wrote that the "present Crop of Wheat being so great that I make No Doubt of purchasing Two Hundred Thousand [bushels] Between this & the Spring." Rutherford had already forwarded a thousand bushels of corn to Fort Pitt. Rutherford and Graham accounted for a drive of at least 350 head of cattle, and in December Walker dispatched a "drove of Hogs Weighing about 24,000 lb of Pork." Butter, cheese, onions, and apples went west as well.[54]

The Virginia Indian trade, largely dormant since the days of Alexander Spotswood, was also energized by the economic magnet of Fort Pitt. By the Easton Treaty, Pennsylvania had agreed to organize a fair and honest trade with the Indians. Late in 1758 the Pennsylvania Assembly established a provincial monopoly over this commerce and called for official stores to be set up at western forts. There missionaries and schoolmasters would supposedly civilize, Christianize, and educate the natives. But capital shortages and poor planning delayed the establishment of the store at Fort Pitt until the following September. Meanwhile, the commander of the garrison welcomed many small traders and farmers from Virginia eager to dispatch their produce and whiskey. In Winchester, George Mercer moved quickly. He wrote to at least six merchants he knew in eastern Virginia "to encourage their sending out Goods for the Indians to Pitsburg," but he soon discovered that this was a "trade We have so long been deprived of, that they cant get a sortable cargo." Winchester merchants, however, appeared more daring, and by late August, Mercer had "engaged two very good, honest, industrious young Merchts here, to go out to Pitsburg with about £500 of Indian Goods." It was, Mercer observed, their "first Venture." With the dispatch of their wagon about the middle of the next month, Mercer advised Bouquet that "upon their Report of the Affair, depends many others going out." Instability and unrest during the Cherokee War and Pontiac's War no doubt discouraged the Indian trade, but that some Winchester merchants hazarded it was testimony to flush times and economic optimism following the success of British-American arms in the West.[55]

· ⚘ ·

Despite the outpouring of goods from Winchester and Opequon during the summer and fall of 1759 and the venturesome spirit of local merchants, all was not well in the western trade with the army and the Indians. Ultimately, the market created by this commerce would run afoul of the difficulties that Mercer described to Bouquet: the deep cultural conservatism of farmers steeped in the traditions of European mixed agriculture and their dependence upon the caprices of nature and human capacity. The flour trade caused the most egregious problems. Flour was as essential to the British army as gunpowder, and Henry Bouquet could not imagine victualing his force without the means of making bread. Wheat or flour could enter the exchange economy whenever a household had a little extra to trade, but substantial quantities of flour were often not available until water from winter or spring rains was sufficient to drive mills. Bouquet had reason to hope that his complement of flour from Virginia would arrive in time to insure a successful wintering for his army deep in the snows of the Ohio Country. "I have engag'd the people to make the best Flour our Mills can produce," William Ramsay assured him in late September, "& have given an extraordinary price for that purpose." But the Virginia contractor cautioned, "New Wheat to thrash out, Seeding time & the dry Weather hath prevented me from having it on the Road at this time ... but we may hope for Rain soon." A full month later, however, Mercer was still complaining that "it is not more than a Fortnight now, since there has been a sufficient Rain to work four or five of the Mills." Believing incorrectly at one point that relief was at hand, an exasperated Bouquet exclaimed that the "Eternal Pack Horses from Winchester are at last on the Roads."[56]

More letdowns were to follow. "I have been equally disappointed by the Virga Pack Horses," Bouquet wrote to his commander John Stanwix, "which being loaded the first Trip with very coarse Meal, in lieu of flour lefft their loads at Cumberland." Flour at Fort Pitt, not meal (coarse, unbolted flour) at Fort Cumberland, was what Bouquet needed. Thomas Walker explained the situation: "The Flour Made in the upper parts of the Colony was Chiefly Consumed Among the Farmers who Are So frugal as to eat the Midlings Mixed With the Flour gennerly, and Many use the Shorts in the Same Manner that It was found uneces[sary] for the Millers to go to the Expence of Merchant Boutting [bolting, or sifting] Cloths." Farmers in the Shenandoah Valley were clearly growing wheat and grinding coarse flour mixed with the bran and germ of the wheat kernel only for domestic use, not for sale. "You may remember that I contracted wth Mr. Ramsay for merchantable flour, and not meal," Bouquet retorted. "Add the disapointmnt in point of quantity & time, & you may imagine what I must think of Mr. Ramsay."[57]

Unfamiliarity with producing for a market like the one created by the British army also led Thomas Rutherford to run afoul of Henry Bouquet. Not only was the commander at Fort Pitt frustrated with the tardiness of the pack-horses, but they were also poorly equipped and not up to the task of hauling heavy loads over the mountains of western Virginia. George Mercer explained: "Being quite unacquainted with that particular Branch of Business," the hapless contractor had "employed Persons, he thought he coud trust, to fit out his Pack Horses, and the Saddles were so badly made, that many of the Horses Backs are much hurt." Inexperience in business was also Richard Graham's undoing. Contracted to supply the army with salt, Graham proceeded to purchase cattle, too. Bouquet was incensed: "Mr. Graham has intirely mistaken me. I made a Contract in writing for Salt, But never any for Cattle." Graham's problems multiplied when he engaged thirty-two wagons to haul his salt to the forks of the Ohio. Mercer was to have any surplus wagon space, but the deputy quartermaster general reported to his superior in late October 1759 that "on the 18th late in the Night arrived Mr Graham's Waggon Master here with two waggons, and upon my not receiving him very civily after such a Disappointment, he went off and has left Me to transact Mr Graham's Business for him."[58]

Mercer was not pleased. Nor was Bouquet happy with the traditional ways in which the people at Opequon responded to the demands of the army and the market it was attempting to "settle." "Never was any Person more chagrined then myself at the Disappointments in the Flour & Salt Contracts," Mercer complained. "Indeed I believe the Gentlemen were not much acquainted with the Business they undertook, and tis not a very easy Matter among the extraordinary Set of Mortals We have to deal with here to establish a Character & Credit imediately." By October 1759 Bouquet must have decided that these extraordinary mortals were not worth the trouble—nor was the Virginia trade. By the end of November he had resolved that "as soon as I see the Salt forwarded, I Shall proceed to Winchester to finish if I can forever with all those worthy Gentlemen." Presently he reported to John Stanwix that "we must therefore for the future have our Sole dependance for Bread from Pensilva."[59]

A frustrated Henry Bouquet left the Shenandoah Valley in late December 1759. Dry weather, bad saddles, insufficient wagons, and ancient customs of threshing grain in November or eating whole-grained bread had thwarted his efforts to provision his troops. But these attempts had had their effects. From the labors and the lands of Opequon households flowed a cornucopia of wheat, flour, beef, pork, and other essentials sufficient apparently for both the British army and the local population. An injection of gold and silver into the exchange economy had initiated this flow. If the eighteen thousand or more that Bouquet reported spending in 1759 was distributed equally among white tithables in Frederick and Augusta Counties, then each of these nearly four thousand men would have received more than four and one-half pounds. This sum represented almost two months' work for a farm laborer or more than a month's salary for a mason. Because most households had several tithables, families saw more money than they ever had before. As the subsequent actions of Henry Heth and Adam Stephen indicate, this much wealth moving in the economy did change the way people behaved.[60]

· ☩ ·

Winchester tavern keeper and merchant Henry Heth was among the primary beneficiaries of the Virginia Regiment's stay in Winchester. One of Washington's favored tavern keepers, he kept the business of quartering soldiers when others lost it for selling drink to them. The court compensated him for sessions held at his establishment, and Washington, too, paid him well for treating the voters with abundant wine and rum at the July 1758 elections. Heth was probably also trading at Fort Pitt through his son William, who resided there. Sometime after the British army pulled its commissary operations out of Winchester, Heth began to explore other commercial opportunities with Falmouth merchant William Allason. Like other eastern merchants, Allason knew about the money flooding the western part of the state, and he sought a way to channel it into his eastern Virginia store trade with tobacco planters and Glasgow merchants. In 1760 he reported that "farmers 70 miles back of this place, has brought down quantitys of Flower to this place, from the last crop of Wheat and sold at 12 / 6 p 100 [12s. 6d. per hundredweight]." Allason's contacts in Norfolk promised that an "advantageous trade might be carried on provided that article [flour] cou'd be had on easeyer Terms then 11 / pr ct [hundredweight] delievered here in Barrells." To Heth, Allason then proposed sending down "50 or 100 Barrells on the above terms as soon as you can and I Believe you may get a return Load." Thomas Rutherford and others, moreover, had a "quantity of Salt laying here, which could help make up a back cargo for the Valley."[61]

What Allason was extending to Heth was a link to the international trade in flour that would in the decades to come transform the economy of the Shenandoah Valley and profoundly influence the shape of a town and country landscape. "As this Trade is but new and no one has made anything considerably in it as yet," Allason went on, I "imagine we might carry it on to our mutual advantage." For his part, Allason would "willingly supply you with goods on as easey terms as you buy of any one else, and you undoubtedly wou'd let me have a living Profit on the Flour." Alternatively, Allason offered to sell what flour Heth could send him "for the Common Commission." In either case, Allason hinted that "we might do a good deal of Business before that other People wou'd attempt it." On the same day Allason made a similar offer to John Briscoe, a Shenandoah Valley farmer and physician with more than three thousand acres to work and a medical practice to attend. Briscoe had been trading with Allason in butter. Like others who had once produced surplus grains to feed the British army, he was now looking for new markets for his wheat.[62]

Adam Stephen was thinking along the same lines as Heth, Briscoe, and Allason. Stephen had taken command of the Virginia Regiment in August 1761, near the end of its existence. During the preceding decade he had amassed more than seventeen hundred acres in the northern part of the Opequon settlement not far from Briscoe. In February 1762 Stephen was "expecting the Virga Regiment will soon be broke [disbanded]," as he confessed in a letter to Henry Bouquet. Since "all my Views are turned towards farming & trade," Stephen sought Bouquet's "concurrence & assistance in any scheme which will Raise the Value of our Lands in the Back parts." What Bouquet could do at this point is not clear, but Stephen's "present design . . . [was] to fix a market for the produce of them, and to Establish flour & Hemp our Staple Commodities."[63]

Allason's next move was to send his brother David to the Shenandoah Valley to set up a store. With one brother, Richard, in Glasgow and another on the Virginia frontier, Allason was clearly positioning his family and trading firm as a critical link in the chain of a burgeoning Atlantic economy. During the fall following his initial contact with Heth, Allason wrote Richard that he proposed "very soon to Send David about 70 miles up the Country with a few Goods with a view to engage Customers as there is large quantity of Tobacco made there, likewise Flower, Butter, Cheese & Hemp." The store lasted only until 1763, when William called his brother home, blaming a slack trade on Indians, who were "again committing outrages on our back Settlers." These difficulties, however, would soon be resolved, and by the mid-1760s the Shenandoah Valley would once again be at peace. Flour quickly became the most dynamic aspect of the region's commerce, providing farmers with a source of profit and linking them to the Atlantic economy. In this empire of goods a revolution in consumption was providing the means for families at Opequon to rebuild and reshape their landscape and to breathe new vitality into the economy of towns as marketplaces. Winchester was making the transition from strategic to central place.[64]

Chapter 7

Town and Country

ON DECEMBER 5, 1774, Nicholas Cresswell crossed the Blue Ridge, "a high barren mountain," and headed into the Shenandoah Valley. Staying with Jacob Hite and other friends in the neighborhood of the Hopewell Quaker meeting, he explored the lower Valley and found "some of the finest land I ever saw either for the plough or pasture." In Alexandria, before venturing west, this young man had seen huge quantities of wheat and flour pour in from the backcountry. Now, witnessing for himself how the land "produces good Wheat and Barley," he knew he had arrived at the objective of his journey. At age twenty-four Cresswell had left the large sheep farm of his father in Derbyshire, England, and departed Liverpool for America. Educated and with some means, he was intent on seeking his fortune there and finding the best possible place to take up farming.[1]

Cresswell, however, was no Jost Hite, his host's father; nor was he a Philip Windle, an Alexander Ross, or a Samuel Glass. These were men who had come to unorganized territory—waste land or wilderness, as they saw it—surveyed it, cleared it, built subsistence farms, and pursued a competency. "I am well convinced," Cresswell admitted, "that I could have lived much better and made more money, as a Farmer in this Country, with five hundred pound [invested], than I can in England, with two thousand." He wanted land for the profits it would yield growing wheat, and he found it in the Shenandoah Valley, where "limestone in general, abounds with Shumack, Walnut, and Locust trees which are certain indications that the Lands are rich." Riding around the vicinity of Winchester all day on December 9 confirmed that the land was "good, the country healthy and a good neighborhood." Winchester itself was "one of the largest towns I have seen in the Colony. . . . Regularly laid out in squares, the buildings are of limestone." Town and country, then, were ripe for the kind of commercial grain farming Nicholas Cresswell had in mind. "I am exceedingly pleased with these two Counties [Frederick and Berkeley]," he concluded, "and am determined to settle in one of them, if ever these times are settled."[2]

The times, however, were anything but settled. A decade and a half earlier George Mercer had declared that "we must settle the Market ourselves," and Adam Stephen had laid out his "design . . . to fix a market for the produce of" the Shenandoah Valley. Little of this seemed possible now. The same spring that Cresswell left England, Parliament passed the Coercive Acts to punish the people of Massachusetts for the Boston Tea Party. Uncowed, most Americans rallied to defend the traditional rights of English peoples and to uphold the authority of their own colonial governments. While Cresswell was wandering through Virginia on his way to the Shenandoah Valley, the people of the back-country met at the Anglican church in Winchester and resolved that the Coercive Acts were "not only . . . repugnant to the fundamental law of natural justice, . . . but also a despotic exertion of unconstitutional power, calculated to enslave a free . . . people." Enforcing the acts, moreover, "by a military power, will have a necessary tendency to raise a civil war." Unrest would spoil Cresswell's plans: "I am afraid it will be some time before this hubbub is settled and there is nothing to be done now. All trade is almost at a stand, everyone seems to be at a loss in what manner to proceed." In the end he conceded, "I am sorry it is not in my power to settle here."[3]

Almost a quarter of a century later, another traveler described the Shenandoah Valley as a "fine country, inhabited by an industrious and active people; a country, formed by nature to be rich." The produce, he said, "consists chiefly of flour . . . the backcountry . . . abound[s] in wheat; mills are very numerous." Wheat production and the marketing of flour was bringing great profits not only to farmers but also to millers and anyone who touched this commerce—coopers who made barrels for flour and wagoners who carted it to markets; blacksmiths, wheelwrights, and joiners who made the wagons; and so forth. Merchants profited from the sale of imported goods, the demand for which rose rapidly with wheat profits. These profits rippled through the regional economy, sustaining varied trades and professions, from teaching school, to ministering, to dressmaking, and even to silversmithing or instrument making. In other words, wheat and flour came to shape and define both the economy and the economic geography. Whereas the early settlement of Opequon had been characterized by the dispersal of farm households and the services they required at scattered mills, shops, and stores, the landscape of the Shenandoah Valley at the end of its settlement century had evolved to the final phase, which wove town and country into a complex fabric of geographic relationships.[4]

· ☙ ·

Wheat production and flour consumption had, of course, always been central to the traditional way of life that farm families brought to the Shenandoah Valley from Europe. For example, the wheat belonging to James Vance when he died in 1751 constituted 13 percent of the value of his estate, which also included various quantities of flax, hemp, barley, oats, and corn. His relative Andrew Vance had six acres planted in wheat when he died three years later. But in inventories, estate records, or book accounts, wheat rarely appeared in quantities sufficient to suggest any value beyond its worth in local exchange, and ground with the bran, flour brought little profit.[5]

The emergence of wheat as the most dynamic element in the exchange economy at Opequon in the 1760s was once again—like so many forces shaping the Shenandoah Valley landscape—linked to large-scale developments throughout the Atlantic world. Certainly military demand during the Seven Years' War encouraged farmers to shed traditional patterns of agriculture by threshing grain in the late summer and grinding white, bolted flour. The sources of landscape transformation in the Shenandoah Valley during the final third of the eighteenth century, however, can be traced to England in the 1740s, when this island nation was becoming less and less able to feed itself. The rate of population growth more than doubled during that decade. Meanwhile, rising wealth from manufacturing meant more laborers and fewer food producers, greater consumer demand, and basic changes in foreign trade. A craving for sugar, for instance, led to a dramatic increase in West Indian sugar imports. These developments converged to lift wheat prices throughout the Atlantic economy. Great Britain went from a net exporter of wheat and flour to a nation dependent upon foreign shipments of breadstuffs for its livelihood. Because southern Europe—the Iberian Peninsula and the western Mediterranean—had relied on British flour, its food needs now increased demand on alternative markets. West Indian planters, meanwhile, began to seek new sources for provisions as they cut back on food production and purchased additional slaves to make more sugar.[6]

As the price of wheat on English markets more than doubled between 1740 and 1770, demands on American markets increased apace. From a low point in 1745 of one and one-half shillings per bushel for wheat and five shillings per hundredweight for flour, Philadelphia prices rose to five shillings for wheat and twelve for flour a quarter century later. Meanwhile, flour exports increased sixfold, and tonnage clearing this rapidly growing middle-Atlantic port for the West Indies doubled. Four times as many Philadelphia vessels went to Europe in 1768 as in 1733, while the reach of the Philadelphia market extended farther and farther west during this same interval. The needs of the British army created a boom on the Philadelphia provisions market during the

Seven Years' War, while the navy increased the number of mouths to feed in the West Indies by adding Tobago, Dominica, St. Vincent, and Grenada to the British chain of Caribbean Island possessions. It was, of course, during the war boom that Philadelphia merchants also began to ply their wares in back-country towns such as Winchester.[7]

How did these developments look, then, from the perspective of Henry Heth—eager to establish an export flour trade from Winchester—or merchants Alexander Wodrow, John Greenfield, and Bryan Bruin, or farmers John Briscoe and Adam Stephen, who were intent on fixing a market for their produce? The cost of carting flour one hundred seventy miles to Philadelphia was simply too high. But price rises from the 1750s to the late 1760s extended the geographical range at which wheat or flour profits could offset transportation expenses from about thirty miles to more than sixty—precisely the distance from the lower Shenandoah Valley to Alexandria. Early trade in Alexandria had centered on the shipment of tobacco to Great Britain. Like Winchester, the town grew during the 1750s, when it became the seat of Fairfax County and benefited from the commissary trade of the Seven Years' War. At the close of this conflict, the Potomac River port was shipping one thousand bushels of wheat annually and virtually no flour. Then, between 1764 and 1766, these figures shot up to seven thousand bushels for wheat and 3,500 barrels for flour. At this point merchant Henry Piper reported that the townspeople were "running mad" for flour and "going out of Town before Day to meet the waggons to buy." Nicholas Cresswell's enthusiasm for the grain trade was so great that he hoped to procure a commission for purchasing wheat, commenting that "great quantities of this article is brought down from the back Country in waggons to this place, as good Wheat as ever I saw in England. . . . Great quantities of Flour are likewise brought from there." He reported the export of one hundred thousand bushels of wheat and fourteen thousand barrels of flour the year before his stay. Recognizing that the roads to the Shenandoah Valley backcountry were, in Cresswell's words, "cut to pieces with the waggons," the Virginia Assembly authorized the Frederick, Berkeley, Loudoun, and Fairfax County Courts to levy as much as forty-five pounds on tithables to pay for road repairs.[8]

Despite the vitality of Alexandria's wheat and flour trade, Philadelphia remained the organizational center of middle-Atlantic commerce. John Carlyle was one of the few Alexandria merchants to trade overseas on his own account and risk. More typical were the activities of Daniel Jenifer and Richard Hooe. Between January 1775 and April 1776, this firm dispatched fifteen ships to the West Indies and southern Europe carrying a total of more than a million pounds of flour, forty-three thousand bushels of wheat, and various quantities of corn, bread, rye, beans, peas, beeswax, and oak staves. All of these ventures stood on the order and account of other firms, such as John Howell of Barbados or Gregory and Guille of Barcelona. Most of Jenifer and Hooe's business, however, ran through the accounts of Willing and Morris of Philadelphia, with consignments to Lisbon, Barcelona, and Gibraltar at a 2.5 percent commission. This aggressive Philadelphia firm scoured the countryside of Maryland, Virginia, New Jersey, and Delaware purchasing crops at farmers' doors or flour directly from millers. A significant amount of Philadelphia's flour originated in the Shenandoah Valley, where, on the eve of the American Revolution, Frederick and Berkeley Counties each produced one million pounds. Another Philadelphia merchant, Clement Biddle, kept a schooner plying back and forth between the Delaware and the Potomac Rivers and had shipping arrangements directly with millers near Winchester.[9]

Success soon invited competition, especially from merchants in Baltimore. Founded in 1729 on a branch of Maryland's Patapsco River and surrounded by barren or poor tobacco lands, this Chesapeake port grew slowly. It was, according to one historian, a "totally insignificant place" in 1750, but the grain trade soon transformed it into one of the most dynamic economies on the East Coast. As trade rivals—not subsidiaries—to Philadelphia firms, Baltimore merchants captured 15 to 20 percent of the commerce of the Chesapeake's eastern shore and were exporting one hundred thousand barrels of flour annually by the time of the American Revolution. More and more of this flour came from the Shenandoah Valley, where its production was reshaping the landscape.[10]

· ⚘ ·

By the end of the eighteenth century the reshaping process would constitute a transformation, but during the 1760s the establishment of a commercial grain economy was slow and halting. The end of the Seven Years' War and a lack of cash stymied Henry Heth's efforts to launch a grain trade with William Allason. By May 1761 Heth "had Flour made Ready to send down." Allason, however, had insisted that Heth pay for the barrels in which it was to be shipped. But Heth's margin was so thin that the 2s. 6d. cost of each cask consumed his profits. Moreover, "the want of Cash prevented my Going down as intended," Heth complained, "the troop not being paid off at this place [Winchester] has disapointed many." The replacement of military payments by market mechanisms would not be complete until after the American Revolution. In the meantime, Winchester merchants sought other methods to underwrite their trade. Bryan Bruin, for instance, continued to operate his tavern on the north end of Winchester on Loudoun Street, near Fort Loudoun. He also conducted a considerable store trade in goods acquired on credit from Philadelphia firms like that of Quaker merchants Owen Jones and Daniel Wister. James Wood was a constant customer, as was James Jr. after the death of his father in late fall 1759. Between 1761 and 1766 the younger Wood acquired "Single Channd. Pumps," "Womens Mourning Gloves," "Shammey Gloves," "Silver Sleeve Buttons," handkerchiefs, various teas and spices, different types of fabric, a horse, a scythe, and numerous other goods plus tavern debts totaling £103 9s. 11¼d. In 1763 Wood balanced four-fifths of his account by deeding Bruin two Winchester lots.[11]

What happened next demonstrates how men like Bruin responded to opportunities created by the grain trade as well as the challenges it presented. As in his dealings with Wood and other customers, Bruin acquired land—a lot of land in town lots and rural tracts—to settle his local debts. The land then served as collateral for mortgages with merchants in Philadelphia and Baltimore to underwrite credit for store goods. James Wood Jr.'s two Winchester lots, for example, ended up in a mortgage with three additional lots and eighty acres of rural land to Baltimore merchants Benjamin Howard and Hercules Courtney. After paying off this mortgage, the lots from Wood were combined with a total of thirty-five rural tracts and an additional four town lots in a sale to Baltimore merchants Thomas Ashburner and Thomas Place for £2,105 12s. 10d. in 1773. Bruin also relied on mortgages to resolve his tangled affairs with Jones and Wister. In August 1763 Jones wrote to Bruin that "on considering of the several proposals thou hast made in order to satisfy us, . . . the most agriable to us (Except receiving the Cash) Is to give us Mortgages for so much of thy Lands, as will fully secure thy debt to us." But Pontiac's War—or in Jones's words, "the present Trouble given by the Indians"—ruined the land market, and less than a year later the Philadelphia merchant was remonstrating his backcountry associate: "I don't want nor never did to be concerned in lands there. . . . Therefore pray to be so kind as to send me the money." Unfortunately, surviving accounts fail to reveal how Bruin settled with Jones and Wister. But the former ended up with some of Bruin's Shenandoah holdings in any case because Bruin had mortgaged several Winchester lots, including the one where his tavern was located, together with such personal property as ten feather beds, a billiard table, "Seventy Pictures painted on glass," a half-dozen chairs, ten tables, and a "negro woman named Hegar" to John Mitchell, a Spotsylvania County merchant, in 1762, and Mitchell sold the mortgage on the land to Jones five years later.[12]

Although complex, these arrangements were not unusual. In 1767 Henry Heth mortgaged his house lot in Winchester, the appended outlot, and two rural tracts totaling four hundred acres to merchants John Carlyle and John

Dalton of Alexandria for a debt of £300. Carlyle, Dalton, and a third partner, Robert Wilson, had earlier received a mortgage from Winchester merchant and tavern keeper William Cochran for a £400 debt. Daniel Bush and Robert Rutherford had also mortgaged property to eastern Virginia merchants. That Bush and his brother Philip maintained ties to the Philadelphia trade was indicated by their mortgages to Henry Keple and John Bell, both merchants there.[13]

Thus a merchant community began to emerge in Winchester. Bruin, Heth, Greenfield, and Wodrow had set up shop in the town during the boom years of the Seven Years' War, when military money flowed freely. Others followed in the 1760s to take advantage of the backcountry trade, primarily in grains. But as supplies of cash dried up, an economy in which wheat was exported from Potomac River ports in eastern Virginia and store goods acquired in Philadelphia or Baltimore created geographical discontinuities difficult to overcome. Continued fighting with the Indians did little to improve commercial prospects. The Shenandoah Valley was, however, rich in land, and local landowners would exchange land for goods with town merchants, who would then mortgage these lands to obtain credit with merchants in coastal ports. Cumbersome as this process was, land did secure the long-distance legs of the import-export trade and allow the exchange economy to function both locally and regionally. Economic change, however, was due to grain production in the countryside.

· ⚘ ·

By the second half of the 1760s farmers could seek a profit in growing surplus quantities of wheat, grinding it into flour at local mills, transporting the flour to Alexandria, and selling it through commission merchants on the Atlantic market. These surpluses began to appear everywhere in barns, in fields, and in mills. When early Opequon settler Robert Allen died in 1769, he had thirty bushels of wheat worth £4 10s. in his possession, along with basic accouterments for growing grain—a harrow, plow irons, a harness, nine horses, and a wagon. Similarly situated was Samuel Glass's son-in-law John Beckett, who died about the same time possessed of a mow of wheat worth £14 waiting to be threshed in his barn. Some threshed wheat was already in bags, and there was flour in casks in addition to a harrow, plow irons, scythes, sickles, a harness, and a wagon. Quantities of wheat or flour in estate inventories tended to be small, but added together, they could easily total the millions of pounds Frederick and Berkeley County farmers produced during the early 1770s. Other measures of a staple economy directing greater and greater energy toward market production appeared from the 1750s to the 1760s in increased frequency in inventories: horses, from 91 percent to 94 percent; plows, from 35 percent to 48; wagons, from 19 to 30; and book debts, from 43 to 63.[14]

Nicholas Cresswell's observations provide another measure of a developing commercial economy in the Shenandoah Valley during the years before the American Revolution. He visited the region with the idea of setting himself up as a commercial farmer. "Agriculture," he said, "is in such an infant state and the value of land so low that anyone with the least spark of industry might make what money they please." Accordingly, he composed an "Estimate of the cost and profit of an Estate containing 500 acres" in Frederick or Berkeley Counties. At forty shillings an acre the land would require £1,000. Livestock, including breeding mares, an imported stallion, cows, oxen, cattle, sheep, and hogs, would add an additional £1,190. Labor—five manservants and two women—plus their clothing totaled £160. Harrows, plows, a wagon, and other implements brought the grand total, including quitrents and tithes, to a little more than £2,400. Expected annual revenues, however, reached £600, or 25 percent of the initial investment. The sale of livestock plus the stallion's stud fees accounted for most of this sum, but not insignificant was the £45 earned from "30 acres of wheat at 12 bushels to the acre sold @ 2/6."[15]

Cresswell reckoned profits from no farm crops except wheat, but other Shenandoah Valley farmers were still growing hemp and tobacco for sale as they had before the Seven Years' War. A new hemp bounty in the 1760s soon made Virginia the leading hemp producer in North America. The Shenandoah Valley played no small role in this development, as "Philo Virginia" made clear in the *Virginia Gazette:* "As I was travelling some months ago through several of the back counties in Virginia, I observed with pleasure that a great number of the inhabitants, encouraged by the offered bounty, had for a year or two past raised a considerable quantity of hemp." Between 1764 and 1769, Valley farmers produced 650 tons of hemp, and in the upper Valley, Philip Fithian found that "Great Quantities" were raised. A farm household could earn £13–15 a year from hemp, and a rope walk for the production of hempen cord was operating in Winchester by 1767.[16]

Comparable profits in tobacco could also be had in the Shenandoah Valley. David Allason collected £50,000 annually during his brief stay in the early 1760s. By the time of the Revolution, perhaps three hundred fifty to four hundred acres, mostly in the lower Valley, were devoted to the crop, and according to Samuel Kercheval, its cultivation "was first introduced and pursued by immigrants from the eastern counties of Virginia." One of these was Nathaniel Burwell, the master of Carter's Grove, near Williamsburg. Burwell, who had inherited 5,325 acres of land near the Shenandoah River in the lower Valley, purchased another twenty-five hundred acres. In the years before and after the Revolution, he developed his land in tenancies or satellite plantations called quarters, which were worked by a small group of slaves under the management of an overseer. Twenty-seven percent of his total profits and half of his tobacco came from the Valley in 1774. The next year two Valley quarters, Marsh and River, yielded thirty-two thousand pounds of tobacco and revenues of £754 against £270 in expenses for overseers' wages and provisions for the slaves. Burwell was one of several prominent Tidewater planters who inherited large quantities of land in the Shenandoah Valley from a common ancestor, Robert Carter, the land agent for Lord Fairfax. Many, including Burwell, Thomas T. Byrd, and John, Robert, and Matthew Page would move to the Valley after the Revolution with large numbers of slaves to grow wheat, not tobacco.[17]

Livestock and livestock products constituted another source of income for Valley farmers. According to Nicholas Cresswell, "Great numbers of Hogs and cattle of all sorts are bred and fed here." In adding that the "range for stock is unlimited," Cresswell indicated that open spaces across property boundaries and between fenced enclosures still functioned as a commons where livestock grazed freely. As in Washington's day, drovers continued to drive Valley cattle to northern markets, and Philadelphia butchers continued to buy them. The market for dairy products also thrived, as one Staunton merchant demonstrated by sending five and a half tons of butter, 812 pounds of cheese, and two hundred pounds of tallow to buyers in eastern Virginia.[18]

The £14 of John Beckett as an average—or the £4 10s. of Robert Allen and the £45 of Nicholas Cresswell as a range—was what farmers could begin to expect as profits in growing grain in the 1760s. But how could they make use of these sums? Allen's £4 or £5 could readily purchase a horse or mare. At Allen's own estate sale it could have bought a table, twelve chairs, three dishes, twelve plates, six basins, ten spoons, and three tin cups, or it could have furnished a chamber with a chest and bedstead, sheets, two double blankets, a quilt, and a rug. Anyone with that sum could put cash down on Bryan Bruin's counter in Winchester and take away ten pounds of green tea, ten yards of white jean cloth, two gallons of Madeira wine, plus a fiddle. Various imported or manufactured items, such as tea kettles or Delft plates and bowls, began to appear in rural households. These items and the ability to purchase them did not yet constitute a consumer revolution, but one was clearly in the making.[19]

During the decade and a half before the American Revolution, essential elements for significant economic development fell into place in the Shenandoah Valley. Rising prices in the Atlantic economy created a market for wheat that penetrated into interior areas at least as far west as the Shenandoah Valley. Farmers there could transport flour long distances and still come out ahead.

Wheat profits produced a demand across the countryside for manufactured and imported goods. To organize the trade in these goods, a merchant community emerged in Winchester. This triad of wheat profits, consumer demand, and merchant trade would transform the landscape geography of the Shenandoah Valley during the last quarter of the eighteenth century. At the same time that the American Revolution disrupted this process, it also created the conditions that would intensify it. The result would be the landscape of enclosed farms and market towns that became the signature of the Shenandoah Valley in the nineteenth century. Its interpretation—like its development—is complex.

· ৶ ·

How this landscape worked, therefore, requires explanation. How could towns function when wheat, the source of regional wealth, was produced on thousands of farms scattered over hundreds of square miles? How could widely dispersed farmers transform flour profits into consumer demand that could be realized in the shops of town merchants? How could merchants conduct a trade when the staple export was handled at mills dispersed on streams across the countryside or when they procured their stock in trade hundreds of miles away in Atlantic ports? How, in other words, did the pieces of this landscape fit together and function relationally?

If, in the years before the American Revolution, the elements of economic development in the Shenandoah Valley began to align, the war itself slowed and deepened the process of change. No fighting took place in the Valley, but George Washington had received his military education there, and the region also provided for the home, if not the nurture, of such other leaders as Daniel Morgan, Horatio Gates, Charles Lee, and Adam Stephen. Grassroots support for the patriot cause betrayed none of the suspicion or resistance demonstrated by county militias during the Seven Years' War. On arriving in the Shenandoah Valley in June 1775, Philip Fithian reported that "Mars, the great God of Battle, is honored in every Part of this spacious Colony, but here every Presence is warlike, every Sound is martial! Drums beating, Fifes & Bag-Pipes playing, & only sonorous & heroic Tunes." As early as 1772 Adam Stephen counted twenty-two hundred Valley men armed and ready to fight. How different from the time when Washington had carped that "you may, with almost equal success, attempt to raize the Dead to Life again, as the force of this County."[20]

What had changed was the nature of the conflict. Many people of the backcountry had seen the earlier war as an imperial struggle—a king's war—which threatened their property, their farms, their households, and the competency they had worked so hard to achieve. Recall the militia captain who explained to Washington that, because "his Wife, Family, and Corn was at stake, [and] so were those of his Soldrs," it was not possible to answer the royal call to arms. A revolution against the king was, of course, another matter, and Shenandoah Valley militias mustered two decades later for what they saw as the defense of their lands against a threat to the very commerce and political autonomy that made competency possible. Immediate and palpable fears for the fate of market opportunities that had developed during the previous fifteen years surfaced in Fithian's further comment that "Country Produce of all kinds has no Price with the Merchants—& is exchanged through the Country, commonly without Money, where need calls.—The best Wheat is not sold for more than three Shillings." Evidently, however, the exchange economy survived and sustained the community in an economic and political crisis as it had in the earlier hardships of settlement.[21]

Like the Seven Years' War, the Revolution had its economic effects on the Shenandoah Valley. The military demands of the conflict coaxed more and more wheat from Valley soils. Because hemp was critical for cordage, the state of Virginia became a major hemp buyer during the war years, and output in the Shenandoah Valley doubled. Conversely, the market dropped out from under tobacco. But army quartermasters spent thousands of pounds on livestock products, and some farmers sold more than seven thousand pounds of beef to the military. After the war military demand relaxed, inflation eased, commodity prices dropped, hemp markets stagnated, and what little tobacco was grown in the Valley went largely to pay taxes. Wheat prices, however, doubled during the postwar decades, making it the premier crop of the region.[22]

· ☙ ·

The Revolution also had important strategic consequences for the Valley. Disputes with Native Americans brought a series of western actions, first in Dunmore's War and later in the campaigns of George Rodgers Clark and John Sullivan, which crippled Indian resistance west of the Appalachians as far north as Iroquoia. In the effort to assert authority over western territory, the Virginia legislature also established Kentucky County in 1776 and approved a land law three years later that provided for the survey and conveyance of the state's trans-Appalachian lands. Diplomacy and war would not only deprive Native Americans of much of the Ohio Valley by the mid-1790s but would also open to American occupation this vast region won from Great Britain in the Revolution. Opportunities in trans-Appalachia would touch off one of the great folk migrations in American history.

The consequences of American victory in the Revolution reverberated throughout the Shenandoah Valley during the economic depression of the mid-1780s. After the 1783 Peace of Paris, British merchants flooded American markets with trade goods on easy credit to meet a pent-up demand caused by wartime shortages. The new nation's trade deficit soon ballooned from less than a million pounds sterling to 2.7 million by 1784. The consequent flow of gold and silver coin eastward across the Atlantic to balance this trade nearly crippled the American economy. These problems were compounded by Great Britain's ban of American ships from its West Indian ports and Spain's closure of the Mississippi to American commerce. Imports plummeted and exports stagnated for much of the remaining decade.[23]

If the Shenandoah Valley escaped the fighting during the Revolution, it hardly remained unscathed by postwar economic troubles. The stagnating foreign trade and the refusal of European powers to conclude commercial treaties with the United States almost destroyed wheat markets. Meanwhile, extensive state powers over domestic trade under the Articles of Confederation led to Virginia-imposed duties on goods brought overland from other states. The costs of doing business in Philadelphia or Baltimore for Shenandoah Valley merchants soared. New state taxes, including a levy on the stock in trade of merchants, hurt backcountry commerce further. The exchange economy buffered household competence against the immediate effects of declining markets and restricted trade, but even the ability of this economy to absorb debt was strained. From 1782 to 1784 the number of debt cases before the Frederick County Court increased by 221 percent. Augusta County debtors were double the number in Frederick.[24]

Several mitigating factors, however, softened the economic blows of the 1780s. While the exchange economy sustained local trade, the settlement of the trans-Appalachian West provided new sources of economic growth. From 1783 to 1790 the population of Kentucky swelled from twelve thousand to more than seventy-three thousand, and by the latter year the aggregate population of the Kentucky and Tennessee territories outnumbered that of any of the three smallest states, Delaware, Rhode Island, or Georgia. Many migrants took the Valley route west—the wagon road up the Shenandoah Valley, then Daniel Boone's Wilderness Road west to the new territories. The needs of these people for food and provisions, wagon repairs, and all the necessities of life proved to be a boon for the people of the Shenandoah Valley. One observer estimated that travelers numbered four thousand annually, and in 1789 the editor of a Winchester newspaper exclaimed that in "the rage for Kentucky . . . the number of families which have passed through this town for the last four or five weeks, on their way to that distant region is almost incredible."[25]

Hard times in the 1780s, however, were not to stay, and the last decade of the eighteenth century was one of the most prosperous in American economic history. The new federal government, armed with the commerce clause of the Constitution, broke down state barriers to domestic trade and concluded commercial treaties with European powers in 1795, thus freeing the trade of the new nation from constraints at home and abroad. Meanwhile, population growth in Europe hopelessly outpaced staple production, and the European wars following the French Revolution rapidly increased the demand for foodstuffs while allowing American merchants to capture the trans-Atlantic shipping trade. The value of United States exports, which remained fairly static in the early 1790s, fluctuating between $19 million and $20 million annually, jumped to $26 million in 1793, then almost doubled within the next two years, and climbed steadily thereafter until reaching $70 million by the end of the decade. Imports, however, grew apace and consistently exceeded exports. Although the excess of imports over exports in 1800 equaled export totals ten years earlier, the trade deficit was more than offset by earnings in the shipping and shipbuilding trades. Americans in the 1790s could, therefore, import huge quantities of European goods without increasing indebtedness and replicating the economic problems of the previous decade.[26]

The domestic economy grew in ways that specifically benefited the Shenandoah Valley. While the United States population grew by 35 percent in the 1790s, the number of people in Kentucky and Tennessee multiplied at almost six times that rate. It was not only prosperity that fueled western migration during that decade but also new agreements between the federal government and the Ohio tribes—Delawares, Shawnees, and others represented at the long-ago 1753 Winchester council. Defeated at the Battle of Fallen Timbers in 1794, these western peoples conceded all of eastern, central, and southern Ohio to American settlement. "There is but little occasion for arms now that peace has been made with the Indians," commented one Shenandoah Valley traveler, "but formerly it used to be a very serious undertaking to go by this route to Kentucky." Peace and security explained the "great numbers of people from Kentucky and the new state of Tenassee going towards Philadelphia and Baltimore, and . . . many others going in a contrary direction, 'to explore,' as they call it, that is, to search for lands conveniently situated for new settlements in the western country."[27]

Because as one Shenandoah Valley resident put it, the "emigration . . . to Kentucky is astonishing," the number of people in the Valley grew by only 12 percent during the 1790s. But outmigration relieved population pressure on the land, easing conditions for those who stayed behind. Farm productivity increased during the decade—so much so that by 1810 Frederick County stood third in Virginia flour production and would lead the state ten years later. The amount of capital devoted to labor also grew, as measured in a 27 percent expansion of the slave population during the 1790s. Slave hiring provided the means of deploying bound labor flexibly amid the diverse work regimes of mixed agriculture. Gains in productivity and labor meant more wealth for the white population. The average value of probate inventories in Frederick County, for instance, jumped from £165 to £198 from the 1770s to the 1790s, while the frequency of those who died with cash on hand grew from 36 to 40 percent. Although the percentage of Shenandoah Valley households lacking assets in slaves, horses, or cattle escalated from six in 1782 to twenty-five eighteen years later, other indicators suggest that new wealth was not concentrating unduly in the hands of the better-off. In Frederick County, the percentage of the taxable population that owned no land changed very little between 1782 and 1800, while the percentage of total real property owned by the wealthiest decile increased from forty-seven to only fifty-three during the same period and declined thereafter.[28]

. ⚤ .

Trade, commerce, and general prosperity created the context in which the Shenandoah Valley began to take on the garb of a town and country landscape. From the outbreak of the Revolution to the end of the century, at least fourteen new towns were laid out (fig. 7.1). Many received legislative charters. New counties, spawned from existing ones, accounted for the founding of three new towns as county seats: Martinsburg (Berkeley County) and Lexington (Rockbridge County) in 1778, and Harrisonburg (Rockingham County) in 1780. Woodstock, established in 1761, became the county seat of Dunmore County (later Shenandoah County) after its creation in 1772. These county towns all lay along the Valley Road, as did Darkesville, Middletown, and New Market, each surveyed in the 1790s. Another group of more than a half-dozen new towns, including Charles Town, Berryville, Front Royal, and Waynesboro, lay on connectors to the Valley Road, intensifying the trellis pattern of road development. By the end of the eighteenth century, therefore, most Valley people lived within a half-day's journey to the nearest stores and shops.[29]

What emerged from this complex of settlement configurations, then, was a hierarchy of towns intricately woven into the earlier pattern of open-country neighborhoods. Historical geographer Robert D. Mitchell calls this arrangement a "settlement continuum" to stress the continuities of rural and urban worlds in the preindustrial landscape. By the end of the eighteenth century, settlement neighborhoods such as Opequon, Hopewell, Mill Creek, and North Mountain had lost their geographical distinctiveness as intervening

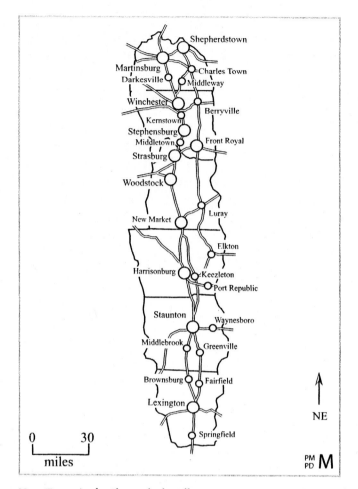

FIG. 7.1. New Towns in the Shenandoah Valley, 1780–1800. Economic growth during the final decades of the eighteenth century produced a wave of town founding in the Shenandoah Valley. New towns assumed positions on the Valley Road, and others formed along the growing number of connecting roads leading east and west. Based on Mitchell, *Commercialism and Frontier*, 192, fig. 25.

spaces were settled, but their social cohesion survived. Along the drains of the upper Opequon, for instance, the Hites, Glasses, Vances, Willsons, Marquises, and others were still on the land. For the most part, their holdings remained undivided or distributed among family members. Parents in some cases left their holdings to children in shares, not subdivisions, with the expectation that the money expended by one or two offspring in consolidating family lands would underwrite the establishment of other children in commerce or a craft. Alternatively, it could fund their move farther west.[30]

What was new in the urban geography of the late-eighteenth-century Shenandoah Valley was a hierarchy of hamlets, villages, and towns. In contrast to open-country neighborhoods, hamlets, according to Mitchell, were "more clustered settlement forms that might include an occasional agricultural unit but were distinguished by supporting three or four nonfarm functions, such as those expressed in a store, artisan's shop, mill, or residence of a local justice, minister, or school teacher." Slightly larger were villages "of one or two streets that contained no farm units and a greater number of functions and occupations, likely including more stores, a church or meeting house, post office (after 1800), an inn and tavern, and residences of several professional people." Neither hamlets nor villages would have been set apart by incorporation, and the life ways of residents were linked more directly to the economy of the countryside than to the commerce of the Atlantic world. Most houses in these settlements backed onto open fields or pastures, worked by many residents for at least a part of their livelihood. Pasturing a cow or two and maintaining kitchen gardens kept village life in step with the rhythms of life in the country.[31]

Towns, according to Mitchell, "constitute 'urban' settlement, based on additional population and a wider range of functions." They were "distinguished . . . by a recognized legal status that permits self-government and a commercial status that encompasses extensive local and regional service areas." Winchester was the only Shenandoah Valley town thus incorporated by the Virginia legislature during the eighteenth century, although Staunton received town status in 1801. The 1779 Winchester act empowered the "mayor, recorder, aldermen, and common councilmen . . . to make bye laws and ordinances for the regulation and good governance of the said town." These officials, to be elected by the "freeholders and house-keepers" of the town, would possess the "power to hold and keep within the said town annually, two market days in every week of the year, the one on Wednesday and the other on Saturday, and from time to time to appoint a clerk of the market, who shall have assize of bread, wine, beer, wood, and other things." Empowered as a corporation to conduct commerce, Winchester clearly dominated the urban hierarchy of the lower Shenandoah Valley by the end of the eighteenth century. As the count de Castiglioni, who visited the area in 1785, saw it, "Winchester, for commerce, is one of the most important towns of Virginia." The lower Valley's fifty-three thousand people in 1800 supported 14 percent of their number in hamlets, villages, or towns. Between one-third and one-quarter of the nonrural population lived in Winchester.[32]

The settlement continuum from open-country neighborhoods through hamlets and villages to towns such as Winchester represented more than a simple hierarchy of size. Functional relationships within the economic geography—patterns in how many people made a living—knit all these components into a landscape. By comparison to eastern Virginia, this was a town-rich landscape, a spatial composition of dispersed farmsteads drawn together by roads into networks of millers and artisans clustering at hamlets or villages and merchants, artisan specialists, and professionals congregating in towns.

· ⚘ ·

Key to understanding this landscape—to unraveling the meaning of its various interrelated elements—were three crucial features: farms, mills, and shops. To some extent farmers, millers, and merchants traded in straightforward cash transactions carrying wheat to the mill, cash to the merchant, and so forth. But the quantity of cash in this economy was never sufficient for its operation, and, as in the past, cash itself was regarded more as a commodity than as a means of exchange. The exchange economy, which had rendered the settlement of the Shenandoah Valley by Europeans viable since the 1730s, still underlay the landscape, allowing it to function as a complex machine for production, distribution, and consumption. The town-rich environment of the region and the settlement continuum from open-country neighborhoods to market centers such as Winchester worked because of the ancient system of reckoning debits and credits in book accounts maintained over long periods of time.

By the end of the eighteenth century, little had changed in the mix of farm activities: wheat, rye, oats, barley, corn, flax, hemp, and tobacco could all be seen growing on Shenandoah Valley farms; horses, cattle, sheep, and pigs ranged the land. The emphasis, however, clearly lay on wheat. According to Isaac Weld, wheat was "produced in as plentiful crops as in any part of the United States"; fifteen to twenty-five bushels to the acre is what the duc de La Rochefoucauld-Liancourt estimated. By 1790 lower Shenandoah Valley farmers produced four million pounds of flour annually and more than two and one-half times that amount ten years later. Samuel Glass's son Robert was a farmer who certainly took advantage of opportunities to grow wheat on his 544 acres along the upper Opequon. When he died in 1797, he had a 26-acre field of wheat in the ground, a quantity of "light wheat" already harvested, and ten barrels of flour worth in all more than £43. With the exception of his horses and cattle, no other possession was so valuable. Robert's brother and neighbor, Joseph, passed away at about the same time possessed of 100 bushels of wheat. Its value, appraised at more than £26, exceeded the sum affixed to all the hay and corn in his barn. So attractive was the culture of wheat, that Thomas Bryan Martin, who in the 1760s had asserted that "tobacco . . . is our all," now could query a relative in England: "Are you all starving that you give such prices for our flour, farming is now my object, Tobacco not worth raising."[33]

Wheat changed the landscape. In 1800 the Valley supported more people than ever before. Although outmigration meant a minimum of subdivision, land clearance proceeded at a rapid rate. "In the neighbourhood of Winchester," according to Isaac Weld, "it is so thickly settled, and consequently so much cleared, that wood is now beginning to be thought valuable; the farmers are obliged frequently to send ten or fifteen miles even for their fence rails." A sale notice for a farm on the Opequon Creek four miles from Winchester in 1791 provides a good description of how property "in as fine a settlement as any in the State" might appear: "There are upwards of 100 acres cleared and under fence—10 acres of meadow, chiefly timothy, which may be watered at very little expence.—There are on the premises, a good orchard and an excellent spring, a good dwelling-house, kitchen, spring house, and two new barns." As farmers cleared more land, they struggled to increase its productivity and make their own operations more efficient. Rationalization of the landscape dictated the relocation of dwellings and farmsteads from initial settlement locations on stream terraces to upland areas more central to property holdings. Wells had to be dug and roads realigned. In the absence of archaeological evidence, little can be said about farmstead layout, but it undoubtedly tended toward the rectilinear patterns of the nineteenth century, in which the roof lines of dwellings, barns, and outbuildings either aligned or formed interconnected yards at right angles. As the cultivated landscape was reorganized for greater productivity and profit, it also expanded into previously undeveloped areas. Charged with the responsibility for leasing the mountain lands of the Fairfax Proprietary, Thomas Bryan Martin found that by 1791 he was "easily renting . . . [the] land, the mountains are stripping their ancient dress, instead of trees in view I behold rocks and plantations and Cash coming in. Dear and wolves disposessed of their former retreat, and beings in human form supplying their place."[34]

Thus the landscape created by the drive for competence became the landscape of improvement. Farmers built new houses, farmyards became compounds with structures for every agricultural purpose, and fields increased in size. On the Hollingsworth farm, along the original Philadelphia Wagon Road near Winchester, there was "about 100 acres of cleared land, nearly the same quantity of wood land, and 30 acres of meadow, well-watered." There was also a "convenient stone dwelling-house, a merchant-mill, a saw mill and fulling-mill, a good barn and other out houses." Robert Allen and his son Montgomery had improved family land along the upper Opequon so extensively that by 1794 there were "about 150 acres of upland, cleared and in good repair, and about 25 acres of good meadow, a considerable quantity, more of which may be made; 125 acres of woodland, well-timbered, a good apple orchard, and a number of cherry and peach trees; and has on it several never failing springs; a stream of water runs through a part there of, sufficient for a mill; there are likewise . . . two tolerable dwelling houses, two good kitchens and smoke house, one still house, large enough for three or four stills, two good barns, stables, and other necessary houses." According to the survey Jonathan Clark conducted to resolve the legal disputes of the Fairfax Proprietary, William Vance, son of James and Elizabeth Vance, possessed 338 acres, of which he cultivated 86, maintained 14 in meadow, and preserved sufficient space for a thirty-tree orchard. In addition, he built a log shop, stable, still house, meat house, and two log dwellings—one with a shed addition on the back and a front shaded by a seven-foot-wide porch. And to make good his intention to establish flour as one of the "Staple Commodities" of the Valley, Adam Stephen owned extensive lands by the 1790s and cultivated 184 of 400 acres on one parcel alone.[35]

Breeding and fattening livestock also required landscape improvements. The open range that Cresswell described survived into the nineteenth century, but it was rapidly giving way to fenced pasture. As one prominent eastern Virginia planter wrote to his overseer in the Valley, "I can not see why Cattle shou'd not be penned all Summer tho', as well up the Country as down—I shou'd be glad if you wou'd fall upon a Method of having them got up every Night, both here and in Frederick." In the central Valley La Rochefoucauld-Liancourt found that cattle were "constantly kept in the woods," but on approaching Winchester he remarked that "considerable numbers of cattle are reared, and more particularly fattened in pastures, and then, as well as the sheep and pigs, which are also very numerous, sent to the markets of Baltimore and Philadelphia."[36]

As in earlier landscapes in which roads knit together all the places where exchanges so necessary to economic competence took place, roads linked farm households not only to each other but also to nearby mills, hamlets, and villages, as well as to Winchester (fig. 7.2). It was by road and wagon, of course, that farmers took the first step in transforming their wheat crops into flour profits. Mills were dispersed upon the landscape by their necessary dependence on waterpower. The consequent and critical association of mills and roads had been recognized in colonial legislation that required mills to be "erected at convenient places" and mill dams be wide enough to accommodate "neerer roads." Just as millers had to dam streams to tap the power contained in falling water, so these streams formed a kind of power grid stretched with all the erratic regularity of nature across the landscape. Unlike grids of electric power delivering energy practically anywhere people need it today, the eighteenth-century power grid was fixed by topography, and people had to tap its energy only where landforms afforded proper mill seats. People came to the power, not power to the people, and roads overspread the land in dense, interconnecting networks.[37]

Geology also influenced the economic geography. A mill required at least four or five feet of falling water for a breast-shot wheel, and a large overshot

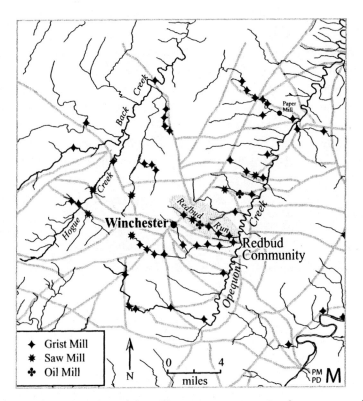

FIG. 7.2. Winchester, Roads, and the Milling Economy, 1800. Road patterns reveal the town of Winchester as the geographic hub for the lower Shenandoah Valley at the end of the eighteenth century. Mills upon which the economy of the town depended, however, were dispersed across the countryside. Many appeared along the rapidly descending streams of the shale lands adjoining the Opequon Creek. The five mills clustered along a two-mile segment (shaded) of Redbud Run were recognized as a community named after the creek. Based on Charles Varlé, *Map of Frederick, Berkeley, and Jefferson Counties in the State of Virginia* (Philadelphia: Benjamin Jones, 1809).

wheel needed as much as twenty feet of fall. Depending on stream gradient, either requirement could necessitate mill races as long as a mile or more. On shale lands in the central Shenandoah Valley, where surface runoff was swift and streams dropped steeply, mills could be stacked practically one after another along a waterway. Although less productive for agriculture, shale lands had been called the "poor hills," where farmers lived mostly by herding and occupied "only small and wretched habitations," in the words of La Rochefoucauld-Liancourt. But just as wheat farming produced improved landscapes in limestone regions of the Shenandoah Valley, grinding wheat into flour brought improvement to shale lands by the end of the eighteenth century. Eleven of fourteen mills along two streams east of Winchester, for instance, were built between 1791 and 1815. One two-mile stretch of Redbud Run—a region of industrial development so dense it was called the community of "Red-bud"—supported five mills, which produced flax fibers, linseed oil, lumber, paper, and wrought iron, as well as flour.[38]

Fewer mills appeared along the upper branches of the Opequon, where the earliest settlement community had taken root three-quarters of a century earlier. A gentler slope to the land could only accommodate mills spaced about one and one-half miles apart. Jost Hite and Samuel Glass had built mills early in the history of the area, and Glass's son Joseph followed his father in developing a large saw- and gristmill complex requiring a several-acre impoundment. Along the five-mile stretch of creek separating Glass and Hite, two to four mills operated at various times during the eighteenth century. Throughout the entire Valley the number of mills doubled during the last quarter of the century, reaching a total of 400 in the lower Valley alone.[39]

Much of the millers trade was custom work for local farmers. A farmer could haul wheat to the mill and exchange it at the ratio of five bushels for a barrel of flour with a one-eighth toll as the miller's share. John Kercheval, at Greenwood Mills on Abrams Creek, for instance, advertised that "for the convenience of those who favor him with their custom, he will always have flour on hand to give for wheat when it is delivered." Some millers, however, were flour merchants purchasing flour from farmers. Thus Kercheval also gave "cash for Wheat or Rye delivered at his mills near Winchester, or at his store in Battle-Town [Berryville]." He would also contract with a farmer for an entire crop of grain. Merchant mills became sites of varied enterprise. At Greenwood, Kercheval owned a "valuable merchant mill, a handsome dwelling house, barn, distillery, and other conveniences." John Koontz and Richard Ober at Millsgrove, nine miles east of Winchester along the Opequon, not only kept ten wagons plying back and forth to Alexandria while employing several coopers but also advertised a "large assortment of European, East and West India Goods" available at their mill store. Here "Country Store-Keepers and private families will find it their interest to visit." Blacksmiths, harness makers, and other artisans often congregated at mill sites, which became small hamlets with associated dwellings and farmsteads.[40]

Millers conducted most of their trade in cash, but at mills, as elsewhere in an exchange economy, cash served primarily to balance debits and credits in book accounts. The commerce of wheat thus organized economic relationships in complex patterns over large stretches of the landscape in a manner familiar to practically every resident of the Shenandoah Valley. Take, for example, George Stubblefield, who, between August 1799 and January 1800, brought forty-seven barrels of corn and ninety bushels of wheat worth £67 15s. to Philip Earhart's mill on Chapel Run, a tributary of the Shenandoah River. Little of this cash, however, ever found its way into Stubblefield's pockets, because he also took home salt, herrings, sugar, coffee, oysters, and cloth, which Earhart had hauled back from marketing trips to Alexandria. To the account Earhart also added thirty-one gallons of whiskey, two gallons of brandy, and enough flour for Stubblefield's family and twenty-one slaves.[41]

When Philip Earhart recorded a credit for wheat received from George Stubblefield in his account book and Stubblefield documented this same transaction as a debit in his accounts, the two notations effectively created transferable wealth in Stubblefield's crop. This wealth could be traded immediately for salt, herrings, and other commodities, but it could also be kept almost indefinitely and drawn upon in an ongoing exchange of goods and services. It could, moreover, order economic exchanges across the landscape. Stubblefield, for instance, acquired credit with Berryville merchant Bushrod Taylor in April and May 1800 for sixty-seven barrels of flour at Earhart's mill and another sixty-two barrels deposited in Alexandria. By writing orders on his credit with Taylor, Stubblefield then acquired various goods and services from other farmers and artisans living throughout his neighborhood. Shoes came from Moses, a slave artisan belonging to Thomas Stribling, blacksmithing from Richard Shirkliff, calf and sheepskins from tanner Thomas McCormick, and sixty and one-half yards of cloth from weaver Henry Bradford. Similarly, at John Kercheval's Berryville store, Stubblefield procured sugar, linen, sickles, stockings, cheese, raisins, and dry goods on an account that in one year also included credit for more than eighty-four bushels of wheat. Stubblefield's accounts readily extended to Winchester, where he dealt with merchants William Groverman, William Holliday, and Cornelius O'Laughlin, as well as artisans Peter Kehoe and George Kiger. By reckoning debits and credits through time and across space, George Stubblefield demonstrated how keeping book accounts knit together the key elements of the landscape: the farm, the mill, and the town.[42]

· ☖ ·

Roads, of course, completed the connections of farm and mill to town (fig. 7.3). On the road to Winchester in 1775, Philip Fithian had observed that "the Country Road . . . to this Town is thick inhabited—The Land is good, the Country pleasant, the Houses in general large." Thirteen years, a revolution, and a federal Constitution later, another traveler, Samuel Vaughan, followed this same "good road" through "Rich land" to Winchester. There he found a "Borough town" with a "Court house Gaol, Market Assembly room . . . Lutheran Calvinist Episcopal, many Baptist & Methodist Churches. an Accademy & gramr. Schools 400 houses above 2000 Inhabitants, a flourishing town of great trade."[43]

The plan of streets and blocks had changed little since the expansions of the 1750s. The nucleus of the town was in the public square and the new buildings it boasted by the end of the eighteenth century (fig. 7.4). In the mid-1780s the Frederick County Court removed the old courthouse and constructed a new one fifty by forty feet, two stories high, with a bell. The new church that the Anglican vestry had called for in 1761 was completed in 1766. Built of coursed stone, with four windows on each side, it opened onto Loudoun Street with a double door and a sixty-foot steeple. Inside, a canopy surmounted a raised pulpit. Below the altar was a communion table and fourteen wainscoted pew boxes. By the 1780s, however, this imposing structure was no longer a public building. Virginia had broken ties with the Church of England in 1776 and withdrawn the vestry's power to impose tithes. Ten years later, Thomas Jefferson's "Statute of Virginia for Religious Freedom" formally severed the remaining ties between church and state, and in 1789 Anglicans organized the Protestant Episcopal Church of America as a private, voluntary body. Although in 1802 the state confiscated all its property previously purchased with public funds, the Episcopal church remained on the public square until it removed to Boscawen and Washington Streets later in the nineteenth century. The jail also stood on the public square. By the 1760s the old jail no longer served the needs of county justice, and the court called for the construction of a new, forty-by-thirty-four-foot stone prison with three-foot walls and a two-inch grid of iron bars over the single window in each of four rooms. Two rooms were reserved for the jailer, another for debtors, and a fourth for "criminals of every description and Sex." A twelve-foot stone wall surrounded the jail and a separate kitchen building in a sixty-by-eighty-foot enclosure. It is

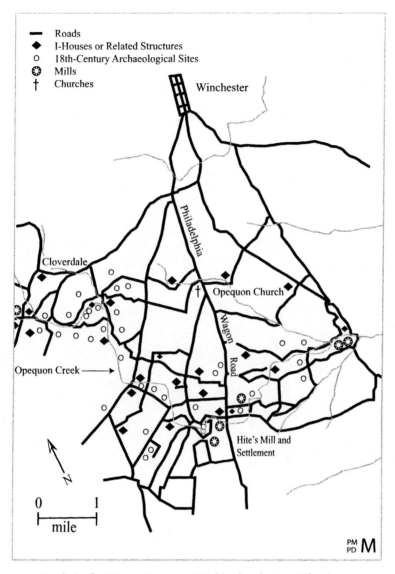

FIG. 7.3. Roads in the Upper Opequon Neighborhood, 1800. The dense pattern of roads throughout the old open-country neighborhood along the upper Opequon Creek demonstrates the importance of connections between farms and mills for economic activity in improved landscapes of the late eighteenth century. The spokelike roads leading to Winchester also testify to the significance of market towns to rural life. Based on road orders in Frederick County Court Orders, Frederick County Courthouse, Winchester, and field survey by the author.

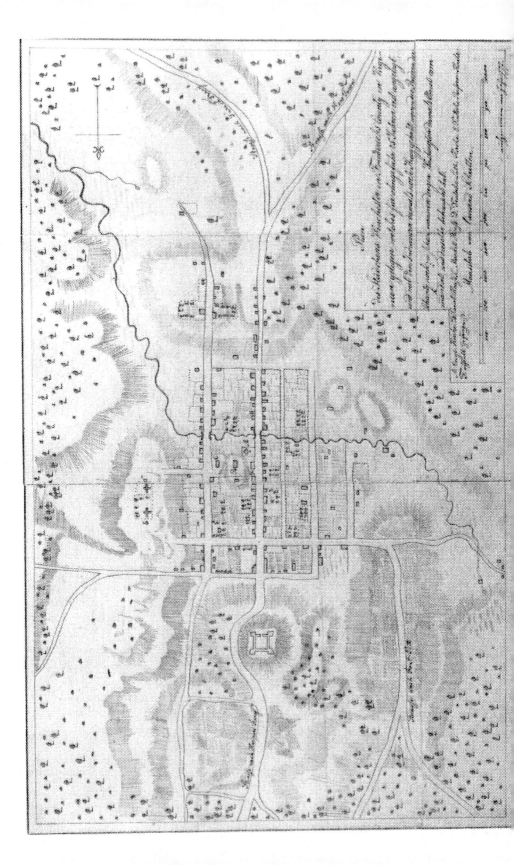

unclear if the whipping post and stocks survived, but the ducking stool had been repaired as late as November 1766. But perhaps the market house was the most significant new building for the role the town was assuming in the regional economy. Built in the 1760s, it actually predated the incorporation of the town and the establishment of the Winchester public market in the next decade. With the lower arcade devoted to space for market stalls, the upstairs chambers served the needs of town government and public functions. Elections were held there for town offices in the 1790s.[44]

The public square and main streets of the town lay in the basin that Philip Fithian had described as so "disagreeable." Many other features defining the town were situated on the surrounding hills. Although the outlots had come to be called the commons, and some townspeople grazed livestock there, others had fenced their five acres or subdivided them into one-half-acre town lots. "Wasted & crumbled down by Time," according to Fithian, old Fort Loudoun still occupied the prominence immediately to the north of the town. Offsetting the military with the religious, hills to the east of town supported a line of churches for Presbyterian, German Lutheran, and German Reformed congregations. Through these hills snaked the roads that connected Winchester northward and eastward to distant markets in Pennsylvania, Maryland, or eastern Virginia. To the south and west roads led toward the new trans-Appalachian settlements. But as countryside gave way to town, these sinuous routes became straight streets and the corridors of urban commerce.[45]

Commercial activity clustered along Loudoun and Cameron Streets, especially around the public square (fig. 7.5). When La Rochefoucauld-Liancourt visited Winchester in the mid-1790s, he counted "upwards of thirty well-stocked stores, or shops" and estimated their total trade at more than six hundred thousand dollars. Mechanics, too, were "found in abundance; even a coach-maker, and several watch-makers." In addition to smiths, weavers, potters, hatters, saddlers, and shoemakers, Harry Toulmin took note of clock-

Facing page

FIG. 7.4. Andreas Wiederholdt, "Plan of the Town of Winchester in Frederick County, Virginia, 1777." A Hessian soldier, Wiederholdt was imprisoned in Winchester when he sketched this map in 1777. Despite the additions to the town during the Seven Years' War, commercial, residential, and public structures clustered along its two main streets, which connected directly to country roads. According to Wiederholdt's key, the letters on the map refer to (A) English Church, (B) Court House, (C) Market House, (D) German Lutheran Church, (E) German Reformed Church, and (F) Public Jail. Andreas Wiederholdt, Map of Winchester, 1777, Dewey manuscript 973.3 R723.3, Rare Book and Manuscript Library, University of Pennsylvania.

makers, cabinetmakers, painted-chair makers, gunsmiths, and coachmakers practicing their specialty crafts in town. "The stores, or shops, are numerous and considerable," he commented. For the two years following 1792, at least thirty-three separate artisans advertised in Winchester newspapers. The largest number represented the textile or clothing trades, not the storage, transport, or marketing of flour, which was dispersed at mills throughout the countryside. Taverns, too, were plentiful. Eight advertised their accommodations in the newspapers, and La Rochefoucauld-Liancourt counted "ten or twelve inns, large and small, which are often full." Winchester, according to this eyewitness, lay "in the way of all travellers who proceed to the back parts of Virginia, to Tenessee, or to the mineral springs in the counties of Augusta and Berkeley." As a county town, Winchester supported more than twenty lawyers, who "find constant practice, and are in thriving circumstances."[46]

Loudoun, Cameron, and Boscawen Streets became Main, Market, and Water Streets in the nineteenth century, a change that suggests their commercial importance to the town. The eighteenth-century streetscape, however, was far more irregular than the well-articulated, three-story commercial blocks surviving today in main-street towns would suggest. "In entering main street," one visitor commented, "I was particularily struck with the narrowness of the street, which, on this account, has a very disagreeable appearance." Mixing commercial and residential activities, townspeople built stores, shops, and residences on property lines to give the street a confined, linear appearance. Lots were not completely built out, gaps existed between buildings, and roof lines jumped jaggedly from story to story and between gable ends and eave sides. Some structures combined shop and house, and in back lots could be found a hodgepodge of kitchens, stables, warehouses, smokehouses, and ovens.[47]

Fire insurance policies provide a detailed view of commercial and residential Winchester during the 1790s (fig. 7.6). Merchant James Gamul Dowdall, for instance, lived and conducted business on his Loudoun Street lot near the bridge over Town Run. At a two-story store and dwelling, he had "ready for sale, a large complete assortment of Merchandise bought on cash on very ad-

Facing page

FIG. 7.5. Winchester, Virginia, 1800. Loudoun and Cameron Streets were the center of commercial activity in late-eighteenth-century Winchester, as indicated by this composite map based on fire insurance policies. Chartered in 1794, the Mutual Assurance Society of Virginia quickly insured more than seventy inhabitants of the town against fire. Based on transcription by Paul Davis, Mutual Assurance Society of Virginia Papers, Library of Virginia.

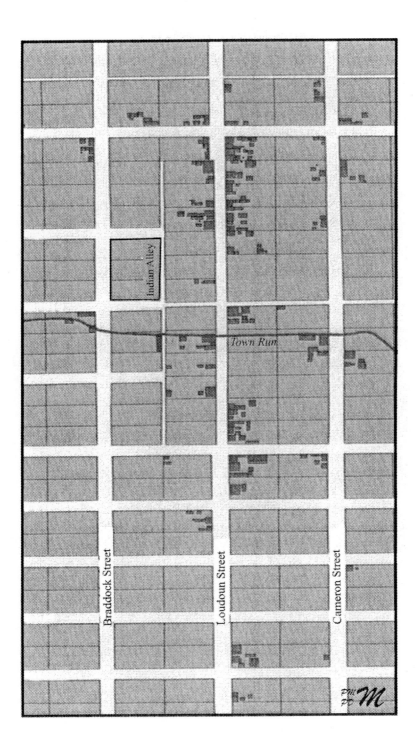

vantageous terms, in the city of Philadelphia." Under construction next door was a large, thirty-eight-by-forty-eight foot, two-story stone house, and in between lay a single-story warehouse. A kitchen and granary occupied the back lot, and a large wooden barn and stable stood across Indian Alley. On the corner of Loudoun and Piccadilly Streets, merchant James Holliday oversaw similar congeries of structures, including a one-story store-dwelling with both shed and ell additions at the rear connecting to a second dwelling, a wooden kitchen and warehouse featuring a porch and another shed addition, and finally a nineteen-by-twenty-foot stable.[48]

Artisans often attached their shop to an end of their house. With the "experience he has had in England, Ireland, and America [that] will enable him to execute work so as to deserve encouragement," shoemaker Peter Kehoe, for example, announced in 1793 that he had "removed to Cameron Street near the Market House," where he maintained a "general assortment [of] ready made" shoes on hand. His two-story wooden house had two rooms separated by a central hallway on each floor. A fifteen-foot addition to the north gable wall served as a shoemaking shop, and a fifteen-foot-square kitchen was connected to the rear of the central passage by a covered walkway. A free-standing wooden stable also occupied the back lot. Perhaps the most complex structures in commercial Winchester were taverns. Philip Bush maintained a stone dwelling house and tavern, a wooden dwelling, two kitchens, and two stables at the Golden Buck on Cameron Street. On the southern end of Loudoun Street nine buildings constituted Peter Lauck's Red Lion tavern: the two-story stone tavern and adjoining stone dwelling house, a wooden single-story dwelling at the end of the lot, and in the back lot another dwelling, a kitchen, a stable, a granary, a smokehouse, and a storage shed (figs. 7.7, 7.8).[49]

Little manufacturing took place in Winchester. Merchant James Holliday did operate a scythe factory and made potash in the "suburbs" of the town, and another member of the Holliday family, Richard, managed a hemp manufactory, where "all kinds of twine, bed-cords, well-ropes and mill ropes may be had on the shortest notice." By the late 1780s a twelve-by-twenty-six-foot building erected on the public lots beside the church sheltered a nail-making operation. Winchester was first and foremost a market town whose commerce revolved around—but did not house—the production, processing, storage, transporting, and marketing of wheat and flour. Most manufacturing was dispersed across the countryside as dependence upon waterpower dictated, and what manufacturing did take place in town, especially scythe and rope making, clearly supported a staple economy. It was the merchant trade centered in Winchester that organized the vast spatial and temporal extent of this economy.[50]

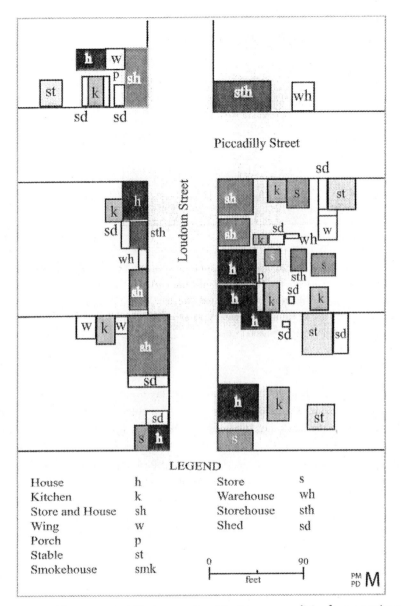

FIG. 7.6. Building Types in Winchester, 1800. Fire insurance policies for properties at the corner of Loudoun and Piccadilly Streets in Winchester describe the wide variety of building types found on commercial lots in the town. Based on transcription by Paul Davis, Mutual Assurance Society of Virginia Papers, Library of Virginia.

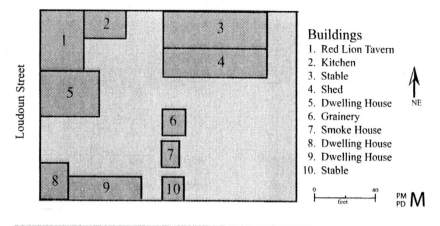

FIG. 7.7. Peter Lauck's Lot, 1796. As proprietor of the Red Lion Tavern in Winchester, Lauck insured a variety of structures against fire with the Mutual Assurance Society in March 1796. His lot depicts the variegated streetscapes of Shenandoah Valley market towns at the end of the eighteenth century. Based on policy of Peter Lauck, transcribed by Paul Davis, Mutual Assurance Society of Virginia Papers, Library of Virginia.

Even so, very little of the merchant trade lay directly in wheat. The activities of John Conrad provide a good example of the conduct of this trade and its power over the landscape. Conrad was the son of Frederick Conrad, a German immigrant who arrived in the British colonies in 1750 and soon set up trade as a tanner in Winchester. John married Betsy Rutherford, the daughter of the now-elder merchant Robert Rutherford, and established himself in trade on Loudoun Street. On the shelves of his store could be found a wide variety of goods, including numerous bolts of brown and white Irish linens, osnaburgs, bagging, and fine broadcloths, as well as ink powder, rifle locks, snuff boxes, looking glasses, screws, spectacles, hinges, corkscrews, tableware, sets of china, coffeepots, decanters, goblets, salad dishes, pudding dishes, butter boats, and many more dry-good or hardware items (fig. 7.9).

Facing page

FIG. 7.8. Mutual Assurance Society of Virginia Policy for Peter Lauck, 1796. Lot plans on policies depicted uninsured as well as insured structures along with information about building type, construction material, size, and roof covering. Peter Lauck, policy, Mutual Assurance Society of Virginia Papers, Library of Virginia.

N.º 20.

Form of the Declarations for Assurance.

I the underwritten *Peter Lauck* residing at *Winchester* in the county of *Frederick* do hereby declare for Assurance in the Mutual Assurance Society against Fire on Buildings of the State of Virginia, established the 26th December, 1795, agreeable to the several acts of the General Assembly of this state, to wit:

My *eight* Buildings on *Loudoun Street* at *Winchester* now occupied by *myself & others* situated between *the lots of Lewis Wolfe* and *Jacob Gerber of Gretchen* in the county of *Frederick* Their dimensions, situation and contiguity to other buildings or wharves, what the walls are built of, and what the buildings are covered with, are specified in the hereunto annexed description of the said Buildings on the plat, signed by me and the appraisers, and each valued by them as appears by their certificate here under, to wit:

The *Tavern* marked A. at *3000* Dollars, say *Three thousand* Dollars
The *Dwellinghse* do. B. at *2200* do. *Two thousand two hundred* do.
The *Kitchen* do. C. at *500* do. *Five hundred* do.
The *Stable* do. D. at *700* do. *Seven hundred* do.
The *Granary* do. E. at *100* do. *One hundred* do.
The *Stable 2* do. F. at *150* do. *One hundred* do.
The *Dwellinghouse* do. G. at *300* do. *Three hundred* do.
The *ditto* do. H. at *200* *Two hundred* do.

Say *Seven thousand Five hundred* Dollars in all.

I do hereby declare and affirm that the above mentioned property is not, nor shall be insured elsewhere, without giving notice thereof, agreeably to the policy that may issue in my name, upon the filing of this declaration, and provided the whole sum do not exceed four-fifths of the verified value, and that I will abide by, observe, and adhere to the Constitution, Rules and Regulations as are already established, or may hereafter be established by a majority of the insured, present in person, or by representatives, at a general Meeting to be agreed upon for the said Assurance Society. Witness my hand and seal at *Winchester* the *twenty eighth* day of *March* 1796.

Peter Lauck (Seal)

WE the underwritten, being each of us House-Owners, declare and affirm that we have examined the above mentioned Property of *Peter Lauck* and that we are of opinion that it would cost in cash *Seven thousand five hundred* Dollars to build the same, and is now actually worth *Seven thousand One hundred* Dollars in ready money; and will command the same as above specified to the best of our knowledge and belief.

Winchester &c.
The foregoing valuation *sworn to* in due form before me, a Magistrate for the said *Town* of *Winchester* Given under my hand this *28th* day of *March* in the year 1796.

Peyton
Chs. Laird Residing in *Winchester*

Abraham Britt

Loudoun Street

Conrad kept accounts with more than fifty people in Winchester and the surrounding community in the early 1790s, relying upon the same system of reckoning debits and credits that his predecessors Benjamin Perreyra and Peter Tostee had used half a century earlier. Subtle differences, however, marked basic tendencies of economic change. Conrad usually debited customers for "Sundries" in amounts ranging regularly between one to three pounds. Most credits, however, were for cash, received typically within six months of

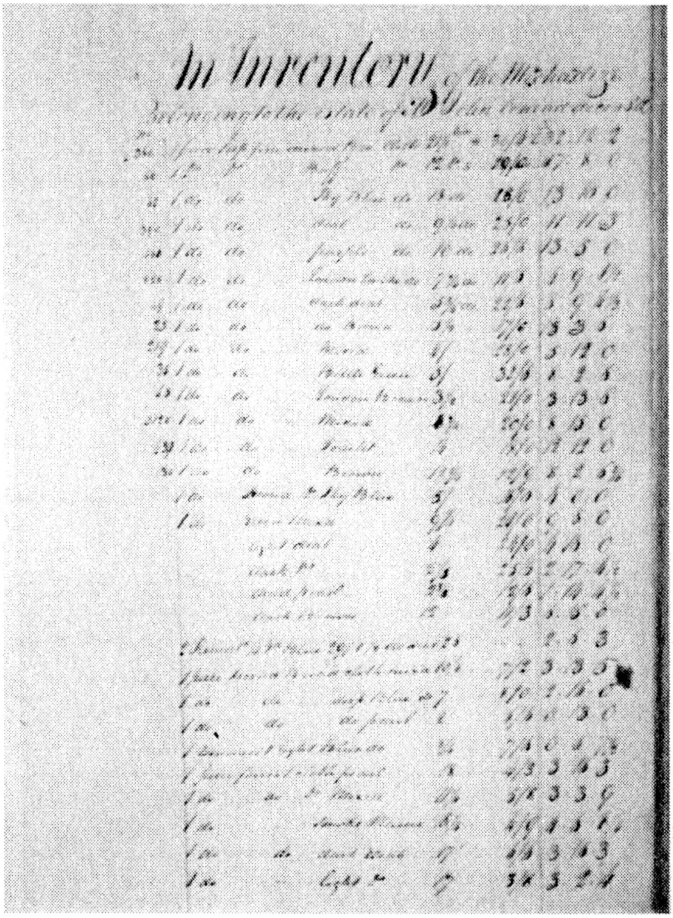

FIG. 7.9. John Conrad's Estate Inventory, 1794. When Conrad died, his store on the corner of Loudoun and Cork Streets contained a wide variety of goods, mostly from Philadelphia merchants, as detailed in this extensive inventory required for the settlement of his estate. Inventory of John Conrad, Sept. 24, 1794, Frederick County Wills, 6:150, Frederick County Courthouse.

the initial transaction. Conrad, for instance, debited Samuel Glass 15s. 2d. "to Sundries pr your wife" on May 10, 1792. This Samuel Glass, the son of Robert Glass, farmed 200 hundred acres his father had given him on the Opequon Creek. On October 22 Glass reciprocated with 15s. 2d. "by Cash in full."[51]

Cash, however, was not the basis of Conrad's commerce. Some customers still paid in goods or services. Peter Windle brought iron and shot to Conrad and worked for him to settle accounts. Other customers coopered barrels for the merchant, worked on door locks, shaved him, fixed his watch, made him a coffin, hauled logs, mended a cart, and set up stills for a still house, or gave him fish, salt, cordwood, and a bird cage. On occasion Conrad accepted country produce, several times receiving oats, for instance, from John Stonebridge in return for whiskey dispensed a gallon at a time. Tobacco, blacksnake root, butter, beef, ginseng, potatoes, and hay also came to Conrad by way of trade. If cash transactions were the salient feature of Conrad's trade, then wheat was distinguished by its absence. The largest wheat deal Conrad concluded was with Benjamin Johnson, who brought in a total forty-eight and three-quarter bushels in March and May 1792 and settled in full for cash by June. Three other direct transactions for wheat netted only a total of fifteen bushels. Clearly, Conrad was not collecting wheat in exchange for store goods. But wealth acquired in wheat elsewhere could be used in Conrad's store. On one occasion Conrad debited customer John Kneester for an order drawn on Eben Parkins, son of miller Isaac Parkins. A month later Conrad credited Kneester by drawing on Parkins's account, thus facilitating transactions between Kneester and Parkins outside his store. Conrad occasionally debited his customers for cash, effectively lending it to them much as a banker would—there would be no banks in Winchester for another twenty years. Conrad also traded goods and cash back and forth with other Winchester merchants, at one time accumulating debits and credits with William Groverman totaling more than £68.[52]

Cash was such an important part of Conrad's store trade because he relied upon it in distant port towns to make payments to merchants who supplied his stock. In many years Conrad made spring and fall trips to Philadelphia, where he acquired goods worth as much as £1,000. From May 10–22, 1792, the Winchester merchant did business with eighteen Philadelphians for sums ranging from £1 3s. 1½d. for cinnamon with Griffith Edwards to £387 18s. 2¼d. with Andrew Clow for fabrics. Taking some days off but on others visiting as many as five merchants, he acquired books, spices, tea, fabrics, paper, porter, beer, hardware, paint, glue, furniture, snuff, and tablewares. His account with the High Street dry-goods firm of Wister and Aston was typical. On May 12 Conrad acquired thirty-four items, including fustian, holland, calico, silk, and muslin fabrics, as well as cravats, handkerchiefs, binding, and a trunk. He was, however, already deep in Wister and Aston's debt. By spring 1791 he owed more than £300 to the firm. Cash to the sum of almost £270 paid during the next year was offset by some £140 in "Sundries" acquired during the same period. When the two merchants balanced accounts in spring 1792, Conrad came up £315 11s. 16d. short, against which he paid additional cash before leaving Philadelphia and signed a sixty-day note for almost £278. By carrying nearly £200 forward in his account at the same time, Conrad perpetuated an economic relationship with Wister and Aston in the traditional pattern of an exchange economy.[53]

Conrad's business was much the same in Baltimore as in Philadelphia, although by 1789 he was transferring much of it from the former to the latter. Thereafter, trips to Baltimore became shorter and more sporadic. Visits to Alexandria were also brief and irregular, but the trade there differed. Conrad balanced accounts with cash but carried home mostly bulk items, such as sugar, salt, rum, coffee, and molasses. Perhaps to minimize breakage by shortening the carriage distance, most of Conrad's stock of glassware and tableware also came from Alexandria. Conrad died in 1794, and during the next twelve years, his executors paid at least sixty-six bonds, notes, and book debts while collecting on more than eighty-eight accounts, all balancing at close to £4,000.[54]

John Conrad's accounts demonstrate the close relationships between landscape and economy as well as the way in which these relationships were changing. The economic activity of farmers, millers, and merchants was still dependent upon keeping accounts. The Newtonian mentality of balancing debits and credits in economic equilibrium survived to the end of the eighteenth century and continued to govern how most people saw social relations in the world around them. Reckoning and forwarding accounts organized both time and space for the founders of the Opequon settlement as well as for their successors. Keeping book allowed the landscape to work, whether for economic competence or profit and improvement. Cash, though still only one element in balancing accounts, was nonetheless growing in importance and appeared more frequently in transactions.

· ☿ ·

The growing volume of cash in the economy was facilitating a transition from an exchange economy to a commercial economy. In a commercial economy, production was substantially in excess of subsistence, and substantial exchange occurred beyond the local community sustained by the exchange economy. External markets came to affect prices, supply, and demand significantly, not only for staple exports but also for manufactured imports. The enlarging area over which an expanding volume of goods and services flowed required more and more cash to achieve a balance of trade. Cash slowly began to replace accounts as a means of organizing time. Although subject to inflation or deflation, cash could be accumulated free from the social dependencies of debit and credit. Insofar as amassing cash, or capital, was synonymous with the increasing volume of transactions, economic growth came to erode static notions of economic stability and dispel suspicions of entrepreneurial activity. Entrepreneurs came increasingly to be seen as the creators of new wealth.

Spatial arrangements changed under these conditions, as well. Reckoning accounts in an exchange economy allowed for economic activity to overspread large areas of dispersed producers and consumers. Towns formed primarily under the impetus of political necessity or military strategy. In a commercial economy, those intent on accumulating wealth located where the flow of cash was greatest even if that flow was initiated by political or military spending. The number of customers a merchant, artisan, or tavern keeper could attract was simply greater in towns at which population was already concentrated, to which people of the countryside were growing accustomed to looking for trade, and through which transportation arteries flowed.

In the Shenandoah Valley, the primary commodity—the staple—which initiated the ever-increasing flow of goods, services, and cash, was wheat. The production of wheat, its manufacture into flour, and the transportation, storage, and marketing of flour required the services of many artisans—millwrights, joiners, masons, wheelwrights, wagon makers, blacksmiths, harness makers, wagoners, coopers, iron makers, and so forth. Many of these trades could be practiced anywhere in the countryside, as Shenandoah Valley artisans proved throughout the eighteenth and nineteenth centuries. But the profits of the trade in wheat and flour also generated demand in the countryside for the more refined goods marketed by merchants or manufactured by tailors, silversmiths, furniture makers, coach makers, or other specialists who located in towns because the area commanded by their services was larger and people were willing to travel greater distances to their stores and shops.

All of these developments took place in a time of transition from an exchange to a commercial economy. Many characteristics of the exchange economy, such as rendering cash as a commodity in balancing accounts and trading goods and services throughout the countryside, survived. But the Conrad accounts demonstrate that merchants and artisans were literally becoming more central to the nexus of landscape and economy. And as they grew more central, towns became more central to the landscape.

As John Conrad's accounts bear out, Winchester merchants facilitated economic activity locally in an Atlantic-wide commercial economy in various ways. Most important in local exchanges were relations between merchants and customers. Merchants accepted country produce in trade. Thomas Cantwell, for instance, advertised that "for accommodation of his customers he will receive in payment Wheat, Rye, Corn, Oats, Tobacco, Flour, Skins, Furs, Public-Paper, Bees Wax, [and] domestic distilled spirits." Many merchants were so eager for business that they readily bought entire crops from farmers. John Kercheval promised to "contract with any gentleman for three crops of wheat and rye, payable in cash or goods as may best suit the seller." The frequency of cash transactions in Conrad's accounts, however, demonstrated the growing importance of money to a commercializing and spatially expanding economy. "Shopkeepers and craftsmen . . . must pay cash for their wares at Baltimore," one visitor to Winchester observed in the 1780s. The traveler La Rochefoucauld-Liancourt reinforced this point more than a decade later: "Winchester carries on a considerable trade for its inland position. . . . It sends to Alexandria the whole produce of the upper country, and draws from Baltimore, but especially from Philadelphia, all sorts of dry goods: the traffic, both in buying and selling, is carried on with ready money." Some merchants, such as John Koontz and Richard Ober, asked for "immediate remittances." To attract cash, many merchants offered goods at a lower price for cash transactions. "By experience," James Gamul and John Dowdall found "so great an advantage in selling for READY MONEY . . . [they were] determined to dispose of them [store goods] as low as any sold in this town for many years, and give a considerable discount for cash paid at the time of purchasing." Charles O'Neal was blunter. He operated a "Ready Money Store," where "Wet and Dry Goods . . . will be sold very cheap, for cash only."[55]

Artisans, too, wanted cash. George Deibler made saddles and harnesses in a shop next to James Gamul Dowdall's store on Loudoun Street. "In order to accommodate he will take in country produce, at market price," he advertised—but added, "if cash is not convenient." As shoemaker Peter Kehoe explained to his customers, "the materials used in his business, are not to be got without ready money, [therefore] it is out of his power to give any credit." Cash not only facilitated Kehoe's distant transactions with suppliers but also allowed for the immediate balancing of local transactions. "Persons of the country, who may hereafter incline to favor him with their commands," he cautioned, "will please to notice, that his terms of dealing in the future will be cash, or country produce, paid when the work is taken away."[56]

In calling for immediate cash transactions, men such as Charles O'Neal and Peter Kehoe were looking into the future, to developments that would only come to pass in the nineteenth century; but in the 1790s book accounts still organized economic activity across a dispersed landscape. Merchants like John

Kercheval owned stores in town and a mill or two in the country so that store credit could readily be granted to anyone delivering wheat to a mill. Farmers who brought their harvest to Kercheval's Greenwood Mills could also charge goods at John McAlister's store at the sign of the tobacco hogshead opposite the bridge in Winchester. Dowdall accepted "merchantable wheat delivered at his store, or any of the neighboring mills." A simple transfer of debits and credits made these transactions possible. Merchants kept accounts with both millers and farmers. When a farmer brought wheat to a mill, the merchant simply entered the value of the wheat, or its equivalent in flour, as a credit in the farmer's account and as a debit in the miller's.[57]

The accounts of partners Richard Galloway and William Vance indicate how the activities of a general merchandise firm in Winchester could organize exchange over a large area. On January 20, 1807, they credited Hugh Kenedy £15 for fifty bushels of wheat delivered to David Carlisle's mill and £15 for an equal quantity of wheat at Benjamin Touchstone's mill. The next day they debited the £15 against David Carlisle's account but waited until June to complete the bookkeeping process for Kenedy's transaction with Touchstone. A month later, however, the "neat proceeds of flour" offset Touchstone's debit, and in October, Carlisle received credit "by 13 Barrels of Superfine flour sold Anderson Nutt and Co." in Alexandria. By these accounts, wheat traveled from Kenedy's farm to Carlisle's and Touchstone's mills, where it was ground to flour, and the flour was transported to Alexandria merchants. All parties profited in some way by these arrangements: Kenedy from goods in Galloway and Vance's store, or in credit transferred by order to other merchants and artisans; the millers by their toll; Galloway and Vance by the sale of the flour acquired for the credit advanced Kenedy; and Alexandria merchants by their commission. If Galloway and Vance exchanged the value of the flour for bulk goods in the Alexandria trade, then bookkeeping alone would have made all of these transactions possible. Cash, however, would constitute an increasing part of the back trade from Alexandria.[58]

As the accounts of John Conrad and others indicate, cash was also vital to the Philadelphia and Baltimore trades in manufactured and imported goods. Winchester merchants, according to Harry Toulmin, "obtain their goods from Philadelphia, Baltimore, and Alexandria, but principally from Philadelphia, and dispose of them to people of the town, of the neighborhood, and of the back country." But why depend on such a distant port for a stock in trade? "From the greater wealth possessed by the merchants of that city, they are able to give longer credit," La Rochefoucauld-Liancourt explained. "They receive the goods from the first hands, and consequently can sell them cheaper; their warehouses being plentifully stocked with merchandize, the buyers can also suit themselves better—circumstances, none of which take place at Alexandria, and which being less combined at Baltimore than at Philadelphia, caused the latter to be resorted to in preference to the former." In the midst of a controversy over Virginia's imposition of import duties, a correspondent to a Winchester newspaper pointed out that the "business of Philadelphia is on a better regulation than in any town in Virginia. The advantages resulting from the establishment of a bank and corresponding circumstances, are sufficient to claim our partiality." That Conrad's accounts with Philadelphia merchants, although conducted in cash and goods, often ran for years and were settled only with his death substantiates the points about "longer credit" and "better regulation" available in Philadelphia than in other Atlantic ports. Many other Winchester merchants took advantage of these conditions. In 1791, for instance, Robert Grey advertised a "general assortment of the best Goods that could be collected from the first wholesale Warehouses in Philadelphia," and the firm of Sherrard and Alexander wished to "respectfully inform their friends and the public at large that they have just received from Philadelphia . . . a very large and beautiful assortment of well chosen Merchandise."[59]

Despite Philadelphia's advantages, Baltimore was the rising star of the late-eighteenth-century Atlantic trade. According to one traveler in Winchester, "a large part of the trade of Philadelphia has shifted to Baltimore, which before the [Revolutionary] war was no more than a village." Unlike counterparts in Alexandria, Baltimore merchants traded on their own risk and account, and thanks to local streams and rivers, their town was rapidly becoming a milling center. Some Shenandoah Valley merchants, for example, Galloway and Vance, chose to send flour to Baltimore and acquire store goods in a single trip. Another, William Holliday, advertised that he had "just received from Baltimore a large and most beautiful assortment of all kinds of Goods . . . to sell on lower terms than Goods of equal quality has been sold for in this place these ten years past." Artisans also turned to Baltimore for raw materials and imported goods to supplement what they produced. Shoemaker Alex Porter, for instance, "laid in from Baltimore a large assortment of boot and bootee legs" in September 1794.[60]

Proximity was Alexandria's primary advantage in the Shenandoah trade. "The carriage from Philadelphia to Winchester costs from four to five dollars per hundred weight," La Rochefoucauld-Liancourt calculated, "and from Winchester to Alexandria, two dollars and a half." Most Shenandoah Valley flour was carried to Alexandria by wagon; only a portion was floated down the Shenandoah and Potomac Rivers, where it could also end up at Georgetown. Thus roads and ferries remained a critical interest to everyone engaged in the flour trade. In 1786 Winchester merchants Philip Bush, Robert Sherrard, William Holliday, James Holliday, John Conrad, John McAlister, James Gamul Dowdall, and others petitioned the Virginia legislature for additional ferries across the Shenandoah River, "there not being ferries enough upon the river at the brisk time of carrying down the produce, to dispatch half the Waggons" of Frederick and Berkeley Counties. The movement to improve roads to Alexandria culminated with the establishment of turnpikes in the early nineteenth century. Alexandria merchant Elisha Janney notified "millers and the public in general that he hath rented a large and convenient warehouse in the town of Alexandria . . . and will store and sell flour for a commission of two percent." A few merchants in Alexandria imported manufactured goods directly from Europe. One was William Lowrey, who notified the people of Winchester when he received a cargo "from the several Manufactories of England." According to Isaac Weld, however, "more than two thirds of the goods which are sent from thence to the back country" were procured "second hand only, from Baltimore and Philadelphia." "Heavy merchandize, such as grocery," La Rochefoucauld-Liancourt chimed in, was "sent by sea from Philadelphia to Alexandria, whence it is conveyed to Winchester in waggons." Thus the sugar, salt, rum, coffee, and molasses that John Conrad had on store came from Alexandria, and no Winchester merchant advertised the sale of manufactured goods from Alexandria as they did those from Philadelphia or Baltimore.[61]

How merchants in Winchester, Alexandria, Baltimore, and Philadelphia conducted their local and long-distance trades indicates that the Shenandoah Valley lay within a complex regional system in which the primary agricultural commodity—flour—flowed into the Atlantic marketplace through Alexandria, and imported goods, for which the sale of flour created a demand in the countryside, entered through Philadelphia and Baltimore. Cash became increasingly important to the operation of this system as the means of balancing payments from Alexandria and to Philadelphia. But better credit terms gave an advantage to Philadelphia over Baltimore, which reveals the persistent role that keeping accounts played in the regional economy. No evidence exists that Winchester merchants ever acquired goods in either Philadelphia or Baltimore by regularly paying cash in full. All merchants entered cash in accounts as debits and credits, settling them from time to time and carrying balances forward from year to year.

· ⚜ ·

This system of reckoning both cash and goods as debits and credits in book accounts, which organized trade across a broad middle-Atlantic region in late-eighteenth-century America, also helps explain the geographical hierarchy of central places within this region. The spatial pattern of hamlets, villages, and towns capped by Winchester in the lower Shenandoah Valley was an expression of economic function and the interrelationships of trade and account keeping spread across the countryside. Connections between Winchester and Charles Town exemplify the hierarchical nature of this pattern. The Virginia legislature established Charles Town in 1787 on a proposal by George Washington's brother Charles to lay out "eighty acres of his land in the County of Berkeley into convenient Lots Situate on the great Leading way from Winchester [and] the west and South western frontiers of this State to the city of Philadelphia the Towns of Baltimore, and Alexandria." By 1800 the town supported a population of 568, larger than Stephensburg but smaller than Woodstock. To La Rochefoucauld-Liancourt's eye it was in 1796 a "small place, built within these ten or twelve years, consisting of about forty houses. . . . The culture of wheat extends five or six miles beyond Charlestown. The fields are all of a vast extent, and the crops of Indian corn are remarkably fine. The meadows are also very rich, but they are few in number." Still, Charles Town was dependent upon Winchester: "The whole produce is disposed of in the same manner as that of the environs of Winchester, and Strasburgh, &c. &c. But it is from Winchester that the stores or shops of Charlestown receive their supplies: none of the shop-keepers is sufficiently rich to draw merchandise directly from the sea-ports." Some Winchester merchants, such as Gabrielle Norse and the partnership of Andrew and Hamilton Cooper, moved to Charles Town and its vicinity in the early 1790s, as the town began to grow. The business of the latter firm demonstrates La Rochefoucauld-Liancourt's point. Accounts kept from December 1792 to November 1794 describe a trade in agricultural commodities sent to Baltimore and Alexandria and general merchandise acquired on credit from seven Winchester merchants, among them John Conrad, Cornelius O'Laughlin, and Richard Holliday. These accounts were usually settled in cash.[62]

The hierarchical relations among central places were also evident in the commercial activities Winchester merchants maintained in smaller communities. In addition to their store on Loudoun Street, the Dowdall brothers also did business in nearby Stephensburg. John Conrad had a partnership with George Hite, who traded in Berryville, and John McAlister operated stores both in Winchester and near Marlboro, an iron-making community about ten miles from town. In addition to a retail trade with customers, at least seven Winchester firms operated as wholesalers for merchants in smaller communities. For instance, James Gamul Dowdall pledged to "make a considerable abatement to those who buy to sell again" and promised that "Country Merchants and others will find their advantage in purchasing of him."[63]

Thus, the town and country landscape that had emerged in the Shenandoah Valley by the end of the eighteenth century expressed functional relationships extending to Atlantic ports and more broadly throughout the entire Atlantic economy. Because of the connections of its merchants to these ports, Winchester held the primary position in the urban hierarchy of the lower Shenandoah Valley. The primacy of Winchester was also evident in the rise in the value of land near the town. "The plantations increase both in number and size, as we approach Winchester," observed La Rochefoucauld-Liancourt in 1796. Another traveler asserted that "cleared ground, on which a few sheds have been built, brings from three to four <u>pounds</u> (an acre). Such is the price of the plantation near <u>Winchester</u>; but the farther away you go, the cheaper the land becomes. Twelve miles from that town a planter would offer a plantation at the rate of fifty shillings an acre."[64]

. ⚱ .

As Winchester emerged as the primary town center in a hierarchical settlement system, it also assumed the mantle of a civic community. It was a corporation not simply in governing itself but also in binding individuals together for a common economic purpose. The civic community thus resided in the traditions and institutions of collective life in which the interests of individuals were linked in the public arena. Anyone keeping accounts in the town— and presumably everyone did—could readily see how trade drew all citizens together. John Conrad's accounts provide a vivid picture of how embedded he was in a large web of economic and social relations. He was portrayed at his death in 1794 as "humane and charitable, a loving husband, a tender father and sincere friend; an upright dispenser of justice, a lover of virtue, morality and order; a friend to religion; a dispiser of bigotry." Virtue in Conrad's time meant the ability to place public interest above self-interest, and it was often equated with civic virtue because civic life meant public life. When demonstrated through exemplary individuals, it indeed brought morality and order to the community. This order was embodied in many of the ceremonies and institutions that defined Winchester's civic community.[65]

Perhaps the most vivid portrait of the town as an ordered civic community appeared in the celebrations following the ratification of the federal Constitution in 1788. Believing that it was the critical ninth state that would bring the new national government into being, Virginia ratified on June 26. The news reached Winchester three days later, on a Sunday. Many people in Winchester, as throughout the Shenandoah Valley, supported the Constitution because it created a federal government with national economic authority to regulate trade and commerce. It thus released Virginia's western regions from the grasp of a state legislature that restricted the flow of goods across state lines when domestic trade in the interior hurt the interests of eastern merchants. The import duties imposed by the state had threatened the Valley's trade with Philadelphia and Baltimore throughout the 1780s. Thus it was with "extreme joy . . . sparkling eyes and elated spirits" that the people of Winchester greeted the news of ratification. The following day, the militia met on the parade ground and fired "nine volleys in honor of the *nine pillers* which now support the glorious *American Fabric.*" More volleys followed during a march through town. That evening, a "large quantity of combustables were collected and conveyed to *Federal Hill,* by the *Federal Waggon,* drawn by nine horses" for a "large and beautiful bonfire . . . which was seen for many miles in the vicinity." At a public dinner that followed numerous toasts commemorated George Washington, the United States, the "Patrons of Freedom," and the "friends of the Federal Constitution." Militia volleys, bonfires, dinners, and toasts were all part of a civic ceremony designed to reinforce what the Constitution's supporters felt was a collective victory benefiting the trade and welfare of the town.[66]

The "Grand Procession" that took place a few days later, on the Fourth of July, shows how the town's public life was ordered. At noon the "different crafts, consisting of upwards of two hundred" headed by the militia assembled at the courthouse. "Each craft bearing implements suitable to their several occupations" followed in the "ORDER of PROCESSION," which included farmers with sheaves of wheat, bakers and brewers, butchers, coppersmiths, white- and blacksmiths, tanners, saddlers, shoemakers, masons, hatters, tailors, watchmakers and silversmiths, wheelwrights, carpenters and joiners, painters, potters, weavers, barbers, combmakers, printers, merchants, doctors, clergy, and members of the bar. The procession put the occupational organization of the town on display. Absent in Winchester, as elsewhere in North America, were guilds, which brought political structure to contemporaneous European towns and collectively regulated craft production and market activity. But when called upon to celebrate the formation of a new national government, local townspeople came together by their trades, ordered themselves into a procession, and marched together along the streets of the town.[67]

The procession, volleys, dinners, toasts, the "jovial bowl," and other aspects of civic ceremony all emphasized for the people of Winchester that they were a corporation—that as individuals they possessed the legal power to act together for their mutual benefit. The 1779 act of incorporation had constituted the mayor, recorder, alderman, and common council as a "body corporate and politick" with authority "to make bye laws and ordinances for the regulation and good government of the said town." Not surprisingly, John

Conrad, William Holliday, Jacob Kiger, and Philip Bush, among other artisans and merchants, dominated town offices. They acted to improve the town by prohibiting porches that obstructed streets, requiring the construction of stone sidewalks, and ordering the removal of all wood, stone, or lumber from streets except for purposes of construction. Clearing the public streets was protecting public space.[68]

The corporation had the power to regulate the market to ensure that buying and selling were conducted fairly and in public. Although the economy of the Shenandoah Valley was changing rapidly—as the increasing adoption of cash was to demonstrate—the operation of a regulated market for the public exchange of goods essential to survival, especially bread and meat, betrayed the traditional suspicion of private trading in an economy of scarcity in which wealth was reduced to the collective means of subsistence at a constant value. Public trading in a regulated market suppressed competition for these means and assured that no ambitious individual could corner the market on any essential good. Corporations, therefore, prevented individuals from engrossing all the goods available in a certain trade, from acting aggressively as middlemen by purchasing commodities directly from farmers to sell again privately, and from buying or selling certain commodities outside the public market.

Due as much to high productivity on local farms as to the oversight of Winchester's market clerk, the public market in Winchester appeared to be a great success. La Rochefoucauld-Liancourt described a "well-stocked market . . . held there twice a week," and Harry Toulmin counted more than sixty items for sale. The town government acted on its corporate powers when, in 1794, it set prices of bread at four shillings for a two-pound loaf and subjected any swindlers to a one hundred shilling fine. Confiscated bread was to be given to the poor. At the same time the town forbid "any person selling any kind of marketing at any other place in this Borough, on the [market] days . . . than [at] the Market-house." The hustings, or town, court on at least one occasion investigated bakers on charges of extortion. These actions, however, were often made in the breach, and as developments during the nineteenth century would demonstrate, the movement toward private enterprise was unstoppable. As Toulmin reported, "at all times provisions are to be purchased at private houses."[69]

Other public institutions included a poorhouse, but the civic community of the town came increasingly to revolve around private, voluntary organizations. Many, for example, the newly established Episcopal Church, were religious. La Rochefoucauld-Liancourt counted five churches in Winchester during his stay in 1796: Episcopal, Presbyterian, German Lutheran, Catholic, and Methodist. But Bayard quipped that "nearly all the inhabitants of <u>Winchester</u> are Presbyterians." After hearing a sermon by a Presbyterian minister that "turned entirely upon the principles of the evangelical doctrines," he "noticed that doors of the houses were closed . . . throughout the day. . . . Everyone seemed lost in meditation." Other accounts suggest that piety and Protestant doctrine played less of a role in ordering the Sabbath. "An Enemy of Vice & Immorality" complained in the *Virginia Centinel; or, the Winchester Mercury* about children playing in the streets on Sundays who "committ outrages during the time of divine service." "All idlers, gamblers, fornicators and adulterers," he warned, "will be deligently sought after, and every legal method taken to check their diabolical proceedings." His concerns may not have been unfounded if the complaints of several town justices against Michael Laubinger, Thomas Clark, and Angus McDonald, for riotously assembling on a Sunday at the home of William Holliday and refusing to disperse, were valid. The problem of observing the Sabbath was severe enough that the corporation of Winchester resolved in 1788 that "no person spend the Sabbath in the exercise of any unlawful game or amusements." Whether or not all the citizens of Winchester passed the Sabbath in sober religious reflection, the townspeople clearly considered the observance of this day a public function within the civic community. Proper conduct on Sundays was debated in public and was subject to public regulation. And at the same time that merchant William Holliday could play host to riotous amusements, he joined merchants James Holliday and Robert Sherrard in a committee of Presbyterians formed to oversee the construction of a new church. On other occasions townspeople banded together behind a lottery to buy an organ for the Lutheran Church and supported Peter Kehoe in collecting subscriptions for a Catholic chapel.[70]

The townspeople also came together in the interest of education. Merchants regularly took the lead in educational efforts. Charles O'Neal, for example, who ran the "Ready Money" store, was educated at the universities of Dublin and Glasgow and taught Latin and Greek at the Winchester Seminary, where James Gamul Dowdall, Frederick Conrad, and Samuel May were subscribers. Other merchants or tavern keepers, such as Joseph Holmes and Philip Bush, supported the Winchester Academy. From time to time various individuals also opened schools that offered "a proper English education" or in which young ladies could be instructed in "marking sewing and reading" or writing, arithmetic, or "elements of history, geography, and the use of globes." Boys could master English, Latin, Greek, geography, arithmetic, surveying, and oratory.[71]

Other cultural endeavors marked the civic community of the town. On November 9, 1787, Edward McGuire summoned all those "who wish to encourage the Winchester Dancing Assemblies" to meet at his tavern on the next Monday. These assemblies commenced at the end of November and continued during succeeding winters until at least 1790. Theater, too, came to Winchester. During spring 1791, the McGrath Company performed *The Miser* by Molière and Richard Sheridan's *School for Scandal*. One performance was a benefit for repairing the Episcopal church. Demands for a library appeared as early as 1788, although one did not open for another fifteen years. The townspeople held horse races on the town common and formed a "Society for the detection of Horse-Thieves" to apprehend rustlers. Fourth of July celebrations continued at the race ground throughout the 1790s, and on at least one occasion the militia staged a "sham fight" there. As additional indications of a civic community, the town boasted two newspapers, a post office, and a municipal water supply.[72]

· ⚶ ·

The corporate quality of life in Winchester's civic community by no means suppressed diversity or overrode tensions among townspeople. To Harry Toulmin the town's "1,660 inhabitants . . . [were] a motley set of Germans, Irish, Scots, and Anglo-Americans." In addition small numbers of Dutch, French, and Welsh people lived in or near town. Scots-Irish and Germans, however, predominated, and one visiting Scottish nobleman condemned the town as "inhabited by a spurious race of mortals known by the appelation of Scotch-Irish." Germans were so numerous that publisher Matthias Bartgis not only produced German-language newspapers and almanacs but also printed in both German and English for customers.[73]

Harmony among ethnic groups did not always prevail. The founder of American Methodism, Francis Asbury, commented on visiting Winchester in 1783 that the "inhabitants are much divided; made up, as they are, of different nations, and speaking different languages, they agree in scarcely anything, except it be to sin against God." The trustees of the Winchester Academy would certainly have concurred, attributing their difficulty in raising funds to the "various religions and languages which prevail among the people preventing their union, in support of this useful institution." Tensions sporadically broke out in violence. On one occasion in 1759 a "certain disturbance and affray arose" between groups of German and Scots-Irish inhabitants. As a result of the fracas, the Germans were "much beaten and hurt." Litigation of the so-called Winchester riot eventually rose to Virginia's General Court, although its resolution is uncertain. Not so, however, in the rather fanciful case of ethnic conflict and its folk culture described by Samuel Kercheval:

> The national prejudices which existed between the Dutch and Irish produced much disorder and many riots. It was customary for the Dutch on St. Patrick's Day, to exhibit the effigy of the saint, with a string of Irish potatoes around his neck, and his

wife Shelley, with her apron loaded also with potatoes. This was always followed by a riot. The Irish resented the indignity to their saint, and his holy spouse, and a battle followed. On St. Michael's Day the Irish would retort, and exhibit the saint with a rope of sour knout about his neck. Then the Dutch, like the Yankee, "felt chock full of fight" and at it they went pell-mell, and many a black eye, bloody nose, and broken head, was the result.[74]

Conflict, however, might have been more the exception than the rule for the people of Winchester. According to Baptist minister James Ireland, "persecution was not a reigning principle among them, and they lived in a common state of sociability, it gave them an opportunity of being acquainted with each other's principles and practices." And Frances Asbury might have moderated his opinion of Winchester when, in 1786, he took a "leisurely" ride through town and "preached under some spreading trees on a hill . . . to many white and black people. It was a solemn, weighty time," he observed; "all was seriousness and attention." Perhaps the single greatest factor promoting interethnic and interracial accommodation was the regular interaction of people within the civic community. Men from all ethnic groups sat together on governing bodies in the town. Similarly, ethnic diversity characterized the trustees of various educational or cultural organizations. Race was a more complicated issue, but 348 African or African American slaves lived in Winchester in 1800, constituting 16 percent of the population. There was a smaller, but significant, number of free blacks. Asbury's experience indicated that at evangelical churches whites and blacks worshiped together, and in commenting that "Negroes are very numerous in Winchester; but white laborers are not easily procured," La Rochefoucauld-Liancourt gave no indication that conflict existed in what must have been a racially competitive labor market. Blacks, moreover, played music at Winchester dances. That Ireland could proclaim a "common state of sociability" after one of his own slaves attempted to poison his family, succeeding with his youngest child, suggests that the oppression of slavery more than the divide of race motivated interracial violence.[75]

The extent to which violence presided over the heart of slavery aside, the exchange economy underpinning the civic community incorporated both whites and blacks. Take, for instance, the trade that Ann Frame conducted from her store in Charles Town at the end of the eighteenth century. In accounts very similar to those of Winchester merchants, she exchanged foodstuffs, dry goods, and hardware procured largely from Baltimore, for cash in the main but also for labor or such local commodities as hops, corn, rye, wheat, and tobacco, wagoned primarily to Alexandria. Most interesting, however, were the 123 accounts she kept with African Americans in her "Black Ledger." About two-thirds of these customers appeared in her ledger by first name and owner's name, for example, "Browns Julius," " Rutherfords Cuffee," or "Williamsons Betty," mixing classical, African, and English nomenclature. Some, like "Charles at the mill" or "Hanah at Stephensons," were indicated by location and a few, including "Will the weaver," by trade. "Free Mime," "Free Dolly," "Dugless a Free man," and "Elleth Row free man" had obviously escaped the clutches of slavery. There were more women than commonly appeared in other merchant accounts.[76]

That most of Ann Frame's black customers procured nonsubsistence, specialty items suggests that they lived in a plantation regime, which provided the basics of food and clothing. They were neither hired out nor living on their own. Whiskey, sugar, and chocolate were the most popular items among black men and women, but salt, pepper, coffee, molasses, tea, snuff, textiles, and dry goods from Ann Frame's store could also be found in their homes. The cash with which they balanced accounts derived from the informal economy that functioned on their plantations or in their neighborhoods, where extra work could be performed on evenings or weekends. Some traded under the order of their master or by credit from another customer for whom some service had been rendered. Others brought in corn, tobacco, beef, soap, hogs, apples, flax, shad, or barley; worked a day or two for Frame; or helped transport her goods. In a large majority of accounts credit had been carried over from a previous book and extended into the next. Take, for instance, Davenport's Davy. From Frame he acquired coating, thread, two penknives, chocolate, pepper, a hat, and one almanac. In partial exchange he brought in a pair of shoes, sweet potatoes, a fowl, flax, and on one occasion he provided "Carriage of goods," leaving a balance carried over of more than £3. In the picture that emerges in these accounts, free and enslaved African Americans worked for goods, credit, or cash in the local economy and traded on their own account in town shops. Few would have claimed that the exchange economy was color blind—Frame, after all, recorded the distinctive nature of this trade in a separate ledger—but certainly the reasoned process of keeping accounts and extending credit over time did not exclude blacks from the world of commercial goods.

· ⚜ ·

From the primary town of Winchester the civic community overspread the landscape to take in communities at all levels of the urban hierarchy and, by a complex system of roads, to incorporate virtually every household on the rural end of the settlement spectrum. The public nature of town life was most evident on streets and at the market. It was no accident that a merchant, John Conrad, helped organize a lottery for paving Loudoun Street in 1791. Just as commerce was a solvent of ethnic and racial difference, so did it shape the inclusive nature of public life. Trading in the market was public, to forestall competition and ensure a right to competence for everyone. Merchants, of course, traded in their shops, and as Harry Toulmin pointed out, provisions could be had at private homes. Merchants, however, often lived in their shop buildings and thus mixed public commercial with private residential space. That houses, stores, and shops all stood on a common street line was a metaphor for equal access to the commerce of public space. Moreover, by building stoops into the street—even though the town required their removal—householders and shopkeepers expressed a desire to link public and private space physically. And if travelers noticed that doors were closed on Sundays, then open doors on weekdays extended the public space of the street literally into the house along the central passage or hallway, which was becoming so common in domestic architecture by the end of the eighteenth century. Sitting on stoops or in doorways—in the portal between public and private space—was apparently a common practice.[77]

Even though they curved around encircling hills, the streets of Winchester extended directly into the countryside. Every one of the town's primary streets was, in fact, a country road straightened and woven into the town grid. A person walking from any point in town could be in the countryside within minutes. There, too, of course, people built houses, mills, taverns, and artisan shops directly on roads, thereby connecting themselves to the public space upon which the commerce of the countryside flowed and linking themselves to the commercial life of the town. "The habitations do not stand at a great distance from the road," observed La Rochefoucauld-Liancourt. The countryside as it emerged in settlement was described as a landscape of competence. In taking up the land and transforming waste land into private property through metes and bounds surveys, settler families had captured the resources in field and forest, stream and road necessary to live independently from the will of others but also interdependently among themselves. At the end of the eighteenth century, farmers still constructed houses on roads because interdependence now extended to town and the economic lifeblood of merchant commerce. Moreover, the civic community of the town overspread the countryside through the public space of roads.[78]

The civic community also overspread ethnic diversity in the inclusive landscape of improvement, which had come to replace the earlier landscape of competence. "Many of the Irish here can scarcely speak in English," observed one traveler in the 1780s, "and thousands of the Germans understand no language but High Dutch; however they are all very laborious, and extremely industrious, having improved this part of the country beyond conception." Toward the end of the century, the landscape began to change in ways that reflected the newfound and widespread prosperity of grain agriculture. Families cleared more land for wheat and located houses in the interior of tracts for better access to fields. Roads crisscrossed this landscape, bisecting property boundaries. Men and women literally recreated their built environment. "As the country improved in population and wealth," observed Samuel Kercheval, "there was a corresponding improvement in the erection of buildings. When this improvement commenced, the most general mode of building was with hewn logs, a shingle roof and plank floor." Another traveler described the settler's next step, of building "an addition to his cabin; this is done with hewed logs; . . . his floors are made of boards; his roof is made of what are called clapboards. . . . This house is divided by two floors." Finally, and this happened in the Shenandoah Valley by the end of the eighteenth century, a farmer began "improvements by building a commodious dwellinghouse, suited to the improvements and value of the plantation." Improvement, moreover, paralleled the transition from an exchange economy to a commercial economy and was driven by the burgeoning Atlantic market in grain and the international revolution in the distribution of goods.[79]

At the end of the eighteenth century a new aesthetic was sweeping the Atlantic world in conjunction with the market revolution in grains and the consumer revolution in manufactured goods. Called Georgian, after the Hanoverian kings of England and later neoclassicism, it drew primarily upon the art, architecture, and philosophy of the ancient world as brought initially to modernity through Renaissance Italy and to England in the seventeenth century by artists and architects who had studied in Italy. By century's end, historical and archaeological investigations were allowing the moderns to experience the ancient world directly. Like the order created in the Newtonian world of eighteenth-century bookkeeping, this aesthetic stressed balance and symmetry to achieve a sense of harmony in design and form. In Georgian architecture, façade features, such as bays of aligned windows and doors, were poised equally around a central axis. Exterior balance and symmetry were intended as public statements reflecting the primacy of reason and order over the raw materials of irregular nature—wood, stone, or brick—and by architectural example, the dominance of civilization over nature itself. Georgian architecture was preeminently the architecture of civic culture and the town, especially a backcountry town such as Winchester, so recently carved out of a wilderness "whose Surface was Rocks & Mountains, & it's Inhabitants Wildbeasts or Hostile Indians." The improved landscape of the countryside, however, was also the embodiment of the farmer's triumph over nature in agriculture. Here, too, Georgian aesthetics came to embody the meaning of the farmer's success in achieving a competence and then rendering it profitable.[80]

Linked together in town and country, families everywhere in the settlement continuum began rebuilding their homes, sometimes by rearranging features, sometimes by addition, and sometimes by new construction. The one- or two-room structures of early settlement were inherently irregular, with a door on the eave side located as far as possible from the hearth. But Georgian requirements of a central door with an equal number of flanking windows, or bays, could be met if a log crib was built the width of a central passage away from an existing gable and the whole enclosed with roof and wall. Raised two stories, such a structure achieved both vertical and horizontal symmetry (fig. 7.10). Visiting a house near Winchester in 1791, Ferdinand Bayard encountered "on a rather small hill, near the road . . . a white house with green blinds; . . . It consists of two rooms on the first floor and of an equal number on the second floor. The door is in the center. Between the two parloirs (parlors) there is a rather large hall open at both ends to maintain a current of air during the excessive heat of dog-days." The hall, or central passage—also in the spirit of Georgian rationalism—served to regulate the passage of people through the dwelling and mediate between the public space beyond the door and the interior private space of parlors and chambers. Thus, the hall represented the public space of the street or road extended directly into the house. Parlors were themselves new room types intended for refined entertainment and the display of consumer goods. The kitchen—with its smells, heat, and danger of fire, all previously contained within the single room of a cabin— was now moved outside the main dwelling to a separate backyard structure or to a rear ell addition. At the house Bayard visited, the kitchen was "separated from the main building only by a covered passageway," much as in the arrangement at Peter Kehoe's dwelling and shop on Cameron Street.[81]

Georgian dwellings were structures conceived from the outside in. Even as private residences, they were public structures insofar as they were meant to be seen from the road. They were overt testimonies to success, to the competence and independence of the household and to the improvements profits made possible. Germanic *Flürkuchenhauses,* such as Jost Hite's or those built at the Massanutten settlement of Jacob Stover, posed distinct challenges to ra-

Facing page

FIG. 7.10. Cloverdale. The three-bay, stucco-over-log portion of Cloverdale, in Frederick County, Virginia, provides an excellent example of a Georgian house and its evolution. Construction of the eastern log crib preceded the addition of the western crib and the enclosure of the central passage. The stone kitchen was attached later. Photo: By the author.

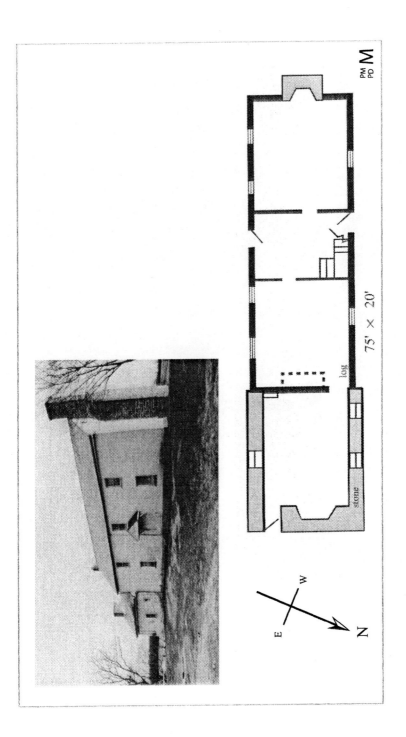

M
PD
PM

$75' \times 20'$

log

stone

N
E W

FIG. 7.11. Pennsylvania Bank Barns, Frederick County, Virginia. The combination of
an overhanging forebay above an animal lot and a wagon ramp to a second-story threshing floor made the Pennsylvania bank barn into an icon of improved and intensified
grain-livestock agriculture during the late eighteenth and nineteenth centuries. Photos:
Ben Ritter.

tionalization, or Georgianization. The central chimney and asymmetrical arrangement of rooms—*Küche*, *Stube*, and *Kammer*—around it presupposed an irregular façade, one conceived according to interior spatial arrangements. Under the impetus of the same drive for reason and improvement symbolized in an architectural order of balance and harmony, German householders often undertook the massive project of removing central chimneys in favor of gable-end chimneys and balancing fenestration around a central doorway or, if symmetry demanded, two central doors. Many Germans simply abandoned imperfect solutions and constructed new dwellings on Georgian lines.[82]

The rationalization of space in the Georgian dwelling had its counterpart in the countryside. By the end of the eighteenth century the forebay bank barn had become the dominant feature of the agricultural landscape of southeastern Pennsylvania. It combined, in a distinctive form, a variety of functions all critical to intensive grain-livestock farming (fig. 7.11). Built on a slope, or bank, or with a banked earthen ramp constructed to the upper story, the structure allowed direct access at each floor. The lower level accommodated the stabling and winter feeding of livestock; the story above contained a threshing floor and storage space for grains and feed. The forebay extended this space and provided access to the animal yard below. Large rectangular structures with balanced, three-part eave sides and symmetrical gables, forebay bank barns were as much a part of the machinery of agriculture as farmyards, field systems, road patterns, or milling operations, but they also served as the symbolic embodiment of the same desire for system, balance, and reason reflected in the Georgian dwelling. More and more in the late eighteenth century and increasingly in the nineteenth, this agricultural archetype appeared among all ethnic groups in the Shenandoah Valley for the same reasons of agricultural intensification and economic development that made it so emblematic of Pennsylvania.[83]

Whether it was found among people who could trace their ancestry to Ireland, England, the Rhine Valley, or elsewhere in Europe, this new architecture of balance and reason created a powerful symbol of the ordered world of civic culture that spread across the landscape of town and country in the Shenandoah Valley at the end of the eighteenth century. It would be this world—this symbol—that would overspread the geography of middle America in a landscape of dispersed farms and market towns during the next century and come to embody what was quintessentially American in small-town, main-street communities, many of which still populate the land today.[84]

Chapter 8

The Future of New Virginia

AN EPILOGUE

WHEN Nicholas Cresswell visited Winchester in December 1774 he called the town the "capital of this Colony." The settlements west of the Blue Ridge must have stuck this ambitious young man as separate and distinctive enough to constitute a colony within a colony with its own "capital" city. It was this region, of course, that would come to be called New Virginia after the American Revolution. Wandering about the town, he took note of the limestone buildings, the churches, the remains of Fort Loudoun, and the grid plan of the streets, all of which set off the regularity of the town from the seeming irregularity of the countryside. The town and the market opportunities it represented were crucial to Cresswell's plans to set himself up as a commercial farmer in the neighborhood, but what he said about a group of four Shawnee Indians he met during his visit to Winchester suggests that the town also represented civic order on the edge of the wilderness:

> Saw four Indian Chiefs of the Shawnee Nation, who have been at War with the Virginians this summer, but have made peace with them, and they are sending these people to Williamsburg as hostages. They are tall, manly, well-shaped men, of a Copper colour with black hair, quick piercing eyes, and good features. They have rings of silver in their nose and bobs to them which hang over their upper lip. Their ears are cut from the tips two thirds of the way round and the piece extended with brass wire till it touches their shoulders, in this part they hang a thin silver plate, wrought in flourishes about three inches diameter, with plates of silver round their arms and in the hair, which is all cut off except a long lock on the top of the head. They are in white men's dress, except breeches which they refuse to wear, instead of which they have a girdle round them with a piece of cloth drawn through their legs and turned over the girdle, and appears like a short apron before and behind. All the hair is pulled from their eyebrows and eyelashes and their faces painted in different

parts with Vermilion. They walk remarkably straight and cut a grotesque appearance in this mixed dress.[1]

That Imcatewhaywa, Wissesspoway, Genusa, and Neawah looked grotesque to Cresswell was no doubt owing to their incongruous dress and body ornament. This conclusion would only have been accentuated by their role as hostages in Virginia's latest conflict with the Ohio Indians known as Dunmore's War. As a result of the encroachment of white settlers on Indian lands west of the Kanawha River and a series of attacks by whites and Indians on each other, John Murray, earl of Dunmore and governor of Virginia, had personally led colonial forces to the Ohio River, where a detachment of Valley men under Andrew Lewis defeated a force of Shawnees at Point Pleasant on October 10, 1774. In the resulting Treaty of Camp Charlotte, concluded nine days later, the Ohio Indians agreed to surrender four hostages as a guarantee to appear the following year at Fort Pitt to resolve differences with Virginia over Ohio land claims. The hostages were on their way to Williamsburg when Cresswell encountered them.[2]

Events at Point Pleasant, Camp Charlotte, and Fort Pitt were soon overshadowed by the American Revolution and largely lost to the larger narrative of American history. To Shawnees, Delawares, and other Native Americans in the Ohio Valley, however, the developments of 1774–1775 represented a turning point in their efforts to secure a homeland on what was rapidly becoming the American frontier. Point Pleasant was the first battle the Ohio Indians fought against white settlers on their own territory, and at Camp Charlotte for the first time they ceded their own land by agreeing not to contest American settlement south of the Ohio River. Throughout the conflicts of the 1740s, 1750s, and 1760s the Ohio Indians had proved remarkably resilient in self-defense, but Dunmore's War initiated a long downward slide of Native American power in the American interior, which would culminate in the destruction of Indian society there in less than a half century.[3]

What struck Cresswell as grotesque about the hostages in Winchester might also have derived from the contrast they presented to popular European ideals of noble savages, free and independent in American woodland homes. The abject state of the four bound men on their way to Virginia's capital would have stood out vividly against the image of Indian life Jonnhaty and his party of Oneidas and Onondagas represented during their visit to the Shenandoah Valley just thirty-two years earlier. Jonnhaty's men had spent upwards of two months freely wandering through the Opequon settlements, hunting, fishing, and visiting in the land they called Jonontore. Jonnhaty saw no towns, not even a crossroads settlement of any significance. He would have had to search out a justice of the peace in his home for a pass to travel in Virginia. In the absence of county government, no courthouse or public square marked a center of political power in the region. Needing food, Jonnhaty's men simply hunted deer or the settlers' livestock in the woods; the presence of markets or market places never entered into their calculus of subsistence. Amid dispersed settlements strung along creeks or streams and bound together into open-country neighborhoods by networks of kinship and trade, Jonnhaty would have found a familiar world. He would have understood the "lazy life" that hunters lived at Opequon. What we have called a landscape of competence overspreading the Virginia backcountry could also be said to describe Indian homelands in Iroquoia and the Ohio Valley. By contrast, in the improved landscape of the Shenandoah Valley, emerging so quickly at the time of the American Revolution and appealing so strongly to Nicholas Cresswell, the Indians seemed almost grotesquely out of place. It was the spread of this landscape westward that so profoundly threatened Native American life.[4]

· ✸ ·

For more than three-quarters of a century the interaction of Native American and European American peoples and cultures had shaped the regional history of the Shenandoah Valley. Although no evidence exists for sustained Indian occupation of the Valley during the eighteenth century and the absence of Indians might have quickened European settlement, it was the movement of northern and southern Indians through the region and the political instability this movement provoked in Virginia that led to the migration of foreign Protestants into the Valley after 1730. Encounters between Indians and Europeans determined the course of landscape evolution thereafter in bounding the land within counties, centering counties in county towns, and stimulating economic development in these towns as garrisons during the Seven Years' War. The memories of these encounters and the relics of Indian occupants, however, would continue to shape the identity of the Valley and the manner in which nineteenth-century residents would construct their history.

During the opening decades of that century, ofttimes merchant and tavern keeper Samuel Kercheval collected the reminiscences of "aged individuals now living" about the pioneering period of the region. In his *History of the Valley of Virginia*, published in 1833, he documented extensive remains of earlier Native American occupants, including twenty-foot burial mounds as large as sixty feet in diameter and even more extensive remnants of palisaded villages. The "oral statements of several aged individuals of respectable character" confirmed for Kercheval's generation that "Indians and white people resided in the same neighborhood for several years after the first settlement commenced, and that the Indians were entirely peaceable and friendly." Skeletal remains, moreover, suggested to Kercheval that the earlier occupants of the Valley were a race of giants, some seven feet tall. Reminders of these peoples were quickly disappearing, however, as their "burying places [were] broken up, their bones torn up with the plow, reduced to dust, and scattered to the winds." To Kercheval the loss of these "lasting monuments in the history of our country" was a source of "melancholy regret." Indians were only a memory constructed to reflect their earlier significance. Kercheval's mirror of nostalgia and myth contrasted starkly with the forced removal of Native Americans by the federal government from the entire region east of the Mississippi River in the 1830s.[5]

The turning point in Native American history at Camp Charlotte was also a defining moment in the transition of the Shenandoah Valley from a backcountry to a forecountry. The emergence of a landscape of dispersed farms and market towns, which required a full half century on Virginia's first interior frontier, would be replicated in little more than a decade on the new frontiers of Kentucky, Tennessee, and Ohio in the 1780s and 1790s and then with ever greater speed as American settlement overspread the immense valley of the Mississippi and Ohio Rivers. The two-story, one-room-deep Georgian dwelling, whose symmetrical façade made a public statement of order and control, would quickly become the most common house type throughout this region and the most powerful symbol of a town and country landscape. So pervasive would this cultural statement become that when geographers discovered it in the twentieth century, they dubbed it an "I-house" because it dominated the landscape of the "I-states": Indiana, Illinois, and Iowa. Forebay bank barns appeared throughout this middle-American region, as well.[6]

In the nineteenth-century Shenandoah Valley as elsewhere, the I-house would undergo modifications according to various revival styles—Gothic, Italianate, Victorian—but the basic house in 1900 would remain as strong a representative of agricultural success—the competence of the farm household and the comfort achieved in a commercial economy—as it had at the time of its emergence a century earlier (fig. 8.1). The stability of the I-house is largely attributable to the enduring prosperity that wheat production in a mixed-farm economy brought to the Shenandoah Valley throughout the nineteenth century. Town and country became a kind of landscape machine for the production of agricultural commodities.

The world of wheat touched virtually every aspect of life in the region. Social relations; patterns of economic growth; labor systems, including slavery; politics, especially the politics of sectionalism; religion and religious pluralism; and attitudes toward nature and the environment were all shaped by the dominant culture of wheat and its cycles of cultivation, harvest, and sale. So efficient and so productive was this landscape machine that not even the devastation worked by the Civil War would seriously impede its operation. In a scorched-earth campaign Union forces burned barns and mills from Strasburg to Staunton, but Valley farmers marketed more wheat in 1870 than they had in 1860. And as measured in wheat yields per acre and per capita, the Valley outproduced the twelve north-central wheat-belt states, including Kansas and Nebraska, during the three decades before 1900.[7]

Notable in this story of stability and stasis is what did not happen in the nineteenth-century Shenandoah Valley that transformed America elsewhere. Unlike New England, where textile production initiated the Industrial Revolution in America as early as the 1790s; unlike Pennsylvania, made over by the iron and steel industries during the nineteenth century; and unlike the Midwest, where food and lumber processing built the great cities of Cincinnati and Chicago, no major industries developed in the Valley. Great, or even large, cities were notably absent in this region, where market towns—Winchester, Harrisonburg, Staunton, Lexington—surrounded by a hierarchy of villages and hamlets still defined the landscape in 1900 as they had in 1800. The world of wheat would become a "world we have lost" only after World War II, when wheat production in the Shenandoah Valley declined precipitously in the face of the Green Revolution and deep changes in world markets.[8]

Despite—or perhaps as a contribution to—stability in the nineteenth-century world of wheat, cash proliferated. Keeping accounts and balancing debits and credits in interdependent social networks survived, but the mechanisms of an exchange economy increasingly gave way to the simpler methods of trading in cash and keeping running accounts of income and expenditures. Accounts not unlike today's bank or credit card accounts replaced the old daybooks and ledgers as merchants, artisans, millers, and farmers sequentially recorded money received for goods sold and money expended for goods received in running accounts or cash books. The sum at any one time was a ready measure of profit or loss that was unavailable to men and women keeping track of innumerable transfers of goods and services as a balance of debits and credits. If the slow infusion of cash in the exchange economy of the eighteenth century served as an engine of town growth, then the expanding role of cash in the next century helps explain the continued expansion of towns. From 1800 to 1860, the population of Winchester increased from 2,130 to 4,477, and by 1900 the town boasted 5,161 inhabitants. Meanwhile, the percentage of the population living in towns throughout the lower Valley region increased from eleven to twenty-six. Banks as instruments of cash accumula-

FIG. 8.1. Gardner House, Frederick County, Virginia. By the nineteenth century the basic elements of the I-house had been incorporated into numerous revival styles. Nonetheless, the Gothic Revival Gardner House maintains the three-bay, single-pile plan that evolved in the eighteenth century as a symbol of order, balance, and rationalism. Frederick County Rural Landmarks Survey.

tion and capital distribution appeared for the first time in the Shenandoah Valley in 1812 and proliferated thereafter. In 1830 two of the four banks chartered in Virginia were located in the Valley, where 16 percent of the state's bank capital also resided.[9]

· ⚘ ·

The role of cash, the exchange economy, European settlement, encounters between whites and Indians, the founding of towns, military affairs, and many, many other subjects treated in this volume compose a braided narrative of contingent events. Narrative provides the primary organizing principle, or methodology, for explaining the emergence of a town and country landscape in the Shenandoah Valley from 1700 to 1800. The first phase of the narrative described the dispersal of yeoman farm families under the press of imperial conflict over the North American interior, a region Native Americans also defended as their homeland and colonial authorities feared would become a haven for runaway slaves. The narrative traced how the transformation of wilderness or waste land into private property and the aggregation of property holdings bounded the land into counties. The commissioning of courts and the founding of county towns provided the first centralizing forces in this landscape of dispersal. As the case of Winchester demonstrates, however, towns remained poorly integrated into the countryside in this second phase of landscape evolution; or, put differently, the economy of what happened in towns differed little from economic relations in the exchange economy, which spatially organized the quest for competence in the countryside.

In the developing imperial conflicts of the 1740s and 1750s, Winchester became a strategic place before it became a central place. The economy of the town as well as its distinctiveness from the countryside grew with its designation as a garrison town for the Virginia theater of the Seven Years' War and with the money that flowed into it from military coffers. The final phase of landscape evolution was ushered in by this infusion of cash, coinciding with a huge expansion of demand for wheat throughout the Atlantic economy and a consumer revolution in the marketing of domestic goods, fueled at least in part by higher prices for grain and flour. From 1760 to the end of the eighteenth century this commercial dynamo of grain production and the consumption of manufactured goods organized economic relations on expanding scales, from personal exchanges between farmer and miller or merchant in the Shenandoah Valley, to the long-distance trade from the Valley to eastern entrepôts at Philadelphia, Baltimore, and Alexandria, and finally, to the entire Atlantic world. At the same time, this dynamo structured the spatial relations of town and country and stimulated town growth in a rural landscape shaped more and more by the quest for improvement.

Narrative provides powerful techniques for interpreting history, but the results are not always as neat as they are in fiction. The story of town and country in the Shenandoah Valley is braided because characters, ideas, themes, and events weave in and out, leaving an occasional loose end or incomplete strand. The imperial struggles crucial to the episode on European settlement, for instance, become largely irrelevant after the 1760s, as the global forces behind landscape evolution shifted from the military to the economic. What is constant in this story, however, is the scale upon which it must be conceived. Answers to questions about why Europeans moved into so isolated a place as the Shenandoah Valley in the 1730s or how towns developed out of dispersed farm settlements require a perspective that embraces the entire Atlantic world from the beginning of the eighteenth century until its end. Similarly, the European settlement story cannot be told without recourse to Native American or African American history, but over time, the Indian side of the narrative shifted to new arenas, whereas the braid of slavery and freedom extended well beyond 1800.

Casting events as contingent also serves to integrate the various theoretical approaches to town formation described in the introduction to this volume. Landscape narrative does indeed explain the timing of Winchester's founding and growth, so problematic in central-place theory. Similarly, narrative incorporates the morphology, or distinctive appearance, of the town as crucial, not just as the setting for the story, but as itself the story of deepening relationships among producers, consumers, distributors, and marketers of goods and services in the moral geography of competence and improvement. The civic community of the town, in other words, reflected values deeply embedded in the landscape. And finally, this narrative of town formation demonstrates that the establishment of towns in so distant and isolated a place as the Virginia backcountry in the 1740s is inextricably related to long-distance trade throughout the Atlantic economy and the imperial system that sustained it. The subsequent growth of towns, moreover, reflected an increasing reliance on cash in regional exchanges.

The braiding of contingent events into a narrative provides a powerful analytical tool, but it raises questions about representativeness. Stories are by definition unique; if not, they would lack interest. As the emergence of a town-rich landscape in the Shenandoah Valley unfolds in this volume, the focus tightens on the lower Valley and its principal town, Winchester. Does the story of Winchester and its countryside explain anything that happened elsewhere in the geography of American history? Much of this story is indeed particular only to its region. Settlement in the Shenandoah Valley resulted very quickly in the 1730s from a singular conjunction of forces posed by French, Spanish, and English imperialism, Native American territorialism, the assertion of proprietary land claims, and growing fears about black maroonage in the Virginia mountains. The specific history of imperial wars, moreover, explains the establishment of Winchester as a strategic place in the 1740s and a garrison town in the 1750s. And although the late-eighteenth-century rise in grain prices and the consequent shift to wheat production was felt universally throughout the Atlantic economy, the extraordinary concurrence of excellent soils and mixed-farm agricultural traditions in the Shenandoah Valley allowed its people to respond with remarkable speed and effectiveness to these developments.

If indeed the Shenandoah Valley became the forecountry to emerging western backcountries after the Revolution and the pattern of landscape evolution in the Valley was quickly replicated beyond the Appalachians, then would not common factors explain the sequential reemergence of this landscape? Everywhere in the geography of American mixed-agricultural settlement, property in farms was created and bounded in counties, counties were centered in county towns with courts and markets, and economic activity was leavened by the yeast of political and legal business in these towns. Whether these developments took place in eastern Kentucky, around the Great Lakes, or along the Mississippi River, they all unfolded within strategic political or military contexts. What drove American settlement westward beyond the Appalachians and across the Mississippi was, first, the commercial revolution so significant to the Shenandoah Valley, and then the market, industrial, and urban revolutions of the nineteenth century. All of these upheavals precipitated territorial conflicts, primarily with Native Americans but also with Mexico, Spain, and Great Britain. Thus, every settlement story was an imperial story, and strategic considerations played tangible roles in the founding of many western towns.

· ⚓ ·

If the distinctive features of landscape change in the Shenandoah Valley fit into broad patterns of American history, what was new in this story? In other words, why the "new" in New Virginia? Clearly, the town-rich geography west of the Blue Ridge was new in the Virginia experience. An absence of towns continued to characterize Old Virginia throughout the nineteenth century, when the downward cycle of declining tobacco production discouraged economic centralization. Today, large areas of Tidewater and Southside Virginia lie under dense pine forests and the dominance of the wood products industry, and many county towns in the eastern part of the state outside the metropolitan areas of Northern Virginia, Richmond, and Virginia Beach remain small places marked only by a courthouse, lawyers row, a few stores, and scattered dwellings.

What struck so many people as new in western Virginia at the end of the eighteenth century, however, came from more than a prosperous countryside, thriving market towns, a vibrant grain economy, and a town and country landscape. For many, this landscape depicted the reality of republican society and hence the promise of American life. In the anxieties that led to its settlement, in the family settlement requirements imposed on its developers, and in the belief that freehold-farm families would defend their property and hence the empire by force of arms, there arose a people who, in seeking competence, did indeed liberate themselves from the webs of dependence that hobbled European society. These people were citizens, not subjects, whose virtue derived from labor on their own land and the consequent capacity to vote, hold office, and act politically in freedom from the controlling influence of landlords, employers, or aristocrats. Or so a group of European travelers saw it during the great era of republican revolutions that redefined history at the end of the eighteenth century.

The Shenandoah Valley still holds a mystique for vacationers who envision beautiful rolling farmland, majestic mountains, misty mornings, flourishing towns, and friendly people contented with their measure of earth's bounty. For many travelers two centuries and more ago, the Valley also held a mystique. All were inspired by the American Revolution, and many had fought in it. They were seeking out the social consequences of republican government established in the states during the conflict and in the nation by the Constitution of 1787. These people visited the centers of American governance in New York, Philadelphia, and eventually Washington, D.C., and they communed with Washington at Mount Vernon or Jefferson at Monticello. But, more importantly, they wanted to observe people firsthand in the natural state of freedom from the oppressive hand of aristocracy.

Most travelers made a point of visiting the Shenandoah Valley because they had heard about its beauty, its fertile land, and its industrious people, who reaped the rewards of their own labor free from rents, high taxes, or the machinations of landlords and government officials. These were certainly the sentiments of Andrew Burnaby when he sojourned in the lower Valley in 1760 and found that he "could not but reflect with pleasure on the situation of these people." "If there is such a thing as happiness in this life," he exclaimed, "they enjoy it." He painted the landscape as embracing the "most delightful climate," the "richest soil imaginable," "majestic woods," and "beautiful prospects and sylvan scenes." But the landscape was important only insofar as it gave rise to a people who were "generally robust" and "live in perfect liberty." "They are ignorant of want, and acquainted with but few vices. Their inexperience of the elegancies of life precludes any regret that they possess not the means of enjoying them: but they possess what many princes would give half their dominions for, health, content, and tranquility of mind." Fanciful as these descriptions sound, they were repeated often by later travelers deeply influenced by republican revolutions in France as well as America.[10]

Like Burnaby, Isaac Weld connected land and social structure to republican society. In his early twenties when he visited the United States between 1795 and 1797, this Dubliner was third in his family line to bear the name Isaac, after Sir Isaac Newton, a close associate of his greatgrandfather, Dr. Nathaniel Weld. Arriving in Philadelphia, Weld visited York, Lancaster, Baltimore, Alexandria, Mount Vernon, and Norfolk before journeying from Richmond westward across the Blue Ridge and into the Shenandoah Valley. He carefully compared eastern to western Virginia, observing that the "cultivated lands" of the Valley "are mostly parcelled out in small portions." "There are no persons here," he continued, "as on the other side of the mountains possessing large farms; nor are there any eminently distinguished by their education or knowledge from the rest of their fellow citizens. Poverty also is as much unknown in this country as great wealth." The republican social order of independent citizens was, in Weld's mind, based on private property and a concept of competence that discouraged greed and acquisitiveness: "Each man owns the house he lives in and the land which he cultivates, and every one appears to be in a happy state of mediocrity, and unambitious of a more elevated situation than what he himself enjoys." Mediocrity, to Weld, described a middling class of propertied farm families in which modest, broadly distributed wealth produced substantial comfort but few distinctions of class or status.[11]

Ferdinand Bayard was twenty-three in 1791, when he, his young wife, and infant son left France to see America and escape the turmoil of the French Revolution. Bayard was, nonetheless, a committed republican who looked to America for a model of what liberty, equality, and fraternity might mean at home. He sought out Americans "under their rustic roofs, in the solitude of their forests, on the high summits of their mountains"—in other words, as natural persons in their own landscapes. Only there could he "comprehend their character traits." He avoided cities, "where everything is imitation, where the inhabitants, communicating constantly with Europe, remain still imbued with English prejudices, and reveal in their customs as in their opinions, the traces of the irons which they had the courage to break." Instead, he journeyed to the Shenandoah Valley, "this fertile region," because "beneath skies almost always serene, the inhabitants cultivate a bountiful land, which rewards liberally the slightest effort of human labor." He came to the Valley to find people whose dependence upon the land freed them from the shackles of aristocratic privilege, and his search did not go unrewarded. Twelve miles from Winchester he came upon "well-kept meadows [that] foretold the proximity . . . of some intelligent planter." By the side of the road stood a "pretty little house, painted red . . . where Negro children and white children were playing games of their age." Surrounding the house were familiar trees, "poultry and suckling pigs," a garden, and a large meadow. This to Bayard was a "delightful place," where the "sexagenarian couple" who received him were "two human beings, as they really are, when their wants are not beyond their power." Republican simplicity was a trait that Bayard also found in Richard Kidder Meade. An officer in the Continental army, Meade had retreated to the Shenandoah Valley after the Revolution and set himself up as a farmer along the lines planned by Nicholas Cresswell. At dinner Meade talked "with pleasure about his home industries; everything was made in the home; and . . . he owed his independence to those industries which included all the articles of domestic economy."[12]

That travelers such as Burnaby, Weld, Bayard, and others found in the Shenandoah Valley a society of propertied farmers living in republican simplicity and virtue was to a large measure a self-fulfilling prophecy. They found what they wanted to find. They did not, for instance, comment that in 1790 one in seven Valley residents was a slave or that in some counties this proportion might reach one in four by century's end. So strong was the yearning for republican virtue that Bayard could extol it and at the same time overlook elections that he himself described as "days of reveling . . . and . . . drunkenness." Bayard also praised the freehold farmer as the bedrock of equality but described at great lengths the "land merchants" who "have gotten rich speculating in land."[13]

Stronger than what they did not see or what they noted and criticized was a conviction among travelers that in the Shenandoah Valley they were looking into the future of the United States. This future lay in the industry of the people, in the prosperity and independence they could derive from private property, and in the landscape they had created in the pursuit of competence and improvement. Bayard, for instance, called the Valley a "promised land, from whose bosom is arising an innumerable population of well-to-do and happy men, who passing very soon beyond the confines of the valley, will overflow all the surrounding country and will make vast wildernesses productive." Bayard could not have foretold the harsh realities of the American move west—the spread of slavery, the competition and conflicts over land, the wanton exploitation of natural resources, and the near annihilation of native peoples in a rapidly developing liberal economic state. The vision of a republican society these men put forth, however, was premised on the close integration of people, politics, culture, and environment in a landscape of market towns and family farms that combined both competency and improvement into what was *new* in New Virginia. And it was this landscape upon which they rested the future of the new republic.[14]

♫Notes

1. Charles E. Kemper, "Documents Relating to Early Projected Swiss Colonies in the Valley of Virginia, 1706–1709," *Virginia Magazine of History and Biography* 29 (Jan. 1921): 11, 2–3; key to fig. I.1 on 2. For additional material on Michel, his explorations, and his proposals for a Swiss colony in the Virginia backcountry, see Robert D. Mitchell, *Commercialism and Frontier: Perspectives on the Early Shenandoah Valley* (Charlottesville: UP of Virginia, 1977), 25–26; and Klaus Wust, *The Virginia Germans* (Charlottesville: UP of Virginia, 1969), 17–20. Accounts of Shenandoah Valley prehistory are largely confined to archaeological site reports, but for a popular interpretation, see William M. Gardner, *Lost Arrowheads and Broken Pottery: Traces of Indians in the Shenandoah Valley* (N.p.: Thunderbird Museum, 1986).

2. Scholarly accounts of Shenandoah Valley economy and society at the end of the eighteenth century are confined to two studies. See Freeman H. Hart, *The Valley of Virginia in the American Revolution, 1763–1789* (Chapel Hill: U of North Carolina P, 1942); and Mitchell, *Commercialism and Frontier.* For comparison, see Richard R. Beeman, *The Evolution of the Southern Backcountry: A Case Study of Lunenburg County, Virginia, 1746–1832* (Philadelphia: U of Pennsylvania P, 1984); and Charles J. Farmer, *In the Absence of Towns: Settlement and Country Trade in Southside Virginia, 1730–1800* (Lanham, Md.: Rowman & Littlefield, 1993).

3. The social history of early New England has been investigated for at least the past thirty years through the medium of town studies. These studies are legion, but for the best examples, see Philip J. Greven, *Four Generations: Population, Land, and Family in Colonial Andover, Massachusetts* (Ithaca: Cornell UP, 1970); Robert A. Gross, *The Minutemen and Their World* (New York: Hill & Wang, 1976); Kenneth A. Lockridge, *A New England Town: The First Hundred Years: Dedham, Massachusetts, 1636–1736* (New York: W. W. Norton, 1970); and Michael Zuckerman, *Peaceable Kingdoms: New England Towns in the Eighteenth Century* (Westport, Conn.: Greenwood Press, 1983). The scholarship on the colonial South tends to focus on either urban or rural society exclusively; see Carville V. Earle, *The Evolution of a Tidewater Settlement System: All Hallow's Par-*

ish, Maryland, 1650–1783, University of Chicago, Department of Geography, Research Paper, no. 170 (Chicago: U of Chicago P, 1975); Carville V. Earle and Ronald Hoffman, "Staple Crops and Urban Development in the Eighteenth-Century South," in *Perspectives in American History*, vol. 10, ed. Donald Fleming and Bernard Bailyn (Cambridge: Harvard UP, 1976): 7–78; Earle and Hoffman, "The Urban South: The First Two Centuries," in Blaine A. Brownell and David R. Goldfield, eds., *The City in Southern History: The Growth of Urban Civilization in the South* (Port Washington, N.Y.: Kennikat Press, 1977), 23–51; Joseph A. Ernst and H. Roy Merrens, "'Camden's turrets pierce the skies!': The Urban Process in the Southern Colonies during the Eighteenth Century," *William and Mary Quarterly*, 3d ser., 30 (Oct. 1973): 549–74; James O'Mara, *An Historical Geography of Urban System Development: Tidewater Virginia in the Eighteenth Century*, Geographical Monographs no. 13 (Downsview, Ont.: Department of Geography, Atkinson College, York University, 1983); John W. Reps, *Tidewater Towns: City Planning in Colonial Virginia and Maryland* (Williamsburg: Colonial Williamsburg Foundation, 1972); Reps, *Town Planning in Frontier America* (Princeton: Princeton UP, 1969); and Hermann Wellenreuther, "Urbanization in the Colonial South: A Critique," *William and Mary Quarterly*, 3d ser., 31 (Oct. 1974): 653–68.

4. No modern comprehensive study of colonial land policy exists, but for Virginia, see Warren R. Hofstra, "Land Policy and Settlement in the Northern Shenandoah Valley," in Robert D. Mitchell, ed., *Appalachian Frontiers: Settlement, Society, and Development in the Preindustrial Era* (Lexington: UP of Kentucky, 1990), 105–26; and Manning C. Voorhis, "The Land Grant Policy of Colonial Virginia, 1607–1774" (Ph.D. diss., University of Virginia, 1940).

5. The best account of the plantation of northern Ireland is Philip R. Robinson's *The Plantation of Ulster: British Settlement in an Irish Landscape, 1600–1670* (Dublin: Gill & MacMillan, 1984; New York: St. Martin's Press, 1984; Belfast: Ulster Historical Foundation, 1994). For a comparative context for English colonization in Ireland and America, see the works of Nicholas Canny, esp. "The Ideology of English Colonization: From Ireland to America," *William and Mary Quarterly*, 3d ser., 30 (Oct. 1973): 575–98, and *Kingdom and Colony: Ireland in the Atlantic World, 1560–1800* (Baltimore: Johns Hopkins UP, 1988).

6. For variations of this argument applied to the Shenandoah Valley, see Mitchell, *Commercialism and Frontier*, 16–19; and Wust, *The Virginia Germans*, 28–30.

7. On the distinction between Old and New Virginia, the early nineteenth-century writer James K. Paulding commented that the "people of whom I am writing, call those east of the mountain Tuckahoes, and their country Old Virginia. They themselves are the Cohees, and their country New Virginia," as quoted in Willard F. Bliss, "The Tuckahoe in the Valley" (Ph.D. diss., Princeton University, 1946), 202; see also Bliss, "The Tuckahoe in New Virginia," *Virginia Magazine of History and Biography* 59 (Oct. 1951): 387–96. Perhaps the earliest reference to "New Virginia" occurred in 1755, when cartographer Lewis Evans wrote in the analysis to his *Map of the Middle British Colonies* that, "as for the Branches of Ohio, which head in New Virginia, I am particularly obliged to Mr. Thomas Walker." See Evans, *Geographical, Historical, Political, Philosophical and Mechanical Essays. The First, Containing an Analysis Of a General Map of*

the Middle British Colonies in America . . ., as quoted in Richard W. Stephenson and Marianne M. McKee, *Virginia in Maps: Four Centuries of Settlement, Growth, and Development* (Richmond: Library of Virginia, 2000), 56. Describing New Virginia, the duc de La Rochefoucauld-Liancourt pointed out that in this "part of the State the population is not so great as in that which is called Old Virginia." See François Alexandre Frédéric, duc de La Rochefoucauld-Liancourt, *Travels through the United States of North America . . . in the Years 1795, 1796, and 1797,* 4 vols., 2d ed., trans. H. Neuman (London: R. Phillips, 1800), 3:222. Sectionalism in Virginia is a topic awaiting further study, but for traditional accounts, see Charles H. Ambler, *Sectionalism in Virginia from 1776 to 1861* (Chicago: U of Chicago P, 1910; New York: Russell & Russell, 1964); and Virginius Dabney, *Virginia: The New Dominion* (Garden City, N.Y.: Doubleday, 1971), 211–23.

8. Gooch was actually lieutenant governor serving under Gov. George Hamilton, earl of Orkney, who remained in England. He was, however, commonly referred to as governor, as were Alexander Spotswood and Robert Dinwiddie, who also served as lieutenant governors under Orkney, or his successor, William Keppel, earl of Albemarle.

9. Achieving economic independence or competency has been interpreted by a number of historians as a determining element in the settlement evolution of eighteenth-century North America; see Jack P. Greene, "Independence, Improvement, and Authority: Toward a Framework for Understanding the Histories of the Southern Backcountry during the Era of the American Revolution," in Ronald Hoffman, Thad W. Tate, and Peter J. Albert, eds., *An Uncivil War: The Southern Backcountry during the American Revolution* (Charlottesville: UP of Virginia for the United States Capitol Historical Society, 1985), 3–36; Greene, *Pursuits of Happiness: The Social Development of Early Modern British Colonies and the Formation of American Culture* (Chapel Hill: U of North Carolina P, 1988), 15–16, 98, 195–97; James A. Henretta, "Families and Farms: *Mentalité* in Pre-Industrial America," *William and Mary Quarterly,* 3d ser., 35 (Jan. 1978): 18–19; and Daniel Vickers, "Competency and Competition: Economic Culture in Early America," *William and Mary Quarterly,* 3d ser., 47 (Jan. 1990): 3–29.

10. The development of alternative political cultures in backcountry communities is more fully treated by Albert H. Tillson Jr. in *Gentry and Common Folk: Political Culture on a Virginia Frontier, 1740–1789* (Lexington: U of Kentucky P, 1991). The Council also served as the upper branch of the Virginia legislature and the high court for the colony.

11. The best treatment of the Philadelphia trade and its implications for the economy of the Virginia backcountry is Thomas M. Doerflinger's *A Vigorous Spirit of Enterprise: Merchants and Economic Development in Revolutionary Philadelphia* (Chapel Hill: U of North Carolina P for the Institute of Early American History and Culture, 1986). For contemporary accounts of this trade, see Harry Toulmin, *The Western Country in 1793: Reports on Kentucky and Virginia,* ed. Marion Tinling and Godfrey Davies (San Marino, Calif.: Huntington Library, 1948), 57; La Rochefoucauld-Liancourt, *Travels,* 3:202–4; and Clement Biddle and Co. Letterbook, 1769–1770, Clement Biddle Papers, and Owen Jones Letterbook, 1759–1781, Owen Jones Papers, 1759–1824, Historical Society of Pennsylvania, Philadelphia.

12. For a discussion of flour prices and market ranges, see Earle and Hoffman, "Staple Crops," 68–78. The shift to wheat production in southern colonial agriculture is

treated in a variety of sources; see Doerflinger, *Spirit of Enterprise*, 108–14; Earle and Hoffman, "Staple Crops," 28–30; Paul W. Gates, *The Farmer's Age: Agriculture, 1815–1860*, vol. 3 of *Economic History of the United States* (New York: Holt, Rinehart & Winston, 1960), 159; Lewis C. Gray, *History of Agriculture in the Southern United States to 1860*, 2 vols. (Washington, D.C.: Carnegie Institute, 1933; reprint, 1 vol., New York: Augustus M. Kelly, 1973), 161–66, 881, 908; David Klingaman, "The Significance of Grain in the Development of the Tobacco Colonies," *Journal of Economic History* 29 (June 1969): 268–78; and Jacob Price, "Economic Function and the Growth of American Port Towns in the Eighteenth Century," in *Perspectives in American History*, vol. 8, ed. Donald Fleming and Bernard Bailyn (Cambridge: Harvard UP, 1974): 151–56.

13. For a discussion of the consumer revolution, see T. H. Breen, "An Empire of Goods: The Anglicization of Colonial America, 1690–1776," *Journal of British Studies* 25 (Oct. 1986): 467–99; Cary Carson, Ronald Hoffman, and Peter J. Albert, eds., *Of Consuming Interests: The Style of Life in the Eighteenth Century* (Charlottesville: UP of Virginia, 1994); Thomas M. Doerflinger, "Farmers and Dry Goods in the Philadelphia Market Area, 1750–1800," in Ronald Hoffman, John J. McCusker, Russell R. Menard, and Peter J. Albert, eds., *The Economy of Early America: The Revolutionary Period, 1763–1790* (Charlottesville: UP of Virginia, 1988), 166–95; Greene, *Pursuits of Happiness*, 108–9; Neil McKendrick, John Brewer, and J. H. Plumb, *The Birth of a Consumer Society: The Commercialization of Eighteenth-Century England* (Bloomington: Indiana UP, 1985); and Carole Shammas, "Consumer Behavior in Colonial America," *Social Science History* 6 (winter 1982): 67–86.

14. Accounts of the remarkable development of a plantation society in the Shenandoah Valley are surprisingly few. In addition to the author's own works on this subject, see Willard F. Bliss, "Tuckahoe in the Valley," and Bliss, "Tuckahoe in New Virginia," 387–96.

15. William W. Hening, ed., *The Statutes at Large: Being a Collection of All the Laws of Virginia, from . . . 1619 . . .*, 13 vols. (Richmond, New York, and Philadelphia: 1819–23), 10:35–37, 172–76.

16. U.S. Census Office, Second Census, 1800, *Return of the Whole Number of Persons within the Several Districts of the United States . . .* (Washington, D.C., 1801), 21.

17. Bonnie Barton, "The Creation of Centrality," *Annals of the Association of American Geographers* 68 (Mar. 1978): 34; Walter Christaller, *Central Places in Southern Germany*, trans. C. W. Baskin (Jena: Gustav Fisher, 1933; Englewood Cliffs, N.J.: Prentice Hall, 1966); August Lösch, *The Economics of Location*, trans. William H. Woglom (New Haven, Conn.: 1954); and Lösch, "The Nature of Economic Regions," *Southern Economic Journal* 5 (1938): 71–78. See also H. Beguin, "Christaller's Central Place Postulates: A Commentary," *Annals of Regional Science* 26 (1992): 209–29; Brian J. L. Berry and J. Parr, *Market Centers and Retail Location: Theory and Applications* (Englewood Cliffs, N.J.: Prentice Hall, 1988); Martyn Bowden, B. L. La Rose, and B. Mishara, "The Development of Competition between Central Places on the Frontier," *Proceedings of the Association of American Geographers* 3 (1971): 32–38; and James T. Lemon, *The Best Poor Man's Country: A Geographical Study of Early Southeastern Pennsylvania* (Baltimore: Johns Hopkins UP, 1972; New York: W. W. Norton, 1976), 102–49.

18. The terminology of town-rich and town-poor landscapes was developed by August Lösch; see *Economics of Location* and "Nature of Economic Regions." The best discussion of staple theory as applied to questions of town development appears in Earle and Hoffman, "Staple Crops," 7–77; John J. McCusker and Russell R. Menard, *The Economy of British America, 1607–1789* (Chapel Hill: U of North Carolina P for the Institute of Early American History and Culture, 1985), 10–34; and Price, "Economic Function and the Growth of American Port Towns," 123–86.

19. The functionalist argument about town geography is developed in Ernst and Merrens, "Urban Process in the Southern Colonies," 549–74, and O'Mara, *Historical Geography of Urban System Development.* For a critique of this approach, see Wellenreuther, "Urbanization in the Colonial South," 653–68.

20. For a discussion of long-distance trade theory, see James E. Vance Jr., *The Merchant's World: The Geography of Wholesaling* (Englewood Cliffs, N.J.: Prentice Hall, 1970).

CHAPTER 1. Empire and Encounter: A Prologue

1. Thomas McKee, deposition, Jan. 24, 1743, in Samuel Hazard, ed., *Minutes of the Provincial Council of Pennsylvania*, 16 vols. (Harrisburg: Theo. Fenn, 1838–53), 4:631. The term *opickin Settlement* appears in *Bringhurst v Blackburn*, May 1744, Ended Causes, 1743–1909, Frederick County Court Papers, Library of Virginia, Richmond. For the term *Jonontore*, see Conrad Weiser, Report of his Journey to Shamokin, Jan. 30–Feb. 9, 1743, in Hazard, *Provincial Council of Pennsylvania*, 4:640–46. Until the early 1720s, when the Tuscaroras formally joined the Mohawks, Oneidas, Onondagas, Cayugas, and Senecas, the Six Nations were known as the Five Nations.

2. William J. Hinke and Charles E. Kemper, eds., "Moravian Diaries of Travels through Virginia," *Virginia Magazine of History and Biography* 11 (Apr. 1904): 372; and Samuel Kercheval, *A History of the Valley of Virginia*, 5th ed. (Strasburg, Va.: Shenandoah Publishing House, 1973), 36. On settlement in western Pennsylvania and Maryland, see James T. Lemon, *The Best Poor Man's Country: A Geographical Study of Early Southeastern Pennsylvania* (Baltimore: Johns Hopkins UP, 1972; New York: W. W. Norton, 1976), 42–70; and Frank W. Porter III, "From Backcountry to Country: The Delayed Settlement of Western Maryland," *Maryland Historical Magazine* 70 (winter 1975): 329–49. Charles Friend's settlement near the mouth of Conococheague Creek appears on "A Map of the Northern Neck in Virginia, according to an actual survey begun in the year 1736, and ended in the year 1746," by Peter Jefferson and Robert Brooke and Others, CO 700/Virginia 11, Colonial Office Papers, Public Record Office (hereafter PRO), London. When a delegation of Shawnees failed to appear at a prearranged meeting, Charles Calvert, governor of Maryland, designated "Israel Friend [to] be sent up immediately to the said Indians" to remind them that the governor "came with no other View or Intention but to Confirm a lasting Peace and setled Friendship with them." Instructions to Israel Friend, Aug. 6, 1725, in William Hand Browne, ed., *Proceedings of the Council of Maryland, 1698–1731*, vol. 25, *Archives of Maryland* (Baltimore: Maryland Historical Society, 1905), 450–51.

3. Opequon in the 1730s and 1740s had no precise boundaries. Settlements in the vicinity of Opequon Creek certainly fell within the community, but for the purpose of this discussion it consisted of all the tracts patented or identified before 1736 as later included within the Northern Neck Proprietary of Thomas, sixth lord Fairfax. On population estimates, see Robert D. Mitchell, *Commercialism and Frontier: Perspectives on the Early Shenandoah Valley* (Charlottesville: UP of Virginia, 1977), 30. The evolution of Native American societies in the Shenandoah Valley is most comprehensively treated in William M. Gardner, *Lost Arrowheads and Broken Pottery: Traces of Indians in the Shenandoah Valley* (N.p.: Thunderbird Museum, 1986). See also Mary Ellen N. Hodges, "The Archaeology of Native American Life in Virginia in the Context of European Contact: Review of Past Research," in Theodore R. Reinhart and Dennis J. Pogue, eds., *The Archaeology of Seventeenth-Century Virginia*, Special Publication no. 30 (Courtland: Archeological Society of Virginia, 1993): 1–65; Warren R. Hofstra and Clarence R. Geier, "Native American Settlement within the Middle and Upper Drainage of Opequon Creek, Frederick County, Virginia," *Quarterly Bulletin of the Archeological Society of Virginia* 54 (Sept. 1999): 154–65; Michael J. Klein and Thomas Klatka, "Late Archaic and Early Woodland Demography and Settlement Patterns," in Theodore R. Reinhart and Mary Ellen N. Hodges, eds., *Late Archaic and Early Woodland Research in Virginia: A Synthesis*, Special Publication no. 23 (Courtland: Archeological Society of Virginia, 1991): 139–83; Douglas C. McLearen, "Virginia's Middle Woodland Period: A Regional Perspective," in Theodore R. Reinhart and Mary Ellen N. Hodges, eds., *Middle and Late Woodland Research in Virginia: A Synthesis*, Special Publication no. 29 (Courtland: Archeological Society of Virginia, 1992): 39–63; and E. Randolph Turner III, "Paleoindian Settlement Patterns and Population Distribution in Virginia," in J. Mark Wittkofski and Theodore R. Reinhart, eds., *Paleoindian Research in Virginia: A Synthesis*, Special Publication no. 19 (Courtland: Archeological Society of Virginia, 1989): 71–93.

4. The spacing between farmsteads and other issues concerning landscape dispersal are covered more fully elsewhere in this volume as well as in Warren R. Hofstra, "Land, Ethnicity, and Community at the Opequon Settlement, Virginia, 1730–1800," *Virginia Magazine of History and Biography* 98 (July 1990): 423–48, reprinted in H. Tyler Blethen and Curtis W. Wood Jr., eds., *Ulster and North America: Transatlantic Perspectives on the Scotch-Irish* (Tuscaloosa: U of Alabama P, 1997), 167–88; Hofstra, "Adaptation or Survival? Folk Housing at Opequon Settlement, Virginia," *Ulster Folklife* 37 (1991): 36–61; Hofstra and Robert D. Mitchell, "Town and Country in Backcountry Virginia: Winchester and the Shenandoah Valley, 1730–1800," *Journal of Southern History* 59 (Nov. 1993): 619–46; Mitchell and Hofstra, "How Do Settlement Systems Originate? The Virginia Backcountry during the Eighteenth Century," *Journal of Historical Geography* 21 (Apr. 1995): 123–47; and Clarence R. Geier and Hofstra, "An Archaeological Survey of and Management Plan for Cultural Resources in the Vicinity of the Upper Opequon Creek" (Richmond: Virginia Department of Historic Resources, 1991).

5. John Bartram, *Observations on the Inhabitants, Climate, Soil, Rivers, Productions, Animals . . .* (London: Whiston & White, 1751), 42, 14; and "Diary of the Journey of Br. Cammerhoff and David Zeisberger to the Five Nations from May 3–14 to August 6–17,

1750," in William M. Beauchamp, ed., *Moravian Journals Relating to Central New York, 1745–66* (Syracuse, N.Y.: Onondaga Historical Association, 1916), 60. On the dispersal of Native American settlements, see Michael N. McConnell, *A Country Between: The Upper Ohio Valley and Its Peoples, 1724–1774* (Lincoln: U of Nebraska P, 1992), 25; and Daniel K. Richter, *The Ordeal of the Longhouse: The Peoples of the Iroquois League in the Era of European Colonization* (Chapel Hill: U of North Carolina P for the Institute of Early American History and Culture, 1992), 257–62.

6. George Clarke speech to Six Nations, June 15, 1742, in Edmund Bailey O'Callaghan and Berthold Fernow, eds., *Documents Relative to the Colonial History of the State of New-York*, 15 vols. (Albany: Weed, Parsons, 1853–87), 6:217; and John Armstrong, "Scheme of an Expedition to Kittanning," Miscellaneous Manuscript Collections, American Philosophical Society, Philadelphia, as quoted in McConnell, *A Country Between*, 25.

7. On Native American views toward surveying, see Thomas A. Lewis, *For King and Country: The Maturing of George Washington, 1748–1760* (New York: HarperCollins, 1993), 53; and McConnell, *A Country Between*, 90.

8. On Brooke's appointment to survey lands in the Shenandoah Valley, see William P. Palmer, Sherwin McRae, Raleigh Colston, and H. W. Flourney, eds., *Calendar of Virginia State Papers and Other Manuscripts, 1652–1781*, 12 vols. (Richmond, 1875–93; New York: Kraus Reprint, 1968), 1:217–18; H. R. McIlwaine, Wilmer L. Hall, and Benjamin J. Hillman, eds., *Executive Journals of the Council of Colonial Virginia*, 6 vols. (Richmond: Virginia State Library, 1925–66), 4:321; and Sarah S. Hughes, *Surveyors and Statesmen: Land Measuring in Colonial Virginia* (Richmond: Virginia Surveyors Foundation and Virginia Association of Surveyors, 1979), 98–99. See also Robert Brooke Survey Book, 1732–34, Thornton Tayloe Perry Collection, Virginia Historical Society, Richmond. The patent for Brooke's Falling Water tract can be found in Virginia Land Patents (hereafter VLP), 17:461, Patents, 1623–1774, Library of Virginia. On June 12, 1716, Spotswood announced the discovery of the passes over the Blue Ridge to the Virginia Council and visited them several months later to assess the threat they posed to the colony's security. See McIlwaine et al., *Executive Journals of the Council*, 3:428; Leonidas Dodson, *Alexander Spotswood: Governor of Colonial Virginia, 1710–1722* (Philadelphia: U of Pennsylvania P, 1932), 238–40; John Fontaine, *The Journal of John Fontaine: An Irish Huguenot Son in Spain and Virginia, 1710–1719*, ed. Edward P. Alexander (Williamsburg: Colonial Williamsburg Foundation, 1972); and Warren M. Billings, John E. Selby, and Thad W. Tate, *Colonial Virginia: A History* (White Plains, N.Y.: KTO Press, 1986), 183–84.

9. Charles E. Kemper, ed., "Documents Relating to a Proposed Swiss and German Colony in the Western Part of Virginia, 1706–1709," *Virginia Magazine of History and Biography* 29 (Jan. 1921): 2; and *The Journal of Philip Vickers Fithian, 1775–1776*, ed. Robert G. Albion and Leonidas Dodson (Princeton: Princeton UP, 1934), 107. The discussion of forest species is derived from Robert D. Mitchell, Edward F. Connor, and Warren R. Hofstra, "European Settlement and Land-Cover Change: The Shenandoah Valley of Virginia during the Eighteenth Century," report to the National Geographic Society, June 1993, Washington, D.C.; and Mitchell, Hofstra, and Connor, "Recon-

structing the Colonial Environment of the Upper Chesapeake Watershed," in Philip E. Curtin, Grace S. Brush, and George W. Fisher, eds., *Discovering the Chesapeake: The History of an Ecosystem* (Baltimore: Johns Hopkins UP, 2001), 167–90. For an account of "savanae," see John Lederer, *The Discoveries of John Lederer*, ed. William P. Cumming (London: Samuel Herick, 1672; Charlottesville: UP of Virginia, 1958).

10. Fithian, *Journal*, 91, 19; and John Smith, *The Generall Historie of Virginia, New-England, and the Summer Isles* (Glasgow: J. MacLehose; New York: Macmillan, 1907) as quoted in William Condit Robinson, "Cultural Plant Geography of the Middle Appalachians" (Ph.D. diss., Boston University, 1960), 127. In a revealing marginal note Smith commented that Indians "cannot travell but where the woods are burnt."

11. Charles Butts, *Geology of the Appalachian Valley in Virginia*, Virginia Geological Survey Bulletin 52 (Richmond: Division of Purchase and Printing, 1940; Charlottesville: Virginia Division of Mineral Resources, 1973), 1–210; Charles Butts and Raymond S. Edmundson, *Geology and Mineral Resources of Frederick County*, Virginia Division of Mineral Resources Bulletin 80 (Charlottesville: Virginia Division of Mineral Resources, 1966), 1–33; and Geier and Hofstra, "Archaeological Survey," 8–12.

12. McIlwaine et al., *Executive Journals of the Council*, 4:229.

13. John Bartram to Peter Collinson, July 18 [1739], in Edmund Berkeley and Dorothy Smith Berkeley eds., *The Correspondence of John Bartram, 1734–1777* (Gainesville: UP of Florida, 1992), 121–22; William W. Hening, ed., *The Statutes at Large: Being a Collection of All the Laws of Virginia, from . . . 1619 . . .*, 13 vols. (Richmond, New York, and Philadelphia, 1819–23), 5:60–63; and William Gooch to Board of Trade, Feb. 22, 1739, CO 5/1324, PRO.

14. Joseph Doddridge, *Notes, on the Settlement and Indian Wars, of the Western Parts of Virginia and Pennsylvania . . .* (Wellsburgh, Va., 1824), 126–27; Stephen Aron, *How the West Was Lost: The Transformation of Kentucky from Daniel Boone to Henry Clay* (Baltimore: Johns Hopkins UP, 1996), 5–28; and John Mack Faragher, *Daniel Boone: The Life and Legend of an American Pioneer* (New York: Henry Holt, 1992), 19–22. Portions of Doddridge's text also appear in Kercheval, *History of the Valley*, 183–301.

15. Doddridge, *Notes*, 115.

16. Cecil O'Dell, *Pioneers of Old Frederick County, Virginia* (Marceline, Mo.: Walsworth, 1995), 88–93. On Indian roads in the Shenandoah Valley, see Kercheval, *History of the Valley*, 38; and O'Dell, *Pioneers of Old Frederick County*, 517–19.

17. Weiser, Report, in Hazard, *Provincial Council of Pennsylvania*, 4:644; McIlwaine et al., *Executive Journals of the Council*, 4:318–19; and William H. B. Thomas, "Courthouses of Orange County," *Virginia Cavalcade* 18 (summer 1969): 32–37.

18. George Webb, *The Office and Authority of a Justice of Peace . . .* (Williamsburg: William Parks, 1736), 49–51.

19. Webb, *Office and Authority of a Justice*, 50. On Morgan's appointment as militia captain, see O'Dell, *Pioneers of Old Frederick County*, 176; and Orange County Court Orders, 3:344, Orange County Courthouse (hereafter OCCO), Orange, Virginia.

20. Weiser, Report, in Hazard, *Provincial Council of Pennsylvania*, 4:644; Minutes, East Nottingham Monthly Meeting, Mar. 18, 1734, as quoted in *Hopewell Friends History, 1734–1934, Frederick County, Virginia* (Strasburg, Va.: Shenandoah Publishing House,

1936), 45. On Ross, his land grant, and his land dealings, see William Couper, *History of the Shenandoah Valley*, 3 vols. (New York: Lewis Historical Publishing, 1952), 1:217–27; and VLP, 16:320; and McIlwaine et al., *Executive Journals of the Council*, 4:229, 347.

21. *Hopewell Friends History*, 52. On the use of oaths and affirmations in Pennsylvania, see Sally Schwartz, "Religious Pluralism in Colonial Pennsylvania," in Robert D. Mitchell, ed., *Appalachian Frontiers: Settlement, Society, and Development in the Preindustrial Era* (Lexington: U of Kentucky P, 1990), 52–68.

22. Thomas Chalkley to the "friends of the monthly meeting at Opequon," July 21, 1738, in Thomas Chalkley, *A Collection of the Works of That Antient, faithful Servant of Jesus Christ, Thomas Chalkley* (London: Luke Hind, 1751), 308–11, also quoted in Kercheval, *History of the Valley*, 46–47. On Quaker wealth in Pennsylvania, see Lemon, *Best Poor Man's Country*, 188–93.

23. Kercheval, *History of the Valley*, 38.

24. John Frost survey [Oct. 1734], Robert Brooke Survey Book, 64; *Hopewell Friends History*, 28–39; OCCO, 3:8, 198; and Anne Brush Miller, *Orange County Road Orders, 1734–1739* (Charlottesville: Virginia Highway and Transportation Research Council, 1984), 60, 74.

25. Butts and Edmundson, *Geology of Frederick County*, 5–6; and Robert L. Holmes and David L. Wagner, *Soil Survey of Frederick County Virginia* (Washington, D.C.: U.S. Department of Agriculture, Soil Conservation Service, 1987), 2–3.

26. John Bartram, folder 41, vol. 1, Bartram Papers, Historical Society of Pennsylvania, Philadelphia; John F. D. Smyth, *A Tour in the United States of America*, 2 vols. (London: G. Robinson, 1784; New York: New York Times and Arno Press, 1968), 2:73; *The Journal of Nicholas Cresswell, 1774–1777* (New York: Dial Press, 1924), 49; and Foote, "Genealogy of the Glass Family in Virginia," 7, typescript, Archives Room, Handley Regional Library, Winchester.

27. "The Treaty Held with the Indians of the Six Nations, at Lancaster in Pennsylvania, in June, 1744" (Williamsburg: William Parks, n.d.), enclosure in William Gooch to Board of Trade, Dec. 21, 1744, CO 5/1325, PRO.

28. In August 1742 the Orange County Court directed that George Hollingsworth serve as overseer for the road from John Littler's dwelling to Abraham Hollingsworth's mill and Robert Willson, from Hollingsworth's to Jost Hite's mill, see OCCO, 3:198; and Miller, *Orange County Road Orders*, 74. Hite had been appointed to the court with Hobson, Morgan, John Smith, and Benjamin Borden on April 23, 1734; see McIlwaine et al., *Executive Journals of the Council*, 4:318–19. On Hite and the Palatinate immigrants, see Henry Z. Jones, Ralph Conner, and Klaus Wust, *German Origins of Jost Hite: Virginia Pioneer, 1685–1761* (Edinburg, Va.: Shenandoah History, 1979); and Philip Otterness, "The New York Naval Stores Project and the Transformation of the Poor Palatines, 1710–1712," *New York History* 75 (Apr. 1994): 133–56.

29. *John Hite et al. v Lord Fairfax et al.*, Additional Manuscript 15317, British Museum, London, transcript by Hunter Branson McKay, 1521, 1519, Archives Room, Handley Regional Library; and McIlwaine et al., *Executive Journals of the Council*, 4:253. In addition to the 100,000-acre land orders to himself and Robert McKay, Hite purchased rights to another 40,000 acres previously granted to John and Isaac Van Meter. See

McIlwaine et al., *Executive Journals of the Council*, 4:223–24. On Hite's recruitment of settlers, see *Hite v Fairfax*, transcript by McKay, 1523, 1662–63; and Stuart E. Brown Jr., *Virginia Baron: The Story of Thomas Sixth Lord Fairfax* (Berryville, Va.: Chesapeake Book Co., 1965), 74–75.

30. VLP, 15:343. On Hite's tavern, mill, and road petition, see Hinke and Kemper, "Moravian Diaries," 11:373–74, 12:142; OCCO, 1:439, 2:3; and Miller, *Orange County Road Orders*, 36, 39.

31. On the *Flürkuchenhaus*, or *Ernhaus*, see Edward A. Chappell, "Acculturation in the Shenandoah Valley: Rhenish Houses of the Massanutten Settlement," *Proceedings of the American Philosophical Society* 124 (1980): 55–89; K. Edward Lay, "European Antecedents of Seventeenth and Eighteenth Century Germanic and Scots-Irish Architecture in America," *Pennsylvania Folklife* 32 (1982): 2–43; and William Woys Weaver, "The Pennsylvania German House: European Antecedents and New World Forms," *Winterthur Portfolio* 21 (1986): 243–64.

32. Christopher Windle deposition, Feb. 8, 1787, *Christopher Windle v Rep. of Jost Hite et al.*, fol. 742, folder 175, Clark-Hite Papers, Filson Historical Society, Louisville, Ky.; Hinke and Kemper, "Moravian Diaries," 11:373–74; and Kercheval, *History of the Valley*, 56–57.

33. For deeds from Jost Hite to Stephen Hotsinpiller, Thomas Wilson, James Wood, William and Mary Reed, Robert Allen, John Harrow, David Vance, Abraham Wiseman, Peter Mauk, John Hite, Samuel Glass, and James Vance, see Orange County Deeds, 1:431, 442; 2:304, 4:9; 6:165, 170, 174, 249, 258; 8:22, 38, 46, Orange County Courthouse, Orange, Va.; and to Joseph Colvin (Colvill) and John Poker, see Frederick County Deeds, 1:68; 2:90, Frederick County Courthouse, Winchester.

34. The reference to survey lines run from creeks into woodlands appears in many surveys along the upper Opequon. For examples, see Northern Neck Land Grants, 1690–1874, H:282, 294, 529, Library of Virginia. The reference to big timbers appears in Thomas K. Cartmell, *Shenandoah Valley Pioneers and Their Descendants: A History of Frederick County, Virginia* (Winchester, Va.: Eddy Press, 1909; Bowie, Md.: Heritage Books, 1989), 53.

35. Kercheval, *History of the Valley*, 150; and *William Dobbin v Duncan O'Gullion*, Oct. 1747, Ended Causes, 1743–1909, Frederick County Court Papers. References to thatch roofs can be found in the Jonathan Clark Notebook, July–Aug. 1786, Clark-Hite Papers.

36. James Vance inventory, Feb. 12, 1752, Frederick County Wills (hereafter FCW), 2:17, Frederick County Courthouse, Winchester. For buckwheat, see John Beckett inventory, Apr. 6, 1769, FCW, 3:488–89; and for spelt, see ibid. and Edward Hoge inventory, Nov. 12, 1782, FCW, 4:549–51.

37. This discussion of ethnic, kinship, and landholding patterns at Opequon is drawn from Hofstra, "Land, Ethnicity, and Community," 423–48.

38. James Vance will, Feb. 26, 1750, FCW, 1:495; Elizabeth Vance will, Nov. 12, 1781, FCW, 5:110; and Thomas, lord Fairfax, to Elizabeth Vance, grant, Aug. 7, 1752, Northern Neck Land Grants, H:191.

39. See Warren R. Hofstra, "Ethnicity and Community Formation on the Shenan-

doah Valley Frontier, 1730–1800," in Michael J. Puglisi, ed., *Diversity and Accommodation: Essays on the Cultural Composition of the Virginia Frontier* (Knoxville: U of Tennessee P, 1997), 59–81. Stoever's records are compiled in William E. Eisenberg, *This Heritage: The Story of Lutheran Beginnings in the Lower Shenandoah Valley, and of Grace Church Winchester* (Boyce, Va.: Carr Publishing, 1954), 312–21. On the marriage of Barbara Willson and Peter Stephens, see Robert Willson to Peter Stephens, deed of gift, Mar. 4, 1767, Frederick County Deeds, 11:330; and Robert Willson will, Nov. 1777, FCW, 4:444.

40. Hinke and Kemper, "Moravian Diaries," 12:144; and Fithian, *Journal*, 137. On the Indians' arrival in the Irish tract, see James Patton to William Gooch, Dec. 23, 1742, enclosure in Gooch to Board of Trade, Feb. 14, 1743, CO 5/1325, PRO.

41. On November 20, 1743, Leonhard Schnell and Robert Hussey visited Jost Hite, and one of them "asked him for the way to Carolina. He told me of one, which runs for 150 miles through Irish settlements, the district being known as the Irish tract." Hinke and Kemper, "Moravian Diaries," 11:374. On the land activities of William Beverley and Benjamin Borden, see McIlwaine et al., *Executive Journals of the Council*, 4:336, 346, 351, 375–76, 408–9; and Mitchell, *Commercialism and Frontier*, 31–36.

42. Samuel McDowell to Arthur Campbell, July 27, 1808, 4ZZ3, Draper Manuscripts, State Historical Society of Wisconsin, Madison; Arthur Campbell to Allen Magruder, June 3, 1809, 4ZZ2, Draper Manuscripts; and Turk McCleskey, "Across the First Divide: Frontiers of Settlement and Culture in Augusta County, Virginia, 1738–1770" (Ph.D. diss., College of William and Mary, 1990), 249–50.

43. Weiser, Report, in Hazard, *Provincial Council of Pennsylvania*, 4:644; and Kercheval, *History of the Valley*, 53, 57.

44. McIlwaine et al., *Executive Journals of the Council*, 5:95; and William Gooch to Board of Trade, July 31, 1742, CO 5/1325, PRO.

45. Council held at Philadelphia, minutes, July 7, 1742, and Oct. 13, 14, in Hazard, *Provincial Council of Pennsylvania*, 4:570, 90–95. On Iroquois claims to the Shenandoah Valley by right of conquest over the Susquehannocks, see Gardner, *Lost Arrowheads and Broken Pottery*, 89–90. Logan never admitted to writing to Maryland on behalf of the Six Nations, but the governor of that colony produced Logan's letter in 1742; see James Logan to Samuel Ogle, Dec. 20, 1736, in William Hand Browne, ed., *Proceedings of the Council of Maryland, 1732–1753*, vol. 28, *Archives of Maryland* (Baltimore: Maryland Historical Society, 1908), 271–72.

46. Browne, *Proceedings of the Council of Maryland, 1732–1753*, 257–60. On Indian plans to trade land for arms and ammunition in Philadelphia, see Jacob Pattasahook deposition, June 30, 1742, in ibid., 262.

47. Council held at Philadelphia, minutes, July 6, 7, 1742, in Hazard, *Provincial Council of Pennsylvania*, 4:566–72.

48. Ibid., July 7, 1742, in ibid., 569–72.

49. Hazard, *Provincial Council of Pennsylvania*, 4:586–87. Convening the Maryland Council on July 23, Samuel Ogle presented James Logan's 1736 letter along with Canasetego's speech, which was enclosed in George Thomas's letter of July 10. The Council ordered Ogle to consult with William Gooch as soon as possible to coordinate a re-

sponse that included both defensive measures and diplomatic initiatives. See Browne, *Proceedings of the Council of Maryland, 1732–1753*, 271–74. For the Virginia reaction, see McIlwaine et al., *Executive Journals of the Council*, 5:94–95; and Gooch to Board of Trade, July 31, 1742, CO 5/1325, PRO.

50. McKee, deposition, and Weiser, Report, in Hazard, *Provincial Council of Pennsylvania*, 4:632, 644.

51. Weiser, Report, in ibid., 645; McDowell to Campbell, July 27, 1808, Draper Manuscripts; and James Patton to William Gooch, Dec. 23, 1742, enclosure in Gooch to Board of Trade, Feb. 14, 1743, CO 5/1325, PRO.

52. James Patton to William Gooch, Dec. 18, 23, 1742, enclosures in Gooch to Board of Trade, Feb. 14, 1743, CO 5/1325, PRO.

53. McIlwaine et al., *Executive Journals of the Council*, 5:113; and William Gooch to George Clarke, Jan. 3, 1743, in O'Callaghan and Fernow, *Documents Relative to the Colonial History of New-York*, 6:230.

54. Gooch to Board of Trade, Feb. 14, 1743, CO 5/1325, PRO; and McKee, deposition, in Hazard, *Provincial Council of Pennsylvania*, 4:631, 32.

55. George Thomas to Conrad Weiser, Jan. 26, 1743, in ibid., Hazard, *Provincial Council of Pennsylvania*, 4:635–37. For the Indian version, see McKee, deposition, and Weiser, Report, in ibid., 632, 644.

56. Weiser, Report, in ibid., 645.

57. Thomas to Weiser, Jan. 26, 1743, in ibid., 635–37; and Pennsylvania Assembly to George Thomas in ibid., 637. McDowell to Campbell, July 27, 1808, Draper Manuscripts.

58. Commissioners of Indian Affairs, minutes, Mar. 20, 1743, in O'Callaghan and Fernow, *Documents Relative to the Colonial History of New-York*, 6:234; George Clarke to Commissioners of Indian Affairs, Apr. 27, 1743, in ibid., 6:236; Commissioners of Indian Affairs to Clarke, May 30, 1743, in ibid., 6:240; and Clarke to William Gooch, June 16, 1743, in ibid., 6:241–42. On Gooch's letter to Clarke, see McIlwaine et al., *Executive Journals of the Council*, 5:112–13; and Clarke to Gooch, May 2, 1743, in O'Callaghan and Fernow, *Documents Relative to the Colonial History of New-York*, 6:237. See also *Pennsylvania Gazette*, Jan. 27, 1743.

CHAPTER 2. Peopling an Empire

1. Several recent works have made the point that the way of life Europeans led on the eighteenth-century frontier in North America drew heavily upon the culture of Native Americans. See Stephen Aron, *How the West Was Lost: The Transformation of Kentucky from Daniel Boone to Henry Clay* (Baltimore: Johns Hopkins UP, 1996); and John Mack Faragher, *Daniel Boone* (New York: Henry Holt, 1992).

2. Frederick Jackson Turner introduced the concept of free land into the historiography of the American frontier. He was also the foremost spokesman for the idea of the frontier as the advance of Anglo-American civilization. See Frederick Jackson Turner, "The Significance of the Frontier in American History," in *The Frontier in American History* (New York: Holt, Rinehart & Winston, 1920), 1–38.

3. Robert Dinwiddie to the Board of Trade, Jan. 1755, in Robert A. Brock, ed. *The Official Records of Robert Dinwiddie . . .*, 2 vols. (Richmond: Virginia Historical Society, 1883), 1:389, as quoted in Chester Raymond Young, "The Effects of the French and Indian War on Civilian Life in the Frontier Counties of Virginia, 1754–1763" (Ph.D. diss., Vanderbilt University, 1969), 12. The term *open-country neighborhood* was first applied to dispersed small-farm communities by Conrad Arensburg. See Arensburg, "American Communities," *American Anthropologist* 57 (Dec. 1955): 1143–62.

4. On the economic diversity and cultural pluralism of the Virginia backcountry, see Richard R. Beeman, *The Evolution of the Southern Backcountry: A Case Study of Lunenburg County, Virginia, 1746–1832* (Philadelphia: U of Pennsylvania P, 1984); Freeman H. Hart, *The Valley of Virginia in the American Revolution, 1763–1789* (Chapel Hill: U of North Carolina P, 1942); Warren R. Hofstra, ed., *George Washington and the Virginia Backcountry* (Madison, Wis.: Madison House, 1998); James G. Leyburn, *The Scotch-Irish: A Social History* (Chapel Hill: U of North Carolina P, 1962); Turk McCleskey, "Across the First Divide: Frontiers of Settlement and Culture in Augusta County, Virginia, 1738–1770" (Ph.D. diss., College of William and Mary, 1990); Robert D. Mitchell, *Commercialism and Frontier: Perspectives on the Shenandoah Valley* (Charlottesville: UP of Virginia, 1977); Mitchell, ed., *Appalachian Frontiers: Settlement, Society, and Development in the Preindustrial Era* (Lexington: UP of Kentucky, 1990); Michael J. Puglisi, ed., *Diversity and Accommodation: Essays on the Cultural Composition of the Virginia Frontier* (Knoxville: U of Tennessee P, 1997); Albert H. Tillson Jr., *Gentry and Common Folk: Political Culture on a Virginia Frontier, 1740–1789* (Lexington: U of Kentucky P, 1991); and Klaus Wust, *The Virginia Germans* (Charlottesville: UP of Virginia, 1969), 17–199.

5. Turner, "Significance of the Frontier," 3–4; Hart, *The Valley of Virginia*, 5–7; and Mitchell, *Commercialism and Frontier*, 16–19. For more on the argument that the settlement of the southern backcountry was driven by demands for land by settlers, see Oscar Theodore Barck Jr. and Hugh Talmage Lefler, *Colonial America*, 2d ed. (New York: Macmillan, 1968), 255–56; Carl Bridenbaugh, *Myths and Realities: Societies of the Colonial South* (Baton Rouge: Louisiana State UP, 1952; Westport, Conn.: Greenwood Press, 1981), 122; Johanna Miller Lewis, *Artisans in the North Carolina Backcountry* (Lexington: UP of Kentucky, 1995), 19, 22, 33, 49–50; Leyburn, *Scotch-Irish*, 184–223; and Wust, *Virginia Germans*, 28–30.

6. Thomas Perkins Abernethy, "The First Transmontane Advance," in *Humanistic Studies in Honor of John Calvin Metcalf*, University of Virginia Studies, vol. 1, ed. James S. Wilson (New York: Columbia UP, 1941), 137–8; and Richard L. Morton, *Colonial Virginia*, 2 vols. (Chapel Hill: U of North Carolina P for the Virginia Historical Society, 1960), 2:540. See also Abernethy, *Three Virginia Frontiers* (Baton Rouge: Louisiana State UP, 1940), 29–62; and W. Stitt Robinson, *The Southern Colonial Frontier, 1607–1763* (Albuquerque: U of New Mexico P, 1979), 139–50.

7. William Gooch to Board of Trade, Apr. 2, 1729, CO 5/1321, Colonial Office Papers, Public Record Office (hereafter PRO), London; and H. R. McIlwaine, Wilmer L. Hall, and Benjamin J. Hillman, eds., *Executive Journals of the Council of Colonial Virginia*, 6 vols. (Richmond: Virginia State Library, 1925–66), 5:50. On one occasion in

1738 the Council expressed its fear that "divers persons of small Substance in Combination with the Surveyors have made Seperate Entries for large quantities of Land lying Contiguous to one Another without such Licence." McIlwaine et al., *Executive Journals of the Council*, 4:430–31. On the control of land granting by the Virginia elite, see Sarah S. Hughes, *Surveyors and Statesmen: Land Measuring in Colonial Virginia* (Richmond: Virginia Surveyors Foundation and Virginia Association of Surveyors, 1979), 84–85, 107; Turk McCleskey, "Rich Land, Poor Prospects: Real Estate and the Formation of a Social Elite in Augusta County, Virginia, 1738–1770," *Virginia Magazine of History and Biography* 98 (July 1990): 449–86; Charles S. Sydnor, *Gentlemen Freeholders: Political Practices in Washington's Virginia* (Chapel Hill: U of North Carolina P for the Institute of Early American History and Culture, 1952); and Manning C. Voorhis, "Crown versus Council in the Virginia Land Policy," *William and Mary Quarterly*, 3d ser., 3 (Oct. 1946): 499–514.

8. Spotsylvania County was established in 1720, with its western boundary along the Shenandoah River. Not until Orange County was created in 1734 did the Shenandoah Valley come under county organization. Northern Neck counties Stafford and Prince William were at this time unbounded to the west, but neither possessed any jurisdiction beyond the Blue Ridge. See Fairfax Harrison, *Landmarks of Old Prince William: A Study of Origins in Northern Virginia* (Richmond: Old Dominion Press, 1924), 1:311–14, and William W. Hening, ed., *The Statutes at Large: Being a Collection of All the Laws of Virginia, from . . . 1619 . . .* , 13 vols. (Richmond, New York, and Philadelphia, 1819–23), 4:77–79, 303, 450–51.

9. George Thomas to Gooch, Apr. 25, 1743, in Samuel Hazard, ed., *Minutes of the Provincial Council of Pennsylvania*, 16 vols. (Harrisburg: Theo. Fenn, 1838–53), 4:653; George Clarke to Gooch, May 2, 1743, in Edmund Bailey O'Callaghan and Berthold Fernow, eds., *Documents Relative to the Colonial History of the State of New-York*, 15 vols. (Albany: Weed, Parsons, 1853–87), 6:237; and Board of Trade to Gooch, Aug. 2, 1744, Entry Book for Virginia, 1728–1756, CO 5/1365, PRO. For a discussion of the "connection between settlement and issues of colonial defense and economy" in the Virginia Piedmont, see David A. Rawson, "The Anglo-American Settlement of Virginia's Rappahannock Frontier," *Locus* 6 (spring 1994): 93–117.

10. McIlwaine et al., *Executive Journals of the Council*, 3:428, 399; Alexander Spotswood to Board of Trade, May 9, 1716, in Robert A. Brock, ed., *The Official Letters of Alexander Spotswood, Lieutenant-Governor of the Colony of Virginia, 1710–1722*, 2 vols. (Richmond: Virginia Historical Society, 1882–85), 2:150, and Memorial of the Virginia Indian Company, Apr. 23, 1716, CO 5/1317, PRO.

11. Spotswood to Board of Trade, May 9, 1716, in Brock, *Letters of Spotswood*, 2:149; and McIlwaine et al., *Executive Journals of the Council*, 3:428.

12. Warren M. Billings, John E. Selby, and Thad W. Tate, *Colonial Virginia: A History* (White Plains, N.Y.: KTO Press, 1986), 173; U.S. Bureau of the Census, *Historical Statistics of the United States: Colonial Times to 1970* (Washington, D.C.: GPO, 1975), pt. 2:1168, 1172; James R. Bugg Jr., "The French Huguenot Frontier Settlement of Manakin Town," *Virginia Magazine of History and Biography* 61 (Oct. 1953): 359–94; McIlwaine et al., *Executive Journals of the Council*, 2:172–77; and Hening, *Statutes*, 3:204–9.

See also John M. Hemphill II, *Virginia and the English Commercial System, 1689–1733: Studies in the Development and Fluctuations of a Colonial Economy under Imperial Control* (New York: Garland, 1985), 14–25, and Robinson, *Southern Colonial Frontier*, 121–27.

13. On the contest among England, France, Spain, and Native Americans for the Southeast, see Charles M. Andrews, *The Colonial Period of American History*, vol. 3, *The Settlements* (New Haven: Yale UP, 1937), 235–36; Verner W. Crane, *The Southern Frontier, 1670–1732* (Durham, N.C.: Duke UP, 1928; New York: W. W. Norton, 1981), 47–70; W. J. Eccles, *France in America* (East Lansing: Michigan State UP, 1990), 107–9; Daniel H. Usner Jr., *Indians, Settlers, and Slaves in a Frontier Exchange Economy* (Chapel Hill: U of North Carolina P for the Institute of Early American History and Culture, 1992); and David J. Weber, *The Spanish Frontier in North America* (New Haven: Yale UP, 1992), 147–58.

14. Richard Aquila, *The Iroquois Restoration: Iroquois Diplomacy on the Colonial Frontier, 1701–1754* (Detroit: Wayne State UP, 1983), 205–45; Billings, Selby, and Tate, *Colonial Virginia*, 175–76; Francis Jennings, *The Ambiguous Iroquois Empire: The Covenant Chain Confederation of Indian Tribes with English Colonies from Its Beginnings to the Lancaster Treaty of 1744* (New York: W. W. Norton, 1984), 210–12; Michael N. McConnell, *A Country Between: The Upper Ohio Valley and Its Peoples, 1724–1774* (Lincoln: U of Nebraska P, 1992), 15–17; James H. Merrell, *The Indians' New World: Catawbas and Their Neighbors from European Contact through the Era of Removal* (Chapel Hill: U of North Carolina P for the Institute of Early American History and Culture, 1989), 25, 41–42, 78, 89, 97–98, 113–22, 135–36, 149–67, 244–45; Daniel K. Richter, *The Ordeal of the Longhouse: The Peoples of the Iroquois League in the Era of European Colonization* (Chapel Hill: U of North Carolina P for the Institute of Early American History and Culture, 1992), 32–38, 236–80; and Ian K. Steele, *Warpaths: Invasions of North America* (New York: Oxford UP, 1994), 148–50, 166–67.

15. Spotswood to Board of Trade, Nov. 16, 1713, in Brock, *Letters of Spotswood*, 2:42, as quoted in Richter, *Ordeal of the Longhouse*, 239. See also Aquila, *Iroquois Restoration*, 209–10; Jennings, *Ambiguous Iroquois Empire*, 262; McIlwaine et al., *Executive Journals of the Council*, 3:291; Gregory H. Nobles, *American Frontiers: Cultural Encounters and Continental Conquest* (New York: Hill & Wang, 1997), 73; Robinson, *Southern Colonial Frontier*, 107–10; Richter, *Ordeal of the Longhouse*, 238–39; and Steele, *Warpaths*, 159–60.

16. H. R. McIlwaine, ed., *Journals of the House of Burgesses of Virginia, 1712–1714, 1715, 1718, 1720–1722, 1723–1726* (Richmond: Virginia State Library, 1912), 80, 116. See also Billings, Selby, and Tate, *Colonial Virginia*, 180–81, 185; Leonidas Dodson, *Alexander Spotswood: Governor of Colonial Virginia, 1710–1722* (Philadelphia: U of Pennsylvania P, 1932), 82–99; and Merrell, *Indians' New World*, 49–91.

17. McIlwaine, *Journals of the House of Burgesses [1712–1726]*, 47, 79–80; McIlwaine et al., *Executive Journals of the Council*, 3:363–64, 366, 368. See also Billings, Selby, and Tate, *Colonial Virginia*, 175, 179–80; and Dodson, *Alexander Spotswood*, 76–78.

18. McIlwaine, *Journals of the House of Burgesses [1712–1726]*, 79, 47. See also Spotswood to Board of Trade, Nov. 16, 1713, in Brock, *Letters of Spotswood*, 2:41–43; Billings, Selby, and Tate, *Colonial Virginia*, 179–80; Dodson, *Alexander Spotswood*, 228–32; Wust, *Virginia Germans*, 20–25; and A. G. Roeber, *Palatines, Liberty, and Property: Ger-*

man Lutherans in Colonial British America (Baltimore: Johns Hopkins UP, 1993), 101–9. The concept of employing settlement for strategic purposes was not entirely new to Spotswood. Throughout his administration he consistently focused land-granting activities on the Virginia frontier. Moreover, in one of the first acts of his administration he proposed a means of extending settlement westward along the James River. "Whereas the ffrench are endeavouring to settle a communication between Canada and their late Settlements on Mississippi," Spotswood argued to the Board of Trade, "our people would, by pushing on their settlem'ts in one straight Line along the banks of James River, be able to cutt off that communication and fix themselves so strongly there that it would not be in the power of the French to dislodge them." Spotswood never pursued the project further, nor did he envision employing foreign Protestants for purposes of defense. See Spotswood to Board of Trade, Dec. 15, 1710, in Brock, *Letters of Spotswood*, 1:40; Dodson, *Alexander Spotswood*, 237–38; and Rawson, "Anglo-American Settlement of Virginia."

19. McIlwaine et al., *Executive Journals of the Council*, 3:400–401, 396; and McIlwaine, *Journals of the House of Burgesses [1712–1726]*, 189.

20. John Fontaine, *The Journal of John Fontaine: An Irish Huguenot Son in Spain and Virginia, 1710–1719*, ed. Edward P. Alexander (Williamsburg: Colonial Williamsburg Foundation, 1972), 105–6.

21. Billings, Selby, and Tate, *Colonial Virginia*, 184; Brock, *Letters of Spotswood*, 1:36–43; 2:149–50, 295; Crane, *Southern Frontier*, 177, 221; and Dodson, *Alexander Spotswood*, 239–40.

22. Spotswood to Board of Trade, Aug. 14, 1718, in Brock, *Letters of Spotswood*, 2:295. Lieutenant governor of Maryland John Hart warned the board that Indians indicated to him that the lakes lay "eight s[uns], that is 240 miles" away, admittedly a "better confirm[ation] from what Colonel Spotswood" had provided. Hart's estimate was more accurate: On a straight line Lake Erie lies slightly less than three hundred miles northwest of the earliest-discovered passes over the Blue Ridge. See Hart to Board of Trade, Aug. 8, 1720, CO 5/717, PRO, and Dodson, *Alexander Spotswood*, 241 n. 65.

23. Richard Berresford to Board of Trade, Dec. 4, 1717, CO 323/7, PRO, and Crane, *Southern Frontier*, 208–9.

24. Spotswood to Board of Trade, Aug. 14, 1718, in Brock, *Letters of Spotswood*, 2:296–97.

25. McIlwaine et al., *Executive Journals of the Council*, 3:442; Spotswood to Paul Methuen, May 30, 1717, in Brock, *Letters of Spotswood*, 251; and Dodson, *Alexander Spotswood*, 88, 99–100.

26. McIlwaine et al., *Executive Journals of the Council*, 3:450–51, 446.

27. Ibid., 452, 457; Spotswood to Joseph Addison, Aug. 27, 1717, Spotswood to Board of Trade, Aug. 29, 1717, Feb. 27, 1718, in Brock, 2:25–65; and Dodson, *Alexander Spotswood*, 101.

28. McIlwaine, *Journals of the House of Burgesses [1712–1726]*, 250.

29. Ibid., 254; H. R. McIlwaine, ed., *Legislative Journals of the Council of Virginia*, 3 vols. (Richmond: Virginia State Library, 1918–19, 1979), 2:641; and Hening, *Statutes*, 4:77–79.

30. Hening, *Statutes*, 4:77–79.

31. Board of Trade to Spotswood, June 13, 1720, Entry Book for Virginia, 1717–27, CO 5/1365, PRO; McIlwaine, *Journals of the House of Burgesses [1712–1726]*, 262, 301; and McIlwaine et al., *Executive Journals of the Council*, 3:533–34.

32. McIlwaine et al., *Executive Journals of the Council*, 3:552–54; Propositions made to the Five Nations of the Indians, Aug. 29–Sept. 12, 1722, in *History of the Dividing Line and Other Tracts from the Papers of William Byrd of Westover, in Virginia, Esquire*, 2 vols. (Richmond: Virginia Historical Society, 1866), 2:253; O'Callaghan and Fernow, *Documents Relative to the Colonial History of New-York*, 5:635–39; McIlwaine, *Journals of the House of Burgesses [1712–1726]*, 319–20, 323; and McIlwaine, *Legislative Journals of the Council*, 2:660, 666, 668, 670, 674, 676.

33. Spotswood to Board of Trade, June 11, 1722, CO 5/1319, PRO.

34. McIlwaine et al., *Executive Journals of the Council*, 3:549–50.

35. Billings, Selby, and Tate, *Colonial Virginia*, 204–5; Bureau of the Census, *Historical Statistics*, 1172; John J. McCusker and Russell R. Menard, *The Economy of British America, 1607–1789* (Chapel Hill: U of North Carolina P for the Institute of Early American History and Culture, 1985), 135–37; and Edmund S. Morgan, *American Slavery, American Freedom: The Ordeal of Colonial Virginia* (New York: W. W. Norton, 1975), 295–315.

36. McIlwaine et al., *Executive Journals of the Council*, 3:234–35, 242–43, 246, 573–74.

37. Ibid., 4:20, 31; Propositions made to the Five Nations, in *History of the Dividing Line and Other Tracts*, 264; and William Hand Browne, ed., *Proceedings of the Council of Maryland, 1698–1731*, vol. 25, *Archives of Maryland* (Baltimore: Maryland Historical Society, 1905), 394–95, 450–51.

38. Board of Trade to the king, Sept. 8, 1721, CO 324/10, PRO.

39. James Stanhope to Board of Trade, July 7, 1715, CO 5/1264, PRO, and Board of Trade to Stanhope, July 19, 1715, CO 5/383, PRO, as quoted in Crane, *Southern Frontier*, 207.

40. William Keith to Alured Popple, Feb. 16, 1719, CO 5/1265, PRO; James Logan, "Account of the French Trade," enclosure in Patrick Gordon to Board of Trade, Mar. 15, 1731, CO 5/1268, PRO; and Crane, *Southern Frontier*, 223–24.

41. John Barnwell, "A True State of the Case between the Inhabitants of South Carolina, and the Lords Proprietors," CO 5/1265, PRO, as quoted in Crane, *Southern Frontier*, 218.

42. Crane, *Southern Frontier*, 224–26; Eccles, *France in America*, 173–74; and Pierluigi Portinaro and Franco Knirsch, *The Cartography of North America, 1500–1800* (New York: Crescent Books, 1987), 223.

43. Spotswood to Board of Trade, Feb. 1, 1720, in Brock, *Letters of Spotswood*, 2:329–30; Robert Johnson to Board of Trade, Jan. 12, 1720, CO 5/1265, PRO; and Crane, *Southern Frontier*, 227.

44. Crane, *Southern Frontier*, 229–31.

45. South Carolina's first major slave rebellion in 1720 was described to the Board of Trade as a "designe to destroy all the white people in the country and then to take the

towne [Charles Town] in a full body." Letter to [Joseph] Boone, June 24, 1720, CO 5/358, PRO. See also Crane, *Southern Frontier*, 215; Peter H. Wood, *Black Majority: Negroes in Colonial South Carolina from 1670 through the Stono Rebellion* (New York: Alfred A. Knopf, 1974; New York: W. W. Norton, 1975), 298–99, 303–26; and Gary B. Nash, *Red, White, and Black: The Peoples of Early North America*, 3d ed. (Englewood Cliffs, N.J.: Prentice Hall, 1992), 169–70, 185, 293–95.

46. *Journal of the Commissioners for Trade and Plantations from November 1718 to December 1722* (London: HMSO, 1925), 315, 316–20; Board of Trade to the king, Sept. 8, 1721; Crane, *Southern Frontier*, 232–34; and Ian K. Steele, *Politics of Colonial Policy: The Board of Trade in Colonial Administration, 1696–1720* (Oxford: Clarendon Press, 1968), 167–70.

47. Board of Trade to the king, Sept. 8, 1721.

48. Philip S. Robinson, *The Plantation of Ulster: British Settlement in an Irish Landscape, 1600–1670* (Dublin: Gill & MacMillan; New York: St. Martin's Press, 1984; Belfast: Ulster Historical Foundation, 1994), and Roeber, *Palatines, Liberty, and Property*, 40, 95–113.

49. Stephen Saunders Webb claims that colonial governors during the early eighteenth century encouraged "farm families to settle closely in self-sustaining settlements. Such settlements could support a numerous militia, capable of self-defense and subject to garrison-government discipline." Thus these governors, many of whom were schooled in garrison government under the duke of Marlborough during European wars, actively pursued a settlement strategy of frontier defense based on classical military precepts. They then helped write this concept into the report of 1721. See Webb, *The Governors-General: The English Army and the Definition of the Empire, 1569–1681* (Chapel Hill: U of North Carolina P for the Institute of Early American History and Culture, 1979), 452. On the matter of farm size, Robert Mitchell demonstrates that approximately 95 percent of landholdings acquired from the crown in Augusta County between 1736 and 1779 contained four hundred or fewer acres. See Mitchell, *Commercialism and Frontier*, 66. With an estimated population of more than sixty-eight hundred in 1760, Augusta County had only 60 blacks. In Frederick County at the same time there were 611 blacks, but they still constituted only 6 percent of the population. See Young, "The Effects of the French and Indian War," 432, 436. On the settlement initiatives adopted by South Carolina in 1716, see Crane, *Southern Frontier*, 214–15.

50. Board of Trade to the Lords Justices, Aug. 30, 1720, as quoted in Wood, *Black Majority*, 220, and McIlwaine et al., *Executive Journals of the Council*, 3:549–50.

51. Board of Trade to Privy Council, May 26, 1732, CO 5/401, PRO; Instructions to Robert Johnson enclosure in Board of Trade to duke of Newcastle, June 10, 1730, CO 5/400, PRO; and Board of Trade to Lord Harrington, Dec. 5, 1734, CO 4/383, PRO. On the colonizing projects of Daniel Hintze, see Hintze to Alured Popple, May 1, 1729, CO 5/870, PRO; and Board of Trade to Privy Council, May 14, 1729, CO 5/916, PRO. And on similar efforts by Jean Pierre Purry, see CO 5/359, 361–65, 383, 387–88, 393, 400–401, PRO. See also Crane, *Southern Frontier*, 283–87; and Roeber, *Palatines, Liberty, and Property*, 210–11.

52. Hugh Drysdale to Board of Trade, June 6, 1724, CO 5/1319, PRO; and Gooch to Board of Trade, Apr. 2, 1729, CO 5/1321, PRO. On land grants in Spotsylvania County, see Ulysses P. Joyner Jr., *The First Settlers of Orange County, Virginia* (Baltimore: Gateway Press, 1987), 265–71; and on the Privy Council restriction on these grants, see W. L. Grant, James Munro, and Almeric W. Fitzroy, eds., *Acts of the Privy Council of England, Colonial Series,* 6 vols. (London: HMSO, 1910–12; Nendeln, Liechtenstein: Kraus Reprint, 1966), 3:23; and Manning C. Voorhis, "The Land Grant Policy of Colonial Virginia, 1607–1774" (Ph.D. diss., U of Virginia, 1940), 145–51.

53. McIlwaine et al., *Executive Journals of the Council,* 4:126; Robert Carter to Board of Trade, Aug. 1727, CO 5/1320, PRO; and Gooch to Board of Trade, Mar. 26, 1729, CO 5/1321, PRO.

54. For histories of the Northern Neck Proprietary and its struggle with the colony over land rights, see Stuart Brown, *Virginia Baron: The Story of Thomas Sixth Lord Fairfax* (Berryville, Va.: Chesapeake Book Co., 1965), 26–100; Douglas Southall Freeman, *George Washington: A Biography,* 7 vols. (New York: Charles Scribner's Sons, 1948–57), 1:447–525; and Morgan, *American Slavery, American Freedom,* 244–45.

55. McIlwaine et al., *Executive Journals of the Council,* 4:205; and Gooch to Board of Trade, June 29, 1729, CO 5/1322, PRO. For grants on the Blue Ridge, see McIlwaine et al., *Executive Journals of the Council,* 4:180–81.

56. Gooch to Board of Trade, June 29, 1729, CO 5/1322, PRO.

57. For information on Stover, Harlan, and their proposals, see Jacob Stover's application for land, Apr. 6, 1713, in William Henry Egle, ed., *Minutes of the Board of Property of the Province of Pennsylvania,* Pennsylvania Archives, 2d ser., vol. 19 (Harrisburg: E. K. Meyers, 1893), 552; Survey for Jacob Stauber, Mar. 26, 1714, Survey D78–85, Bureau of Land Records, Pennsylvania State Archives, Harrisburg; Charles E. Kemper, ed., "Documents Relating to a Proposed Swiss and German Colony in the Western Part of Virginia, 1706–1709," *Virginia Magazine of History and Biography* 29 (Apr. 1921): 183–90, (July 1921): 287–91; Ann V. Strickler Milbourne, ed., "Colony West of the Blue Ridge, Proposed by Jacob Stauber and Others, 1731, etc.," *Virginia Magazine of History and Biography* 35 (Apr. 1927): 175–90, (July 1927): 258–66, and 36 (Jan. 1928): 54–70; Mitchell, *Commercialism and Frontier,* 26–28; and Wust, *Virginia Germans,* 30–32.

58. Petition of Stauber and Others to Board of Trade, Mar. 30, 1731, in Kemper, "Documents Relating to a Proposed Swiss and German Colony," 29:287–90.

59. McIlwaine et al., *Executive Journals of the Council,* 4:224. The progress of Stover's proposal can be traced through the deliberations of the Board of Trade in the *Journal of the Commissioners for Trade and Plantations from January 1728–9 to December 1734* (London: HMSO, 1928), 180, 188, 189, 191, 197, 232, 234, 241, 246, 256, 265, 272, 306, 318–19, 419. Additional partners included John Ocks, Thomas Gould, and William Keith himself.

60. McIlwaine et al., *Executive Journals of the Council,* 3:581; Billings, Selby, and Tate, *Colonial Virginia,* 177; Leonard Woods Labaree, *Royal Instructions to British Colonial Governors, 1670–1776,* 2 vols. (New York: D. Appleton-Century, 1935), 2:589–90; and Voorhis, "Land Grant Policy of Colonial Virginia," 106–28.

61. Keith to Board of Trade, Apr. 6, 1730, in Kemper, ed., "Documents Relating to a Proposed Swiss and German Colony," 29:188–90. See also Keith to Board of Trade, Aug. 30, 1731, in Milbourne, "Colony West of the Blue Ridge," 35:185–87.

62. McIlwaine et al., *Executive Journals of the Council*, 4:223–24, 229, 253.

63. Gooch to Board of Trade, May 24, 1734, CO 5/1323, PRO. For grants in the Shenandoah Valley, see McIlwaine et al., *Executive Journals of the Council*, 4:223–24, 229, 249–50, 253, 270, 295.

CHAPTER 3. Settling the Shenandoah

1. Writing at the beginning of the nineteenth century, Samuel Kercheval listed the Bowmans, Chrissmans, Fromans, McKays, Greens, Duffs, and Stephens among the sixteen families accompanying Hite. By the end of the century this group was exalted in the writing of local historian Thomas Cartmell, who opened his book with the statement that "the first families to settle in the Lower Shenandoah Valley, were generally known as the *sixteen families* who came with Joist Hite." See Samuel Kercheval, *A History of the Valley of Virginia*, 5th ed. (Strasburg, Va.: Shenandoah Publishing House, 1973), 49; and Thomas K. Cartmell, *Shenandoah Valley Pioneers and Their Descendants: A History of Frederick County, Virginia* (Winchester, Va.: Eddy Press, 1909; Bowie, Md.: Heritage Books, 1989), 1.

2. *John Hite et al. v Lord Fairfax et al.*, Additional Manuscript 15317, British Museum, London, transcript by Hunter Branson McKay, pp. 1568, 1519, Archives Room, Handley Regional Library, Winchester; and Richard K. MacMaster, *The History of Hardy County, 1786–1986* (Salem, W. Va.: Hardy County Public Library, 1986), 1–5. The uncertain nature of Indian relations on the Pennsylvania frontier might have encouraged Hite's interest in removing to Virginia. See Petition of the Inhabitants of Colebrookdale, 1728, in Samuel Hazard, ed., *Pennsylvania Archives*, 1st ser. (Philadelphia: Joseph Severns, 1852), 1:213–14.

3. McIlwaine, Wilmer L. Hall, and Benjamin J. Hillman, eds., *Executive Journals of the Council of Colonial Virginia*, 6 vols. (Richmond: Virginia State Library, 1925–66), 4:253; and Transcript of the Record in the case, *Jost Hite and Robert McCoy v Lord Fairfax 1749–*, fol. 713, folder 100, Clark-Hite Papers (hereafter C-HP), Filson Historical Society, Louisville, Ky.

4. *Hite v Fairfax*, transcript by McKay, 1521; Benjamin Burden, Andrew Hampton, and David Griffith survey, Apr. 23, 1734, Robert Brooke Survey Book, 1732–34, p. 26. Thornton Tayloe Perry Collection, Virginia Historical Society, Richmond; Paul A. W. Wallace, *Indian Paths of Pennsylvania* (Harrisburg: Pennsylvania Historical and Museum Commission, 1993), 105, 177; and Cecil O'Dell, *Pioneers of Old Frederick County, Virginia* (Marceline, Mo.: Walsworth, 1995), 488–91. Although the location of Hite's crossing over the Potomac cannot be known with precision, several histories locate it between present-day Harpers Ferry and Shepherdstown, and Robert Brooke's 1734 survey for Isaac Garrison records a "Waggon Road Ford" in this area. See Cartmell, *Shenandoah Valley Pioneers*, 1; Kercheval, *History of the Valley*, 49; Isaac Garrison survey, Apr. 4, 1734, Robert Brooke Survey Book, 16.

5. *Hite v Fairfax*, transcript by McKay, 1521; Charles Butts and Raymond S. Edmundson, *Geology and Mineral Resources of Frederick County*, Virginia Division of Mineral Resources Bulletin 80 (Charlottesville: Virginia Division of Mineral Resources, 1966); and O'Dell, *Pioneers of Old Frederick County*, 488–91.

6. Virginia Land Patents, 15:336, 338, Patents, 1623–1774, Library of Virginia, Richmond; Orange County Deeds (hereafter OCD), 1:436, 3:186, Orange County Courthouse, Orange, Va.; and O'Dell, *Pioneers of Old Frederick County*, 309, 316, 322–23, 349–51, 411–13.

7. For the deeds Hite issued along the Opequon, see OCD, 1:431, 442, 2:304, 4:9, 6:165, 170, 174, 249, 258, 8:22, 38, 46; and Frederick County Deeds, 1:68, 2:90, Frederick County Courthouse, Winchester.

8. McIlwaine et al., *Executive Journals of the Council*, 4:229; and Virginia Land Patents, 16:320. For Ross's land sales, see OCD, 2:465, 5:149; Frederick County Deeds, 1:75; and *Hopewell Friends History, 1734–1934* (Strasburg, Va.: Shenandoah Publishing House, 1936), 15–16.

9. Charles E. Kemper, "Documents Relating to Early Projected Swiss Colonies in the Valley of Virginia, 1706–1709," *Virginia Magazine of History and Biography* 29 (Jan. 1921): 3; Robert S. Grumet, *Historic Contact: Indian People and Colonists in Today's Northeastern United States in the Sixteenth through Eighteenth Centuries* (Norman: U of Oklahoma P, 1995), 283–87; Michael N. McConnell, *A Country Between: The Upper Ohio Valley and Its Peoples, 1724–1774* (Lincoln: U of Nebraska P, 1992), 5–20; and Daniel K. Richter, *The Ordeal of the Longhouse: The Peoples of the Iroquois League in the Era of European Colonization* (Chapel Hill: U of North Carolina P for the Institute of Early American History and Culture, 1992), 50–66, 256.

10. McConnell, *A Country Between*, 45.

11. Examination of Jonah Davenport, Oct. 29, 1731, in Hazard, *Pennsylvania Archives*, 1st ser., 1:299–300; Examination of James Letort, 1731, in ibid., 300–301; Number of Indians, 1731, in ibid., 301–2; Message of Shawnee Chiefs to Gov. Gordon, June 7, 1732, in ibid., 329–30; and McConnell, *A Country Between*, 20–22.

12. Board of Trade to the king, Sept. 8, 1721, CO 324/10, Colonial Office Papers, Public Record Office (hereafter PRO), London; and George Clarke to William Gooch, June 16, 1743, in Edmund Bailey O'Callaghan and Berthold Fernow, eds., *Documents Relative to the Colonial History of the State of New-York*, 15 vols. (Albany: Weed, Parsons, 1853–87), 6:242.

13. Shawnee Chiefs to Patrick Gordon, 1732, in Hazard, *Pennsylvania Archives*, 1st ser., 1:329, as quoted in Francis Jennings, *The Ambiguous Iroquois Empire: The Covenant Chain Confederation of Indian Tribes with English Colonies from Its Beginnings to the Lancaster Treaty of 1744* (New York: W. W. Norton, 1984), 301–2; Samuel Hazard, ed., *Minutes of the Provincial Council of Pennsylvania*, 16 vols. (Harrisburg: Theo. Fenn, 1838–53), 3:274, as quoted in Richter, *Ordeal of the Longhouse*, 273; and McConnell, *A Country Between*, 16–20.

14. John Bartram, *Observations on the Inhabitants, Climate, Soil, Rivers, Productions, Animals, and other matters worthy of Notice Made By Mr. John Bartram, in his Travels from Pensilvania to Onondago, Oswego and the Lake Ontario, In Canada* (London: Whis-

ton & White, 1751), 42; McConnell, *A Country Between*, 25; William M. Beauchamp, ed., *Moravian Journals Relating to Central New York, 1745–66* (Syracuse, N.Y.: Onondaga Historical Association, 1916), 60; and Examination of Davenport, Examination of Letort, and Number of Indians, 1731, in Hazard, *Pennsylvania Archives*, 1st ser., 1:300–302.

15. Council held at Philadelphia, Oct. 14, 1736, in Hazard, *Provincial Council of Pennsylvania*, 4:93.

16. Ibid., 94.

17. "The Treaty Held with the Indians of the Six Nations, at Lancaster in Pennsylvania, in June, 1744" (Williamsburg: William Parks, n.d.), enclosure in William Gooch to Board of Trade, Dec. 21, 1744, CO 5/1325, PRO.

18. In the seventeenth century the legislatures of Virginia and Massachusetts required the systematic processioning of land by parish and town inhabitants. See Allan Kulikoff, *From British Peasants to Colonial American Farmers* (Chapel Hill: U of North Carolina P, 2000), 112; and William H. Seiler, "Land Processioning in Colonial Virginia," *William and Mary Quarterly*, 3d ser., 6 (July 1949): 416–36.

19. Alexander Spotswood, "A Proclamation declaring her Majties Pleasure Concerning ye Granting of Land," Dec. 8, 1710, in McIlwaine et al., *Executive Journals of the Council*, 3:580–81; and Manning C. Voorhis, "The Land Grant Policy of Colonial Virginia, 1607–1774" (Ph.D. diss., University of Virginia, 1940), 106–28.

20. Edward T. Price, *Dividing the Land: Early American Beginnings of Our Private Property Mosaic* (Chicago: U of Chicago P, 1995).

21. Sarah S. Hughes, *Surveyors and Statesmen: Land Measuring in Colonial Virginia* (Richmond: Virginia Surveyors Foundation and Virginia Association of Surveyors, 1979), 29–30.

22. Hughes, *Surveyors and Statesmen*, 30–66.

23. Copy of a Surveyor of a County's Commission, in "Public Officers in Virginia, 1680," *Virginia Magazine of History and Biography* 1 (Jan. 1894): 241, as quoted in Hughes, *Surveyors and Statesmen*, 63. On the association of the College of William and Mary with the appointment of surveyors, see ibid., 23–27, 71, 73, 75, 93–94, 96–98, 105, 119.

24. Warren M. Billings, John E. Selby, and Thad W. Tate, *Colonial Virginia: A History* (White Plains, N.Y.: KTO Press, 1986), 40–41; Hughes, *Surveyors and Statesmen*, 62; and Voorhis, "Land Grant Policy of Colonial Virginia," 44–86, 115–19.

25. Spotswood, "Proclamation Concerning ye Granting of Land," in McIlwaine et al., *Executive Journals of the Council*, 3:581–82. On the role of the county surveyor in shaping the social composition of Virginia's landowning classes, see Turk McCleskey, "Rich Land, Poor Prospects: Real Estate and the Formation of a Social Elite in Augusta County, Virginia, 1738–1770," *Virginia Magazine of History and Biography* 98 (July 1990): 449–86.

26. McIlwaine et al., *Executive Journals of the Council*, 4:229, 253; and *Hite v Fairfax*, transcript by McKay, 1707.

27. William Keith to Board of Trade, Apr. 6, 1730, in Charles E. Kemper, ed., "Documents Relating to a Proposed Swiss and German Colony in the Western Part of Virginia, 1706–1709," *Virginia Magazine of History and Biography* 29 (Apr. 1921): 189–90;

Transcript of the Record, *Hite and McCoy v Fairfax*, fol. 717, folder 100 C-HP, and *Hite v Fairfax*, transcript by McKay, 1588-89.

28. Keith to Board of Trade, Apr. 6, 1730, in Kemper, "Documents Relating to a Proposed Swiss and German Colony," 29:189-90; and *Hite v Fairfax*, transcript by McKay, 1547.

29. Mr. White's statement of Hite's claims, Land Papers, 1741-1760, folder 110a, C-HP; *Hite v Fairfax*, transcript by McKay, 1547, 1791; William W. Hening, ed., *The Statutes at Large: Being a Collection of All the Laws of Virginia, from . . . 1619 . . .*, 13 vols. (Richmond, New York, and Philadelphia, 1819-23), 4:450-51. On Hume's refusal to survey lands west of the Blue Ridge, see Hughes, *Surveyors and Statesmen*, 98-99; and for additional material on Brooke's surveys and his dispute with Wood, see Robert Brooke Survey Book; and McIlwaine et al., *Executive Journals of the Council*, 4:426-27.

30. *Hite v Fairfax*, transcript by McKay, 1521. On the population of the Shenandoah Valley and adjoining counties, see Chester Raymond Young, "The Effects of the French and Indian War on Civilian Life in the Frontier Counties of Virginia, 1754-1763" (Ph.D. diss., Vanderbilt University, 1969), 431-40, tables 28, 29, 31, 32, 33, 36, 37.

31. Joseph Doddridge, *Notes, on the Settlement and Indian Wars, of the Western Parts of Virginia and Pennsylvania . . .* (Wellsburgh, Va., 1824), 103. Stephen Aron makes a similar point about the settlement of Kentucky using Doddridge; see Aron, *How the West Was Lost: The Transformation of Kentucky from Daniel Boone to Henry Clay* (Baltimore: Johns Hopkins UP, 1996), 74-75. For a useful account of economy and society in early Kentucky, see Ellen Eslinger, *Citizens of Zion: The Social Origins of Camp Meeting Revivalism* (Knoxville: U of Tennessee P, 1999).

32. On competence in North American rural societies in the eighteenth and nineteenth centuries, see Jack P. Greene, "Independence, Improvement, and Authority: Toward a Framework for Understanding the Histories of the Southern Backcountry during the Era of the American Revolution," in Ronald Hoffman, Thad W. Tate, and Peter J. Albert, eds., *An Uncivil War: The Southern Backcountry during the American Revolution* (Charlottesville: UP of Virginia for the United States Capitol Historical Society, 1985), 3-36; Greene, *Pursuits of Happiness: The Social Development of Early Modern British Colonies and the Formation of American Culture* (Chapel Hill: U of North Carolina P, 1988), 15-16, 98, 195-97; and Daniel Vickers, "Competency and Competition: Economic Culture in Early America," *William and Mary Quarterly*, 3d ser., 47 (Jan. 1990): 3-29.

33. For the literature of this debate, see Christopher Clark, "The Household Economy, Market Exchange and the Rise of Capitalism in the Connecticut Valley, 1800-1860," *Journal of Social History* 13 (winter 1979): 169-89; Clark, "Rural America and the Transition to Capitalism," *Journal of the Early Republic* 16 (summer 1996): 223-36; Paul Gilje, "The Rise of Capitalism in the Early Republic," *Journal of the Early Republic* 16 (summer 1996): 159-81; James A. Henretta, "Families and Farms: *Mentalité* in Pre-Industrial America," *William and Mary Quarterly*, 3d ser., 35 (Jan. 1978): 3-32; Allan Kulikoff, "The Transition to Capitalism in Rural America," *William and Mary Quarterly*, 3d ser., 46 (Jan. 1989): 120-44; Kulikoff, *The Agrarian Origins of American Capitalism* (Charlottesville: UP of Virginia, 1992); Michael Merrill, "Cash Is Good to Eat: Self-Sufficiency and Exchange in the Rural Economy of the United States," *Radical*

History Review 3 (winter 1977): 42–69; Merrill, "Putting 'Capitalism' in Its Place: A Review of Recent Literature," *William and Mary Quarterly*, 3d ser., 52 (Apr. 1995): 315–26; Gregory H. Nobles, "Capitalism in the Countryside: The Transformation of Rural Society in the United States," *Radical History Review* 41 (1988): 163–77; Bettye Hobbs Pruitt, "Self-Sufficiency and the Agricultural Economy of Eighteenth-Century Massachusetts," *William and Mary Quarterly*, 3d ser., 41 (July 1984): 333–64; Winifred B. Rothenberg, "The Market and Massachusetts Farmers, 1750–1858," *Journal of Economic History* 41 (June 1981): 283–314; Rothenberg, "The Emergence of a Capital Market in Rural Massachusetts, 1730–1838," *Journal of Economic History* 45 (Dec. 1985): 781–808; and Rothenberg, "The Emergence of Farm Labor Markets and the Transformation of the Rural Economy: Massachusetts, 1750–1855," *Journal of Economic History* 48 (Sept. 1988): 537–66.

34. Gen. 1:28.

35. Richard Hakluyt, *Principal Navigations, Voyages, Traffiques, and Discoveries of the English Nation*, Hakluyt Society Publications, Extra Series, 12 vols. (Glasgow: J. MacLehose, 1903–5), 8:53–54, as quoted in Patricia Seed, "Taking Possession and Reading Texts: Establishing the Authority of Overseas Empires," *William and Mary Quarterly*, 3d ser., 49 (Apr. 1992): 185.

36. Board of Trade to the king, Sept. 8, 1721.

37. *Hite v Fairfax*, transcript by McKay, 1791.

38. "Trustees for the Pennsylvania Land Company in London v. Christian Stover," Pennsylvania Land Grants, vol. 9, Penn Papers, 213, 215, as quoted in James T. Lemon, *The Best Poor Man's Country: A Geographical Study of Early Southeastern Pennsylvania* (Baltimore: Johns Hopkins UP, 1972; New York: W. W. Norton, 1976), 57; and John Locke, *Two Treatises of Government*, ed. Peter Laslett (New York: New American Library, 1965), 308, as quoted in Kathy Squadrito, "Locke and the Dispossession of the American Indian," *American Indian Culture and Research Journal* 20 (1996): 156.

39. Kercheval, *History of the Valley*, 43, 45; and Locke, *Two Treatises of Government*, 309, as quoted in Squadrito, "Locke and the Dispossession of the American Indian," 155.

40. Thomas Chalkley to the "friends of the monthly meeting at Opequon," July 21, 1738, in Thomas Chalkley, *A Collection of the Works of That Antient, faithful Servant of Jesus Christ, Thomas Chalkley* (London: Luke Hind, 1751), 308–11; and Kercheval, *History of the Valley*, 45. For William Penn's policy on purchasing Indian lands prior to settlement, see Lemon, *The Best Poor Man's Country*, 31, 60.

41. Kercheval, *History of the Valley*, 41, 43.

42. Ibid., 42–45; William Byrd, *The History of the Dividing Line betwixt Virginia and North Carolina run in the year of our Lord 1728* (1929; New York: Dover Publications, 1967), 218.

43. William M. Gardner, *Lost Arrowheads and Broken Pottery: Traces of Indians in the Shenandoah Valley* (N.p.: Thunderbird Publications, 1986), 1–70; and Victor Carbone, "Environment and Prehistory in the Shenandoah Valley" (Ph.D. diss., Catholic University of America, 1976).

44. Gardner, *Lost Arrowheads and Broken Pottery*, 71–98.

45. Clarence R. Geier and Warren R. Hofstra, "An Archaeological Survey of and

Management Plan for Cultural Resources in the Vicinity of the Upper Opequon Creek" (Richmond: Virginia Department of Historic Resources, 1991), 70–73, table 1.

46. John R. Stilgoe, *Common Landscape of America, 1580 to 1845* (New Haven: Yale UP, 1982), 138–49. The literature of travel and exploration cannot be used to reconstruct the mental outlook of settlers without considerable caution. Travelers were often highly selective in determining subjects for their accounts, neglecting some topics of considerable interest today and treating others with anything but objectivity. Travelers who wrote with a commercial eye to the land often presented very different accounts of the landscape than did those whose purpose was political or literary. Because some travelers journeyed to America explicitly to observe a self-consciously republican society emerging after the Revolution, many accounts were encumbered by prejudices against rural poverty, slavery, social democracy, or other American institutions. Considering all the biases that affected travel accounts, landscape depictions were probably least distorted. Insofar as travelers knew their taxonomy, geology, or geography, their accounts can be relied upon as reasonably accurate records of actual landscapes. The degree to which the observations of a literate minority reflected the mentality of common people immigrating to new lands, however, cannot be determined with precision. But there is no reason to believe that astute travelers would have read the land any differently than did those intending to live upon it.

47. Kemper, "Swiss Colonies in the Valley of Virginia," 29:2; Durand of Dauphiné, *A Huguenot Exile in Virginia* (1687; Baltimore: Johns Hopkins Press, 1932; New York: Press of the Pioneers, 1934), 125, as quoted in William C. Robison, "Cultural Plant Geography of the Middle Appalachians" (Ph.D. diss., Boston University, 1960), 155; William M. Darlington, ed., *Christofer Gist's Journals with Historical, Geographical and Ethnological Notes* (Pittsburgh: J. R. Weldin, 1893), 67, as quoted in ibid., 149; and Andrew Burnaby, *Travels through the Middle Settlements in North America in the Years 1759 and 1760*, 3d ed. (London: T. Payne, 1798; New York: Augustus M. Kelley, 1970), 74.

48. François Jean, marquis de Chastellux, *Travels in North America in the Years 1780, 1781 and 1782*, 2 vols., trans. Howard C. Rice Jr. (Paris: Prault, 1786; Chapel Hill: U of North Carolina Press for the Institute of Early American History and Culture, 1963), 2:407; John Bartram, Bartram Papers, folder 54, vol. 1, Historical Society of Pennsylvania, Philadelphia; *The Journal Philip Vickers Fithian, 1775–1776*, ed. Robert G. Albion and Leonidas Dodson (Princeton: Princeton UP, 1934), 137, 180; and Thomas Coke, "Missionary Journeys of Dr. Coke: 1785–1791," in *Travels in Virginia in Revolutionary Times*, ed. A. J. Morrison (Lynchburg, Va.: J. P. Bell, 1922), 77.

49. Robert D. Mitchell, Warren R. Hofstra, and Edward F. Connor, "Reconstructing the Colonial Environment of the Upper Chesapeake Watershed," in Philip E. Curtin, Grace S. Brush, and George W. Fisher, eds., *Discovering the Chesapeake: The History of an Ecosystem* (Baltimore: Johns Hopkins UP, 2001), 179–83.

50. John F. D. Smyth, *A Tour in the United States of America*, 2 vols. (London: G. Robinson, 1784; New York: New York Times and Arno Press, 1968), 1:93; 2:73; and *The Journal of Nicholas Cresswell, 1774–1777* (New York: Dial Press, 1924), 68–69. On the wide variety of forest species in the middle Atlantic, see Burnaby, *Travels through the Middle Settlements*, 157–59.

51. Isaac Weld, *Travels through the States of North America*, 2 vols. (London: John Stockdale, 1807; New York: Johnson Reprint, 1968), 1:46; Smyth, *A Tour in the United States of America*, 1:289; and James Kirke Paulding, *Letters from the South*, 2 vols. (New York: James Eastburn, 1817; New York: AMS Press, 1973) 1:134.

52. Cresswell, *Journal*, 48, 64; John Lederer, *The Discoveries of John Lederer*, ed. William P. Cumming (London: Samuel Herick, 1672; Charlottesville: UP of Virginia, 1958), 11; Smyth, *A Tour in the United States of America*, 1:320; and Bartram, Papers, folder 66, vol. 1.

53. Jacques Pierre Brissot de Warville, *New Travels in the United States of America, 1788*, ed. Durand Echeverria, trans. Mara S. Vamos and Durand Echeverria (Paris: Buisson, 1791; Cambridge: Belknap Press of Harvard UP, 1964), 358; G. L. Gillespie, "Map of the Upper Potomac from McCoy's Ferry to Conrad's Ferry and Adjacent Portions of Maryland and Virginia," in George B. Davis, Leslie J. Perry, and Joseph W. Kirkley, eds., *The Official Military Atlas of the Civil War* (Gettysburg: National Historical Society, 1978), plate 69, 1; Diary of the Journey of the First Colony of Single Brethren to North Carolina, Oct. 8–Nov. 17, 1753, in William J. Hinke and Charles E. Kemper, eds., "Moravian Diaries of Travels through Virginia," *Virginia Magazine of History and Biography* 12 (Oct. 1904): 144; Burnaby, *Travels through the Middle Settlements*, 37; and Smyth, *A Tour in the United States of America*, 1:203.

54. C. W. Alvord and Lee Bidgood, *The First Explorations of the Trans-Allegheny Region by the Virginians, 1650–1674* (Cleveland: Arthur H. Clark, 1912), 188; Cresswell, *Journal*, 63; Fithian, *Journal*, 107; and Smyth, *A Tour in the United States of America*, 1:309–10. Smyth also found a savanna along the Clinch River in southwest Virginia, see Smyth, *A Tour in the United States of America*, 1:317.

55. Smyth, *A Tour in the United States of America*, 1:140–41; and Fithian, *Journal*, 91.

56. Smyth, *A Tour in the United States of America*, 1:141; François Alexandre Frédéric, duc de La Rochefoucauld-Liancourt, *Travels through the United States of North America . . . in the Years 1795, 1796, and 1797*, 4 vols., 2d ed., trans. H. Newman (London: R. Phillips, 1800), 3:195; and Paulding, *Letters from the South*, 1:153.

57. Lederer, *Discoveries*, 34; and John Fontaine, *The Journal of John Fontaine: An Irish Huguenot Son in Spain and Virginia, 1710–1719*, ed. Edward P. Alexander (Williamsburg: Colonial Williamsburg Foundation, 1972), 91.

58. Bartram, Papers, folder 54, vol. 1; Benjamin Smith Barton, "Journal of Benjamin Smith Barton on a Visit to Virginia, 1802," *Castenea* 3 (Nov.–Dec. 1938): 99; and Francis Asbury, *Journal of Rev. Francis Asbury*, 3 vols. (New York: Lane & Scott, 1852), 1:473.

59. Cresswell, *Journal*, 86; and Fithian, *Journal*, 147.

60. Cresswell, *Journal*, 63; Fithian, *Journal*, 91; Barton, "Journal," 92; and Bartram, Papers, folder 41, vol. 1.

61. Weld, *Travels through the States of North America*, 1:162; Johann David Schoepf, *Travels in the Confederation, 1783–1784*, 2 vols., trans. and ed. Alfred J. Morrison (Erlangen: Johann Jacob Plam, 1788; New York: Bergman Publishers, 1968), 2:73; Hugh Jones, *The Present State of Virginia* (Chapel Hill: U of North Carolina P for the Virginia Historical Society, 1956), 56; and Lederer, *Discoveries*, 26–27.

62. Lederer, *Discoveries*, 10; Fontaine, *Journal*, 104–5; and Smyth, *A Tour in the United States of America*, 1:242–43.

63. Alvord and Bidgood, *First Explorations*, 192; Fithian, *Journal*, 107; Smyth, *A Tour in the United States of America*, 1:151; Burnaby, *Travels through the Middle Settlements*, 92; and Weld, *Travels through the States of North America*, 1:152.

64. Ferdinand M. Bayard, *Travels of a Frenchman in Maryland and Virginia with a Description of Philadelphia and Baltimore in 1791*, 2d ed., trans. Ben C. McCary (Paris: Batilliot Frères, 1798; Ann Arbor: Edward Bros., 1950), 68; Fontaine, *Journal*, 104; Weld, *Travels through the States of North America*, 1:132; and Cresswell, *Journal*, 199.

65. Transcript of the Record, *Hite and McCoy v Fairfax*, fol. 717, folder 100, C-HP.

66. Deposition of Thomas Branson, June 25, 1761, *Hite v Fairfax*, transcript by McKay, 1586; Deposition of John Dyer, Mar. 19, 1762, ibid., 1586–87; *Hite v Fairfax*, transcript by McKay, 1550; and Order in Council, Apr. 11, 1745, CO 5/1325, PRO. For the Privy Council's order halting land granting in the territory disputed by Fairfax and the Virginia government, see Order in Council, Nov. 29, 1733, CO 5/1323, PRO. The best treatments of this dispute appear in Stuart Brown, *Virginia Baron: The Story of Thomas Sixth Lord Fairfax* (Berryville, Va.: Chesapeake Book Co., 1965), 45–100; and Douglas Southall Freeman, *George Washington: A Biography*, 7 vols. (New York: Charles Scribner's Sons, 1948–57), 1:501–13.

67. *Hite v Fairfax*, transcript by McKay, 1547. The full record of the suit *Hite et al. v Fairfax et al.* was transmitted to England in 1772 by John Murry, earl of Dunmore, governor of Virginia, upon appeal from the Virginia General Court; see Additional Manuscript 15317, British Museum. Not until after the American Revolution did Hite's heirs receive a final affirmation of their case; see *Hite et al. v Fairfax et al.*, 4 Call 42 (1786). Many of the suit documents have survived in the Clark-Hite Papers (C-HP). The best discussion of the case appears in Brown, *Virginia Baron*, 110–17, 163, 166–67.

68. Answer of Joseph Langdon, Mar. 30, 1754, *Hite v Fairfax*, transcript by McKay, 1578, 1713; and Deposition of Henry Funk, Mar. 24, 1789, *John Feller v Rep. of Jost Hite et al.*, 1789, fols. 534–35, folder 149, C-HP.

69. Deposition of Lewis Stephens, Aug. 19, 1789, *Joseph Barnes and Ruth Whitson v Rep. of Jost Hite et al.*, 1770–90, fol. 452, folder 137, C-HP; Deposition of Andrew Falkenburg, Feb. 10, 1787, *Solomon Huddle v Rep. of Jost Hite et al.*, 1787–92, fols. 559–60, folder 152, C-HP; and Deposition of Lewis Stephens, 1787, *Benjamin Layman et al. v Rep. of Jost Hite et al.*, fol. 604, folder 155, C-HP.

70. Transcript of the Record, *Hite and McCoy v Fairfax*, fol. 713, folder 100, C-HP; *Hite v Fairfax*, transcript by McKay, 1521; Answer of George Wright, Apr. 11, 1760, ibid., 1580; Answer of William Rogers, Jan. 26, 1754, ibid., 1575; and *Augustine Windle v Rep. of Jost Hite et al.* 1790, fol. 734, folder 174, C-HP.

71. Answer of William Rogers, *Hite v Fairfax*, transcript by McKay, 1575–76, 1713; and O'Dell, *Pioneers of Old Frederick County*, 432.

72. Answer of Joseph Langdon, *Hite v Fairfax*, transcript by McKay, 1578–79.

73. Answer of William Ewing, Apr. 11, 1760, *Hite v Fairfax*, transcript by McKay, 1582; Answer of George Wright, ibid., 1580–81; Deposition of Andrew Falkenburg,

Huddle v Rep. of Hite. On Ewing's land, see O'Dell, *Pioneers of Old Frederick County,* 308–9; and Northern Neck Grants, 1690–1874, H:731, Library of Virginia.

74. Deposition of Christopher Windle, Feb. 8, 1787, *Christopher Windle v Rep. of Jost Hite et al.,* 1787–90, fol. 742, folder 175, C-HP. See also, Deposition of Valentine Windle, Feb. 8, 1787, *Windle v Rep. of Hite,* 1787, fols. 751–52, folder 176, C-HP; and Bill of Augustine Windle, and Brief in the case of Augustine Windle, *Windle v Rep. of Hite,* 1790, fols. 726–27, 729, folder 174, C-HP.

75. For the survey of the North Mountain tract indicating its first settlers, see *Windle v Rep. of Hite,* fol. 731, folder 174, C-HP. See also *Hite v Fairfax,* transcript by McKay, 1627–30. The Virginia Council took up the Privy Council order of Nov. 29, 1733, on Nov. 1, 1735, see McIlwaine et al., *Executive Journals of the Council,* 4:361.

76. For environmental information on the North Mountain tract, see the survey in *Augustine Windle v Rep. of Hite;* and Eugene K. Rader and Thomas H. Biggs, *Geology of the Strasburg and Toms Brook Quadrangles, Virginia,* Virginia Division of Mineral Resources Report of Investigations 45 (Charlottesville: Virginia Division of Mineral Resources, 1976). For comparison to the Opequon tract, see Charles Butts, *Geology of the Appalachian Valley in Virginia,* Virginia Geological Survey Bulletin 52 (Richmond: Division of Purchase and Printing, 1940; Charlottesville: Virginia Division of Mineral Resources, 1973); and Butts and Edmundson, *Geology of Frederick County.*

77. Deposition of Valentine Windle, *Valentine Windle v Rep. of Hite;* and Jonathan Clark, Legal Papers, Miscellaneous, 1774–1812, fol. 382, folder 87, C-HP.

78. Deposition of Christopher Windle, *Christopher Windle v Rep. of Hite.*

79. Deposition of Henry Funk, Mar. 24, 1789, *John Feller v Rep. of Jost Hite et al.,* 1789, fols. 536–37, folder 149, C-HP. On Parrot and Rinehart, see Statement of Augustine Borden's case, *Henry Wolfe et al. v Rep. of Jost Hite et al.,* fols. 756–57, folder 177, C-HP.

80. Reference to Ben Allen's path appears on James Wood's survey of the North Mountain tract, see *Windle v Rep. of Hite;* and on Allen, see O'Dell, *Pioneers of Old Frederick County,* 461.

81. On Windle's complaint, see Brief in the case of Augustine Windle, *Windle v Rep. of Hite.*

82. Survey of North Mountain tract, in ibid.

CHAPTER 4. Bounding the Land

1. Decretal Order of High Court of Chancery, Richmond, Va., May 8, 1786, fol. 897, folder 108, Clark-Hite Papers (hereafter C-HP), Filson Historical Society, Louisville, Ky.

2. Order of High Court of Chancery, May 8, 1786, C-HP; Jonathan Clark Notebook, July–Aug. 1786, fols. 903–60, folder 185, C-HP. Placing a value on improvements was what made Clark's survey such a useful contribution to the historical record. For an analysis of Clark's notebook, see George M. Smith, "Family and Commercial Farms of Virginia's Lower Valley in 1786: A Preliminary Analysis of the Commission Survey Books, *Hite et al. v Fairfax et al.,*" 1969, George Smith Collection, Archives Room, Handley Regional Library, Winchester.

3. Jonathan Clark Notebook, C-HP; and Cecil O'Dell, *Pioneers of Old Frederick County, Virginia* (Marceline, Mo.: Walsworth, 1995), 371–72.

4. *John Hite et al. v Lord Fairfax et al.*, Additional Manuscript 15317, British Museum, London, transcript by Hunter Branson McKay, p. 1550, Archives Room, Handley Regional Library. For land grants of North Mountain settlers, see Northern Neck Grants, 1690–1874, G:375, 376, 378, 385, H:92, 209, 210, N:174, 210, O:52, 56, Library of Virginia, Richmond.

5. Jonathan Clark Notebook, C-HP.

6. On American log construction and its European origins, see Terry G. Jordan, *American Log Buildings: An Old World Heritage* (Chapel Hill: U of North Carolina P, 1985); and Terry G. Jordan and Matti Kaups, *The American Backwoods Frontier: An Ethnic and Ecological Interpretation* (Baltimore: Johns Hopkins UP, 1989). The best treatments of Germanic houses in early America appear in Edward A. Chappell, "Acculturation in the Shenandoah Valley: Rhenish Houses of the Massanutten Settlement," *Proceedings of the American Philosophical Society* 124 (Feb. 1980): 55–89; and William Woys Weaver, "The Pennsylvania German House: European Antecedents and New World Forms," *Winterthur Portfolio* 21 (1986): 243–64. On Germanic structures at Hite's Opequon tract, see Clarence R. Geier and Warren R. Hofstra, "An Archaeological Survey of and Management Plan for Cultural Resources in the Vicinity of the Upper Opequon Creek" (Richmond: Virginia Department of Historic Resources, 1991): 73.

7. Alan Gailey, *Rural Houses of the North of Ireland* (Edinburgh: John Donald, 1984), 148, 35–40; and John B. Rehder, "The Scotch-Irish and English in Appalachia," in Allen G. Noble, ed., *To Build in a New Land: Ethnic Landscapes in North America* (Baltimore: Johns Hopkins UP, 1992), 95–118.

8. Jonathan Clark Notebook, C-HP.

9. Ibid.; and Robert F. Ensminger, *The Pennsylvania Barn: Its Origin, Evolution, and Distribution in North America* (Baltimore: Johns Hopkins UP, 1992), 1–10, 25, 52.

10. Jonathan Clark Notebook, C-HP.

11. United States Census Office, First Census, 1790, *Return of the whole number of persons within the several districts of the United States, . . .* (Philadelphia: Childs & Swaine, 1791), 48; and Frederick County Land Tax Lists, 1790, Library of Virginia.

12. Jonathan Clark Notebook, C-HP; and Thaddeus M. Harris, *Journal of a Tour into the Territory Northwest of the Alleghany Mountains* (Boston: Manning & Loring, 1805), as quoted in Carl Lounsbury, ed., *An Illustrated Glossary of Early Southern Architecture and Landscape* (New York: Oxford UP, 1994), 55–56.

13. Jonathan Clark Notebook, C-HP.

14. Ibid.; and John Smith survey, Mar. 25, 1734, Robert Brooke Survey Book, 1732–34, p. 11, Thornton Tayloe Perry Collection, Virginia Historical Society, Richmond. Five references to mill runs or mill creeks appear in Brooke's surveys.

15. William W. Hening, ed., *The Statutes at Large: Being a Collection of All the Laws of Virginia, from . . . 1619 . . .*, 13 vols. (Richmond, New York, and Philadelphia, 1819–23), 2:260–61, 4:53–55, 5:31–5, 6:64–69.

16. On the public privileges and restrictions placed upon millers by statute, see Hening, *Statutes*, 1:301, 485, 2:127, 242, 260–61, 286–87, 3:359–62, 401–4, 5:352, 7:100.

17. Robert Brooke Survey Book, 26, 4, 5, 16, 18; and O'Dell, *Pioneers of Old Frederick County*, 486–91.

18. John Frost, n.d., Robert Brooke Survey Book, 64. Other references to paths can be found in ibid., 24, 26, 64.

19. Petition to Orange County Court, 1738, as quoted in William J. Hinke and Charles E. Kemper, eds., "Moravian Diaries of Travels through Virginia," *Virginia Magazine of History and Biography* 12 (1905): 142. On April 27, 1738, the court of Orange County issued an ordinary license to Jost Hite, see Orange County Court Orders, 1:293, Orange County Courthouse, Orange, Va.; and Ann Brush Miller, *Orange County Road Orders, 1734–1749* (Charlottesville: Virginia Highway and Transportation Research Council, 1984), 30. Deposition of Peter Wolf, Mar. 6, 1754, *Hite v Fairfax*, transcript by McKay, 1582–1583; and O'Dell, *Pioneers of Old Frederick County*, 489.

20. O'Dell, *Pioneers of Old Frederick County*, 496–98, 506–14; and Miller, *Orange County Road Orders*, 59, 65, 70, 73, 74.

21. H. R. McIlwaine, Wilmer L. Hall, and Benjamin J. Hillman, eds., *Executive Journals of the Council of Colonial Virginia*, 6 vols. (Richmond: Virginia State Library, 1926–66), 4:326, 347. In a decree issued in 1771, the Virginia General Court determined that Hite had fulfilled the settlement requirement of forty families stipulated in the orders he had purchased from John and Isaac Van Meter and that under Hite's own one-hundred-thousand-acre order 54 families had been settled. See Stuart Brown, *Virginia Baron: The Story of Thomas Sixth Lord Fairfax* (Berryville, Va.: Chesapeake Book Co., 1965), 166–67. If five was the average family size at the time, the total of 164 families would have yielded a population of about eight hundred.

22. McIlwaine et al., *Executive Journals of the Council*, 4:318–19.

23. Hening, *Statutes*, 4:450–51. The legislation can be traced through the Assembly of Virginia in H. R. McIlwaine, ed., *Journals of the House of Burgesses of Virginia, 1727–1734, 1736–1740* (Richmond: Virginia State Library, 1910), 184, 193, 195, 197, 209, 234; and McIlwaine, *Legislative Journals of the Council of Colonial Virginia* (Richmond: Virginia State Library, 1918–19, 1979), 758, 821, 824.

24. Richard Aquila, *The Iroquois Restoration: Iroquois Diplomacy on the Colonial Frontier, 1701–1754* (Detroit: Wayne State UP, 1983), 217.

25. McIlwaine et al., *Executive Journals of the Council*, 4:368, 370, 398, 404; William Gooch to James Logan, Sept. 3, 1737, in Samuel Hazard, ed., *Provincial Council of Pennsylvania*, 16 vols. (Harrisburg: Theo. Fenn, 1838–53), 4:245–46, 203–4; and Gooch to Board of Trade, Sept. 20, 1738, CO 5/1324, Colonial Office Papers, Public Records Office (hereafter PRO), London.

26. McIlwaine et al., *Executive Journals of the Council*, 4:414, 443; *Virginia Gazette*, June 6, Apr. 7, July 21, 1738; Gooch to Board of Trade, Sept. 20, 1738, CO 5/1324, PRO; "Journals of the Council of Virginia in Executive Sessions, 1737–1763," *Virginia Magazine of History and Biography* 14 (Apr. 1907): 344; Aquila, *Iroquois Restoration*, 218; and George Clarke to Board of Trade, Nov. 10, 1740, in Edmund Bailey O'Callaghan and Berthold Fernow, eds., *Documents Relative to the Colonial History of the State of New-York*, 15 vols. (Albany: Weed, Parsons, 1853–87), 6:171–72.

27. William Gooch, Address to House of Burgesses, Nov. 1, 1738, in McIlwaine,

Journals of the House of Burgesses [1727–1740], 320–21, 333, 337, 340, 344, 349, 386; and Hening, *Statutes*, 5:24, 4:197–204.

28. McIlwaine, *Journals of the House of Burgesses [1727–1740]*, 373; Hening, *Statutes*, 5:57–58; and John Ochs and Jacob Stover, Petition to Board of Trade, in Ann V. Strickler Milbourne, ed., "Colony West of the Blue Ridge, Proposed by Jacob Stauber and others, 1731, etc.," *Virginia Magazine of History and Biography* 35 (Apr. 1927): 184.

29. McIlwaine, *Journals of the House of Burgesses* [1727–1740], 330, 337–38, 386–87; Hening, *Statutes*, 5:78–80; and William Gooch to Board of Trade, Feb. 22, 1739, CO 5/1324, PRO.

30. Gooch to Board of Trade, Feb. 8, 1733, CO 5/1323, PRO; and McIlwaine et al., *Executive Journals of the Council*, 4:414.

31. Gooch to Board of Trade, Feb. 22, 1739, CO 5/1324, PRO; Hening, *Statutes*, 5:78–80; Petition of the Inhabitants of "Frederica" County, item 2, folder 41, Colonial Papers, Library of Virginia; William P. Palmer, Sherwin McRae, Raleigh Colston, and H. W. Flourney, eds., *Calendar of Virginia State Papers and Other Manuscripts, 1652–1781*, 12 vols. (Richmond, 1875–93; New York: Kraus Reprint, 1968), 1:233; McIlwaine, *Legislative Journals of the Council*, 887; and McIlwaine et al., *Executive Journals of the Council*, 5:47.

32. William Gooch to Board of Trade, Feb. 15, 1739, CO 5/1324, PRO.

33. Board of Trade to George Clarke, Dec. 6, 1738, in O'Callaghan and Fernow, *Documents Relative to the Colonial History of New-York*, 6:137–38; Clarke to Board of Trade, May 24, 1739, in ibid., 6:143; Commissioners of Indian Affairs to Clarke, June 7, 1739, in ibid., 6:146; Clarke to duke of Newcastle, June 15, 1739, in ibid., 6:144–45; Clarke to Board of Trade, June 15, 1739, in ibid., 6:144–45; and Aquila, *Iroquois Restoration*, 218–20.

34. McIlwaine et al., *Executive Journals of the Council*, 5:62–63; Aquila, *Iroquois Restoration*, 220–21; William Gooch to Board of Trade, Aug. 1, 1739, CO 5/1324, PRO; George Clarke to Board of Trade, Aug. 30, 1739, in O'Callaghan and Fernow, *Documents Relative to the Colonial History of New-York*, 6:147–48; and Conference with the Cherokee and Catawba Indians, May 23, 1741, enclosure in William Bull to George Clarke, June 1741, in ibid., 6:210–11. The Cherokees later met with headmen of the Six Nations to confirm the peace, but the Catawbas apparently renounced the agreement, sending instead a message that the Iroquois were "but Women; that they were men and double men for they had two P——s; . . . and would be always at War" with the Six Nations. See Minutes of a Treaty Held at the Town of Lancaster, June 22–July 4, 1744, in Hazard, *Provincial Council of Pennsylvania*, 4:721.

35. Examination of Jemmy Smalhommoney, June 25, 1742, in William Hand Browne, ed., *Proceedings of the Council of Maryland, 1732–1753*, vol. 28, *Archives of Maryland* (Baltimore: Maryland Historical Society, 1908), 257–60; and Aquila, *Iroquois Restoration*, 221–22.

36. William Gooch to George Clarke, Jan. 3, 1743, in O'Callaghan and Fernow, *Documents Relative to the Colonial History of New-York*, 6:230; Gooch to Board of Trade, Feb. 14, 1743, CO 5/1535, PRO; George Thomas to Pennsylvania Assembly, Jan. 25, 1743, in Hazard, *Provincial Council of Pennsylvania*, 4:634; Pennsylvania Assembly to

Thomas, Jan. 26, 1743, in ibid., 4:637; Gooch to Thomas, n.d., in ibid., 4:640; Conrad Weiser, Report of his Journey to Shamokin, Apr. 5, 1743, in ibid., 4:640; and Clarke to Commissioners of Indian Affairs, Apr. 5, 1743, in O'Callaghan and Fernow, *Documents Relative to the Colonial History of New-York*, 231–32.

37. McIlwaine et al., *Executive Journals of the Council*, 5:116–17. The Council met in March 1743 for the first time after having received news of the skirmish in Augusta County, but it lacked a quorum (ibid., 114). On offices held by James Wood, see ibid., 5:2; and H. R. McIlwaine, ed., *Journals of the House of Burgesses of Virginia, 1742–1747, 1748–1749* (Richmond: Virginia State Library, 1909), 49–51.

38. Hening, *Statutes*, 5:78.

39. Minutes of the Proceedings of the Commissioners of Indian Affairs, May 2, 1743, in O'Callaghan and Fernow, *Documents Relative to the Colonial History of New-York*, 6:239, 240; Commissioners of Indian Affairs to George Clarke, May 30, 1743, in ibid., 6:240; Clarke to William Gooch, May 2, 1743, in ibid., 4:237; Clarke to Gooch, June 16, 1743, in ibid., 6:241–42; and Clarke to Commissioners of Indian Affairs, Apr. 27, 1743, in ibid., 6:235–37.

40. William Gooch to George Thomas, Feb. 8, 1743, in Hazard, *Provincial Council of Pennsylvania*, 4:646; and Conrad Weiser, Report of his Journey to Shamokin, Apr. 21, 1743, in ibid., 4:647, 650.

41. Francis Jennings, *The Invasion of America: Indians, Colonialism, and the Cant of Conquest* (Chapel Hill: U of North Carolina P for the Institute of Early American History and Culture, 1975; New York: W. W. Norton, 1976), 148–49; and Daniel K. Richter, *The Ordeal of the Longhouse: The Peoples of the Iroquois League in the Era of European Colonization* (Chapel Hill: U of North Carolina P for the Institute of Early American History and Culture, 1992), 32–33, 39–41.

42. Hazard, *Provincial Council of Pennsylvania*, 4:651; and George Thomas to William Gooch, Apr. 25, 1743, in ibid., 4:653–54.

43. William Gooch to George Thomas, May 7, 1743, in Hazard, *Provincial Council of Pennsylvania*, 4:654–55.

44. Conrad Weiser, Report of his Journey to Onondago on the affairs of Virginia, Sept. 1, 1743, in Hazard, *Provincial Council of Pennsylvania*, 4:662–65.

45. Ibid., 666–68.

46. Minutes of a Treaty Held at the Town of Lancaster, in Hazard, *Provincial Council of Pennsylvania*, 4:700.

47. Ibid., 726–27; and Francis Jennings, *The Ambiguous Iroquois Empire: The Covenant Chain Confederation of Indian Tribes with English Colonies from its beginnings to the Lancaster Treaty of 1744* (New York: W. W. Norton, 1984): 360–62.

48. Minutes of a Treaty held at the Town of Lancaster, in Hazard, *Provincial Council of Pennsylvania*, 4:713, 718; and *The Treaty Held with the Indians of the Six Nations, at Lancaster, in Pennsylvania, in June, 1744* (Williamsburg: William Parks, n.d.), 75–79.

49. William Gooch, Address to the House of Burgesses, Sept. 4, 1744, in McIlwaine, *Journals of the House of Burgesses [1742–1747]*, 76.

50. Ibid.

51. McIlwaine et al., *Executive Journals of the Council*, 5:134, 172–73.

52. Kenneth P. Bailey, *The Ohio Company of Virginia and the Westward Movement, 1748–1792: A Chapter in the History of the Colonial Frontier* (Glendale, Calif.: Arthur H. Clark, 1939), 17–31; Alfred P. James, *The Ohio Company: Its Inner History* (Pittsburgh: U of Pittsburgh P, 1959), 1–27; and Manning C. Voorhis, "The Land Grant Policy of Colonial Virginia, 1607–1774" (Ph.D. diss., University of Virginia, 1940), 166–80.

CHAPTER 5. Centering the County

1. Frederick County Court Orders (hereafter FCCO), 1:3, Frederick County Courthouse, Winchester.

2. FCCO, 1:60; and Thomas K. Cartmell, *Shenandoah Valley Pioneers and Their Descendants: A History of Frederick County, Virginia* (Winchester, Va.: Eddy Press, 1909; Bowie, Md.: Heritage Books, 1989), 126–27.

3. *The Journal Philip Vickers Fithian, 1775–1776*, ed. R. G. Albion and L. Dodson (Princeton: Princeton UP, 1934), 13; François Alexandre Frédéric, duc de La Rochefoucauld-Liancourt, *Travels through the United States of North America, . . . in the Years 1795, 1796, and 1797*, 4 vols., 2d ed., trans. H. Neuman (London: R. Phillips, 1800), 3:202; and FCCO, 2:79, 1:97, 2:192.

4. Cartmell, *Shenandoah Valley Pioneers*, 126; and List of Bonds for the Lots, James Wood Commonplace Book [1745], James Wood Papers, Glen Burnie Museum, Winchester, [6].

5. FCCO, 1:455; Cartmell, *Shenandoah Valley Pioneers*, 24–25; FCCO, 1:224, 2:18, 108, 198, 342, 3:164, 186, 447, 4:59; Account of Stephen Minor and Daniel Sutherland, Nov. 19, 1744, James Wood Account Book, James Wood Papers, Glen Burnie Museum, 11; and Receipt of John Hardin to Justices of Frederick County, Aug. 9, 1745, James Wood Sr., Agreements, James Wood Collection, 711 THL, Archives Room, Handley Regional Library, Winchester. Whether the courthouse was constructed of stone or log is uncertain. Duncan O'Gullion was a stone mason, and no evidence survives that he ever constructed log buildings. But on May 9, 1754, the court ordered "Workmen to rake down the Logs in the Court house to white wash and to finish the same." See FCCO, 5:463.

6. FCCO, 1:4, 2:198, 1:224, 2:193.

7. FCCO, 1:3; 2:1, 18, 22, 138, 139, 352, 496, 499.

8. Account of Stephen Minor and Daniel Sutherland, Nov. 19, 1744, James Wood Account Book, James Wood Papers, 11; FCCO, 1:87, 207, 2:1, 18; and George Webb, *The Office and Authority of a Justice of Peace* . . . (Williamsburg: William Parks, 1736).

9. FCCO, 1:76; and William W. Hening, ed., *The Statutes at Large: Being a Collection of All the Laws of Virginia, from . . . 1619 . . .*, 13 vols. (Richmond, New York, and Philadelphia, 1819–23), 5:78–80.

10. Hening, *Statutes*, 6:259; Frederick Parish Vestry Book, transcript, Cunningham Chapel Parish, Millwood, Va., 9–10, 14–16; Orange County Court Orders, 2:461, Orange County Courthouse, Orange, Va.; Ann Brush Miller, *Orange County Road Or-*

ders, *1734–1749* (Charlottesville: Virginia Highway and Transportation Research Council, 1984), 59; Account of Thomas Rutherford, Aug. 1745, James Wood Account Book, James Wood Papers, 3; FCCO, 2:88, 313; and *Maryland Gazette*, Dec. 3, 1761.

11. Petition of inhabitants of Opeckan and Shenandore to Orange County Court, 1736, in John Frederick Dorman, *Orange County, Virginia, Deed Books 1 and 2, 1735–1738, Judgments, 1735* (Washington, D.C., 1961), 101; and William Gooch to the Justices of the Court of Orange County, Aug. 29, 1737, in ibid., 107–8. Frederick County Deeds, 1:247, Frederick County Courthouse, Winchester; and *Hopewell Friends History, 1734–1934* (Strasburg, Va.: Shenandoah Publishing House, 1936), 144–49.

12. Synod of Philadelphia to William Gooch, May 30, 1738, and Gooch response, May 28, 1739, in William Couper, *History of the Shenandoah Valley*, 3 vols. (New York: Lewis Historical Publishing Co., 1952), 1:286–88.

13. Richard Pillsbury, "The Urban Street Pattern as a Culture Indicator: Pennsylvania, 1682–1815," *Annals of the Association of American Geographers* 60 (Sept. 1970): 428–46; and John W. Reps, *Tidewater Towns: City Planning in Colonial Virginia and Maryland* (Charlottesville: UP of Virginia, 1972).

14. FCCO, 1:89, 130–31, 343, 383, 445, 443, 2:311; and Cartmell, *Shenandoah Valley Pioneers*, 24.

15. FCCO, 1:56, 1–221; George Washington, Mar. 16, 1748, *The Diaries of George Washington*, 6 vols., ed. Donald Jackson and Dorothy Twohig (Charlottesville: UP of Virginia, 1976–79), 1:10–11; Hening, *Statutes*, 4:406–7, 5:78–80; Account of David Vance with John Hopes, Nov. 17, 1746–Dec. 9, 1748, *Hope v Vance*, Feb. 1751, Ended Causes, 1743–1909, Frederick County Court Papers, Library of Virginia, Richmond; and Account of John Hopes, Mar. 12, 1745–June 25, 1747, Accounts, 1736–55, James Wood Family Papers, 173 WFCHS, Archives Room, Handley Regional Library.

16. On the rural economy as a "dispersed general store," see Joseph S. Wood, "Elaboration of a Settlement System: The New England Village in the Federal Period," *Journal of Historical Geography* 10 (Oct. 1984): 331–56 (quote on 338); and Wood, "Village and Community in Early Colonial New England," *Journal of Historical Geography* 8 (Oct. 1982): 333–46. Information about James Wood's store and the business conducted there can be found in Account of William Glover, Mar. 29, 1746, James Wood Account Book, James Wood Papers, 8; Account of James Bruce, May 20–June 28, 1746, ibid., 10; Account of Stephen Minor and Daniel Sutherland, Jan. 1746, ibid., 11; Account of John Rich, Apr. 3, 1748–June 10, 1749, ibid., 36; Account of Benjamin Perreyra, Jan. 22, 1746, James Wood Commonplace Book [14]; John Carlyle to Daniel Hart, Jan. 21, 1747, Daniel Hart folder, James Wood Collection; *Perreyra v Robbins*, Sept. 1747, Ended Causes, 1743–1909, FCCP; and Account of Joseph Carrel with Benjamin Perreyra, Nov. 1747, Accounts, James Wood Papers, Glen Burnie Museum.

17. Account of Benjamin Perreyra, Oct. 5, 1746, James Wood Account Book, James Wood Papers, 13; Account of Lyman Lipman with Benjamin Perreyra, Apr. 15, 1747–Sept. 5, 1748, *Perreyra v Lipman*, Nov. 1749, Ended Causes, 1743–1909, FCCP; Account of Lyman Lipman with Ulrich Poker, 1747, *Poker v Lipman*, May 1750, ibid.; and Account of Richard Cronk with Lyman Lipman, Dec. 4, 1746–July 23, 1747, *Lipman v Cronk*, Aug. 1748, ibid.

18. William J. Hinke and Charles E. Kemper, eds., "Moravian Diaries of Travels through Virginia," *Virginia Magazine of History and Biography* 22 (July 1904): 141; Account of Peter Tostee, May 6, 1748, James Wood Account Book, James Wood Papers, 37; Note of Thomas Rennick to Tostee, Mar. 3, 1746, *Tostee v Rennick*, Mar. 1747, Ended Causes, 1743–1909, FCCP; Account of William Linwell with Tostee, Feb. 2, 1738, *Tostee v Linwell*, Dec. 1747, ibid.; Agreement of Peter Tostee with Thomas How, June 3, 1748, James Wood Sr., Agreements, James Wood Collection; Complaint of William Dobbins against Duncan O'Gullion, Dec. 27, 1744, *Dobbins v O'Gullion*, Oct. 1747, Ended Causes, 1743–1909, FCCP; Account of William Dobbins, Mar. 10, 1745–Dec. 18, 1747, James Wood Account Book, James Wood Papers, 7; Receipt of Dobbins, Dec. 18, 1747, Accounts, 1736–1755, James Wood Family Papers; Account of Abraham Hite with Dobbins, Aug. 18, 1747–Jan. 12, 1750, *Dobbins v Hite*, Aug. 1750, Ended Causes, 1743–1909, FCCP; List of Bonds for the Lots, James Wood Commonplace Book, James Wood Papers [6]; and Deed of Dobbins to Thomas and Mary How, Jan. 23, 1749, FCD, 1:447.

19. Hening, *Statutes*, 6:268–70; Stuart Brown, *Virginia Baron: The Story of Thomas Sixth Lord Fairfax* (Berryville, Va.: Chesapeake Book Co., 1965), 101–23. Local tradition holds that James Wood named the town he surveyed *Winchester* after his home town in England. In the absence of documentary evidence to support this contention, however, the naming of the town after Fairfax's military mentor seems more likely.

20. Hening, *Statutes*, 6:268–70. On colonial legislation restricting the free ranging of hogs in Winchester, see, ibid., 7:411–12.

21. Andrew Burnaby, *Travels through the Middle Settlements in North America in the Years 1759 and 1760*, 3d ed. (London: T. Payne, 1798; New York: Augustus M. Kelley, 1970), 45; and Johann D. Schoepf, *Travels in the Confederation, 1783–1784*, 2 vols., trans. and ed. Alfred J. Morrison (Erlangen: Johann Jacob Plam, 1788; New York: Bergman Publishers, 1968), 2:59. On the absence of towns in eastern Virginia, see Lois Green Carr, "'The Metropolis of Maryland': A Comment on Town Development along the Tobacco Coast," *Maryland Historical Magazine* 69 (summer 1974): 124–45; Carville V. Earle and Ronald Hoffman, "Staple Crops and Urban Development in the Eighteenth-Century South," in *Perspectives in American History*, vol. 10, ed. Donald Fleming and Bernard Bailyn (Cambridge: Harvard UP, 1976), 7–78; Ronald E. Grim, "The Absence of Towns in Seventeenth-Century Virginia: The Emergence of Service Centers in York County" (Ph.D. diss., University of Maryland, 1977); Kevin P. Kelly, "'In dispers'd Country Plantations': Settlement Patterns in Seventeenth-Century Surry County, Virginia," in *The Chesapeake in the Seventeenth Century: Essays on Anglo-American Society*, ed. Thad W. Tate and David L. Ammerman (Chapel Hill: U of North Carolina P for the Institute of Early American History and Culture, 1979), 183–205; John C. Rainbolt, "The Absence of Towns in Seventeenth-Century Virginia," *Journal of Southern History* 35 (Aug. 1969): 343–60; and Edward M. Riley, "The Town Acts of Colonial Virginia," *Journal of Southern History* 16 (Aug. 1950): 306–23.

22. Account of Timothy Holdway, 1737–Jan. 3, 1739, Accounts, 1736–55, James Wood Family Papers; Receipt of Jonathan Littler, Mar. 11, 1737, James Wood Sr., Accounts, James Wood Collection; Receipt of James Wood to colonial secretary, Ac-

counts, James Wood Papers; Account of Wood with Harmer and King, Mar. 28, 1739–June 10, 1740, Accounts, 1736–55, James Wood Family Papers; Account of Wood with W. McKay, July 23, 1740, ibid.; Receipts to Wood, 1739–50, James Wood Sr., Indentured Servants, James Wood Collection; and Receipt of Mr. Rutherford, Apr. 30, 1742, Blacks folder, ibid.

23. Account of [William] Wilson, Aug. 26, 1745, James Wood Commonplace Book, James Wood Papers [10]; Receipt of Nicholas Mercer, July 9, 1742, Receipts, 1738–56, James Wood Family Papers; Account of Jacob Dye with James Wood and Robert Green, 1743–44, Accounts, 1736–55, ibid.; Account of Nicholas Fry, Mar. 21, 1747, James Wood Commonplace Book, James Wood Papers [25]; Account, May 18, 1745–May 23, 1746, Accounts, 1736–55, James Wood Family Papers; Account of James Carter, 1744–47, ibid.; Account of James Carter, June 16, 1747–Apr. 20, 1748, ibid.; Memorandum, Mar. 17, 1747, James Wood Commonplace Book, James Wood Papers [25]; Memoranda, June 6, 12, 16, 28, 1746, ibid. [18–19]; and Account of William Hand, Aug. 2, 1746, James Wood Account Book, James Wood Papers, 14.

24. Receipt of Joseph Lupton, Nov. 21, 1744, Receipts, 1738–56, James Wood Family Papers; Agreement with John O'Neal, Aug. 4, 1746, James Wood Commonplace Book, James Wood Papers [20]; Account of John O'Neal, Aug. 2–4, 1746, James Wood Account Book, James Wood Papers; Memorandum, Apr. 28, 1748, James Wood Commonplace Book, James Wood Papers [35]; Account of Jacob Nisewanger, Mar. 1746, James Wood Account Book, 5; Account of Joseph Lupton, May 24–Nov. 2, 1742, Accounts, 1736–55, James Wood Family Papers; Receipt of Joseph Lupton, Dec. 30, 1743, ibid.; Receipt of William Burk, Oct. 20, 1744, Receipts, 1738–56, ibid.; Cecil O'Dell, *Pioneers of Old Frederick County, Virginia* (Marceline, Mo.: Walsworth, 1995), 205; Memorandum regarding work of James, George, and Jonathan Bruce on meat house, Jan. 15, 1745, James Wood Commonplace Book, James Wood Papers [1]; Account of Hugh Parrell, Mar. 4, 1746, ibid. [16]; and Account of John Howard, July 17–Sept. 30, 1751, James Wood Account Book, 63.

25. Receipt of Michael Ewrey, May 7, 1744, Receipts, 1738–56, James Wood Family Papers; Account of James Gardener, Aug. 6, 1747, James Wood Account Book, James Wood Papers, 23; Account of William Wilson, Apr. 30, 1746, James Wood Account Book, 7; and Account of James Coulter, 1751–Aug. 1753, ibid., 76, 98.

26. Account of Benjamin Perreyra, Nov. 15, 1745–Jan. 22, 1748, Accounts, 1736–55, James Wood Family Papers; Account of Peter Tostee, July 3, 1746–June 16, 1747, and July 8, 1747–June 31, 1748, ibid.; Account of Benjamin Perreyra, 1746–Jan. 2, 1749, James Wood Account Book, James Wood Papers, 13; and Account of Peter Tostee, Apr. 18, 1746–Oct. 28, 1749, ibid., 8, 16, 37.

27. Account of Joseph Lupton, May 24, 1742, Accounts, 1736–55, James Wood Family Papers; Account of Lupton, Nov. 4, 1749–Aug. 1751, James Wood Account Book, James Wood Papers, 43; Receipt of Lupton, Dec. 30, 1743, Accounts, 1736–55, James Wood Family Papers; Receipt of Lupton, Nov. 24, 1744, Receipts, 1738–56, ibid.; Account of Lupton, n.d., ibid.; and O'Dell, *Pioneers of Old Frederick County*, 240–41.

28. Receipt of William Glover, Apr. 13, 1742, James Wood Sr., Accounts, James Wood Collection; Account of William Gilliam, Mar. 18, 1749–June 1751, James Wood

Account Book, James Wood Papers, 38; and O'Dell, *Pioneers of Old Frederick County,* 236–37, 244, 254.

29. Account of William Jolliffe, Oct. 5, 1742, Accounts, 1736–55, James Wood Family Papers; Account of Jonathan McMachen, Nov. 1743, ibid.; Account of Reuben Paxton, Mar. to June 30, 1748, James Wood Account Book, James Wood Papers, 31; O'Dell, *Pioneers of Old Frederick County,* 205–6; 247–48; and Northern Neck Grants, 1690–1874, H:635, K:27, 152, Library of Virginia.

30. Account of Samuel Pritchard, May 25, 1752, James Wood Account Book, James Wood Papers, 86; Account of Joseph Simons, Apr. 20, 1748, Accounts, 1736–55, James Wood Family Papers; and Account of Thomas, n.d., James Wood Account Book, 71.

31. Account of John Crowson with Thomas Chester, Dec. 3, 1744, *Chester v Crowson,* May 1745, Ended Causes, 1743–1909, FCCP; Account of John Davison with Bucket, Dec. 15, 1749–Sept. 20, 1750, *Bucket v Davison,* May 1751, ibid.; Inventory of James Vance, Feb. 12, 1752, Frederick County Wills (hereafter FCW), 2:17, Frederick County Courthouse, Winchester; Will of James Vance, Feb. 26, 1750, ibid., 1:495; and Account of William Branson with Lawrence Stephens, July 28, 1752–June 11, 1753, *Stephens v Branson,* Jan. 1753, Ended Causes, 1743–1909, FCCP.

32. Account of James Davis with John Shearer, Oct. 10, 1745–Aug. 1746, *Warth v Davis,* Feb. 1752, Ended Causes, 1743–1909, FCCP; and Account of Edward Rogers with Richard Rogers, 1746, *Rogers v Rogers,* Aug. 1747, ibid.

33. Account of David Jaycox with Jonathan Jaycox, 1744–46, *Jaycox admr. v Jaycox admr.,* May 1750, Ended Causes, 1743–1909, FCCP; Account of William Perkins with William Ramsay, Aug. 8, 1744–Mar. 9, 1746, *Ramsay v Perkins,* June 1752, ibid.; Account of Edward Rogers with Lewis Stevens, June 1743, *Stevens v Rogers,* Mar. 1746, ibid.; and Note of John Hardin to Christopher Holmes, Jan. 5, 1747, *Earle v Hardin,* Mar. 1753, ibid.

34. Note of John Self to John Hardin, n.d., *Hardin v Self,* Apr. 1745, Ended Causes, 1743–1909, FCCP; Note of Robert Edge to Hardin, Jan. 31, 1744, *Hardin v Edge,* Aug. 1748, ibid.; Account of Stephen Sebastian, May 1750–June 25, 1750, James Wood Account Book, James Wood Papers, 54; and Account of Philip Babb with Jonathan Heath, 1750–51, *Heath v Babb,* Dec. 1752, Ended Causes, 1743–1909, FCCP.

35. Order of Duncan O'Gullion to John Hardin, Aug. 8, 1744, *McCarmich v Hardin,* Nov. 1745, Ended Causes, 1743–1909, FCCP; O'Dell, *Pioneers of Old Frederick County,* 109; Bill of sale of John Hammond to Hardin, May 6, 1745, FCD, 1:211; Account of Jacob Hammon with Hardin, July 5, 1748–July 5, 1749, *Hardin v Hammon,* Sept. 1745, Ended Causes, 1743–1909, FCCP; Note of John Huston to Hardin, Mar. 18, 1745, *Hardin v Huston,* Aug. 1748, ibid.; and Note of Patrick Casey to Edward Nelson, Sept. 7, 1746, *Hardin v Casey,* Aug. 1749, ibid.

36. William Gooch to Board of Trade, July 3, 1739, CO 5/1324, Colonial Office Papers, Public Records Office (hereafter PRO), London; and Account of John Russell with John McCormick, n.d., *McCormick v Russell,* Aug. 1748, Ended Causes, 1743–1909, FCCP. On flax cultivation and the linen trade, see Kenneth W. Keller, "From the Rhineland to the Virginia Frontier: Flax Production as a Commercial Enterprise," *Virginia Magazine of History and Biography* 98 (July 1990): 487–511; and Robert D. Mit-

chell, *Commercialism and Frontier: Perspectives on the Early Shenandoah Valley* (Charlottesville: UP of Virginia, 1977), 135–42.

37. Inventory of James Colvill, Oct. 23, 1777, FCW, 4:373; and Inventory of Robert Glass, Sept. 4, 1797, FCW, 6:287. On flax production and processing at the Opequon settlement, see Warren R. Hofstra, "The Opequon Inventories, Frederick County, Virginia, 1749–1796," *Ulster Folklife* 35 (1989): 59–60. Inventories used in this study dated as late as the 1790s, but the items in them reflected a lifetime of productivity beginning in the 1730s and 1740s.

38. Account of John Smith Jr. with William Green, Nov. 1–3, 1746, *Green v Smith*, May 1751, Ended Causes, 1743–1909, FCCP; Account of Robert Eadmeston with Mary Ross, n.d., *Ross v Eadmeston*, May 1745, ibid.; Account of John Collings with George Keith Gibbons, 1748, *Gibbons v Collings*, Aug. 1750, ibid.; O'Dell, *Pioneers of Old Frederick County*, 156, 174; FCCO, 1:5; Account of Patrick Reily with Ferrol Reily and Tarrence Reily, 1745–46, *Reily v Reily*, Sept. 1749, Ended Causes, 1743–1909, FCCP; Account of Duncan O'Gullion with George Brown, 1748, *Brown v O'Gullion*, Aug. 1750, ibid.; and Account of O'Gullion with James Jackson, 1752, *Jackson v O'Gullion*, Mar. 1753, ibid.

39. Account of John Frost with Andrew Ross, Nov. 30, 1743, *Ross v Frost*, Sept. 1745, Ended Causes, 1743–1909, FCCP; Account of Lyman Lipman with Benjamin Perreyra, Apr. 15, 1747–Sept. 5, 1748, *Perreyra v Lipman*, Nov. 1749, ibid.; Account of Robert Lemon with Peter Tostee, July 25, 1748–Feb. 3, 1749, *Tostee v R. Lemon*, June 1749, ibid.; Account of James M. McCoy with Peter Tostee, Oct. 31–Dec. 19, 1748, *Tostee v McCoy*, June 1749, ibid.; Account of James Lemon with Tostee, July 18–Dec. 3, 1748, *Tostee v Lemon*, Dec. 1749, ibid.; Account of George Brown with Tostee, Dec. 1, 1747–Aug. 29, 1749, *Tostee v Brown*, Feb. 1750, ibid.; Account of Murty Hanly with Tostee, Apr. 5–Oct. 2, 1749, *Tostee v Hanly*, May 1750, ibid.; Account of Robert Hutchings with Tostee, Oct. 17, 1749, *Tostee v Hutchins*, May 1750, ibid.; Account of John Lane with Tostee, Oct. 31, 1747–July 4, 1749, *Tostee v Lane*, June 1750, ibid.; and Account of William Bennet with Peter Tostee, Sept. 1, 1748–Jan. 30, 1750, *Tostee v Bennet*, Oct. 1752, ibid.

40. Note of Richard Mercer to Abraham Hollingsworth, Oct. 1744, *Hollingsworth v Mercer*, Aug. 1746, Ended Causes, 1743–1909, FCCP; Note of John Lemon to Phillip Babb, June 10, 1749, *Babb v Lemon*, Sept. 1749, ibid.; Note of John Nealand to Jost Hite, Jan. 13, 1742, *Hite v Nealand*, Sept. 1744, ibid.; Note of Nealand to Isaac Hite, Feb. 18, 1744, *Hite v Nealand*, Sept. 1744, ibid.; Note of John Nealand to Jost Hite, Aug. 17, 1742, *Hite v Nealand*, Sept. 1744, ibid.; Note of Thomas Rennick to Waller Drenen, Feb. 1, 1744, *Drenen v Rennick*, Aug. 1746, ibid.; and Account of Moses Downor with Epharim McDowell, n.d., *McDowell v Downor*, Sept. 1747, ibid.

41. Hening, *Statutes*, 4:96–99, 301–2, 5:357–59; Inventory of James Vance, Feb. 12, 1752, FCW, 2:17; H. R. McIlwaine, ed., *Journals of the House of Burgesses of Virginia, 1742–1744, 1748–1749* (Richmond: Virginia State Library, 1909), 298–99; and Mitchell, *Commercialism and Frontier*, 162–67.

42. Complaint of Joseph Colvill against John Buller, 1749, *Colvin* (Colvill) *v Buller*, June 1750, Ended Causes, 1743–1909, FCCP; Account of Duncan O'Gullion with Ed-

ward Rogers, Sept. 12, 1745, *Rogers v O'Gullion,* Aug. 1749, ibid.; and Hofstra, "Opequon Inventories," 64. On fence law in eighteenth-century Virginia, see Hening, *Statutes,* 3:279–82; 6:38–40.

43. Richard Poulston to Richard Snowden, May 7, 1743, *Snowden v Poulston,* Sept. 1746, Ended Causes, 1743–1909, FCCP; George Washington to Robert Dinwiddie, Aug. 4, 1756, *The Papers of George Washington,* 10 vols., Colonial Series, ed. W. W. Abbot et al. (Charlottesville: UP of Virginia, 1983–95), 3:318; Account of James Rutledge with Robert Willson, n.d., *Willson v Rutledge,* Feb. 1744, ibid.; and Account of Hugh Parker with Andrew Campbell, Sept. 8, 1746–Aug. 1, 1747, *Parker v Campbell,* Oct. 1752, ibid.

44. Note of Absalom Haworth to Mathias Elmore, Jan. 11, 1744, *Elmore v Haworth,* Mar. 1748, Ended Causes, 1743–1909, FCCP; Account of John Burris with Andrew Campbell, Dec. 23, 1741–Jan. 20, 1745, *Campbell v Burris,* May 1745, ibid.; FCD, 1:215; Account of Solomon Hedges with Peter Tostee, May 16, 1746–Oct. 14, 1747, *Tostee v Hedges,* Aug. 1750, ibid.; Account of Richard Morgan with Tostee, Jan. 27, 1750–Aug. 14, 1751, *Tostee v Morgan,* Aug. 1752, ibid.; and Account of Tostee with Morgan, Aug. 25, 1750, *Morgan v Tostee,* Feb. 1752, ibid.

45. Account of Enoch Anderson with William Mitchell, Oct. 20, 1739–Feb. 13, 1740, *Mitchell v Anderson,* Sept. 1744, Ended Causes, 1743–1909, FCCP; Account of Hugh Ferguson with Bryan Roark, Aug. 16–Oct. 2, 1745, *Roark v Ferguson,* Aug. 1748, ibid.; Account of John Nealand with Edward Nelson, 1750, *Nelson v Nealand,* Aug. 1752, ibid.; Account of Neal Thompson with Ralph Falkner, Nov. 29, 1743, *Falkner v Thompson,* Apr. 1745, ibid.; Account of Reuben Paxton with Thomas Doster, Dec. 1, 1747–May 3, 1748, *Doster v Paxton,* June 1749, ibid.; Account of Edward Mercer with Jonathan Littler, 1743, *Littler v Mercer,* Mar. 1745, ibid.; Account of William Howell, 1750, *Earle v Howell,* May 1751, ibid.; Agreement of John Wilcocks with Gresham Keys, 1758, *Wilcocks v Keys,* Jan. 1758, ibid.; Account of Joseph West with John Nealand, 1748, *Nealand v West,* Aug. 1748, ibid.; and Account of Duncan O'Gullion with George Brown, 1748, *Brown v O'Gullion,* Aug. 1750, ibid.

46. Account of William Senter with Robert Lemon, May 25–Aug. 20, 1751, *Lemon v Senter,* Aug. 1752, Ended Causes, 1743–1909, FCCP; Account of Barnett Lynsey with Samuel Walker, 1743–45, *Walker v Linsay,* May 1745, ibid.; and Account of Stepto Clark with Peter Tostee, June 29–July 16, 1750, *Tostee v Clark,* June 1752, ibid.

47. Account of James Willson with Jeremiah Cloud, Nov. 1748, *Cloud v Willson,* May 1751, Ended Causes, 1743–1909, FCCP; and Account James Rutledge with Thomas Rennick, 1745, *Rennick v Rutledge,* Aug. 1749, ibid.

48. John Bartram to Peter Collinson, July 18 [1739], *The Correspondence of John Bartram, 1735–1777,* ed. Edmund Berkeley and Dorothy Smith Berkeley (Gainesville: UP of Florida, 1992), 122; and William Gooch to Board of Trade, Feb. 22, 1739, CO 5/1324, PRO.

49. H. R. McIlwaine, Wilmer L. Hall, and Benjamin J. Hillman, eds., *Executive Journals of the Council of Colonial Virginia,* 6 vols. (Richmond: Virginia State Library, 1925–66), 4:349, 371; Hening, *Statutes,* 5:54–57, 355–57, 3:356–58; Commission from William Gooch to James Wood as collector of duties on skins and furs, Apr. 8, 1739, in Katherine Glass Greene, *Winchester, Virginia and Its Beginnings, 1743–1814* (Strasburg,

Va.: Shenandoah Publishing House, 1926), 18–19. On the movement of Native Americans into the Ohio Valley beginning in the 1720s, see Michael N. McConnell, *A Country Between: The Upper Ohio Valley and Its Peoples, 1724–1774* (Lincoln: U of Nebraska P, 1992), 5–46; and Daniel K. Richter, *The Ordeal of the Longhouse: The Peoples of the Iroquois League in the Era of European Colonization* (Chapel Hill: U of North Carolina P for the Institute of Early American History and Culture, 1992), 256, 270, 273–75.

50. Charles Dick to Daniel Hart, Feb. 26, 1748, Dr. Daniel Hart folder, James Wood Collection; Note of James McCoy and James McKee to Peter Tostee, Aug. 4, 1746, *Tostee v McCoy et al.*, Sept. 1747, Ended Causes, 1743–1909, FCCP; and Account of Hugh Ferguson, Oct. 2, 1745, *Roark v Ferguson*, Aug. 1748, ibid. On the payment of duties on skins and furs by Hite, Tostee, and others at Opequon, see accounts by name in James Wood Account Book, James Wood Papers, 7, 8, 11, 12, 13, 16, 31, 32. On Andrew Campbell's activities, see FCCO, 1:74, 143; Account of Campbell, Oct. 1745, James Wood Account Book, James Wood Papers, 2; Account of Peter Bradford, Jan. 1–Feb. 29, 1744, *Campbell v Bradford*, Aug. 1746, Ended Causes, 1743–1909, FCCP; and Account of Campbell with Tostee, Dec. 7, 1747, *Campbell v Tostee*, Oct. 1752, ibid.

51. Account of William Howell with Samuel Earle, 1750, *Earle v Howard*, May 1751, Ended Causes, 1743–1909, FCCP; and Account of William Goodchild with Robert Pearis, June 14, 1752–Aug. 29, 1753, *Pearis v Goodchild*, Nov. 1752, ibid. On the number and variety of artisans, see the Ended Causes, 1743–1909, FCCP, the James Wood Papers, the James Wood Family Papers, the James Wood Collection, and the Index of Early Southern Artists and Artisans, Museum of Early Southern Decorative Arts, Winston-Salem, N.C.

52. Account of John Russell with John McCormick, n.d., *McCormick v Russell*, Aug. 1748, Ended Causes, 1743–1909, FCCP; Account of Duncan O'Gullion with James Jackson, 1752, *Jackson v O'Gullion*, May 1753, ibid.; Account of Benjamin Perreyra with Mary Bailey, Aug. 3, 1748, *Bailey v Perreyra*, Aug. 1749, ibid.; Account of Peter Tostee with John Wilcock, May 8, 1749, *Wilcock v Tostee*, May 1749, ibid.; Account of O'Gullion with George Brown, 1748, *Brown v O'Gullion*, Aug. 1750, ibid.; Account of O'Gullion with Roger Burkum, 1743, *Burkum v O'Gullion*, Feb. 1744, ibid.; and Account of William Randles with Barnett Warde, n.d., *Warde v Randles*, May 1751, ibid.

53. Petition of Rose Bignal to the Frederick County Court, n.d., and Account of Rose Bignal with Thomas Williams, 1746, *Williams v Bignal*, June 1746, Ended Causes, 1743–1909, FCCP; Account of John Casey, loose paper, Sept. 1748, ibid.; and Complaint of Isabella Rob against Richard Rogers, Nov. 1745, and Account of Rob with Rogers, 1745, *Rogers v Rob*, Mar. 1746, ibid.

54. Account of Frederick Gabbard with Thomas Gray, Dec. 1745, *Gray v Gabbard*, Mar. 1747, Ended Causes, 1743–1909, FCCP; Account of Neale Ogullin with Harvey Porter, May 25, 1750, *Porter v Ogullin*, May 1751, ibid.; Note of Thomas Rutherford to Jacob Penington, Jan. 3, 1746, *Penington v Rutherford*, Aug. 8, 1748, ibid.; and FCD, 3:16.

55. Complaint of Isaac Baker against John Nealand, 1745, *Baker v Nealand*, Apr. 1745, Ended Causes, 1743–1909, FCCP; A List of Tithables in the Dominion of Virginia, 175[4], CO 5/1328, PRO; Raymond Chester Young, "The Effects of the French and Indian War on Civilian Life in the Frontier Counties of Virginia, 1754–1763"

(Ph.D. diss., Vanderbilt University, 1969), 436; Complaint of William McMachen against Dorothy Cartmell, 1745, *McMachen v Cartmell*, Oct. 1746, Ended Causes, 1743–1909, FCCP; Complaint of Thomas Chester against Cartmell, Jan. 6, 1746, *Chester v Cartmell*, Apr. 1748, ibid.; and Will of Cartmell, Apr. 20, 1749, FCW, 1:412.

56. Complaint of Duncan O'Gullion against James Lemon, 1758, *O'Gullion v Lemon*, Feb. 1758, Ended Causes, 1743–1909, FCCP; Account of Ralph Humphreys with William Picket, 1741, *Picket v Humphreys*, Aug. 1748, ibid.; and Account of Charles Buck with Daniel Hart, 1748, *Wood and Calmes, Extr. v Charles Buck*, Aug. 1749, ibid. Although it was not common, Indian slavery did exist in Frederick County. See Account of John Ramsey with William Mitchell, 1745, *Mitchell v Ramsey*, Nov. 1751, ibid.

57. Note of Alice Anderson to Ralph Falkner and John Muschett, n.d., *Falkner v Anderson*, Sept. 1745, Ended Causes, 1743–1909, FCCP; and Note of Ann Johnson to William Picket, Mar. 18, 1747, *Picket v Johnson*, Mar. 1748, ibid. On the doctrine of *feme covert*, William Blackstone stated that "by marriage the husband and wife are one person in law: that is, the very being or legal existence of the woman is suspended during the marriage, or at least is incorporated and consolidated into that of the husband: under whose wing, protection, and *cover*, she performs every thing." See William Blackstone, *Commentaries on the Laws of England, Book the First*, 4th ed. (Dublin: John Exshaw, Henry Saunders, Boulter Grierson, & James Williams, 1771), 442.

58. Account of Gilbert Parker with Margaret Ramsey, n.d., *Ramsey et ux v Parker*, admr., May 1751, Ended Causes, 1743–1909, FCCP; Account of John Stewart with Sarah Williamson, Feb. 1752, *Williamson v Stewart*, Apr. 1753, ibid.; Note of John Burris to Sarah Shepherd, 1744, *Shepherd v Burris*, June 1745, ibid.; Account of James McCracken with Ann Lilburn, 1745, *Lilburn v McCracken*, June 1745, ibid.; Account of Robert Eadmeston with Mary Ross, n.d., *Ross v Eadmeston*, May 1745, ibid.; Account of Rachel Hood with William Griffiths, Nov. 24, 1743, *Griffiths v Hood*, Oct. 1744, ibid.; and Account of Sarah Davis with Peter Tostee, Oct. 29, 1750, *Tostee v Davis*, June 1752.

59. Considering the importance of keeping accounts for economic activity in early America, scholarship on the subject is surprisingly sparse. See W. T. Baxter, "Accounting in Colonial America," in A. C. Littleton and B. S. Yamey, eds., *Studies in the History of Accounting* (New York: Arno Press, 1978), 272–87; Stuart Bruchey, "Success and Failure Factors: American Merchants in Foreign Trade in the Eighteenth and Early Nineteenth Centuries," *Business History Review* 32 (autumn 1958): 272–92; Michael Chatfield, *A History of Accounting Thought* (Huntington, N.Y.: Robert E. Krieger, 1977), 32–43; Peter A. Coclanis, "Bookkeeping in the Eighteenth-Century South: Evidence from Newspaper Advertisements," *South Carolina Historical Magazine* 91 (Jan. 1990):23–31; A. C. Littleton, *Accounting Evolution to 1900* (New York: American Institute Publishing, 1933; New York: Garland, 1988), 41–122; John J. McCusker and Russell R. Menard, *The Economy of British America, 1607–1789* (Chapel Hill: U of North Carolina P for the Institute of Early American History and Culture, 1985): 344–46; Gary John Previts and Barbara Dubis Merino, *A History of Accountancy in the United States: The Cultural Significance of Accounting* (Columbus: Ohio State UP, 1998), 25–27; and Winifred Barr Rothenberg, *From Market-Places to a Market Economy: The Transformation of Rural Massachusetts, 1750–1850* (Chicago: U of Chicago P, 1992), 61–65.

60. For acts passed by the House of Burgesses for encouraging the founding of towns, see Hening, *Statutes*, 2:172–76, 471–78, 508, 3:53–69, 108–9, 186–89, 404–19. In contrast to Shenandoah Valley towns, Camden, South Carolina, is described by Joseph A. Ernst and H. Roy Merrens as a collecting point for the regional export of agricultural commodities. See Ernst and Merrens, "'Camden's turrets pierce the skies!': The Urban Process in the Southern Colonies during the Eighteenth Century," *William and Mary Quarterly*, 3d ser., 30 (Oct. 1973): 549–74.

61. Account of Mary Hoge with George Hoge, 1750, and Account of George Hoge with Mary Hoge, 1750, *Hoge v Hoge*, Aug. 1751, Ended Causes, 1743–1909, FCCP; Account of Edward Mercer with Jonathan Littler, 1743, *Littler v Mercer*, Mar. 1745, ibid.; O'Dell, *Pioneers of Old Frederick County*, 49, 193–95, 309–13, 344; and Account of Edward Rogers with Lewis Stevens, June 1743, *Stevens v Rogers*, Mar. 1746, ibid.

62. The role of accounting in the history of science and reason in the early modern world is a partially explored field of great potential. See Bruce G. Carruthers and Wendy Nelson Espeland, "Accounting for Rationality: Double-Entry Bookkeeping and the Rhetoric of Economic Rationality," *American Journal of Sociology* 97 (July 1991): 31–69; Barry E. Cushing, "A Kuhnian Interpretation of the Historical Evolution of Accounting," *Accounting Historians Journal* 16 (Dec. 1989): 1–41; Littleton, *Accounting Evolution*, 12–40; and Previts and Merino, *History of Accountancy*, 19–21.

63. James Wood Account Book, James Wood Papers, 8, 16, 27, 49.

64. Note of Richard Abell to Michael Campbell, Aug. 29, 1747, Account of Richard Abell with Michael Campbell, Oct. 11, 1745–Aug. 29, 1747, and Note of Richard Abell to Robert Hamilton, Feb. 28, 1745, *Campbell v Abell*, Sept. 1749, Ended Causes, 1743–1909, FCCP.

65. Order of William Mitchell to Richard Morgan, Feb. 2, 1748, *Morgan v Mitchell*, Aug. 1748, Ended Causes, 1743–1909, FCCP; and Account of Daniel O'Neill with Stephen Hotsinpiller, 1748, *Hotsinpiller v O'Neill*, Feb. 1751, Ended Causes, 1743–1909, FCCP.

66. Account of Thomas Balch with John Arnold, n.d., *Arnold v Balch*, Aug. 1751, Ended Causes, 1743–1909, FCCP; and Account of John Smith Jr. with William Green, Nov. 13, 1746, *Green v Smith*, May 1751, ibid.

67. Account of Samuel Dark with Thomas Hart, Dec. 11, 1747–Apr. 30 1751, *Hart v Dark*, Nov. 1751, Ended Causes, 1743–1909, FCCP; O'Dell, *Pioneers of Old Frederick County*, 115–16; Petition of John Carson to Frederick County Court, Oct. 1743, *Carson v Hart*, Nov. 1743, ibid.; Note of Thomas Hart to Joseph Shippen, 1743, *Shippen v Hart*, May 1744, ibid.; and Receipt of Thomas Rutherford to Joseph Shippen, May 13, 1745, *Shippen v Rutherford*, Oct. 1752, ibid.

68. Account of Edward Shippen, 1744 to June 3, 1747, James Wood Account Book, James Wood Papers, 2; Note of Joseph Cloud to John Harris, Oct. 9, 1739, *Harris v Cloud*, May 1745, Ended Causes, 1743–1909, FCCP; O'Dell, *Pioneers of Old Frederick County*, 76, 361–62, 396–97; Account of Charles Kellar with Shippen, Jan. 7, 1737–Aug. 17, 1738, *Shippen v Kellar*, May 1744, ibid.; Note of John Ellis to John Harris, June 7, 1740, *Harris v Ellis*, Sept. 1745, ibid.; Account of Thomas Williams with Ulrich Poker,

Aug. 9, 1745, *Poker v Williams*, May 1747, ibid.; and Account of Lyman Lipman with Ulrich Poker, 1747, *Poker v Lipman*, May 1750, ibid.

69. Account of Thomas Rutherford with William Ramsay, Mar. 19, 1749–Aug. 1750, *Ramsay v Rutherford*, Feb. 1752, Ended Causes, 1743–1909, FCCP; Account of Benjamin Borden Jr. with Robert Rae, May 31, 1742–Nov. 8, 1743, *Ray and Campbell v Burden*, Nov. 1752, ibid.; Note of Daniel Burnett to John Carlyle, Feb. 18, 1745, *Carlyle v Burnett*, Mar. 1746, ibid.; Account of John Wood with Andrew Cochrane and Company, Nov. 6, 1751–June 2, 1752, *Cochrane and Co. v Wood*, Sept. 1752, ibid.; Account of John Wood with Daniel and Alex Campbell, Oct. 15, 1748–May 12, 1749, *Campbell v Wood*, Sept. 1752, ibid.; and T. M. Devine, *The Tobacco Lords: A Study of the Tobacco Merchants of Glasgow and Their Trading Activities* (Edinburgh: Edinburgh UP, 1990), 36, 178–79.

70. Account of Richard Cronk with Robert Lowther, Nov. 1749, *Cronk v Lowther*, Aug. 1746, Ended Causes, 1743–1909, FCCP; Account of Robert Shedden with John Bozier, n.d., *Robert and Thomas Dunlop v Bozier*, Aug. 1751, ibid.; Note of Cronk to Shedden, June 27, 1744, *Shedden v Cronk*, June 1745, ibid.; Note of Cronk to Daniel Campbell, Apr. 18, 1744, *Shedden v Simmons*, June 1745, ibid.; and Account of Cronk with John Neil, 1744, *Neil v Cronk*, Mar. 1745, ibid.

71. Throughout the eighteenth century, double- and single-entry accounting served more often for tracking debits and credits in personal accounts than for analyzing economic performance or decision making. See Chatfield, *Accounting Thought*, 56–61; Littleton, *Accounting Evolution*, 84–85; Basil S. Yamey, "Scientific Bookkeeping and the Rise of Capitalism," *Economic History Review*, 2d ser., 1 (1949): 99–113; and Yamey, "Accounting and the Rise of Capitalism: Further Notes of a Theme by Sombart," *Journal of Accounting Research* 2 (autumn 1964): 117–36.

CHAPTER 6. From Strategic Place to Central Place

1. William W. Hening, ed., *The Statutes at Large: Being a Collection of All the Laws of Virginia, from . . . 1619 . . .*, 13 vols. (Richmond, New York, and Philadelphia, 1819–23), 6:268–70; and Northern Neck Grants, 1690–1874, H, K, L, W, S, Library of Virginia, Richmond.

2. William J. Hinke and Charles E. Kemper, eds., "Moravian Diaries of Travels through Virginia," *Virginia Magazine of History and Biography* 22 (July 1904): 141.

3. William M. Beauchamp, ed., *Moravian Journals Relating to Central New York, 1745–66* (Syracuse, N.Y.: Onondaga Historical Association, 1916), 18; Francis Jennings, *Empire of Fortune: Crowns, Colonies, and Tribes in the Seven Years War in America* (New York: W. W. Norton, 1988), 54–58; and Michael N. McConnell, *A Country Between: The Upper Ohio Valley and Its Peoples, 1724–1774* (Lincoln: U of Nebraska P, 1992), 39–40.

4. William Fairfax, "Report as a faithful narrative of my proceedings with certain chiefs of the six United Nations of Indians and their Allies," in Josiah Look Dickinson, *The Fairfax Proprietary* (Front Royal, Va.: Warren Press, 1959): 137.

5. Ibid., 137–38.

6. Ibid., 148, 144, 143.

7. Samuel Hazard, ed., *Minutes of the Provincial Council of Pennsylvania*, 16 vols. (Harrisburg: Theo. Fenn, 1838–53), 5:537, as quoted in McConnell, *A Country Between*, 94; Robert Dinwiddie to Thomas Cresap and William Trent, Feb. 10, 1753, in Robert A. Brock, ed., *The Official Records of Robert Dinwiddie . . .*, 2 vols. (Richmond: Virginia Historical Society, 1883), 1:22–24; Dinwiddie to James Glen, Apr. 15, 1754, in ibid., 1:129; Dinwiddie to Board of Trade, Mar. 12, 1754, in ibid., 1:99; Dinwiddie to Thomas Robinson, June 18, 1754, in ibid., 1:201–5; and Robert Orme, "Journal," in Winthrop Sargent, *The History of an Expedition against Fort Du Quesne in 1755 under Major-General Edward Braddock* (Philadelphia: J. B. Lippincott for the Historical Society of Pennsylvania, 1856), 287, 309. See also Louis Knott Koontz, *Robert Dinwiddie, His Career in American Colonial Government and Westward Expansion* (Glendale, Calif.: Arthur H. Clark, 1941; Freeport, N.Y.: Books for Libraries Press, 1970), 195, 255, 314–17.

8. James Patton to John Blair, Jan. 1753, Draper Manuscripts, 1QQ175, State Historical Society of Wisconsin, Madison, Wis., as quoted in Kenneth P. Bailey, *The Ohio Company of Virginia and the Westward Movement, 1748–1792: A Chapter in the History of the Colonial Frontier* (Glendale, Calif.: Arthur H. Clark, 1939), 22–24; and Otis K. Rice, *The Allegheny Frontier: West Virginia Beginnings, 1730–1830* (Lexington: UP of Kentucky, 1970), 34.

9. Petition of John Hanbury to the king, 1748, CO 5/1327, Colonial Office Papers, Public Record Office (hereafter PRO), London, as quoted in Koontz, *Robert Dinwiddie*, 166; Bailey, *Ohio Company of Virginia*, 23–29; and Alfred P. James, *The Ohio Company: Its Inner History* (Pittsburgh: U of Pittsburgh P, 1959), 9–27.

10. Minutes of the Ohio Company, June 21, 1749, as quoted in James, *Ohio Company*, 24; and Minutes of the Ohio Company, Jan. 29, 1750, as quoted in ibid., 33–34. See also ibid., 36–80; and Bailey, *Ohio Company of Virginia*, 17–82.

11. W. L. Grant, James Munro, and Almeric W. Fitzroy, eds., *Acts of the Privy Council of England, Colonial Series*, 6 vols. (London: HMSO, 1910–12; Nendeln, Liechtenstein: Kraus Reprint, 1966), 4:134.

12. Roland-Michel Barrin, marquis de La Galissonnière, to Chev. de Longueuil, Oct. 1748, in Edmund Bailey O'Callaghan and Berthold Fernow, eds., *Documents Relative to the Colonial History of the State of New-York*, 15 vols. (Albany: Weed, Parsons, 1853–87), 10:161, as quoted in McConnell, *A Country Between*, 82–83; George Croghan to [?], July 3, 1749, in Samuel Hazard, ed., *Pennsylvania Archives*, 1st ser. (Philadelphia: Joseph Severns, 1852), 2:31, as quoted in ibid., 90. See also McConnell, *A Country Between*, 61–62, 74–77.

13. George Washington, Mar. 16, 1748, in Donald Jackson and Dorothy Twohig, eds., *The Diaries of George Washington*, 6 vols. (Charlottesville: UP of Virginia, 1976–80), 1:10–11; Washington to Dinwiddie, Apr. 27, 1756, in *The Papers of George Washington*, 10 vols., Colonial Series, ed. W. W. Abbot et al. (Charlottesville: UP of Virginia, 1983–95), 3:59; and Washington to Richard [1749–50], in ibid., 1:44. On Washington's landholdings, see Philander D. Chase, "A Stake in the West: George Washington as

Backcountry Surveyor and Landholder," in *George Washington and the Virginia Backcountry*, ed. Warren R. Hofstra (Madison, Wis.: Madison House, 1998), 177.

14. Douglas Southall Freeman, *George Washington: A Biography*, 7 vols. (New York: Charles Scribner's Sons, 1948–57), 1:268, 273, 2:111–13.

15. Instructions from Robert Dinwiddie, Aug. 14, 1755, in Abbot et al., *Papers of George Washington*, 2:5; Adam Stephen to George Washington, Oct. 4, 1755, in ibid., 2: 272; and Washington to Dinwiddie, Oct. 11, 1755, in ibid., 2:101.

16. Washington to Dinwiddie, Oct. 11, 1755, in Abbot et al., *Papers of George Washington*, Oct. 11, 1755, 2:103–4.

17. Ibid., 101, 104; and Washington to John Robinson, Apr. 16, 1756, in ibid., 3:6.

18. Washington to Dinwiddie, Apr. 24, 1756, in ibid., 3:45; and Washington to John Bacon, Oct. 26, 1755, in ibid., 2:137. On the need for Indian allies, see Washington to Christopher Gist, Oct. 10, 1755, and Washington to Andrew Lewis, Oct. 27, 1755, in ibid., 2:98–99, 140–41.

19. Washington to Stephen, Nov. 18, 1755, in Abbot et al., *Papers of George Washington*, 2:172; Dinwiddie to Washington, May 16, 1757, in ibid., 4:153; Freeman, *George Washington*, 2:198, 218, 249–50, 303, 309, 310; Hening, *Statutes*, 6:544–50; and Washington to John Blair, Apr. 9, 1758, in Abbot et al., *Papers of George Washington*, 5:113–14.

20. Washington to Dinwiddie, Apr. 7. 1756, in Abbot et al., *Papers of George Washington*, 2:334; Washington to John Robinson, Apr. 24, 1756, in ibid., 3:49–49; and Hening, *Statutes*, 7:9–20.

21. Washington to Robinson, Apr. 24, 1756, in Abbot et al., *Papers of George Washington*, 3:48–50; Washington to Dinwiddie, Apr. 27, 1756, in ibid., 3:60–61.

22. H. R. McIlwaine, ed., *Journals of the House of Burgesses of Virginia, 1752–1755, 1756–1758* (Richmond: Virginia State Library, 1909), 393; Dinwiddie to Washington, May 3, 1756, in Abbot et al., *Papers of George Washington*, 3:85; Washington to Fairfax, June 26, 1756, in ibid., 4:260; and Washington to Dinwiddie, May 23, 1756, in ibid., 3:173. For the act calling for the construction of a fort at Winchester, see Hening, *Statutes*, 7:26–33.

23. Washington, orders, July 25, 1756, in Abbot et al., *Papers of George Washington*, 3:291; and Andrew Burnaby, *Travels through the Middle Settlements in North America in the Years 1759 and 1760*, 3d ed. (London: T. Payne, 1798; New York: Augustus M. Kelley, 1970), 74–75. Fort Loudoun was named for John Campbell, earl of Loudoun, governor of Virginia, 1756–59, and commander in chief of British forces in America. Dinwiddie was technically lieutenant governor in the place of Loudoun.

24. Washington, orders, Aug. 7, 1756, in Abbot et al., *Papers of George Washington*, 3:339; Washington to Charles Lewis, June 4, 1756, in ibid., 3:198; Washington, orders, July 30, 1756, in ibid., 3:300; and Washington, orders, June 1, 1756, in ibid., 3:188. William Peachy, 1729–1802, served as captain in the Virginia Regiment from September 1755 until July 1757.

25. Washington, orders, Apr. 24, 1756, in Abbot et al., *Papers of George Washington*, 3:44; Washington to Stephen, May 18, 1756, in ibid., 3:157; Receipt Book, 1755–58, 5r, Virginia Colonial Militia Accounts, George Washington Papers, Series 5, Library of

Congress, Washington, D.C. (hereafter Receipt Book); and Memorandum respecting Militia, May 16, 1756, in Abbot et al., *Papers of George Washington*, 3:137–38. Daily wages paid to carpenters, masons, and smiths were fixed by the House of Burgesses in legislation regulating the affairs of the Virginia Regiment. See Hening, *Statutes*, 7:26–33; and Receipt Book. For payments to Kennedy, Riddle, and Vauts, see Receipt Book, 3v, 72r.

26. Hening, *Statutes*, 7:19.

27. Account of Benjamin Perreyra with George Brown, 1749, *Brown v Perreyra*, Dec. 1749, Ended Causes, 1743–1909, Frederick County Court Papers, Library of Virginia; Account of John Russell with John McCormick, n.d., *McCormick v Russell*, Aug. 1748, ibid.; Account of Mathias Ardis with Isaac Hite, Feb. 23–June 25, 1747, *Hite v Ardis*, Aug. 1749, ibid.; Account of Duncan O'Gullion with George Brown, 1748, *Brown v O'Gullion*, Aug. 1750, ibid.; and Account of Robert Worthington with David Crage, Mar.–July 1744, *Crage v Worthington*, June 1749, ibid.

28. Washington to Dinwiddie, June 27, 1757, in Abbot et al., *Papers of George Washington*, 4:264–65; Washington, orders, June 1, 1756, in ibid., 3:189 n. 1; Washington to Dinwiddie, Nov. 24, 1756, in ibid., 4:29–30; and Return of the Virginia Regiment, Jan. 1, 1757, in ibid., 4:76–77.

29. Washington to Joshua Lewis, June 6, 1757, in Abbot et al., *Papers of George Washington*, 4:181; Washington to Dinwiddie, Oct. 11, 1756, in ibid., 2:106; Washington to Thomas Walker, Nov. 11, 1755, in ibid., 2:167–68; Raymond Chester Young, "The Effects of the French and Indian War on Civilian Life in the Frontier Counties of Virginia, 1754–1763" (Ph.D. diss., Vanderbilt University, 1969), 218, 239–45; and Account of John Buchanan, Sept. 29, 1757, Draper Manuscripts, 1QQ142–45. Even before the Virginia Regiment was formed, Shenandoah Valley residents attempted to profit from the procurement of provisions for the military. A member of the Hite family, for instance, had a contract with Charles Dick to supply five hundred beef cattle to General Braddock's army. See Dinwiddie to Edward Braddock, May 23, 1755, in Brock, *Records of Dinwiddie*, 2:40–42; Orme, "Journal," 315; and Young, "Effects of the French and Indian War," 222–23.

30. Receipt Book, 7v, 5r, 51r, 43r, 75r, 60r, 62r, 6v, 63r, 60r, 5v; Washington to Walker, Jan. 10, 1756, in Abbot et al., *Papers of George Washington*, 2:270; and Washington, orders, Aug. 7, 1756, in ibid., 3:339. Opportunities for soldiers in the Virginia Regiment to earn extra income continued after the fall of Fort Dusquesne in 1758. In 1761 Daniel Morgan, of Revolutionary War fame, received £1 4s. for carrying messages between Forts Pitt and Venango. See Receipt of Daniel Morgan, Jan. 28, 1761, Accounts and receipts relating to Fort Pitt, Penn., 1760–61, Robert Monckton Papers, 1742–1834, vol. 40, Northcliffe Collection, National Archives of Canada, Ottawa.

31. Receipt Book, 78r, 81r.

32. Charles Dick and Fielding Lewis to John Greenfield, deed, Aug. 30, 1757, Frederick County Deeds, 4:293, Frederick County Courthouse, Winchester; John Greenfield and Mary, his wife, to Charles Smith, deed, May 26, 1758, in ibid., 4:362; James Pitcher to Alexander Wodrow and John Nelson, deed, Aug. 24, 1756, in ibid., 4:13; Mary Wood to Wodrow, deed, Aug. 31, 1761, in ibid., 6:384; John Nevil to James Craik,

Charles Smith, Robert Phillips, and Wodrow, deed, Dec. 2, 1761, in ibid., 6:446; Council of War, July 10, 1756, in Abbot et al., *Papers of George Washington*, 3:246, 402–3 n. 5; Receipt Book, 47r, 6v; Frederick County Poll Sheet, 1758, in Abbot et al., *Papers of George Washington*, 5:334; and ibid., 1:152–53 n. 4, 9.

33. Greenfield to Bryan Bruin, deed, Feb. 9, 1758, FCD, 5:135; Owen Jones Letterbook, 1759–1781, Owen Jones Papers, 1759–1824, Historical Society of Pennsylvania, Philadelphia; and Thomas M. Doerflinger, *A Vigorous Spirit of Enterprise: Merchants and Economic Development in Revolutionary Philadelphia* (Chapel Hill: U of North Carolina P for the Institute of Early American History and Culture, 1986), 96–97. For details of Bryan Bruin's extensive activities buying and selling land, see FCD, 4–21.

34. List of Bonds for the Lots, James Wood Commonplace Book [1745], James Wood Papers, Glen Burnie Museum, Winchester [6]. For records of ordinary licenses, see Frederick County Court Orders (hereafter FCCO), 1–8, Frederick County Courthouse; and James Wood Account Book, James Wood Papers.

35. Washington, orders, Sept. 15, 1755, in Abbot et al., *Papers of George Washington*, 2:39; Washington, orders, July 22, 1756, in ibid., 3:281–82; FCCO, 7:97, 135; Washington, orders, Aug. 7, 1756, in Abbot et al., *Papers of George Washington*, 3:338–39; Washington to Dinwiddie, Sept. 23, 1756, in ibid., 3:417; Inventory of James Lemon, Aug. 2, 1757, Frederick County Wills, 2:272; Young, "Effects of the French and Indian War," 238; and Matthias Calman to Henry Baker, deed, Mar. 9, 1761, FCD, 6:202. Stewart and Sowers received ordinary licenses from the county court during the fall of 1755 and regularly thereafter. See FCCO, 6:404, 7:3; and see also James Wood Account Book, James Wood Papers.

36. Robert Stewart to Washington, Sept. 27, 1757, in Abbot et al., *Papers of George Washington*, 4:424; and Return of Alexander Wodrow of "Goods supposed to be felloniously stolen from the public," Sept. 27, 1757, in ibid., 4:425–26 n. 4.

37. Washington to Dinwiddie, Oct. 9, 1757, in Abbot et al., *Papers of George Washington*, 5:10, 12; and Gabriel Jones to Washington, Oct. 9, 1757, in ibid., 7–8.

38. Washington to Dinwiddie, Oct. 9, 1757, in Abbot et al., *Papers of George Washington*, 5:12; Account of George Brown with Henry Brinker, n.d., *Brinker v Brown*, Nov. 1751, Ended Causes, 1743–1909, Frederick County Court Papers; Account of O'Gullion with James Lemon, Mar. 26, 1751 to Oct. 1752, *Lemon v O'Gullion*, Dec. 1752, ibid.; and Account of Samuel Divinny with John Hopes, Feb. 1745–Nov. 1746, *Hopes v Divinny*, May 1749, ibid.

39. Account with Henry Brinker, July 24[–25], 1758, in Abbot et al., *Papers of George Washington*, 5:332; Account with Henry Heth, July 24[–26], 1758, in ibid., 5:333; Account with Alexander Wodrow, July 24, 1759, in ibid.; and Account with John Funk, July 24[–26] in ibid., 5:332–33.

40. "Two Journals of Western Tours," by Charles Frederick Post, in Rueben Gold Thwaites, ed., *Early Western Journals, 1748–1765*, vol. 1 of *Early Western Travels, 1748–1846*, ed. Rueben Gold Thwaites (Cleveland: Arthur H. Clark, 1904), 212, 214 as quoted in McConnell, *A Country Between*, 130–31. On the Easton Treaty, see ibid., 126–32; and Jennings, *Empire of Fortune*, 274–78.

41. Burnaby, *Travels*, 7–8, 63, 66, 67, 73–74.

42. Young, "Effects of the French and Indian War," 235–36, 296–99, 310, 315–19, 436, tables 16, 18, 33.

43. George Mercer to Washington, Sept. 16, 1759, in Abbot et al., *Papers of George Washington*, 6:345; H. R. McIlwaine, ed., *Journals of the House of Burgesses of Virginia, 1758–1761* (Richmond: Virginia State Library, 1908), 17, and Hening, *Statutes*, 7:234–36, 314–17. For deeds for lots on the lands of Isaac Hollingsworth and William Cochran, see FCD, 5–6, 8, 9–11.

44. Richard Pillsbury, "The Street Name Systems of Pennsylvania before 1820," *Names* 17 (Sept. 1969): 214–22; and Garland R. Quarles, *Winchester, Virginia: Streets-Churches-Schools* (Winchester: Winchester–Frederick County Historical Society, 1996), 37–87.

45. Robert D. Mitchell, *Commercialism and Frontier: Perspectives on the Early Shenandoah Valley* (Charlottesville: UP of Virginia, 1977), 155–56, 195–96; Hening, *Statutes*, 7:284–86, 473–76; and FCD, 5–7.

46. Hening, *Statutes*, 7:406–7, 473–76; Jacob Funk to Peter Stover, deed, May 2, 1749, FCD, 2:8; and ibid., 7–8.

47. Hening, *Statutes*, 7:598–600; and FCD, 9.

48. McIlwaine, *Journals of the House of Burgesses, 1758–1761*, 16–17.

49. Fred Anderson, *Crucible of War: The Seven Years' War and the Fate of Empire in British North America, 1754–1766* (New York: Alfred A. Knopf, 2000), 284–85; Dora Mae Clark, "The British Treasury and the Administration of Military Affairs in America, 1754–1774," *Pennsylvania History* 2 (Oct. 1935): 197–204; Lawrence Henry Gipson, *The Great War for the Empire: The Victorious Years, 1758–1760*, vol. 7 of *The British Empire before the American Revolution* (New York: Alfred A Knopf, 1949), 328–70; and McConnell, *A Country Between*, 145–48.

50. John St. Clair, advertisement and circular letter, Jan. 4, 1759, in S. K. Stevens, et al., eds., *The Papers of Henry Bouquet*, 5 vols. (Harrisburg: Pennsylvania Historical and Museum Commission, 1951–84), 3:14–16; Thomas Rutherford to Henry Bouquet, July 31, 1759, in ibid., 3:466; and Mercer to Bouquet, Aug. 28, 1759, in ibid., 3:630. Premarket prices often varied and diverged considerably. Mercer was suggesting that the British army ought to enforce price convergence as a means of market formation.

51. Mercer to Bouquet, Aug. 28, 1759, in ibid., 3:629.

52. Mercer to John Stanwix, Sept. 19, 1759, in ibid., 4:125; and Young, "Effects of the French and Indian War," 230–32.

53. Walker to Stanwix, Oct. 12, 1759, in Stevens et al., *Papers of Henry Bouquet*, 4:222; Mercer to Bouquet, Oct. 9, 1959, in ibid., 4:203; Bouquet to Stanwix, Dec. 20, 1759, in ibid., 4:372; and Bouquet, account as deputy adjutant general, May 24, 1760, in ibid., 4:574.

54. Bouquet to Stanwix, Sept. 28, 1759, in ibid., 4:152; Mercer to Bouquet, Sept. 28, 1759, in ibid., 4:157; Walker to Bouquet, Oct. 12, 1759, in ibid., 4:220; Bouquet to Stanwix, Dec. 20, 1759, in ibid., 4:373; Mercer to Bouquet, Oct. 1759, in ibid., 4:174; Rutherford to Bouquet, Sept. 30, 1759, in ibid., 4:170; and Richard Graham to Adam Hoops, Sept. 21, 1759, in ibid., 4:133.

55. Mercer to Bouquet, Sept. 8, 1795, in ibid., 4:56; Mercer to Bouquet, Aug. 28, 1759, in ibid., 3:630; Mercer to Stanwix, Sept. 19, 1759, in ibid., 4:125; and Anderson, *Crucible of War*, 325–28. In October, quartermaster Lewis Ourry wrote to Bouquet that the wagon with "Indian goods" was the "private property of Mesrs Lemmon & Buch of Winchester," referring probably to Thomas Lemon, son of Winchester tavern keeper James Lemon, and Philip Bush, whose tavern George Washington recommended as the "best House in Winchester." See Ourry to Bouquet, Oct. 15, 1759, in Stevens et al., *Papers of Henry Bouquet*, 4:231; and Washington to St. Clair, May 11, 1758, in Abbot et al., *Papers of George Washington*, 5:178.

56. William Ramsay to Bouquet, Sept. 27, 1759, in Stevens et al., *Papers of Henry Bouquet*, 4:149; Mercer to Stanwix, Oct. 27, 1759, in ibid., 4:264; and Bouquet to Stanwix, Sept. 28, 1959, in ibid., 4:152.

57. Bouquet to Stanwix, Sept. 21, 1759, in ibid.; Walker to Bouquet, Oct. 12, 1759, in ibid., 4:220; and Bouquet to Mercer, Oct. 25, 1759, in ibid., 4:253.

58. Mercer to Stanwix, Sept. 19, 1759, in ibid., 4:124; Mercer to Hoops, Oct. 6, 1759, in ibid., 4:189; and Mercer to Stanwix, Oct. 27, 1759, in ibid., 4:264.

59. Mercer to Stanwix, Oct. 27, 1759, in ibid., 4:266; Bouquet to Stanwix, Nov. 26, 1759, in ibid., 4:330; and Bouquet to Stanwix, Dec. 20, 1759, in ibid., 4:373.

60. The white tithable population for Frederick County in 1759 was 2,111, and for Augusta County, 1,732, producing a total of 3,843. See Young, "Effects of the French and Indian War," 432, 436, tables 29, 33. At wage rates reported earlier in this chapter, farm laborers would have had to work forty-seven days and masons, thirty-one days to earn a proportionate share of British army expenditures in Virginia.

61. William Allason to John Schaw, Sept. 20, 1760, Letter Books, 1757–1793, David and William Allason Papers, 1722–1847, Library of Virginia; Allason to Heth, Feb. 28, 1761, ibid.; George Kerr to Bouquet, Dec. 29, 1760, in Stevens et al., *Papers of Henry Bouquet*, 5:219–20 n. 1; and "List of Houses and Inhabitants at Fort Pitt," in ibid., 5:407–11.

62. Allason to Heth, Feb. 28, 1761, Letter Books, 1757–1793, David and William Allason Papers; Allason to John Briscoe, Feb. 28, 1761, ibid.; and Cecil O'Dell, *Pioneers of Old Frederick County, Virginia* (Marceline, Mo.: Walsworth, 1995), 149–50.

63. Stephen to Bouquet, Feb. 21, 1761, in Stevens et al., *Papers of Henry Bouquet*, 5:305. On Adam Stephen's landholdings, see Virginia Land Patents, H:184, 185, 274, 398, Patents, 1623–1774, Library of Virginia; and FCD, 2:103.

64. William Allason to Robert Allason, Sept. 13, 1761, Letter Books, 1757–93, David and William Allason Papers; and William Allason to Alexander Knox, July 10, 1763, ibid. See also Shenandoah Store Ledgers, 1761–63, David and William Allason Papers.

CHAPTER 7. Town and Country

1. *The Journal of Nicholas Cresswell, 1774–1777* (New York: Dial Press, 1924), v–viii (Samuel Thornely's foreword), 48, and 49.

2. Ibid., 195, 49, 50.

3. George Mercer to Henry Bouquet, Aug. 28, 1759, in S. K. Stevens et al., eds., *The Papers of Henry Bouquet*, 5 vols. (Harrisburg: Pennsylvania Historical and Museum Commission, 1951–84), 3:630; Adam Stephen to Bouquet, Feb. 21, 1761, in ibid., 5:305; Frederick County Resolves, June 8, 1774, ed.. J. Dallas Robertson, in *Men and Events of the Revolution in Winchester and Frederick County, Virginia* (Winchester: Winchester–Frederick County Historical Society, 1975), 1; and Cresswell, *Journal*, 44, 60. According to Cresswell, "the cultivation of this article [wheat] is not altogether profitable, because the market is precarious"; see ibid., 198.

4. François Alexandre Frédéric, duc de La Rochefoucauld-Liancourt, *Travels through the United States of North America . . . in the Years 1795, 1796, and 1797*, 4 vols., 2d ed., trans. H. Neuman (London: R. Phillips, 1800), 3:216, 204.

5. Inventory of James Vance, Feb. 14, 1752, Frederick County Wills (hereafter FCW), 2:17, Frederick County Courthouse, Winchester; and Inventory of Andrew Vance, May 7, 1754, ibid., 2:125.

6. Thomas M. Doerflinger, *A Vigorous Spirit of Enterprise: Merchants and Economic Development in Revolutionary Philadelphia* (Chapel Hill: U of North Carolina P for the Institute of Early American History and Culture, 1986), 108–14; Carville V. Earle and Ronald Hoffman, "Staple Crops and Urban Development in the Eighteenth-Century South," in *Perspectives in American History*, vol. 10, ed. Donald Fleming and Bernard Bailyn (Cambridge: Harvard UP, 1976), 7–78; Marc Egnal, *New World Economies: The Growth of the Thirteen Colonies and Early Canada* (New York: Oxford UP, 1998): 25–77; Paul W. Gates, *The Farmer's Age: Agriculture, 1815–1860*, vol. 3 of *Economic History of the United States* (New York: Holt, Rinehart & Winston, 1960), 159; Lewis C. Gray, *History of Agriculture in the Southern United States to 1860*, 2 vols. (Washington, D.C.: Carnegie Institute, 1933; reprint, 1 vol., New York: Augustus M. Kelly, 1973), 161–66, 881, 908; David Klingaman, "The Significance of Grain in the Development of the Tobacco Colonies," *Journal of Economic History* 29 (June 1969): 268–78; and Jacob Price, "Economic Function and the Growth of American Port Towns in the Eighteenth Century," in *Perspectives in American History*, vol. 8, ed. Donald Fleming and Bernard Bailyn (Cambridge: Harvard UP, 1974), 151–56.

7. Egnal, *New World Economies*, 46–77; and Price, "Economic Function and the Growth of American Port Towns," 151–56.

8. Harry Piper Letterbook, 1767–75, Albert and Shirley Small Special Collections Library, Alderman Library, University of Virginia, Charlottesville, as quoted in Thomas M. Preisser, "Alexandria and the Evolution of the Northern Virginia Economy, 1749–1776," *Virginia Magazine of History and Biography* 89 (July 1981): 289, 287; Cresswell, *Journal*, 47, 27; Earle and Hoffman, "Staple Crops," 77–78; Robert D. Mitchell, *Commercialism and Frontier: Perspectives on the Early Shenandoah Valley* (Charlottesville: UP of Virginia, 1977), 149–52, 189–95; Preisser, "Eighteenth-Century Alexandria, Virginia, before the Revolution, 1749–1776" (Ph.D. diss., College of William and Mary, 1977), 135–37; and Edward Graham Roberts, "The Roads of Virginia, 1607–1840" (Ph.D. diss., University of Virginia, 1950), 33–36. According to the legislation that permitted funding road repairs with tax revenues, the "public roads leading from the north western parts of this colony to the towns of Alexandria and Colchester,

in the county of Fairfax, by means of the great number of waggons which use the same, are rendered almost impassible." See William W. Hening, ed., *The Statutes at Large: Being a Collection of All the Laws of Virginia, from . . . 1619 . . .* , 13 vols. (Richmond, New York, and Philadelphia, 1819–23), 8:549.

9. Preisser, "Alexandria and the Evolution of the Northern Virginia Economy," 284–86, 289–91; Preisser, "Eighteenth-Century Alexandria," 140–60; Freeman H. Hart, *The Valley of Virginia in the American Revolution, 1763–1789* (Chapel Hill: U of North Carolina P, 1942), 10 n. 22; and Doerflinger, *Vigorous Spirit of Enterprise,* 113–14. Robert D. Mitchell states that Hart's sources do not support his claims about wheat production in the lower Shenandoah Valley on the eve of the American Revolution. See Mitchell, *Commercialism and Frontier,* 174 n. 34.

10. Price, "Economic Function and the Growth of American Port Towns," 171; and Earle and Hoffman, "Staple Crops," 49–50.

11. Henry Heth to William Allason, May 22, 1761, Letters and Papers, 1761–63, David and William Allason Papers, 1722–1847, Library of Virginia, Richmond; Account of James Wood with Bryan Bruin, Aug. 31, 1760–Nov. 27, 1766, James Wood Jr. Accounts, 1741–1814, James Wood Collection, 711 THL, Archives Room, Handley Regional Library, Winchester; and Deed of Wood to Bruin, June 2, 1763, Frederick County Deeds, 8:474.

12. Owen Jones to Bryan Bruin, Aug. 9, 1763, Owen Jones Letterbook, 1759–81, Owen Jones Papers, 1759–1824, Historical Society of Pennsylvania, Philadelphia; Jones to Bruin, Sept. 28, 1763, ibid.; Mortgage of Bruin to Benjamin Howard and Hercules Courtney, Aug. 5, 1771, FCD, 15:46; Deed of Bruin to Thomas Ashburner and Thomas Place, Dec. 7, 1773, FCD, 16:302; Deed of Bruin to John Mitchell, Aug. 5, 1762, FCD, 8:258; and Mortgage of Mitchell to Jones, Sept. 12, 1767, FCD, 12:82.

13. Mortgage of Henry Heth to John Carlyle and John Dalton, Nov. 4, 1767, FCD, 13:3; Mortgage of William Cochran and Mary Cochran to Carlyle, Dalton, and Robert Wilson, Apr. 7, 1762, FCD, 7:69; Mortgage of Daniel Bush and Dinah Bush to John Orr, July 11, 1764, FCD, 10:17; Mortgage of Robert Rutherford and Mary Rutherford to Charles Yates, Nov. 7, 1767, FCD, 12:355; Mortgage of Philip Bush and Catherine Bush to Henry Kepple, Dec. 20, 1764, FCD, 10:352; and Mortgage of Daniel Bush and Dinah Bush to Philip Bush, Sept. 1, 1766, FCD, 11:167.

14. Inventory of Robert Allen, Mar. 7, 1771, FCW, 4:77; Inventory of John Beckett, Apr. 5, 1769, FCW, 3:488; and Mitchell, *Commercialism and Frontier,* 115, table 12; 118, table 14.

15. Cresswell, *Journal,* 195, 196.

16. *Virginia Gazette* (Williamsburg), Jan. 14, 1768; *The Journal Philip Vickers Fithian, 1775–1776,* ed. R. G. Albion and L. Dodson (Princeton: Princeton UP, 1934), 138; Hening, *Statutes,* 8:354–57; G. Melvin Herndon, "Hemp in Colonial Virginia," *Agricultural History* 38 (Apr. 1963): 86–93; and Mitchell, *Commercialism and Frontier,* 162–67.

17. Samuel Kercheval, *A History of the Valley of Virginia,* 5th ed. (Strasburg, Va.: Shenandoah Publishing House, 1973), 153; and Mitchell, *Commercialism and Frontier,* 178–81. On the movement of Tidewater planters to the Shenandoah Valley and their activities there, see Warren R. Hofstra, "These Fine Prospects: Frederick County, Vir-

ginia, 1738–1840" (Ph.D. diss., University of Virginia, 1985), 137–49; and Hofstra, *A Separate Place: The Formation of Clarke County, Virginia* (White Post, Va.: 1986; Madison, Wis.: Madison House, 1999), 9–12.

18. Cresswell, *Journal*, 267, 50; and Mitchell, *Commercialism and Frontier*, 183–87.

19. Inventory of John Beckett, Apr. 5, 1769, FCW, 3:488; Inventory of Robert Allen, Mar. 7, 1771, ibid., 4:77; Cresswell, *Journal*, 196; and Account of James Wood Jr. with Bryan Bruin, Aug. 31, 1760–Nov. 27, 1766, James Wood Jr. Accounts, 1741–1814, James Wood Collection.

20. Fithian, *Journal*, 24; and George Washington to John Augustine Washington, May 28, 1755, in *The Papers of George Washington*, 10 vols., Colonial Series, ed. W. W. Abbot et al. (Charlottesville: UP of Virginia, 1983–95), 1:289; and Hart, *Valley of Virginia*, 77.

21. Washington to Robert Dinwiddie, Oct. 11, 1755, in *The Papers of George Washington*, 2:204; and Fithian, *Journal*, 135.

22. Mitchell, *Commercialism and Frontier*, 167–72, 173–76, 179–81, 184.

23. U.S. Bureau of the Census, *Historical Statistics of the United States: Colonial Times to 1970* (Washington, D.C.: U.S. GPO, 1975), pt. 2:1176; and Cathy Matson, "The Revolution, the Constitution, and the New Nation," in Stanley L. Engerman and Robert E. Gallman, eds., *The Cambridge Economic History of the United States*, vol. 1, *The Colonial Era* (Cambridge: Cambridge UP, 1996), 372–82.

24. Hening, *Statutes*, 10:165–71, 271–72, 500–517; and Hart, *Valley of Virginia*, 124.

25. *Virginia Centinel; or, the Winchester Mercury*, Oct. 21, 1789; Otis K. Rice, *Frontier Kentucky* (Lexington: UP of Kentucky, 1993), 111; Bureau of the Census, *Historical Statistics*, pt. 1:24–37; and La Rochefoucauld-Liancourt, *Travels*, 3:208.

26. Bureau of the Census, *Historical Statistics*, pt. 2:284–86; and Matson, "Revolution, Constitution, and New Nation," 388–401.

27. Isaac Weld, *Travels through the States of North America*, 2 vols. (London: John Stockdale, 1807; New York: Johnson Reprint, 1968), 1:233–34; and Bureau of the Census, *Historical Statistics*, pt. 1:8, 24–37.

28. Thomas Bryan Martin to Philip Martin, June 28, 1790, Wykeham-Martin Papers, 1672–1820, M-1124.2 Microforms Collection, John D. Rockefeller Jr. Library, Colonial Williamsburg Foundation, Williamsburg; Robert D. Mitchell, "The Settlement Fabric of the Shenandoah Valley, 1790–1860: Pattern, Process, and Structure," in Kenneth E. Koons and Warren R. Hofstra, eds., *After the Backcountry: Rural Life in the Great Valley of Virginia, 1800–1900* (Knoxville: U of Tennessee P, 2000), 36; U.S. Census Office, Third Census, 1810, *A Statement of the Arts and Manufactures of the United States of America for the Year 1810*, ed. Tench Cox (Philadelphia, 1814), 112; U.S. Census Office, Fourth Census, 1820, *Digest of Accounts of Manufacturing Establishments in the United States and Their Manufactures* (Washington, D.C., 1823), 21; Mitchell, *Commercialism and Frontier*, 99, 109–21; and Hofstra, "These Fine Prospects," 374–76.

29. William Couper, *History of the Shenandoah Valley*, 3 vols. (New York: Lewis Historical Publishing Co., 1952), 2:1091–172; and Thomas K. Cartmell, *Shenandoah Valley Pioneers and Their Descendants: A History of Frederick County, Virginia* (Winchester, Va.: Eddy Press, 1909; Bowie, Md.: Heritage Books, 1989), 228–43.

30. Mitchell, "Settlement Fabric"; and Warren R. Hofstra, "Land Ethnicity, and Community at the Opequon Settlement, Virginia, 1730–1800," *Virginia Magazine of History and Biography* 98 (July 1990): 423–48, reprinted in H. Tyler Blethen and Curtis W. Wood Jr., eds., *Ulster and North America: Transatlantic Perspectives on the Scotch-Irish* (Tuscaloosa: U of Alabama P, 1997), 167–88.

31. Mitchell, "Settlement Fabric," 34.

32. Ibid., 34–35, 38; Hening, *Statutes*, 10:174, 172, 175; and for Luigi Castiglioni's observations on Winchester, see A. J. Morrison Jr., ed., *Travels in Virginia in Revolutionary Times* (Lynchburg, Va.: J. P. Bell, 1922), 69.

33. Weld, *Travels through the States of North America*, 1:230; Thomas Bryan Martin to Edward Martin, Aug. 20, 1768, and Thomas Bryan Martin to Denny Martin, Mar. 10, 1791, Wykeham-Martin Papers; La Rochefoucauld-Liancourt, *Travels*, 3:197; Mitchell, *Commercialism and Frontier*, 177; Inventory of Robert Glass, Sept. 4, 1797, FCW, 6:287; and Inventory of Joseph Glass, Apr. 8, 1795, ibid., 6:29.

34. Weld, *Travels through the States of North America*, 1:231; *Virginia Gazette and Winchester Advertiser*, Aug. 17, 1791; and Thomas Bryan Martin to Denny Martin, Mar. 10, 1791, Wykeham-Martin Papers. For a discussion of landscape changes during the late eighteenth century, see Clarence R. Geier and Warren R. Hofstra, "An Archaeological Survey of and Management Plan for Cultural Resources in the Vicinity of the Upper Opequon Creek" (Richmond: Virginia Department of Historic Resources, 1991), 75.

35. *Virginia Centinel and Gazette; or, the Winchester Repository*, Jan. 6, and Mar. 31, 1794; Stephen to Bouquet, Feb. 21, 1761, in Stevens et al., *Papers of Henry Bouquet*, 5:305; and Jonathan Clark Notebook, July–Aug. 1786, fols. 903–60, folder 185, Clark-Hite Papers, Filson Historical Society, Louisville, Ky.

36. Hugh Nelson to Battaile Muse, Feb. 10, 1779, Battaile Muse Papers, Duke University Rare Book, Manuscript, and Special Collections Library, Duke University, Durham, N.C.; and La Rochefoucauld-Liancourt, *Travels*, 3:185, 197–98.

37. Hening, *Statutes*, 2:260, 4:53–55, 5:31–35, 6:64–69.

38. G. L. Gillespie, "Map of the Upper Potomac from McCoy's Ferry to Conrad's Ferry and Adjacent Portions of Maryland and Virginia," in George B. Davis, Leslie J. Perry, and Joseph W. Kirkley, eds., *The Official Military Atlas of the Civil War* (Gettysburg: National Historical Society, 1978), plate 69, 1; La Rochefoucauld-Liancourt, *Travels*, 3:209; *Virginia Gazette; or, the Winchester Advertiser*, Aug. 20, 1788; Warren R. Hofstra and Clarence R. Geier, "The Abrams Creek–Redbud Run Project: A Cultural Resource Inventory Study of Archaeological Sites in the Shale Area East of Winchester, Virginia" (Richmond: Virginia Department of Historic Resources, 1992), 88–96; and *Hopewell Friends History, 1734–1934* (Strasburg, Va.: Shenandoah Publishing House, 1936), 168–70.

39. Leila Wood, "Industrial Mills," in Geier and Hofstra, "Archaeological Survey," 64–70; and Mitchell, *Commercialism and Frontier*, 175.

40. *Virginia Centinel and Gazette: or, the Winchester Political Repository*, Oct. 15 and July 30, 1792; and *Virginia Centinel and Gazette; or, the Winchester Repository*, Apr. 21, 1794 and June 3, 1793.

41. General Account Book [George Stubblefield Account Book], 1791–1802, Account Book Collection, 916 THL/WFCHS, Archives Room, Handley Regional Library.

42. Ibid.

43. Fithian, *Journal*, 13; and Samuel Vaughan Diary, 1787–1796, Manuscript Division, Library of Congress, Washington, D.C.

44. Report of the "Persons appointed to examine & report the situation of the Public Goal," Sept. 8, 1789, Frederick County Superior Court Order Book, 1789–93, pp. 38–39, Frederick County Courthouse; *Virginia Journal and Alexandria Advertiser*, Apr. 14, 1785; Frederick County Court Orders (hereafter FCCO), 23:499; Bond of Charles Smith, Feb. 9, 1762, Frederick County Vestry Book, 1764–80, pp. 18, 25; Bond of Simon Taylor, Aug. 10, 1764, FCD, 9:362; Order to John Neavill, Feb. 7, 1770, FCCO, 14:580; Order to John Greenfield and Angus McDonald, Nov. 5, 1766, ibid., 13:252; *Maryland Gazette*, Dec. 3, 1761; and *Virginia Centinel and Gazette; or, the Winchester Political Repository*, Jan. 7, 1793.

45. Fithian, *Journal*, 13. On the use of the Winchester outlots, see *Virginia Centinel and Gazette; or, the Winchester Repository*, Nov. 11, 1793 and May 19, 1794; and Petition of Thomas Edmondson, Nov. 23, 1782, Winchester City, Legislative Petitions, 1774–1865, Library of Virginia.

46. La Rochefoucauld-Liancourt, *Travels*, 3:204, 208; and Harry Toulmin, *The Western Country in 1793: Reports on Kentucky and Virginia*, ed. Marion Tinling and Godfrey Davies (San Marino, Calif.: Huntington Library, 1948), 57. La Rochefoucauld-Liancourt's count of stores might have been high. A 1787 legislative petition enumerated twenty-one, and twenty-four merchants received commercial licenses in 1798. See Memorial of the Merchants and Traders of the Town of Winchester, Nov. 6, 1787, Winchester City, Legislative Petitions, 1774–1865; and List of Merchants who have obtained Licenses from Obed Waite, 1798, Winchester City, Personal Property Taxes, 1782–1927, Library of Virginia.

47. W. L. McAtee, ed., "Journal of Benjamin Smith Barton on a Visit to Virginia, 1802," *Castanea* 3 (Nov.–Dec. 1938): 89.

48. *Virginia Centinel and Gazette; or, the Winchester Political Repository*, Jan. 28, 1792; Policy of James Gamul Dowdall, Mar. 30, 1796, no. 33, Frederick County, Mutual Assurance Society of Virginia Papers, Business Records Collection, Library of Virginia; and Policy of James Holliday, Mar. 30, 1796, no. 44, ibid.

49. *Virginia Centinel; or, the Winchester Mercury*, Dec. 31, 1788; *Virginia Centinel and Gazette; or, the Winchester Repository*, Apr. 29, 1793, and Apr. 21, 1794; Policy of Peter Kehoe, June 15, 1796, no. 81, Frederick County, Mutual Assurance Society of Virginia; Policy of Philip Bush, Mar. 29, 1796, no. 41, ibid.; and Policy of Peter Lauck, Mar. 28, 1796, no. 20, ibid.

50. *Virginia Centinel and Gazette; or, the Winchester Repository*, Aug. 11, 1794; *Virginia Centinel and Gazette; or, the Winchester Political Repository*, Jan. 28, 1792; *Virginia Gazette and Winchester Advertiser*, Dec. 30, 1789; Permit for nail manufactory, Feb. 5, 1788, Frederick County Court Minutes, 1786–90, p. 117, Frederick County Courthouse; and *Virginia Gazette and Winchester Advertiser*, Apr. 16, 1788.

51. Account of Samuel Glass with John Conrad, May 10 to Oct. 22, 1792, Unidentified Ledger C [John Conrad Account Book], 1791–93, p. 37, Business Records/Corporations/Partnerships, Frederick County Court Records, Library of Virginia; Garland R. Quarles, *Some Worthy Lives* (Winchester: Winchester–Frederick County Historical Society, 1988), 71–72; and Inventory of John Conrad, Sept. 24, 1794, FCW, 6:150. Conrad's store was located on the corner of Loudoun and Cork Streets on lot 12 in the original James Wood survey of Winchester. See FCD, 39:473.

52. Unidentified Ledger C [John Conrad Account Book], 1791–93.

53. Invoice Book, 1787–94, John Conrad Records, 635 THL, Archives Room, Handley Regional Library.

54. Ibid.; and Estate Accounts of John Conrad, 1794, FCW, 8:192.

55. *Virginia Centinel and Gazette; or, the Winchester Political Repository*, Oct. 1 and July 30, 1792; Johann D. Schoepf, *Travels in the Confederation, 1783–1784*, 2 vols., trans. and ed. Alfred J. Morrison (Erlangen: Johann Jacob Plam, 1788; New York: Bergman Publishers, 1968), 2:26; La Rochefoucauld-Liancourt, *Travels*, 3:202; *Virginia Centinel and Gazette; or, the Winchester Repository*, June 3, 1793; and *Virginia Centinel and Gazette; or, the Winchester Political Repository*, July 16 and Jan. 28, 1792.

56. *Virginia Centinel and Gazette; or, the Winchester Political Repository*, Jan. 14, 1793; and *Virginia Centinel and Gazette; or, the Winchester Repository*, Apr. 21, 1794, and Apr. 29, 1793.

57. *Virginia Centinel; or, the Winchester Mercury*, Nov. 17, 1789; and *Virginia Centinel and Gazette; or, the Winchester Political Repository*, Aug. 6, 1792.

58. General Merchandise Ledger [Richard Galloway and William Vance Account Book], 1804–8 (quotations on 85, 94), Account Book Collection.

59. Toulmin, *Western Country*, 57; La Rochefoucauld-Liancourt, *Travels*, 3:203; *Virginia Gazette and Winchester Advertiser*, Sept. 14, 1787; and *Virginia Centinel and Gazette; or, the Winchester Political Repository*, Jan. 7 and Sept. 10, 1791.

60. Jacques Pierre Brissot de Warville, *New Travels in the United States of America, 1788*, ed. Durand Echeverria, trans. Mara S. Vamos and Durand Echeverria (Paris: Buisson, 1791; Cambridge: Belknap Press of Harvard UP, 1964), 340; *Virginia Centinel and Gazette; or, the Winchester Repository*, Nov. 25, 1793, and Sept. 8, 1794; and General Merchandise Ledger [Richard Galloway and William Vance Account Book], 1804–8.

61. La Rochefoucauld-Liancourt, *Travels*, 3:203; Petition of the subscribers, citizens of the Counties of Loudoun, Berkeley, and Frederick, Nov. 24, 1786, Loudoun County, Legislative Petitions, 1774–1865, Library of Virginia; *Virginia Centinel and Gazette; or, the Winchester Political Repository*, Dec. 3, 1792, and Dec. 15, 1790; and Weld, *Travels through the States of North America*, 1:71.

62. Petition of Charles Washington and others, Nov. 22, 1780, Berkeley County, Legislative Petitions, 1774–1865, Library of Virginia; La Rochefoucauld-Liancourt, *Travels*, 3:210–13; Mitchell, *Commercialism and Frontier*, 198; *Virginia Centinel and Gazette; or, the Winchester Repository*, Oct. 21, 1793, and Aug. 25, 1794; and White House Store Ledger, Manuscript Division, Alderman Library, University of Virginia, Charlottesville.

63. *Virginia Centinel and Gazette; or, the Winchester Repository*, Nov. 11, 1793, and

June 23, 1794. On merchant connections between Winchester and smaller communities, see *Virginia Centinel and Gazette; or, the Winchester Political Repository,* Jan. 28, May 7, June 18, and Aug. 6, 1792; *Virginia Centinel and Gazette; or, the Winchester Repository,* Mar. 18, June 10, Oct. 21, and Dec. 30, 1793, and Feb. 10, Apr. 7, 21, and Aug. 25, 1794.

64. La Rochefoucauld-Liancourt, *Travels,* 3:201; and Ferdinand M. Bayard, *Travels of a Frenchman in Maryland and Virginia with a Description of Philadelphia and Baltimore in 1791,* 2d ed., trans. Ben C. McCary (Paris: Batilliot Frères, 1793; Ann Arbor: Edward Bros., 1950), 89.

65. *Virginia Centinel and Gazette; or, the Winchester Repository,* Aug. 18, 1794.

66. *Virginia Gazette; or, the Winchester Advertiser,* July 2, 1788; and *Virginia Centinel; or, the Winchester Mercury,* July 9, 1788.

67. Ibid. Although New Hampshire ratified the Constitution as the ninth state on June 21, 1788, news of this action did not reach Virginia until after June 26.

68. *Virginia Centinel; or, the Winchester Mercury,* July 9, 1788; Hening, *Statutes,* 10:173, 174; and *Virginia Centinel and Gazette; or, the Winchester Repository,* May 5, 1794. Election of town officers was regularly reported in local newspapers.

69. La Rochefoucauld-Liancourt, *Travels,* 3:208; *Virginia Centinel and Gazette; or, the Winchester Repository,* May 5, 1794; Toulmin, *Western Country,* 45–47 (quotation on 45); and Order of May 5, 1778, FCCO, 16:491.

70. Bayard, *Travels,* 92, 87; *Virginia Centinel; or, the Winchester Mercury,* May 20, 1789; *Virginia Gazette; or, the Winchester Advertiser,* May 21, 1788; La Rochefoucauld-Liancourt, *Travels,* 3:204–5; Complaint of Edward McGuire and James G. Dowdall, June 1, 1790, FCCM, 1786–90, p. 393; *Virginia Centinel; or, the Winchester Mercury,* July 30, 1788; *Virginia Centinel and Gazette; or, the Winchester Repository,* Nov. 25, 1793; and *Virginia Centinel and Gazette; or, the Winchester Political Repository,* May 14, 1792.

71. *Virginia Gazette and Winchester Advertiser,* Nov. 2, 1787; *Virginia Centinel and Gazette; or, the Winchester Repository,* Feb. 24 and Jan. 6, 1794; *Virginia Gazette and Winchester Advertiser,* Sept. 28, 1787; and Petition of the trustees of the Winchester Academy, Oct. 27, 1786, Winchester City, Legislative Petitions, 1774–1865.

72. *Virginia Gazette and Winchester Advertiser,* Nov. 9 and 23, 1787; *Virginia Centinel and Gazette; or, the Winchester Repository,* Aug. 12, 1793, and July 7, 1794; *Virginia Centinel and Gazette; or, the Winchester Political Repository,* Nov. 10, 1790. On the theater in Winchester, see *Virginia Gazette and Winchester Advertiser,* May 21, 28, June 4, and 18, 1791; on the library, see *Virginia Centinel; or, the Winchester Mercury,* Apr. 15, 1788; and Henry St. George Tucker to St. George Tucker, Feb. 14, 1804, Tucker-Coleman Papers, Manuscript Division, Swem Library, College of William and Mary, Williamsburg; and on the races, see the account of the 1794 Fourth of July celebration in *Virginia Centinel and Gazette; or, the Winchester Repository,* July 7, 1794.

73. Toulmin, *Western Country,* 57; Adam Gordon as quoted in Maldwyn A. Jones, "The Scotch-Irish in British America," in Bernard Bailyn and Philip D. Morgan, eds., *Strangers within the Realm: Cultural Margins of the First British Empire* (Chapel Hill: U of North Carolina P for the Institute of Early American History and Culture, 1991), 284. On the German language press in Winchester, see *Virginia Gazette; or, the Winchester Advertiser,* Oct. 1 and Dec. 3, 1788, and July 1 and Dec. 9, 1789.

74. Francis Asbury, *Journal of Rev. Francis Asbury*, 3 vols. (New York: Lane & Scott, 1852), 1:461; Petition of the trustees of the Winchester Academy, Nov. 10, 1788, Winchester City, Legislative Petitions, 1774–1865; Winchester riot, July 11, 1759, Bonds, Qualifications, and Commissions, 1782–1904, Frederick County Court Papers; and Kercheval, *History of the Valley*, 176.

75. James Ireland, *The Life of the Rev. James Ireland*, . . . (Winchester: J. Foster, 1819), 184; Asbury, *Journal*, 1:512; La Rochefoucauld-Liancourt, *Travels*, 3:208; U.S. Census Office, Second Census, 1800, *Return of the Whole Number of Persons within the Several Districts of the United States* . . . (Washington, D.C., 1801), 21; *Virginia Gazette; or, the Winchester Advertiser*, Oct. 8, 1788; and *Virginia Centinel and Gazette; or, the Winchester Political Repository*, May 21, 1792.

76. Account Book, 1798–1812, Daybook, 1800–1808, Account Book, 1801, Account Book, "The Black Ledger," 1802, Mrs. Ann Frame Papers, 1798–1812, Thornton Tayloe Perry Collection, Virginia Historical Society, Richmond.

77. Petition of the inhabitants of the Borough of Winchester, Oct. 21, 1791, Winchester City, Legislative Petitions, 1774–1865. While visiting Lancaster, Pennsylvania, in 1778, Thomas Anburey observed that "most of the houses before the door have an elevation, to which you ascend by steps from the street, resembling a small balcony with benches on both sides, where the inhabitants sit and enjoy the fresh air, and view the people passing." Thomas Anburey, *Travels through the Interior Parts of America*, 2 vols. (London: W. Lane, 1789; Boston: Houghton Mifflin, 1923), 2:175.

78. La Rochefoucauld-Liancourt, *Travels*, 3:184.

79. John F. D. Smyth, *A Tour in the United States of America*, 2 vols. (London: G. Robinson, 1784; New York: New York Times and Arno Press, 1968), 2: 258; Kercheval, *History of the Valley*, 150; and Warville, *Travels*, 266, 268.

80. Transcript of the Record in the case, *Jost Hite and Robert McCoy v Lord Fairfax, 1749–*, fol. 717, folder 100, Clark-Hite Papers.

81. Bayard, *Travels*, 62.

82. Edward A. Chappell, "Acculturation in the Shenandoah Valley: Rhenish Houses of the Massanutten Settlement," *Proceedings of the American Philosophical Society* 124 (1980): 55–89.

83. Robert F. Ensminger, *The Pennsylvania Barn: Its Origin, Evolution, and Distribution in North America* (Baltimore: Johns Hopkins UP, 1992), 107–46.

84. The symmetrical Georgian dwelling in a three- or five-bay, single pile configuration was first documented as a house type in Indiana, Illinois, and Iowa by geographer Fred B. Kniffen. See Kniffen, "Folk Housing: Key to Diffusion," *Annals of the Association of American Geographers* 55 (Dec. 1965): 549–77.

CHAPTER 8. The Future of New Virginia: An Epilogue

1. *The Journal of Nicholas Cresswell, 1774–1777* (New York: Dial Press, 1924), 49–50.

2. *Virginia Gazette*, Dec. 22, 1774; Warren M. Billings, John E. Selby, and Thad W. Tate, *Colonial Virginia: A History* (White Plains, N.Y.: KTO Press, 1986), 337–38; Michael N. McConnell, *A Country Between: The Upper Ohio Valley and Its Peoples, 1724–*

1774 (Lincoln: U of Nebraska P, 1992), 268–75; and John E. Selby, *The Revolution in Virginia, 1775–1783* (Williamsburg: Colonial Williamsburg Foundation, 1988), 16–18.

3. McConnell, *A Country Between,* 280–82.

4. John Bartram to Peter Collinson, July 18 [1739], in Edmund Berkeley and Dorothy Smith Berkeley, eds., *The Correspondence of John Bartram, 1734–1777* (Gainesville: UP of Florida, 1992), 121–22.

5. Samuel Kercheval, *A History of the Valley of Virginia,* 5th ed. (Strasburg, Va.: Shenandoah Publishing House, 1973), 52 n. 53, 44–45.

6. Fred Kniffen, "Folk Housing: Key to Diffusion," *Annals of the Association of American Geographers* 55 (Dec. 1965): 549–77; and Robert F. Ensminger, *The Pennsylvania Barn: Its Origin, Evolution, and Distribution in North America* (Baltimore: Johns Hopkins UP, 1992), 147–80.

7. Kenneth E. Koons, "'The Staple of Our Country': Wheat in the Regional Farm Economy of the Nineteenth-Century Valley of Virginia," in Koons and Warren R. Hofstra, eds., *After the Backcountry: Rural Life in the Great Valley of Virginia, 1800–1900* (Knoxville: U of Tennessee P, 2000), 3–33, tables 1.1, 1.2.

8. For reference to the "world we have lost," see Peter Laslett, *The World We Have Lost* (New York: Charles Scribner's Sons, 1966).

9. Robert D. Mitchell, "The Settlement Fabric of the Shenandoah Valley, 1790–1860: Pattern, Process, and Structure," in Koons and Hofstra, *After the Backcountry,* 38, 44–45, tables 3.3, 3.4; Samuel Thomas Emory Jr., "The Economic Geography of Clarke and Frederick Counties, Virginia" (Ph.D. diss., University of Maryland, 1964), 46, table 2; Thomas K. Cartmell, *Shenandoah Valley Pioneers and Their Descendants: A History of Frederick County, Virginia* (Winchester, Va.: Eddy Press, 1909; Bowie, Md.: Heritage Books, 1989), 112–13; and Charles H. Ambler, *Sectionalism in Virginia from 1776 to 1861* (Chicago: U of Chicago P, 1910; New York: Russell & Russell, 1964), 238 n. 64. On the use of cash books and running accounts, see W. T. Baxter, "Accounting in Colonial America," in A. C. Littleton and B. S. Yamey, eds., *Studies in the History of Accounting* (New York: Arno Press, 1978), 272–87. For an example, see Nathaniel Burwell Disbursements, 1794–1804, 232 CCHA, Clarke County Historical Association Archives, Berryville, Va.

10. Andrew Burnaby, *Travels through the Middle Settlements in North America in the Years 1759 and 1760,* 3d ed. (London: T. Payne, 1798; New York: Augustus M. Kelley, 1970), 73–74.

11. Isaac Weld, *Travels through the States of North America,* 2 vols. (London: John Stockdale, 1807; New York: Johnson Reprint, 1968), 1: xix–xx (Roth intro.), 232–33.

12. Ferdinand M. Bayard, *Travels of a Frenchman in Maryland and Virginia with a Description of Philadelphia and Baltimore in 1791,* 2d ed., trans. Ben C. McCary (Paris: Batilliot Frères, 1793; Ann Arbor: Edward Bros., 1950), vii (McCay intro.), 1, 58–59, 81.

13. Bayard, *Travels,* 65, 90; and Mitchell, *Commercialism and Frontier,* 99, table 9.

14. Bayard, *Travels,* 1.

Index

Note: Page numbers in *italics* refer to illustrations.

Abell, Richard, 230
Abernethy, Thomas Perkins, 54
account statements, *199*, 206, 227–31, *228*,
    304–5
Ardis, Mathias, 250
affluence in Anglo-American society, 28.
    See also wealth
agriculture, corn, bean, and squash, 105, 123
Alexandria, trade with, 232, 275, 278, 306,
    310–11
Allason, David, 271, 279
Allason, Richard, 271
Allason, William, 270–71, 276
Allen, Ben, 138–39
Allen, James, 252
Allen, Montgomery, 289–90
Allen, Robert, 99, 278, 289–90
ambition, view of, 117–18
American Revolution, 281–83
Anderson, Alice, 223
Anderson, Enoch, 216–17
Anglican Church, 184–85, 294
Annapolis, plan of, 186, *188–89*
armed force, 28–29
Armstrong, John, 106
Arnold, John, 231
Articles of Confederation, 283
artifact: as lines defining tract, 112–13; as
    object created by culture, 116–17

artisans: Baltimore and, 310; cash and, 308;
    exchange economy and, 219–20; mill
    sites and, 293
Asbury, Francis, 129, 317, 318
Ashburner, Thomas, 277
Ashby, John, 199
Aspinal, Alice, 201
Augusta County, 8, 164, 387n. 60
avian habitat, human settlement compared
    to, 107–8, *109*

Babb, Philip, 208, *209*, 214
backcountry: as buffer zone, 4–5, 7, 56,
    163–64; cultural manifestations on land
    of, 39, 51–55; settlers in, 81–84; transition
    of to forecountry, 329, 333–34. *See also*
    dispersal in backcountry; frontier
Bailey, Mary, 220
Baker, Henry, 254
Baker, Isaac, 222
Baker, Joshua, 248
Balch, Thomas, 231
Baltimore, 276, 309–10
banks, 330–31
barley, 207
barns: double-crib construction, 153;
    ground, 151, *152*; in Opequon, 149; Penn-
    sylvania bank, *324*, 325; Wood and, 200
Barnwell, John, 70, 71
barrens, 127
barter economy, 224–25
Bartgis, Matthias, 317

397

· *About the Author* ·

WARREN R. HOFSTRA was born in 1947 in Staten Island, New York, and raised in Detroit and Lansing, Michigan, and Bethesda, Maryland. He received an undergraduate degree in history from Washington University, St. Louis, a master's degree in history from Boston University, and his doctorate in history from the University of Virginia. He is the recipient of numerous awards, including a fellowship from the National Endowment for the Humanities and successive Mellon fellowships at the Virginia Historical Society. He is the author of *A Separate Place,* editor of *George Washington and Virginia Backcountry,* and co-editor of *After the Backcountry: Rural Life in the Great Valley of Virginia, 1800–1900* and *Virginia Reconsidered: New Histories of the Old Dominion.* In 1977, Hofstra joined the faculty of Shenandoah University in Winchester, Virginia, where he is now the Stewart Bell Professor of History.

Charles S. Aiken, *The Cotton Plantation South since the Civil War*

Larry Anderson, *Benton MacKaye: Conservationist, Planner, and Creator of the Applachian Trail*

Brian Black, *Petrolia: The Landscape of America's First Oil Boom*

Warren Boeschenstein, *Historic American Towns along the Atlantic Coast*

Robert F. Ensminger, *The Pennsylvania Barn*

Richard Harris, *Unplanned Suburbs: Toronto's American Tragedy, 1900 to 1950*

Michael Holleran, *Boston's "Changeful Times": Origins of Preservation and Planning in America*

Cathy D. Knepper, *Greenbelt, Maryland: A Living Legacy of the New Deal*

Gabrielle M. Lanier and Bernard L. Herman, *Everyday Architecture of the Mid-Atlantic: Looking at Buildings and Landscapes*

Robert Lewis, *Manufacturing Montreal: The Making of an Industrial Landscape, 1850 to 1930*

Carolyn S. Loeb, *Entrepreneurial Vernacular: Developers' Subdivisions in the 1920s*

Martha J. McNamara, *From Tavern to Courthouse: Architecture and Ritual in American Law, 1658–1860*

Richard L. Nostrand and Lawrence E. Estaville, editors, *Homelands: A Geography of Culture and Place across America*

David Schuyler, *Apostle of Taste: Andrew Jackson Downing, 1815–1852*

James E. Vance, Jr., *The North American Railroad: Its Origin, Evolution, and Geography*

Alexander von Hoffman, *Local Attachments: The Making of an American Urban Neighborhood, 1850 to 1920*

Joseph S. Wood, *The New England Village*

Printed in the United States
34809LVS00002BC/2